HUMANKIND EMERGING

HUMANKIND EMERGING

EIGHTH EDITION

BERNARD G. CAMPBELL

JAMES D. LOY
University of Rhode Island

Allyn and Bacon

BOSTON ■ LONDON ■ TORONTO ■ SYDNEY ■ TOKYO ■ SINGAPORE

Editor-in-Chief: Karen Hanson
Marketing Manager: Brooke Stoner
Series Editor: Sarah L. Kelbaugh
Editorial Assistant: Jennifer DiDomenico
Full Service Production Manager: Valerie Zaborski
Project Coordination and Text Design: Elm Street Publishing Services, Inc.
Electronic Page Makeup: Elm Street Publishing Services, Inc.
Photo Researcher: Mira Schachne
Manufacturing Buyer: Megan Cochran

Copyright © 2000 by Allyn & Bacon
A Pearson Education Company
160 Gould Street
Needham Heights, MA 02194

www.abacon.com

Library of Congress Cataloging-in-Publication Data

Campbell, Bernard Grant.
     Humankind emerging / Bernard G. Campbell, James D. Loy. — 8th ed.
          p. cm.
     Rev. ed. of: Humankind emerging. 7th ed. c1996.
     "Adapted in part from materials published by Time-Life Books in two
series: The emergence of man and The Life nature library"—T.p. verso
     Includes bibliographical references and index.
     ISBN 0-321-02274-2 (pbk.)
     1. Human evolution. 2. Prehistoric peoples 3. Physical anthropology.
I. Loy, James. II. Humankind emerging. III. Title.
GN281.C36   2000
599.93'8—DC21   99-12135
                                                                              CIP

Printed in the United States of America

10 9 8 7 6 5 VH 04 03

Contents

PART I EVOLUTION
Chapter 1 THE SEARCH FOR HUMAN ORIGINS 1

Chapter 2 EVOLUTIONARY MECHANISMS 33

PART II THE ORIGIN OF HUMANKIND
Chapter 3 HUMANS AMONG THE PRIMATES 75

Chapter 4 THE BEHAVIOR OF LIVING PRIMATES   113

Chapter 5 APES AND OTHER ANCESTORS: PREHOMINID EVOLUTION   166

Chapter 6 THE TRANSVAAL HOMINIDS   202

Chapter 7 EAST AFRICA: THE AUSTRALOPITHECINE FOSSILS   232

Chapter 8   EAST AFRICA: THE ADVENT OF *HOMO*   278

Chapter 9   THE EVOLUTION OF HOMINID BEHAVIOR   294

PART III THE EVOLUTION OF HUMANKIND
Chapter 10 DISCOVERING *HOMO ERECTUS* 323

Chapter 11   ENVIRONMENT AND TECHNOLOGY OF *HOMO ERECTUS*   364

Chapter 12   HUNTING, GATHERING, AND THE EVOLUTION OF SOCIETY   391

Chapter 13 THE EVOLUTION OF LANGUAGE AND THE BRAIN   412

PART IV MODERN HUMANITY
Chapter 14 *HOMO HEIDELBERGENSIS* AND THE NEANDERTALS: SUCCESSORS TO *HOMO ERECTUS*   446

Chapter 15   *HOMO HEIDELBERGENSIS* AND THE NEANDERTALS: CULTURE AND ENVIRONMENTS   481

Chapter 18   THE HUMAN CONDITION   578

APPENDICES

PREFACE

Humankind Emerging, first published in 1976, is one of the longest-running anthropology texts. You hold in your hands the eighth edition of this book, which generations of students have found useful in introductory anthropology, physical anthropology, and human evolution courses. The product of the collaboration between a paleoanthropologist (Bernard G. Campbell) and a primatologist (James D. Loy), *Humankind Emerging,* treats all the subdisciplines of physical anthropology as well as several related fields but focuses mainly on paleoanthropology—the science concerned with the collection and interpretation of the fossil and cultural evidence of human evolution. Through the book's eighteen chapters, the reader learns what we know of how, when, and where humans came to exist. The investigation of our past is exciting, and *Humankind Emerging* conveys this excitement to students who are studying physical anthropology for the first time.

In this new edition, we have made every effort to remove outdated material and to add the latest discoveries and theories. The latter aspect of this revision has been a particular challenge, since reports of new fossils and new analyses appear constantly in scholarly journals and monographs. Nonetheless, we believe we have incorporated the main paleoanthropological developments through the early months of 1999. Significant additions and changes to the book include:

- Revision of the genetics chapters, with new material on natural selection, genetic drift, and the mechanisms of speciation.
- New information from primate field studies, especially those focused on the behavior and ecology of the various ape species.
- Updated speculations about the characteristics of humans' last ape ancestor.
- Descriptions of the latest discoveries of fossil primates, particularly as they pertain to the early apes' evolution of knuckle-walking and/or suspensory locomotion.
- A taxonomic revision of the Hominidae that sinks the taxon "archaic *Homo sapiens*" and recognizes or describes the following species for the first time: *Ardipithecus ramidus, Australopithecus anamensis, Australopithecus bahrelghazali, Homo heidelbergensis,* and *Homo neanderthalensis.*
- Detailed lists of technical diagnostic traits for each of the hominid species (this material is organized into an end-of-book appendix).
- Descriptions of the latest hominid fossil finds, including australopithecine material from Chad, *Homo erectus* specimens from Ceprano (Italy) and Venta Micena (Orce, Spain), and the oldest *Homo heidelbergensis* remains from Gran Dolina (Atapuerca, Spain).
- Expanded treatments of the various theories that account for the appearance of anatomically modern humans, including information on Neandertal mtDNA analyses, Y-chromosome studies, and the genetic ancestry of modern Chinese populations.
- A revised discussion of race and anthropologists' varying views on the applicability of this biological concept for humans.

As in previous editions, the extensive illustrations provide students with important visual supplements for learning physical anthropology. To this end, more than fifty new photos, figures, drawings, and tables have been added. Of particular interest are the new tables that present data on the comparative anatomy of apes and humans. Also, a third color photo essay has been added that profiles a selection of current anthropologists, allowing students to "put a face" on the discipline.

Finally, we have tried to make the new edition of *Humankind Emerging* an improved teaching tool through the addition of several new pedagogical features. These include:

- A series of boxed items that describe the relevancy of physical anthropology for students' everyday lives.
- "Mini-Timelines" in the Overview sections at the start of most chapters that alert students to significant fossil discoveries or other events and give their geologic age or date in history.
- An expanded running glossary and end-of-book definitions.
- Lists of pertinent Internet (WWW) sites and search terms at the end of each chapter.
- Supplementary reading lists at the end of each chapter.

Humankind Emerging was originally developed from material first published in Time-Life Books' *Emergence of Man* series and *The Life Nature Library*. *Humankind Emerging,* Eighth Edition, continues to benefit from the use of certain aspects of this material. Our thanks go to the authors, editors, and consultants who worked on this edition. Teachers and students who used earlier editions of the text have provided constructive suggestions for change. Many friends and colleagues were generous with their time, comments, and materials, and among them special thanks go to Tim White and Mark Schmidt for providing color photographs. Several anthropologists helped especially by sharing their thoughts in careful and detailed reviews. These reviewers included:

George J. Bey III, *Millsaps College*
James R. Bindon, *University of Alabama*
George Gill, *University of Wyoming at Laramie*
Bruce LaBrack, *University of the Pacific*
Carol Lauer, *Rollins College*
Ann Palkovich, *George Mason University*
John Pryor, *California State University-Fresno*
Mary Sandeford, *University of North Carolina at Greensboro*
Jeffrey Schwartz, *University of Pittsburgh*
William A. Stini, *University of Arizona*
Ian Tattersall, *American Museum of Natural History*

Finally, we would like to thank our wives, Susan Campbell and Kent Loy, whose companionship and love sustain us, whose help is indispensable, and who have the humanity to pry us away periodically from our word processors.

Bernard G. Campbell
James D. Loy

INTRODUCTION

Know then thyself, presume not God to scan;
The proper study of mankind is man.
Placed on this isthmus in a middle state,
A being darkly wise, and rudely great:
With too much knowledge for the skeptic side,
With too much weakness for the Stoic's pride,
He hangs between; in doubt to act or rest;
In doubt to deem himself a God, or beast;
In doubt his mind or body to prefer;
Born but to die; and reas'ning but to err;
Alike in ignorance, his reason such,
Whether he thinks too little or too much;
Chaos of Thought and Passion, all confused;
Still by himself abused, or disabused;
Created half to rise, and half to fall;
Great Lord of all things, yet a prey to all;
Sole judge of truth, in endless error hurled;
The glory, jest, and riddle of the world!

ALEXANDER POPE, 1688–1744.
Essay on Man, Ep. II, 1, 1–18.

These profound and brilliant lines by the English poet and satirist Alexander Pope describe the paradox of human nature. Throughout history, people have been puzzled and exasperated by humankind's strange duality—half animal, half angel—and much of religious and philosophical teaching has been an attempt to understand and integrate these two sides of our being. Neither priest nor philosopher has offered us an explanation that has proved either intellectually satisfactory or (in modern jargon) operationally effective. The writings of the wise throughout the ages have not enabled most of us to come to terms with our dual nature, however much we may have thought about these things or faced the moral dilemmas that are our inheritance. We carry the marks and needs of an animal, but we also find ourselves alienated and unsure in the natural world and in the face of our own biology. In our imagination, we travel far beyond the bounds of both our own environment and our biological nature, and yet we still feel rooted to them in a way that seems to constrict the highest reaches of our humanity. Our forces tend to be ranged opposite each other like the poles, and we find ourselves torn between them, caught in a conflict that has been cruelly sharpened by the demands of every culture in every age.

Humanity has, quite logically, looked to the past to explain the present and in so doing has developed numerous mythological accounts of human origins. In the Judeo-Christian tradition, for example, our duality is explained by the Biblical story of a stern God who placed a perfect man and a perfect woman in paradise and then expelled them when they disobeyed His commands. This story of humankind's fall from perfection has been used in Western cultures to account for the darker side of human nature.

Today the sciences, particularly geology, biology, and anthropology, have a different and naturalistic explanation to help us understand our duality. This scientific account began to be written with the work of the Scottish geologist James Hutton, who demonstrated in 1795 that the world was vastly older than previously had been believed. As this remarkable scientific deduction became generally accepted, humanity's presumably short past was stretched a thousandfold, and to the future, present, and immediate past of the historical period was added prehistory. Understanding this new dimension of humanity's story has become a major requirement for understanding our present.

Humankind Emerging is about this relatively newly discovered prehistoric dimension. It recounts the extraordinary story of the discovery of, and the evidence for, humanity's long past. It reveals to us the nature of our distant ancestors, who began the long evolutionary journey from the African forests to today's modern cities. It brings prehistory to bear upon the present-day human condition and thus gives us an entirely new way of approaching and understanding ourselves. The evolutionary perspective, which we owe to the genius of Charles Darwin and Alfred Russel Wallace, illuminates not only the physical origin of humankind but also the light and dark sides of our behavior. But that is not all: This perspective also shows us the integrated and dynamic evolution of both psychological aspects and their essentially interlocking relationship. The evolutionary perspective gives us profound insights into humanness and shows us that our duality arises not from two warring halves but from two interdependent aspects of an integrated whole—or what should and could be an integrated whole if we saw ourselves as we truly are, instead of as we have mistakenly believed ourselves to be.

This new view of human nature is just one small part of the revolution in knowledge and understanding brought about by the work of Charles Darwin and his successors. Our past has created us and influences or determines every part of our lives. Our present condition is a consequence not just of our individual life histories, important though they may be, but of the whole history of the human species. We are, in this sense, a product both of our childhood and of our prehistory.

The theory of evolution by the Darwin/Wallace mechanism of natural selection has now been developed over more than a century as a result of an enormous amount of painstaking research. The evidence that living organisms have evolved over many millions of years is today very strong and convincing. Science builds up such hypotheses or theories on the basis of a vast range of accumulated evidence derived from experiment and observation. Each new piece of evidence has corroborated the central theory. No evidence currently known either falsifies or undermines the theory of organic evolution by natural selection.

This book applies the Darwin/Wallace evolutionary model to the development of humankind, and thus it advocates a *naturalistic* explanation for our physical and behavioral attributes. But does this mean that we are setting out to disprove the existence of God or any role one or more divine forces might have played in the production of modern human beings? No. It is simply that such *supernaturalistic* explanations of human origins are beyond the bounds of scientific investigation and testing, and physical anthropologists like to keep their feet on the ground. Our only real argument with religion is when it attempts to masquerade as science, as in the present-day "creation science" movement (more on this at the end of Chapter 1). Science and religion may both be legitimate ways of "knowing" about the world, but they have very different modes of operation and thus should be neither confused nor mixed. Only evolution provides us with a truly scientific hypothesis about human origins.

Nonetheless, as we hope the following chapters will demonstrate, an evolutionary explanation of the origin of species, particularly our own, can be just as awe-inspiring and full of wonder as religious explanations. Indeed, this point was not lost on Charles Darwin who in 1859 ended his book *On the Origin of Species* with these words:

> There is a grandeur in this view of life, with its several powers, having been originally breathed into a few forms or into one; and that, whilst this planet has gone cycling on according to the fixed law of gravity, from so simple a beginning endless forms most beautiful and most wonderful have been, and are being, evolved.

THE SEARCH FOR HUMAN ORIGINS

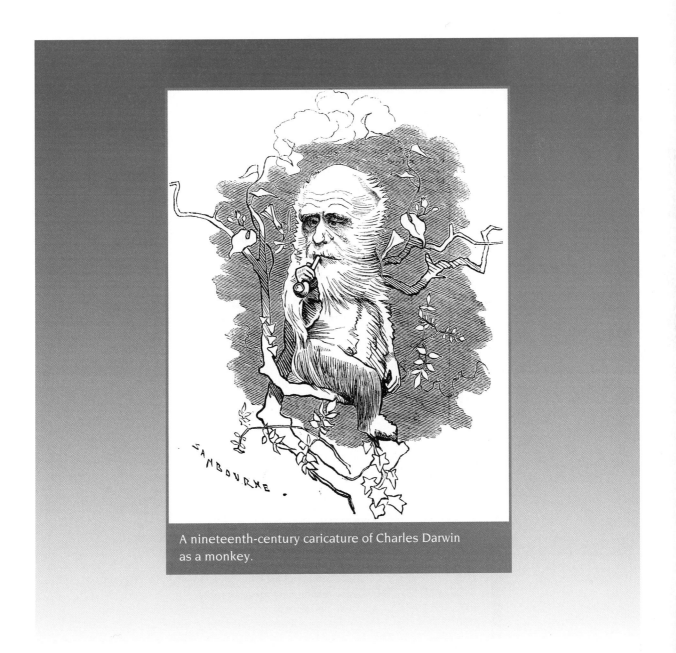

A nineteenth-century caricature of Charles Darwin as a monkey.

I would not be ashamed to have a monkey for my ancestor, but I would be ashamed to be connected with a man who used great gifts to obscure the truth.

THOMAS HENRY HUXLEY, 1825–1895. *Defending Darwin's theory against the attack of Bishop Samuel Wilberforce.*

OVERVIEW

Paleoanthropology the study of the fossil and cultural remains and other evidence of humans' extinct ancestors.

This is a book about **paleoanthropology**, the study of humans' physical evolution and the origins of modern behavior. Along with students of humankind's current biological variation, most paleoanthropologists can be classified more broadly as *physical anthropologists*. While other anthropological researchers focus mainly on humans' social and behavioral patterns (*cultural anthropologists* if their subjects are living; *archaeologists* if they study extinct societies) or on speech and language (*linguistic anthropologists*), physical anthropologists primarily concern themselves with our biology and its evolutionary development. Today, paleoanthropologists pursue the search for human origins within the Western scientific tradition, and therefore some knowledge of that tradition is necessary to understand current theories and discoveries. Toward that end, this opening chapter describes a series of historical events and scientific developments that contributed to our modern views on evolution. Beginning with the seventeenth century—when Europeans' opinions were shaped by the Biblical creation story and belief in a young earth—we will review sequentially the accumulation of geologic evidence for "deep time" (that is, for an ancient earth); the development of Charles Darwin's theory of evolution; Gregor Mendel's research into the problem of heredity; and finally, the (relatively recent) formulation of the modern synthetic theory of evolution. A short timeline is given below to help you learn the chronology of these developments. Important concepts in the chapter include creationism, deep time, James Hutton's "world machine" model, catastrophism, extinction, uniformitarianism, evolution, natural selection, particulate inheritance, genotype-phenotype, dominance-recessiveness, homozygosity-heterozygosity, Mendel's principles of segregation and independent assortment, mutation, and the modern synthesis.

 Mini-Timeline

YEARS A.D.	CONCEPT OR DEVELOPMENT
1930s–1940s	Modern synthetic theory of evolution
1880s–1920s	Mutation vs. natural selection controversy
1900	Gregor Mendel's work rediscovered
1866	Mendel publishes his work on heredity
1859	Charles Darwin publishes his theory of evolution by natural selection
1700s and 1800s	Evidence accumulates for "deep time"
1600s and 1700s	Antiquarians begin to recover evidence of ancient humans
1650	Bishop Ussher publishes his date of creation

PRESCIENTIFIC THEORIES OF HUMAN ORIGINS

Creation Myths and Bishop Ussher's Young Earth

For thousands of years, the question of human origins has preoccupied people of all cultures. Where did we come from? What forces have shaped our bodies, behaviors, and societies? How do we fit within the wide world of nature? This book attempts to answer these ancient questions from a modern, anthropological perspective, but for millennia the only available answers came from the **creation myths** of the world's various cultures and religions. These prescientific myths—always beautiful, imaginative, and often poetic—typically went beyond purely naturalistic explanations and described humans as the result of supernatural and divine creative acts. The creation story told in the Bible (Genesis 1; see Figure 1–1) is a particularly pertinent case in point because of the strong influence it exerted on

Creation myth a story describing the origins, usually supernatural, of the earth and life (including humans).

FIGURE 1–1 A woodcut from Schedel's *World Chronicle of 1493* depicting God's creation of woman from Adam's rib as told in Genesis.

thought in Western Europe, the geographic region destined to be the cradle of modern evolutionary theory.

According to the Genesis account, God created the earth and all of its inhabitants, including the first people, during six days of labor. Humans, created in God's own image, were then blessed, given dominion over all the other species, and directed to be fruitful and multiply. These two themes, our divine origins and earthly dominion, were stressed by the Christian church and widely accepted throughout post-Renaissance Europe. The Bible was generally taken quite literally—to do otherwise might have meant condemning oneself to a fiery Hell—and church teachings affected the world views of people at all levels of society. Finally, on top of everything else, it was believed that God's burst of creativity had occurred rather recently and that the earth was only a few thousand years old.

The notion of a young earth was universal and supported by the Irish Archbishop James Ussher (1581–1656), who in 1650 A.D. published his calculated date for the creation of the world. Based partly on biblical references, Bishop Ussher determined that the year of creation was 4004 B.C, not quite 5700 years before his own day! Subsequently, this date was inserted as a footnote to authorized versions of the Bible, and before long it acquired the infallibility of Scripture itself. Furthermore, the validity of a young earth must have seemed assured when the Reverend John Lightfoot, who was working independently but following in Ussher's footsteps, confirmed 4004 B.C. as the creation date and added the detailed information that it happened on October 23 at nine o'clock in the morning. The few discoveries from nature that suggested a greater antiquity for the earth—the fossilized remains of marine shellfish collected from high mountain slopes, fossil bones unlike those from any living creature, petrified wood—were generally explained away either as the chance results of natural forces imitating life or as the remains of unlucky creatures drowned in Noah's flood.

EARLY NATURALISTS BEGIN TO QUESTION HUMAN ANTIQUITY

Ancient Bones and Tools Found Together

Even in the seventeenth century, however, there were a few brave souls in Europe who dared to challenge orthodox views. The early antiquarian Isaac de la Peyrère (1594–1676), for example, concluded that certain chipped stones gathered from the French countryside had been made by primitive humans living at a time before Adam. Unfortunately, de la Peyrère's suggestion that the world might have gone through a period of pre-Adamite existence was too audacious for the times and his book was burned publicly in 1655. Happily, by the next century the pressure to conform to church teachings had relaxed somewhat, and in 1797 John Frere (1740–1807) announced his discovery from Hoxne, England, of apparently ancient stone tools associated with the bones of extinct animals. Frere concluded that the stone implements (Figure 1–2; now recognized as Acheulean tools, see Chapter 11) must have been "used by a people who had not the use of metals" [and who probably lived in] "a very remote period indeed; even beyond that of the present world." Scholars still weren't ready to accept the idea of prehistoric humans, how-

FIGURE 1–2   An example of the Acheulean stone tools recovered from Hoxne, England.

ever, and although Frere's published report didn't draw the same sort of censorship as de la Peyrère's, it did go largely ignored for more than half a century until Jacques Boucher de Perthes and others began to construct an undeniable case for ancient human life.

Boucher de Perthes (1788–1868) was a French customs official who began in the 1830s to collect curiously chipped flints from the terraces along the Somme River—terraces that also contained the remains of extinct animals. He became convinced that his ever-growing collection of flints were tools shaped by the hands and brains of early humans (they are now classified as more examples of Acheulean tools, see Chapter 11), but in 1847 when he published his findings under the title *Antiquites Celtiques et Antediluviennes*, Boucher de Perthes gained not a single convert. Equally unappreciated was the work of the Catholic priest, Father J. MacEnery (1796–1841). In 1829, MacEnery conducted excavations in a cave called Kent's Hole in southeastern England. Digging through an unbroken layer of stalagmite—and thus into quite old cave deposits—MacEnery found mammoth, rhinoceros, and cave bear bones, along with several unmistakable flint tools. Unfortunately, when he reported his find, MacEnery found himself opposed by another antiquarian cleric with a greater reputation, namely William Buckland (1784–1856), Dean of Westminster. Buckland argued that MacEnery's discovery was best interpreted as the result of early, but definitely post-Adamite, Britons digging ovens through the stalagmite layer and then accidentally dropping some of their stone tools into the holes. MacEnery's protests fell on deaf ears, which was unfortunate since he was right and Buckland was wrong about the evidence from Kent's Hole. And, as it turned out, Buckland's interpretation of his own discoveries at the Welsh site called Goat Hole (Figure 1–3) was just as wrong. Buckland simply was not prepared to accept any evidence of ancient human life.

But for several reasons we should not be too harsh on scholars such as Buckland who were skeptical about the accumulating proof for prehistoric human life. For one thing, contemporary procedures for site excavation and data analysis were woefully lacking in scientific rigor. This made it easy for critics to argue that chipped stone tools and extinct animal remains could have come together by accident. Furthermore, the early antiquarians were still generally laboring under the

FIGURE 1–3 Excavation of the cave called Goat Hole in Wales took William Buckland many years. Although a human skeleton that he found there has since been dated to about 25,000 years B.P. (before the present), Buckland insisted that the bones were no older than Roman times. He described his finds in his book *Reliquiae Diluvianae* (1823), from which this figure comes.

impression that the earth was only a few thousand years old—a belief that essentially precluded theories about biological or cultural histories with any time depth.

In any event, scholarly views on human prehistory changed rather abruptly in the mid-nineteenth century, and the shift was especially clear in England. In 1858, the paleontologist Hugh Falconer (1808–1865) examined Boucher de Perthes' collection of stone tools and became convinced of their authenticity. Falconer then persuaded Joseph Prestwich (1812–1896) to examine the geology of the Somme valley—an exercise that resulted in strong proof of the commingling of chipped flint tools and extinct animals' bones on river terraces older than the modern geologic epoch. By 1863, Sir Charles Lyell (1797–1875), then one of England's leading geologists, was sufficiently convinced of the case for ancient humans to write a volume called *The Antiquity of Man* synthesizing the evidence. And finally, in 1865, the naturalist and archaeologist John Lubbock (1834–1913) proposed a classification scheme that separated the oldest and most primitive flaked implements—such as those found by Boucher de Perthes—from younger stone tools attributed to Celtic (pre-Roman) Europe. Lubbock coined the terms **Paleolithic** and **Neolithic** for the respective tool types.

This shift of attitudes alone could not carry human history very far into the past, however. For 200 years, belief in Bishop Ussher's model of a young earth had firmly capped the limits of prehistory at just a few thousand years. But, in fact, by the mid-nineteenth century, that model had very nearly collapsed under the weight of new geological discoveries and theories. It is to those developments that we must now turn our attention.

Paleolithic the Old Stone Age; the earliest stage of stone tool making, beginning about 2.5 million years ago.

Neolithic the New Stone Age; a late stage of stone tool making that began about 10,000 years ago.

GEOLOGY COMES OF AGE: THE THEORY OF DEEP TIME

Comte de Buffon

The heretical notions that the earth might be quite old (today often called the theory of **deep time**) and that it might have originated in a way different from the Genesis story actually had a few European advocates as early as the mid-eighteenth century. These scholars had to be cautious with their opinions, however, and sometimes they risked paying a high price for their theories. For example, the French naturalist Comte de Buffon (1707–1778) suggested in his 1749 work *Histoire Naturelle* that the earth had slowly and gradually developed from the matter produced when a comet collided with the sun. The forces that molded the globe, Buffon argued, were everyday processes such as erosion by wind and water, volcanic activity, and earthquakes. For his rashness, Buffon found himself threatened with excommunication from the Catholic Church and he publicly retracted his views.

Deep time the theory that the earth is billions of years old and thus has a long history of development and change.

James Hutton and the World Machine

With advances in geology, however, came increasing evidence in favor of deep time. As geologists read the accumulating "testimony of the rocks," some began to suspect that the extensive sedimentary deposits already discovered—layers of river gravels, sands, and marine limestones, sometimes dozens of feet thick and piled one on top of another—must have been laid down over long periods of time. One of the men working on this problem was the Scot James Hutton (1726–1797), who produced an important model of the world's formation even though he was more of an armchair theorist than a field worker. In 1795, Hutton published a book entitled *Theory of the Earth* in which he described the earth as a constantly decaying and self-renewing machine. His world machine model involved ordinary geological processes operating in an endless three-stage cycle. First, Hutton wrote, terrestrial surfaces decay through weathering and erosion, with the erosional products then being carried to the sea. Second, erosional products are laid down as horizontal marine deposits, which eventually solidify into rocks. And third, sooner or later, forces within the earth cause the marine rocks to be uplifted as new continents, at which point erosion and decay come into play once again. Hutton's proof that his world machine worked relied on features such as the unconformity shown in Figure 1–4. Here the deepest (and therefore, oldest) rock layers have been tilted into a vertical position (in contrast to their original, horizontal layering on the sea floor) and then eroded (which bears testimony to the fact that they were high and dry at that point). Then the area was once again submerged, allowing the horizontal layers of (young) rock near the surface to be deposited. That uplift has occurred once again is obvious from the scene of present-day countryside. Hutton's view of the immensity of deep time is neatly captured in his famous closing dictum: "No vestige of a beginning—no prospect of an end."

Georges Cuvier and Catastrophism

By no means was all of the geological action taking place in the British Isles, however. At about the same time that James Hutton was publishing his decay-and-restoration model, French paleontologist Georges Cuvier (1769–1832; Figure 1–5)

FIGURE 1–4 This engraving was published by James Hutton in 1795 in his book *Theory of the Earth*. It shows an unconformity—an ancient eroded surface—between the underlying vertical strata and the overlying horizontal strata of marine sediments at Jedburgh, Scotland. Since all these water-laid strata must have been deposited flat, it follows that the underlying sequence had arisen horizontally. Thus we know that the lower strata were uplifted and tilted through 90 degrees. The land so formed was then eroded and produced the horizontal surface of the unconformity itself. Later the land subsided (or the seas rose), and further marine strata were deposited. Finally, the land again rose (or the sea subsided), so that the strata formed a new land surface. Thus, from this single exposure of rock, Hutton was able to deduce that the land at this place had undergone two periods of marine deposition and two periods of uplift, the first very dramatic, the second gentle. Hutton had the genius to recognize the breathtaking significance of the sight: the immense antiquity of the earth.

FIGURE 1–5 Georges Cuvier, whose proof of extinction allowed fossils to be used as historical markers.

and others were discovering the bones of ancient elephants, mammoths, whales, and other exotic and apparently long-dead species in the rocks near Paris. (Cuvier recognized each species by its members' shared physical traits. See Chapter 2 for a discussion of modern definitions of species.) Cuvier also proved to be a genius at reconstructing the long-dead animals from their fragmentary remains, an ability that inspired novelist Honoré de Balzac to exclaim: "Is Cuvier not the greatest poet of our century? Our immortal naturalist has reconstructed worlds from bleached bones. He picks up a piece of gypsum and says to us 'See!' Suddenly stone turns into animals and another world unrolls before our eyes."

In all, Cuvier was able to show that at least 90 of the species he had recovered, as well as several genera (groups of similar species), apparently had disappeared entirely from the face of the earth. This was an extremely important discovery, because proving that extinction is a common fate of species opened the way for fossils to be used as historical markers in the geologic record (Figure 1–6). But how could this massive loss of life have occurred, Cuvier wondered? What destructive forces led to extinction of the species and what restorative forces controlled their replacement by later life forms? In order to answer these questions, Cuvier enlisted the aid of mineralogist Alexandre Brongniart (1770–1847) and together they began a detailed study of the mechanisms of fossil deposition and the record of ancient environments in the Paris countryside. They studied one geologic column (sequence of rock layers) after another, and found the strata to be variously filled with marine fossils, freshwater or land shells, the bones of terrestrial animals, or no

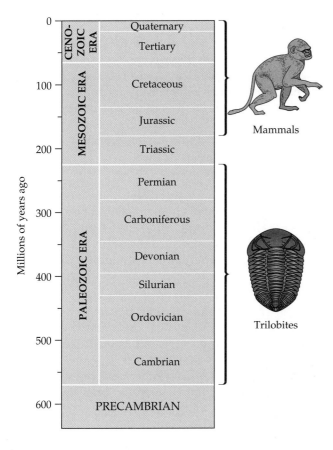

FIGURE 1–6 The use of fossils as historical markers became possible in the late 1700s and early 1800s, after scientists such as George Cuvier proved the reality of extinction. For example, trilobites were marine arthropods that were common on the world's sea floors during the Paleozoic Era. After a period of decline, trilobites disappeared completely about 245 million years ago. Thus, trilobite-bearing rock strata are easily recognized as older than those containing the fossilized remains of mammals, here represented by a modern monkey. (Note: Although a primate icon is used here, that particular order of mammals did not make its evolutionary appearance until the early Cenozoic Era; see Chapter 5.)

fossils at all. What sense could be made of this bewildering sequence of the comings and goings of life forms? Cuvier concluded that the history of life, in the Paris area and elsewhere, had been disrupted routinely by geologic "revolutions"—earthly convulsions related to buckling of the globe's crust as the world continued to cool down from an originally very hot state. These revolutions sometimes caused the seafloor to be raised and laid dry, or alternately, the dry land to be submerged. Such catastrophes (Cuvier's theory was dubbed **catastrophism**) were thought to have occurred suddenly and to have caused great loss of life and extinction of species over quite large areas. Following each catastrophe, Cuvier argued, devastated areas were repopulated by migrations of organisms, some entirely new for that locale, coming in from unaffected regions (some of Cuvier's followers elaborated on the basic theory by proposing that God might also have created a few new species to aid in each post-catastrophe repopulation). Significantly, Cuvier did not see these changes in plant and animal communities as the results of **evolution** (he was strongly opposed to the evolutionary theories of his compatriot Jean Baptiste de Lamarck), but nonetheless his work provided much new evidence in favor of deep time. For Cuvier, the world was not only ancient, but it had been shaped by a series of sudden and catastrophic shocks. On this last point, Cuvier was destined to be opposed by the gradualist model of change developed by Scottish geologist Charles Lyell.

Catastrophism Georges Cuvier's theory that vast floods and other disasters wiped out ancient life forms again and again throughout the earth's history.

Evolution cumulative changes in the average characteristics of a *population* generally thought to occur over many generations.

Charles Lyell and Uniformitarianism

By far the most influential nineteenth century statement on the antiquity of the earth and the forces that have shaped the globe was produced by Charles Lyell (Figure 1–7), who strongly countered Cuvier's views with his own gradualist model of earthly change. His three-volume work, *Principles of Geology*, published between 1830 and 1833, synthesized the available evidence for deep time and, building on the earlier work of Hutton and others, established a theoretical position quickly named **uniformitarianism**. Although Lyell applied his uniformitarian tenets primarily to geology, the young Charles Darwin read the *Principles*, adopted Lyell's theoretical model, and later applied it to the organic world.

In the *Principles*, Lyell made four uniformitarian claims:

Uniformitarianism Charles Lyell's theory that the forces now affecting the earth—water and wind erosion, frost, volcanism—had acted in a similar way in the past, and that change is always gradual and nondirectional.

1. *Uniformity of law:* Through space and time, natural laws remain constant.
2. *Uniformity of process:* When possible, past phenomena should be explained as the results of processes now in operation.
3. *Uniformity of rate:* Change usually occurs slowly and steadily.
4. *Uniformity of state:* Change, although continuous, is nondirectional and nonprogressive.

Lyell's world was thus one of constant and gradual, but nonprogressive, change produced by processes that could be identified and understood. And although his uniformitarian model provided the vast time needed for organic evolution to produce the diversity of living species, Lyell rejected such notions. The idea of evolution was "in the air" during the early nineteenth century, however, primarily because of the efforts of a French scientist, Jean Baptist de Lamarck.

FIGURE 1–7   Sir Charles Lyell in 1863. Lyell's gradualist model of change was adopted by Charles Darwin and applied to organic evolution.

THE ADVENT OF EVOLUTIONARY THEORIES

Lamarck

The French naturalist Jean Baptiste de Monet, Chevalier de Lamarck (1744–1829), was a friend of Buffon and provided the first persuasive theory that could account for the process of organic evolution. In his *Système des Animaux* (1801) and later books, Lamarck developed his theory of the means by which animal species had been transformed. He recognized that animals and plants were finely adapted to their environments and that their relationship was dynamic, with environmental change generating biological change and adaptation. He suggested that in their daily lives animals recognized certain needs, and that, through altered behavior patterns and the action of "subtle fluids" within the body, forces were generated that stimulated the development and growth of organs, even completely novel ones. Thus the evolution of the species was a response to need, to use, or to disuse of organs, and the changes produced in each generation were inherited. This theory is sometimes described as that of the "inheritance of acquired characteristics."

Although Lamarck's ideas were to be discredited, they were extremely important in the early part of the nineteenth century and had a small place in evolutionary biology until recently. The theory, however, is generally discounted because it has not been possible to prove the validity of Lamarck's main mechanism of evolutionary change that characteristics acquired during the lifetime of an individual are in fact passed on genetically to the succeeding generation.

Charles Darwin

Lyell's great work, *Principles of Geology*, was published in the early 1830s. Among its readers was a young man named Charles Darwin (1809–1882), who was destined to publish an even more revolutionary book, a book that combined Lyell's uniformitarianism with a valid mechanism of evolutionary change. Darwin's student life at Cambridge was undistinguished except in one respect: he was passionately interested in natural history and in collecting birds, butterflies, spiders, flowers, and even rocks—there was nothing in nature that did not fascinate him. While a student he became a great friend of the Reverend J. S. Henslow (1796–1861), the professor of botany, who gave him much encouragement. When Darwin heard of the sailing of one of the navy's survey ships, HMS *Beagle*, he joined first as the captain's companion, later as the ship's naturalist, and sailed around the world observing and collecting for nearly five years. The *Beagle* left Devonport on December 27, 1831, and returned to Falmouth on October 2, 1836. Three-and-a-half years were spent surveying and collecting along the coasts of South America, five weeks were spent in the Galapagos Islands of Ecuador, and a year was spent returning home via Tahiti, New Zealand, Australia, and South Africa (Figure 1–8). This voyage offered Darwin a priceless opportunity to carry his observations to foreign lands, and it gave him a brilliant panorama of the variety of organic life. One of the most important parts of the voyage for the later development of Darwin's ideas was the visit to the Galapagos or Enchanted Islands 600 miles off the coast of Ecuador.

Soon after his arrival there, Darwin wrote in his journal, "Here, both in space and time, we seem to be brought somewhere near to that great fact—that mystery of mysteries—the first appearance of new beings on this earth." Later he wrote, "It was most striking to be surrounded by new birds, new reptiles, new shells, new insects, new plants, and yet by innumerable trifling details of structure, and even by the tones of voice and plumage of the birds, to have the temperate plains of ... Patagonia, or the hot dry deserts of northern Chile, vividly brought before my eyes." Struck by the basic similarities yet subtle differences that linked the Galapagos fauna to that of the mainland, Darwin later learned that many species differed slightly from island to island, even though many of the islands were only 50 or 60 miles apart. From an analysis of his bird collections later made by John Gould (1804–1881), Darwin learned that the Galapagos finches constituted distinct species on the various islands but were all obviously related. On one island they had strong thick beaks used for cracking big nuts and seeds; on another the beak was smaller and used for catching insects; on another the beak was elongated for feeding on flowers and fruit (Figure 1–9). One species used a cactus spine to probe grubs out of holes in tree trunks and branches. Clearly the birds had found different foods on different islands and through successive generations had adapted in some manner so that they were better able to survive in their own particular environments. All this evidence was critically important in the development of Darwin's ideas.

When, in 1859, Charles Darwin published his revolutionary book *On the Origin of Species by Means of Natural Selection*, he presented a theory that was the product of many years of thought and observation. Darwin was encouraged to publish by

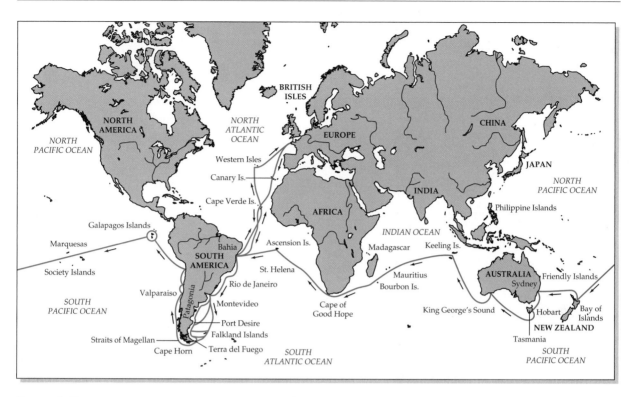

FIGURE 1-8 Charles Darwin left Devonport, England, in December 1831 and returned to Falmouth in October 1836. Out of the nearly five years spent on the voyage in HMS *Beagle*, Darwin spent more than three years in South America and its islands. The voyage was completed with visits to New Zealand, Australia, the Keeling (Cocos) Islands, the Cape of Good Hope, and St. Helena. Darwin's experience on this voyage was a rich and fertile source of observation and inspiration in the development of his ideas.

seeing the work of Alfred Russel Wallace (1823–1913), who, working independently, had come to similar conclusions (Figures 1–10 and 1–11). Both men had traveled widely and had observed in great detail the variation that exists within animal and plant species. Members of species, they noted, are not identical but vary in size, strength, health, fertility, longevity, behavior, and many other characteristics. Darwin realized that humans use this natural variation when they selectively breed plants and animals; a breeder selects to interbreed only particular individuals possessing the desired qualities.

FIGURE 1-9 These four species of Galapagos finch show some of the variety of form into which the beak evolved. The left species is most powerfully equipped and is adapted to crack big seeds and nuts. That on the right is adapted to feed from flowers and fruit. These species are all close relatives and all the descendants of an original South American ancestor.

FIGURE 1–10 Charles Darwin as a young man. In his *Autobiography* he wrote, "In September 1858 I set to work by the strong advice of Lyell and Hooker to prepare a volume on the transmutation of species, but was often interrupted by ill-health.... [The book] cost me thirteen months and ten days of hard labour." Darwin was an intermittent invalid for 40 years, but he found that invalidism had some advantages: "Even ill-health, though it annihilated several years of my life, has saved me from the distractions of society and amusement." He lived to the age of 73.

FIGURE 1–11 Alfred Russel Wallace was a complete contrast to Darwin in both background and character. Whereas Darwin did not need to work for a living, Wallace earned his way by collecting rare tropical plants and animals for private collectors and museums. As a result, he traveled far more widely than Darwin in both South America and Southeast Asia. Later in his life he wrote a number of books on evolution. Although of considerable interest, they do not have the originality and intellectual integrity of Darwin's writings.

Both Darwin and Wallace saw that a kind of *natural* selection was at work, and an understanding of the means by which selection operates in nature came to both from the same source. The first edition of *An Essay on the Principle of Population* by an English clergyman, T. R. Malthus (1766–1834), appeared in 1798. In his book Malthus showed that the reproductive potential of humankind far exceeds the natural resources available to nourish an expanding population. In a revised version of his essay, published in 1830, Malthus began, "In taking a view of animated nature, we cannot fail to be struck with the prodigious power of increase in plants and animals ... their natural tendency must be to increase in a geometrical ratio— that is, by multiplication." He continued by pointing out that, in contrast, subsistence can increase only in an arithmetical ratio: "A slight acquaintance with numbers will show the immensity of the first power in comparison of the second." And he had written in 1798, "By that law of our nature that makes food necessary to the life of man, the effects of these two unequal powers must be kept equal. This implies a strong and constantly operating check on population from the difficulty of subsistence." As a result, he argued, the size of human populations is limited by disease, famine, and war and that, in the absence of "moral restraint," such factors alone appear to check what would otherwise be a rapid growth in population.

Both Darwin and Wallace read Malthus's essay, and, remarkably, both men recorded in their diaries how they realized that in that book lay the key to understanding the evolutionary process. It was clear that what Malthus had discovered of human populations was true of populations of plants and animals: the reproductive potential vastly exceeds the rate necessary to maintain a constant population size. They realized that the individuals that do survive must be in some way better equipped to live in their environment than those that do not survive. It follows that, in a naturally interbreeding population, any variation that increased the organism's ability to produce fertile offspring would most likely be preserved and passed on to future generations, while the variations that decreased that ability would most likely be eliminated.

Darwin had carried these ideas for some years; he wrote a short sketch in 1842 and a more extended *Essay* in 1844 but was not prepared to publish either. He knew he would shock the public and his family; he could hardly face the implications of his thoughts. Wallace was held back by no such inhibitions, and early in 1858, after he read Malthus, the idea of natural selection occurred to him. He immediately sent a short paper on the subject to Darwin. Darwin received this paper on June 18. He was quite astounded and wrote in his diary, "I never saw a more striking coincidence; if Wallace had my MS sketch written out in 1842, he could not have made a better short abstract."

The Basis of Darwin's Theory

As the Harvard zoologist Ernst Mayr has recently shown, Darwin's theory of evolution through **natural selection**, as presented in *On the Origin of Species*, is based on five facts and three inferences (Figure 1–12). From Malthus, Darwin took the elements of organisms' potential superfecundity (Fact 1) and the limitations placed on population expansion by limited environmental resources (Fact 3). He combined these elements with the observation that most natural populations tend to remain stable in size rather than to constantly expand (Fact 2). From these three facts, Darwin (following Malthus) inferred that individual organisms (especially members of the same species) are in strong competition with one another (Inference 1). Combining this inference with the observation that individuals

Natural selection the principle mechanism of Darwinian evolutionary change, by which the individuals best adapted to the environment contribute more offspring to succeeding generations than others do. As more of such individuals' characteristics are incorporated into the *gene pool*, the characteristics of the *population* evolve.

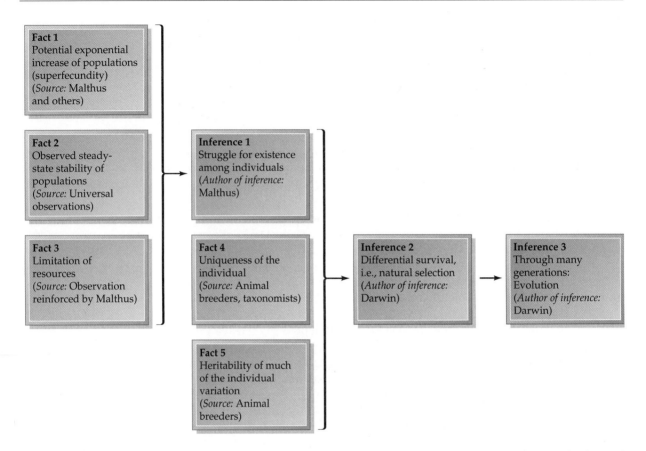

FIGURE 1–12   Zoologist Ernst Mayr has reduced Darwin's explanatory model of evolution through natural selection to five facts and three inferences.

Conspecifics members of
the same *species*.

(including **conspecifics**) show spontaneous variations in physical and behavioral traits (Fact 4) and the observation that parents often pass their individual variations on to their offspring (Fact 5) allowed Darwin to reach a second inference, that organisms experience differential survival and reproduction based on the possession of traits that are adaptive in their particular environment (Inference 2; this is the statement that we recognize as natural selection). Finally, Darwin argued that through the action of natural selection over many generations a species could slowly, but surely, *evolve* (Inference 3).

Thus natural selection was presented as a process by which adaptive traits are preserved (through the survival and reproduction of their carriers) and maladaptive (or *less* adaptive) traits are winnowed out of species. This process occurs in both plants and animals, and true to Lyell's uniformitarian principles, Darwin described the evolutionary process as extremely slow and gradual. Such a process clearly could not have been responsible for species diversity on Bishop Ussher's 6,000-year-old earth, but by the mid-nineteenth century, Hutton, Cuvier, Lyell, and others had provided ample evidence for deep time.

The first presentation of the Darwin/Wallace evolutionary model was made at the Linnaean Society in London over a year prior to the *Origin's* publication. On July 1, 1858, a paper entitled "On the Tendency of Species to Form Varieties, and on the Perpetuation of Varieties and Species by Means of Selection" was read before the fellows of the society. This was the first publication to the world of Darwin's and Wallace's theory, and the world has not been the same since that day. Neither Darwin nor Wallace was present.

It is impossible today to recreate the atmosphere of intellectual and moral shock that swept England when Darwin's book was published the following year (Figure 1–13). It was not that the evolution of plants or animals was so hard to swallow. After all, humans themselves had been responsible, through selective breeding, for the evolution of a number of domestic animals and a great variety of crops. Then there were those peculiar dinosaur bones that people had been digging up; they had to be explained, as did the growing evidence that the earth was not simply thousands of years old but hundreds of thousands, perhaps hundreds of millions. No, those things were not really the problem. What was so hard to accept

FIGURE 1–13 This 1861 *Punch* cartoon, which appeared two years after Darwin's publication of *On the Origin of Species*, typifies the contemporary reaction of shock to the idea that humans could be descended from apes.

was the implied suggestion that human beings were descended from a bunch of "repulsive, scratching, hairy apes and monkeys."

Those awful monkeys! As one Victorian lady is reported to have said, "My dear, let us hope that it is not true, but if it is, let us pray that it will not become generally known."

The genius of Charles Darwin's evolutionary theory becomes apparent when one considers that he constructed it despite the lack of two critical pieces of information. Darwin knew neither the sources of spontaneous variation within each generation (the basis of Fact 4) nor the mechanisms of intergenerational inheritance (the basis of Fact 5). (As it happens, a contemporary researcher, Gregor Mendel, was hard at work on those very problems, but Darwin was unaware of Mendel's findings. See the next section for more on Mendel's work.) Furthermore, Darwin was very careful about the way he presented his theory to the world, doing all he could to minimize giving offense to his readers. Of prime importance, in *On the Origin of Species*, Darwin refrained from mentioning the question of human origins with the exception of a single timid sentence near the end: "Light will be thrown on the origin of man and his history." But, the implication was plain, and nobody missed it.

In 1863, Thomas H. Huxley (1825–1895), a friend of Darwin and an ardent propagandist for his theory, published *Evidence as to Man's Place in Nature*. This was the first book to address itself in an orderly and scientific way to the problem of human origins. By making many telling anatomical comparisons between humans and the apes, Huxley established that, of all animals on earth, the African great apes—the chimpanzee and gorilla—are most closely related to humans (Figure 1–14). He further stated that the evolutionary development of apes and humans had taken place in much the same way and according to the same laws. From this it followed that, if prehuman fossils were ever found, older and older humanlike fossils would be found, leading eventually to types that would turn out to be

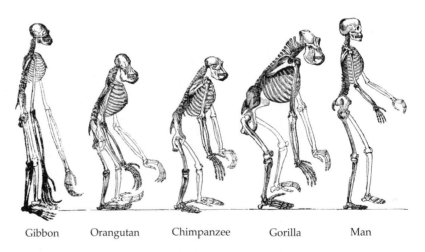

Gibbon   Orangutan   Chimpanzee   Gorilla   Man

FIGURE 1–14   In 1863, Thomas H. Huxley published this drawing of the skeletons of the four apes and a human to illustrate their extraordinary similarity. He wrote, "Whatever part of the animal fabric might be selected for comparison, the lower apes (monkeys) and the Gorilla would differ more than the Gorilla and the Man." All drawings are to the same scale except the gibbon, which is drawn to twice the scale.

ancestral to both apes and humans. And these common ancestors would probably be found in Africa.

Darwin, confronted by the same relationship of fossil species to living ones, saw that the latter were the modified descendants of the former. Carrying the case to its full conclusion in *The Descent of Man*, published in 1871, Darwin propounded the theory of an unbroken chain of organisms that began with the first forms of life and evolved to humans. Here was a true scientific theory, a theory of evolution subject to proof. But where was the proof? Where were the bones of this multitude of organisms? Surely many of them should have survived in the earth, yet the fossils found up to Darwin's day supplied only the most fragmentary evidence. Where were the missing links? It was a painful time for the evolutionists. Despite all the logic in Huxley's and Darwin's views, they were difficult to support, because in Africa, or indeed anywhere else, there was an embarrassing lack of fossils resembling human beings.

At this turning point in the history of human knowledge, there had emerged two great and related ideas about the origin of nature and of humankind: the earth is extremely ancient, long populated by many kinds of animals, some of which are no longer living, and humans themselves, mutable creatures like the animals, have their ancestors far back in time. But how far back and who those ancestors were nobody had even the slightest notion. Almost everything we know about our ancestry we have learned in the past one hundred and thirty years, much of it during the past four decades.

GREGOR MENDEL AND THE PROBLEM OF HEREDITY

Charles Darwin deduced the operation of natural selection even though he was missing two major pieces of the evolutionary puzzle, namely the sources of variation and the mechanisms of heredity. From personal observations and reading, Darwin knew that all species contain a variety of individuals in every generation and, additionally, he shared the common knowledge that offspring often inherit parental traits. Folk wisdom in Darwin's day held that blood was intimately involved in the passage of traits from parent to child, a belief that resulted in sayings such as "Blood will tell." Mother's and father's bloods (and therefore, traits) were thought to be coalesced somehow in each of their children, but logical as it may have seemed, this notion of **blending inheritance** raised some formidable problems. After all, if each child is a blend of the parents' characteristics, the long-term effect should be an overall loss of variation within the population. That is, new individuals should be born increasingly alike in each succeeding generation as individual differences are diluted through blending. And yet the opposite is true: In sexually reproducing species, variability is maintained over time and often increases.

Unknown to Darwin, the problems that proved so intractable for him—variation and inheritance—were beginning to yield their secrets to an Augustinian monk named Gregor Johann Mendel (1822–1884; Figure 1–15). Born in a small village in what is now the Czech Republic, Mendel was, in his own words, "addicted to the study of Nature" from his youth. He learned much about plants and horticulture from his father, Anton, who was renowned for his fine fruit trees. Later, after enter-

Blending inheritance an outmoded theory stating that offspring receive a combination of all characteristics of each parent through the mixture of their bloods; superseded by Mendelian genetics.

ing the Augustinian monastery at Brunn at the age of twenty-one, Mendel combined his religious studies with a lengthy series of botanical experiments designed to elucidate the natural laws that control variation and inheritance.

The Experiments

True breeding (breeding true) situation in which the members of a genetic strain resemble each other in all important characteristics and show little variability.

Reviewing earlier studies of plant hybridization, Mendel realized that most had been poorly designed and rather haphazardly carried out. He realized that success depended not only on systematic work done on a large scale, but of equal importance, on selecting the right species for study. For his inheritance work, he needed **true-breeding** plants, plants that showed little spontaneous variation from gener-

FIGURE 1–15 Gregor Mendel's country childhood gave him a deep knowledge and sympathetic understanding of the plant world. As a monk with some leisure, he took up plant breeding in the monastery garden, with remarkable and brilliant results.

Box 1-1

CURRENT ISSUE: The Relevance of Paleoanthropology

Reviewers of earlier versions of this book indicated that students are interested in learning how its contents can have everyday relevance. To that end , we have created a series of Current Issue boxes that appear throughout the text. Other topics of present-day interest are discussed in the Postscripts at the end of each chapter.

It may not be immediately obvious what possible relevance ancient bones and stones can have to our present occupations and problems. Almost any branch of science can immediately be seen to have a greater impact on the present world than the study of human evolution.

This is not, however, a realistic assessment of the value of our study. We all know now that we are the product of our genes and our environment, and have been fashioned over millions of years to be as we are. Life has been evolving for more than two billion years, and we are one of its most remarkable products. It follows that we are the product of our past experience as a species. To a great extent, our bodies are adaptations to past environments and our minds are no different. The fact that we have evolved some degree of free will is the single factor that tends to free us a little from the stamp of history and prehistory. But our genes hold our personalities on a leash and we cannot stray far from the anchor of our genetic blueprint.

Our study of bones and stones tells us how we were made: It is as simple as that. If you want to understand a complex mechanism, you find out how it is made and the principles that underlie its design. To understand ourselves, it is essential to understand how we were made, and the principles that operated during our formation. That is, it is necessary to study and plot in detail the evolution of our bodies and behavior.

Why do we need to understand ourselves? Because this is the only way that we will be able to develop a world society that is capable of sharing and preserving this planet in peace. To give a few examples, if we want to live free of the threat of destruction at the hand of maverick politicians, we need to understand the driving forces that are operating in their lives and the lives of people generally. If we want to solve the problems of crime in our countries, we need to understand what drives people to criminal acts. If we want to preserve the world and its resources into the next century and beyond, we need to understand how we became creatures who "live for the moment," but have little demonstrated talent in planning for the distant future.

You may answer that many of these issues fall within the purview of psychologists, not of paleoanthropologists. Up to a point that is true, but without the historic and prehistoric evidence, the psychologists can never fully understand their subject. All biological research must be done under the rubric of evolution. This is the essential and revealing key that alone can deliver the understanding we need.

The logic is inescapable. To understand ourselves, we must understand the past. That is why the study of human evolution, seemingly so far from everyday problems, is really the most basic and fundamental science of all. It lies at the root of all human studies, from psychology to political science, and from medicine to management. ■

ation to generation. He also needed a species whose pollination he could control easily, for otherwise systematic cross-fertilizations would be impossible. Mendel ended up choosing the common garden pea for most of his experimental work.

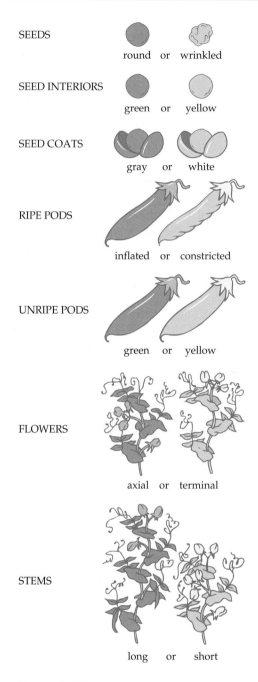

SEEDS
round   or   wrinkled

SEED INTERIORS
green   or   yellow

SEED COATS
gray   or   white

RIPE PODS
inflated   or   constricted

UNRIPE PODS
green   or   yellow

FLOWERS
axial   or   terminal

STEMS
long   or   short

FIGURE 1–16 Mendel's pioneering observations of the pea plant were based on a comparison of these seven easily identifiable characteristics.

The garden pea was a good choice because it presents several traits that are easily observed and manipulated. Mendel chose seven characteristics for systematic investigation (illustrated in Figure 1–16), the most important of which, for the following discussion, were pea form and pea color—round or wrinkled, green or yellow. He was now ready to begin producing hybrids and he started with a simple cross between wrinkled-pea and round-pea plants grown from seeds he had bought, taking great care to prevent accidental pollination from plants outside his study and removing the anthers or stigma of each flower (the male and female organs) to avoid self-fertilization. After the necessary time for fertilization, growth, and pea development, Mendel was able to observe the results of his experiment. Upon opening the pods, he found only round peas (Figure 1–17). The wrinkled trait, which had existed in half of the parent plants, seemed to have disappeared completely! (Similar disappearances of one variant or the other were found in Mendel's other first-generation hybrids—green pea color disappeared after a green-yellow cross, and short plant height disappeared after a short-tall cross.)

After due consideration, Mendel decided to call the characteristic that prevailed (such as roundness in Figure 1–17) **dominant**, and the one that apparently disappeared, **recessive**. But what, Mendel wondered, would happen to the dominant and recessive traits if the hybrids were allowed to self-fertilize as they would normally? He made the experiments and waited. When at last he could examine the traits of second generation plants, Mendel found that the recessive characteristics had reappeared! In the round-wrinkled cross, for example, wrinkling was back in about one-third of the peas (Figure 1–18), and round and wrinkled peas could be found side by side in the same pod. In general, dominant traits outnumbered their recessive counterparts by a 3:1 ratio in the second generation.

Dominant describes a trait that is expressed in the *phenotype* even when the organism is carrying only one copy of the underlying hereditary material (one copy of the responsible *gene*).

Recessive describes a trait that is expressed only when the organism is carrying two copies of the underlying hereditary material (two copies of the responsible *gene*).

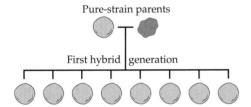

Pure-strain parents

First hybrid | generation

FIGURE 1–17 This diagram shows the results obtained when Mendel crossed a plant produced by round seeds with one produced by wrinkled seeds. The hybrid seeds show the character of only one parent (round); this character Mendel termed *dominant*. Mendel obtained similar results with the other six pairs of characteristics.

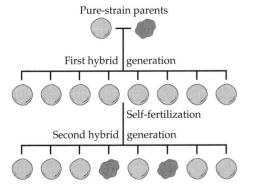

Pure-strain parents

First hybrid | generation

Self-fertilization

Second hybrid | generation

FIGURE 1–18 The production of a second hybrid generation by the self-fertilization of plants produced by the seeds in Figure 1-17 showed that the first-generation hybrids had carried the characteristics of both their parents, but with the wrinkled characteristic hidden. The new generation of seeds was made up of both kinds (like the pure-strain parents), but came in the proportion of three round ones to one wrinkled.

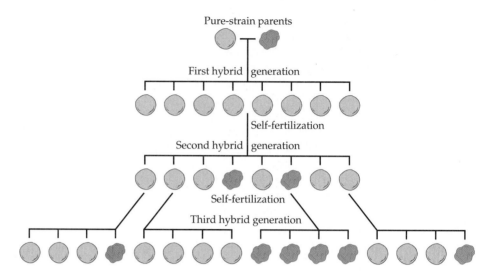

Pure-strain parents

First hybrid generation

Self-fertilization

Second hybrid generation

Self-fertilization

Third hybrid generation

FIGURE 1–19   Mendel found the explanation of the 3:1 proportion shown in Figure 1-18 when he allowed the second generation plants to self-pollinate. In the third hybrid generation, he found new combinations of characteristics. The wrinkled seeds had bred true (and would always do so); some of the round peas also bred true, while others repeated the 3:1 ratio.

Phenotype the observable characteristics of a plant or an animal; the expression of the *genotype*.

Genotype the genetic makeup of a plant or animal; the total information contained in all *genes* of the organism.

Gene an hereditary unit that codes for a particular trait; see Chapter 2 for additional—and more detailed—definitions.

Homozygous having identical versions of a *gene* (*alleles*) for a particular trait.

Heterozygous having different versions of a *gene* (*alleles*) for a particular trait.

And there were more surprises in store. When Mendel planted his second generation of peas and then allowed those plants to self-fertilize, he obtained mixed results. Recessive characteristics always bred true (for example, plants grown from wrinkled peas produced only wrinkled peas). Plants with dominant traits, however, came in two types: one-third were true-breeding, but two-thirds acted like hybrid seeds of the first generation and produced both dominant and recessive offspring at a ratio of 3:1 (Figure 1–19). Pondering these results, Mendel drew several conclusions that took him a long way toward solving the riddle of heredity. First, he reasoned that an organism's visible characteristics (now called its **phenotype**) are not always an accurate representation of its set of hereditary qualities (now, its **genotype**). This discovery not only explained why some plants with dominant traits could produce mixed descendants, but it also forced a second major conclusion: that hereditary qualities are nonreducible *particles*. These particles (now called **genes**) are not blended during sexual reproduction, but rather retain their identities as they are passed from parents to offspring. And third, Mendel's mathematical results—his ratios of offsprings' traits—suggested that hereditary particles generally function as pairs, with a particle expressing its trait unless it is blocked (dominated) by its partner.

A simple way to visualize the connection between hereditary pairs (genotype) and visible traits (phenotype) is shown in Figure 1–20. Here dominant particles are labeled *A* and recessive ones *a*. With regard to the form of Mendel's peas, hybrids with *Aa* genotypes would be round (of course, so would all *AA* individuals). Crossing two such hybrids could potentially produce three different genotypes (*AA*, *Aa*, and *aa*) and both possible phenotypes (round and wrinkled). Today, individuals with similar genes for a trait (*AA* and *aa*) are said to be **homozygous**, while those with different genes (*Aa*) are described as **heterozygous**.

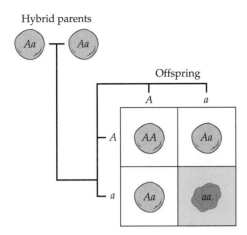

FIGURE 1–20   The experiment described in
Figure 1-18 was explained by Mendel in this way:
Using the letters *A* and *a* for the characters smooth
and wrinkled, he accounted for the 3:1 proportion
by proposing that *A* is always dominant to *a* in
every hybrid.

Mendel's Hereditary Principles

Mendel eventually looked at much more complex cases than just single contrasting
characteristics. As shown in Figure 1–21, simultaneously studying two traits—pea
form (round, wrinkled) and pea color (green, yellow)—produced a greatly enlarged
set of possible genotypes reducible to four phenotypes with a 9:3:3:1 ratio. In addition, Mendel identified a few traits (for example, flower color in beans) that seemed
to be controlled by two pairs of hereditary particles rather than one. In all, his work
allowed Mendel to formulate several important biological laws:

1. Heredity is transmitted by a large number of independent, nonreducible
   particles that occur as pairs in individual organisms. These hereditary particles retain their distinctive identities regardless of the nature of their pair-
   partners. This is the *principle of particulate heredity*, and it disproved the old
   notion of heredity as a matter of blending.
2. Each hereditary pair is split during the production of sex cells (sperm and
   eggs, or pollen and ovules) so that a sex cell has only one particle from any
   pair. This is the *principle of segregation*. New pairs are formed, of course, as
   a result of fertilization.
3. Hereditary particles for different traits generally are inherited independently of one another. This is the *principle of independent assortment* (see
   Figure 1–21 for an illustration).

These principles, along with the detailed results of Mendel's long years of
work, were read to the Brunn Society for the Study of Natural Science in 1865 and
published in that society's proceedings in 1866. Unfortunately, Mendel's work
found few interested readers, and virtually no one at the time recognized how far
he had gone toward answering the basic questions about heredity. It would be the

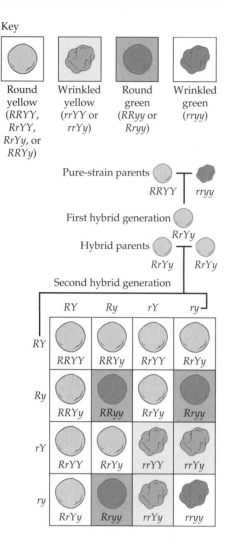

FIGURE 1–21 The Punnett square shows Mendel's law of independent assortment. A pea with two dominant characteristics (roundness and yellowness, *RR* and *YY*) is crossed with a pea having two recessive characteristics (wrinkledness and greenness, *rr* and *yy*). The hybrid combines all four genes of its parents (*RrYy*). If these hybrids are crossed, their genes produce the combinations shown: four kinds of peas appearing in a ratio of 9:3:3:1.

turn of the century before Mendel's work was rediscovered, and in the meantime, the man now widely viewed as the "father of genetics" devoted the rest of his life to leadership duties as abbot of his monastery.

TURN OF THE CENTURY: MENDEL REDISCOVERED, NATURAL SELECTION OUT OF FAVOR

Hugo De Vries and the Mutationists

The decades following Darwin's and Mendel's deaths in the 1880s found scientists in general agreement about the occurrence of evolutionary change, but at odds concerning such basic questions as the sources of spontaneous phenotypic variation and the effectiveness of natural selection. The confusion among biologists was

Figure 1–22 Hugo De Vries was a Dutch botanist of great distinction. From his observations of the evening primrose, *Oenothera lamarckiana*, De Vries developed a theory of mutation that was to prove important in our understanding of genetics. He was also the first to recognize the importance of Mendel's observations—thirty-five years after Mendel announced them.

compounded by the fact that Mendel's detailed work on inheritance, having never gained much recognition when it was published, had been forgotten.

Among the workers caught in this muddle was Hugo De Vries (1848–1935; Figure 1–22), a botanist at the University of Amsterdam. De Vries accepted Darwin's thesis that descent with modification is the main law of change among organisms, but he wondered how large differences between species could ever be produced by natural selection, picking and choosing among small, individual variations. De Vries had a hunch that **mutations**, spontaneous (and sometimes substantial) changes in an organism's characteristics, are more important than natural selection in directing the path of evolution. Darwinians recognized the occasional sudden appearance of new traits—so-called *sports of nature*—but credited them only with secondary importance. For his studies of mutations, De Vries chose to work with the evening primrose, a plant capable of wide variations in each generation. His observations carried out for more than a decade reinforced De Vries's confidence in the power of mutations, and also led him to several of the same conclusions that Mendel had formulated thirty-five years earlier, especially the conclusion that hereditary units are "distinct, separate, and independent" particles. Indeed, as De Vries conducted a literature search in 1900 prior to publishing his primrose data, he came across Mendel's long-lost paper, and only then realized that much of his work had been anticipated by the Moravian monk. (By a remarkable coincidence, Mendel's paper was also rediscovered by two other researchers,

Mutation generally, a spontaneous change in the chemistry of a *gene* that can alter its phenotypic effect. The accumulation of such changes may contribute to the *evolution* of a new *species* of animal or plant.

one German and one Austrian, in that same year.) Behaving honorably, De Vries gave full credit to Mendel, whose discoveries were at last given the scientific acclaim they deserved.

And so, as the twentieth century got underway, Mendel's principles of inheritance had not only been rediscovered, but also confirmed. The controversy between mutationists like De Vries and traditional Darwinians (believers in natural selection as the main evolutionary mechanism) continued to rage, however, with a new line of mutationist evidence being advanced: the evidence of mimicry in nature. Probably the most striking cases of mimicry involve cross-species matches in appearance, as demonstrated for butterflies in Figure 1–23. Often mimics gain a degree of protection against predators, for example, by becoming the look-alikes of tough or bad-tasting prey species. The mutationists claimed that such wonderful resemblances could have arisen only by mutation since intermediate types—quarter-mimics or half-mimics that had abandoned their own original camouflage but had achieved only a portion of the model's protective coloration—would be maladaptive. How, except by mutation, could the elaborate markings and other bodily designs of mimics ever have come into being? Mimicry, the mutationists argued, is *the* outstanding proof of the power of mutations, a power that might even extend to the relatively instantaneous production of entirely new species through **macromutations**. (Such large-scale mutations—that may involve doubling or tripling the original genotype—are more common in plants than in animals, although not unknown among the latter.) For their part, the Darwinians vigorously disagreed with the idea of saltatorial (jumpy) evolution, and they backed up their arguments with a new weapon: mathematics.

Macromutation a large and genetically inherited change between parent and offspring.

The Emergence of the Modern Synthesis

That natural selection is, in fact, the primary mechanism of evolution was demonstrated in the early twentieth century by Ronald Aylmer Fisher (1890–1962), J. B. S. Haldane (1892–1964), Sewall Wright (1889–1988) (Figure 1–24), and other mathe-

FIGURE 1–23 Mimicry occurs quite widely among animals (and even some plants). In this example, the monarch butterfly *Danais plexippus* (top) is mimicked by the viceroy butterfly *Limenitis archippus* (bottom). Both butterflies have an orange ground and black and white markings. Experiments have demonstrated the function and effectiveness of this mimicry: The monarch butterfly is protected from predators by its unpalatability; the viceroy is protected by mimicking it.

[a] Ronald Aylmer Fisher (1890–1962)

[b] J. B. S. Haldane (1892–1964)

[c] Sewall Wright (1889–1988)

FIGURE 1–24

matically inclined biologists. Fisher, in particular, zeroed in on the mutationists' pet phenomenon, mimicry. He proved conclusively that natural selection acting on small variations is the only force that could bring about the intricate matches of mimic to model. The coincidental occurrence of the same traits in mimics and models due to random mutations is so unlikely as to be mathematically impossible. Besides, said Fisher, the mutation theory explained neither why mimics and models are always found in the same regions and during the same season, nor why mimicry is usually only "skin deep" (involves no more copying of traits than is necessary). In the end, the mathematical arguments prevailed and, in accordance with Darwin's original position, natural selection reemerged as the main force driving evolutionary change. Mutation took on the role as the primary source of new genetic material. Thus, mutations contribute to phenotypic variations that are then either rejected or, more rarely, preserved and molded by the action of natural selection.

Progress in the newly formed science of Mendelian genetics continued during the first two decades of the twentieth century. It was not until the 1930s and 1940s, however, that Darwin's theory of natural selection was finally combined with Mendel's theory of heredity to produce a genetically based evolutionary model. Fisher, Haldane, and Wright were all part of this development, along with other scientists such as Julian Huxley (1887–1975; the grandson of T. H. Huxley) and Ernst Mayr (1904–present). The new model was dubbed the *synthetic theory of evolution* or, following the title of an important book by Julian Huxley, the *modern synthesis* (it is also occasionally called *neo-Darwinism*). The modern synthesis has proved remarkably resilient to subsequent testing and refinement, and as we enter the twenty-first century, it prevails as the universally accepted evolutionary paradigm. The next chapter presents more detailed information about genetics and the ways populations of organisms evolve.

SUMMARY

During the past four centuries, our understanding of the earth's origin—and our own—has changed dramatically. In the seventeenth century, the Christian creation myth of a divine origin was widely accepted in Europe, as was Bishop Ussher's calculation of the young age of the earth. The young earth theory fell victim to geological discoveries during the next two hundred years, however, and, in addition, in 1859 Charles Darwin published a convincing theory of evolution by natural selection that was quickly applied to the question of human origins. Darwin developed his theory without much knowledge about the source of phenotypic variations or the mechanisms of inheritance, but Mendel's work (which marked the beginning of the science of genetics) went a long way toward correcting that lack of knowledge. Building on Mendel's achievements, De Vries, Fisher, Haldane, Wright, and others produced a series of further discoveries in genetics. Finally, during the 1930s and 1940s, Darwin's theory of natural selection was united with Mendelian genetics to produce the synthetic theory of evolution, a theory that still guides the work of biologists (including physical anthropologists) today.

POSTSCRIPT

Fundamental Judeo-Christian beliefs and Biblical literalism are alive and well in the United States and several other parts of the world. A 1993 Gallup poll found that 49 percent of adult Americans believe that humans are the result of special creation by God within the last 10,000 years. While **creationism** is believed in by only a tiny minority of scientists, its acceptance by a substantial portion of the American populace has important implications. Creationists argue that their Bible-based explanation of human origins is as valid as the evolutionary explanation and thus deserves equal time in public school curricula. They insist that their studies are based on sound scientific principles and even refer to their work as *creation science*. Anthropologists, geologists, and other traditional scientists have responded to the fundamentalists' challenge by arguing that "creation science" is a sham and no science at all. The argument goes like this: Traditional science works through the development of *theories* (broad sets of principles that explain bodies of facts) and *hypotheses*. Scientific theories are constantly tested by generating hypotheses (falsifiable research predictions), which are then tested by laboratory experimentation or field observations. If most of the predictions (hypotheses) generated by a theory prove to be correct, then the validity of the entire theory is supported. On the other hand, if one's hypotheses consistently prove to be wrong, the validity of one's theory is destroyed. Based on the results of hypothesis testing, scientific theories are maintained unchanged, are modified, or are discarded. The theory of evolution, for example, has been subjected to repeated tests ever since Darwin's day, and though extended and modified in places, it has survived essentially intact.

Scientists argue that the problem with creation science is that the fundamentalists' basic theory—that God created the world and its inhabitants recently and in a short time span—is not really open to falsification. Creationists may formulate hypotheses and gather data, but since their theory is truly an article of faith, there is no possibility of changing or discarding it, regardless of their results.

Creationists continue to press local school boards and textbook publishers to include their views. And traditional scientists continue to argue that, while material on creationism may be included legitimately in Bible courses or studies of comparative religion, it does not belong in the science classroom. What do you think? Your stand on this question could well affect your children's future public education.

> **Creationism** the belief that humans and all life forms were specially created by God or some other divine force.

REVIEW QUESTIONS

1. Describe the effects of Christian beliefs on the development of evolutionary theory and studies of human prehistory.
2. Discuss the development of deep time within European science. What were the implications of this development for evolutionary theory?
3. Georges Cuvier and Charles Lyell had very different ideas about the pattern and pace of geologic change. Compare Cuvier's catastrophism with Lyell's theory of uniformitarianism.
4. Describe how competition and natural selection are related in Charles Darwin's evolutionary model.
5. Explain how Gregor Mendel's work refuted the old concept of blending inheritance.

6. Since offspring in sexually reproducing species are the result of mother's egg uniting with father's sperm, it seems that children should have twice as many genes as either parent. But, of course, they don't. What does this have to do with Mendel's principle of segregation?

7. What is the synthetic theory of evolution? When was it developed and what are its constituent parts?

SUGGESTED FURTHER READING

Darwin, Charles. *On the Origin of Species* (facsimile of 1st ed.). Harvard University Press, 1996.

Eisley, Loren. *Darwin's Century: Evolution and the Men Who Discovered It.* Doubleday, 1958.

Fisher, Ronald. *The Genetical Theory of Natural Selection.* Clarendon Press, 1930.

Gould, Stephen J. *Time's Arrow, Time's Cycle.* Harvard University Press, 1987.

Huxley, Thomas. *Man's Place in Nature.* University of Michigan Press, 1959.

Mayr, Ernst. *The Growth of Biological Thought: Diversity, Evolution, and Inheritance.* Harvard University Press, 1982.

Price, Peter. *Biological Evolution.* Saunders College Publishing, 1996.

Ridley, Mark. *Evolution*, 2nd ed. Blackwell Science, 1996.

INTERNET RESOURCES

ENTER EVOLUTION: THEORY AND HISTORY
http://www.ucmp.berkeley.edu/history/evolution.html
(This web site provides biographical sketches of several scientists who contributed to "deep time" and/or evolutionary theories.)

MENDELWEB
http://www.netspace.org/MendelWeb
(Information about the life and work of Gregor Mendel and the origins of classical genetics.)

NATIONAL CENTER FOR SCIENCE EDUCATION
http://www.natcenscied.org/
(Information about the continuing controversy over teaching evolution and "creation science" in the public schools.)

VICTORIAN SCIENCE: AN OVERVIEW
http://www.stg.brown.edu/projects/hypertext/landow/victorian/science/sciov.html
(Part of The Victorian Web, this site provides background information about Charles Darwin and other nineteenth-century scientists.)

USEFUL SEARCH TERMS (FOR YOUR OWN WEB EXPLORATIONS):
Charles Darwin
creationism
evolution
history of geology
phylogeny

Chapter 2

EVOLUTIONARY MECHANISMS

RNA strands (lateral branches) shown being synthesized on DNA (vertical line).

E*volution is always happening. What [geneticists mean by that is] the genes of this generation are not precisely what they were in the preceding generation. Nor will they be precisely the same in the next. And evolution is that change. And it is almost a certainty, a mathematical certainty, that the genes will never be the same.*

PETER GRANT, quoted in J. Weiner's *The Beak of the Finch* (1994).

OVERVIEW

Chapter 2 provides a primer on the science of genetics and the mechanisms of evolutionary change. Taking its lead from the modern synthetic theory of evolution, the chapter focuses mainly on change at the level of the population, but attempts throughout to show how the survival and reproduction of individuals contributes to the characteristics of the population. The chemistry (DNA, RNA) and functioning of genes are described, including the role genes play in protein synthesis. Next comes a discussion of the contributions of mutation and crossing-over to phenotypic variation at the level of the population, followed by material on the nature (and definition) of species. Gene flow, an important non-Darwinian mechanism, is examined as part of the biological species concept, and this is followed by descriptions of the evolutionary effects of natural selection, genetic drift, and the founder effect. The Hardy-Weinberg theorem, one of population geneticists' most useful tools, is then described. The chapter ends with discussions of speciation (particularly allopatric speciation), extinction, and the question of progress in evolution. Important concepts from this chapter include the gene pool, collective phenotype, fitness, adaptation, chromosomes, DNA, RNA, meiosis, crossing-over, point mutations, heritability, species, biological species concept, gene flow, natural selection (directional and stabilizing), genetic drift, founder effect, balanced polymorphism, genetic load, Hardy-Weinberg theorem, sexual selection, allopatric speciation, phyletic transformation, extinction, and progress in evolution.

LEVELS OF SELECTION AND CHANGE

The modern synthetic theory of evolution proposes that changes in species' traits are the results of altered frequencies of Mendel's hereditary particles—that is, altered gene frequencies. In strong contrast to the mutationists' theory, which focused on the spontaneous modifications of *individual* organisms as the basis of evolutionary change, the modern synthesis focuses on genetic changes produced by natural selection working within **populations** of plants and animals. (Typically, a population is a subunit of a *species*. Further information about the connection between populations and species is given on pages 46 through 49. For now, just think of a population as a geographically localized breeding group of conspecifics.) Evolutionary biologist Ernst Mayr has described the emergence of the modern synthesis as a shift to "population thinking," and one of the main goals of this chapter is to get you used to thinking about biological change in this way. A second goal is to make sure that you understand how natural selection (aided by certain

Population usually, a local or breeding group; a group in which any two individuals have the potential of mating with each other.

other processes) shapes groups of organisms over time. This primer on the mechanisms of evolutionary change is a necessary prerequisite for applying Darwinian theory to the specific case of human origins.

Of course, the mutationists were partially right in their belief that individual organisms contribute fundamentally to evolutionary change. But contributing to evolution is not the same as actually evolving personally. By definition, individuals cannot evolve, only populations can do that. That is, only populations can show the sort of intergenerational changes in genes and traits that qualify as evolution. Individuals make their contributions by surviving (or not), reproducing (or not), and getting their genes into the next generation (or not). And as certain individuals succeed and others fail, the population itself is modified over time. Therefore, in order to understand evolution fully, you must learn to pay attention simultaneously to two levels of biological activity: individual organisms, each trying to survive and reproduce, and populations, each reflecting the cumulative results of its members' efforts. At first, this sort of two-level awareness may seem difficult, but it gets easier with practice. As a framework to get you started, we can identify three types of linkage between individuals and their populations, as shown in Table 2-1.

Genes, Genotypes, and Gene Pools

Every living creature is characterized by its genotype, its own entire set of **genes**. (Note: some scientists prefer the term *genome* here, using genotype to refer only to subsets of genes linked to specific traits. We prefer the broader meaning of genotype.) The vast majority of genes are located in the nuclei of the individual's cells (Figure 2–1), where they are organized into structures called **chromosomes**. (This term, which means "colored bodies," refers to the fact that at certain stages of cell growth the chromosomes can be stained by researchers and viewed microscopically; see Figure 2–2). A few genes can also be found outside the nucleus within organelles called **mitochondria** (Figure 2–1), where they take the form of closed loops of hereditary material. Of the two types, nuclear and mitochondrial, nuclear genes are infinitely more important in the production of an organism's phenotypic traits (mitochondrial genes seem to be related mainly to the organelles' own functioning and to general cell chemistry). Nonetheless, mitochondrial genes may have the potential to help scientists date evolutionary events and analyze taxonomic relationships (more on this topic in Chapters 14 and 16).

Genes provide, in effect, a blueprint for the construction, operation, and maintenance of individual organisms. So-called "structural genes" tend to produce, and thus end up being named for, particular traits. For example, humans have eye color genes, skin color genes, and even genes that determine our susceptibility to certain diseases. Additionally, there is an important set of "regulatory genes" that

Genes primarily, functional units of the *chromosomes* in cell nuclei, controlling the inheritance of phenotypic traits; some genes also occur in *mitochondria*.

Chromosomes coiled, threadlike structures of *DNA*, bearing the *genes* and found in the nuclei of all plant and animal cells.

Mitochondria granular or rod-shaped bodies in the cytoplasm of cells that function in the metabolism of fat and proteins. Probably of bacterial origin.

TABLE 2-1   *A Framework for Understanding Darwinian Evolution*

INDIVIDUAL	POPULATION
Genotype	Gene pool
Phenotype	Collective phenotype
Fitness	Degree of adaptation

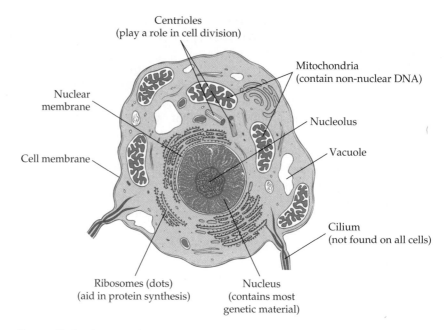

Centrioles
(play a role in cell division)

Nuclear
membrane

Cell membrane

Mitochondria
(contain non-nuclear DNA)

Nucleolus

Vacuole

Cilium
(not found on all cells)

Ribosomes (dots)
(aid in protein synthesis)

Nucleus
(contains most
genetic material)

FIGURE 2–1   This simplified diagram of an animal cell shows the nucleus (containing the gene-bearing chromosomes) separated from the remainder of the cell's contents (the cytoplasm) by the nuclear membrane. Important structures to note within the cytoplasm include the ribosomes, which contribute to protein synthesis, and the mitochondria, which contain nonnuclear DNA.

control the metabolic, energetic, and biosynthetic activities of the body. The genetic blueprint is rather flexible, however, and the details of the resulting phenotype—which specific traits make up an individual's phenotype—are always dependent on complex interactions between the organism's genes and its environment. An obvious example in this connection is body size. Genes for large body size may not be expressed fully when coupled with environmental factors such as poor nutrition or disease during development, and, as a result, the adult individual will be smaller than its genetic potential for growth. The gene-and-environment relationship is expressed in the following simple, but important, formula:

Genotype + Environment = Phenotype

Gene pool all of the *genes* of a *population* at a given time (summing genes within a species yields the species' gene pool).

Following Table 2-1, summing the genotypes of the members of a population yields information about the **gene pool**. A full inventory of a population's gene pool would list all of the various genes and their frequencies. This ideal situation has not yet been achieved for humans or any other species, however, and population geneticists can usually draw conclusions only about the frequencies of a few well-studied genes. A good example of this kind of study is shown in Figure 2–19 (p. 62) and it involves calculations of the M and N blood type genes among the Quinault Indians, a Native American tribe from Washington State. Of the MN blood genes of the Quinaults, 63 percent are gene *M*, while the remaining 37 percent are gene *N*. If one could show a clear shift in these percentages over time, it

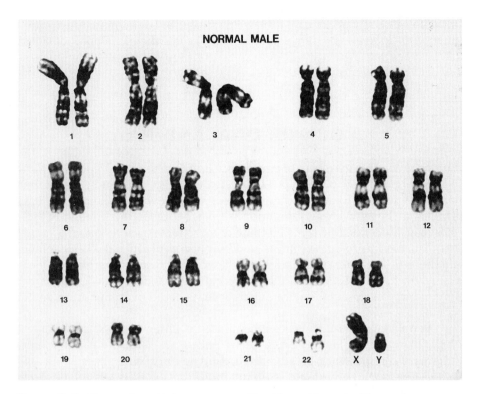

NORMAL MALE

FIGURE 2–2 Humans have 46 chromosomes as 22 or 23 matching pairs. The sex chromosomes (labeled X and Y) are indicated in this photograph from a male human. Only males have the small Y chromosome, and so in this sex, the twenty-third pair cannot be matched. Females have two similar X chromosomes.

would be strong proof of evolution. Indeed, *documenting change in the composition of a population's gene pool is the very best way to show that evolution has occurred.*

Phenotypes and Collective Phenotypes

There is a second, although somewhat less satisfactory, way to show that evolution has taken place, and that is to document transgenerational phenotypic change. As described in Chapter 1, individual organisms possess not only genotypes, but also phenotypes. If we pool the trait data for all members of a population, we can draw conclusions about the population's **collective phenotype**. For continuous traits, such as body weight, statements about the collective phenotype take the form of a mean value plus a measure of variation around that mean (humans' average weight = 128 ± 2 lb [58 ± 1 kg]; the variation is best measured in standard deviations). For discontinuous traits, such as blood types, collective phenotype statements express the percentages shown by the various phenotypic states. The blood-group data in Figure 2–19 once again provide a good example. Among the Quinault Indians, almost exactly 50 percent of individuals show the MN blood *type* (note that blood types are different from blood genes), just over 38 percent show type M, and about 11 percent show type N. When aspects of a population's collective phenotype show clear evidence of change across generations, scientists are justified in concluding that evolution has probably occurred. Such a conclusion is warranted even though we may lack information about the population's genetic

Collective phenotype the set of phenotypic averages and norms that characterize a *population* or *species*.

makeup—as is always the case for fossil populations. To summarize, evolution can only be documented by demonstrating changes in either gene pools or collective phenotypes.

GENES, DNA, AND RNA

But we're about to get ahead of ourselves. Clarifying how genotypes are related to gene pools, and how phenotypes are related to collective phenotypes, are important steps toward understanding the workings of evolution under the modern synthesis. The third linkage identified in Table 2-1 relates the "fitness" of individuals (usually defined by some measure of reproductive success) to the "adaptedness" of their populations (measured by phenotypic match to environmental conditions). These are key concepts and deserve full discussions, but first we need to backtrack and get a more thorough grounding in modern genetics. Of particular importance is a closer look at the details of genes' location, composition, and functioning.

As noted earlier, most genes occur as part of chromosomes, those interesting threadlike structures found in cell nuclei. Each living species has a characteristic number of chromosomes, the so-called **diploid number** (symbolized $2n$). This is the full chromosomal count and it occurs in all *somatic* cells (all cells except the **gametes**, eggs, and sperm). Gametes, or sex cells, in contrast, possess a **haploid number** of chromosomes, or half of the full count (symbolized n). Diploid numbers for some well-studied species include 14 in Mendel's pea plants, 40 in house mice, 42 in baboons, 48 in chimpanzees and gorillas, and 46 in humans. Careful readers will have noticed that diploid numbers are always even. This is because somatic cells primarily contain pairs of **homologous chromosomes**—pairs that resemble each other in shape, size, and their sequence of genes (see Figure 2–2). The pair of **sex chromosomes**, however, is an exception to this rule. The X and Y chromosomes that determine femaleness or maleness are quite different in shape, size, and genetic contents (Figure 2–2). Among mammals, inheriting two Xs results in development as a female, while an XY combination results in development as a male. Obviously, in sexually reproducing species, babies' diploid numbers are produced by the union of haploid egg with haploid sperm at conception.

The possibility that the chromosomes might contain the cell's hereditary material was first suggested in 1902 by Walter Sutton in the United States and Theodor Boveri in Germany. Numerous discoveries since then have amply confirmed this suggestion and collectively give us a detailed picture of the chemistry of chromosomes and genes. We now know that chromosomes consist of long, spiraling strands of **DNA** (*deoxyribonucleic acid*), a substance that was first discovered in 1869 by Friedrich Miescher and whose composition and structure were worked out by Francis Crick, Rosalind Franklin, James Watson, and Maurice Wilkins in 1953 (Figure 2–3). Another way to understand genes, then, is to view them as basic functional subunits of DNA—segments of DNA that can be identified with particular phenotypic effects—that tend to occur at particular chromosomal locations or loci (singular, **locus**). But it's a little more complicated than that. A gene at a particular locus may show several different forms and these variants are called **alleles**. Alleles influence the same phenotypic trait, only differently. Gregor Mendel's work, described in Chapter 1, provided several examples of alleles and their pair-

Diploid number the full *chromosome* count in somatic cells (all cells except *gametes*)

Gametes reproductive *haploid* cells generated by *meiosis*, which fuse with *gametes* of the opposite sex in reproduction; in animals, eggs and sperm.

Haploid number the number of *chromosomes* carried by *gametes*; one-half of the full count carried by somatic cells.

Homologous chromosomes *chromosomes* that are similar in shape, size, and sequence of *genes*.

Sex chromosomes *chromosomes* carrying *genes* that control gender (femaleness or maleness).

DNA (deoxyribonucleic acid) chemical substance found in *chromosomes* and *mitochondria* which reproduces itself and carries the *genetic code*.

Locus the position of a nuclear *gene* on a *chromosome*; each locus can carry only one *allele* of a gene.

Alleles *genes* occupying equivalent positions on paired *chromosomes*, yet producing different phenotypic effects when *homozygous*; alternative states of a gene, originally produced by *mutation*.

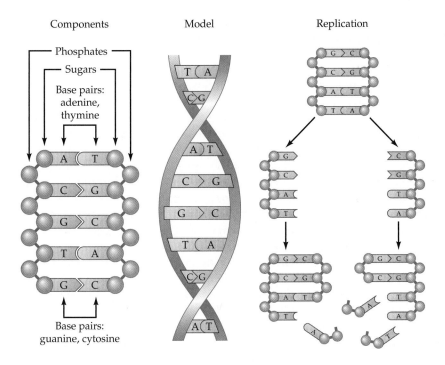

Components Model Replication

FIGURE 2–3 The DNA molecule is a double spiral (or helix) linked by four interlocking chemical subunits: the base pairs. Replication and protein synthesis take place by the splitting of the double helix: each separate strand replicates by synthesizing its mirror image from the unit molecules floating in solution, as shown here.

wise interactions. As shown in Figure 1-21, *R* and *r* represent alleles (variant types) of the gene for pea form. Depending on the combination of alleles that a new plant inherits during fertilization, it can be homozygous dominant (*RR*, producing round peas), heterozygous (*Rr*, also producing round peas), or homozygous recessive (*rr*, producing wrinkled peas). So far so good, but how do genes actually go about producing phenotypic traits? To answer that question, we must literally unravel the DNA molecule.

The DNA of a chromosome consists of two long, interlocking polynucleotide chains arranged in a double helix (Figure 2–3). The backbone of each chain is a series of linked sugar and phosphate molecules (deoxyribose phosphates), and each sugar-phosphate unit is bonded to a single **nucleotide** base. These bases come in four varieties—(A) adenine, (T) thymine, (G) guanine, and (C) cytosine—and the two chains are held together in a helical structure by the bonds between complementary nucleotide pairs (A with T, G with C). If the two chains are separated for individual analysis, each can be described by its sequence of nucleotide bases, for example, ACGTTGCAA. The nucleotides work in groups of three adjacent bases (e.g., ACG; such a triplet is called a **codon**) to code for the production of particular **amino acids** as part of protein synthesis within the cell (this is the first step in the production of phenotypic traits). Each gene consists of a long sequence of codons (humans' genes range in size from a few hundred to tens of thousands of base pairs) that work together to produce a particular protein.

The DNA double helix actually becomes partially unraveled into two individual chains in two circumstances. First, this occurs as part of chromosomal replication (sometimes called gene replication) during both forms of cell division. During

Nucleotides organic compounds, consisting of bases, sugars, and phosphates; found in cells either free or as part of polynucleotide chains.

Codon a *nucleotide* triplet that codes for the production of a particular *amino acid* during *protein* production.

Amino acids a group of organic compounds that act as building blocks for *proteins*.

mitosis, the normal division process of somatic cells, all of the chromosomes form replicas (thus temporarily doubling the genes in the nucleus) and then the cell divides once. This results in identical twin copies of the original diploid cell. In contrast, during *meiosis*, the process of reduction division that results in gametes, a single act of chromosomal replication is followed by two episodes of cell division. This produces haploid sex cells (see Figure 2–9; meiosis is described in greater detail in a later section concerned with the sources of phenotypic variation). In any event, during both types of cell division, each polynucleotide chain serves as a template for the formation of its partner from newly synthesized sugar-phosphate-base units (Figure 2–3). The second circumstance of DNA unraveling is during the transcription of DNA information into **RNA** (*ribonucleic acid*) as a step toward protein synthesis (Figure 2–4). A brief look at protein synthesis reveals more details of the structure of genes and the process of phenotype production.

Proteins are complex molecules composed of long chains of amino acids. They take a variety of forms, and collectively they coordinate and control our basic life processes, being involved in growth, development, reproduction, and bodily maintenance (one researcher has remarked that proteins "breathe life" into the information contained in genes). Examples of proteins include hemoglobin (responsible for oxygen and carbon dioxide transport throughout the body), collagen and keratin (building blocks of connective tissues and hair), the antibodies active within our immune system, and the enzymes that catalyze our biochemical reactions. The cellular process that results in protein synthesis begins with partial unwinding of the DNA helix (Figure 2–5). Transcription of the DNA information then starts as a strand of "messenger RNA" (mRNA) and is synthesized by complementary base pairing onto the DNA template. Interestingly, only certain portions of each gene's DNA, called **exon** segments, actually code for protein production. Long stretches of noncoding DNA, called **intron** segments, must therefore be removed from the mRNA template after transcription is completed. This is done through a process called *splicing* that leaves the mRNA with only exon information (Figure 2–6).

Once a gene is completely transcribed, the mRNA strand is released, and the DNA helix re-forms. Messenger RNA is then engaged by particles called **ribosomes** that move along the mRNA chain and catalyze the translation of proteins, triplet codon by triplet codon (Figure 2–7). A key element in this process is the action of another form of RNA—"transfer RNA" (tRNA)—in engaging amino acids

RNA (ribonucleic acid) a compound found with *DNA* in cell nuclei and chemically close to DNA; transmits the *genetic code* from DNA to direct the production of *proteins*. May take two forms: messenger RNA (mRNA) or transfer RNA (tRNA).

Proteins molecules composed of chains of *amino acids*.

Exons segments of a *gene's* DNA that code for *protein* production.

Introns segments of a *gene's* DNA that do not code for *protein* production (so-called noncoding DNA).

Ribosomes cellular organelles that contribute to *protein* synthesis.

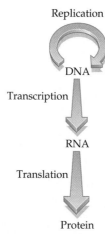

FIGURE 2–4 The relationships between DNA and RNA that function during gene replication and protein synthesis.

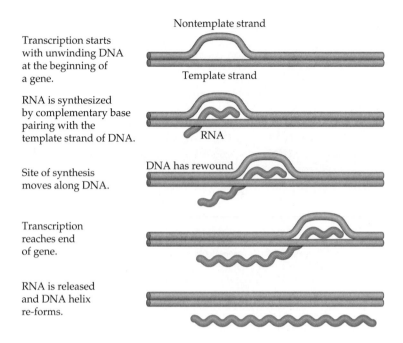

Transcription starts with unwinding DNA at the beginning of a gene.

Nontemplate strand

Template strand

RNA is synthesized by complementary base pairing with the template strand of DNA.

RNA

Site of synthesis moves along DNA.

DNA has rewound

Transcription reaches end of gene.

RNA is released and DNA helix re-forms.

FIGURE 2–5   The basic sequence of events during DNA-to-RNA transcription.

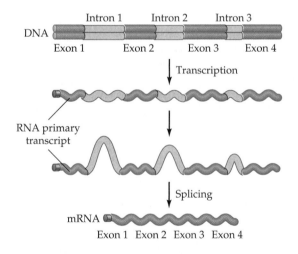

Intron 1   Intron 2   Intron 3

DNA

Exon 1   Exon 2   Exon 3   Exon 4

Transcription

RNA primary transcript

Splicing

mRNA

Exon 1   Exon 2   Exon 3   Exon 4

FIGURE 2–6   RNA splicing after transcription removes the noncoding introns and leaves only exon information.

and then positioning them on the mRNA template. Bit by bit, amino acids are assembled into long protein chains, all of which will contribute to the formation or operation of the organism's phenotype.

Two final points need to be made before we end this section on the chemistry of genes. First, it bears repeating that by no means does all of a cell's nuclear DNA actually contribute to protein (and therefore, phenotype) production. Introns are noncoding sequences and, surprisingly, they account for much more DNA than do exons. Furthermore, at certain points on chromosomes, tandem repetitions of DNA sequences (called **satellite DNA**) tend to accumulate, and these are also likely to be

Satellite DNA tandem repetitions of *DNA* sequences that accumulate at certain locations on *chromosomes* and usually are noncoding.

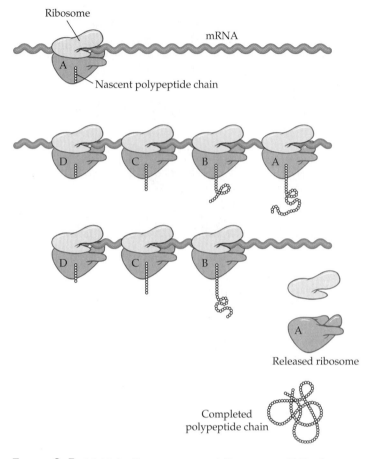

FIGURE 2–7 Multiple ribosomes sequentially engage mRNA after transcription and, aided by tRNA (not shown), catalyze the translation of the polypeptide chains that will form proteins. When a ribosome has completed its portion of polypeptide synthesis, it is released from the mRNA chain.

noncoding. Current estimates of the total proportion of humans' DNA that is noncoding range from 75 to 90 percent. Just think how much sorting and splicing (Figure 2–6) is required to extract our (relatively few) exon sequences from all of the noncoding material surrounding them! Scientists have yet to learn precisely how and why the "silent" sequences of DNA accumulated, and what functions (if any) they serve. One idea is that the noncoding DNA may have a structural function, to keep the genes correctly spaced within the three-dimensional DNA molecule. Alternately, the extra DNA may just be noncoding "junk." Future studies should lead to the resolution of this issue.

The second point concerns the universal occurrence of the DNA genetic code (Appendix I). Scientists have found that in virtually all life forms the same 61 DNA triplets encode the same 20 amino acids. Furthermore, one triplet (ATG) functions universally as a "start" codon marking the beginning point for a protein coding sequence, while three triplets (TAA, TAG, TGA) function as "stop" markers. This remarkable discovery argues as powerfully as the entire fossil record that all life has evolved from a single ancestral source. If Charles Darwin could come back to life and read these words, he would chuckle and say, "I told you so!"

SOURCES OF GENETIC AND PHENOTYPIC VARIATION

A resurrected Darwin would also be keenly interested in modern information about the sources of trait variation among conspecific organisms. Remember that Darwin formulated his evolutionary theory without the slightest notion as to why variation occurs in every new generation—he simply knew that you could count on it. Today, evolutionary biologists consider two distinctly different processes to be the main sources of phenotypic variation: gene mutations and chromosomal mixing and recombination during gamete production (meiosis and crossing-over).

Mutations

Modern humans are estimated to carry about 100,000 genes per haploid gamete, which multiplies into 200,000 alleles per diploid somatic cell. As in all living creatures, spontaneous changes in humans' DNA sequences occur constantly and randomly. Such changes, called **point mutations**, can change the allelic identity of genes and influence an offspring's phenotype if they are carried on gametes and thus inherited. (Mutations in somatic cells also occur, but they cannot be inherited. Somatic mutations may contribute to the development of diseases such as cancer, however.) Although mutations occur constantly, in humans they have a low average rate of about 1 mutation per 100,000 copies of a gene (rates vary for different genes, with some genes mutating at one-third this speed and others ten times as fast). The mutation rate of an organism's genes may be increased, however, through exposure to environmental stimuli such as radiation and certain chemicals (the rate also increases with age). H. J. Muller won the Nobel Prize in 1946 for his work on X-ray–induced mutations in fruit flies.

Point mutations may be as small as the substitution, addition, or loss of a single nucleotide base. Many point mutations are never expressed phenotypically because of DNA's ability for self-repair back to the original condition. (Specialized enzymes exist for DNA repair. Single-strand damage, such as missing or mismatched bases, is repaired using the undamaged strand as a template. Double-strand damage can be repaired after chromosomal recombination during meiosis [see next section] provides unaltered DNA as a template.) Even when expressed, mutations do not necessarily produce completely new alleles and monstrous traits, although these do occur occasionally as shown by the fruit fly in Figure 2–8 that has developed legs in place of antennae. Many mutations simply alter a gene from one known allele (and trait) to another, as in the case of humans' normal blood-clotting allele mutating into the allele that causes hemophilia, a pathological condition characterized by bleeding due to inadequate clotting. Sometimes, of course, entirely new genetic variants *are* produced, and therefore mutations must be ranked as the primary source of new alleles in a species' gene pool.

But are constantly occurring point mutations responsible generation after generation for the vast amount of individual phenotypic variation seen in all species? Probably not. First of all, the mutation rates are too low. And second, most new mutant alleles are quickly lost from the gene pool. In some cases they are eliminated by natural selection, being selected against because they code for deleterious traits. Given the random nature of mutation, it is unusual for the process to produce beneficial genetic changes (just as a random adjustment inside a computer is unlikely to improve its performance, a random addition to a species' gene pool is

Point mutation usually the substitution of one *nucleotide* in a single *codon* of a *gene* that affects *protein* synthesis and *genotype*; gene *mutation*.

FIGURE 2–8 Due to a mutation, this fruit fly has grown legs in front of its eyes in place of antennae. (Image magnified 140x.)

unlikely to be useful to anyone who inherits it). In many other cases, mutant alleles disappear through chance loss alone. It has been calculated that even mutant alleles with small selective advantages stand a 90 percent chance of disappearing within thirty generations. Mutations do not serve, therefore, as the main source of phenotypic variation in each generation. A much better candidate exists for that important role: meiosis, the cell division process that produces eggs and sperm.

Meiosis and Crossing-over

The reduction division process of meiosis is remarkable in many ways. Not only does it reduce the chromosome count of gametes to the haploid number, but it also provides the basis for extensive phenotypic variation in every generation by producing genetically unique sex cells. While mutation stands as the ultimate source of new alleles and allelic variation, meiosis must be viewed as the primary (and proximate) source of genotypic variety among individuals.

Meiosis involves one chromosomal replication and two cell divisions (Figure 2–9). Before the first cell division, each chromosome replicates itself to produce two **chromatids**. The duplicated chromosome with its two elements then pairs with its homologous partner, and this pairing yields clusters of four chromatids called *tetrads*. As the tetrads line up at the equator of the fibrous spindle that stretches between the **centrioles** (Metaphase I), the chromatids in each may overlap at points called **chiasmata**. **Crossing-over**, or the exchange of sections between homologous chromosomes, may then take place at these sites (Figure 2–10). During the next stage (Anaphase I), the homologous chromosomes (each still consisting of two chromatids) separate and move toward opposite poles of the spindle (technically, the two halves of the dividing cell are now haploid, since we count chromosomes, not chromatids). At this point, any or all of the four chromatids formerly making up a tetrad may contain a different mixture of genetic material from their original condition.

The first meiotic division is then completed, and the second begins (in females of some species—such as our own—the first division in potential egg cells begins prenatally, is suspended between birth and puberty, and is then completed—along with the second division—by a few cells every month between puberty and menopause). The second meiotic division occurs without further replication of the genetic material and involves the separation of chromatids (Anaphase II). The potential result of meiosis is the production of four haploid "daughter" cells (this

Chromatid one of the two elements in a duplicated *chromosome*.

Centrioles minute granules present in many cells outside the nuclear membrane. The centriole divides in cell division, and the parts separate to form the poles of the spindle.

Chiasmata points where the *chromatids* of a tetrad overlap and segment exchange may occur; crossover points (singular, chiasma).

Crossing-over the exchange of sections between *homologous chromosomes*.

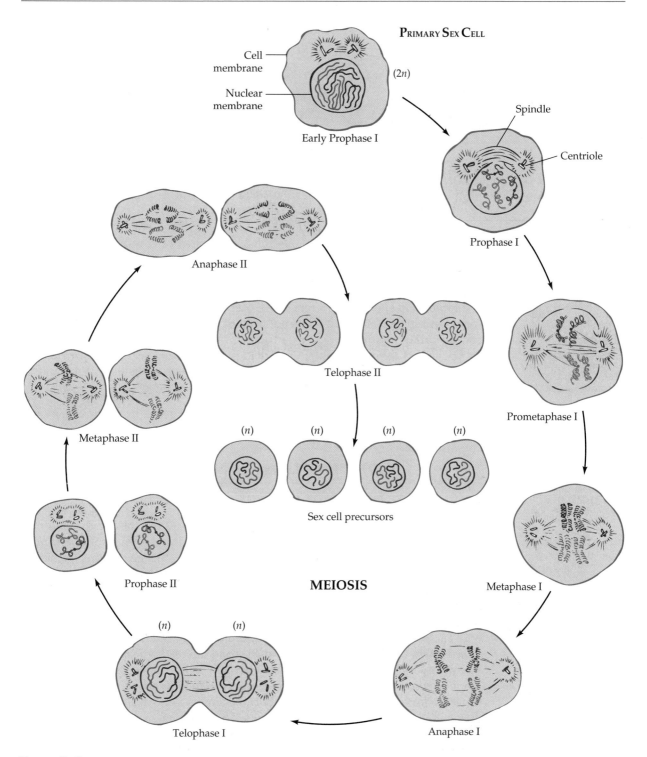

Primary Sex Cell

Cell membrane

Nuclear membrane

(2n)

Early Prophase I

Spindle

Centriole

Prophase I

Prometaphase I

Metaphase I

Anaphase II

Telophase II

(n)   (n)   (n)   (n)

Sex cell precursors

MEIOSIS

Metaphase II

Prophase II

(n)   (n)

Telophase I

Anaphase I

FIGURE 2–9 Meiosis. The single replication of genetic material occurs in Prophase I. Crossing-over within the tetrad takes place in Metaphase I, producing numerous reconstituted chromosomes. Two cell divisions then follow that (potentially) result in four haploid gamete precursors.

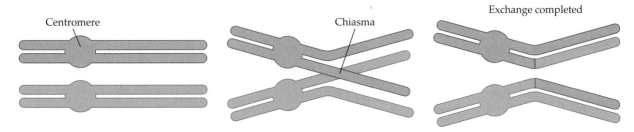

FIGURE 2–10 A simple example of crossing-over and segment exchange among the chromatids of a tetrad.

term is used for both sperm and egg cells), each genetically unique. This potential is realized in men (four sperm cells from each original parent cell), while in women only one energy-rich egg is produced from every parent cell.

Evolutionary change via natural selection can proceed only if conspecifics vary phenotypically and trait differences are based, at least partially, on genetic differences (within a population, the proportion of phenotypic variance attributable to genetic variance is referred to as a trait's level of **heritability**). Meiosis, with its genetic and chromosomal mixing, provides the basis for gene-based phenotypic variations. The stage is now set for evolution at the levels of the population and the species.

Heritability a property of phenotypic traits; the proportion of a trait's interindividual variance that is due to genetic variance.

POPULATIONS AND SPECIES

Various Definitions of Species

As we discussed earlier in the chapter, the modern synthetic theory of evolution is based on "population thinking." Although individuals' contributions to evolution through the generation of variation are acknowledged, the focus is on population-level changes in gene frequencies and phenotypic traits. Now, populations have several interesting characteristics, the first being that they are usually identifiable in nature. That is, at any point in time, a population consists of a finite collection of conspecific individuals living in the same area and having the potential of mating with each other (these breeding communities are also called **demes**). Populations are anything but closed, however, and a second interesting feature is their permeable community boundaries that allow communication between neighboring populations through the (occasional or regular) exchange of members. In sexually reproducing creatures, these member exchanges almost always result in the movement of genes between populations. This phenomenon, call **gene flow**, has the obvious result of decreasing differences (both genetic and phenotypic) *between* populations, while increasing variation of both sorts *within* each deme. In other words, thanks to gene flow, populations within a species are homogenized, both genetically and in their traits. If a new and advantageous mutation crops up in one population, sooner or later it will be spread to all of the others. The occurrence of gene flow is what most evolutionary biologists would say binds a set of populations into a **species** (Figure 2–11).

Deme the community of potentially interbreeding individuals at a locality.

Gene flow the transmission of *genes* between *populations*, which increases the variety of genes available to each and creates or maintains similarities in the genetic makeup of the populations.

Species following the *biological species* concept, a group of interbreeding natural *populations* that are reproductively isolated from other such groups.

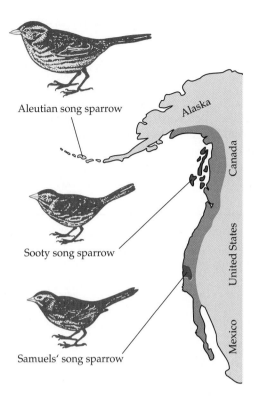

Aleutian song sparrow

Sooty song sparrow

Samuels' song sparrow

FIGURE 2–11 Shown here are representatives of 3 of the 34 subspecific populations of the song sparrow (*Passarella melodia*). Lines indicate the approximate breeding ranges of the illustrated subspecies, while those of 14 other distinct populations are shown by medium shading. Although birds at the northern and southern extremes of the geographic range do not interbreed directly, the unity of the species is maintained by extensive gene flow between neighboring populations all along the Pacific coast.

If the presence of gene flow demonstrates permeable population boundaries *within* a species, does its absence reflect relatively impenetrable boundaries *between* species? Most biologists would say yes, and this is indeed the basis for the classical *biological species* concept which defines a species as "a group of interbreeding natural populations that are reproductively isolated from other such groups." Here conspecifics are recognized not from the fact that they look alike (although this is almost always true as well), but from the fact that they mate exclusively (or almost exclusively, see below) with one another. In virtually every case, one or more *isolating mechanisms* have evolved that have rendered organisms unable, or unwilling, to reproduce outside of their own species. Common isolating mechanisms that separate species include morphological differences (body shape, size, coloration, etc.), genetic and chromosomal differences (e.g., distinctive chromosome numbers and shapes), and, perhaps most important of all, behavioral differences. Typical behavioral mechanisms include differences in breeding seasons and courtship patterns. Courtship, in particular, often involves complicated ritualistic behavior that is important in species recognition. (It should be noted that the word *natural* is very important to the biological species concept. The definition was never meant to apply to species that are naturally separated geographically but can interbreed in captivity. African lions [*Felis leo*] and Asian tigers [*Felis tigris*] may hybridize in zoos to produce "tiglons," but this does not mean that the two parent species are, in fact, one.)

The biological species definition is probably the best, but by no means the only, way to conceptualize and recognize species. Morphological definitions (the so-called *phenetic species* concept, based on looking alike) were popular in Darwin's

BOX 2-1

CURRENT ISSUE: The Upside and Downside of Genetics Research

Hardly a week goes by without a new break-through in biomedical science. Premature infants who would have died only a few decades ago are now saved. Immunizations protect us from many serious diseases. Organ transplants allow life-saving replacements for people with kidney and heart disease. In genetics, we've gained much understanding about inherited predispositions to diseases and pathologies, and this knowledge, along with new techniques for detecting "bad" genes, allows informed counseling of high-risk individuals (people at personal risk of gene-related illness or would-be parents likely to pass detri-mental genotypes to children). With the new knowledge, however, come new problems and dif-ficult decisions. Consider an example.

Researchers have discovered that women with mutations in two genes—the so-called BRCA1 and BRCA2 genes—almost certainly run an elevated risk of breast and ovarian cancers. One recent study suggested that carriers of mutations at both loci—mainly Jewish women of eastern or central European ancestry—have a 56 percent chance of breast cancer and a 16 percent chance of ovarian cancer by age 70 (average risks for noncarriers are 8 percent and 2 percent for the two cancers, respec-tively). Laboratory tests have been developed to identify people with mutated BRCA1 and BRCA2 genes, but the personal dilemma is how to respond to positive test results. Ideally, the genes themselves could be altered somehow and the risk of disease therefore reduced. Unfortunately, such "genetic engineering" is still only a possibility for the future and the options presently available for cancer-gene carriers are less than appealing. One can choose to do nothing and simply live with the risks, in the hope that further discoveries will allow the neces-sary gene therapy. Or one can opt for prophylactic removal of the breasts and ovaries, procedures that can dramatically reduce the risk of the cancers (some

researchers are urging women with mutant genes to consider at least removal of the ovaries). But how is one to choose? Modern Americans grow up expect-ing to live to a ripe old age *and* to do so with normal, healthy bodies. We're not used to thinking of our bodies as our own worst enemies. We have no guidelines for deciding whether to coexist with an internal time bomb such as a cancer gene or to get rid of its likely target, despite the physical, emotional, and reproductive costs. Which path would you choose for yourself? Which would you choose for a loved one?

To take this example one step further, consider some of the possible "ripple effects" of increased biomedical knowledge. Imagine the case of a cancer gene carrier's medical history becoming known to a prospective employer or an insurance company. Do you think she ethically could be denied either a job or insurance coverage based solely on her *risk* of cancer? And if you don't think this sort of thing can happen, consider the follow-ing actual incident, reported by Joseph Levine and David Suzuki in their recent book, *The Secret of Life.*

> One couple who knew that they were CF (cystic fibrosis) carriers asked their HMO (health main-tenance organization) to pay for a genetic test on their unborn child during pregnancy. They were told that if the child tested positive, the HMO would cancel their health plan unless they agreed to an abortion. Only threatened legal action induced the HMO to withdraw that demand.

What's the take-home message? The Pandora's box of biomedical knowledge is wide open. Future discoveries will have both upside and downside effects, and the latter will test our wisdom and courage as individuals and our ethics as a society. ■

day and they are still preferred by some scientists. The primary weakness of phenetic definitions is the arbitrariness of trait selection for species classifications. Different phenetic yardsticks may result in researchers recognizing different numbers and patterns of species. Other definitions, such as the *ecological species* concept, try to distinguish between species based on their different **ecological niches** (the set of resources and habitats exploited by each species). Like phenetic definitions, this approach also has problems, including the fact that in widespread species there can be extensive niche diversification among demes (which would therefore have to be redefined as individual species). Overall, the biological species concept seems to be the best approach to species recognition, but even it has drawbacks.

Ecological niches the set of resources and habitats exploited by a *species*.

Perhaps the greatest weakness of the biological species definition is that it makes the reproductive barriers between species sound too solid and universal. In fact, fertile hybridization (crossing) between widely recognized species is quite common among plants and occurs at least occasionally among animals. About 40 percent of duck and geese species have been known to hybridize, grey wolves (*Canis lupus*) produce fertile hybrids with coyotes (*Canis latrans*), and in the Awash National Park in Ethiopia, New York University anthropologist Clifford Jolly and his colleagues have documented anubis baboons (*Papio cynocephalus anubis*) cross-breeding with hamadryas baboons (*Papio hamadryas*). Even Ernst Mayr, one of the strongest supporters of the biological species concept, has noted recently that "a leakage of genes occurs among many good 'reproductively isolated' species." By "gene leakage," he means the transmission of genes from one species to another through hybridization followed by hybrids back-crossing with one of the original parent species. Mayr argues, however, that the biological species definition is by no means invalidated by this "messiness" in nature. In his view, despite the fact that reproductive "isolating mechanisms do not always prevent the *occasional* interbreeding of non-conspecific individuals . . . they nevertheless prevent the complete *fusion* of such species" (emphasis added). And so it appears that despite occasional gene leakage from one species to another, most of the time **assortative mating** (the tendency for creatures with similar phenotypes to mate with one another) and other behavioral and genetic mechanisms ensure species' integrity.

Assortative mating the tendency of like to mate with like.

A second weakness of the biological species concept, and one that plagues evolutionary biologists, is that it is difficult to apply to fossil species since we can never be sure about their reproductive behavior. Thus when scientists try to identify and sort extinct species, they are forced to fall back on phenetic similarities and differences as the best indicators of reproductive isolation. Types and amounts of morphological distinctiveness needed for the identification of fossil species is usually based on studies of their closest living evolutionary relatives. For example, knowledge about morphological variation among modern humans, as well as that found among the living ape species, allows anthropologists to make informed decisions about the species of early human ancestors (see Chapter 7).

Darwinian Evolution: How Natural Selection Shapes Populations

Despite continuing disagreements among specialists over the precise definition(s) of species, it is clear that they do exist in nature and that they usually can be subdivided into identifiable populations. (Very small species, with limited geographic ranges, may consist of only a single population. In this case, the species and the population are identical. Presumably, all new species that have resulted from the splitting or branching of an evolutionary lineage began as a single-population species.

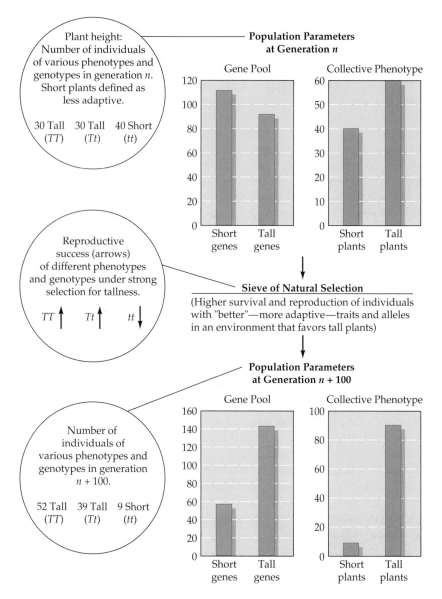

FIGURE 2–12 A model of evolution by natural selection. In this example, pea plant height has two alleles, *T* (dominant) and *t* (recessive). The effects of selection for tallness from generations *n* to *n*+100 are shown. Population size is held at 100 plants throughout the example.

Species formation by branching is discussed at the end of this chapter.) Once in existence, a species may be stable or it may change with time (most species that last for a reasonable period probably experience both stability and change). And of the handful of mechanisms that produce evolutionary change, the force that Charles Darwin dubbed *natural selection* is still widely regarded as the most important.

As noted in Chapter 1, natural selection is a straightforward and remarkably obvious concept once you begin to think about it (we have tried to diagram its operation in Figure 2–12). In a nutshell, each population consists of individuals who vary in their genotypes and traits (remember the contributions that mutation and meiosis make to variation) and who are living under a distinct set of environ-

| | (a) $s = 0.05$ | | (b) $s = 0.01$ | |
| | GENE FREQUENCY | | GENE FREQUENCY | |
GENERATION	A	a	A	a
0	0.01	0.99	0.01	0.99
100	0.44	0.56	0.026	0.974
200	0.81	0.19	0.067	0.933
300	0.89	0.11	0.15	0.85
400	0.93	0.07	0.28	0.72
500	0.95	0.05	0.43	0.57
600	0.96	0.04	0.55	0.45
700	0.96	0.04	0.65	0.35
800	0.97	0.03	0.72	0.28
900	0.97	0.03	0.77	0.23
1000	0.98	0.02	0.80	0.20

FIGURE 2–13 The results of a simulation of changes in the frequencies of alleles A and a during 1000 generations of selection against the recessive allele. (a) Selection coefficient of 0.05 (*aa* individuals have a relative chance of survival of 95 percent, compared with 100 percent for *AA* and *Aa* individuals). (b) Selection coefficient of 0.01 (*aa* individuals have 99 percent chance of survival, compared to 100 percent for *AA* and *Aa*). (Adapted from M. Ridley, 1996, *Evolution* (2nd edition). Reprinted by permission of Blackwell Science, Inc.)

mental conditions (broadly defined to include physical conditions, food, water, and competing organisms). Individuals simply try to survive and reproduce, and—other things being equal—those lucky few who possess traits that "work" in that environment succeed at both. Reproductively successful individuals pass their genes and traits on to the next generation, while nonreproducers obviously do not. Thus, with each passing generation, reproducers' alleles tend to increase in relative frequency (compared to the genes' alternate forms—alleles at the same loci—that were carried by nonreproducers) within the population gene pool and reproducers' phenotypic traits tend to become more common. The effects of natural selection can be measured as changes in the population's gene pool (Figure 2–13) and/or shifts in the collective phenotype (Figure 2–14). Charles Darwin envisioned natural selection as a process that operates slowly and that requires great stretches of time (and many generations) to perform its work. This may be true most of the time, and the results in Figure 2–13 show how small differences in the survival rates of different alleles (more correctly, the survival rates of the carriers of different alleles) can produce dramatic genetic shifts given enough time. Nonetheless,

FIGURE 2–14 A common measure of evolution is change in the average expression of any characteristic in a species. A simple case is the lengthening of the necks of the ancestors of giraffes. Because long-necked giraffes have more reliable and extensive food sources in trees than short-necked ones, they are more successful and have more offspring over time. As a result, the average neck length slowly increases. Eventually all individuals are relatively long-necked. In contrast, Lamarck would have seen this change as a response of the individual to need and continual stretching of the neck.

recent studies of fish, lizards, and even Darwin's Galapagos finches have demonstrated that under sufficiently strong environmental pressures, natural selection can move rapidly on occasion to transform a population or species.

Natural selection does not always change things, however. The example given in Figure 2–14 shows **directional natural selection**: as long-necked giraffes are selected for (and short-necked ones are selected against), average neck length in the population is altered in the direction of the tallest phenotypes. But at times (probably often) natural selection acts to preserve current gene frequencies and phenotypic distributions. Such **stabilizing natural selection** occurs when the environment is relatively constant (unchanging), and it operates by selecting against all individuals that deviate from the prevailing phenotypic norms (Figure 2–15). Periods of **stasis** in the his-

Directional natural selection *natural selection* that operates in response to environmental change and produces shifts in the composition of a *population*'s *gene pool* and *collective phenotype*.

Stabilizing natural selection *natural selection* that operates during periods when the environment is stable and maintains the genetic and phenotypic status quo within a *population*.

Stasis a period of evolutionary equilibrium or inactivity.

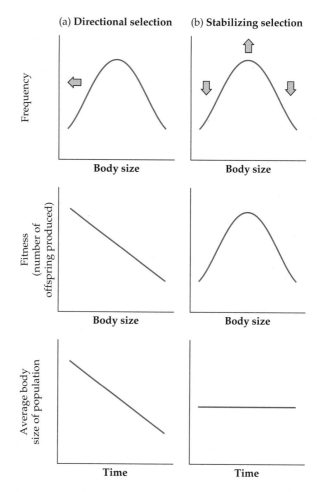

FIGURE 2–15 Diagrams of (a) directional natural selection and (b) stabilizing natural selection. Top row shows the frequency distribution in a hypothetical population of body size (*vertical axis:* Bottom, few/Top, many; *horizontal axis:* L, small/R, large). Most individuals are of medium size, with some considerably smaller or larger. Arrows show the forces of selection. Middle rows show individuals' "fitness," as measured by number of offspring (axes as in top row). Bottom row shows the average body size in the population (*vertical axis:* Bottom, small/Top, large; *horizontal axis:* L, present/R, present + *n* generations). Note that as directional selection favors smaller individuals, the average size drops over time. During stabilizing selection, however, medium-sized individuals have higher fitness than individuals at both size extremes, and mean size remains the same over time. (Adapted from M. Ridley, 1996, *Evolution* (2nd edition). Reprinted by permission of Blackwell Science, Inc.)

Box 2-2

THREE EXAMPLES OF NATURAL SELECTION AT WORK

1. FUR COLOR IN MICE

In 1962, a mutant strain of house mice (*Mus musculus*) was discovered in a farm population in Missouri. Because of the effects of a single recessive allele, mutant animals had pink eyes and pale yellow fur in contrast to the dark eyes and dark (agouti) fur of normal mice. Mutants interbred freely with normal mice, and the two strains lived together in a granary used to store corn. The solid construction of the granary prevented the farm's numerous cats from entering.

In order to determine the relative proportions of mutants and normals, researchers periodically live-trapped the granary mice and released them (see Table below). At the first trapping, the mutants accounted for about 28 percent of the population, and their representation increased steadily throughout 1962. In January 1963, because of an increase in the mouse population, the farmer made an opening in the granary wall to provide access for his cats. The cats immediately began to prey on the mice, and the pale yellow animals soon proved to be much more vulnerable to predation than their agouti conspecifics (probably because of greater visibility in the dimly lit corn crib). Percentages of mutants in the population fell to zero soon after the cats began their deadly work.

The allele responsible for the mutant coloration had not been completely removed from the population, however. In September 1963, at the urging of the researchers, the farmer sealed off the cats' entrance, and within three months the pale-colored mice had rebounded to about 5 percent of the population. In this example from nature, heritable differences in fur color were strongly affected by predator pressure. (Data from L. N. Brown, 1965, *Journal of Mammalogy* 46:461–465.)

2. BODY SIZE AND BILL DIMENSIONS IN DARWIN'S FINCHES

A species of Darwin's finch (*Geospiza fortis*) was studied on the Galapagos island of Daphne Major between 1975 and 1978. Birds were trapped and measured regularly, and data were collected on their feeding patterns (they ate mostly seeds of various sorts and sizes).

In 1977 Daphne Major experienced a severe drought that resulted in a sharp food shortage for the finches. Seeds of all sorts declined in abundance, but small seeds declined faster than large ones, and the result was a strong overall increase in the average size and hardness of the available seeds (averages for the "size-hardness index" for the seeds increased from a predrought figure of just over 4 to about 6 during the drought). In response to these environmental changes, the finches suffered an 85 percent drop

Date	Total Mice Trapped	Mutants as Percentage of Trapped Mice
Apr. 1962	32	28.1
Aug. 1962	44	40.1
Dec. 1962	58	46.6
(Jan. 1963—cats allowed into granary)		
Apr. 1963	22	0.0
Aug. 1963	29	0.0
(Sept. 1963—cats excluded from granary)		
Dec. 1963	37	5.4

BOX 2-2 *(continued)*

in population size. Small birds suffered greater decimation than large ones, apparently because the smaller birds (with their smaller bills) had difficulty cracking and eating large, hard seeds. That is to say, smaller birds were strongly "selected against" because of the drought-related changes in food. Measurements taken after the drought (1978, see Table below) showed the effects of natural selection: average body size in the population had increased, as had average bill size.

3. ADAPTATIONS TO WITHSTAND FAMINE AND EXTREME COLD IN HUMANS

During the winter of 1846, the Donner Party—87 pioneers headed to California—became snowbound in the Sierra Nevada. Food supplies were soon depleted, the weather was brutal, and before rescuers could reach the group in April of the next year, 40 people had died. Death did not occur randomly, however; it came most often to those who were least adapted biologically to survive famine and cold. Thus the pattern of death and survival in the Donner Party serves as a small-scale example of natural selection in humans.

The first factor to be considered in this retrospective analysis is sex. Overall, women are better adapted to survive famine and cold than are men. This better adaptation is due primarily to the fact that women carry somewhat more body fat than men and, importantly, they have a higher proportion of fat stored subcutaneously (thus providing insulation for the body's core). Despite having a higher body surface-to-mass ratio than men (which should increase heat loss), in response to extreme cold women experience smaller reductions in core temperature and smaller increases in metabolic rate, and they lose body heat at a lower rate than do men. Other things being equal, therefore, one would predict that in the face of cold and famine, women should outsurvive men by a significant margin.

A second important factor is age. Generally speaking, the very young and the very old are at much greater risk under conditions of cold and famine than are prime-aged individuals. The reason is that youngsters have few nutrients stored in the form of fat, while older people have a diminished capacity to respond metabolically to cold conditions. Thus a second prediction can be made: Under conditions of cold and famine, prime-aged individuals should outsurvive both the very young and the very old.

The following Winter 1846 figures show that natural selection decimated the Donner Party pretty much according to retrospective predictions made from knowledge of differential biological adaptations. Females (age classes combined) proved to be much more "fit" than males under the harsh conditions and lost only 29.4 percent of their number. In contrast, 56.6 percent of males died (age classes combined). With regard to age, prime individuals outsurvived both the youngest and the oldest members of the group. More than 60 percent of the children between 1 and 4 years old died, as did more than 80 percent of the individu-

FINCH TRAITS	PREDROUGHT MEAN	POSTDROUGHT MEAN
Weight (g)	15.59	16.85
Bill length (mm)	10.68	11.07
Bill depth (mm)	9.42	9.96

(Data from P. T. Boag and P. R. Grant, 1981, *Science* 214:82–85.)

> Box 2-2 *(continued)*
>
> als older than 50. Although other variables, such as family size, also affected survival within the Donner Party, the biological correlates of sex and age seem to have been of major importance in differentiating fit and unfit individuals. Natural selection favored females over males and prime individuals over the young and old during that grisly winter of 1846.
>
> | BEFORE WINTER 1846 (PERCENTAGE) | AFTER WINTER 1846 (PERCENTAGE) |
> | --- | --- |
> | Proportion of females = 39.1 | Proportion of females = 51.1 |
> | Proportion of males = 60.9 | Proportion of males = 48.9 |
> | Proportion 1–4 years old = 18.4 | Proportion 1–4 years old = 12.8 |
> | Proportion 5–49 years old = 74.7 | Proportion 5–49 years old = 85.1 |
> | Proportion 50 or older = 6.9 | Proportion 50 or older = 2.1 |
>
> (Data from D. K. Grayson, 1993, *Evolutionary Anthropology* 2:151–159.)

tory of a species, when little or no evolutionary change occurs, are generally periods of stabilizing selection.

Natural selection is not the only evolutionary mechanism, but it ranks at the top of the list. In order to ensure your understanding of this important process, three clear examples of directional selection—including one from humans—are given in Box 2-2. In addition, a later section of this chapter explains the action of natural selection on humans' hemoglobin alleles, and Chapter 18 describes how the process has contributed to biological diversity among living people.

Non-Darwinian Evolutionary Mechanisms

Although of primary importance, natural selection is not the only force in nature shaping the genes and traits of populations and species. At least five other processes can be identified and assigned to a category called non-Darwinian evolutionary mechanisms: mutation, chromosomal recombination during meiosis (crossing-over), gene flow, the **founder effect**, and **genetic drift**. (The label "non-Darwinian" simply means that Charles Darwin was unaware of the biological processes in question. Their discoveries—mainly in the twentieth century—followed the development of the science of genetics.) The first three phenomena, mutation, crossing-over, and gene flow, have been described already and require little discussion here. All three of these processes produce random genetic and phenotypic variability within populations—variability that can then be shaped by natural selection. The last two phenomena—founder effects and genetic drift—also affect variability and thus feed natural selection, but, they also may sometimes produce evolutionary change on their own.

The founder effect and genetic drift are both special factors operating in very small populations. These small communities either may be the remnants of larger populations that have gone through size-reducing *bottlenecks* (for example, decimation by disease) or they may be *founder populations* started by a few individuals splintering off to establish a new breeding colony. Small, descendant populations

Founder effect genetic difference between a newly founded, separated *population* and its parent group. The founding population is usually different because its *gene pool* is only a segment of the parent group's.

Genetic drift genetic changes in *populations* caused by random phenomena rather than by *natural selection*.

often are not typical samples of the parent species. That is, just by chance alone, these populations may, from the very start, carry different gene frequencies and phenotypic norms than the parent species. In particular, the small populations' gene pools will probably not contain the full assortment of alleles found among their parents. This is true because of the slim chance that carriers of all of the parents' rare alleles will be represented in either post-bottleneck or colonial populations. The term founder effect can be used to describe the altered genetic and phenotypic qualities of small, descendant populations, evolutionary differences that may then be enhanced by natural selection.

Small populations also become good candidates for yet another evolutionary mechanism: *genetic drift*. This mechanism involves chance variations in allele frequencies between the generations of small populations (Figure 2–16). In such populations rare alleles may be quickly lost or "fixed" (widespread) in the gene pool because of several chance factors. For example, rare alleles may be lost when their few carriers die accidentally (no natural selection is involved here, just pure chance). Or perhaps the carriers survive but because of chance alone, fail to reproduce. Or finally, perhaps heterozygous individuals with rare alleles are lucky enough to survive and reproduce, but then just by chance the alleles are absent from the particular sperm or egg cells involved in reproduction. In a similar way, these examples could be reworded to explain how rare alleles may become fixed by chance alone. Studies suggest that weak environmental selection pressures are critical in the operation of genetic drift. Thus alleles with neutral or weak selective values should be good candidates for the effects of drift.

Evidence for genetic drift has been obtained from experiments with small populations of the fruit fly *Drosophila*, but more interesting examples from natural populations can be found in the literature on human blood groups. (The nature and frequency of A, B, O, and other genetically determined blood groups are discussed in Chapter 18, but we shall refer to them here briefly in this connection.) An interesting instance of drift has been shown to have occurred among the polar Eskimos who lived near Thule in northern Greenland. This small band, which numbered no more than 271 people at any time, was isolated for generations. Another related band of Eskimos from Baffin Island spent several years trying to reach them, and when they made contact, the isolated band had come to believe that they were the only people in the world. In 1956 the American physical anthropologist William Laughlin took blood samples from both the isolated band and the parent population, and he showed that they differed quite significantly from their nearest relatives in two of their blood group frequencies. Other small and isolated communities have shown the same response, including some of the aboriginal tribes in Australia, the Dunker religious sect in eastern North America, and the Jewish community in Rome. These data are of interest because we believe that during much of human evolution the species consisted of small bands of between 200 and 500 individuals.

In summary, it seems clear that founder effects and genetic drift—along with the other non-Darwinian mechanisms and, of course, natural selection—have made important contributions to the evolution of populations and species, including the human species. Mutation, crossing-over, and gene flow all produce increased variability within populations (so does simple population growth, since an abundance of individuals means an abundance of new mutations). Natural selection and founder effects have acted to decrease variation. Genetic drift, being a random process, can either enhance variability (when rare alleles become established or "fixed" in a gene pool) or reduce it (when rare alleles are lost). The interplay of all these processes determines the evolutionary potential of an evolving lineage.

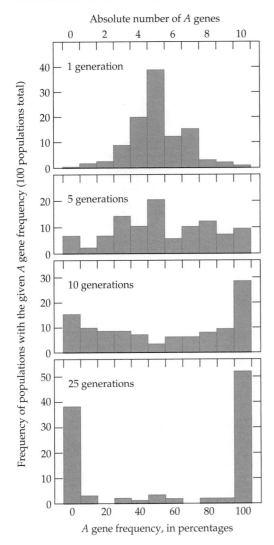

FIGURE 2–16 Computer simulations of genetic drift show how random changes across several generations may lead to either the elimination or the fixation of alleles in small populations. One hundred simulations for two alleles (*A*, *a*) at a single locus were conducted, and the figure shows the randomly generated frequency distribution of one allele (*A*) at generations 1, 5, 10, and 25. Population size was set at five diploid individuals (10 genes) with *A* and *a* equally represented initially. (Data from L. L. Cavalli-Sforza and W. F. Bodmer, 1971, *The Genetics of Human Populations*, Freeman, San Francisco).

Interestingly, however, even these various powerful forces acting in combination are usually unable to bring populations into perfect genetic and phenotypic harmony with their environments (that is, produce perfectly adapted populations). This is due to several factors, but high on the list is the extreme difficulty of eliminating detrimental recessive alleles completely, particularly if they are protected by the condition known as *balanced polymorphism*.

Polymorphism and Genetic Load

All populations of plants and animals (and hundreds of millions of people) carry harmful unexpressed recessive genes. These are termed the **genetic load**. The genes constituting the genetic load are expressed only in the relatively rare recessive homozygote, when they may bring about a physical malformation or a fatal genetic disease. An example of such a phenomenon is **sickle-cell anemia**. Persons who are homozygous for the recessive sickle-cell allele (*Hb*^{S}) are characterized by anemia due to red blood cells that become crescent-shaped when oxygen levels are

Genetic load *recessive genes* in a *population* that are harmful when expressed in the rare *homozygous* condition.

Sickle-cell anemia a genetically caused disease that can be fatal, in which the *red blood corpuscles* carry insufficient oxygen.

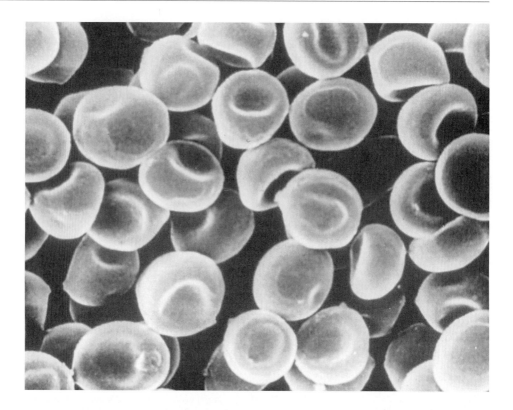

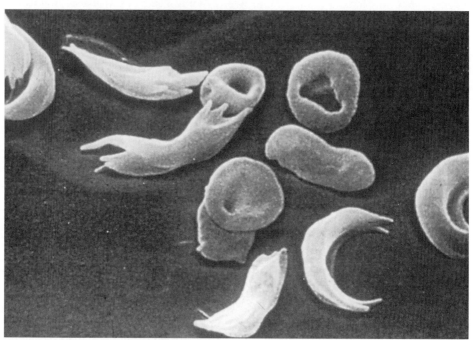

FIGURE 2–17 The sickle-cell trait is due to abnormal hemoglobin, which differs from normal hemoglobin in only 1 amino acid out of nearly 300 that constitute the protein. The red blood corpuscles in the top photograph appear normal; the bottom photograph shows the distortion that gives sickle-cell anemia its name.

low (Figure 2–17). Homozygotes for the normal allele (Hb^A) have round red blood cells. Sickle-cell disease is a life-threatening condition that is common in certain regions of West and Central Africa (Figure 2–18). In many Central African populations, from 20 to 40 percent of individuals are $Hb^A Hb^S$ heterozygotes; 1 to 2 percent are $Hb^S Hb^S$ homozygotes, who usually die soon after birth.

Because natural selection would ordinarily select out such an undesirable trait, we have to ask why such a high frequency of the Hb^S gene is maintained. In 1954, A. C. Allison, a British doctor, showed that the sickle-cell trait in its heterozygote condition affords protection against malarial infection, and that the distribution of the Hb^S gene coincides with the distribution of the *Anopheles* mosquito, which carries malaria. The Hb^S gene was maintained by natural selection according to the balanced advantages and disadvantages that it offered: protection from disease for the $Hb^A Hb^S$ carrier and death for the $Hb^S Hb^S$. This is an example of **balanced polymorphism**. *Polymorphism* usually refers to the expression of two or more alleles of a single gene in a population in more or less constant proportions. The human blood groups constitute further well-known examples.

Balanced polymorphism maintenance in a *population* of different *alleles* of a particular *gene* in proportion to the advantages offered by each (e.g., sickle-cell and normal *hemoglobin*).

Today in the United States we live in an environment free of malaria, yet approximately 10 percent of Americans of African origin still carry the Hb^S gene. Thus it has become a complete liability and, in the rare homozygous state, is still a serious and often lethal condition. Clearly, a lifesaving adaptation in one environment is part of humankind's genetic load in another.

We can see, then, that the survival value of genes is determined by the environment in which they are expressed. We can see, too, how natural selection acting on genetic variability will often compromise between advantages and disadvantages, so that ordinarily lethal phenotypes are maintained in a population in balance with advantageous phenotypes. Of course, many rare recessive lethal genes are simply carried along in the gene pool because they are almost never expressed in a homozygote. Between balanced polymorphisms and rare recessives, it appears that most species will always bear the burden of a genetic load. But look on the bright side. Perhaps our genetic load represents a potential for variability that may in the future be necessary for survival, as it may have been in the past. Natural selection operates on phenotypes, that is, only on the expression of a proportion of the genotype. Hidden genetic variability is, to some extent, our insurance against environmental change.

The term genetic load also refers to the normal mutation rate that most commonly reduces fitness. In human populations, genetic birth defects may affect up to 4 percent of births. Research has shown that in Britain 12 to 15 percent of all pregnancies that continue longer than four to five weeks end in spontaneous abortion before the end of the twenty-seventh week, and that more than 2 percent result in stillbirths. Some of these deaths may be due to external factors, but most are due either to inherited genetic factors or recent mutations in the germ cells. The latter may often be chromosomal abnormalities such as Down's syndrome, in which the individual has an extra chromosome (46 + 1); Turner's syndrome, in which the Y chromosome (the sex chromosome that determines maleness) is missing (46 − 1); or Klinefelter's syndrome, in which individuals are XXY (phenotypic males with two female X chromosomes; surviving individuals are sterile). Other chromosomal abnormalities include individuals who are XXX (super females with three X chromosomes) or XYY (super males with two male Y chromosomes). Such abnormal chromosome numbers are often associated with mental disorders.

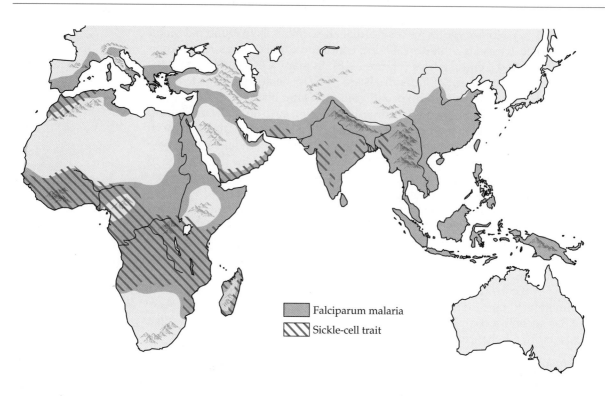

FIGURE 2–18 Coincidence of the sickle-cell trait and malaria in parts of the Old World led us to understand why the abnormal hemoglobin *Hb*^{s} appears in these areas. Though disadvantageous elsewhere, in malarial areas the sickling gene gives considerable protection against the dangerous malarial parasite. The two hemoglobin forms are in balance according to the advantages and disadvantages they offer. Therefore, this instance of the phenomenon of polymorphism is termed *balanced polymorphism*. Other genes give similar protection in other parts of the world where malaria occurs.

Hardy-Weinberg Theorem

The preceding sections have established that evolution is a population-level phenomenon. Within their environments living creatures strive to survive and reproduce, and their success or failure in getting their genes into succeeding generations determines the evolutionary trajectories of their populations. The examples in Box 2-2 illustrate rapid evolutionary change in small populations, but in fact, most of the time populations (particularly large ones) are probably in stasis, with little or no change occurring as long as the environment remains constant. It would obviously be very useful to be able to determine whether a population is in equilibrium (stable) for specific phenotypic traits, and geneticists have developed a procedure for this purpose: the Hardy-Weinberg test.

In 1908, English mathematician G. H. Hardy and German physician W. Weinberg independently developed a formula for describing the proportions of a pair of alleles within a stable population. This formula allows researchers to calculate the expected frequencies of genotypes and phenotypes once they have obtained information about allele frequencies. Here's how it works. Imagine the simplest possible condition: a trait that is controlled by a single pair of alleles (*A, a*).

If we symbolize the frequency of the dominant allele (A) as p and that of the recessive allele (a) as q, then we can develop the equation:

$$\text{(1) } p + q = 1$$

This is true since the total proportion of the alleles at any given locus is equal to 100 percent. Furthermore, this equation can be expanded to produce the frequencies of the three possible genotypes (AA, Aa, and aa) that would be expected in a population at equilibrium:

$$\text{(2) } (p + q)^2 = 1$$

$$\text{(3) } p^2 + 2pq + q^2 = 1$$

Substituting the genotypes for their mathematical symbols, we get:

$$\text{(4) } AA + 2Aa + aa = 1$$

In other words, the frequencies of both homozygotes (AA and aa), plus the total frequency of the heterozygotes ($2Aa$), equal 100 percent of the population for the trait in question. Of course, with regard to their phenotypes, in this example both the AA homozygotes and the heterozygotes (Aa) would show the dominant form of the trait. Only the aa homozygotes would show the recessive phenotypic condition.

The genius of Hardy and Weinberg was to realize that under a certain set of conditions the allele frequencies p and q will reach equilibrium in one generation and, assuming the conditions are maintained, remain in equilibrium indefinitely. The necessary conditions, sometimes summarized by the term *random mating*, include infinitely large population size, no mutations, no selection, and no gene flow. Although these conditions may seem impossibly stringent at first glance, in fact, the Hardy-Weinberg theorem is rather robust and fits a number of natural populations rather well despite their failure to meet one or more of the criteria.

For simple single recessive allele traits, the frequency of q can be easily determined from the occurrence of individuals showing the rare phenotype. And once q is known, p (and thus all genotypic frequencies) can be readily calculated. For example, a rare disorder caused by a single recessive allele in modern human populations is Tay-Sachs disease. Most common in Jews of eastern European descent, Tay-Sachs sufferers experience nervous system degeneration, convulsions, and death at a young age. Although the frequency of Tay-Sachs disease varies strongly between populations, its global incidence is about 1 per 100,000 births, or 0.00001 ($= q^2$). The value of q is therefore 0.0032, making the frequency of the recessive Tay-Sachs allele 0.32 percent. From these figures p can be calculated as 0.9968 and p^2 (homozygous dominants) as 99.36 percent of living humans. Finally, of critical importance in the development of programs for the prevention and cure of Tay-Sachs disease, the frequency of unafflicted carriers of the disease (the heterozygotes, $2pq$) can be calculated as 0.0064, or about 1 person in 157 worldwide.

The Hardy-Weinberg theorem can also be used to test whether a population is at or near equilibrium with regard to particular phenotypic frequencies. One does this test by first determining p and q values, and then using those figures to calculate "expected" or predicted frequencies of the various phenotypes (p^2, $2pq$, and q^2).

PHENOTYPE	
Blood type	No. of persons
M	77
N	23
MN	101
Population totals	201

ALLELES PRESENT				
		No. of alleles	M	N
M homozygotes	2×77	154	154	0
N homozygotes	2×23	46	0	46
MN heterozygotes	2×101	202	101	101
			402 = 255 + 147	

Therefore frequency of allele $M = \dfrac{255}{402} = 63\%$ or 0.63

and frequency of allele $N = \dfrac{147}{402} = 37\%$ or 0.37.

Is the population in equilibrium with respect to MN blood types?

Using the formula: $p^2 + 2pq + q^2 = 1$ let p = allele M, and q = allele N.

Then $0.63^2 + (2 \times 0.63 \times 0.37) + 0.37^2 = 0.397 + 0.466 + 0.137 = 1$.

The frequency of each phenotype is therefore predicted (expected) to be:

$0.397 \times 201 = 80$ M
$0.137 \times 201 = 28$ N
$0.466 \times 201 = 94$ MN

Now compare *actual* and *predicted* numbers:

Actual	M 77	N 23	MN 101

Predicted	M 80	N 28	MN 94

The population is in equilibrium.

FIGURE 2–19   The Hardy-Weinberg theorem is a probability statement that predicts the phenotype frequencies in a population given the allele frequencies. Thus the Hardy-Weinberg theorem may be used to determine whether a population is undergoing change. Here we see the computation of such frequencies based on an actual example published by Frederick Hulse. The *M* and *N* blood group genes constitute a simple two-allele trait, neither of which is dominant to the other. Genetic stability in these traits is indicated by the fact that the observed frequencies are not significantly different from those predicted.

The set of predicted phenotypic frequencies can then be statistically tested against "observed" or actual frequencies found in the population. If the two sets of frequencies are statistically indistinguishable, the population is regarded as being at equilibrium for the trait. An example of this sort of equilibrium testing is shown in Figure 2–19, which uses data on the *M* and *N* blood group genes among the

Quinault Indians of Washington State. In this case, *M* and *N* are alternate alleles at a single locus but they are **co-dominant** (neither is dominant to the other) and thus there are three distinct phenotypes: blood types M, N, and MN. Here *p* is simply assigned to *M* and *q* to *N*. Statistical testing of the predicted versus the actual phenotypic proportions proved the population to be in Hardy-Weinberg equilibrium.

Although all of the above examples were genetically simple, the Hardy-Weinberg formula can be expanded to cover cases with multiple alleles at a locus. This theorem has proved to be of exceptional value to population geneticists.

Co-dominant the term for *alleles* that, in *heterozygous* combination, produce a *phenotype* distinct from either type of homozygote.

Sexual Selection

In discussing the action of selection and the transmission of characteristics in a population, and also in our discussion of the Hardy-Weinberg theorem, we have assumed that mating occurs randomly between members of the opposite sex of a population or species. Rarely is this so in practice, however, and a number of mating patterns can often be recognized. When struggle or choice enters into mating, we have what Darwin described as **sexual selection**. In 1871, he defined two kinds of sexual selection.

The first kind was the result of competition among members of one sex (usually males) for the opposite sex. Good examples are found among the higher primates, such as some multimale baboon groups (Chapter 4) where the alpha male may have primary sexual access to most females in a troop as they near ovulation. This reproductive pattern of behavior will select the genes for powerful and impressive males.

Darwin's second kind of sexual selection involves differential choice by members of one sex for members of the opposite sex: this usually takes the form of the females' choice of some males in preference to others and is well known among both birds and primates (see Chapter 4). Both these phenomena are most commonly observed among polygamous species and play a much smaller part in a purely monogamous species in which every individual has a mate.

The role that sexual selection has played in human evolution is not yet understood, but it is clearly not a significant factor in a monogamous society with a 50:50 sex ratio. Insofar as human societies permit polygamy (and very many do), and insofar as the historical pattern was probably not monogamous (Chapter 9), it is possible that sexual selection has indeed brought about the evolution of traits that are not the product of natural selection (and that in theory could become non-adaptive if developed to excess). The kind of characteristics in humans that may be a product of sexual selection are those which appear to advertise sexuality, such as hair patterns and types, body shape and breast development in women, and penis size in men. The second type of selection (differential choice of mate) has probably been more important in human evolution than the first. The elucidation of this problem depends on knowledge of the mating patterns of early peoples—information that is probably unobtainable. Were matings a result of free choice, or were they arranged by parents or elders for political and economic reasons? The present arrangements may not tell us much about the past.

Sexual selection a category including intrasexual competition for mates (usually aggressive and among males) and intersexual mate selection (usually of males by females).

Other nonrandom mating systems found in animals and humans are **inbreeding** and **outbreeding**. Inbreeding occurs when sexual partners share a recent

Inbreeding mating among related individuals.

Outbreeding mating among unrelated individuals.

common ancestor (that is, when they are genetically related to some degree). In small, isolated animal and human populations, inbreeding may be the typical pattern, but it has its costs. It often results in the homozygous pairing of recessive genes, so that the recessive trait becomes expressed in the phenotype. As we have seen, recessive genes are often harmful, and in due course they will tend toward numerical reduction or elimination by natural selection. Until then, their expression may be accompanied by increased disease and higher mortality rates, both of which have been predicted and observed in inbred animal populations (in humans the frequency of stillbirths is much higher for related parents).

Outbreeding is characteristic of human groups with extensive incest taboos, such as those groups that insist on marriage with members of other clans for political and economic reasons. Outbreeding has the opposite genetic effect of inbreeding: Variation increases, and lethal recessives remain unexpressed, and possibly accumulate, although the population may show improved health and lower mortality.

The mating system is therefore an important characteristic of a species and is linked not only to the species' social life as a whole, but, as we shall see, to many of its most striking anatomical adaptations.

Measures of Fitness

We began this chapter with a table that identified three different types of linkage between individual organisms and their populations (Table 2-1). Two of those linkages—genotypes and gene pools, phenotypes and collective phenotypes—already have been discussed, and now is an appropriate time to describe the third: the relationship between individuals' **fitness** and their population's degree of *adaptation*.

Fitness individuals' relative degrees of success in surviving and reproducing, and thus in gaining genetic representation in succeeding generations.

Traditionally, fitness has been measured in terms of individual reproductive success, that is, how many offspring an organism produces and successfully rears. Since each offspring carries 50 percent of each parent's genes (in most organisms) and many parental traits, individual reproduction is a primary path to evolutionary fitness. (Obviously, survival to adulthood is necessary for individual reproductive success, but surviving without reproducing does not equal fitness as measured here. Equally obviously, simply possessing traits that are likely to lead to survival, such as strength, stamina, and general good health—the popular meaning of "being fit"—doesn't qualify as evolutionary fitness.)

Inclusive fitness the sum total of an organism's individual reproductive success (number of offspring) plus portions of the reproductive success of genetic kin.

Recently, the definition of evolutionary fitness has been extended in important ways. Thanks to the work of W. D. Hamilton and many others, we now realize that individual reproductive success is only one component of an organism's **inclusive fitness**. A second important component is the reproductive success of one's genetic kin. After all, in diploid organisms, parents and offspring and full siblings have 50 percent of their genes in common, half-sibs 25 percent, first cousins 12.5 percent and so on. Assisting a relative to survive and reproduce is therefore a perfectly good way to get copies of one's own genes into future generations. This realization also appears to explain several previously puzzling aspects of animals' (and perhaps humans') behavior. Animals often appear to behave altruistically, doing things that benefit others while inflicting a cost on the actor (there are many examples, such as alarm calling, intervening in fights, and sharing food). But if the recipients of such **bioaltruism** are the actor's kin, then acts that appear to be altruistic may in fact reap a genetic reward for the actor by helping relatives survive and reproduce. This insight is the basis for yet another evolutionary mechanism known

Bioaltruism behavior that appears to be altruistic, but that in fact is believed to benefit the animal indirectly, by increasing its *inclusive fitness*.

as **kin selection**. Kin selection may well be the process by which behaviors that are apparently altruistic, but that in reality are likely to serve genetic self-interest, may have evolved.

In any event, as individuals possessing advantageous traits (those that contribute to survival and successful reproduction within the prevailing environment) demonstrate their fitness by passing many copies of their genes into the next generation (in the form of offspring, grand-offspring, nieces, nephews, etc.), they drive up the frequencies of good-trait alleles relative to alleles that code for less advantageous traits. Thus, in the next generation, the population's collective phenotype will be shifted (slightly or strongly, depending on selection pressures) toward "good" traits. In other words, the population, viewed as a whole, will be *better adapted* to its environment than before. In this way, the actions of individuals as they face each day's challenges—feeding, survival, reproduction, parenting, aiding kin—contribute to the evolution of their population and species.

Kin selection the selection of characteristics (and their *genes*) that increase the probability of the survival and reproduction of close relatives.

Speciation

Only three topics remain to be discussed in this chapter, but they are essential for an understanding of evolution. We need to look first at **speciation**, the processes by which new species come into existence, second at **extinction**, the processes by which species are lost, and finally at the notion of *progress* in evolution.

There appear to be two primary ways that new species are formed: **phyletic transformation** (also called *phyletic evolution*, *phyletic gradualism*, or *anagenesis*) and **cladogenesis**. In its purest form, phyletic transformation involves the evolutionary conversion of an entire species into a species of phenetically (phenotypically) different descendants (Figure 2–20, top). Here, transformation within an evolving lineage results from the slow accumulation of adaptive changes wrought by natural selection. After sufficient phenetic change has built up, a new species

Speciation the production of new *species*, either through the gradual transformation, or the splitting or branching, of existing species.

Extinction the loss of a *species* due to the deaths of all its members.

Phyletic transformation the conversion (mainly through *natural selection*) of an entire *species* into a new species.

Cladogenesis branching evolution involving the splitting of a *species* or lineage.

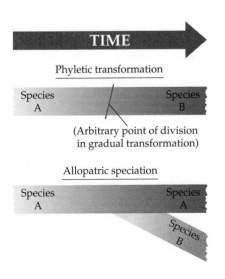

FIGURE 2–20 Phyletic transformation involves the gradual conversion (mainly through natural selection) of an entire species into a new species. While it occurs in nature, it is not a true form of speciation because it does not lead to an increase in species diversity. In contrast, allopatric speciation involves branching of an existing species (usually due to the isolation of one or more populations) with the result that the total number of species is increased.

name is deemed necessary by scientists studying the lineage, and so they coin one; in Figure 2–20, species A gradually converts into species B. Phyletic evolution thus involves losing one old species for each new one that is added. There is no increase in species diversity here, a fact that has led some researchers to balk at calling this process true speciation. A further problem with phyletic transformation—at least for taxonomists trying to assign specimen names unambiguously—is that it complicates the identification of species in a lineage since their phenetic boundaries are largely arbitrary (Figure 2–20). Sometimes, for ease of communication, researchers resolve the confusion by identifying **chronospecies**, lineage subdivisions that are as strongly time defined as they are trait defined (Chapter 16 discusses chronospecies in human evolution). Criticisms aside, however, it is clear that phyletic transformations occur in nature and, furthermore, that anagenesis plays an important supporting role in cladogenetic speciation, increasing the divergence of populations that are splintering from their parent species.

The second speciation mode—cladogenesis—increases the diversity of life forms through the splitting or branching of existing species. Almost certainly its most important form is **allopatric speciation** (the name means "different localities" and refers to speciation among populations with different ranges; see Figure 2–20, bottom, and also Figure 2–21). Allopatric speciation is thought to begin, typically, with the formation of a physical barrier between a peripheral population and the rest of its species. Such *geographic isolation*—perhaps produced by the formation of a new mountain range, volcanoes, geologic faults, a river changing its course, or some other topographic alteration—results in the interruption of gene flow between the separated population and the parent species. The maintenance of genetic and phenotypic continuity between the population and the parent species ends, and thereafter, mutations occurring on either side of the barrier will make the two units progressively different. Of course, thanks to the founder effect, the chances are good that the population and the parent species are substantially different genetically the instant that geographic isolation becomes effective. The population's much smaller gene pool probably lacks a good number of the rare alleles found in the species' gene pool, as well as having different frequencies of even the common ones, and all of this will result in phenotypic differences in short order. Furthermore, if the isolated population is small (as seems generally to be the case in nature) genetic drift may add to its accumulating allelic differences from the parent species. And finally, natural selection will occur among the population's phenotypes (and associated genotypes) as it adapts the isolated community to its new environment, an environment that may differ significantly from that of the parent species.

The combination of all of these evolutionary forces—no gene flow, accumulating mutations, founder effect, genetic drift, and natural selection working within a different environment—leads to increasing differences between the isolated population and the parent species. When the two have become sufficiently different so that they cannot, or will not, interbreed should they meet again (due to the disappearance of the barrier or to migration), they qualify as good species under the biological species concept, distinct breeding communities that are *reproductively isolated* from one another. How long this might take—for a geographically isolated population to become reproductively isolated from its parent species—undoubtedly differs from case to case. Some organisms mature and reproduce rapidly, while others are much slower. With all factors working at top speed, it seems likely that

Chronospecies the sort of "species" that are created when an unbroken evolutionary continuum is arbitrarily divided into time-defined units.

Allopatric speciation the production of new *species* through the splitting or branching of existing ones. The process begins with the geographic isolation of one or more *populations* from the bulk of the parent species.

1. The original frogs in this area interbreed with each other and constitute a single species.

2. Changes in the topography and drainage conditions of the region eventually create two distinct regions–swamp and forest–with a barrier between the two that the frogs cannot cross.

3. Over a long period of time, the frogs in the swamp and those in the forest adapt to their different environments. As they adapt and remain isolated from each other, the frogs in the two areas become different.

4. So many differences have now been selected in the two populations that the frogs do not interbreed even if they meet; they do not recognize foreigners as potential mates.

FIGURE 2–21 A simplified visual description of allopatric speciation in an imaginary frog population. In the last stage, two separate and independent gene pools now exist, eventually constituting two species where one had existed.

complete speciation might be achieved in several hundred to a few thousand generations.

There are other forms of cladogenesis, including **sympatric speciation** (the name means "same locality") in which populations living in the same or overlapping ranges separate by adapting to different ecological niches, and **parapatric speciation** (which separates populations of sedentary organisms living in adjacent

Sympatric speciation speciation among *populations* with the same or overlapping geographic ranges.

Parapatric speciation speciation among *populations* of sedentary organisms with adjacent ranges.

Hybrid speciation speciation through hybridization
between two good *species*.

ranges). There is even a noncladogenetic process call **hybrid speciation** in which hybrids between two good species find themselves at an adaptive advantage in a particular ecological situation and therefore thrive. Nonetheless, most scientists think these processes have been much less important in the history of life than the allopatric production of new species. But enough about the birth of species. Let's turn our attention to how species die.

Extinction

The term *extinction* is applied most commonly to the loss of species due to the disappearance of all of their members. (It can also be applied to the loss of larger biological units such as genera or "families"—in zoology, collections of related genera.) We need to begin with a clarification, however, because there are at least two ways for species to disappear. When a species becomes truly extinct, all of its members die—and their genes die with them. In contrast, when a species is phyletically transformed (Figure 2–20), its genes don't cease to exist, but simply end up being housed in a different kind of creature. Phyletic transformation produces a type of pseudoextinction of species that should not be confused with the real thing. (Unfortunately, the two are sometimes devilishly hard to distinguish in the fossil record.)

In any event, disappearance, either by true extinction or the false extinction of phyletic transformation, is the inevitable fate of all species (humans included). While animal species typically last about 4 million years (among humans and our ancestors, the average is closer to 1 million years), it still remains true that the vast majority of all species that have ever lived are now extinct. But why do species become extinct? Is it, as D. M. Raup asked in a recent book, a matter of "bad genes or bad luck"? Raup tends to side with bad luck, and there is a good deal of evidence supporting this point of view. It appears that, regardless of how well a species is adapted to its normal environment, sooner or later it will be exposed to such extraordinary biological or physical stresses that it will die. Examples of possible extinction-causing stressors include new and intense interspecific competition; extreme environmental changes due to fluctuations in sea level, global climate, and large-scale volcanism; and environmental and ecological disasters resulting from collisions of the earth with extraterrestrial objects (comets and asteroids). Raup favors the collision hypothesis as an explanation for many mass extinction events, particularly the event that killed off the dinosaurs 65 million years ago (see Figure 5–5 for the dates of the five largest mass extinctions).

The data on extinction—and especially the mass events—suggest that contrary to the teachings of Lyell and despite a day-to-day appearance of regularity and predictability, when one views the earth over geological time it is clearly a dangerous and rather unpredictable place, periodically liable to large-scale, devastating environmental fluctuations. The extinctions that result from such fluctuations have played an important part in shaping the history of life on earth, and the existence of each living species is the result of a unique history of adaptation, speciation, and extinction. While natural selection has tended to improve species' adaptations to their normal environments and has combined with processes such as genetic drift to produce new species, extinction has operated to reduce species' diversity and to open up ecological niches. Happily for humans, vacating ecological niches tends to open the way for new evolutionary experimentation. Had the dinosaurs not become extinct, mammals might never have diversified, and primates (including humans) might never have evolved.

Progress in Evolution

For most educated people, including the vast majority of scientists, the fact of evolution cannot be denied. Evolutionists often differ considerably, however, in their interpretations of pattern and meaning in the history of life. Among the commonly asked interpretative questions are these: Has evolution shown any broad trends? Has evolution been moving life toward some identifiable goal? Is evolution progressive, producing ever-better organisms over time? Interestingly, Charles Darwin would probably have answered "no" to most, if not all, of these questions. In his books and personal correspondence, Darwin repeatedly expressed the view that natural selection works locally, producing a sequence of adaptive adjustments to changing local environments. Natural selection cannot "see" beyond the local level in order to produce broad trends, thought Darwin, and thus he resisted the notion of progress in life's history. For many people, however, progress and evolution have become synonymous, and they argue that there have been broad increases—progressive trends—in such variables as animals' size and overall organic complexity (including intelligence) throughout life's history.

Unfortunately for believers in evolutionary progress, a close examination of the evidence fails to provide strong support for their position. First, on the issue of size, recent tests of the so-called Cope's rule (named after its 1871 formulator, paleontologist Edward Drinker Cope), which states that body size tends to increase in an animal lineage during its evolution, have produced mixed results. While the inadequacy of Cope's rule has been demonstrated for marine organisms, fossil mammal species (particularly those whose members are already large) do show a tendency to increase about 9 percent in size over their immediate ancestors. Interestingly, humans have shown a significant intraspecific decrease in body size over the last 50,000 years, a change that cuts against the grain of the general mammalian trend. Second, with regard to organic complexity, recent studies suggest that the occasional evolution of creatures with increased complexity was predictable from random change alone, given the utter simplicity of the earliest living creatures, the bacteria. That there has been no overall trend toward increased organic complexity is shown by the fact that bacteria are still the predominant form of life on earth. And finally, concerning the evolution of intelligence, a widely accepted theory is that intelligence (and the correlated trait of brain enlargement) has evolved repeatedly among social animals as an adaptation for remembering and manipulating social relationships (see Chapters 9 and 13). Most mammals are social (that is, group-living) creatures and this is particularly true for humans and our closest animal relatives, the primates (monkeys, apes, etc.). Therefore, humans' big brains—viewed against a background of big-brained mammalian and primate ancestors—become understandable as an extreme form of a common adaptation for life in a complex society. The fact that among modern people brain functioning includes self-consciousness may be simply a fluke, an accidental stroke of luck that was in no way preordained.

The persistence of the idea of progressive evolution seems, in the end, to be mainly the result of humans' egocentric nearsightedness (see Box 2-3). People who believe that humans are the acme of evolution usually find it hard to accept the notion that life wasn't moving from the start toward the production of our

Box 2-3

SOME THOUGHTS ON EVOLUTION AND PROGRESS

For many modern people, reflection on the long journey that our ancestors have made from single-celled organisms to big-brained, self-aware creatures inevitably leads to the conclusion that evolution is progressive. As we argue in the text, however, this conclusion is more illusory than real, and here's why.

Both evolutionary theory and an obsession with progress are relatively recent developments, dating mainly from the nineteenth century. In medieval times, life seemed to continue more or less the same from generation to generation. There was no reason to expect scientific breakthroughs or significant philosophical developments. Alchemists still had not managed to make gold from lesser metals, try as they would. The created world was constant and stable. The concept of evolution brought the idea of progress into social consciousness, and to humans, who stood at the top of the "chain of being," it seemed to confirm their natural superiority.

The reality is not quite so simple, however. Evolution is a process, operating in time, driven primarily by natural selection, which has produced a whole range of organisms from viruses to humans. The fact that some recently evolved creatures are large and complex is counterbalanced by the survival and diversification of older and simpler forms of life. The plant kingdom has achieved a dominant position on earth without the added sophistication of a nervous system or musculature. Our greatest competitors on earth today are minute and relatively simple viruses, bacteria, and protozoa. As disease organisms, they still play a major part in shaping human history.

It follows that evolution cannot be described as progressive; the process is characterized by change, the sole result of which is survival. The success of a species could be measured in terms of its numbers, or the gross weight of its biomass, or its stability and longevity in time, its variety of adaptations, or its geographical range. We humans have a rapidly increasing population and biomass, yet these can hardly be called signs of progress, since this very increase puts the whole species in danger. Compared with the dinosaurs that ruled the world for more than 100 million years, we are merely upstarts and have no cause for self-congratulation on the basis of stability or longevity. We are a variable and widespread species, but that seems only to make the population explosion more dangerous, for there is now little wilderness remaining for the survival of many of those other species with which we share the planet and upon which we depend. No, none of these characteristics constitutes evolutionary success for humanity. The dinosaurs appear to have done better, though extinction was their ultimate fate.

So in what way are we special? In what way could we be called the most successful and progressive species in the history of the planet? If we look at *Homo sapiens*, we see, for example, that the species is very complex (especially the nervous system) and is fully self-conscious (which is probably unique in the animal world). It has also intentionally altered its environment in a drastic manner. But we cannot be sure that it is necessarily progressive to be complex, or self-conscious, or to alter the environment; any of these characteristics could prove disastrous to its possessor and so to humankind. But human history does exemplify one evolutionary trend which appears to be truly progressive: *an increase in the range and variety of adjustments that the organism is capable of making in response to its environment.* This is the secret of our adaptation.

In order to respond to the environment, animals require a range of sense organs, a powerful brain to process the

---

Box 2-3 *(continued)*

sensory inputs, and efficient and effective mechanical systems to bring about a whole range of responsive behavior. In *Homo sapiens*, we find a greater range of sensory input (we know more about our environment), more analytic processing of that input (a far more complex brain), and a greater range of motor outputs (i.e., of behavior and communication) than in any other species. This much lies in our biology, but our culture has taken this trend much, much further. Microscopes, telescopes, a variety of sensors, and amplifiers of many kinds have vastly increased the range of environmental inputs. Books and computers aid memory, analysis, and prediction. Transportation and tools of every description help us amplify our behavior and satisfy our needs with increasing success. It is in this sense that we are more complex and in this sense that we are more adaptable than other species. If we are more adaptable, we are more likely to survive, and maybe more likely to achieve long-term success.

The story of human evolution is a tale of increasing interaction with and control over our environment. Perhaps unfortunately, our adaptation has become so potent that we now run the risk of destroying the environment and ourselves with it. We must learn to control our unprecedented abilities for short-term manipulation and exploitation of the earth's resources. Clearly, we still have some way to travel on the evolutionary journey before we can call ourselves, without qualification, a successful and progressive species.

kind of creatures. For those who will see, however, the scientific evidence is clear: Like all living species, humans are the result of a series of (for us, happy) contingent events and despite our many marvelous qualities, in the final analysis, we are the result of chance.

SUMMARY

During the present century, the science of genetics has yielded numerous secrets that allow us to understand the workings of evolution. Phenotypic traits are encoded in genes—hereditary units, consisting of DNA, that occur on chromosomes within the nucleus of the cell. Offspring tend to look like their parents because of inherited genes, but because of genetic mixing during gamete production, offspring never look exactly like their parents or each other (with the single exception of identical siblings). This heritable variation in every generation allows natural selection to improve the degree of adaptation of populations.

Working along with other factors, such as geographic isolation, mutation, founder effect, and genetic drift, natural selection can lead to speciation. Species exist for varying amounts of time—some for many millions of years—but ultimately all species disappear. Some (several?) mass extinction events have probably been caused by comets or asteroids hitting the earth. Every species has a unique history of speciation, adaptation, and, in the end, extinction.

Finally, a variety of recent studies have confirmed that evolution is indeed a contingent process with few, if any, general trends encompassing large numbers of species. Despite the persistent human hope that we are the pinnacle of evolution and that evolution's flow has moved inexorably toward our morphology and self-conscious intelligence, all available evidence suggests that humans—like all other species—are the result mainly of chance and the action of natural selection.

POSTSCRIPT

Every passing year brings an increase in humans' control over their own evolutionary future. Technological advances now enable many of the world's people to effectively short-circuit natural selection as we use new means of controlling our environment, health, survival, and reproductive success. Is a geographic region too hot or cold or dry or humid for comfortable human living? No problem. We simply build artificial environments featuring cooling, heating, humidifying, or dehumidifying systems that allow easy living in any climate regardless of one's phenotype. Poor vision is corrected with eyeglasses, poor hearing with hearing aids, and lost teeth with dentures. Light-skinned people live and work safely in areas of high solar radiation thanks to clothing and sunscreen creams.

Today, medical advances allow the birth, survival, and reproduction of people with physical and mental impairments that would have been fatal in the past. At the same time, we are gaining genetic knowledge that, in combination with amniocentesis, may enable us at some future point to scan and even *tailor* genotypes prenatally, thus preventing unwanted traits—including impairments—from being expressed phenotypically. Indeed, for better or worse, we may soon be able to **clone** humans entirely! We are thus rapidly gaining control over both of the factors—genes and environment—that determine the fitness of individuals and the evolution of populations. But increased control brings its own uncertainties. Consider the following questions:

Clone a genetically identical organism asexually reproduced from an ancestral organism.

- What are the implications of assisting increasing numbers of genetically and/or physically impaired people to be born and to reproduce? Will the genetic load of the species increase? Would the denial of medical assistance to *any* impaired individual (fetal or postnatal) be consistent with humane behavior?
- Should we attempt to eliminate undesirable human traits and develop desirable ones? If the answer is yes, who should decide which traits are which and how should the decisions be made? Should genetic tailoring be allowed for strictly cosmetic reasons (e.g., to alter skin color or projected height)? How should "species engineering" be accomplished? (Humans have a very checkered history of such eugenics projects.) Are there long-term disadvantages in reducing genetic and phenotypic variability within our species?

Although the traditional set of evolutionary mechanisms (natural selection, mutation, gene flow, and genetic drift) continues to have some effect on modern humans (more on some populations than on others), it is clear that we are becoming something of a special case with regard to further evolution. Ever-increasing control over our evolutionary trajectory promises to bring a plethora of challenging questions for scientists, physicians, theologians, **bioethicists**, and laypersons alike.

> Bioethicist a person who specializes in exploring the ethical dimensions of biological decisions.

REVIEW QUESTIONS

1. What are genes, how do they determine phenotypic traits, and what happens when they mutate?
2. Describe the contributions made by point mutations and meiosis (crossing-over) to phenotypic variability in populations.
3. Describe the biological species concept. How must this concept be adjusted to account for the occasional case of "gene leakage" between species?
4. Explain how natural selection operates to shape the gene pools and collective phenotypes of populations. How does the fitness of individuals contribute to the degree of adaptation of the population?
5. How does allopatric speciation work? Why isn't phyletic transformation considered to be true speciation? Are there any other ways new species can come into existence?
6. Discuss the possibility of the extinction of our species. What circumstances could result in the extinction of humans?
7. Discuss the implications of humans being the result of chance, rather than the inevitable result of progressive evolution. Does this alter the way you look at yourself and your species?

SUGGESTED FURTHER READING

Gould, S. J. *Full House*. Harmony Books, 1996.
Leakey, R. and R. Lewin. *The Sixth Extinction*. Doubleday, 1995.
Raup, D. M. *Extinction: Bad Genes or Bad Luck?* W. W. Norton, 1991.
Singer, M., and P. Berg. *Genes and Genomes*. University Science Books, 1991.
Strickberger, M. W. *Evolution*, 2nd. ed. Jones and Bartlett, 1996.
Weiner, J. *The Beak of the Finch*. Vintage Books, 1994.

INTERNET RESOURCES

FRANK POTTER'S SCIENCE GEMS – LIFE SCIENCE I
http://www-sci.lib.uci.edu/SEP/SEP.html
  (Links to more than 2,000 web sites dealing with topics such as molecular genetics, evolution, and ecology.)

PRIMER ON MOLECULAR GENETICS (DEPARTMENT OF ENERGY)
http://www.bis.med.jhmi.edu/Dan/DOE/intro.html
  (Basic information on genes, chromosomes, DNA, etc.)

THE TALK.ORIGINS ARCHIVE

http://www.talkorigins.org/

(Good starting point for material on genetics, evolutionary processes, speciation models, and extinction. Search the archive for numerous topics related to evolution—particularly human evolution—and creationism.)

USEFUL SEARCH TERMS:

evolution

extinction

human genome

natural selection

population genetics

speciation

HUMANS AMONG THE PRIMATES

A baby orangutan (*Pongo pygmaeus*) and friend.

What a piece of work is a man! How noble in reason! How infinite in faculties! In form and in moving, how express and admirable! In action how like an angel! In apprehension how like a god! The beauty of the world! The paragon of animals!

WILLIAM SHAKESPEARE, 1564–1616. *Hamlet*, II, ii.

OVERVIEW

The order Primates—that subgroup of mammals that includes prosimians, monkeys, apes, and humans—is quite ancient and this chapter is devoted to its description. First appearing at least 60 million years ago, the order is represented today by more than 200 widely diverse species. Originally shaped by life in the trees and an insectivorous diet, primates have evolved an array of distinctive adaptations, including freely moving limbs with grasping hands and feet, keen vision, and (at least among the anthropoids) complex brains. Humans are in many ways typical primates, and our distinctive features can be best appreciated when considered against the primate background. Human specialities include habitual bipedal locomotion, extreme brain complexity, language and speech, and a cultural way of life. Thanks to cultural adaptations, humans have gained considerable control over their evolutionary future. Important topics in the chapter include classification systems, general primate characteristics, prosimian traits, anthropoid traits, the arboreal theory, the visual predation theory, and the numerous distinctive traits of humans. Particular attention is given to the ways humans differ from their close evolutionary relatives, the apes.

NAMES AND CLASSIFICATIONS

Homo sapiens among living *primates,* the scientific name for modern humans; members of the *species* first appeared about 130,000 years ago.

The first two chapters have shown how evolution works, but before we can start examining our past, we must first learn something about what we are like today. We cannot completely—or even partially—answer this question until we have answered simpler questions about our similarities to and differences from other animals. Humankind is biologically classified under the Latin name ***Homo sapiens***; *Homo* means "man," and *sapiens* "wise." The human has been called the thinking animal. The human has also been labeled a political animal, a tool-using animal, a social animal, a speaking animal, and the animal that is aware of itself. We are all these things, and more.

The Latin name *Homo sapiens* was coined by the great Swedish biologist Carl von Linné (1707–1778) as part of his classification of all plants and animals. Though a practicing doctor for part of his life, Linnaeus (the Latinized form of his name, by which he is more commonly known) collected plants and animals in Europe and received specimens from collectors throughout the world. He began to develop a system for naming and classifying most of the then-known living organisms. He used a binomial (two-name) system to label each one, choosing Latin for the names because it was a convenient international language. He published his system of names in his famous book *Systema Naturae*, which ran to twelve editions between 1735 and 1766.

It was already clear to biologists that some creatures were more similar to each other than to others; they seemed to be created on the same general plan. Linnaeus grouped the similar ones in classes and orders to form a hierarchic arrangement. In 1735, Linnaeus had put *Homo* in his first class of Quadrupeds in the order Anthropomorpha, with the apes (Simia) and the sloth. In the tenth edition (1758) he called humans *Homo sapiens* and placed them with monkeys and apes in the order called *Primates*. Although not based on a theory of evolution, this classification indicated anatomical similarities—similarities that disturbed Linnaeus, among others. In 1766 he wrote: "It is remarkable that the stupidest ape differs so little from the wisest man."

Linnaeus's classification scheme is still used because his method has proved to be of immense value. An international system of nomenclature (the rules of naming) has become essential in the development of the biological sciences, and the Linnaean system has survived the development of evolutionary biology since Darwin. The use of a language, such as Latin, that is no longer spoken, means that

---

Box 3-1

VARYING APPROACHES TO HUMAN AND GREAT APE TAXONOMY

Phenetic, cladistic, and traditional evolutionary classifications provide three different ways of arranging the taxonomy of modern humans and the great apes. The basis for each classification scheme is described below.

PHENETIC CLASSIFICATION

Phenetic classification schemes are based simply on overall morphological similarities and differences among organisms. In a phenetic scheme, humans are separated from the four ape species, which are clustered together. This arrangement reflects the fact that the apes share such traits as long arms and short legs, grasping feet, projecting canine teeth, and relatively small brains, while humans have short arms and long legs, nonprehensile feet, short canines, and enormous brains. See Figure 3-1a.

(Fig. 3–1a) Phenetic Classification

Humans   **Great Apes**
                      Chimpanzees, bonobos,
                      gorillas, orangutans

CLADISTIC CLASSIFICATION

Cladistic systematists attempt to arrange organisms in groups that reflect their history of evolutionary branching. See Figure 3-1b. Members of a related cluster (or **clade**) are recognized by the possession of shared, derived traits. Furthermore, in cladistic classifications all traits are treated equally (i.e., viewed as being equally useful in establishing evolutionary relationships), and sister groups are always given equal taxonomic rank. A look at the division of great apes and humans shows how this system works.

(Fig. 3–1b) Cladistic Classification

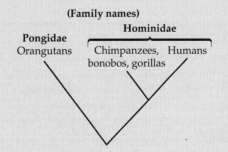

(Family names)

Pongidae   **Hominidae**
Orangutans   Chimpanzees, Humans
                      bonobos, gorillas

Clade members of an evolutionary cluster (e.g., sister species) plus their common ancestor.

Box 3-1	*(continued)*

Among the numerous traits shared by humans and the African apes are the following features: a broad nasal opening, square orbits that are often broader than they are high, and widely spaced eyes. In contrast, the orangutan is characterized by a nasal opening that is higher than it is broad, small oval orbits that are higher than they are broad, and closely spaced eyes. These and many other features support the conclusion that humans and the African apes share a recent common ancestor to the exclusion of orangutans. The two sister groups (orangutan versus African apes plus humans) must have the same rank, and here they are placed at the family level.

TRADITIONAL EVOLUTIONARY CLASSIFICATION

Traditional evolutionary systematists differ from cladists in several important ways. First, they routinely place different weights on morphological traits since they maintain that some features are more useful than others in revealing evolutionary relationships. Second, traditional evolutionary systematists do not feel constrained to place sister groups at the same taxonomic level. In this scheme, sister groups are often ranked differently, in a ranking that reflects dif-

ferent amounts of change from the common ancestral condition. Species that show extreme degrees of change from the ancestral condition are often described as having attained a new evolutionary **grade** compared to their near relatives. In the classification in Figure 3-1c, humans are placed in a different evolutionary grade from the apes because of their enlarged skull and brain, skeletal adaptations for bipedalism, incisiform canines, a fully **opposable thumb**, and so on. In contrast, ape-grade creatures share smaller brain size, skeletons adapted for some combination of quadrupedalism and suspension, elongated canines, and imperfectly opposable thumbs.

(Fig. 3–1c) Traditional Evolutionary Classification

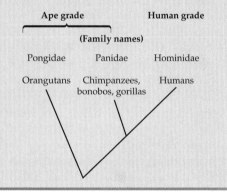

the terms do not undergo the changes through time that are characteristic of spoken languages. The theory of evolution changed the basis of the system, however, making it clear that the similarities seen by Linnaeus and others were in many cases a result of evolutionary or phylogenetic relationships. Groups based on anatomical likeness often proved to share a common ancestor. The form of the system of classification remained but its meaning altered. The hierarchy came to reflect relationship, the species became variable and adaptable. The species was no longer the expression of an ideal type created by God, which Linnaeus believed it to be, but the changing product of natural selection.

Today we attempt in our classifications to reflect the evolutionary process so that the **taxonomy** we use is a **phylogenetic classification**. Where we lack knowledge of relationships, classifications can be based only on similarities and differences between species. Such a grouping scheme is called a **phenetic classification**. Linnaeus's system was phenetic, and it proved to require relatively little change with the coming of evolutionary biology because similarities do in fact often reflect relationship—but not always.

The contrast between a phenetic arrangement of species and one that is phylogenetic can be seen in the different ways one can group humans and the so-called great apes: chimpanzees, bonobos, gorillas, and orangutans (Box 3-1). A traditional phenetic arrangement based on overall morphological similarity separates these creatures into two groups: humans on the one hand and the four apes on the other. In contrast, when traits are treated in evolutionary terms and primitive features (ancestral and ancient traits, broadly shared) are distinguished from *derived* features (recent innovations, shared by a small number of close species), orangutans are separated from the more closely related quartet of chimpanzees, bonobos, gorillas, and humans. But not all evolution-based classifications are alike. **Cladistic classification** views traits as having equal classificatory value and insists that **sister groups** be given the same taxonomic rank; that is, sister groups cannot

Cladistic classification evolution-based *taxonomy* that gives equal weight to traits and requires *sister groups* to be similarly ranked.

Sister groups in *cladistics*, the groups resulting from a dichotomous evolutionary branching event; initially ranked as sister species, these groups may change rank due to subsequent branching, but must always maintain the same *taxonomic level*.

TABLE 3-1   *Classification of Humankind*

TAXONOMIC CATEGORY	GROUP INCLUDING HUMANS	PRIMARY CHARACTERISTICS	MEMBERS
Kingdom	Animalia	Organisms that move, and that feed by the mouth	Vertebrates and all other animals (e.g., insects)
Phylum	Chordata	Possession of a notochord at some stage of life	All animals with backbones, plus sea squirts, amphioxus, etc.
Subphylum	Vertebrata	Bilaterally symmetrical animals with flexible, internal segmented backbones and other bony skeletal structures	Mammals and all other animals with backbones (e.g., fish, birds, reptiles)
Class	Mammalia	Class of Vertebrates characterized by fur, warm blood, the feeding of live-born young by means of milk glands, and maternal care of young	Primates and all other warm-blooded furry animals that suckle their young (e.g., dogs, elephants)
Order	Primates	Order of Mammalia distinguished by grasping hands and feet, nails on digits, flexible limbs, and highly developed visual sense	Anthropoidea and Prosimii (lower primates; tarsiers, lorises, lemurs)
Suborder	Anthropoidea	Suborder of the Primates with evolved social organization, daytime activity, and notable development of intelligence and ability to learn	Hominoidea, Old World monkeys (e.g., rhesus), and New World monkeys (e.g., spider monkey)
Superfamily	Hominoidea	Superfamily of the Anthropoidea characterized by relatively erect posture, loss of tail, development of arms and shoulders for climbing, and (generally) five-cusped lower molars	Hominoidea, Pongidae (orangutans), Panidae (chimpanzees, bonobos, gorillas), and Hylobatidae (gibbons, siamangs)
Family	Hominidae	Family of the Hominoidea characterized by bipedalism, canine reduction, and a trend toward brain enlargement	Genera *Homo*, *Ardipithecus*, *Australopithecus*, and *Paranthropus*
Genus	*Homo*	Genus of the Hominidae characterized by a relatively large brain, skillful hands, and evolving traditions of tool use, tool-making, and culture	*Homo habilis, H. rudolfensis, H. erectus, H. heidelbergensis, H. neanderthalensis*, and *H. sapiens*
Species	*Homo sapiens*	Species of the genus *Homo* characterized by a large brain, an advanced culture, technology, and language and speech	Modern humans

be placed at different levels (say, genus versus family) within a classification. In contrast, traditional evolutionary systematists routinely give different weights to traits (that is, view some as more important than others in elucidating relationships) and argue that sister groups most definitely can occupy different taxonomic levels. Throughout this book, we rely primarily on traditional evolutionary taxonomies.

The close relationships of humans and the great apes with each other and with the lesser apes (the gibbons) has never been in question. The point was clearly made by T. H. Huxley in 1863 (Figure 1–14). Today they are all placed in the superfamily Hominoidea. As noted, Linnaeus classified this group (or taxon) with the monkeys and some other animals under the name Primates. Linnaeus then grouped the primates with other furry, warm-blooded creatures that suckled their young in the class Mammalia. We mammals have backbones and share an even more general structure with such animals as fish and birds, with whom we constitute the subphylum Vertebrata. Humans' position in the grand hierarchy of the animal kingdom is summarized in Table 3-1.

TABLE 3-2   *Major Characteristics of Primates*

A. CHARACTERISTICS RELATING TO MOTOR ADAPTATIONS

1. Retention of ancestral mammalian limb structure, with five digits on hands and feet, and free mobility of limbs with unfused radius and fibula.
2. Evolution of mobile, grasping digits, with sensitive friction pads and nails replacing claws. Palmar surfaces with friction skin.
3. Retention of tail as an organ of balance (except in humans, apes, and a few monkeys) and as a grasping "limb" in some New World monkeys.
4. Evolution of erect posture in many groups with extensive head rotation.
5. Evolution of nervous system to give precise and rapid control of musculature.

B. CHARACTERISTICS RELATING TO SENSORY ADAPTATIONS

1. Enlargement of the eyes, increasing amount of light and detail received.
2. Evolution of retina to increase sensitivity to low levels of illumination and to different frequencies (that is, to color).
3. Eyes that look forward with overlapping visual fields that give stereoscopic vision.
4. Enclosure of eyes in a bony ring in all living groups, and a full bony socket in anthropoids.
5. Reduction in olfactory apparatus, especially the snout.
6. Internal ear structures enclosed within petrosal bone.

C. DENTAL CHARACTERISTICS

1. Simple cusp patterns in molar teeth.
2. In most groups, 32 or 36 teeth.

D. GENERAL CHARACTERISTICS

1. Lengthened period of maturation, of infant dependency, and of gestation, compared with most mammals. Relatively long life span.
2. Low reproductive rate, especially among Hominoidea.
3. Relatively large and complex brain, especially those parts involved in vision, tactile inputs, muscle coordination and control, and memory and learning.

THE PRIMATES

The list of animals included in the order Primates has been modified substantially since Linnaeus's time. He had included the bats and *colugos* ("flying lemurs") as primates, but in 1873 these animals were removed by the English scientist St. George Mivart, who also provided a more detailed definition of the order. Mivart defined primates as placental mammals that possess the following traits: claws or nails; collarbones; eye sockets encircled by bone; **heterodont** dentition (specifically, having incisors, canines and molars); posterior lobe of the brain that includes a distinctive groove (the calcarine fissure); thumbs or big toes (or both) that are opposable; flat nail on big toe; caecum (pouchlike portion of the large intestine); pendulous penis; scrotal testes; and two nipples.

Heterodont having several different types of teeth (incisors, *canines*, etc.), each with a different function.

Mivart also arranged the primates in the two suborders of the Prosimii (or "premonkeys") and the Anthropoidea (monkeys, apes, and humans).

During the twentieth century, this anatomical definition of the primates was to a great extent superseded by a definition based on the order's evolutionary trends. According to the English anatomist W. E. Le Gros Clark (as presented in his influential book *The Antecedents of Man* in 1959), primates are characterized by the retention of generalized limbs tipped with five grasping digits; the replacement of claws by nails; retention of a tail; expansion and elaboration of the brain; emphasis on vision; deemphasis on olfaction; loss of some teeth from the ancestral condition; retention of a simple molar cusp pattern; delayed maturation; and reduction of litter size to single infants (Table 3-2).

Today more than 200 species of animals living in Africa, Asia, and the tropical Americas (Figures 3–2 and 3–3) are recognized as primates, and the diversity within the order is staggering. Primates range in size from the gorilla at an average

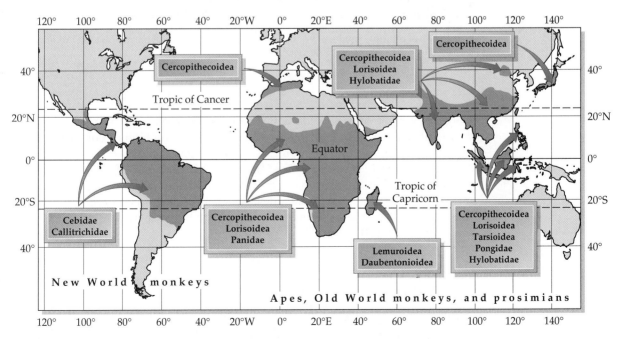

FIGURE 3–2 Worldwide distribution of nonhuman primates by superfamilies and families. Dark areas show the approximate ranges of nonhuman primates. (Adapted from J. Napier and P. Napier, *A Handbook of Living Primates*, London, Academic Press, 1967.)

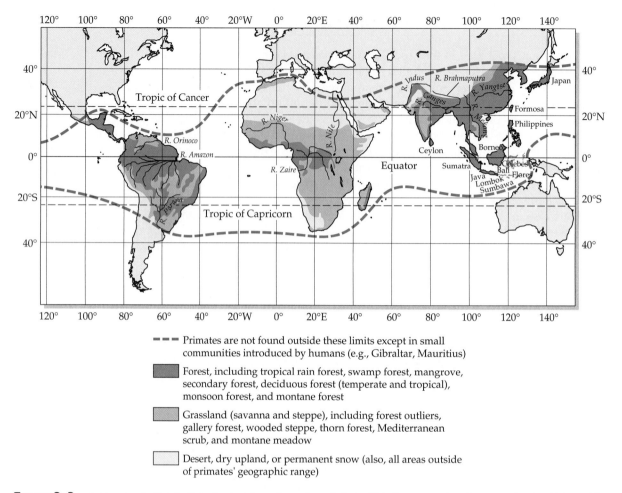

FIGURE 3–3   Approximate distribution of principle regions of vegetation within the range of nonhuman primates. (Adapted from J. Napier and P. Napier, *A Handbook of Living Primates*, London, Academic Press, 1967.)

Diurnal active during the day, as *apes*, humans and *monkeys* are.

Nocturnal active during the hours of darkness.

weight of 258 pounds (117 kilograms) to the tiny Demidoff's dwarf bush baby at 2.3 ounces (65 grams). Some primates are exceedingly intelligent creatures, others seem to have run-of-the-mill mammalian intelligence. Most are very social creatures, but some live solitary lives; most are **diurnal**, but some are **nocturnal**. Dietary specialities range from insects to fruit to leaves (with humans adding a significant amount of animal flesh to the basic primate diet). In order to describe all of this diversity, a complex taxonomy based on the Linnaean classification system is required (Table 3-3).

Prosimians

Following Mivart, the primates are usually divided into two suborders: the prosimians and the anthropoids. Fossil discoveries indicate that the prosimians first evolved at least 60 million years ago (mya) and that this suborder gave rise to the anthropoids some 10 to 15 million years later. Living prosimians include the superfamilies Lemuroidea (the lemurs; Figure 3–4), Daubentonioidea (the aye-aye;

Table 3-3   *Living Genera of the Order Primates*

Suborder	Superfamily	Family	Genus	Common Name	Location
Prosimii	Lemuroidea		9 genera	Lemurs	Madagascar
	Daubentonioidea		1 genus	Aye-ayes	Madagascar
	Lorisoidea		5 genera	Lorises and bush babies	Africa/Asia
	Tarsioidea		1 genus	Tarsiers	Southeast Asia
Anthropoidea	Ceboidea			New World Monkeys	Central/South America
		Callitrichidae	*Callithrix*	Marmosets	South America
			Cebuella	Pygmy marmosets	South America
			Saguinus	Tamarins	Central/South America
			Leontideus	Golden lion tamarins	South America
			Callimico	Goeldi's marmosets	South America
		Cebidae	*Pithecia*	Sakis	South America
			Chiropotes	Bearded sakis	South America
			Cacajao	Uakaris	Central/South America
			Aotus	Douroucoulis	Central/South America
			Callicebus	Titis	Central/South America
			Saimiri	Squirrel monkeys	Central/South America
			Cebus	Capuchins	Central/South America
			Alouatta	Howler monkeys	Central/South America
			Ateles	Spider monkeys	Central/South America
			Lagothrix	Woolly monkeys	South America
			Brachyteles	Woolly spider monkeys	South America
	Cercopithecoidea			Old World Monkeys	Africa/Asia
		Cercopithecidae	*Cercopithecus*	Guenons	Africa
			Erythrocebus	Patas monkeys	Africa
			Cercocebus	Mangabeys	Africa
			Mandrillus	Mandrills	Africa
			Papio	Baboons	Africa
			Theropithecus	Geladas	Africa
			Macaca	Macaques	Asia/Africa
			Cynopithecus	Celebes black ape	Asia
		Colobidae	*Colobus*	Guerezas	Africa
			Presbytis	Langurs	Asia
			Pygathrix	Douc langurs	Asia
			Rhinopithecus	Snub-nosed langurs	Asia
			Nasalis	Proboscis monkeys	Asia
			Simias	Pagai Island langurs	Asia
	Hominoidea			Apes and Humans	Worldwide
		Hylobatidae	*Hylobates*	Gibbons and Siamangs	South/Southeast Asia
		Pongidae	*Pongo*	Orangutans	Southeast Asia
		Panidae	*Pan*	Chimpanzees and bonobos	Africa
			Gorilla	Gorillas	Africa
		Hominidae	*Homo*	Humans	Worldwide

Note: Authors differ in details of primate classification. This table presents a classification that is widely accepted.

FIGURE 3–4   The ring-tailed lemur (*Lemur catta*) is typical of the varied group of prosimian primates (Lemuroidea) from Madagascar. The most striking features of lemurs are large forward-looking eyes and long separated fingers and toes. The ring-tail stands about 15 inches (38 centimeters) high.

Toothcomb a dental specialization of *prosimians* in which the lower front teeth are closely spaced and forwardly inclined.

Figure 3–5), Lorisoidea (lorises and bush babies; Figures 3–6 and 3–7) and, in most classifications, Tarsioidea (tarsiers; Figure 3–8). The tarsiers are actually quite difficult to classify since in many ways they are anatomically intermediate between undoubted prosimians and the anthropoids (monkeys, apes, and humans). In fact, some cladistic systematists prefer to group tarsiers with the anthropoids and refer them all to a suborder called Haplorhines, with lemurs, aye-ayes, and lorises remaining in a sister suborder called Strepsirhines. In this book, we will follow the traditional placement of tarsiers among the prosimians while pointing out tarsiers' distinctive features where appropriate.

Today prosimians are found only in Africa, particularly on the island of Madagascar, and in Asia, and they are characterized by a suite of primitive traits (Table 3-4). In general, prosimians are small-to-medium-sized animals with a well developed olfactory apparatus, visual features that suggest a current or ancestral adaptation to nocturnal activity, claws on some digits, prehensile hands and feet (but poor opposability of the thumb), and a dental specialization called a **toothcomb** that is used for both foraging and grooming. Prosimians are arboreal animals

FIGURE 3–5   The aye-aye is a solitary and nocturnal prosimian with the most unusual dentition of the entire order. It has evolved enormous gnawing incisors, and the rest of its teeth have dwindled or disappeared.

that move about the forests of the Old World in a **quadrupedal** fashion or by cling-ing and leaping from one vertical support to another. On average they are some-what less social than anthropoids, at least insofar as many prosimians forage solitarily or form small social groups (often monogamous breeding units). Prosimians are also more committed to insect eating than the average anthropoid (the only specialized primate insectivores are prosimians), although all eat fruit as well.

Quadrupedal moving on all four limbs.

In several important ways, living prosimians bridge the anatomical gap between anthropoids and the primates' primitive mammalian ancestors. For one thing, most prosimians lack the extensive eye protection found in anthropoids (Figure 3–9). While monkeys and apes show a complete bony eye socket, all prosimians except tarsiers display only a **postorbital bar** of bone extending from brow to cheekbone. Second, while both prosimians and anthropoids show a

Postorbital bar a bar of bone running around the outside margin of the orbits of *prosimians*.

FIGURE 3–6   The loris (*Loris tardigradus*) represents another group of prosimians (Lorisoidea) found in Africa and Asia. Lorises are smaller than lemurs but have very large eyes adapted for hunting insects and other small creatures at night. Lorises' bodies are about 8–14 inches (20–36 centimeters) long.

FIGURE 3–7   Hands are among the most characteristic features of primates. One striking primate adaptation is that of nails replacing claws. Both humans and the bush baby (*Galago*), which is just over 6 inches (16 centimeters) long, carry flat nails on their hands.

FIGURE 3–8   Three species of tarsier occur in Southeast Asia. With their enormous eyes, all are nocturnal, and most are forest living. Their diet consists mainly of insects. They weight only just over 4 ounces (120 grams), but have long and powerful hind limbs adapted for leaping. They appear to have evolved little in 50 million years.

reduction in total tooth count from the ancestral dental formula (Figure 3–10), several prosimian species have retained the ancient three-cusped pattern in their upper molar teeth. Third, prosimians still show the primitive clawed condition on some digits, while anthropoids show nails (usually flat, but sometimes compressed and recurved into "pseudoclaws") on all digits. Fourth, while prosimians show greater divergence of the thumb than nonprimate mammals and have grasping hands and feet, they lack the extensive thumb opposability (and precision gripping) that characterizes most anthropoids (compare Figure 3–11 with Figures 3–23 and 3–24).

Despite the retention of some primitive traits, however, prosimians show the distinctive primate combination of increased emphasis on vision plus grasping hands and feet. This pattern was inherited by the anthropoids, in whom further modifications of the sensory systems—such as a reduction of the olfactory sense—took place. But why did the combination of prehension and keen vision evolve among primates? There are two explanations, one traditional and one recent. The traditional explanation for the primate characteristics, especially grasping hands and feet and good vision, is called the *arboreal theory*. First developed by British scientists G. E. Smith and F. Wood Jones in the early twentieth century, this theory suggests that primate characteristics are essentially adaptations to life in the trees. Grasping extremities are viewed here as evolving for safe and lively movement

TABLE 3-4　*Distinguishing Characteristics of Various Primate Taxa*

PROSIMIANS

Rhinarium the moist, hairless nose characteristics of all *prosimians* except *tarsiers*, and of most nonprimate mammals.

Long muzzle tipped with a **rhinarium** (rhinarium absent in tarsiers)
Tactile vibrissae (sensory whiskers)
Frenulum which anchors upper lip (frenulum absent in tarsiers)
Toilet claw on second toe
Postorbital bar only (tarsiers have a virtually complete eye socket)
Two-part frontal bones
Two-part mandible
Mandibular toothcomb in most species

Frenulum the flap of skin that tethers the upper lip to the jaw in *prosimians*. It is reduced or absent in *anthropoids* and *tarsiers*.

ANTHROPOIDS

Reduced muzzle with a hairy nose (lack of rhinarium)
Lack of prominent whiskers
Reduced or absent frenulum
Nails (flat or modified) on all digits
Complete bony eye socket
Fused frontal bones
Fused mandibular symphysis
Lack of toothcomb
Retina that includes a **fovea** (also present in tarsiers)
Cerebral cortex that includes a central sulcus
Generally, extensive thumb and big toe opposability

Fovea an area of the *anthropoid* retina that allows extremely detailed vision.

HOMINOIDEA

Lack of tail
Broad chest
Shortened lower back
Dorsally placed scapulae (shoulder blades)
Great mobility at shoulders, elbows, and wrists
Higher ratio of brain size to body size than in other primates
Increased complexity of folding of cerebral cortex
Y-5 cusp pattern of lower molars

HOMINIDAE

Reduced canine length
Nonprehensile big toes
Pelvis and legs reflecting habitual bipedalism (short, wide iliac blades; enlarged iliac spines; close-knee stance)
Extreme brain enlargement and elaboration

Stereoscopic vision vision produced by two eyes with overlapping fields, giving a sense of depth and distance; most highly evolved in hunting animals and *primates*.

through the irregular arboreal habitat. Similarly, keen vision is thought to have evolved to facilitate arboreal locomotion—particularly **stereoscopic vision**, with depth perception for judging distance before leaping—and for locating food and danger. The sense of smell was of limited use to arboreal animals, and its supporting structures (a long muzzle and large smell centers in the brain) dwindled.

The logic of the arboreal theory carried the day among anthropologists for more than half a century. In the 1970s, however, American anthropologist Matt Cartmill began to probe that logic and the validity of the arboreal explanation. Cartmill observed that arboreal life does not necessarily select for primatelike characteristics. Many animals are perfectly at home in the trees without looking and

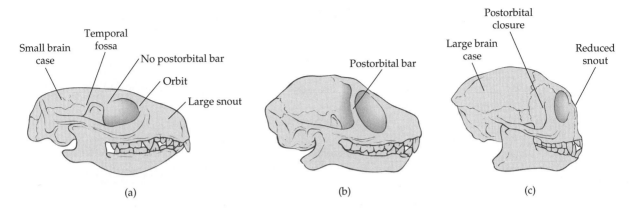

FIGURE 3–9   Comparative skull anatomy reveals several distinctive primate traits. Lateral views of [a] a nonprimate mammal (hedgehog), [b] a lemuroid prosimian, and [c] an anthropoid (New World monkey). Skulls not drawn to scale.

acting like primates. Gray squirrels are a good example. Squirrels skitter about in the trees, moving through the branches and making leaps of many times their body length. Furthermore, they successfully locate food and detect danger in the trees. Squirrels manage all this even though their hands and feet are relatively nonprehensile and their eyes are much more wide-set and laterally oriented than those of a primate, producing poorer depth perception. Moving the eyes closer together and forward produces increased overlap of the left and right visual fields, and increased overlap leads to better stereoscopic depth perception at close range (Figure 3–12).

Cartmill began a series of careful comparisons of primates with other animals and found that relatively close-set, forwardly directed eyes (and thus good close-range depth perception) are characteristic of predators that rely on vision in hunting. Cats, owls, chameleons, and many other animals use their close-set eyes to locate prey and to judge the distance for a capturing leap or grab. For arboreal hunters, grasping feet stabilize the animal on its support, while grasping hands (one or both working together) make the capture.

Based on these discoveries, Cartmill fashioned the *visual predation theory* of primate evolution. This theory holds that, among the primates, grasping extremities and keen vision originally evolved as adaptations for vision-directed predation on insects (such hunting is still common among some prosimians). Deemphasis on the sense of smell—and reduction of the olfactory apparatus—is viewed here as the result of a migration of the eyes in an anterior direction. Approximation of the eyes could have constricted the olfactory connections between the muzzle and the brain and thus could have led to a reduced sense of smell.

Cartmill's theory is currently carrying the day among anthropologists, but it has not gone unquestioned or unmodified. First, follow-up studies identified several diurnal visual predators (e.g., mongooses and some tree shrews) that lack convergent eyes, suggesting that the first primates' nocturnal lifestyle also influenced their visual evolution. Because nocturnal creatures have wide-open irises, orbital convergence both enhances their stereoscopic, close-range depth perception *and* it improves the clarity of objects directly in front of the eyes. (In diurnal creatures, even those with widely spaced eyes, blurred objects are focused by constricting the pupils.) Thus, it was not just hunting, but nocturnal hunting, that

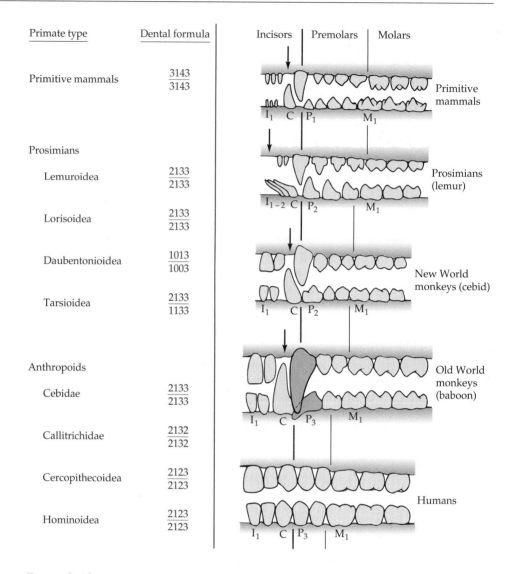

Primate type	Dental formula
Primitive mammals	$\dfrac{3143}{3143}$
Prosimians	
Lemuroidea	$\dfrac{2133}{2133}$
Lorisoidea	$\dfrac{2133}{2133}$
Daubentonioidea	$\dfrac{1013}{1003}$
Tarsioidea	$\dfrac{2133}{1133}$
Anthropoids	
Cebidae	$\dfrac{2133}{2133}$
Callitrichidae	$\dfrac{2132}{2132}$
Cercopithecoidea	$\dfrac{2123}{2123}$
Hominoidea	$\dfrac{2123}{2123}$

FIGURE 3–10   Dental formulae and lateral views of several primate varieties. Dental formulae represent half of the upper dentition over half of the lower and count (from left to right) numbers of permanent incisors, canines, premolars, and molars. In lemurs, I_{1-2} and the lower canines make up the toothcomb. Arrows mark the presence of a **diastema** or gap in the toothrow.

Diastema (pl. diastemata) space in the toothrow that accommodates one or more teeth in the opposite jaw when the mouth is closed.

shaped the primates' traits. Second, American primatologist Robert Sussman has challenged both the behavioral and anatomical evidence underlying the visual predation theory. While he agrees that many living prosimians show considerable insectivory, Sussman argues that they more often locate insect prey by smell or hearing than by sight, and that therefore "visual predation *per se* is not a sufficient explanation of [primates'] visual adaptations." Sussman counterproposes that primate traits first appeared during the Eocene as part of a diffuse coevolutionary interaction with the diversifying angiosperms (flowering plants). In his view, prehensile hands and feet evolved to allow movement in the food-laden terminal branches of angiosperms, while visual changes were adaptations for making fine discriminations among small plant foods. But is this scenario, although based on

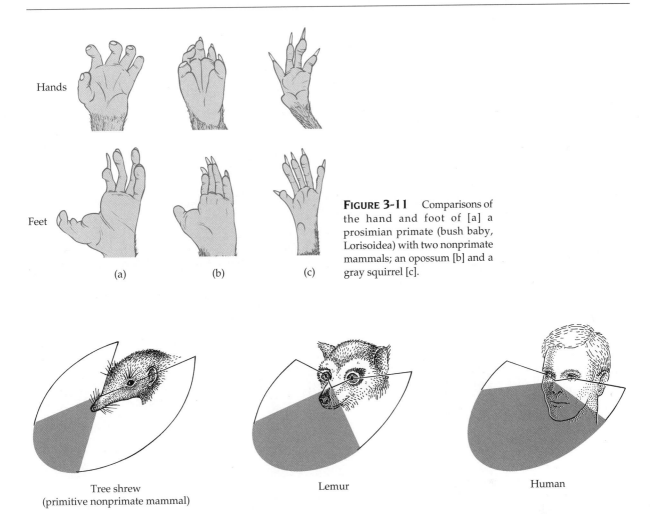

Hands

Feet

(a) (b) (c)

FIGURE 3-11 Comparisons of the hand and foot of [a] a prosimian primate (bush baby, Lorisoidea) with two nonprimate mammals; an opossum [b] and a gray squirrel [c].

Tree shrew
(primitive nonprimate mammal)

Lemur

Human

FIGURE 3–12 Stereoscopic vision is of great importance to primates, probably for both arboreal movement and foraging activities. The primitive tree shrew's eyes look sideways, and the visual fields have small overlap; in the lemur the overlap is greater. In monkeys, apes, and humans the extent of visual field overlap is great. Upright posture permits easy head rotation, which compensates for the loss of backward vision. As the eyes moved to the front of the face in primate evolution and vision became the primary sense, the sense of smell became less important, the snout was reduced, and the face flattened. Heads not drawn to scale.

the latest information on plant and animal evolution, really very different from the older arboreal theory? Not by much, and thus it seems we still have only two major options concerning primate origins.

Careful readers will have noticed, however, that the two theories—arboreal versus visual predation—overlap sufficiently for one to ask whether they are complementary or alternative explanations for primate traits. The most reasonable answer seems to be that they are complementary, with the visual predation theory probably having more explanatory power. After all, Cartmill's visual predators were probably operating in a tree and bush habitat, and thus adaptations for successful hunting would also have satisfied the requirements of arboreal locomotion. Until someone produces evidence to the contrary, it seems that we should tentatively conclude that all living primates—humans included—are the descendants of ancient, prehensile, big-eyed, insect hunters.

Anthropoids

The earliest anthropoid fossils are 45 to 50 million years old. From that early beginning, modification and diversification have led to the living representatives of this suborder, including the monkeys of the New and Old Worlds (respectively, the Ceboidea and the Cercopithecoidea; Figure 3–13) and the hominoids (apes and humans; Figure 3–14).

FIGURE 3–13 Old World monkeys (top): a long-tailed macaque (left) and a mandrill (right), both primarily adapted to terrestrial quadrupedalism. New World monkeys, such as the spider monkey (bottom, left and right), are highly adapted to an arboreal life. Notice the long grasping tail in the New World monkey and its laterally opening nostrils. In contrast, the Old World monkeys' nostrils are downwardly directed.

FIGURE 3–14 Whereas the orangutan (upper left) and the gibbon (upper right) are still primarily arboreal, the gorilla (lower left) and the chimpanzee (lower right) have developed knuckle-walking as the form of locomotion most practical for their ground-based way of life. The fifth living ape, the bonobo, is shown in Figure 4–22.

As shown in Table 3-4, the anthropoids possess numerous anatomical differences from prosimians. Among anthropoids the sense of smell has been further reduced as the muzzle has been shortened and the rhinarium lost. The eyes of anthropoids are close together and forwardly directed, adapted for diurnal vision, and protected by complete bony sockets. With the exception of the tiny marmosets and tamarins of the New World, anthropoids have flat nails on all of their digits. (The small callitrichid monkeys have "reevolved" claws by compressing and curving their nails, and these pseudoclaws are used for moving about in squirrel fashion in the trees. Most anthropoids are large, heavy animals, however, that have only nails; claws cannot bear the weight of a big arboreal animal.) Anthropoids also have lower jaws that are fused at the midline, and their front teeth are vertically implanted (no toothcomb). And finally, as detailed in Chapter 13, anthropoids show increases in the relative size and complexity of the brain. Monkeys, apes, and humans all have a larger and more complexly folded cerebral cortex than prosimians. To some extent this is due to changes in the animals' sensory systems, but it is also related to increased intelligence.

For the purpose of further anatomical comparisons, anthropoids may be divided in several ways. Some authorities distinguish the **platyrrhines** from the **catarrhines**. The first category includes the New World monkeys (superfamily Ceboidea), all of which are marked by round nostrils that are widely spaced and face laterally, and by a total of 12 premolars in the adult dentition. Catarrhines include the Old World monkeys, apes, and humans (superfamilies Cercopithecoidea and

Platyrrhines an infraorder of the *anthropoids* that includes the *New World monkeys*.

Catarrhines an infraorder of the *anthropoids* that includes *Old World monkeys, apes,* and humans.

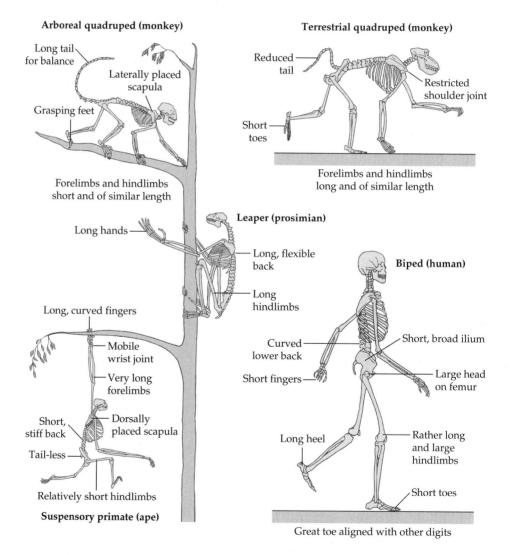

Figure 3–15   Monkeys are generally arboreal or terrestrial quadrupeds, while hominoids engage in arboreal suspensory behavior, knuckle-walking, and bipedalism. This figure shows some of the anatomical features associated with each main type of primate locomotion.

Hominoidea), and they are characterized by compressed, closely spaced, and downwardly directed nostrils, and only eight permanent premolars (see Figure 3–13 for examples of both types). This division of New World versus Old World anthropoids will be useful when we begin to interpret the primate fossil record (Chapter 5), but for now a convenient classification separates all monkeys (Old and New World varieties combined) from all hominoids (apes and humans combined). Monkeys have long backs, narrow chests, laterally placed scapulae (shoulder blades) and a tail (Figure 3–15). Some ceboids have **prehensile** or grasping tails, but none of the cercopithecoids is so equipped. Monkeys also have a smaller range of motion at the shoulder than hominoids (Figure 3–16). These anatomical traits are correlated with habitual quadrupedal locomotion both in the trees and on the ground (Figure 3–15). Generally speaking, monkeys walk, run, and leap about on all fours. This is not to say that monkeys don't or can't do other things—some species show a good deal of hanging and swinging by their arms (or tail)—but the majority of species usually move about quadrupedally along the tops of branches.

The anatomy of hominoids (apes and humans, members of the superfamily Hominoidea) differs significantly from that of monkeys. To start at the top, hominoids have larger brains than monkeys and this larger brain size is correlated with new functional capabilities such as self-recognition (in some species) and learning by insight. Hominoids also have certain distinctive dental traits. Their lower molars show a characteristic arrangement of five cusps and grooves called the **Y-5 pattern**. Old World monkeys, in contrast, show a pattern of molar cusp morphology called **bilophodonty**: four cusps that are arranged in two pairs (front

Prehensile adapted for grasping.

Y-5 pattern an arrangement of the cusps and grooves of lower molars that is characteristic of living *hominoids*.

Bilophodonty the molar cusps pattern of *Old World monkeys*, featuring four cusps arranged in front and rear pairs.

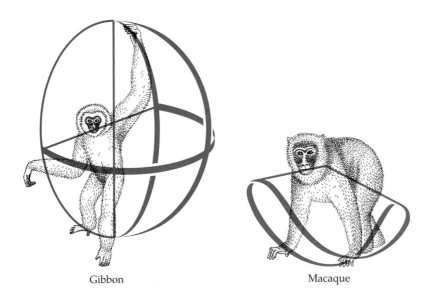

Gibbon   Macaque

FIGURE 3–16   One of the basic differences between apes and monkeys lies in the greater freedom of movement that the former have in their forelimbs. Apes are climbers; many can also swing by their arms in trees and can move their arms freely in all directions (gibbon, left). Most monkeys (such as the Asian macaque, right), by contrast, are true quadrupeds. Since they travel on four limbs, they need move their front legs only backward and forward and a little to the side. They leap and jump in the trees and run across the ground.

Top views

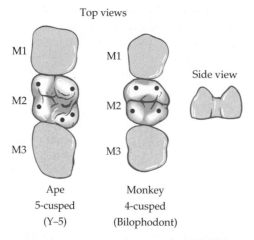

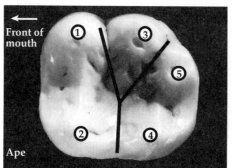
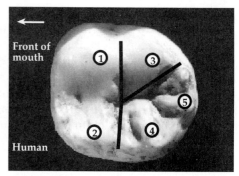

FIGURE 3–17 The cusp patterns of the lower molars enable us to distinguish apes and monkeys with ease. Old World monkeys show four paired cusps (the bilophodont pattern); front and rear cusps are clearly seen in a side view. In contrast, humans are relatively difficult to distinguish from apes on the basis of the molar teeth: both have five cusps following a Y-5 pattern. In some human lower molars, however, the fifth cusp has been lost and it is commonly much reduced.

Postcranial referring to any anatomical feature that is behind the head (in quadrupeds) or below the head (in bipeds).

and rear), with the members of a pair connected by a transverse ridge of enamel (Figure 3–17).

With regard to **postcranial** anatomy, all hominoids show broad chests with dorsal scapulae; short, stiff backs; relatively long arms with mobile wrists, elbows, and shoulders; and no tail. These traits are probably adaptations for suspensory locomotion and posture (arm swinging or hanging), behaviors that are shown to some extent by all living apes, though not by humans. A closer look at the variety of hominoid locomotor patterns, and their associated anatomical variations, is instructive.

The most obvious distinction between apes and monkeys is that apes are built for a different mode of travel, having short, wide, shallow trunks and long, free-swinging arms that rotate at the shoulders. These adaptations allowed apes to reach out in all directions in the trees, climbing arm over arm.

From their probable beginning as efficient climbers, the different families of apes have adapted in different ways. The gibbons and siamangs (Hylobatidae), although they climb much of the time, especially when feeding, have evolved very long arms and hands and in this way are specialized for the horizontal arm-over-

FIGURE 3–18   This photograph shows the hanging locomotion (called *brachiation*) of a gibbon (here photographed brachiating along a rope in a cage).

arm locomotion called **brachiation**. They can throw themselves from hand to hand, swinging under the branches through the treetops, often with their legs tucked up under their bodies. They can travel with considerable speed and extraordinary grace (Figure 3–18).

The orangutan (*Pongo*) moves steadily, climbing through the trees with all four limbs. So flexible are its shoulder and hip joints that its legs are like arms in use: the animal almost appears to be four-armed and four-handed (Figure 3–14). On the ground the orangutan moves quadrupedally with clenched fists and feet, though it occasionally walks on the palms of its hands. Both the gibbons and the orangutans are fully adapted to arboreal life, however, and show no specific terrestrial adaptations.

The African apes (family Panidae), however, do show such adaptations, and the larger species, especially the mountain gorilla, have almost deserted the trees for the ground, though they will still sleep in trees. Although the smaller chimpanzees are good climbers, all species of panids are adapted to terrestrial quadrupedalism, and they walk on the soles of their feet and the knuckles of their hands. The terrestrial skeletal adaptations are seen in the bones of their wrists and hands, which are modified to support the weight of the animals on their knuckles—on the second phalanx counting from the tip of the finger (Figure 3–14). Here, normal hairy skin is replaced by hairless friction skin such as we find on the palms of our hands and the soles of our feet.

Thus the living apes, sharing a common ancestor which we believe was an arboreal climber that underwent a reduction in the tail, have each in their own way modified this original locomotor adaptation together with their skeleton and musculature. The tail was lost because a climber does not need an organ that balances and adjusts the aerodynamics of a leaping animal. Human ancestors have taken a fourth route—to terrestrial bipedalism. Although we are still quite able as climbers, our lower limbs have undergone profound changes in adaptation to **bipedal** walking on the ground.

> **Brachiation** an arboreal locomotor pattern featuring manual swinging from branch to branch.

> **Bipedal** moving erect on the hind limbs only.

Changes in Anatomy

Obviously, the adaptation that gave the apes the ability to climb with their arms and distribute their weight among several branches provided them with an opportunity for increased size. But having been granted this opportunity, what led them to exploit it? What advantage did the apes win by growing bigger?

TABLE 3-5   *Hominoid Comparative Anatomy: Size and Longevity*

TRAIT	HUMANS (Homo sapiens)	CHIMPS (Pan troglodytes)	BONOBOS (Pan paniscus)	GORILLAS (Gorilla gorilla)	ORANGUTANS (Pongo pygmaeus)	GIBBONS (Hylobates species)
Adult body weight: F–M range	100 – 200 lb. (40–70 kg.)	73–132 lb. (33–60 kg.)	73–99 lb. (33–45 kg.)	159–386 lb. (72–175 kg.)	82–179 lb. (37–81 kg.)	11–24 lb. (5–11 kg.)
F body weight as a percentage of M weight	81	78	73	51	46	94
Life span	75 yrs.	>50 yrs.	>50 yrs.(?)	>50 yrs.	>55 yrs.	>30 yrs.(?)

(Data from Fleagle, 1988; Napier and Napier, 1985.)

There was, of course, the competitive advantage that any big animal has over a smaller one when it comes to eating or being eaten. But there is also an extended life span (Table 3-5). Big animals tend to live longer, and their rate of metabolism is slower than that of small animals: their internal organs simply do not have to work so hard and therefore do not wear out as fast.

Any useful change often begets more change along the same line of development: it is a basic rule of evolutionary dynamics. Climbing prompted a series of further changes in the apes that altered the primate anatomy, providing on the one hand the potential for bipedal and tool-using humans and on the other the specialized adaptations of the modern anthropoid apes. As part of their adaptations for arboreal movement, the apes acquired a whole new complex of characteristics in their shoulders, their elbows, and their wrists that combined to make their arm movements much more flexible. Apes can swing their arms out in a wide circle from their shoulders. With their more flexible elbows they can straighten out their arms, and their wrists are much more mobile than a monkey's—more so, in fact, than a human's. An ape can hang from a branch by one hand and rotate its body completely around, thanks to the flexibility of its arm and wrist joints.

Nor did the changes that arose from climbing stop at the apes' arms and shoulders. Ultimately changes affected the whole of their upper bodies, giving them their characteristic short, relatively inflexible spine; the wide, shallow trunk with its resultant different arrangement of the internal organs; and a pelvis splayed out to provide additional room for the attachment of muscles. All these changes helped to produce animals that, from the waist up, physically began to remind us of the apes' evolutionary descendants—humans.

The results of the apes' evolutionary shift from quadrupedalism to climbing and brachiation are profoundly important. If an animal evolves greater erectness and arm flexibility, it can reach farther and grasp, pluck, hold, examine, and carry with greater ease. The more often a hand performs these acts, the better it gets at doing them. Despite their short thumbs, chimpanzees have the manual dexterity to strip the leaves from a twig (in other words, to make an implement) and to deftly insert that twig into a small hole in a termite mound so that they can lick off the termites that cling to the twig when it is pulled out (Figure 3–19). This remarkable act of food gathering requires not only careful manipulation but also intelligence. This is another way of saying that increased dependence on the hands has an evolu-

FIGURE 3–19   Jane Goodall observed chimpanzees fishing with short twigs for termites in mounds. The chimpanzees prepared the twigs by stripping off the leaves and breaking the twigs to a certain length: In fact, they made a tool.

tionary effect on the brain. It is therefore significant that apes are, as a group, more intelligent than monkeys, whose hands are dexterous enough, but whose quadrupedal way of life limits their use and thus limits the feedback that the use of the hands has on the evolution of the brain.

HUMAN CHARACTERISTICS

In the traditional evolutionary classification of Table 3–3, humans are the only living representatives of the primate family Hominidae, that is, the only living *hominids*. An abbreviated list of hominid traits is given in Table 3–4, but this list provides a most incomplete description of the attributes and abilities of modern people. What is it that makes humans different from the other primates? From among all the physical traits that separate humans from all other animals, four have overwhelming significance. The first three are a skeleton adapted for erect bipedalism (upright walking; Figures 3–15 and 3–20); eyes capable of sharp, three-dimensional vision in color; and hands that can both grip powerfully and manipulate things nimbly. These features are found in some degree in many primates; it is their elaboration and special combination with one another that distinguishes us. Controlling and making use of this equipment is humans' fourth significant trait:

FIGURE 3–20   Bipedalism involves split-second balancing feats with precise muscular control. The right foot pushes off from the toe; the left foot bears the full body weight while the right leg moves ahead to land on the heel; then the left foot thrusts off.

the brain—a physical organ itself, but one that introduces the capacity for rational thought and, with the body, makes possible that other most human of all our abilities: speech.

Bipedalism

The four distinguishing attributes uniquely combined in humans interact with one another. It is impossible to say that one led to the next, or that one is necessarily more important than the others. Each reinforces the others and makes improvements in them possible. Nevertheless, one attribute stands out simply because it is so conspicuous: upright walking. It is a remarkably effective method of locomotion, and no animal can use it as consistently as humans can.

For all its apparent simplicity, walking is an adaptation as specialized as flying is to a bat or swimming is to a seal. True, humans are not the only animals able to stand on their hind legs; birds, bears, and a number of our primate cousins occasionally do so. But with the exception of a few flightless birds, such as the ostrich, humans are the only animals that depend exclusively on two legs for locomotion. (The kangaroo, which may seem to be bipedal, actually uses its tail as a third limb and jumps rather than walks.) Using two legs, a human has the endurance to outrun a deer and can carry heavier loads, pound for pound of body weight, than a donkey. Only humans can swim a mile, walk several miles, and then climb a tree. Hominid bipedalism is specialized, yet it allows extraordinary versatility in locomotion.

Like horses, human beings have a variety of gaits; they amble, stride, jog, and sprint. The simple stride, though, is at once the most useful and the most peculiarly human way of getting from one place to another. Probably evolved on the African grassland, or **savanna**, where our early ancestors often covered many miles in a day's food gathering or scavenging, the long, free-swinging stride has taken us to every corner of the earth. Striding is no minor accomplishment. When compared with the way four-legged animals get about, human walking turns out to be a surprisingly complex feat (see Figure 3–20). "Without split-second timing," said John Napier, a British authority on primates, "man would fall flat on his face; in fact with each step he takes, he teeters on the edge of catastrophe." Human walking is

Savanna tropical or subtropical grassland, often with scattered trees (woodland savanna).

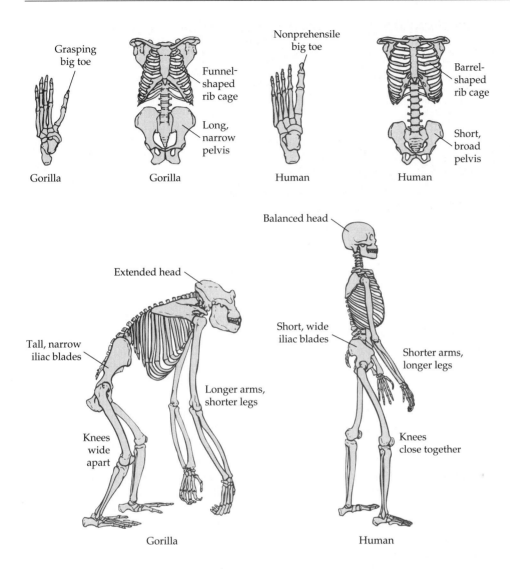

FIGURE 3–21 A comparison of key skeletal features of bipedal humans and quadrupedal apes.

actually a balancing act in which the muscles of the feet, legs, hips, and back are alternately contracted and relaxed according to synchronized orders from the brain and the spinal cord.

As Huxley showed in 1863, the human skeleton is closer in form to that of the African great apes than to that of any other animal. There are nevertheless striking differences between the human and the African ape skeletons—differences almost entirely due to the evolution among hominids of bipedal walking and among apes of quadrupedal knuckle-walking (Figure 3–21; see also Table 3-6). The human foot has lost the ability to grip with the big toe and the toe itself has become long and robust, forming the ball of the foot—an essential pivot for the act of walking. Human arms are short and legs long, in relation to the length of the trunk, while the apes have relatively long arms and short legs, indicating that the arms are more important in locomotion. The human knee has been modified for the transmission

TABLE 3-6 *Hominoid Comparative Anatomy: Limbs and Hips*

TRAIT	HUMANS	CHIMPANZEES	BONOBOS	GORILLAS	ORANGUTANS	GIBBONS
Arms as % of body weight[a]	8	16	16	?	18	20
Arm length × 100 divided by trunk length[a]	148	172	?	172	200	238
Legs as % of body weight[b]	30	18	24	?	18	18
Leg length × 100 divided by trunk length[b]	169	127	?	124	116	140
Ilium width × 100 divided by ilium length	126	66	?	92	74	49
Width of hip socket × 100 divided by ilium length	30	12	?	15	14	11

[a]Note that humans' arms are lighter and shorter than apes' arms.
[b] Humans' legs are heavier and longer than apes' legs.
(Data from Aiello and Dean, 1990; Schultz, 1968.)

of weight and can be locked when extended. Fundamental changes have occurred in the pelvis as well. Compared to apes, our pelvis is shorter (a change that improved bipedal balance) and has a broader blade or *ilium* (giving greater leverage to the muscles that hold the body erect). Additionally, our hip sockets have increased in relative size to match the greater weight they transmit compared to apes. Almost every bone in the body reflects the remarkable evolution of humans' and apes' distinctly different kinds of posture and locomotion.

Balanced bipedalism is uniquely human and strangely beautiful in its sheer efficiency and its superb adaptation of bone and muscle, brain and nerve, to the tricky problem of moving about on two limbs rather than four. Our adaptations for bipedalism have not been perfected, however (Box 3-2). Back trouble, foot ailments, and difficulty in giving birth—common among humans—result partly from upright posture. Indeed, natural selection does not necessarily generate perfection in any trait. If a species survives, natural selection has brought about those traits required for survival and reproduction—nothing more. To our eyes, the results often seem to constitute a kind of perfection, but most traits are compromises.

Vision

Why is it so important to human evolution that we stand erect and walk on two legs? Part of the answer has to do with the human head. The head is where the eyes are, and the taller an animal stands, the more it sees. A dog running through tall grass is forced to leap into the air time and again to get its bearings, but even on a

Box 3-2

CURRENT ISSUE: *Humans' Anatomical Imperfections*

The human body is a marvelous and intricate piece of biological machinery. Indeed, that complexity is so impressive (at least to us) that it is often given as proof that we must be the result of divine design. Surely, the reasoning goes, only God could have made creatures with our intelligence, physical skills, and beauty. As Shakespeare said, "What a piece of work . . .!" Well, lest you get carried away with that logic, let's run down a list of human imperfections related to the switch from quadrupedalism to bipedalism, problems that natural selection has not been able to correct. (See also Price, 1996.)

First, as an adaptation for a fully upright and balanced stance, humans evolved a strong curvature in the small of the back (see Figure 3–15; apes have a straight lower back). Unfortunately, the curved shape and increased pressure on the lower back due to carrying the full weight of the upper body have increased our vulnerability to painful conditions such as pulled muscles, slipped discs, lumbago (rheumatism), and scoliosis (lateral curvature of the spine). Second, expanding brain size in our species has resulted in an increase in the size of a baby's head at birth. Women's average pelvic size has not been able to keep up, however (pelvic width is constrained by the biomechanical requirements of bipedalism), and the ensuing mismatch— newborn head lengths that are slightly bigger than mothers' pelvic widths—has resulted in more difficult deliveries than in other hominoids. Third, humans' upright posture puts much more pressure on the muscles of our lower abdominal wall than is true for quadrupeds and, as a result, we commonly rupture those muscles (producing hernias) during heavy lifting or sometimes even as the result of vigorous coughing. Fourth, because the human heart is so far above the ground, our blood can have a hard time overcoming the pull of gravity to make the return trip from the feet. A result: distended and swollen varicose veins, particularly in older people. Fifth, humans' common complaint of hemorrhoids is related partly to our upright posture bringing extra pressure to bear on the blood vessels supplying the large intestine's lower end. As many sufferers can attest, these vessels can become swollen and quite painful. And finally, bipedalism puts the full weight of the body on our feet alone (as opposed to quadrupeds' hands *and* feet). In the course of a human lifetime, this can result in painful calluses and fallen arches (flat feet), conditions that can be exacerbated by poorly designed or ill-fitting shoes.

And so, the human body *is* marvelous, and also distinctly imperfect. Working with the material at hand, natural selection converted quadruped apes into bipedal humans. But, unfortunately for us, natural selection is concerned with survival, not perfection, and as a result it left us with several annoying and painful rough edges. ∎

smooth surface where no obstacles obstruct vision, the advantage of height is marked. Eyes that are 2 feet (0.6 meters) above ground level can detect low objects about 6 miles (almost 10 kilometers) away; eyes 5 feet (1.5 meters) above the ground can see 9 miles (14 kilometers) farther (Figure 3–22).

The advantage of height is especially important because vision is the most important of our five major senses. Scientists estimate that some 90 percent of the information stored in the brain arrives there through the agency of the eyes. Human eyes are attuned precisely to human needs. In general, they are unsurpassed by any other eyes in the world. A hawk can see more sharply but cannot move its eyes easily and must move its head to follow its prey. A dragonfly can

FIGURE 3–22   More distant information about its environment is available to an animal with eyes 3 or 4 feet (about 1 meter) above ground level (left) than to one of low height (right). These photographs, taken from different heights, are sharp at all distances, but animals other than primates usually can focus only at certain ranges of distance.

follow faster movement but cannot focus a sharp image. A horse can see almost completely behind its head but has difficulty seeing objects straight ahead at close range. Most important, human beings and their nearest primate relatives have the special combination of full stereoscopic vision and color vision (Figure 3–12). Human eyes, placed at the front of the head rather than at the sides, can focus together on an object so that it is perceived as a single three-dimensional image in the brain. And within this image, color vision enables us to pick out details by hue as well as by form, relationship, and brightness.

Taken together, color vision and depth perception bring us enormous advantages over most other animals, the majority of which are either color-blind or have a relatively poor capacity to judge visual distances and to focus in fine detail on particular objects. Though it has stereoscopic vision, a dog sees, when it looks out over an open field, little more than what a black-and-white movie might show, though with some color sense, and the dog's distance focus is limited. The dog is unlikely to spot a rabbit in the field unless the rabbit moves—one reason rabbits and similar prey react to noises by freezing, which conceals them from their enemies. Human hunters, on the other hand, can scan a scene from their feet to the horizon in a few seconds by focusing sharply and selectively on a succession of images. And they see more images than any dog does because their eyes are raised at least 3 feet (almost 1 meter) higher above the ground and their vision is in color.

Hands

Humans stand up partly in order to see and stay up partly because they see so well. But the freedom that this posture gives to their arms, and particularly their hands, has proved even more decisive in distinguishing humans from animals. Chimpanzees, though often upright and occasionally bipedal, are basically quadrupedal animals, and they lack free use of the arms. In an experimental situation they can get around with a bunch of bananas in their arms, but they must always be ready to maintain their balance with the help of a knuckle on the ground. Humans have far less need for caution. Babies may crawl on all fours; old people may rely on canes; but most humans go about with never a thought of support by anything but their two legs. Their hands are free to grab, carry, and manipulate.

Not needing our hands for support, we have been able to use them for more complicated and more creative tasks. With 25 joints and 58 distinctly different motions, the human hand is one of the most advanced mechanisms produced by nature. Imagine a single tool that can meet the demands of tasks as varied as gripping a tool, playing a violin, wringing out a towel, holding a pencil, gesturing, and—something we tend to forget—simple feeling.

Furthermore, while the hand itself may be a marvelous tool, it is used to full value only when it manipulates still other tools. This capacity is a second-stage benefit of upright walking. With our erect posture, our hands are free; with hands free, we can use tools; with tools, we can get food more easily and exploit the environment in other ways to ensure our survival. Humans are not the only animals that use tools, but they are the only ones that have become *dependent* on tools.

There are two distinct ways of holding and using tools: the **power grip** and the **precision grip**, as John Napier termed them (Figure 3–23). Human infants and children begin with the power grip and progress to the precision grip. Think of how a child holds a spoon: first in the power grip, in its fist or between its fingers and palm, and later between the tips of the thumb and the first two fingers, in the precision grip. All primates have the power grip. It is the way they get firm hold of a tree branch. But only catarrhine primates have thumbs that are long enough or

Power grip a grip involving all fingers of the hand equally, as in grasping a baseball.

Precision grip a grip that involves opposing the tip of the thumb to the tips of the other fingers, allowing fine control of small objects.

FIGURE 3–23   The power grip (left) and the precision grip (right) are illustrated in these photographs, together with the uniquely human independent control of the five fingers.

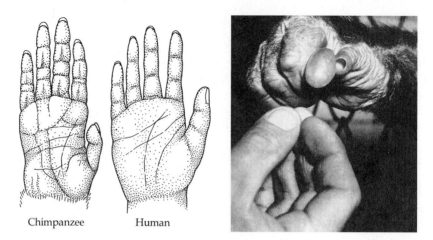

FIGURE 3–24   Though superficially like a human hand, the hand of a chimpanzee has a relatively short thumb and less independent control of the fingers. As the photograph shows, when the chimpanzee picks up an object between finger and thumb, it does not fully oppose the tip of the thumb to the tips of the fingers as do humans. Thus, compared to humans (and Old World monkeys), the ape's precision grip is somewhat impaired.

flexible enough to be completely opposable through rotation at the wrist, able to reach to the tips of all the other fingers and thus provide some degree of precision gripping. Apes and Old World monkeys differ in their grips, however, and, unexpectedly, the monkeys are somewhat more like humans. As an adaptation for arboreal arm-swinging and arm-hanging, apes have evolved greatly elongated fingers, exclusive of the thumb (see the hand length index in Table 3-7). As a result, apes' thumbs are relatively quite short and, despite their potential full opposability, usually produce only an impaired precision grip (Figure 3–24). Humans' long, fully opposable thumbs and the independent control of our fingers make possible

TABLE 3-7   *Hominoid Comparative Anatomy: Hands and Brains*

TRAIT	HUMANS	CHIMPANZEES	BONOBOS	GORILLAS	ORANGUTANS	GIBBONS
Hand length × 100 divided by trunk length[a]	37	49	?	40	53	55
Thumb length × 100 divided by index finger length[a]	65	43	?	47	40	46
Brain size (sexes averaged)	1330 cc	383 cc	?	505cc	377 cc	103 cc
Encephalization quotient (EQ)[b]	7.2	3.0	?	2.4	1.8	2.2

[a] Note that humans have relatively short hands, but long thumbs.
[b] EQ expresses a species' actual brain size relative to the expected brain size calculated from body weight.
(Data from Aiello and Dean, 1990; Schultz, 1968, 1969; Napier, 1970.)

nearly all the movements necessary to handle tools, to make clothing, to write with a pencil, to play a flute.

But the fine precision grip of humans would be a much less extraordinary adaptation without the complex brain that coordinates and directs its use. In the human lineage, manipulation, tool use, and the brain may have developed together. The hand carries out some of the most critical and complex orders of the brain, and as the hand grew more skillful so did the brain.

The Brain

The human brain is not much to look at. On the dissecting table, it is a "pinkish-gray mass, moist and rubbery to the touch . . . perched like a flower on top of a slender stalk" (the spinal cord). An ape's brain does not look very different. But there is a difference, and it is crucial. It lies in the extent of the gray layer called the *cortex*, which constitutes the outer layer of the largest part of the brain, the cerebrum. The cortex, scientists now know, plays the major role in reasoned behavior, memory, and abstract thought—and also supervises the delicate and accurate muscular movements that control the precision grip. The cortex is quite thin, but it represents 80 percent of the volume of the human brain and contains most of the brain's estimated 10 billion nerve cells, or **neurons**. If spread out flat, it would be about the size of a large newspaper page. It fits inside the head only by being compressed like a crumpled rag (the famous "convolutions" of the brain are mainly the folds and overlaps of the cerebral cortex). This compression demonstrates that the cortex has all but outgrown its allotted space. Indeed, the human brain is more than seven times larger than expected for a mammal of our body size. Somehow, the increase in the size of the cortex has helped make our brain the uniquely human thing it is (Figure 3–25 and see Chapter 13).

Neurons nerve cells; the basic units of the nervous system.

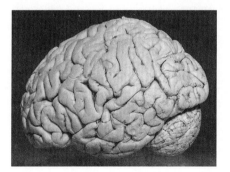

FIGURE 3–25 Conscious mental activity takes place at the surface, or cortex, of the cerebral hemispheres, the two halves of the cerebrum. This cortex has evolved so much in primate evolution that, in apes and humans, it is too large to be smooth, as it used to be, and is deeply folded. This series of diagrams illustrates the importance of the cerebrum and its cortex in humans. The photo shows a freshly dissected human brain.

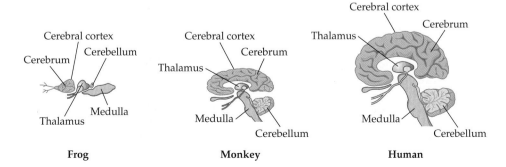

Frog   Monkey   Human

Although many mysteries about the brain remain to be solved, some of its secrets, particularly the importance of the huge cortex, are now well understood. The cortex is not only the seat of intelligence but also, and perhaps more significantly, the part of the brain where sense impressions and memories are stored to be called forth and acted on as circumstances suggest. The working of the human cortex follows no fixed pattern that dictates certain associations between experience and memory, as in some animal brains, and few predetermined responses are generated in the cortex. Among animals, many patterns of action are effectively automatic, performed by inborn programs or through previous conditioning. In humans, these patterns are, to some extent, performed consciously, or refrained from consciously, or replaced by completely new patterns, again consciously. This use of the brain results in what is known as *reasoned behavior*, a phenomenon typically human and rarely seen in other animals.

But of course the most impressive mental ability of humans is not the ease with which we solve problems or reason through behavioral decisions. Rather, it is our ability to look inward and observe our own mental processes: Humans not only think but know they are thinking. We are conscious of what we know, believe, and feel, and we recognize knowledge, beliefs, and emotions in other people (we are also quick to manipulate others' beliefs, emotions, and knowledge to our own advantage). In a word, humans have a *mind*—but is this also true of other primates? Primatologists Dorothy Cheney and Robert Seyfarth have summarized much of what is known about the problem of mind among nonhuman primates in their book *How Monkeys See the World*. They find little evidence of mind among monkeys. Although monkeys know a lot about their physical and social environments, they differ from humans in their failure to use knowledge for personal gain—apparently because they "do not know what they know and cannot reflect upon their knowledge, their emotions, or their beliefs." Monkeys apparently are unable to attribute mental states or impute motives to other individuals, and therefore these concepts do not affect how they behave. Furthermore, monkeys appear to have little if any self-awareness. But, Cheney and Seyfarth continue, apes may be different. Research on apes (primarily chimpanzees) suggests that these animals may be far superior to monkeys in attributing mental states to each other: "There is strong suggestive evidence that chimpanzees, if not other apes, recognize that other individuals have beliefs and that their own behavior can affect those beliefs. Unlike monkeys, chimpanzees seem to understand each others' goals and motives. They deceive each other in more ways and in more contexts than monkeys, and they seem better than monkeys at recognizing both their own and other individuals' knowledge and limitations." In other words, apes may fall squarely between monkeys and humans with regard to the evolution of mind.

Language and Speech

Language the cognitive aspect of human communication, involving symbolic thinking structured by grammar.

Speech the oral expression of *language* (other expressions include signed or written language).

The uniquely large and complex human brain has combined with certain critical bodily modifications to produce our most important innovations: **language** and **speech**. Although virtually all animals communicate with their fellows, only humans think symbolically and transmit their thoughts by talking. Bees dance to direct hive mates to food; wolves warn off intruders by marking their territories with scent; one bird calls to announce danger, another to initiate courtship. Besides using these ancient methods of communication, including bodily movements and simple sounds, humans also use speech, that most common physical expression of language, a repertory of short, contrasting sounds that can be combined in an almost infinite number of ways. While animals communicate emotional state and, on occasion, limited information about their physical or social circumstances, humans routinely engage in complex linguistic exchanges of information or ideas.

Language and speech are so clearly dependent on brainpower that their dependence on the body is often overlooked. The role of the body is most clearly demonstrated by studies of chimpanzees. Chimpanzees have brains that appear to be adequate for some degree of abstract thought and some learning by insight. They can stack several boxes on top of one another to reach a bunch of bananas, a simple act to us, but one requiring the imaginative combination of superficially unrelated elements. They can also produce a wide range of sounds. It seems that they ought, then, to be able to talk. Since the turn of the century scientists have been trying to teach chimpanzees to speak. The best anyone has been able to do, after years of patient tutelage, is to get a chimpanzee to say "mama," "papa," and one or two other infant words. Only recently has the reason for this failure been traced. It involves not simply brain size but other aspects of the anatomy. Chimpanzees and gorillas are indeed able to use very simple sentences—but they cannot speak them. These apes lack the kind of pharynx, mouth, and tongue that enable humans to articulate vowels. With training, they can "speak" somewhat, not with auditory symbols, but with visual ones, specifically, with the symbols of American Sign Language, originally designed for the deaf (see Chapter 13). The human remains the only creature that has developed both the physical structures and the powerful, specialized brain needed to produce speech.

Cultural Adaptation

Language was perhaps the last of our major biological characteristics to evolve. And with the gift of speech, we acquired an immensely powerful tool for the development and continuing evolution of our unique way of life—a way of life based on cultural adaptation. Unlike the other primates, humans are no longer wholly at the mercy of their surroundings. Faced with environmental challenges, we invent cultural solutions rather than evolve biological ones (apes also do this to a very limited extent, as described in Chapter 4). Clothes, shelters, and heating and cooling systems help us deal with harsh climatic conditions. Tools, irrigation systems, and pesticides help us aggressively exploit the environment for food. Medical technology helps us deal with diseases and physical handicaps. Furthermore, thanks to language, human knowledge is cumulative: it increases steadily as each new generation's innovations are added to the summed knowledge passed down to it. Thus **culture** evolves in a Lamarckian fashion, by the inheritance of acquired traits.

Culture humans' systems of learned behavior, symbols, customs, beliefs, institutions, artifacts, and technology, characteristic of a group and transmitted by its members to their offspring.

The importance of humans' evolution of a cultural way of life cannot be overemphasized. Our reliance on cultural adaptation has set us apart from the other primates. For better or worse, we are the only living primate species that exerts significant control over its own evolutionary future.

SUMMARY

The first primates evolved at least 60 million years ago. Today the order is represented by more than 200 species and is characterized by extreme physical and behavioral diversity. The most basic primate traits—grasping hands and feet, and stereoscopic vision with depth perception (plus the neural elaborations that go with these developments)—were most likely originally adaptations for predation on insects in an arboreal habitat. The primate order contains two suborders: Prosimii and Anthropoidea. The prosimians were the first suborder to evolve, and today they are characterized by the retention of several primitive anatomical traits, including a keen sense of smell and relatively unprotected eyes. At present these small (and often nocturnal) creatures are found only in Africa and Asia. The anthropoid suborder, today including monkeys, apes, and humans, first appeared about 45 to 50 million years ago. Compared to prosimians, living anthropoids show a reduced sense of smell, elaborated vision, complete loss of claws, and a more complex brain. Modern monkeys are found in Central and South America (superfamily Ceboidea) and in Africa and Asia (superfamily Cercopithecoidea). Most monkeys show some variety of quadrupedal locomotion in the trees.

The superfamily Hominoidea includes the apes and humans. While humans are found worldwide, apes are limited to Africa (chimpanzees, bonobos, and gorillas) and Asia (gibbons and orangutans). Apes tend to be large, tailless, arboreal arm-swingers and arm-hangers (or their terrestrial descendants), while humans have evolved into terrestrial bipeds. Hominoids display the largest, most complex brains of all primates. Humans have shown unparalleled brain expansion and elaboration, and they are characterized by the unique possession of a fully developed mind. Other unique traits shown by humans include language and speech and cultural adaptation as a way of life. The latter has given humans considerable control over their evolutionary future.

POSTSCRIPT

Along with many other species, nonhuman primates are currently in a state of global emergency. Of the 200-plus primate species, more than 50 percent are considered endangered or in some jeopardy, and one in five is likely to become extinct in just a few years if strict conservation measures are not begun immediately. Among the species at greatest risk are several of Madagascar's prosimians (aye-ayes, hairy-eared dwarf lemurs, golden and greater bamboo lemurs, and Perrier's sifaka), the muriqui monkeys and lion tamarins of South America, the Asian golden snub-nosed and Tonkin snub-nosed monkeys, the lion-tail macaques of India, and Africa's red colobus monkeys. Most of the living apes are endangered to some degree, although mountain gorillas—with only 600 or so individuals left—are clearly at the greatest risk of imminent extinction.

Who is responsible for bringing so many of our evolutionary relatives to the brink of disaster? Unfortunately, we have no one to blame but ourselves. Through our use of primates for food, pets, and research subjects and our destruction of their natural habitats, we have become monkeys', apes' and prosimians' worst enemy. Let's consider the problem.

The global population of humans is currently about 5.6 billion; this figure is predicted to rise to more than 10 billion by the middle of the next century. Population growth is uneven from one country to the next, but the highest rates seem generally to be in underdeveloped tropical countries (around 3 percent annual growth). All of these people need—and demand—food and living space, and in their efforts to meet these needs, they are causing massive habitat destruction. Habitat destruction impinges most directly on primates when it affects the tropical and subtropical forests since, as explained in this chapter, this is where most species naturally occur—and the forests of the world are being ravaged. Every year some 67,000 square miles (more than 173,000 square kilometers) of tropical and subtropical forest are destroyed worldwide—an area almost as big as the state of Washington. About 180 square miles (466 square kilometers) of forests are destroyed every day! The forests are cut down to make space for agriculture and ranching, for fuel to be used locally, and for exportable wood. And as the forests go, so do their primate inhabitants. The primate-rich Amazonian forests are expected to be reduced by half in the next 25 years, while the Congo basin forests will decrease 25 percent in the same period.

In addition to habitat destruction, humans contribute to primate extinction by hunting the animals for food and capturing them to sell. Primates are an important source of food in many parts of tropical South America and Africa. Additionally, even if they are not on the menu, when primates begin to raid farms and gardens they are hunted and killed as agricultural pests. Furthermore, tens of thousands of primates are captured each year for sale as pets or research subjects. Although capturing animals for sale has come under some control in the last few decades, it can still have a major impact on marginal species, and it is terribly inefficient: It has been estimated that traditional capture techniques result in five to ten animals killed for every one that is sold.

What, if anything, can (or should) we do about global habitat destruction and the plight of endangered primates? One response might be that we should do nothing; after all, extinction is a fact of life, and given enough time, the earth will surely adjust to humans' habitat and wildlife depredations. However, is this the wisest course? What do we stand to lose if the forests and their inhabitants are plundered completely? Perhaps we should move quickly to stop the destruction and save the endangered species, but how can we do it? After all, inhabitants of developed countries—comparatively well fed, well housed, and secure—are hardly in a strong moral position to tell people in poor, developing countries to stop destroying the forests and the animals *for the global common good*. Hard questions. And also questions that demand immediate answers and carry high stakes. What's *your* position on these issues?

REVIEW QUESTIONS

1. Review the relative merits of the arboreal and visual predation theories as explanations of the common characteristics of primates.
2. Compare the anatomy of prosimians to that of anthropoid primates. Can anthropoids be said to have progressed beyond the prosimian condition?
3. Why are humans classified as hominoids rather than as monkeys? Describe how human anatomy resembles that of apes and differs from that of monkeys.

4. One can arrange the living primates so that it appears that evolution shaped the creatures to become increasingly humanlike. Discuss this notion of humans being the goal of primate evolution.

5. Do monkeys and apes have minds? Discuss the evidence, and consider the implications of how humans treat these animals.

6. What are the implications of humans now being largely in control of their own evolutionary future?

SUGGESTED FURTHER READING

Bowler, P. J. *Theories of Human Evolution.* The Johns Hopkins University Press, 1986.

Cartmill, M. "New Views on Primate Origins." *Evolutionary Anthropology,* 1, 1992.

Cartmill, M. "Rethinking Primate Origins." *Science,* 184, 1974.

Cheney, D. L., and R. M. Seyfarth. *How Monkeys See the World.* University of Chicago Press, 1990.

Fleagle, J. *Primate Adaptation and Evolution.* Academic Press, 1988.

Napier, J. R., and P. H. Napier. *The Natural History of the Primates.* British Museum (Natural History) and Cambridge University Press, 1985.

Schultz, A. H. *The Life of Primates.* Universe Books, 1969.

Smuts, B., et al., eds. *Primate Societies.* University of Chicago Press, 1987.

Sussman, R. W. "Primate Origins and the Evolution of Angiosperms." *American Journal of Primatology,* 23, 1991.

INTERNET RESOURCES

ELECTRONIC ZOO/NET VET–PRIMATE PAGE
http://www.avma.org/netvet/primates.htm
(Links to primate organizations and information sites.)

PHYSICAL ANTHROPOLOGY WEB SITES
http://www.anth.ucsb.edu/netinfo/netinfo2.html#phys
(Useful links to sites dealing with human evolution, primates, and other topics.)

PRIMATE INFO NET
http://www.primate.wisc.edu/pin
(Maintained by the Wisconsin Regional Primate Research Center, this site provides extensive information about primates, as well as lots of links.)

USEFUL SEARCH TERMS:
apes
human biology
monkeys
physical anthropology
primates
prosimians

THE BEHAVIOR OF LIVING PRIMATES

Studies of living apes such as this orangutan can yield important insights into the early stages of human evolution.

We love animals, we watch them with delight, we study their habits with ever-increasing curiosity; and we destroy them.

KENNETH CLARK, 1903–1983.
Animals and Men, Ch. 5.

OVERVIEW

The fossilized remains of our extinct ancestors provide important direct information about their anatomy, but only limited (and indirect) information about their behavior. In order to make reasonable behavioral reconstructions, researchers often rely on analogies drawn from living human cultures (usually hunting-and-gathering peoples) and nonhuman primates. This chapter presents a broad summary of what scientists have learned about our nonhuman primate kin, including their diets, grouping patterns, social development, sexuality, dominance systems, and affiliative (friendly) relations. Particular emphasis is placed on the various living ape species, since the fossil record makes it clear that humans are descended from ape stock. Important topics in the chapter include social group type, socialization, dominance, sexual behavior, sexual selection, friendly relations, territoriality, and feeding strategies. Also important are the behavioral profiles of baboons, gibbons, orangutans, gorillas, chimpanzees, and bonobos.

STUDYING PRIMATES

Fossils can provide a very good indication of the course of evolution, but they are less good at indicating precisely how evolution came about. This limitation has been a source of frustration to anthropologists for many years—so much so that many are now looking for answers elsewhere than in the fossil record. One alternative field that is fruitful is the study of humankind's primate relatives, the monkeys and apes; closely related to us, they are even more closely related to our ancestors.

Recent developments in biochemistry have shown close similarities of DNA, cell proteins, and blood proteins including hemoglobin between humans and the other primates (Box 4–1). Now, thanks to an upsurge in studies of monkeys and apes in their natural environments, it is becoming clear that in their social behavior, too, they stand much closer to us than we had suspected. Many live in highly organized groups in which following routines and sharing knowledge permit a relatively stable social organization. Others, like chimpanzees, live in more loosely organized groups. Whatever the size or structure of the group, some members are good friends, others dedicated enemies; some are collaborators, others rivals; some are popular, others despised. Infant apes and monkeys, as they grow up, must learn a code of behavior, much as a human child must, and all the members of a group are linked by an elaborate system of communication that uses both sounds and gestures and shows considerable sophistication.

Box 4-1

BIOCHEMICAL RELATIONS BETWEEN HUMANS AND OTHER PRIMATES

Close relationships among humans, apes, and monkeys are demonstrated by our many anatomical similarities, as T. H. Huxley showed in 1863 (Figure 1–14). Within the last forty years, those close relationships have been verified by studies of anthropoids' biochemistry. For example, the figure below shows the results of Vincent Sarich's and Allan Wilson's work on the evolved differences in one protein, serum albumin, for a select set of primates and other mammals. With a total of thirty-two amino acid differences, the serum albumin molecules of humans and rhesus monkeys

are quite distinct (32 = 4 + 12 + 16). This suggests that Old World monkeys and hominoids last shared a common ancestor many millions of years ago (fossil discoveries confirm this; see Chapter 5), and thus the monkey-hominoid fork is placed about a third of the way down the primate branch. In contrast, humans only show seven albumin differences from chimpanzees and gorillas, indicating a much more recent evolutionary divergence, as shown by a higher fork (the two apes are even closer with only six differences separating them).

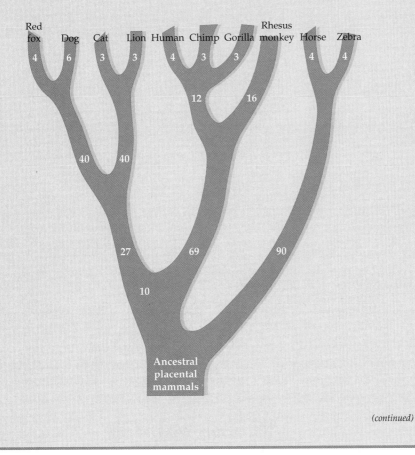

(continued)

Box 4-1 *(continued)*

Other biochemical measures have yielded similar results. As shown in Table 4–1a below, both blood protein immunology and DNA hybridization reveal close evolutionary distances between humans and the African apes, with larger distances separating humans from gibbons (Asian apes), monkeys, and prosimians. (DNA hybridization is a rather complex process that involves splitting a species' double-stranded DNA by heating it, and then comparing the nucleotide sequences on single DNA strands with strands from a second species.) Furthermore, the pooled results of amino acid sequencing studies of several different proteins go beyond the serum albumin evidence and suggest that humans are even closer to chimpanzees than to gorillas. Note that all of the numbers below can be read simply as measures of *relative evolutionary relationship.*

TABLE 4-1A   *Relationships Between Humans and Other Primates Using Biochemical Markers*

BIOCHEMICAL MARKER	CHIMPANZEE	GORILLA	GIBBON	OLD WORLD MONKEY	NEW WORLD MONKEY	PROSIMIAN	SOURCE
Protein immunology	8	8	18	40	70	140	V. M. Sarich and J. E. Cronin (1977)
DNA hybridization	2.3	2.4	6.4	9	15	—	R. E. Beneviste and G. J. Todaro (1976)
Amino acid sequencing	0.3	0.6	2.4	3.8	7.5	11.3	M. Goodman (1975)

Molecular clocks a variety of molecular measures for estimating the time of divergence of living *species* from the common ancestor.

Finally, although there is some disagreement among specialists, it seems reasonable to assume that molecular changes occur at approximately the same rate in different lineages of organisms. This means that measures of accumulated change can be used to estimate the date when lines leading to different living species diverged from their common ancestor. In other words, accumulated change can be used to construct **molecular clocks**. Table 4–1b lists humans' molecular divergence dates from the African ape lineage, as well as from the lines of several other types of anthropoids. Note that these dates are estimates. Many paleontologists still feel that only fossils can give us conclusive evidence of divergence times.

The comparison of ape and monkey behavior with human behavior, of course, must not be pushed too far. Yet, in their daily routine and in many aspects of their relationships with their fellows, the nonhuman primates resemble humans in many surprising ways and throw much light on the roots of human behavior.

Early Work

Although new aspects of the connection between us and our primate kin are continually coming to light, the idea of studying primates is by no means a new one.

> ### Box 4-1 *(continued)*
>
> TABLE 4-1B   *Estimated Times of Evolutionary Divergence Among Higher Primates (in millions of years ago)*
>
> | SPECIES | TIME OF DIVERGENCE BASED ON MOLECULAR CLOCK | TIME OF DIVERGENCE BASED ON FOSSIL EVIDENCE |
> |---|---|---|
> | Humans and *Pan*[a] | 6–7[b] | 5–7 |
> | Humans and gorillas | 8–10[b] | — |
> | Humans and gibbons | 12±3[c] | 12–21 |
> | Humans and Old World monkeys | 20±2[c] | 15–20 |
> | Humans and New World monkeys | ~33[d] | ~27 |
>
> [a]Chimpanzees and bonobos.
> [b]Dates from C. G. Sibley, in *The Cambridge Encyclopedia of Human Evolution* (S. Jones, R. Martin, and D. Pilbeam, eds.), Cambridge, Cambridge University Press, 1992, pp. 313–315.
> [c]Dates from J. E. Cronin, *South African Journal of Science*, 1986, 82:83–85.
> [d]Date from V. Sarich, in *The Cambridge Encyclopedia of Human Evolution* (S. Jones, R. Martin, and D. Pilbeam, eds.), Cambridge, Cambridge University Press, 1992, pp. 303–306.

In the parts of the world where humans live in close contact with monkeys or apes, accounts of their primate neighbors have dotted observers' writings for centuries; the Chinese general Wang Jeñ-yü, for instance, mentioned his pet gibbon Yeh-pin in his memoirs written in the tenth century. Western travelers to foreign lands were especially impressed by monkeys and apes, which in many ways were uncannily similar to themselves. In the mid-1800s, while writers such as Edgar Allan Poe spun tales emphasizing the eerie aspects of the resemblance between ape and human, others who observed monkeys and apes in their natural habitat were awed by what they saw. In 1840 the English naturalist William Charles Martin, observing a female gibbon, wrote, "It is almost impossible to convey in words an idea of the quickness and graceful address of her movements: they may indeed be termed aerial as she seems merely to touch in her progress the branches along which she exhibits her evolutions."

Early in the twentieth century, casual observation of primates began to give rise to more serious study. In the 1920s psychobiologist Robert Yerkes observed captive chimpanzees in the United States and was so impressed by what he saw and so astonished by how little was known about the great apes that he sent two students, Henry Nissen and Harold Bingham, to Africa to study the chimpanzee and the gorilla, respectively. In 1930 Yerkes opened the Laboratories of Primate Biology at Orange Park, Florida, which later moved to Emory University in Atlanta and were renamed the Yerkes Regional Primate Research Center. Behavioral studies, including intelligence tests and other studies of social behavior, as well as studies of stress and other physiological matters, are carried out at the center.

The first systematic investigations of the behavior of apes and monkeys living under natural conditions were made by C. R. Carpenter. In the early 1930s Carpenter journeyed to Barro Colorado Island in Panama to study howler monkeys (*Alouatta palliata*) and then traveled to Southeast Asia to observe gibbons.

Later he set up a colony of rhesus monkeys (*Macaca mulatta*) on Cayo Santiago near Puerto Rico and observed them. Carpenter published some revolutionary findings on monkey behavior. The results he obtained by viewing primates in the wild pointed up the limitations of studying primates in captivity, which had been the practice up to that time.

Around the same period, the South African zoologist Solly Zuckerman was studying baboons—first, hamadryas baboons (*Papio hamadryas*) in the London Zoo and then chacma baboons (*Papio cynocephalus*) in South Africa. Zuckerman was especially interested in what these creatures' behavior might suggest about that of humans. He concluded that sexual behavior was the original force behind social organization among primates, an idea that has since been alternately discredited and somewhat revived. But he was seriously misled by studying baboons in the zoo: their behavior in captivity was quite different from the way they were later found to behave in the wild.

Psychologists, too, took an interest in the behavior of nonhuman primates, particularly that of apes. In Germany, Wolfgang Köhler conducted experiments investigating chimpanzees' capacity to find solutions to problems, such as stacking boxes or using sticks to reach bundles of bananas. In Russia, Nadie Kohts studied chimps' ability to discriminate between objects by size, color, and shape. And in the United States, Harry and Margaret Harlow studied the mother-infant bond in rhesus monkeys. By using artificial surrogate mothers of varying design, the Harlows were able to show that tactile stimuli (i.e., the ability to cling to "mother") was much more important to young monkeys than access to milk. Furthermore, monkeys denied access to their mothers when young showed behavioral problems in adulthood—a finding with important implications regarding humans.

It is exceedingly difficult to do some kinds of experimental work in an animal's natural habitat, for example, surgery, chemical therapy, and experimental separations of mothers and infants. But however useful for gauging an individual animal's response to a specific stimulus or situation it is, observing apes or monkeys in artificial confinement provides only partial insight into normal primate behavior. The other handy spot for observation is the zoo, but there, too, the subjects' behavior is distorted by the abnormal environment (Figure 4–1). Small cages provide scant room for movement, there is no need for ordinary activities such as seeking food, and the crowding found in many zoos transforms the animals' social relationships. For scientists interested in studying normal primate behavior, the only realistic option is to observe monkeys and apes in their natural setting.

A major development in field research occurred after World War II, when primatologists in Japan established the Primate Research Group to study native Japanese macaques (*M. fuscata*) under natural conditions. At Takasakiyama, by setting up feeding stations that a macaque colony with 200-odd members visited regularly, scientists were able to observe one group of monkeys over an extended period. On the island of Koshima, with an isolated macaque population, researchers not only recorded their subjects' customs but to some extent changed them, thereby gaining numerous insights into how the monkeys' behavior and social structure were determined.

Recent Studies

The trend toward studying primates in their native habitats really caught hold in the late 1950s. Led by various anthropologists, a large number of young field workers, including both women and men, began pouring out all over the world from

FIGURE 4–1   Zoos are necessarily extremely unnatural environments for primates, which in nature are gregarious, inquisitive, and extremely active. In these photographs, a gorilla attempts to use dry leaves to build a nest on a concrete floor. Neither hard floor nor dry leaves are present in a tropical forest, where nests are built from soft living vegetation folded to make a comfortable bed.

universities and museums in a dozen countries. In the late 1950s, they began by studying langurs and baboons. During the 1960s, they studied rhesus and langur monkeys in India and gorillas, chimpanzees, and many forest monkeys in Africa. During the 1960s and 1970s, they observed the gibbons and orangutans of Southeast Asia. At various times, studies of New World monkeys have been conducted in Central and South America.

Primates turned out to be much harder to study than anyone had imagined. Many, like the mountain gorilla, live in inaccessible places. Many stay in the tops of trees in dense forest, where they are nearly invisible. Others, like the orangutan, are extremely rare. Most are shy. There is also the problem of what to look for and how to interpret it. Different species act differently in different areas, under different ecological influences, and even in different population densities. Primate behavior is not stereotyped, but complex and highly variable.

Yet, as we shall see, field studies have proved an invaluable source of information. Our knowledge of apes' behavior has greatly increased over the past three decades, thanks to the work of researchers such as Vernon and Frances Reynolds, who studied chimpanzees in the Budongo Forest of Uganda; Adrian Kortland, who studied chimpanzees in West Africa; Jane Goodall, who spent decades at the Gombe Stream chimpanzee reserve in Tanzania; Toshisada Nishida, who studied chimpanzees in the Mahali Mountains of Tanzania; George Schaller, who observed gorillas on the mountain slopes of Central Africa; Biruté Galdikas, who studied orangutans in Kalimantan (Borneo); and the late Dian Fossey, who extended Schaller's work. As each new fact is unearthed, old prejudices are dispelled. The gorilla, whose size and appearance cast it for more than a hundred years as a fearsome forest monster, is now known to be shy and usually gentle. And the chimpanzee is not merely an amiable muncher of bananas but an enthusiastic hunter and a murderous adventurer on occasion.

BASIS OF SOCIAL ORGANIZATION

Although, as shown in Chapter 3, monkeys and apes differ from each other in important ways, they also share many characteristics. Of these, certainly the most interesting is that they are all social species (except the orangutan) and that their societies are highly organized. We first need to ask ourselves several questions: What are the advantages of social life? Why are so many mammal and bird species social and why have the Hominoidea developed this characteristic to such lengths? Four kinds of advantage are usually proposed by zoologists.

1. Several pairs of eyes are better than one in the detection of predators and in their avoidance. Defense by a group is also far more effective. Three or four male baboons constitute an impressive display and can frighten any predator, even a lion. A lone baboon is a dead baboon. ·

2. Competing for large food patches is more successful when done by groups rather than by individuals. We shall see that, in some monkeys, social groups subdivide when food is sparse and widely scattered.

3. Reproductive advantages accrue from social groups because regular access to the opposite sex is ensured.

4. Social groups permit extensive socialization with peers and elders and the opportunity to learn from them. Among animals such as the higher primates, this is a factor of the greatest importance.

These factors are probably the most important in bringing about the selection of social life in animals such as primates. Although considerable variation may occur within a species, especially under different environmental conditions, only a few Old World primate species (including the gibbons and the siamang, a large gibbon) normally live in groups consisting of only an adult male, a female, and their young. The orang is unique in being more-or-less solitary. The remaining Old World monkeys and apes all live in social groups that number as many as 500 individuals but most commonly number between 10 and 50 (see Table 4–2 and Figure 4–2).

But how are these societies organized? Far from being a structureless collection of rushing, squalling animals, primate societies are remarkably complex and stable. Order is maintained in primate societies through a complex interrelationship of several factors. One is the animals' prolonged period of dependence: infant apes and monkeys, like human infants, are far from self-sufficient and maintain a close relationship with their mothers longer than most other animals. During this time they learn some of the roles they will play as adults. Other factors are dominance and hierarchy. In many species the adults of one or both sexes have quite a well-defined social rank within the group. Also important are the other relationships among adults, which to some extent are determined by kinship, friendship, sexual contacts and competition for food, sleeping sites, and any other limited resources.

Thinking about these factors, one quickly sees that they are among the most important regulators of human society as well. Thus, for a very long time (we may assume) and for many species—for humans, for chimpanzees, and for baboons—the problem of life has been, and still is, largely the problem of getting along in a group.

TABLE 4-2 Some Socioecological Characteristics of Old World Monkeys and Apes

	JAPANESE MACAQUES (*Macaca fuscata*)	SAVANNA BABOONS (*Papio cynocephalus*)	HANUMAN LANGURS (*Presbytis entellus*)	WHITE-HANDED GIBBONS (*Hylobates lar*)	EASTERN HIGHLAND GORILLAS (*Gorilla gorilla beringei*)	ORANGUTANS (*Pongo pygmaeus*)	CHIMPANZEES (*Pan troglodytes*)	BONOBOS (*Pan paniscus*)
Group size	35–55	10–185	10–65	Adult pair and 1 or 2 offspring	2–34	2 (mother and offspring)	20–105	50–120
Social structure	Multimale; multifemale	Multimale; multifemale	Multimale, unimale, and possibly age-graded; multifemale	Monogamous families	Unimale or multimale with one dominant silverback male; also lone males; multifemale	Mother and infant; lone males	Multimale; multifemale; dispersed community	Multimale; multifemale, dispersed community
Habitat	Seasonal, deciduous and evergreen and montane and submontane areas	African acacia woodland, short grass savanna, forest	Deciduous to moist evergreen forests; sea level to high Himalayas	Forest	Lowland and mountain rain forests and bamboo forests	Indonesian jungles; herbivorous (mostly frugivorous) diet	Deciduous woodland; omnivorous (mostly frugivorous) diet	Lowland rain forest and swamp forest; omnivorous (mostly frugivorous) diet
Home range	0.1–10.4 mi² (0.27–27 km²)	0.8–15.4 mi² (2.1–40 km²)	0.04–3 mi² (0.1–7.8 km²)	0.08–0.2 mi² (0.2–0.5 km²)	1.9–3.1 mi² (4.9–8.1 km²)	0.2–2.3 mi² (0.4–6 km²)	2–215 mi² (5–560 km²)	7.7–19.3 mi² (20–50 km²)

Sources: Cheney, D. L. "Interactions and Relationships Between Groups," in *Primate Societies*, ed. by B. Smuts, D. Cheney, R. Seyfarth, R. Wrangham, and T. Struhsaker, Chicago, University of Chicago, 1987; Nishida, T., and M. Hiraiwa-Hasegawa. "Chimpanzees and Bonobos: Cooperative Relationships Among Males," in *Primate Societies*, ed. by B. Smuts et al. Chicago, University of Chicago, 1987; Rodman, P. S., and J. C. Mitani. "Orangutans: Sexual Dimorphism in a Solitary Species," in *Primate Societies*, ed. by B. Smuts et al. Chicago, University of Chicago, 1987; Stewart, K. J., and A. H. Harcourt. "Gorillas: Variation in Female Relationships," in *Primate Societies*, ed. by B. Smuts et al. Chicago, University of Chicago, 1987; Melnick, D. J., and M. C. Pearl. "Cercopithecines in Multimale Groups: Genetic Diversity and Population Structures," in *Primate Societies*, ed. by B. Smuts et al. Chicago, University of Chicago, 1987; Doran, D. M., and A. McNeilage. "Gorilla Ecology and Behavior." *Evolutionary Anthropology*, 6, 1998.

Mother + infant; lone males
(e.g., orangutans)

Monogamous family
(e.g., gibbons)

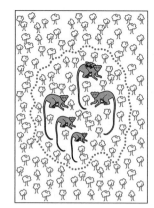

Multimale; unifemale
(e.g., some New World
monkeys [*Saguinus*])

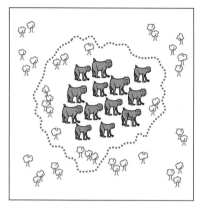

Multimale; multifemale
(e.g., macaques and baboons)

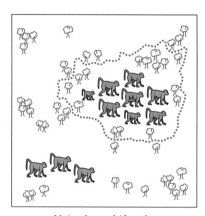

Unimale; multifemale
(e.g., patas monkeys
[*Erythrocebus*] and gorillas)

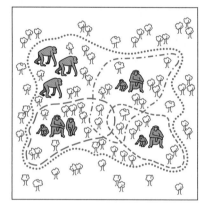

Multimale; multifemale; dispersed
or fusion-fission community
(e.g., chimpanzees and bonobos)

FIGURE 4–2   Illustrations of the different types of primate society. Adult males are shown in color. Dotted and dashed lines indicate home ranges or territorial boundaries, depending on the species.

Learning in Childhood

What is meant by a prolonged period of dependence? A kitten has become a cat by the time it is a year old. A comparably-sized ring-tailed lemur takes about twice as long to reach adulthood. A male baboon takes seven to eight years to reach full social and biological maturity, a chimpanzee needs anywhere from ten to fifteen years, and a human even longer. As a result, family ties—and especially those based on **matrilineal kinship**—among higher primates tend to be strong and lasting. This slow development among a group of supportive relatives is necessary for a higher primate to learn all the things it must to fit itself into the complex society into which it is born. It needs time to learn. In a society in which an individual must deal with many daily choices and varied personal interchange, a long period of youthful learning is an absolute necessity. During this period the vulnerable young animal is protected by its kin and other members of the group.

Matrilineal kinship kinship traced through the maternal line.

FIGURE 4–3 Each night, chimpanzees prepare new nests for themselves by bending tree branches over larger boughs to make a bed.

For a chimpanzee, childhood play is the equivalent of going to school. It watches its mother look for food, and looks for food itself. It watches her make nests and makes little nests of its own—not to sleep in, just for the fun of it (Figure 4–3). Later, during a long adolescence, it picks up from its peers the physical skills it will need as an adult, as well as the more intricate psychological skills required to get along with others: it learns not only how to interpret the moods of other chimpanzees but also how to respond to other individuals. Any chimpanzee that cannot learn to communicate fully with its fellows almost certainly will not live to grow up, for communication is the essential bonding of any society. All this time the learner is finding its own place among its peers, first in play, later in more competitive activity that will help determine its rank as an adult. In sum, two sources of learning and two sets of relationships make up primate society. One of these is the family relationship (usually, mother-infant and other matrilineal kin; occasionally, mother-father-infant-siblings). The other is the larger relationship of the individual to all other members of its social group.

Primate behavior, like that of some other highly evolved mammals, depends heavily on learning, in contrast to the less flexible behavior of simpler animals. For this reason the prolonged learning period is especially significant. The important role of learned behavior among primates also means that the group as a whole has more knowledge and experience than its individual members. Experience is pooled, and the generations are linked. This was demonstrated in the Nairobi game park, where a ranger had had to kill a baboon: for many years afterward, the troop that had lost its member avoided the site of the killing, even though all members of the troop had not witnessed the event.

Studies of Hanuman langurs in India (Figure 4–4) have yielded a wealth of information on how the infants of one monkey species learn. These large monkeys live in groups containing several adult females and one or more adult males (Table

Figure 4–4   A juvenile female langur (left) holds a complaining infant while adult females groom each other. As the infants get older, they become more adventurous (right).

Allomothering typically, care or attention directed toward an infant by a female other than its mother (also called *aunting behavior*).

4–2). The adult females are organized in a dominance hierarchy that is shown by their respective abilities to displace one another from food and other resources. Mothers lavish attention on the distinctively dark new infants, but they also allow other females to hold, carry, and groom the baby—and many females, particularly nulliparous youngsters and pregnant adults, are anxious to engage in such "aunting", or **allomothering**. Mothers must be careful, however, as they sometimes have difficulty reclaiming their infants. When confronted by a high-ranking allomother who refuses to return an infant, a low-status mother can only wait until the "aunt" tires of the baby and deserts it, or watch for an opportunity to snatch back her offspring.

After the infant reaches the age of about five months, its dark coat lightens to the color of an adult langur. Now the females no longer vie to hold it. It follows its mother about, copying her actions, learning to forage. It also spends much of its time in energetic activity, running, climbing, chasing, and wrestling—skills that will be invaluable as it reaches adulthood. As it plays with its fellows, it learns to get along as a member of the group.

Once young langurs are weaned, around the age of fifteen months, they become segregated by sex. The females stay near the center of the group, close to the adults, mixing more and more intimately with the adult females and their infants. Holding the infants and sometimes tending them while the mothers are away, they are gaining experience for their own future role as mothers. The male juveniles, meanwhile, spend most of their free time playing. As they grow older, their play becomes ever more vigorous and wide-ranging, and they drift toward the periphery of the group, away from both the adults and the infants. This is the young males' first step toward eventual emigration.

Other monkeys whose development has been studied include the baboons and the macaques. The patterns they follow illustrate interesting social differences among the various genera in the male attitude toward the infants of a group. In a langur group, adult males are inclined to behave like the traditional Victorian father who kept himself apart from his young children. Langur males in captivity do show an interest in newborns, particularly males, but on the whole young langurs grow up in an almost exclusively matriarchal atmosphere. On the other hand,

Japanese macaque males have been observed to cradle one- and two-year-old infants during the birth season. Paternal attention of this nature, which may persist for some time, is somewhat similar to that of hamadryas baboons. The subadult or young adult hamadryas male in fact acquires females for his eventual one-male (and many-female) family unit by first "mothering" infant females (Figure 4–5). For months—often a year or more—a young female enjoys a protective relationship with a male that is similar to the protection she received from her mother. The male readily carries the young female on his back, helps her over difficult terrain when she walks, and lets her huddle next to him at night. She will in due course become an adult member of his one-male group—his harem of females. In savanna baboon groups, adult males also show an intense interest in infants and associate most closely with the babies of females with whom they share a special relationship. Usually an adult male will approach a mother, smacking his lips to show he means no harm, in order to enjoy the pleasure of playing with the mother's infant. The savanna baboons live in multimale groups in which one male does not control a particular harem of females.

Why these differences? They are adaptations acquired in the interests of survival and reproductive success in different environments. Comfortable as some langur species are on the ground, no langur ventures far from trees. Females do not require a male's protection, and they usually do not get it. If a langur group is alarmed, it is every monkey for itself (although langur males have been known to defend group mates—particularly infants—against humans and hawks). Baboons, on the other hand, are organized differently, perhaps because they frequently range far from trees. Adult male baboons routinely defend infants against attacks from conspecifics. Furthermore, if a predator approaches the troop, the males *may*

FIGURE 4–5 An adult male hamadryas baboon hugs an infant while yawning threateningly. Contacts such as these often mark the start of new one-male family units.

(depending on the degree of danger) position themselves between the threat and their group (including the infants). As noted above, however, the protective patterns of baboon males may reflect more than just a generalized concern for infants. These patterns may be one way the males maintain relationships with the infants' mothers—relationships that later may yield important benefits in the form of mating opportunities.

In summary, we can note that monkey species are finely adapted to what may seem to us minor differences in their environment, such as food distribution (density and clumping), density and type of trees (if any), water resources, and terrain. We can reasonably suppose that hominid adaptations during human evolution have also been finely tuned to the environment. It is in these adaptations that we can detect natural selection at its most precise, as it brings about the endless modification of behavior.

The Dominance Hierarchy

Part of growing up in most monkey societies is establishing one's place in the group's social hierarchy. The concept of a status or **dominance hierarchy** among social animals is well recognized from chickens to gorillas. Sometimes called a "pecking order," the idea is a simple one. But even though dominance of one kind or another is a central factor in the social life of many higher primates, it has proved a rather difficult concept to understand in practice.

We can define dominance simply as the relative social status or rank of an animal, as determined by its ability to compete successfully with other individuals for varying goals. Contested goals might include access to resources such as favorite foods or sleeping sites. Social resources, such as mates or grooming partners, are also contested. Dominant animals can also direct and control their own and others' aggression; in aggressive encounters, dominant animals consistently defeat less dominant animals (Figure 4–6).

Dominance hierarchy rank structuring of a primate group, usually based on winning and losing fights. For some purposes, the ranks within a subset of animals, such as the adult males, may be analyzed separately.

FIGURE 4–6   Confrontations among savanna baboons usually result in one individual's either presenting its rump in defeat or scampering off. For these two well-matched baboons, however, confrontation has resulted in fighting.

In some species dominance relationships are clear-cut and static, and a social hierarchy can be recognized. Sometimes such hierarchies are limited to one sex, but in other species both males and females are integrated into a general hierarchy within which some animals may share a similar rank.

However, dominance hierarchies are always subject to influence by animals' personalities and by social variables, and a particular animal may be dominant or submissive under different circumstances. Successful aggression is not the only behavior that generates high status. An ingratiating personality can gain allies and lead to high status, while an ill-tempered, aggressive animal may get little social support. Alternatively, two or even three individuals may team up as a coalition to hold a top position that none alone could hold. High-ranking animals move confidently through their troop, others deferring to them as a matter of course. Supportive relatives are particularly important in maintaining status, and macaque and baboon mothers will pass down their status from generation to generation through the female line. Adult males, however, have to establish their rank from scratch whenever they move from one troop to another.

Dominance hierarchies are not usually stable for long. In one baboon troop studied over a long period, male ranks altered on average every eight days, while female ranks altered on average every fifty-seven days. Factors that brought about such changes included the movement of males in and out of the troop, births and deaths, and fighting within the troop.

Sex and Status

One of the most interesting questions for the evolutionary biologist is this: Do dominant individuals produce more young than subordinates? At first glance, this seems obviously to be the case for males, because in many species, such as savanna baboons, dominance can increase a male's sexual access to fertile females. In fact, the situation is anything but straightforward. Several studies of baboons have reported positive correlations between male rank and reproduction. For example, American primatologist Glenn Hausfater found that higher-ranked males clearly out-copulated lower-ranked males within his study group. To a large extent, this was due to the alpha male's being able to achieve unequaled access to females on the day of ovulation (determined retrospectively from the date of deflation of the females' **sex swellings**). But results such as these seem to be matched by an equal number of studies that find no correlation between male rank and reproduction. Furthermore, since males of many species change ranks frequently, measuring sexual success rates for ranks may not tell us much about the success of individual animals (or at best we will obtain information on short-term reproductive success). That is, today's alpha male, with his high copulation rate, may well be tomorrow's subordinate male, stuck with a much lower reproductive performance. And males that live for many years may occupy several ranks and experience many fluctuations in their level of reproduction. Until longitudinal studies yield information on males' lifetime histories of rank and reproduction, firm correlations between these factors will remain elusive.

Sex swellings hormone-induced swellings on the hindquarters of certain primate females; generally correlated with ovulation.

It is also important to record that female choice does play a part in any male's sexual achievements, and many males court females for long periods of time in order to win their favors. Dominance is not a ticket to unlimited sexual access, though it certainly helps.

The behavior of chimpanzees is most instructive in this matter and shows how flexible the relations between sex and status can be. Wild chimpanzee males show

Opportunistic mating
mating done whenever and wherever the opportunity presents itself, and with whatever partner is available.

Consortship generally, a period of exclusive sexual association and mating between a female and a male.

at least three mating strategies. If a male is sufficiently high-ranking (typically, the alpha male of the community), he may try to monopolize a sexually attractive female (a female with large sex swellings) by preventing the approach of other males. Such sexual possessiveness is often impossible for lower-ranking males, however, who usually opt for the strategy of frequent **opportunistic mating** (this can involve several males' nonaggressively sharing sexual access to a particular female that copulates promiscuously with them all). Finally a male of any rank may attempt—through skillful social manipulation and sometimes aggressive courting—to form a **consortship** with a female which he then leads away to the periphery of the community range for several days of exclusive mating. Thus wild chimpanzee males attempt to exert their dominance rank for reproductive gains whenever possible, but when this strategy is unworkable, they easily shift to other mating patterns, all of which include some likelihood of fathering infants. While the sexual behavior of captive chimpanzees (such as those at the Arnhem Zoo, to be described in a later section) may be rigidly controlled by male rank, this correlation does not hold in the wild, where animals range and associate freely, and where opportunities for concealment and seclusion are numerous. Indeed, a very recent study of paternity among the chimpanzees of West Africa's Taï Forest revealed that, despite the resident males' best efforts to control mating within their community, a high proportion of infants (seven of thirteen tested) was fathered by alien males—-that is, males from neighboring communities (see Table 4–2 and pp. 147–158 for more about chimpanzee society). This unexpected discovery was attributed to the Taï females' habit of regularly making surreptitious visits to neighboring groups and mating with the males there. Male rank still has some effect on reproduction at Taï, but these new data show clearly that female choice (a form of sexual selection; see Chapter 2 and pp. 133 this chapter) and females' interest in novel partners must also be taken into account for a full understanding of a species' mating patterns.

Savanna baboons have been studied in great detail over many years by Shirley Strum, at Gilgil in Kenya. It is now clear that adolescent males leave their home troops as a matter of course and move to neighboring troops. Here they attempt to become assimilated by making friends with high-ranking females. The approach to the female is made very slowly over a long period of time, and in due course, if the male is accepted, he begins to play with her infant for hours. Males generally make friends with infants as a means of winning female trust and of neutralizing the aggression of other males. If such a male becomes accepted by the female, he courts her and becomes her "friend," thereby becoming a full member of the troop. If he is sufficiently ingratiating and clever in developing his relationships, he may be able to copulate with this female or other females when they are sexually swollen. Recent evidence suggests that, among the Gilgil baboons, sexual conquest can be achieved more effectively by building friendships than by achieving dominance in the male hierarchy.

Males' ranks and reproductive strategies are only half of the story, of course, and primatologists have found that females' dominance and mating patterns are equally fascinating. Longitudinal observations of baboons and better knowledge of kin relationships within the baboon troop have revealed that the long-term stability of the group depends not so much on the males as on high-ranking females that constitute an ongoing aristocracy of their own, based on mother-daughter and sister-sister ties. Once established, this matrilineal aristocracy tends to perpetuate itself: the hierarchy of females is much more stable than that of males. The privileged—and usually related—females groom each other sociably, bringing up their infants in an atmosphere of comfort and security that is denied low-ranking females. The latter are forced to hang about at the edge of the group, alert to the possibility of a bite or a slap if they do not move aside for a higher-ranking animal. Unable to enter permanently into the established matriarchy at the center, they pass their timidity and generally low self-esteem on to their young. Not surprisingly, the young reared by the dominant mothers grow up with a far greater chance of achieving dominance themselves, having learned confidence and assurance from their mothers. Among rhesus and Japanese macaques, an individual's rank within its age group is based on its mother's rank. Among baboons, this is also true within each sex, but males of any age consistently dominate females of similar age.

With regard to the question of female rank and reproductive success, recent studies have shown that the situation is just as complex as among males. Observations of the savanna baboons that inhabit Tanzania's Gombe National Park (best known for Jane Goodall's chimpanzee studies, to be described in a later section) have shown that high-ranking females enjoy significant *short-term* advantages in reproduction compared to low-ranking females. Probably because of greater access to food, dominant females have shorter interbirth intervals, greater infant survival, and accelerated maturation of their daughters. These results seem to provide clear evidence why competition for rank would be beneficial for female baboons.

But short-term benefits can be deceptive, and among the Gombe baboons no overall relationship exists between *lifetime* reproductive success and female dominance. This is because achieving and maintaining high rank takes a significant long-term reproductive toll on many females. Compared to low-ranking animals, dominant females experience a higher incidence of miscarriage and run a greater risk of being chronically infertile. Such stress-related reproductive failure represents the cost females pay for being at the top of the dominance hierarchy—a cost that is probably great enough to prevent female baboons from evolving into hyper-aggressive status-seekers.

In contrast to the baboon studies, however, analyses of thirty-five years of dominance and reproduction data from the female chimpanzees at Gombe *do* suggest lifetime benefits for high-ranking individuals. In a study that parallels many of the baboon findings, primatologists Anne Pusey, Jennifer Williams, and Jane Goodall recently reported that in comparison to lower-ranked individuals, dominant female chimps have significantly higher rates of infant survival, more rapid production of young, and daughters who mature (and thus begin their own reproductive careers) faster. It appears that high rank enables female chimpanzees to gain access to the best food sources, and being better nourished enhances maternal and infant health, as well as daughters' maturation rate. High-ranking female chimps probably escape negative stress effects (such as those identified for female baboons) because chimpanzee communities are dispersed and females typically forage alone (see Figure 4–2).

Overall then, high rank has been shown to produce short-term reproductive benefits for both males and females in many primate species. Lifetime benefits, however, are harder to document, although they do seem to occur among female chimps. In any event, status hierarchies, whether based on conflict and threat (Figure 4–7) or on kinship and personality, represent one means by which natural selection has brought order and organization to primate society. The tendency for an individual to attempt to increase its status is deep-seated and is expressed

FIGURE 4–7   Here a male savanna baboon is threatening the photographer. The main features of a baboon threat are the displays of the immense canine teeth and of the half-closed light-colored eyelids.

among most higher primates, and indeed most social animals. Human societies are no exception: Status is just as pervasive and just as variable in its mode of expression as it is among other primates.

Sexual Physiology and Behavior

As we saw earlier, Solly Zuckerman's observations of hamadryas baboons in the London Zoo during the 1930s led him to conclude that the members of primate groups are bound to each other by the continuous urge to satisfy their sexual needs. In many mammals—deer are among the most familiar examples—males and females are together only during the breeding season, forming separate societies during the rest of the year. Because Zuckerman thought that monkeys were sexually active the year around, he argued that sex was a logical explanation for the monkeys' staying together. This theory was bolstered by the effects of the crowded conditions under which primates were often studied in zoos or laboratories, for in such a situation animals use sexual behavior to establish dominance and submission. Studies of Japanese macaques at the Takasakiyama feeding station, for instance, revealed that a dominant male often mounts an inferior male—as he would when copulating with a female—to assert his right to a choice tidbit.

Actually, as recent field studies have shown, many monkeys—for example, the rhesus and the Japanese macaques—breed only in a specific season, and their closely knit societies continue even when there is no primary sexual activity. Thus, once again, the study of captive animals proved misleading. In the controlled environment of a laboratory, a monkey's endocrine system, which governs its sex hormones, is not subject to seasonal variations, and the monkey may copulate all year around. In the wild, however, its hormones are influenced much more heavily by such external factors as day length, humidity, and diet, and the result is that many species copulate during only a few months of the year. The existence of a mating season is one means of ensuring that the young will be born at an auspicious time, when they are most likely to survive.

All Old World monkeys, apes, and humans share a basically similar sexual anatomy and physiology. The ovarian-uterine cycle is about 28–35 days in length, with ovulation occurring near the middle and menstruation (shedding of the uterine lining) at the end. Counting the interval between periods of menstrual bleeding produces a measure of the **menstrual cycle**. Mapped on top of the menstrual cycle, however, is a pattern of behavioral fluctuation called the **estrus cycle**. In response to the changing levels of their sex hormones (mainly the estrogens and progesterone), primate females show monthly cycles in sexual **attractiveness** and **receptivity**, and in their tendency to initiate mating (this is called their degree of **proceptivity**). A sexually active female—one that is simultaneously attractive, proceptive, and receptive—is commonly labeled as being in **estrus**. (In some species—baboons and chimpanzees, for example, as described earlier—females in estrus also display large, colorful sex swellings around the vulva, but it is behavior and not swelling or color that marks a female as estrous.)

Old World monkey and ape females show great flexibility in the occurrence of sexual behavior throughout the menstrual cycle. Copulations may occur early in the cycle, at ovulation, or near menstruation (pregnant females also continue to mate). Indeed, females seem to have a moderate level of situation dependency in their sexual behavior that allows them to use sex to their advantage (perhaps to fool a potentially infanticidal male or to accommodate a sexually insistent one) regardless of their ovarian or hormonal condition. Nonetheless, among monkeys and apes *most* sex takes place near ovulation during a period of estrus that lasts a week or so.

One of the primary differences between nonhuman primates and humans is the fact that women do not show strong estrus-type peaks in sexual behavior. Extending the sexual flexibility characteristic of monkeys and apes, human sexual behavior is marked by extreme situation dependency and mating throughout the menstrual cycle and during pregnancy. Although humans may retain some mild mid-cycle remnants of estrus (experts disagree on this point), it is clear that our sexual behavior is much more flexible and less controlled by hormones than that of our nonhuman relatives. But it is important not to overstate the contrast. While humans no longer show clear-cut estrus, monkeys and apes seem to anticipate human behavior with their moderate degree of situation dependency. A pair of interesting questions (to be discussed in a later chapter) is how and why hominids evolved such an extremely flexible system of sexual behavior.

The overt activities of nonhuman primate sexual behavior contrast with the covert nature of most human sexual behavior. For example, among nonhuman primates, sexual advances and mountings may occur at any time to reduce tension and appease anger. Male-male, male-female, female-male, and female-female mountings are commonly seen. Touching of genitals may occur as a greeting and is often seen in grooming sessions to solidify social relationships. Homosexual behavior, which is quite distinct from the social mountings mentioned above, has

Menstrual cycle the interval (generally, monthly) between periods of menstrual bleeding; especially characteristic of *catarrhine* females.

Estrus cycle the interval between periods of sexual *attractiveness* and activity of primate females; correlated with ovulation and the *menstrual cycle*, but with great flexibility among *catarrhines*.

Attractiveness in primate studies, the aspect of female sexuality reflected by attention from males.

Receptivity the aspect of female sexuality reflected by cooperating in copulation.

Proceptivity the aspect of female sexuality reflected by inviting copulation.

Estrus the period, usually around ovulation, of sexual *attractiveness* and activity by *primate* and other mammalian females

been described in several species. Sex is indeed a continuous and rich part of primate social life.

Sexual Selection Among Primates

In 1871 Charles Darwin noted that competition for mates is unequal between the sexes of most species. The more vigorously competing sex tends to be bigger, and male/female differences in body form and color, decorative appendages, and behavioral displays may evolve as well. In many primate species, males compete for females, since access to females sets an upper limit on males' reproductive success (this is true of all mammals). This may be the reason that males tend to be larger than females—a form of **sexual dimorphism** that is not uncommon. Great apes, various baboon species, and a number of other monkeys have very considerable differences between the sexes in body size, weight, and size of canine teeth (see Table 3-5). Shoulder breadth and strikingly handsome hair forms are often well developed in the males (Figure 4–8). Sex differences in size may vary from females being 50 percent the size of males among gorillas and baboons, to 78 percent among chimpanzees, 81 percent among humans, and 94 percent—near equality—among gibbons.

It is often claimed that the large, aggressive baboon males are selected as protectors of the troop against predators. If we look at higher primates as a whole, however, we can find a correlation between reproductive system and sexual dimorphism. **Monogynous** species, in which neither sex competes strongly for additional mates (for example, siamangs and gibbons), show little sexual dimorphism. **Polygynous** species (such as savanna baboons), which live in multimale troops and

Sexual dimorphism characteristic anatomical (and behavioral) differences between males and females of a species.

Monogyny in zoology, generally having only one mate.

Polygyny in zoology, the tendency for a male to have regular sexual access to two or more females.

FIGURE 4–8   Hamadryas female with young, and a male. The male is larger and heavier, and he carries a magnificent mane, which makes him look even larger.

offer greater sexual opportunities to powerful, successful males, are quite dimorphic. It seems that in such a dimorphic species both natural selection and sexual selection are generating large males. A comparison of dimorphism and the breeding system in a whole range of primates and other mammals, carried out by biologist Richard Alexander and his colleagues, tends to support this conclusion.

Another possible explanation for sexual dimorphism such as we find among baboons has been proposed: small females may be selected to reduce their nutritional requirements in a poor environment, subject to the requirements of their reproductive physiology. Anthropologist James McKenna summarized his conclusions on this topic as follows: "Body size might best be considered the result of genetic compromise between competing variables, such as male intrasexual competition, female reproductive physiology, infant care-giving patterns, feeding, foraging, and defense strategies." Indeed, the entire animal is just such a compromise. But by including among the variables male-male breeding competition, we are including a factor that is not a product of natural but of sexual selection and as such is of profound interest.

But as Darwin pointed out, sexual selection has two faces, and same-sex competition (such as the male-male competition discussed above) is only one. The second kind of sexual selection involves members of one sex exercising a deliberate choice of certain traits in the opposite sex. If two males fight over a female and the victor then forces his attentions on her, the female cannot be said to have exercised much choice—or she had a "Hobson's choice" at best (mate with any male you choose so long as you choose the winner of the fight). But female primates do much more than make Hobson's choices. Like males, females have sexual strategies shaped by evolution to maximize reproductive success, and an important part of those strategies is playing an active role in mate selection. Primatologist Meredith Small has recently reviewed the patterns of mate selection by primate females, and several of her conclusions are startling. She believes that females are more sexually assertive and less picky about their mates than has traditionally been held. Rather than waiting coyly for a male suitor, females are often sexually aggressive and actively solicit males. Further, females sometimes choose *not to be selective* and, as a result, mate rather promiscuously with the males of their group. Or they may make choices that seem to make little theoretical sense, as when—like the female chimpanzees in the Taï Forest—they prefer outsiders (stranger males characterized by unknown fitness) over well-known male group mates (characterized by "proven" fitness). Small concluded that primate females' main objective is to conserve time within their reproductive careers. "Get pregnant as soon as possible" seems to be the overriding guideline; the identity of the baby's father seems considerably less important. Small's views have aroused a good deal of controversy among primate researchers, but they are of extraordinary value in reminding us that it's not only males who do the sexual choosing.

Grooming and Social Interaction

Perhaps the most commonly observed form of social contact between higher primates is grooming. One monkey or ape grooms another by picking through its fur to clean out dirt, as well as parasites and salt crystals, which it then eats. Physically, grooming is simply a cleaning mechanism, and it is highly effective, as one can see by comparing lions and baboons that inhabit the same area of the East African savanna. Although lions are clean animals, the backs of their necks, where they cannot reach to clean, are thick with ticks, whereas the baboons' hair is totally free of them.

But to primates, grooming is far more than a form of hygiene. It is the most important means of social interaction among members of a group, and it serves a variety of purposes. For example, grooming seems to be an effective instrument for reducing tension of all kinds, as shown by baboons, macaques, and chimpanzees. At other times, it serves simply as an enjoyable pastime when the group is not in search of food. Much as humans gather in conversation groups, monkeys gather in grooming groups. The same function is served: the maintenance of friendly social relations. Being groomed is obviously enjoyable: the groomed animal sits or lies in an attitude of beatific contentment (Figure 4–9). Most grooming is done by females. Mothers regularly groom their young from birth. Equals groom each other in approximately equal amounts, while subordinates groom their social superiors much more frequently than they are groomed in turn. As one might expect, dominant males get much grooming and give little. There is, however, a semblance of reciprocity in a female's grooming of a male: after she has worked over him for perhaps ten minutes, she will turn and sit, inviting him to groom her. The male obliges by grooming her for about thirty seconds, then turns indolently and is groomed by the female for another ten minutes. The significant function of grooming in monkey society is that it cuts across hierarchical lines, establishing friendly

FIGURE 4–9   Grooming has two main functions: to remove parasites and keep the fur clean and to establish and maintain social relationships. Here a relaxed female baboon encourages a dominant male to groom her, while a lower-ranking male watches from a proper distance.

relationships between individuals on various levels of the hierarchy that might not otherwise interact.

It seems clear that the degree of awareness exhibited by chimpanzees and baboons is such that they are not merely conscious of the activities and status of other troop members but see deeper into personality. They show preferences; that is, they prefer to spend time with particular members of the troop, which are often their kin. In both species we see what looks very like friendship; certain pairs and trios (sometimes of different sex, but more often of the same sex) spend much time together and share experiences and food sources. When meat, a rare delicacy, is obtained, chimpanzees will share after the provider has had first pick; baboons will move aside to make room for a friend to get at the kill. It looks as if these primates are in some small way responding to each other's needs, even when they are adult and outside the mother-infant relationship. What we see is the innate bioaltruism that rearing an infant implies being extended to **reciprocal altruism** between adults. Insofar as the members of a troop help one another, this behavior has an obvious adaptive value for the social group as a whole.

The degree of cohesiveness of a group, in fact, directly reflects the potential danger that threatens its members. Gorillas live in comparatively little day-to-day danger, and so individual male gorillas feel free to go off on their own, and many do—even for weeks at a time. The situation among Gombe chimpanzees, which are also in little danger, is somewhat similar. They split into small units whose membership is constantly changing, and individuals often search for food alone, out of sight of the group's members. And chimpanzees seem little concerned about the safety of the group as a whole, because when alarmed, an individual chimpanzee will often run off without even giving a warning call.

One of the most noticeable characteristics of many primate species (from howler monkeys to chimpanzees) is their vocalizations. Most higher primates have a highly evolved means of communication, based on calls, facial expressions, and body postures. Because language is a central characteristic of humans, we discuss primate communication in some detail in Chapter 13. In the present discussion it is sufficient to point out that complex social groups depend on sophisticated communication systems, and higher primate societies are no exception.

Variations in the social behavior of the higher primates are endless. Between species, and even within species, there are wide differences in behavior. It seems that many of the details of social interactions are learned and thus generate what in humans would be called cultural differences between populations within the species. This kind of variability is particularly striking among chimpanzees, which are not only highly intelligent and extroverted animals but occupy a broader environmental and geographical range than the gorilla and the orangutan.

We shall now see in more detail just how environment interacts with social behavior.

TERRITORY AND ECOLOGY

The relationship between the social group and its environment is ultimately determined by the distribution and density of the natural resources essential to the animals' survival, by the density of competing animals (including humans) and by the pressure of predators. The social group becomes associated with a recognizable area of land or forest—called the **home range**—which contains sufficient space, food, water, and safe sleeping sites for all its members. Behavioral mechanisms

> Reciprocal altruism trading of apparently altruistic acts by different individuals at different times; a variety of *bioaltruism.*

> Home range the area a *primate* group uses for foraging, sleeping, and so on in a year.

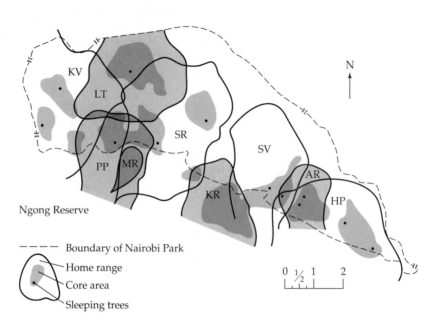

FIGURE 4–10   This plan shows the home ranges and core areas of the baboon troops in the Nairobi Park in 1960. The home ranges overlap considerably, but the core areas, which contain the baboons' sleeping trees, essential to each troop, are quite distinct. The letters refer to the different troops studied by Washburn and DeVore. Scale is in miles.

Core area a portion of the *home range* that is used frequently.

Territory the area occupied and defended by individuals or groups of animals against *conspecifics*.

bring about this spacing, which reduces the possibility of overexploiting the food resources and of having conflict over those resources. The home range of savanna baboons may be partly shared with other groups of the same species; it is always shared with other species, often with other primate species. Within this range, it is usually possible to define smaller areas—called **core areas**—containing resources absolutely essential for survival, in this case sleeping trees (Figure 4–10). A core area becomes defended **territory** when it is actively defended against intruders from neighboring groups.

Different primate species use space in very different ways. In many species, such as savanna baboons (Figure 4–11), some vervet monkeys (*Cercopithecus aethiops*), orangutans, and gorillas, neighbors simply avoid each other by staying at a distance. At the other extreme, gibbons of both sexes display vigorously at the boundaries of their precisely defined territories to demonstrate their occupation of the area and their ferocity. Langur monkeys have also been observed to display at territorial boundaries. Other species, such as chimpanzees, rhesus monkeys, and other macaques, and some baboons, may sometimes interact aggressively if they meet by chance, demonstrating a clear territorial sense.

Why do some species defend a territory while others do not? The answer is uncertain, and a number of factors may be in operation. The resource base seems to be the key, and it appears that, if food is patchy in space and unpredictable in time, an optimum feeding strategy is to form large groups and range over considerable areas of land (e.g., savanna baboons). Where food is concentrated in space and reliable in supply, the smaller groups may occupy a fixed and limited area (e.g., gib-

FIGURE 4–11 The sleeping trees, to which a savanna baboon troop returns each night, are an essential feature in the home range of every troop in open savanna country. In this photograph, the troop has left its grove of acacia trees at dawn and is preparing to move out into the open grasslands to feed.

bons), and it is both possible and worthwhile to defend such an area. In the case of gibbons, the ultimate small group has evolved: a monogynous pair.

For these animals, monogyny and a defended territory reduce individuals' competition for food, and each sex is assured a mating partner. Other monogynous species—siamangs in Southeast Asia and marmosets (*Callithrix*) and titi monkeys (*Callicebus*) in South America—also defend territories and show little sexual dimorphism. These species are also characterized by sexual equality of status and a sharing of social roles not found in other species.

In contrast, savanna baboons and some other monkeys that cover large home ranges are polygynous to **promiscuous,** having multimale groups. They do not defend their extensive home ranges and are not capable of doing so. The contrast in the use of space, the quality of the environment, and reproductive system is clear and significant.

Promiscuous both females and males having multiple sexual partners.

It must be added, however, that food distribution is not the whole story. Other essential resources, such as sleeping trees or cliffs (in open savanna situations) and water supply and forest density may also contribute to how a primate species uses its environment and what form its reproductive system will take. The exact mechanisms operating and the factors involved are still poorly understood. **Socioecology** is, however, a major branch of primate research, and much progress is now being made in this subject.

Socioecology the connection between *species'* ecological relations and their social behaviors; also the study of this connection.

Socioecology of East African Baboons

During the course of human evolution our ancestors have passed through and adapted to a whole range of different environments. An early major adaptation of the hominines—members of the genus *Homo*—was to the relatively dry savannas of Africa, and for this reason it is worth looking in more detail at the adaptations of some well-known monkey species to this habitat.

Baboons are extremely adaptable animals; they have not become as physically specialized as many other species, and they are thus able to suit themselves to a wide variety of living conditions. With no material culture to rely on, however, baboons must change their behavior and social organization in order to adapt to different environmental conditions.

The savanna baboon generally lives in the easiest surroundings: close to trees to which it can flee and in which it can sleep, and in a climate where there is a year-round abundance of food. In this setting, the troop is the all-important social unit; family relationships, except for mother-infant ties, are secondary. The nearest thing to a social father is a dominant male, which as we have seen may exercise authority over troop members or females' male friends.

By contrast, **geladas** (a related genus but not a true baboon) are confined to mountain slopes in Ethiopia. There the climate is harsher, seasonal change is greater, trees are very rare, and food availability is more chancy. Male-female relationships, too, are very different from those which prevail on the savanna. The animals are found in large herds that, in areas or seasons of poor food supply, break down during the day into a number of separate wide-foraging polygynous units, each containing a single adult male with one or more females and assorted young. With this **harem polygyny** social structure, the relationship between a particular male and females is far more durable than it is among savanna baboons. In that respect it resembles the human nuclear family unit more closely than does the organization of the savanna baboon troop. Significantly, when the wet season comes to the dry Ethiopian hills and food starts to be more abundant, the one-male groups coalesce into the larger multi-male troops.

Hamadryas society is different again. This baboon lives in country even drier than the gelada's terrain, in rocky sections of Ethiopia and the near-desert of Somalia. In this environment one-male groups are the rule the year round, though for safety many groups come together at night on the sleeping cliffs. The male-female relationship is more close-knit than among geladas. Each hamadryas male is continuously jealous of his harem, requiring his females to stay very close at all times. When he moves, they move—or get bitten.

Although these baboon adaptations appear at first sight to contradict the considerations of territoriality discussed in the preceding section, the principles enumerated do still apply. The food supply is patchy, widespread, seasonal, and unpredictable, and there is no defended territory. But we have seen that, under the exceptional circumstances of a very harsh and dry environment, where food is extremely widespread, small one-male (polygynous) groups are an appropriate response.

Finally, it is of great interest that there is some reason to believe that the one-male harem may be an ancient and widespread catarrhine pattern. If so, then the savanna baboon's and the chimpanzee's social adaptation of large multimale units may be considered the product of the abundant food supply available to these species.

Gelada species of terrestrial monkey related to *baboons*, found in the mountains of Ethiopia; *Theropithecus gelada*.

Harem polygyny in zoology, a group including one breeding male and multiple females; among humans, one husband and multiple wives and concubines.

THE LIVING APES

After their evolutionary heyday during the Miocene epoch, apes experienced a strong reduction in diversity, until today they are represented by only four genera: *Hylobates* (gibbons and siamangs), *Pongo* (orangutans), *Gorilla* (gorillas), and *Pan* (chimpanzees and bonobos). These remarkable creatures are humans' closest living relatives, and studies of their anatomy, ecology, and behavior promise to yield important insights into our evolutionary development—unless they are pushed over the brink of extinction by hunting and habitat destruction. The following photographs attempt to communicate the intelligent gaze and distinctive personalities of various living apes. ∎

In this painting, entitled *Darwin and Friends*, artist Stephen Nash has depicted a wide variety of living primates. From left to right, one encounters prosimians, monkeys, apes, and humankind represented by Darwin himself.

The white-handed gibbon (*Hylobates lar*) is a monogynous inhabitant of the forests of Southeast Asia. A master brachiator, the gibbon hooks supporting branches with its long fingers as it swings through the trees.

Also an inhabitant of Southeast Asia, a mother orangutan (*Pongo pygmaeus*) is shown with her infant. Once widely spread from India to China and as far south as Indonesia, orangutans are now found only on the islands of Sumatra and Borneo.

An adult male gorilla (*Gorilla gorilla*) munches his way through a leafy meal. So large and powerful that they have few natural predators, gorillas—particularly the eastern "mountain gorillas"—are nonetheless losing the battle for existence because of human activities.

With their lengthy period of sexual activity and frequent bipedal posturing, bonobos (*Pan paniscus*) are thought by some scientists to be the best living models for early hominids. Field studies of these Zairean apes are in their infancy.

An adult male chimpanzee (*Pan troglodytes*) strikes a thoughtful pose. Intelligent and highly social, chimpanzees are without doubt the best hunters and toolmakers among the nonhuman primates, and some anthropologists believe they demonstrate a primitive sort of culture.

This painting by artist R. E. Hynes gives a good idea of the relative sizes of the various hominoid species. Furthermore, a comparison of females (shown on the left for all species except humans) and males demonstrates the amount of sexual dimorphism in body size within each species. From upper left to right the species are gibbons, orangutans, bonobos, chimpanzees, gorillas, and humans.

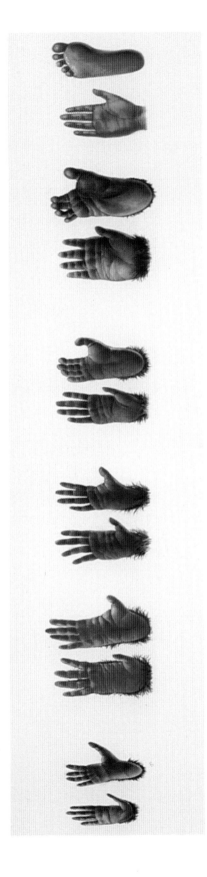

In this illustration R. E. Hynes shows a representative hand and foot for each of the hominoid species. The species are in the same order as on the facing page.

Primate Feeding Strategies

Just as reproductive strategy refers to all those adaptations that maximize reproductive success, so a feeding strategy comprises the anatomical, physiological, and behavioral characteristics that permit animals to obtain energy efficiently by food acquisition. As before, the use of the word "strategy" implies no conscious intent on the part of the individual primate.

The strategy that should be favored by natural selection is the one that is most effective in metabolically converting food resources into energy and that is least expensive in terms of energy expenditure. Thus, to estimate the efficiency of a particular feeding strategy, we would need to know the nutritive, and especially the calorific, value of every food item eaten and the energy required to get it and digest it. A feeding strategy is optimal when, in addition to providing essential nutrients, its net energy yield per unit of time is at its highest.

Several kinds of feeding strategy can be identified among primates, but they all appear to fall, broadly, along a continuum between two extremes. On the one hand we have the generalist-opportunist approach, and on the other hand the specialist approach.

The generalist-opportunist shows selectivity with regard to the energy value of food. It eats according to availability and eats the most nutritive food available at any particular time. Then it moves on to other, sometimes very diverse, food sources. The South American howler monkey is a good example of such a generalist. In some species, opportunism includes the consumption of significant quantities of high-energy insects and meat in addition to plant foods. Baboons, macaques, mangabeys (*Cercocebus*), and chimpanzees have all been observed to eat meat in substantial quantities when the opportunity (sometimes rare) presents itself.

In contrast, specialists concentrate on only a few plant species. These either yield high energy or are abundant enough so that quantity will supplement what may be lacking in caloric density. Specialist strategies necessarily evolve in relatively stable environments where key foods are always available.

Some dietary specialists have evolved specialized digestive organs, such as the large stomach of leaf-eating Colobine monkeys (*Colobus*), which consists of a forestomach (in which cellulose is digested) followed by a series of saclike chambers. The ability to digest both young and mature leaves of common trees places specialist leaf-eating Colobines in a very advantageous position among primates.

Dietary specializations also tend to be correlated with dental differences among primate species. For example, animals such as tarsiers that commonly eat insects usually have enlarged and pointed incisors and canines for killing prey, and tall, sharp cusps on their molars and premolars for shearing insects into tiny, digestible fragments. Specialized leaf-eaters likewise have high-crowned molars and premolars for slicing up foliage (this aids in the digestion of cellulose), but their incisors tend to be rather narrow. And finally, species that eat mainly fruits show yet another combination of traits: large, broad incisors with straight cutting edges (an adaptation for biting off chunks of tough-skinned fruits) and relatively small, low-crowned molars (which are adequate, because the inner flesh of fruit is generally soft and needs little chewing). Information on the dental adaptations of living primates can serve as a basis for inferring the food preferences of fossil species.

The concept of a feeding strategy helps us gain knowledge of how a species actually makes a living in a highly competitive environment. It also helps us to gain insights into early hominid feeding strategies. As shown in later chapters, early hominids were probably both generalist and highly opportunistic feeders.

THE APES

The environmental adaptations of the monkeys and their social organization make their study of interest to us, but it is, of course, not the monkeys but the apes that are our closest relatives among nonhuman primates.

Asiatic Apes: Gibbons and the Orangutan

Gibbons (six species including siamangs) and the orangutan are Asiatic apes. By a great number of external and internal measurements, including genetic ones, they are remarkably different from chimpanzees, bonobos, and gorillas. In fact, they are in some ways less like chimpanzees than are humans. These differences indicate separations far back in time, between 12 and 21 million years ago for gibbons and 13 to 16 million years ago for orangutans—long before the separation of human, gorilla, bonobo, and chimpanzee (see Table 4–1b).

As we have seen, both gibbons and the orangutan are tree-dwelling animals today. Millions of years of climbing and total reliance on the fruits that grow in jungle trees have brought them to an extreme point of arboreal specialization. In the trees, they move superbly, each in its own way. The gibbon (Figure 4–12) is an airy flier that hangs from branches, swinging from one to another in a breathtaking arc, grabbing the next branch just long enough to launch itself in the direction of a third. For this brachiator, arms and hands are everything. Its fingers are

FIGURE 4–12   A gibbon hangs by an arm and steadies itself with a foot while feeding. See also Figure 3–18.

extremely long, specialized to serve as powerful hooks to catch branches. As a result of this finger specialization, the gibbon has the poorest manual dexterity of any ape. And being the smallest ape, it has the smallest brain.

The orangutan is quite different (Figure 4–13). It is much larger: adult males weigh more than 150 pounds (68 kilograms), compared to the gibbons' 11 to 24 pounds (5 to 11 kilograms). Obviously an animal of this size cannot go careening through the branches. Orangutans have developed four prehensile hands well adapted to seizing or holding, and their limbs are so articulated that they can reach in any direction. There is almost nowhere in a tree that an orangutan cannot safely go, despite its great bulk, by careful gripping and climbing.

The grouping patterns and mating systems of gibbons and orangutans are very different. Gibbons form monogynous families that are usually long-lasting. Adult males and females are **monomorphic** in body size and canine tooth length and, as a result, are often codominant (equally dominant). Both sexes actively defend the family's arboreal territory (0.08 to 0.2 miles^2; 0.2 to 0.5 kilometers^2) against encroachment by neighboring families. Subadults of both sexes disperse from their natal units (often after aggression by their same-sex parent) and start their own families.

Monomorphic both sexes showing the same trait (e.g., similar body size).

This traditional picture of stable and cooperative gibbon families is a bit too perfect, however, as shown by recent field studies. Independent observations by anthropologist Ulrich Reichard and psychologist Ryne Palombit have documented

FIGURE 4–13 The orangutan of Indonesian Sumatra and Kalimantan (Borneo) is the most seriously threatened of the great apes. It has immensely long arms and relatively short legs with short thumbs and big toes. It is mainly arboreal but does cover considerable distances on the ground in emergencies. This is a juvenile.

mate desertion by both male and female gibbons (this usually also involves forfeiture of territory), as well as "extra-pair" (in human terms, adulterous) copulations with neighbors. Within three wild gibbon groups in Thailand, Reichard found that extra-pair matings accounted for 12 percent of all copulations. These new data suggest that gibbons continually assess their mates and that both males and females are prepared to copulate adulterously and/or abandon their families in order to improve their personal reproductive prospects. This is a far cry from the old view of gibbons forming life-long nuclear families, and it strongly increases the behavioral similarities between gibbons and humankind.

In contrast to gibbons, adult orangutans of both sexes live solitary lives, and the only real social unit is that of a female and her dependent offspring. Adult males are twice the size of adult females, and males (even as subadults) generally dominate females. Each adult inhabits a large home range (0.6 to 2.3 miles^2, or 1.5 to 6 kilometers^2, for females), with an extensive overlap of males' and females' ranges. Adult males have several mating strategies. Some defend their ranges as territories from other adult males, while pursuing sexual interactions with overlapping females. Other males, both full adults and subadults, do not defend a mating territory; rather, they move over large distances and seek matings opportunistically. Since both males and females have access to multiple sexual partners, the orangutan mating system is best described as promiscuous.

Both gibbons and orangutans are basically frugivorous in their diets. Compared to other ape species, gibbons perform very little object manipulation and may be safely classed as non-tool-users (although there was one observation of a leaf being used as a sponge for water dipping). Wild orangutans, on the other hand, are much more accomplished tool-users. The apes regularly drop twigs and topple snags as part of aggressive displays, and also rub their faces with leaves. Additionally, wild Sumatran orangs have been observed to fashion sticks into tools used to probe seeds from partly opened *Neesia* fruits and to extract insects, bits of insect nests, and honey from tree holes. Stick probes are usually held between the teeth, but occasionally they are hand-held and applied with a power grip (precision gripping has not been observed, perhaps because of orangutans' relatively short thumbs; see Table 3–7). And finally, rehabilitated female orangutans in East Malaysia have been seen to arrange several large leaves into "leaf-vessels" into which they spit partially masticated food. The food is then consumed gradually from the leaf-vessel. In captivity, orangutans have shown quite extensive and complex tool use.

But, as noted earlier, among the living apes, gibbons and orangutans are humans' most distant evolutionary kin. Biochemical and fossil data suggest that the orangutan lineage diverged from that of the other hominoids some 13 to 16 million years ago, with gibbons probably splitting off several million years earlier. In contrast, it appears certain that humans share a common ancestor with some of the African apes as recently as 5 to 7 million years ago (Table 4–1b). Therefore we must examine our hominoid relatives from Africa in somewhat greater detail.

Gorillas: Research of Fossey

Much of what we know of the gorilla comes from the work of Dian Fossey, who began her extensive observations of mountain gorillas in 1967 and founded a research center in Rwanda. Fossey quickly discovered that, far from being the ferocious beasts of legend, gorillas are generally mild-mannered vegetarians who like to mind their own business (Figure 4–14).

While the orangutan and gibbon have evolved into specialized tree-dwellers, the gorilla's development has taken the direction of a great increase in size, along with a dietary switch from the fruit and leaves found in trees to a more general menu of fresh bark, larger leaves, roots, bamboo shoots, and other plants—herbal as much as arboreal vegetation. These two specializations of size and diet go together: we may suppose size and strength have been selected because other animals will not attack the gorilla while it is on the ground eating. And because the gorilla is so large, it needs a great deal of just the kind of coarse vegetation that it finds in large quantities in the places it inhabits. This great ape retains the equipment for climbing and reaching: the long arms, the deft hands, and keen vision. Young gorillas are frisky and venturesome in the trees, but their elders are essentially ground animals. Having carved out a successful niche for themselves there, they have apparently been relatively stable members of the African rain forest community for millions of years.

With no predators to fear except humans, and with plenty of food available, the gorillas Fossey encountered lived most of the time in a state of mild and

FIGURE 4–14 In Central Africa, Dian Fossey walks through the forest near her isolated field station with two young mountain gorillas. She studied this endangered species in its native habitat from 1967 until her death in 1985. (Bob Campbell, © National Geographic Society.)

amiable serenity (Figure 4–15). Most of them live in groups of two to thirty-four, each group led by a powerful silverback male, so called for the saddle of grizzled silver hair that the males grow when they reach the age of ten. His dominance over the group is absolute, but normally genial. Occasionally a young gorilla will get too frolicsome and will be silenced by a glare or a threatening slap on the ground by an adult. Sometimes a couple of females will begin to scream at each other until the leader glares at them, when they promptly quiet down. Except for particularly irascible silverbacks, the leaders are usually quite approachable. Females nestle against them and infants crawl over their huge bodies. When a band of gorillas is at rest, the young play, the mothers tend their infants, and the other adults lie at peace and soak up the sun.

Gorilla groups are not territorial; rather, they move about within nondefended home ranges in search of food and other resources. They do not use tools to obtain food or for any other purpose. The gorilla mating system is one of harem polygyny, and a silverback male typically has several sexual partners, while females have only one. Both males and females routinely emigrate from their natal group

FIGURE 4–15   Here mountain gorillas (the silverback is on the left) relax on a fallen tree after a morning's feeding. The Central African mountain environment in which these animals live has very high rainfall and the vegetation is lush.

as adults, and within a harem the strongest social bonds are between females and their silverback leader. Bonds between females are quite weak.

Like humans, gorillas yawn and stretch when they awake in the morning, and they sit, dangling their legs over the sides of their nests. They pick their noses, scratch themselves when puzzled, and, if nervous or excited, often begin to eat vigorously. Though there is great individual variation of temperament among gorillas, there is about them a curious reserve; they are normally rather quiet creatures and rarely use their immense strength.

Nonetheless, gorillas can exhibit strong feelings, especially when they feel threatened. They scream in alarm and as a warning to other members of the group. They toss leaves in the air. They also beat their chests. All gorillas, even very young ones, do this, rising up on two legs on the ground, or popping up amid the foliage of a tree to give a few brief slaps before fading out of sight. The full performance, however, which is given in response to more serious threat or high anxiety, is put on only by the silverback males. It begins inconspicuously with a series of soft, clear hoots that gradually quicken. Already, the silverback expects to command attention because, if interrupted, he is liable to look around in annoyance. As he continues to hoot, he may stop, pluck a leaf from a plant nearby, and place it between his lips. This curiously incongruous and delicate gesture is a prelude to coming violence, and when they see it, the other gorillas get out of the way. The violence is not immediate. First, the male rises to his full height and slaps his hands on his chest or his belly, on his thigh, or on another gorilla, producing a booming sound that can be heard a mile away. The chest beating over, the violence erupts. He runs sideways for a few steps; then he drops down on all fours and breaks into a full-speed dash, wrenching branches from trees and slapping at everything in his way, including any group members that do not have the wits to keep clear. Finally, there comes the last gesture: the silverback thumps the palm of his hand violently on the ground and then sits back, looking as if he is now ready to hear the applause.

Though gorillas present a mild demeanor to the outside world, protected as they are by their immense strength, they can be aggressive in rivalry between males over females and in other aspects of reproductive behavior. Males reaching full maturity as young silverbacks can form their own family groups only by kidnapping females from other groups, by usurping the position of the dominant silverback male (probably their father) in their own group, or by awaiting his death. Sometimes the females support an up-and-coming male against an older one. The group leaders, in turn, must defend their own females against kidnapping and must maintain their authority over their groups. The kidnapping is usually carried out by stealth as much as by overt aggression, but the takeover of a group from an aging male may be a very unpleasant affair. Sometimes two ambitious young silverbacks fight each other. One or more of the older females may be killed, and quite often the youngest infant or infants are killed by the victorious male. The new male then copulates with the females, which will now rear his progeny rather than the young of his predecessor. In this way, the newly promoted dominant male begins mating and starts his own family without further delay.

Here we see one form of sexual selection in action. The intermale rivalry described by Darwin is selecting sexual dimorphism: gorilla males are about twice as big as females and have powerful jaws and large canine teeth. Thus some features of gorilla dentition are associated not only with diet but also with patterns of behavior that have evolved as part of the social structure of the species.

Infanticide the killing of infants.

The observation of **infanticide** is important. Until 1965 it was believed that the human primate alone had the dubious distinction of sometimes murdering its own infants. In that year, however, the Japanese primatologist Yukimaru Sugiyama observed the takeover of a langur monkey troop by an outside adult male. First, the incoming male chased away the old adult male; then he asserted his dominant position by threatening the females and other troop members. Finally, he set about killing the dependent infants. After a short time, the bereaved females stopped lactating and came into estrus. He copulated with them in turn, and in due course they raised his offspring in place of those they had been nursing before his arrival (Figure 4–16).

Similar observations have since been made among several other primate species. It has been proposed that such behavior is adaptive for the incoming male, which in this way can ensure the production of a large number of offspring at the expense of other males. His young would presumably be old enough by the time of the next takeover to avoid being killed. In other words, infanticide has been proposed as another component of sexual selection in action.

Whether the sexual selection explanation of infanticide is correct is controversial, however. Some workers believe that primate infanticide may be a product of environmental stress, such as overcrowding, or even merely a product of an especially aggressive takeover in which infants are killed more in error than by intent. Furthermore, say skeptics, neither the regularity nor the fitness effects of infanticide have been well documented. Nonetheless, for many primatologists the hypothesis of infanticide as a reproductive strategy is a compelling one. But the evidence so far is limited. Only further observations will help us to resolve this fascinating question.

What Dian Fossey observed among gorillas is valuable evidence that leads toward an understanding of the process by which young males can gain access to females. But Fossey's primary concern in her last years was to protect the remaining mountain gorillas from the deadly work of poachers. Although the gorillas are

FIGURE 4–16   Two older female langurs are chasing away a male that has recently taken over their troop and threatened a black infant. The black infants, less than six months of age, are easily identified as the offspring of the deposed male. Sarah Blaffer Hrdy of the University of California at Davis has studied the Hanuman langurs of Mount Abu near New Delhi. She reports seeing nursing mothers repeatedly try to save their infants from a new dominant male bent on infanticide.

a protected and endangered species, poachers, in order to obtain marketable tourist items, continue to kill them in the Parc National des Volcans in Rwanda. Fossey waged an unceasing war against poachers, doing her best to protect the dwindling numbers of animals in that remote part of Central Africa. In September 1985 she was brutally murdered, presumably by one of the poachers she had caught and punished. Today her successors continue observing the magnificent animals. Her pioneering contribution to our understanding of the gorilla is of priceless value, and her work will be read and discussed for generations to come.

Goodall and the Gombe Chimpanzees

As with the gorilla, long and devoted field observations have helped us understand something of chimpanzee behavior. Paleoanthropologist Louis Leakey knew of a community of chimpanzees that lived in a hilly wooded tract near the Gombe Stream, a river running into Lake Tanganyika in western Tanzania. He was interested in anything that had to do with primates; furthermore, he thought that the present-day stream, with its woodland and grassland environment, closely resembled the environment inhabited by early hominids. He persuaded Jane Goodall to undertake a study of the Gombe chimps.

In 1960, when Goodall arrived in what is now the Gombe National Park, she set up camp near the lakeshore and began to spend her days roaming the hills and valleys, looking for chimpanzees in an area of about 15 square miles (39 kilometers^2). Her plan was to watch the animals discreetly, not getting too close, just accustoming them to her presence, as a preliminary to closer acquaintance. Many months later she was still watching from a distance, still treated with suspicion by the shy chimpanzees. Ultimately, after a period of rejection that would have discouraged a less dedicated person, she was accepted, not by all the chimpanzees, but by many of them (Figure 4–17). She became very friendly with a few of them. Eventually she spent thousands of hours with them, sometimes in actual physical contact—handing out bananas, playing with a baby, and more often just sitting quietly and watching a society of unimagined subtlety and complexity gradually unfold. Goodall's studies (summarized in a book called *The Chimpanzees of Gombe*) reveal the chimpanzee to be an animal whose biology, behavior, and social organization provoke all kinds of speculations about the emergence of humankind (see Box 4-2).

Chimpanzees occur in a broad band across West and Central Africa from Senegal and the Ivory Coast in the west to Uganda and Tanzania in the east (Figure 4–18). Of all the great apes, the chimpanzee is the least specialized. In size it is a neat compromise: small enough to get about in trees, and big enough to take care of itself on the ground against predators, particularly since it usually travels in bands, which are sections of a larger community. As a result, it is at home in both worlds. Although still a fruit eater whose favorite staple is ripe figs, it is a generalist-opportunist and will eat a wide variety of other fruit and vegetation, together with some meat: birds' eggs or fledglings, insects, lizards or small snakes, and occasionally a young baboon, colobus monkey, or bush pig.

Chimpanzee society is not typical of the higher primates. The Gombe animals live in dispersed communities of from forty to sixty individuals, and the bonding between them is loose. The term **fusion-fission** has been applied to chimpanzee society. Individuals of either sex have almost complete freedom to come and go as they wish. The membership of temporary subgroups is constantly changing. Adults and adolescents can and do forage, travel, and sleep alone, sometimes for days at a time. An individual rarely sees all the members of the community on the

Fusion-fission community a society that includes several individuals of both sexes and all ages and is characterized by the formation and dissolution of temporary subgroups.

FIGURE 4–17   Jane Goodall has been a pioneer in the study of wild animals. By undertaking a long behavioral study of wild chimpanzees since 1960, she has contributed greatly to our understanding both of chimpanzees and, by implication, of ourselves.

same day and probably never sees them two days in succession. An animal may travel one day with a large, noisy, and excitable gathering and the next day completely alone. Females may spend many days alone or with their young; males tend to be more gregarious. This flexibility of chimpanzee society is one of its most remarkable characteristics.

In addition to their fusion-fission characteristic, chimpanzee communities can be classed as multimale-multifemale since they contain several adult individuals of each sex. Young females habitually emigrate from their natal community to live and breed elsewhere as adults, while males routinely remain in the community of their birth. Although there is considerable variation among chimpanzee populations, this emigration pattern typically results in relatively weak social bonds between females but strong bonds (often based on kinship) between males. Heterosexual social bonds also appear to be rather weak, and grooming between the sexes is less common than grooming between males.

As noted earlier, male chimpanzees strive to achieve high dominance rank, and within each community one male can be recognized as the alpha animal. Males form strong alliances with one another, and support from allies (often kin) may be

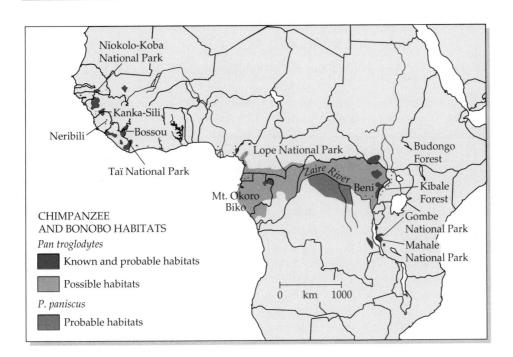

FIGURE 4–18   Chimpanzee and bonobo distribution follows the band of tropical rain forest across Central Africa. A number of study areas are identified. The chimpanzee is today an endangered species because of both poaching and continued logging in forest areas. There is apparently still a world demand for baby chimpanzees, and as long as it continues, the outlook for the species is not good. (Based on Jane Goodall, *The Chimpanzees of Gombe*, Cambridge, Harvard University Press, 1986, Figure 3.1, p. 45.)

crucial to achieving and maintaining high rank. Dominance relations exist among females, but they are not as clear-cut as the male hierarchy, although older females generally dominate younger ones.

Nishida and the Mahale Mountain Chimpanzees

In 1966, not long after Goodall set up camp, Toshisada Nishida and Junichiro Itani, with a small team from Kyoto University in Japan, set out to study another group of chimpanzees not far south of Gombe, in the Mahale Mountains of Tanzania. Since that time they have maintained almost continuous observation of a large community of more than 100 apes. This work constitutes an admirable comparative study that can throw extra light on Jane Goodall's well-known observations. The first most striking impression is that this large community has a far greater density of males, with the result that there is far more intermale rivalry and a much more marked dominance hierarchy. In place of the more easygoing ways of the Gombe males, we see a situation in which the alpha male dominates the matings of all females in season and plays a more central role in all the group's activities. Interactions generally seem to be more intense and more highly structured. We see social behavior responding to a difference in population size and density.

The important result of comparisons of this sort—and we now have studies from parts of West Africa to compare with those of East Africa—is the realization that chimpanzees have a very flexible and adaptable behavior repertoire. There are

Box 4-2

CURRENT ISSUE: *Genetic Relations Between Humans and Chimpanzees*

One often reads the claim that humans and chimpanzees are about 99 percent genetically identical. This startling statistic, which reflects humans' recent evolutionary separation from the chimp-bonobo lineage, excites our interest in several ways. Some people experience increased empathy with chimpanzees and devote themselves to ape conservation efforts. Others ponder the science fiction possibilities of chimp-human hybridization! But what sense can we actually make of the 99 percent claim? After all, humans and chimps *seem* very different. We are taller, smaller toothed, less hairy, bigger brained, and have different limb proportions than chimpanzees. Furthermore, we mature more slowly, live longer, and reproduce more often. And finally, thanks to our large and complex brains, humans have minds, language, and culture—three attributes that chimpanzees may possess partially, but imperfectly (see later sections of this chapter and also Chapter 13). So what's with the claim of genetic near-identity?

As it turns out, there are actually several ways to measure human-chimp genetic relatedness, and the various measures don't necessarily give the same results. For starters, the 99 percent figure is based on comparisons of the amino acid sequences of functionally similar proteins (for example, comparing our hemoglobin *a* protein with that of a chimp). Many such polypeptide chains are absolutely the same in chimps and humans, while others differ by only a single amino acid. In contrast, while functionally similar proteins may be the same across the species, the polypeptide products of alleles at similar chromosomal loci often are not. Electrophoretic comparisons (which involve placing proteins in an electric field and measuring their migration patterns across a starch gel) suggest that humans and chimps are only 52 to 68 percent

identical in their alleles at an average locus. Finally, humans and chimpanzees show several chromosomal differences. As noted in Chapter 2, the species differ in their diploid numbers: forty-six for us and forty-eight for chimps. Our chromosome two is the result of fusing the ancestral ape chromosomes twelve and thirteen, both of which still exist separately in chimpanzees, while other human-chimp chromosomal differences can be traced to inversions (in which stretches of genetic material are reversed on a chromosome) or the addition or loss of chunks of DNA.

The situation, therefore, is considerably more complicated than simply labeling humans and chimps as 99 percent the same. Nonetheless, all of the evidence agrees that *organismal* (anatomical and behavioral) differences between the species have evolved at a much faster rate than *molecular* (chromosomal, allelic, protein) differences. One way this could have happened is if many (most?) of the detectable genetic differences have involved regulatory genes—genes that affect the body's growth, development, and maintenance—rather than structural genes that code for building blocks such as flesh and bones. In other words, humans and chimpanzees may differ not so much in *what* they're made of, as in *how* they're made.

So, the next time you hear the 99 percent measure being bandied about, you might want to point out that while humans and chimps consist of the same bodily bricks and mortar, we differ mightily from chimps when measured by the finished product: the evolved architecture of our bodies, brains, and behavior. These evolved differences clearly preclude gene leakage between the species in nature, and would almost certainly foil the efforts of any scientist mad enough to try creating an ape-human Chimpenstein in the laboratory. ■

subtle (and not so subtle) differences between the behaviors of every community, and it is only by studying a considerable number of different populations, living under slightly different conditions, that we can begin to learn the full repertoire of chimpanzee behavior and come to gain some insight into the total potential of this remarkable and very intelligent animal.

The Chimpanzee as Hunter

Goodall reports that a hunting chimpanzee is unmistakable. Compared with other chimpanzee behaviors, there is something out of the ordinary about hunting behavior, observed much more often among males than among females. There is in it something purposeful, tense, and inward that other chimpanzees recognize and respond to. Sometimes they just watch the hunter intently. Sometimes other chimpanzees move to adjacent trees to cut off the escape of the quarry, a young baboon or a small arboreal monkey. On several occasions observed by Goodall, the quarry was a young baboon whose screams brought adult baboons rushing to its defense. In the ensuing hullabaloo the youngster more often than not escaped. But Goodall saw chimpanzees killing and eating small- to medium-sized animals (monkeys, pigs, small antelopes) often enough to realize that meat is an important part of the apes' diet.

Since Goodall's pioneering work, observations by Nishida at Mahale, Christophe Boesch and Hedwige Bosech-Achermann in the Taï National Park (Ivory Coast), and Craig Stanford at Gombe have added much new information about hunting and meat-eating by chimpanzees. First, we now know that chimps' main prey species is the red colobus monkey (*Colobus badius*), a species that is both smaller and more arboreal than baboons. (Predation on baboons was common early in Goodall's study when she was luring both chimpanzees and baboons into her camp with bananas. Once banana provisioning ceased, baboons became a rare prey item at Gombe.) Chimpanzees hunt red colobus at all three major study sites, and at Gombe, where up to 150 monkeys may be killed during a peak hunting year, the apes have a strong negative effect on colobus population size. Second, we now realize that meat can be a substantial part of the diet for particular populations of chimpanzees. At Gombe, Stanford has estimated that during a good hunting year the chimps may consume more than 270 pounds (600 kilograms) of meat. This would bring the meat consumption of adult males (who hunt much more frequently than females and thus eat more meat) to a point near the low end of the range for human hunters and gatherers (i.e., between 5 to 10 percent of the diet). And finally, scientists have now observed much more complex hunts than those recorded by Jane Goodall, the most intricate of which take place not in Gombe's woodland and grassland habitat, but rather in the dense rain forest at Taï in West Africa.

Observations on the Taï chimps have been made for more than ten years by the husband-and-wife team of Christophe Boesch and Hedwige Boesch-Achermann, primatologists operating out of the Swiss Center for Scientific Research. They have found that red colobus hunts at Taï involve larger groups of chimp males and more complicated strategies than at Gombe. For example, the Taï chimps often take on different roles during colobus hunts: some males function as drivers, others encircle the fleeing monkeys to keep them from dispersing, and yet others race ahead to block the monkeys' arboreal pathway. The chances of a kill are greatly enhanced by larger hunting parties, and after a successful hunt cooperating males may share meat generously. Such regular sharing of the kill presumably encourages future cooperation. Of course, simpler hunts—arboreal pursuits of monkeys by single chimps or pouncing on piglets and fawns when they are discovered hiding in the grass—also occur at all chimpanzee study sites.

Clearly, chimpanzees all across Africa are excited by meat and very fond of it. They chew it long and reflectively, usually with a mouthful of leaves added. Sometimes the carcass is shared in an orderly fashion by the successful hunter(s),

FIGURE 4–19   The upper chimpanzee is holding the rib cage of a small monkey; the two lower chimpanzees are begging. Frequently the hunter will share the remains of the kill.

with bits of meat being torn off and handed out to begging group mates (Figure 4–19). Males tend to share with other males (most often with kin, allies, and co-hunters) and also with estrous females. Indeed, the regularity of chimpanzee males apparently swapping meat for sex has led Craig Stanford to suggest that males "decide to hunt with an awareness that procuring colobus meat may enhance their access to [sexually] swollen females." Females with meat almost never share it with other females. It would be incorrect, however, to give the impression that all transfers of meat are nice and orderly. In fact, immediately after a kill all hell may break loose around a carcass. Individuals with meat may be attacked or threatened by those without, and sometimes fights break out among the throng of have-nots. Such squabbling is not surprising given the high value that chimps place on meat.

The revelation that chimpanzees hunt and eat meat—and share it as well, although sometimes reluctantly—has enormous implications in explaining the development of hunting and sharing among hominids. It now becomes possible to speculate that these traits were brought to the savanna from the forest. We no longer have to puzzle over how a propensity for meat eating began in a creature with a fruit-eating ancestry; it was already there, as we now know it is in most primates. All this propensity needed was encouragement in a new environment.

The First Herbalists?

To this brief section on chimpanzee diet and food strategies, we can now add a most remarkable and unexpected postscript. Jane Goodall's observations and other more recent studies in East Africa by Richard Wrangham of Harvard University and Toshisada Nishida have revealed that on certain occasions chimpanzees will chew the pith or eat a few leaves of particular plants that have been shown to have medicinal properties. The chimps seem to know when they need these plants, and they evidently have the knowledge to select particular species. How do we know they are medicinal? In the first place, they are certainly not part of the chimp's regular diet and are eaten only quite uncommonly and when other more popular food plants are available. The leaves are not particularly palatable, for the chimps do not chew them but swallow them like a pill. Second, the local Tongwa people use some of these same plants, in particular, species of *Aspilia*, in the same way. Finally, the plants turn out on analysis to contain an antibiotic (thiarubrine-A) that is potent against bacteria, viruses, fungi, and even parasitic worms!

Although it has not been proved, it does appear that chimpanzees—and occasionally, gorillas and bonobos as well—are deliberately dosing themselves when they feel unwell, with one or more of a number of species of plants that have very definite medicinal qualities. Research is now proceeding apace, not only to study the chimpanzees' diet more intensively, but to look into any value these plants may have in Western medicine.

Tools and Weapons

One of the most stunning discoveries of the chimpanzee studies is the fact that these apes make and use a wide variety of simple tools (see Table 4–3). Despite their relatively short thumbs and impaired precision grip (see Figure 3–24 and Table 3–7), chimpanzees fish for termites with sticks and stems (Figure 3–19), make sponges of wadded leaves, hammer open nuts with stones, and occasionally use natural objects as weapons. The exact value of these activities to chimpanzees' survival is hard to measure, but it seems clear that they allow the apes to adapt to a variety of habitats and facilitate the extraction of otherwise inaccessible food items. Jane Goodall has

TABLE 4-3 *A Partial List of Tool-Use Patterns Shown By Wild Apes*

TOOL OR BEHAVIOR PATTERN	CHIMPANZEES	BONOBOS	GORILLAS	ORANGUTANS
Sticks as probes for termite (or other insect) fishing or for honey extraction	X			X
Wadded leaf sponges	X			
Leaf-vessels to hold food				X
Leaves as rain hats		X		X
Leaves wiped, rubbed on body	X	X		X
Branches dragged, torn, dropped in display	X	X	X	X
Branches, rocks as hammers for nut cracking	X			
Roots, rocks as anvils for nut cracking	X			
Leaf petiole of oil palms for pestle-pounding in palm crown	X			
Rocks, branches waved, thrown at opponents	X			

shown that each new generation learns tool-using patterns from the previous one. The youngsters have many opportunities to learn: they watch their elders intently, often copying what they do.

Jane Goodall also observed that many members of the Gombe community were good at throwing things. Her accounts reveal that this activity was well established at Gombe; a number of males tried it, and in a variety of circumstances. Even often woefully inaccurate throwing seems useful to a chimpanzee. In chimpanzee life there is a great deal of bluffing and aggressive display. During such activity an animal will jump up and down, wave its arms, hoot, shriek, and charge forward. This behavior looks especially disconcerting if it is accompanied by a shower of sticks, waste, or stones (Figure 4–20). The fact that throwing is useful as an aggressive display explains why it is now established as part of the species' behavior.

At its present stage of throwing development, the chimpanzee is scarcely a star athlete, at least by human standards. Due to lack of practice it cannot throw far or accurately; it cannot count on hitting anything more than 4 or 5 feet (1.5 meters) away. But the performance does not have to impress humans, only other chimpanzees, baboons, leopards, and the like. For such audiences the display is extremely effective. Throwing clearly has selective value, and we can speculate that, if chimpanzees are left to themselves long enough, they may become better throwers than they now are.

Even now, potential for improvement exists among individual chimpanzees. There was one such at Gombe called Mr. Worzle (Goodall named all the chimpanzees as fast as she could recognize them, for ease of identification). Mr. Worzle accomplished the remarkable feat of becoming a superior stone thrower as a result of being exposed to an unusual challenge. As noted earlier, in order to attract the chimps to the camp area, where they more easily could be observed, Goodall made a practice of putting out bananas. This unnatural concen-

FIGURE 4–20   Throwing stones and other objects is typical of chimpanzees trying to scare a threatening intruder or merely letting off steam.

tration of food also attracted baboons that lived in the vicinity, leading to abrasive confrontations. The baboons quickly learned which chimpanzees, mostly females and juveniles, they could intimidate by rushing at them. But they never could dislodge Mr. Worzle, who stood his ground, picking up whatever was handy and throwing it at them. Sometimes it was leaves. Once, to the delight of the baboons, it was a bunch of bananas. But slowly Mr. Worzle learned that rocks were best, and as time went on he depended more and more on rocks and started using bigger and bigger ones. Mr. Worzle's response indicates the ability to improvise that exists in an intelligent and physically adept animal when confronted by a new situation or given an opportunity to deal with an old one in a new way.

More recently, primatologists Yukimaru Sugiyama and Jeremy Koman, who have studied undisturbed chimpanzees near Bossou, in Guinea, West Africa, experienced "aimed throwing" of branches of considerable intensity and accuracy, which repelled everyone present except Sugiyama! These chimpanzees had clearly hit on a most effective way of dealing with predators and other intruders—a technique that surely would have been equally valuable to early hominids.

Bossou is only one of the many new sites, particularly in West Africa, to which chimpanzee studies have been extended. It is now clear that, in different regions of their range, chimpanzees show "cultural" differences in behavior generally, and in tool use. Different kinds of probes are used in "fishing" for termites, and at some sites in Rio Muni, termite hills are very hard and are broken into with much stronger sticks; then the termites are dug out and eaten by hand. The hominid use of digging sticks is foreshadowed by these primates.

In the Taï Forest, chimpanzees have been observed using sticks and stones to break open nuts. At Bossou, chimpanzees used two stones to smash open palm nuts. They placed the nut in the cavity of one flat stone (platform stone) and smashed it with a hammer stone (Figure 4–21). As Sugiyama and Koman, who observed this behavior, pointed out, it is almost identical to that attributed to early hominids, and if these stones had been found in an excavation, they might have been identified as a product of hominid tool use.

Thus among chimpanzees we have evidence of the use of tools as weapons, digging sticks, and nutcrackers, and as implements for the collection of social insects such as termites and ants. Even the use of stone tools—so important in hominid evolution—is seen in chimpanzees' hammer-stone-and-anvil nut processing. But two additional interesting and suggestive observations must be made: female chimpanzees appear to use tools more often and more efficiently than do males. As noted by primatologist W. C. McGrew, most chimpanzee tool use occurs during sessions of insect gathering (termite fishing and ant dipping), and females show much higher levels of insectivory than males. With regard to nutcracking behavior, Boesch-Achermann and Boesch reported that at Taï, chimp females were considerably more efficient than males at opening nuts. Tool use rarely occurs in the context of hunting and eating mammalian prey—which, as noted earlier, are primarily male activities—although occasionally sticks are used to pick marrow from broken bones or leaf wads are used to clean out an opened braincase. Can these findings on sex differences in chimpanzee tool use be applied to early hominids? In McGrew's words, "If the parallels between observed ape and hypothesized proto-hominid data are genuine, then the evolutionary origins of tool-use are more likely to have come from solitary, female gathering and not from social, male hunting." Further data bearing on this point are eagerly awaited.

FIGURE 4–21   Chimpanzee using a hammer stone and an anvil to crack open oil palm nuts.

Murder and War

Observations have revealed that encounters between chimpanzee communities may in fact be sought and may become very aggressive. The best data come from Jane Goodall's observations at Gombe. Here it was observed that parties of up to ten adult males, sometimes accompanied by females and young, might patrol peripheral areas near the boundary of the community territory and actively search for signs of neighboring groups. Contact might result in displays until one or both groups gave up or fled and returned to the core area of their range. When single chimpanzees or very small parties were encountered, they might be chased and even attacked, often brutally. Males have been observed setting out as a small group with the clear intention of stalking a neighbor. They silently moved through the forest, avoiding the crackle of branches or leaves underfoot. Such behavior is known to have resulted in what can only be called brutal murder, clearly cold-blooded and calculated. Goodall has described one four-year period at Gombe as essentially a war, during which an entire community was annihilated, so that the victorious males and their females were able to move into the unoccupied territory. This behavior looks all too familiar, and the whole question of intercommunity relations and aggression among chimpanzees is now a subject of active research. Understanding it is important to those studying the evolution and nature of human violence.

Chimpanzee Politics

Studying chimpanzees and gorillas in the wild may seem the ultimate step in behavioral research, yet it has one serious disadvantage. It is extremely difficult to follow the behavior of groups of individuals for long periods in great detail; trees and undergrowth, the natural shyness of wild animals, and their tendency to move about can interrupt observations at critical moments. On the other hand, observations of captive apes are unreliable insofar as their behavior is distorted in captivity by the unnatural conditions under which they live.

In 1971 an attempt was made to overcome this problem. A large 2-acre (0.8 hectare) moated enclosure was built at the Burghers' Zoo in Arnhem, Holland. Here a group of chimpanzees was settled—males, females, and young—and they have developed into a most successful breeding colony that now numbers twenty-five individuals. Observation platforms were built, and observers were able to watch the behavior of the inmates in extraordinary detail. In his *Chimpanzee Politics*, Frans de Waal describes the social life of these chimpanzees in a way that was never before possible. What he has found is truly remarkable: the chimpanzees exhibit political behavior (defined as social manipulation designed to secure and maintain power status) of a kind previously believed to be found only among humans.

Throughout the past three decades, since Jane Goodall began her research at Gombe, we have been surprised (and delighted) again and again by the extent to which chimpanzees have been found to foreshadow humans in their social behavior: first, the greeting and nursing behavior, then the intermale competition, then the interest in using and making tools, then the enthusiasm for hunting, then the aggression, ambition, and apparent cold-blooded cruelty. Now, de Waal reveals to us that the whole social structure is based on political infighting; that whole passages from Niccolo Machiavelli (1469–1527) describing humans' political manipulations seem to be directly applicable to chimpanzees; and that the struggle for power and the resultant opportunism are so marked among chimpanzees that their social organization seems almost too human to be true. But it is true. The observations are sound, and their interpretation is unavoidable. Not all the political mechanisms seen at Arnhem are necessarily present in all wild communities, but they probably are present, and there is no doubt that the potential for this kind of political maneuvering is indeed part of chimpanzee nature.

The main difference between the wild and the captive chimpanzees is one of leisure time: the wild animals spend most of their waking hours in the quest for food. In contrast, the captive chimpanzees were fed daily, each evening, and therefore had far more time at their disposal to devote to politics and intrigue.

The work at Arnhem has given us important insights into many areas of chimpanzee behavior, which we can only briefly summarize here. In that group there was a clear-cut rank order, at least among the dominant individuals. The urge to power was a primary determinant of all male behavior. Second, female relationships were less hierarchic and much more stable than those of males. Senior females were influential and even mediated between competing males. They occasionally confiscated rocks from the hands of an angry male!

Hidden beneath the power struggle and its resultant hierarchy was a network of positions of influence. Thus the most influential troop members at Arnhem were the oldest male and the oldest female, no longer dominant in the obvious sense, but highly influential and able to pull strings behind the scenes. Newly dominant individuals were usually much less influential and dependent on coalition and alliance.

Thus there is an overt and a covert aspect to chimpanzee politics. Altogether, power politics reigns supreme and is able to give chimpanzee society a logical coherence and even a democratic base. Every individual searches for social significance and continues to do so until a temporary balance is achieved, determining new hierarchic positions. Thus the hierarchy is a cohesive structure and brings stability that makes possible effective child care, play, cooperation, and undisturbed sexual activity. But the balance of power is tested daily and, if found to be weak, is challenged; then the social structure is rebuilt.

At Arnhem, it appears that the rewards of power were more limited than in nature, for food was rationed and fairly distributed among the chimpanzees. Thus the rewards to males of high status were mainly sexual: access to estrous females. This limitation, however, did not prevent the apes from exhibiting almost every political subterfuge known to humans, including dominance networks and coalitions, power struggles, alliances, divide-and-rule strategies, arbitration, confiscation, collective leadership, privileges, bargaining, and frequent reconciliations (which usually took the form of kissing, open-mouthed).

Reconciliation the act of restoring friendly relations.

The importance of **reconciliation** and peacemaking has been stressed by de Waal in a more recent book, where he has extended his studies to three other species, including bonobos. It is clear that peacemaking and other stabilizing social mechanisms of reconciliation are vital for a stable, adaptive, and successful society. Almost all these behaviors have been at least briefly observed or suspected in wild populations, but they were never recorded with the frequency or in the detail made possible at Arnhem. The significance of the Arnhem observations is that they show us yet more of the behavioral potential of an ape such as the chimpanzee.

Bonobos: The Best Evolutionary Model for Early Hominids?

One ape species remains to be described: *Pan paniscus*, the bonobo (pygmy chimpanzee). Although recognized for more than half a century, this species remained essentially unstudied until the last two decades. As data on bonobos have been forthcoming, however, they have been particularly tantalizing for anthropologists, since in some ways these are the apes that most closely resemble humans in their behavior. Some scientists believe, therefore, that bonobos are an especially good model for studies of early hominid evolution.

Bonobos are found in Central Africa, in the lowland rain forests and swamp forests south of the Zaire River (Figure 4–18). They are about the size of the smallest subspecies of chimpanzees (*Pan troglodytes*), although bonobos are somewhat more slender, with narrower shoulders and longer legs. In addition, bonobos have smaller brow ridges and ears and lighter colored lips than chimpanzees, and the hair on their heads is parted down the center (Figure 4–22). As in the other African apes, sexual dimorphism in body size is significant among bonobos, and females' body weight is about three-quarters that of males (see Table 3–5).

Bonobos live in multimale-multifemale communities that are characterized by the fusion-fission subgrouping already described for chimpanzees: females appear to emigrate from their natal communities, but males do not. Interestingly, the tendency of bonobo males to remain in their natal communities is not correlated with strong male-male relationships or clear-cut male dominance, as it is among chimpanzees. The strongest social bonds among adult bonobos are (depending on the study population) either between females or between males and females. Adult males tend not to develop close relations with one another, but rather they remain

Figure 4–22 Bonobo (*Pan paniscus*) female and infant. Bonobos are somewhat more slender than chimpanzees, and their hair is parted in the center.

strongly bonded to their mothers, associating with them frequently. Newly immigrated females use affiliative and sexual interactions (genito-genital rubbing, see below) to establish friendly relationships with resident females, and coalitions of bonded females dominate males and limit males' access to preferred feeding sites. Bonobo females develop distinct dominance relationships, and the support of a high-ranking mother can enhance an adult son's rank among the males. In general, bonobo females have much more influence within their communities—and bonobo males have less—than is true for their chimpanzee counterparts.

A community of bonobos includes between 50 and 120 animals and inhabits a range of about 8 to 19 miles^2 (20 to 50 kilometers^2). The apes spend most of their time in the trees foraging for fruits, a diet supplemented with other plant parts, insects, and some meat. Food is regularly shared. Unlike chimpanzees, bonobos apparently do not use tools to obtain or process either plant or animal foods. Among the few tool-use patterns recorded for bonobos are making rain hats from leafy boughs, wiping feces from their bodies with leaves, and dragging branches in display. In another contrast to chimpanzees, bonobo communities show extensively overlapping home ranges and often fail to defend their ranges as true territories. (Thus, there is much less territorial patrolling than in chimpanzees.) When subgroups from different bonobo communities meet in the forest, they initially display hostility, but may soon begin to interact in a friendly and sexual fashion. First, females from the two communities engage in genital rubbing and then grooming. Youngsters from the different groups begin to play. Finally, adult males may participate in scrotal rubbing with their counterparts from the other group. Amazingly, even copulations between males and females from different communities can take place during these relatively relaxed encounters—something no self-respecting chimpanzee male would ever allow.

Among the similarities claimed for bonobos and humans, most are sexual, but one is postural. Studies of captive animals have suggested that bonobos stand and walk bipedally more often (and with greater ease) than chimpanzees or gorillas (Figure 4–23). While this may be true, no one is claiming that bonobos are habitual bipeds. In fact, a recent field study showed that bipedalism represented less than 2 percent of the total locomotion of its wild bonobo subjects.

The similarities in sexual behavior, however, are more striking and possibly more important. Bonobo females show rather long sexual cycles of thirty-five to forty-nine days, and between menstrual flows they may be maximally sexually swollen for up to 49 percent of the time. This is a considerably longer period of sexual attractiveness and mating activity than is recorded for chimpanzees, whose females are maximally swollen for 27 to 40 percent of their menstrual cycle. Humans, of course, engage in sexual behavior throughout all or most of the men-

FIGURE 4–23   Bonobos stand and move bipedally much more often than chimpanzees.

strual cycle, rather more like bonobos. But the sexual similarities take two more interesting twists. First, while virtually all chimpanzee copulations are ventrodorsal (the male mounts the female from the rear), some 25 to 30 percent of bonobo matings are ventroventral. Of the two sexes, female bonobos seem to be particularly fond of face-to-face sex; several instances have been recorded of females interrupting ventrodorsal copulations in order to change their position and embrace the male ventrally. And second, bonobos are without doubt the most inventive of all the apes in their sexual variations. Bonobos show all of the possible combinations of sexual partners: opposite-sex, same-sex, and old and young. Pairs of females frequently embrace ventrally and rub their genitals together, while males mount one another and occasionally "fence" (mutually rub) with their erect penises. Sex is used by bonobos to reduce tension and resolve conflicts. As Frans de Waal has remarked about this make-love-not-war species, "the chimpanzee resolves sexual issues with power; the bonobo resolves power issues with sex." Indeed, some researchers believe that frequent female-female and male-female sexual contacts explain why these relationships are stronger among bonobos than among chimpanzees.

Studies of bonobos are in their infancy. Assuming that humans allow (and assist) bonobos to avoid extinction, this species promises to yield critical information for interpreting human evolution.

Speculations About Ape-Human Common Ancestors

Studies of chromosomes and DNA are beginning to allow fine-grained distinctions about humans' evolutionary relationships with the African apes (see Box 4–1). Most molecular research suggests that humans, bonobos, and chimpanzees are a clade with a common ancestor that lived about 5 to 7 million years ago—the gorilla lineage having diverged a couple of million years before. These studies further suggest that the chimp and bonobo lines may have separated only within the last 2.5 to 3 million years, so that they are extremely close sister species. Not everyone agrees with this phylogeny, however, and anatomists argue that it implies that knuckle-walking evolved independently twice—once in the gorilla lineage and once in the ancestors of chimps and bonobos after the divergence of hominids—a seemingly unlikely occurrence. Nonetheless, on balance, the molecular evidence seems the more convincing and thus, based on data from living humans, chimpanzees, and bonobos, we can speculate cautiously about the probable characteristics of their last common ancestor (an ape-grade creature whose exact identity has yet to be established).

As summarized in Table 4–4, it seems likely that humans' last ape ancestor formed multimale-multifemale communities that were characterized by fusion-fission subgrouping. Female emigration from the natal community was probably the prevalent pattern, and territorial defense by males probably occurred at least occasionally. Sexual behavior was probably variable and situation-dependent (that is, hormonal control of sex was moderate to low, and mating may have occurred throughout much of the menstrual cycle). Males almost certainly had access to multiple mates, and the same may have been true of females. The common ancestor probably engaged in some tool use (the extent is uncertain), included meat in its diet, and, at least occasionally, shared food. And finally, bipedal standing and walking almost certainly occurred on occasion, although not habitually.

TABLE 4-4   *Characteristics of Chimpanzees, Bonobos, Humans, and Their Common Ancestor*

TRAIT	CHIMPANZEES	BONOBOS	HUMANS	COMMON ANCESTOR
Social group[a]	MM-MF community; fusion-fission	MM-MF community; fusion-fission	MM-MF community; fusion-fission	MM-MF community; fusion-fission
Females or males change groups?	Females	Females	Females more often	Females
Male-male bonds	Strong	Weak	Strong	?
Female-female bonds	Weak	Strong	Weak to moderate	?
Male-female bonds	Weak	Strong	Strong	?
Territorial defense?	Common, by males	Occasional, by males	Common, by males	At least occasional, by males
Mating system	Promiscuity	Promiscuity	Mild polygyny to promiscuity	Multiple mates for males (for females too?)
Sexual swelling?	Yes	Yes	No	?
Sexual activity[b]	27–40%	35–49%	Near 100%	?
Hormonal control of female sexuality	Moderate	Moderate to low	Low	Moderate to low
Copulation pattern	Ventrodorsal	Ventrodorsal > ventroventral	Variable	?
Paternal investment by males	Slight	Slight	Moderate to strong	?
Tool use?	Frequent and variable	Rare	Very frequent and variable	Probably present (variable?)
Meat eating?	Yes	Yes	Yes	Yes
Food sharing?	Routine	Routine	Frequent	Yes
Bipedal stance?	Rare	More common than in chimps	Habitual	At least occasional

[a] MM, multimale; MF, multifemale.
[b] Percentage of menstrual cycle with mating.

Beyond this admittedly sketchy characterization, speculations become very tenuous, but even this incomplete picture of our last ape ancestors is useful in generating evolutionary hypotheses for further testing. Humans appear to be the descendants of social, female-emigrating, moderately territorial, polygynous-to-promiscuous, tool-using apes that relished a bit of meat in the diet and at least occasionally stood and moved upright. But what was involved in the evolutionary transformation of such a creature into a hominid? To begin to answer that question, we need to focus not on shared traits, but on behavioral and anatomical differences between apes and humans. We will examine such differences in the next chapter as we take a look at some fossil candidates for the office of Common Ancestor.

SUMMARY

Knowledge of the behavior of living primates is an important component in the study of human origins and human nature. Since they began in the early part of this century, primate studies have produced much useful information about our evolutionary relatives, the monkeys and apes. As shown in this chapter, primates are extremely social creatures whose complex behavioral repertoires are based mainly on learning. Their societies are structured by several types of relationships, especially dominance relations, kinship, and affiliative relations (the last based commonly on grooming). Patterns of sexual behavior vary from species to species, but the levels of reproductive success and the identities of sexual partners are commonly influenced by dominance and female choice. Among the apes, chimpanzees and bonobos are clearly the closest evolutionary relatives of humans; gorillas rank third. Comparisons among chimpanzees, bonobos, and humans have revealed much about the likely traits of our common ancestor and enable us to formulate numerous evolutionary hypotheses for testing.

POSTSCRIPT

Do chimpanzees have culture? A deceptively simple question perhaps. A knee-jerk answer might be "No, of course not—they're animals!" But how does one classify an animal that makes and uses tools, and that shows regional variation in both tool use and social behavior? The British social anthropologist E. B. Tylor defined culture in 1871 as the "capabilities and habits acquired by man as a member of society." The only kind of culture then known was human culture and it was therefore defined as a specifically human characteristic, dependent on language. Early cultural anthropologists (who produced nearly as many definitions as they themselves numbered) were certain about culture's unique state as a human attribute and did not consider the question of its development from prehistoric times.

The nascent science of archaeology forced the issue of cultural origins in the nineteenth century. Early collectors of stone tools and other artifacts were properly cautious, however, and talked of the beginning of human "material culture." This qualified term reflected the view (since confirmed by animal studies) that simple tools are not always accurate indicators of a total cultural system. This view follows from the fact that toolmaking skills can be learned by observation alone, without language-based instruction. The implication was, and still is, that material culture might well have preceded the full range of cultural manifestations in the course of human evolution.

Modern anthropology has made progress in understanding culture and its definitive features, but there is still room for debate. A modern revision of Tylor describes culture as *the totality of behavior of a social group that is passed down the generations by learning and symbolic means*. This broad definition covers all modern cultural manifestations—rituals, beliefs, material objects, social institutions, and so on—and grounds them in the three key elements of learning, symbolic transmission, and behavior as the property of society.

But to return to the original question: How well do chimpanzees and other nonhuman primates match our current understanding of culture? Following the revised definition, we can recognize some apparently cultural behavior among monkeys as well as among toolmaking chimpanzees. But for many workers, the critical addition of symbolic transmission to the definition seems clearly to distinguish human culture from the nonsymbolic protoculture of nonhuman primates. As most anthropologists—and nearly all cultural anthropologists—understand things, the transition from protoculture to culture came with the evolution of symbolic language.

Not everyone agrees with the prevailing wisdom, however, including W. C. McGrew, primatologist and author of the book *Chimpanzee Material Culture* which takes on the problem of culture among apes. McGrew sets out eight criteria for identifying cultural acts among nonlinguistic creatures such as chimps: innovation, dissemination, standardization, durability, diffusion, tradition, nonsubsistence, and naturalness. He concludes that no single chimpanzee population satisfies all eight conditions, but that all conditions (except perhaps diffusion) are met by the behavior of some chimps in some cases. He also describes differences in grooming patterns between chimp populations that would automatically be described as cultural differences if shown by humans, but that are denied that label when they are shown by apes. McGrew's argument strongly implies that while definitions of culture are important **heuristic devices** for social scientists, they usually also have the unspoken function of separating humans from all nonhumans.

Heuristic devices devices that facilitate or stimulate further investigation and thought.

Of course, the problem with definitions and labels that establish a clean break between humans and nonhumans is that they are hard to reconcile with the fact of evolution. After all, modern people are the descendants of nonhuman ancestors: at least one type of ape and also an entire series of premodern hominid forebears. What sort of terminology should we apply in that gray zone of evolutionary intermediacy? As an example, the earliest known hominid tools (Oldowan tools, about 2.5 million years of age) are only slightly more complex than chimpanzee implements. Should the makers of these tools (presumed by most to be nonlinguistic early *Homo*, probably *H. habilis*) be welcomed as cultural creatures *simply because they are hominids* while chimpanzees are excluded from the fold? Do we gain or lose anything by labeling early *Homo* as protocultural? And how will we ever identify the point where protoculture graded into true culture?

It should be clear that the question of chimpanzee culture is only the tip of a philosophical and terminological iceberg. Rudimentary technology has been documented among living apes and early hominids, but the significance of such discoveries to the origins of what we moderns understand as culture are hard to determine. Furthermore, one can make the case that we are biased toward limiting culture to members of the human family, despite arguments by some researchers that chimpanzees are equally qualified. Are we being anthropocentric and/or practicing poor science in our construction and application of cultural definitions? What do you think?

REVIEW QUESTIONS

1. Studies of primate behavior are commonly conducted both in the field and in captivity. Discuss the strengths and weaknesses of research in these two settings.

2. Why do most primates live in groups? What are the advantages and disadvantages of social living? What mechanisms have the animals evolved to cope with the disadvantages of group life?

3. How does the sexual behavior of primate males and females differ? How is sexual behavior affected by rank, age, kinship, and hormonal condition? What is "situation-dependent" sex?

4. How do primates relate to their habitat? Define and compare the following three concepts: home range, core area, territory.

5. Describe tool use among chimpanzees, and explore the implications of the chimp data for the evolution of tool use among hominids.

6. Why do some anthropologists think that bonobos make a better model for hominid evolution than chimpanzees? Develop some questions about hominid evolution to which one could apply a bonobo model.

7. Describe the (speculative) characteristics of the chimpanzee-bonobo-human common ancestor.

SUGGESTED FURTHER READING

Fossey, D. *Gorillas in the Mist*. Houghton Mifflin, 1983.

Galdikas, B. M. F. *Reflections of Eden: My Years With the Orangutans of Borneo*. Little, Brown, 1995.

Goodall, J. *The Chimpanzees of Gombe*. Harvard University Press, 1986.

Hrdy, S. B. *The Langurs of Abu: Female and Male Strategies of Reproduction*. Harvard University Press, 1977.

Kinzey, W. G., ed.*The Evolution of Human Behavior: Primate Models*. State University of New York Press, 1987.

Loy, J. D., and C. B. Peters, eds. *Understanding Behavior: What Primate Studies Tell Us About Human Behavior*. Oxford University Press, 1991.

McGrew, W. C. *Chimpanzee Material Culture*. Cambridge University Press, 1992.

Nishida, T. *Chimpanzees of the Mahale Mountains*. University of Tokyo Press, 1990.

Smuts, B., et al., eds. *Primate Societies*. University of Chicago Press, 1987.

Stanford, C. B. *The Hunting Apes: Meat Eating Origins of Human Behavior*. Princeton University Press, 1999.

Waal, F. de. *Chimpanzee Politics: Power and Sex Among Apes*. Harper & Row, 1982.

Wrangham, R., and D. Peterson. *Demonic Males*. Houghton Mifflin, 1996.

INTERNET RESOURCES

Internet sites dealing with primates are listed at the end of Chapter 3. The Primate Info Net (PIN), in particular, has numerous links to other sites that describe field studies and/or conservation programs. Additionally, the PIN carries a list of primate-related job openings that may be of interest to some students.

USEFUL SEARCH TERMS:

apes
bonobos
chimpanzees
gibbons
gorillas
monkeys
orangutans
prosimians
primates

APES AND OTHER ANCESTORS: PREHOMINID EVOLUTION

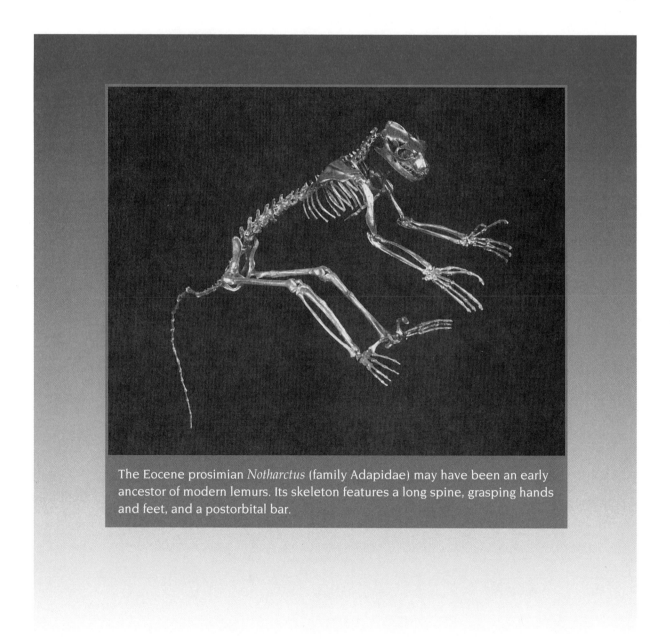

The Eocene prosimian *Notharctus* (family Adapidae) may have been an early ancestor of modern lemurs. Its skeleton features a long spine, grasping hands and feet, and a postorbital bar.

*I*t is an axiom of mine that when you have excluded the impossible, whatever remains, however improbable, must be the truth.
ARTHUR CONAN DOYLE, 1859–1930. *The Adventures of Sherlock Holmes: The Beryl Coronet.*

OVERVIEW

This chapter describes the evolutionary beginnings of the primates, a mammalian order that has been around for at least 60 million years and probably much longer. Judging from the fossil record as currently known, the primate order first evolved in Africa during the Paleocene epoch, and its original representatives were prosimian-grade creatures. Anthropoid primates—with their improved vision, reduced sense of smell, and more complex brains—did not appear for perhaps another 10 million years. Around 20 million years ago (mya)—again in Africa—the superfamily Hominoidea made its evolutionary appearance.

These early hominoids fell into two categories: dental apes, which resembled modern apes only in their dental and cranial traits (postcranially, they were more like monkeys); and suspensory apes, which also showed adaptations for forelimb-dominated locomotion (arm-swinging and arm-hanging). After a period of considerable success, when evolutionary radiations increased their diversity, and geographic expansion carried them into Europe and Asia, the apes began to decline in numbers and variety during a period of late Miocene climatic cooling. It was at this time—some 5 to 7 million years ago—that modern humans' last ape ancestors are thought to have lived, although their precise identity is still unknown. We do know, however, what it took to convert those apes into hominids: primarily the remodeling of quadrupedal creatures into bipeds. And because understanding this conversion is an essential prerequisite to studying the hominid fossil record, the last sections of the chapter are devoted to a description of the anatomy of bipedalism. Important topics in Chapter 5 include the various procedures for dating fossils

 Mini-Timeline

DATE (YEARS AGO OR GEOLOGIC EPOCH)	EVOLUTIONARY EVENTS	IMPORTANT GENERA
5–7 million	First hominids	*Ardipithecus, Australopithecus*
Late Miocene	Apes decline strongly	*Oreopithecus, Gigantopithecus*
Mid Miocene	Apes spread and diversify	*Dryopithecus, Kenyapithecus, Sivapithecus*
Early Miocene (20 million)	First apes; first Old World monkeys	*Morotopithecus, Proconsul*; monkey subfamily Victoriapithecinae
27 million	First New World monkeys	*Branisella, Szalatavus*
Oligocene	Anthropoids diversify	*Aegyptopithecus*
Eocene	First anthropoids; prosimians diversify	*Algeripithecus, Eosimias, Amphipithecus, Siamopithecus, Catopithecus*; prosimian families Adapidae, Omomyidae
Late Paleocene	First primates	*Altiatlasius*

either relatively or absolutely, primate evolution, continental drift, hominoid evolution, ape anatomy, and the anatomy of bipedalism. Important fossils include the plesiadapiforms, *Altiatlasius*, *Algeripithecus*, *Eosimias*, *Amphipithecus*, *Pondaungia*, *Siamopithecus*, the oligopithecines, *Aegyptopithecus*, *Morotopithecus*, *Kenyapithecus*, *Proconsul*, *Oreopithecus*, and *Sivapithecus*.

STUDYING FOSSILS

The study of prehistoric humans is linked inextricably with the study of all other primate fossils. Humans' characteristics evolved out of those of earlier, nonhuman species and so, in order to understand ourselves, we must analyze the remains of ancient prosimians and anthropoids. Luckily, fragments of these creatures are being discovered in ever-increasing numbers and anthropologists can reconstruct (cautiously) their anatomical and behavioral (including socioecological) traits through comparisons with living primates (see Chapters 3 and 4). Additionally, interpretations of fossils are based on estimates of their age, and thanks to advances in **geology**, **paleontology**, and especially atomic physics, scientists usually can determine age with considerable accuracy. Once we have all of the information before us—anatomy, behavior, and age—we can begin to group our primate ancestors into species, genera, and larger lineages and to work out those lineages' evolutionary connections.

At least that's how it works in theory. The tasks of fossil interpretation and the reconstruction of phylogenies are complicated immensely by the simple fact that all primates converge in their various traits as one goes back in time. In other words, telling modern prosimians, monkeys, apes, and humans apart is easy because all have evolved in a somewhat different manner, with different sets of primitive and derived traits (Chapter 3), and so they simply don't look or act alike. But since all living primates are descended from a common ancestor, the farther back we go, the more similar their fossil remains become. Indeed, as later sections of this chapter will show, even the application of such general labels as "monkeys" and "apes" becomes difficult as we move back in time. Looking far back into the past is absolutely necessary, however, because relatively recent developments that led to humankind were made possible only by earlier developments. Much of who and what we are was determined by the evolutionary histories of our prehominid ancestors and so it is to those creatures that this chapter is devoted.

Geology study of the earth's physical formation, its nature, and its continuing development.

Paleontology the study of the fossil remains and biology of organisms that lived in the past.

DATING PROCEDURES

Before we begin analyzing traits and reconstructing evolutionary lineages, however, it is important to say a bit more about what fossils are and how scientists go about dating them. Regarding the first point, fossils are traces of deceased organisms that (typically) are preserved in rock. Most often the hard parts—shells, bones, and especially teeth—are preserved as their original molecules are replaced by minerals. Under certain rare circumstances, traces of the soft parts of ancient organisms (gills, guts, feathers) also may be preserved. Most fossilization takes place as dead organisms are covered by muddy sediments at the bottom of a sea or lake or at the bend of a river. Fossils can also accumulate in caves and sinkholes as dead creatures are covered by rock falls and washed-in or blown-in soil (or, as during the late stages of hominid prehistory, covered by the living debris of subsequent human cave-dwellers). Of course, deliberate burial can also lead to fossilization, but this practice is a very recent one and limited to the human lineage.

In the two centuries that have passed since the work of Cuvier and others began to reveal the importance of the fossil record, many different procedures have been developed to provide dates for ancient remains. Detailed descriptions of several important dating methods are given in Appendix II at the end of the book, but a brief overview of dating is useful here. First of all, within the science of geology the subdiscipline known as **stratigraphy** attempts to interpret the production of rock layers—whether they occurred by the underwater deposition of sediments, by glacial or volcanic action, or by the accumulation of windblown soil—and their subsequent rearrangement, if any, as the result of earth movements and weathering (Figure 5–1). Stratigraphic information allows the **relative dating** of any fossils contained in the various rock layers; in undisturbed strata, the oldest layers are the deepest, and both strata and fossils get younger as one nears the surface. Although stratigraphy alone doesn't tell us a fossil's actual age, simply knowing that one specimen is older or younger than another can be critically important for working out evolutionary sequences. Furthermore, because every species has a finite lifetime between its origin and extinction, well-studied fossil lineages—with known sequences of species dated relative to one another—can be used to date other material by **faunal correlation**. For example, a newly discovered hominid specimen found in the same rock layer as a variety of pig known to be ancient within the pig lineage can properly be assumed to be quite old as well. Better yet, if the actual age of the fossil pig species has been determined (see the methodologies below), that

Stratigraphy the sequence of geologic strata, or layers, formed by materials deposited by water or wind; also, the study of this sequence.

Relative dating estimating the age of geologic deposits (and the fossils in them) by determining their stratigraphic level in relation to other deposits whose relative or absolute age is known. (Compare with *absolute dating*.)

Faunal correlation dating a site by the similarity of its animal fossils to those of another site that may carry a reliable absolute date.

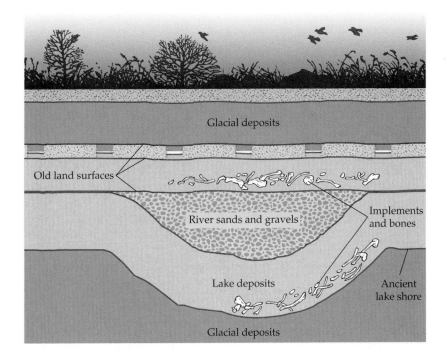

FIGURE 5–1   Fossils are found in deposits formed by the action of glaciers and rivers or laid down in ancient riverbeds, lakes, estuaries, and seas. Some deposits are windblown and may contain volcanic ash. Fossils are laid down in more or less horizontal beds, or strata, as shown here. Stratigraphy is the science that attempts to understand stratigraphic deposition—its form, its sequence, and its age.

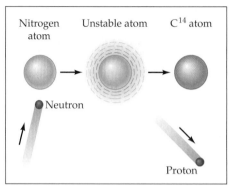

1. Nitrogen atom becomes C^{14} atom in the atmosphere.

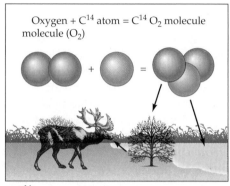

2. C^{14} and oxygen enter live organisms.

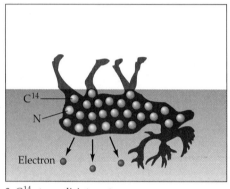

3. C^{14} atoms disintegrate.

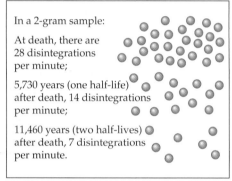

In a 2-gram sample:

At death, there are 28 disintegrations per minute;

5,730 years (one half-life) after death, 14 disintegrations per minute;

11,460 years (two half-lives) after death, 7 disintegrations per minute.

4. C^{14} continues to disintegrate at an orderly, predictable rate.

FIGURE 5–2 Carbon 14, or C^{14}, is an unstable form of carbon (the stable form is carbon 12). A certain proportion of C^{14} exists in the atmosphere and as carbon dioxide (CO_2) is absorbed and incorporated by plants in the form of carbohydrates. Animals absorb C^{14} by eating the plants. Thereafter the C^{14} disintegrates at a known rate (the half-life), and the extent of this disintegration can be measured and related to the amount of C^{14} remaining, and so too the age of the organic material.

Absolute dating determining the actual age of geologic deposits (and the fossils in them) by examining the chemical composition of rock fragments containing radioactive substances which decay at known rates. Also known as *chronometric dating*. (Compare with *relative dating*.)

same age can be attributed to the hominid material. Finally, the claim that fossils from a particular site come from the same rock layer, and therefore are the same relative age, can be tested by analyzing their levels of certain chemicals, usually nitrogen (which is lost during fossilization) and uranium and fluorine (both of which commonly accumulate in bones from groundwater). Noncontemporaneous specimens will show different chemical levels.

Methods for **absolute**, or **chronometric dating**, which provide actual ages for strata and/or fossils, are a much more recent scientific development than stratigraphy. Many of these procedures are based on atomic physics and the natural tendency of one element (or isotope, a variety of a particular element) to decay into some other element (or isotope). For example, carbon 14 (an unstable isotope) and carbon 12 (stable) are present at a known ratio in all living organisms. After an organism's death, C^{14} decays at a known rate and by measuring the ratio between the two carbon isotopes, one can determine how long ago death (usually coincident with fossilization) occurred (Figure 5–2). Somewhat similarly, potassium 40 breaks

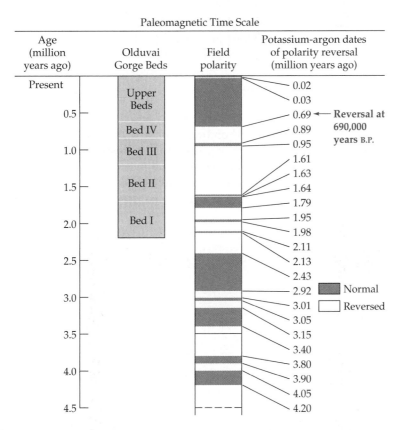

FIGURE 5–3 The left-hand column shows the sequence of beds from Olduvai Gorge, while the right-hand column shows known reversals in world magnetic polarity during the past 4.5 million years. The evidence is obtained by measuring the polarity of volcanic lavas, which can also be potassium-argon dated. Deposits that are only roughly dated by relative methods can often be more accurately dated by the measurement of their magnetic polarity and referral to this chart.

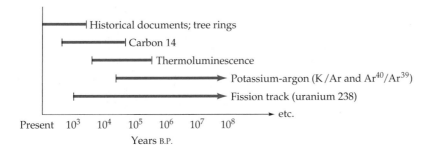

FIGURE 5–4 Approximate ranges of time in which dates can be established by the methods discussed in this chapter. Dates at the limits of any method are less reliable than those toward the center. The time scale is logarithmic.

down into the gaseous element argon in volcanic rocks and measuring the potassium-argon (symbolized K/Ar) ratio provides dates for these strata and any fossils they contain (this procedure is especially important in East Africa, where volcanic activity was widespread in the past). A newly-developed test, the Ar^{40}/Ar^{39} procedure is derived from K/Ar dating.

Several additional dating procedures, many based in one way or another on radioactive decay, have been developed and are described in Appendix II. These include **fission-track dating** (based on tracks made in mineral crystals by spontaneously splitting uranium 238 atoms), **thermoluminescence** (TL, based on the release of trapped electrons from pottery and rocks heated in fires by early humans), **optically stimulated luminescence** (like TL, but measuring the release of trapped electrons from sediments), and **paleomagnetism** (which measures the

Fission-track dating method of dating rocks from tracks left by the spontaneous splitting of uranium 238 atoms.

Thermoluminescence method of dating pottery and stone tools by heating them to release trapped electrons; the electrons produce measurable light.

Optically stimulated luminescence method of dating sediments by stimulating them with intense light; such stimulation causes the sediments to release trapped electrons and thus measurable light.

Paleomagnetism magnetism preserved in rock originally generated by the earth's magnetic field. Past fluctuations in the intensity and direction of this field allow correlation between strata; a form of *relative dating* that can be used for *absolute dating* because the historic pattern of magnetic fluctuations and reversals is known and dated.

Years B.P.	Eras	Period	Epoch	Years B.P.	Main Events
	Cenozoic	Quaternary	Pleistocene	10,000 to 1.6 million	Humans first learn to use and control fire in temperate zones
			Pliocene	1.6 to 5 million	Genus *Homo* appears Age of *Australopithecus, Paranthropus*
			Miocene	5 to 25 million	First hominids First apes
		Tertiary	Oligocene	25 to 35 million	Catarrhines and platyrrhines separate
			Eocene	35 to 58 million	First anthropoids
65 million			Paleocene	58 to 65 million	First primates: prosimians
	Mesozoic	ME Cretaceous		65 to 135 million	First flowering plants Disappearance of large dinosaurs
		Jurassic ME		135 to 180 million	First birds
225 million		Triassic		180 to 225 million	First mammals Age of Reptiles begins
	Paleozoic	ME Permian		225 to 280 million	
		Carboniferous ME		280 to 345 million	First coniferous trees First reptiles
		Devonian		345 to 395 million	First forests First amphibians, insects, and bony fish
		Silurian ME		395 to 430 million	First land plants First fish with jaws
		Ordovician		430 to 500 million	First vertebrates: armored fish without jaws
570 million		Cambrian		500 to 570 million	First shell-bearing animals
	Precambrian			600 million	First multicellular animals
				3.5 billion	First living things: algae, bacteria
				4 billion	Formation of primordial seas
				4.5 billion	Formation of earth

Figure 5–5   Geologic time scales are of such immense duration that it is hard to comprehend fully the great period of time during which nature and humankind have evolved. If the almost 500 million years of vertebrate evolution are symbolized by one hour of time, then primate evolution took seven minutes, and human evolution occurred in the last twelve seconds of that hour. ME=mass extinction event.

"fossilized magnetism" in a rock sample and matches it with a dated history of global magnetic reversals; see Figure 5–3). Altogether, the various relative and absolute dating techniques enable scientists to pinpoint the ages of most (but not all) fossils with considerable precision. And as noted above, such dating is critical for evolutionary interpretations. Figure 5–4 summarizes the effective time spans of some of the most important absolute dating procedures.

THE EARLIEST PRIMATES

As noted in Chapter 3, the oldest known primate fossils are about 60 million years old and are from the late **Paleocene** epoch of geologic time (Figure 5–5). Although this date sounds solid enough, it should be taken only as a rough approximation of the first appearance of primates. The reason is the enormous gaps in our knowledge of the fossil record. The 200-plus fossil varieties currently known represent only 2 to 4 percent of an estimated 5,000 to 7,000 extinct primate species. As additional discoveries are made, it seems inevitable that the origin of our order will be pushed millions of years farther back in time—perhaps even into the late Cretaceous period.

But for now the late Paleocene marks the origin of primates, and those first members of our order emerged into a very different world from today. For one thing, the positioning of the continents was different. Studies of **continental drift** have indicated that the Paleozoic supercontinent Pangaea II (Figure 5–6) split during the Mesozoic to form a large northern landmass—including the modern continents of North America, Europe, and most of Asia—and an even larger southern landmass combining Africa, South America, Antarctica, India, Madagascar, and Australia. By the Paleocene, South America and India had drifted away from Africa, and Africa had been separated from Eurasia by high sea levels. In the north, Eurasia and North America were still contiguous and remained so for several million years (Figure 5–7).

Paleocene the geologic epoch extending from 65 to 58 million years B.P. (before present).

Continental drift a theory that describes the movements of continental landmasses throughout the earth's history.

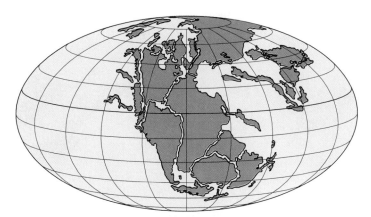

Pangaea II: 200 million years ago

FIGURE 5–6   This reconstruction of the supercontinent Pangaea II at 200 million years B.P. shows the precursors of most of the modern continents. At about this time, Pangaea II split into a northern landmass, Laurasia, and a southern continent, Gondwanaland.

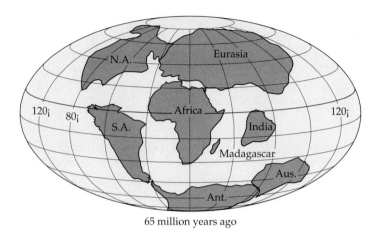

65 million years ago

FIGURE 5–7   By the beginning of the Paleocene epoch, South America and India had separated from Africa, while North America and Eurasia were still linked.

FIGURE 5–8   Tree shrews are found in Southeast Asia. They are primitive mammals and are probably similar to the first primates. Their appearance is somewhat similar to that of the squirrel, but they are quite distinct from any rodent. Their bodies are about 5 inches (13 centimeters) long.

Tree shrew   Slow loris   Macaque

FIGURE 5–9   The hands of a tree shrew, a prosimian, and a macaque monkey are illustrated. The tree shrew, like all insectivores, carries claws. The loris has nails on all digits except its second toe, where a claw has survived for grooming. Macaque monkeys have nails on all digits and relatively long thumbs, giving them a good precision grip.

Not only was the configuration of the continents different during the Paleocene, but in consequence global climate patterns and habitat zones were different as well. Tropical forests spread much farther north and south from the equator; France and Germany were moist, humid jungles, as was much of Africa and nearly everywhere in between. Parts of North America were similarly forested, and the forest avenue between North America and Eurasia allowed extensive mammalian dispersal.

Within this moist, forested world, the first primates arose from some primitive, semiarboreal mammalian ancestor. Although that ancestor's exact identity remains to be discovered, it may well have resembled modern insectivorous tree shrews (Figure 5–8). In response to the challenges of arboreal living and of visual-manual predation on insects (see Chapter 3), the early primates began the order's evolutionary trajectory toward grasping hands and feet (Figure 5–9), keen vision, and a reduced sense of smell.

One diverse group of animals once thought to be basal primates can now be eliminated from the order. The **Plesiadapiformes** from the Paleocene and **Eocene** of North America and Europe have been classified by some authorities as a primate suborder on dental grounds, even though they lacked such defining features as postorbital bars (Figure 5–13). Recent findings, however, have brought this classification into question. For example, some plesiadapiforms are now known to have differed from undoubted primates in the anatomy of the **auditory bulla**. In all true primates, the bulla develops from one particular bone of the skull, while in the plesiadapiform genus *Ignacius* it grew from a different bone entirely. Further evidence comes from the anatomy of the hand. Some plesiadapiforms possessed elongated digital bones that may have served to support webbing between the fingers. From this last discovery, it has been suggested that the plesiadapiforms may be evolutionary relatives of the **colugos**: living nonprimate mammals from Asia known for their arboreal gliding habits and misnamed flying lemurs. In all, despite certain dental similarities, the plesiadapiforms just don't work as basal primates—which leaves the beginnings of our order shrouded in mystery.

Plesiadapiformes fossil mammals of the *Paleocene* and *Eocene* that were once thought to be primitive *primates* but are now classified as relatives of *colugos.*

Eocene the geologic epoch extending from 58 to 35 million years B.P.

Auditory bulla the bulbous bony development that houses the middle ear region.

Colugos nonprimate mammals from Asia known for arboreal gliding; misnamed "flying lemurs."

UNDOUBTED PRIMATE FOSSILS

It is perhaps to be expected that the earliest primate fossils should be difficult to distinguish from related groups, with the result that their status is often controversial. At present, the earliest fossil primates have been found in Morocco at a site named Adrar Mgorn, at the foot of the Atlas Mountains. Here, in late Paleocene sediments, together with remains of twenty-three other mammalian species, have been found ten isolated molar teeth of a very small (2 to 4 ounces; 50 to 100 grams) creature named **Altiatlasius**. Not much to go on, perhaps, but enough to make a case for an African origin for the primate order, for the teeth are undoubtedly the teeth of early prosimians. This claim is supported by later finds from the early Eocene of Algeria, Tunisia, and Egypt.

Altiatlasius the oldest known *primate fossil;* a *prosimian* from the late *Paleocene* of North Africa.

We also have fossils of about this age, or a little later, from Europe, Asia, and North America. It was previously thought that North America contained the earliest fossil primates, and some believe that Asia is a more likely place of origin for the order, but the evidence for an African origin is rapidly accumulating.

Judging from the remains of *Altiatlasius* and many other, more complete fossils, the earliest primates can be classified confidently as prosimians. In clear contrast to the plesiadapiforms and other nonprimate mammals, they possessed forwardly directed eyes, postorbital bars, grasping big toes, and nails on most digits instead of claws. They have been arranged into two extinct families—the **Adapidae** and the **Omomyidae** (Figure 5–10)—and their diversity during the Eocene epoch (we recognize some forty genera) shows that they underwent a strong evolutionary radiation shortly after their origin. Although there is disagreement among paleontologists and more fossil evidence is needed, the adapids appear to be evolutionary predecessors of modern lemurs and lorises, while the omomyids may be ancestral to modern tarsiers and possibly even to anthropoids. *Altiatlasius* has been interpreted as a very early form of omomyid.

Adapidae and *Omomyidae* families of *Eocene prosimians,* now extinct.

The anatomy of the Eocene prosimians indicates that they were agile arborealists that ate a mixed diet of fruit, leaves, and insects. Furthermore, they anticipated one of the main characteristics of modern primates by showing larger brains for their body size than most other Eocene mammals.

But working so far in the past, the evolutionary relationships are admittedly hazy. We need more information from many more fossils before we can determine

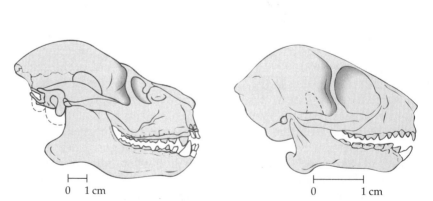

FIGURE 5–10   Representative skulls of early prosimians. Adapid (*Leptadapis magnus*) shown at left and omomyid (*Necrolemur antiquus*) to the right. Both are from European mid-Eocene deposits.

Box 5-1

CURRENT ISSUE: *Old Bones for Sale*

People everywhere are fascinated by evidence of ancient life, be it artifacts from prehistoric cultures or the fossil remains of our human forebears or earlier creatures. Over the centuries, that fascination has taken a rather heavy toll on prehistoric cultural sites with looters doing considerable destruction in search of marketable artifacts, including bits and pieces of ancient monuments. Recently, strong pressure has been brought to bear (mainly by indigenous people claiming descent from specific prehistoric groups) that has helped to slow the archaeological pilfering and bring the human antiquities trade under control.

But what about the nonhuman fossil trade? For better or worse, sales of fossils appear to be growing rapidly. The remains of ancient mollusks, arthropods, fishes, and plants are commonly seen in rock shops and nature stores, and they are also for sale on the World Wide Web, through catalogs, and at auctions. Even the remains of ancient primates sometimes show up in the listings and go to the highest bidder.

The obvious problem here is that fossils that are sold into private collections are usually unavailable for scientific study (even if they end up in public museums, many commercial fossils are of little scientific value since they lack information on geologic context). In the United States, many important fossil deposits are located on federal public lands and collection at those sites historically has been allowed only by permission and for educational and scientific purposes—the rationale being that fossils on federal lands belong to the public at large and thus should not be exploited for private gain (80 to 90 percent of Americans agree with this position).

Within the last few years, however, commercial fossil hunters and their supporters have been trying to open up federal public lands for nonscientific collection and sales. It has become a classic public versus private interest controversy. What's your opinion on this question: Restriction of fossil collecting to specialists working for the (educational and scientific) public good or unrestricted collection and free enterprise? Americans hate to have their activities restricted by government regulations, but should they be free to sell fossil prosimians from public lands? Does every basement collection need an omomyid? ∎

with certainty which (if either) of the two prosimian families gave rise to the anthropoids (see Box 5–1). None of the known adapid or omomyid skulls shows the beginnings of such defining anthropoid traits as complete bony eye sockets or fused frontal bones (Table 3–4), and all of the Eocene prosimians very likely had a rhinarium. Still, by the middle of the Eocene some prosimian variety had given rise to creatures we can recognize as basal anthropoids, creating a major fork in the primate family tree. At first, the emerging anthropoids could not be called anything more than super prosimians, because the differences between them and the older prosimian species were too small to be significant. But as these differences began to build up, by giving a survival advantage to the individuals that had them, the trees became filled with smarter, swifter, defter, altogether abler animals. The surviving prosimians remained nocturnal or died away in many places because they could not compete. Nevertheless, those first Paleocene and Eocene primates do point to the first pieces of the puzzle of humankind's evolution.

THE FIRST HIGHER PRIMATES

Dating the emergence of the anthropoids (higher primates) from prosimian stock is a tricky business. Anthropoids were clearly well established and diversified by the **Oligocene** epoch (35 to 25 million years ago), but their actual origin was probably much earlier. The oldest fossils likely to be anthropoids come from the site of Glib Zegdou in the North African country of Algeria. These remains (consisting of three molar teeth) have been named *Algeripithecus minutus* and date from the middle or even early Eocene. But while the teeth show a number of anthropoid-like features, the fragmentary nature of the fossil argues for a conservative interpretation. At present, the classification of *Algeripithecus* as an anthropoid should be viewed as strictly tentative. If further discoveries—particularly of fossils showing diagnostic anthropoid cranial features—validate the claim, then the appearance of higher primates probably occurred in Africa over 50 million years ago.

The African case is certainly not airtight, however, and there are a number of Asian fossils just slightly younger than *Algeripithecus* that also appear to be anthropoids. Among the most exciting are some very recent discoveries from mid-Eocene deposits in China. In 1994, a joint American-Chinese research team announced the discovery of a rich deposit of fossil primates near the village of Shanghuang. Dating about 45 million years old, the Shanghuang primates include adapids, omomyids, the earliest known tarsiers, and also fossils assigned to a new genus, *Eosimias* ("the dawn ape"). But don't be misled by the name. In fact, *Eosimias* was not an ape at all, but a generalized creature that showed a strong combination of derived (anthropoid) and primitive (prosimian) traits. A very small primate (body weight of 2.4 to 4.8 ounces, or 67 to 137 grams), *Eosimias* shared a number of dental traits with modern anthropoids but still resembled prosimians in its unfused mandibular symphysis (see Table 3–4). Neither a monkey nor an ape, *Eosimias* seems to fill the bill nicely as a basal anthropoid.

Other apparent anthropoids from Asia include *Amphipithecus* and *Pondaungia* from Burma, and the recently discovered *Siamopithecus* from Thailand. All three species date to the late Eocene. The new fossils from Shanghuang, coupled with evidence from Burma and Thailand, suggest to some researchers that the anthropoid suborder originated in Asia, not Africa. *Eosimias* in particular appears to be only slightly younger than *Algeripithecus*, and the dates for both fossils involve considerable estimation. Although Africa may still hold a slight edge in the contest, theories of an Asian origin of anthropoids must be given careful consideration.

But if the early and mid-Eocene glimmers of the anthropoids are faint and confusing, their presence had solidified by the end of the epoch, and for that story we must return to northern Africa and Egypt's Fayum Depression, a region renowned for its fossil remains. In the Fayum, deposits straddling the Eocene-Oligocene boundary have yielded several undoubted anthropoids belonging to an extinct subfamily called the **oligopithecines**. Located in the desert about 60 miles southwest of Cairo, the Fayum Depression is currently one of the driest places on earth—hardly good anthropoid terrain. In Eocene and Oligocene times, however, the Fayum was a tropical and swampy region lying along the southern shore of the Mediterranean. Heavily wooded in parts and laced with rivers, it was a fine place for early anthropoids to live and evolve—and evolve they did, as the diversity of the oligopithecines attests.

The oligopithecines date to the latest Eocene of northern Africa (about 36 million years ago) and include three genera: *Oligopithecus*, *Proteopithecus*, and

Oligocene the geologic epoch extending from 35 to 25 million years B.P.

Algeripithecus tentatively, the oldest known *anthropoid primate* from North Africa's early-middle *Eocene.*

Eosimias probable basal *anthropoid* from the mid-*Eocene* of China.

Amphipithecus and *Pondaungia* possible *anthropoids* from the late *Eocene* of Burma.

Siamopithecus the late *Eocene anthropoid* from Thailand.

Oligopithecines late *Eocene anthropoids*; many have been collected from Egypt's Fayum Depression.

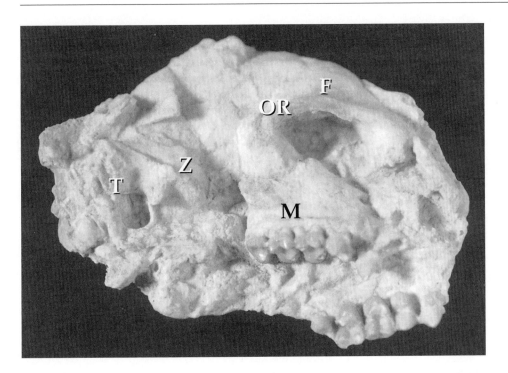

FIGURE 5–11 Distorted fossil skull of *Catopithecus browni,* an oligopithecine anthropoid from the late Eocene of Egypt. Crushing has moved the right orbit over the grinding teeth. The upper teeth P3 through M3 are preserved on both sides. As in this case, fossils are sometimes difficult to interpret because of damage and distortion during fossilization. The key to the skull bones is as follows: F, frontal; M, maxilla; OR, orbital rim; T, temporal; Z, zygomatic.

Catopithecus. All were small-bodied (about 2.2 pounds, or 1 kilogram) forest-dwellers that probably ate a mixed diet of fruit and insects. Among the fossils of *Catopithecus* is a well-preserved skull (Figure 5–11) that demonstrates such diagnostic anthropoid traits as bony eye sockets and fused frontal bones. But the oligopithecines were not typically anthropoid in all of their features. Demonstrating that anthropoid traits evolved in mosaic fashion rather than all at once, the oligopithecines still showed a low ratio of brain size to body size as well as some prosimian-like features in their jaws and teeth. *Catopithecus,* for example, had an unfused mandibular symphysis. Interestingly, the oligopithecines varied somewhat in their dental formulae: while *Catopithecus* had a total of eight premolars, *Proteopithecus* had twelve. Although too generalized to be classified as either monkeys or apes, the oligopithecines give us a good view of the anatomy, diet, and habitat of early, undoubted anthropoids.

Catopithecus a particularly well-known *oligopithecine* from the Fayum in Africa.

Oligocene Anthropoids

By the early Oligocene epoch, anthropoids were enjoying much success in Africa. Several genera had evolved, including *Parapithecus, Propliopithecus* (Figure 5–12), *Apidium* (Figure 5–13), and **Aegyptopithecus** (Figures 5–13, 5–14, and 5–15). Although these creatures showed some advances over their Eocene ancestors, analyses of their total morphological patterns show that they were still very

Aegyptopithecus a basal *catarrhine* from the Fayum in Africa; dated to the *Oligocene* epoch.

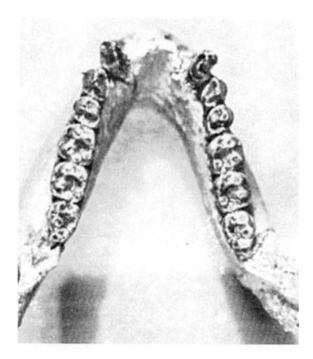

FIGURE 5–12   *Propliopithecus* had a five-cusped pattern on its lower molars. This early primate could possibly have given rise to Old World monkeys, apes, and humans.

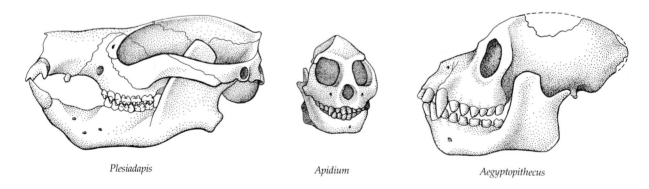

Plesiadapis   *Apidium*   *Aegyptopithecus*

FIGURE 5–13   The orbits of living primates are surrounded by a ring of bone that constitutes a lateral extension of the frontal bone joining the cheekbone. This structure protects the large, forward-pointing eyes. Fossil anthropoids such as *Apidium* had these laterally bounded orbits and also a full bony socket, as did the more advanced *Aegyptopithecus*. In more primitive nonprimate mammals, such as *Plesiadapis*, the orbit was open at the back and side. The scale is 60 percent actual size.

FIGURE 5–14 The palate of *Aegyptopithecus* shows a somewhat apelike dentition and almost rectangular dental arcade. The creature, however, was very small, as indicated by the scale. This specimen was discovered by Elwyn Simons in the Fayum region of Egypt. It is dated about 32 million years B.P.

FIGURE 5–15 Finds of *Aegyptopithecus* bones are now so numerous that a full reconstruction is possible. This drawing of the 12-pound (5.4-kilogram) creature was made under the direction of Elwyn Simons. Notice that this catarrhine carried a long tail.

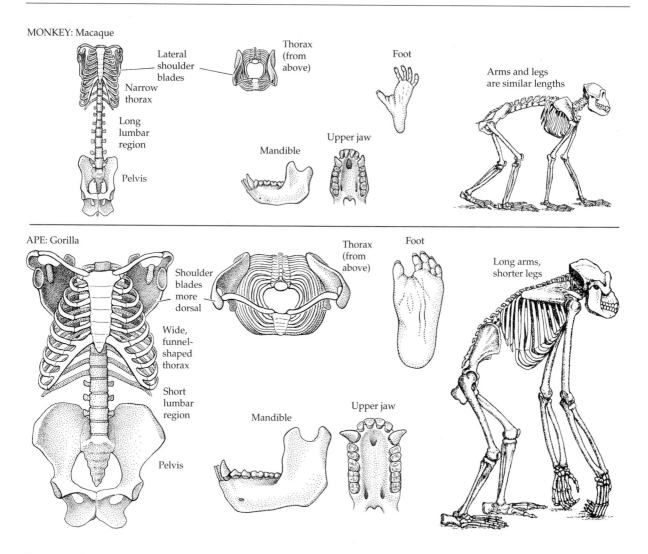

Figure 5–16   Ape and monkey skeletons have much in common. Nonetheless, apes are more like humans than like monkeys in skeletal structure. Note the different proportions of the limbs; the form of the rib cage and shoulder blade; and the use of hands in locomotion. Scale is approximately one-twentieth actual size. Note that the macaque shown has a relatively short tail. See Figure 3–15 for more typical monkey tails.

primitive. *Parapithecus* and *Apidium* are best classified as basal anthropoids that preceded the evolutionary separation of platyrrhines and catarrhines. *Propliopithecus* and *Aegyptopithecus*, on the other hand, can be identified as catarrhines, although both were too primitive to be classified further as either monkeys or apes. A detailed analysis of the total morphology of *Aegyptopithecus* shows how such a conclusion is reached. Although certain dental features suggest that *Aegyptopithecus* had evolved into an ape-grade creature—2123/2123 dental formula, five-cusped molars, rectangular dental arcade (Figure 5–14)—other features are distinctly monkeylike. *Aegyptopithecus* was an arboreal quadruped rather than an arm-hanger or arm-swinger, sported a tail, and had a monkey-shaped skull (Figure 5–15; see also Figure 5–16 for anatomical comparisons of modern monkeys and apes). Thus, given their mosaic anatomy, *Propliopithecus* and *Aegyptopithecus* are best regarded as generalized catarrhines that were, however, on or near the ancestral line for all later anthropoids of the Old World. The stage was set for the evolution of the modern superfamilies of monkeys and apes.

Evolution of the New World Monkeys

Humans are catarrhine primates whose evolutionary origins reside in the Old World. That being the case, the history of the New World monkeys is of rather secondary importance to the story being told here. Nonetheless, the evolutionary appearance of these "second cousins" of ours deserves at least a brief description before we move on to fossil apes.

The oldest fossils of platyrrhine monkeys come from late Oligocene deposits in Bolivia. Two genera are recognized—**Branisella** and **Szalatavus**—and both are about 27 million years old. Thus, on the basis of fossil evidence, anthropoid primates showed up in the New World at least 9 million years later (and possibly as much as 20 million years later) than in Africa. Couple these dates with the present lack of evidence of separate prosimian ancestries for platyrrhines and catarrhines, and one is forced to conclude, although tentatively, that the New World monkeys are descended from African anthropoid stock. But how could they have migrated across the South Atlantic—a sizable span of water even in Oligocene times—to a new neotropical home? It's hard to accept, but the best answer seems to be that they crossed by a combination of island hopping (a series of mid-Atlantic islands may have existed off the coast of Sierra Leone and elsewhere) and rafting aboard floating mats of vegetation. Once in South and Central America, the platyrrhines diversified strongly to produce the great variety of New World monkeys alive today. They made no contribution, however, to the evolution of humankind.

Branisella and *Szalatavus* *Oligocene platyrrhine monkeys from Bolivia.*

The Miocene: Apes at Last

The earliest known members of the superfamily Hominoidea—that is, the first apes—appear in the fossil record from the early **Miocene** epoch and date to about 20 million years of age. The absolutely oldest genera, *Morotopithecus* and *Proconsul*, are from African sites, as are most of the other early Miocene forms (Figure 5–17 and Table 5–1), making an African origin for hominoids a safe conclusion (note that attributing an early Miocene date to the Asian genus *Dionysopithecus* is questionable). Cercopithecoid monkeys apparently evolved at roughly the same time, but details of the evolutionary differentiation of the two living catarrhine superfamilies are unclear at present. The earliest catarrhine monkeys are classed within the extinct subfamily **Victoriapithecinae**, and many species used more open habitats than those favored by the evolving hominoids. Although interesting in their own right (and excellent socioecological models for certain habitats, as shown in Chapter 4), the Cercopithecoidea had little, if any, effect on hominid evolution and therefore they will concern us no further. (Some scientists do speculate that competition from an increasingly diverse and numerous collection of monkeys may have led some African apes to begin adapting to life on the ground, perhaps literally taking the first steps toward hominid status. The idea remains controversial.)

The apes do concern us, however, and during the Miocene they were busy adapting to a warm East African environment covered mostly by forest and woodlands. Most were forest animals who subsisted on a mixed diet of fruit and leaves,

Miocene the geologic epoch extending from 25 to 5 millions years B.P.

Morotopithecus an *ape* from East Africa that lived during the early *Miocene*.

Proconsul an *ape* from East Africa that lived during the early *Miocene* epoch.

Victoriapithecinae extinct subfamily of the earliest *catarrhine monkeys*.

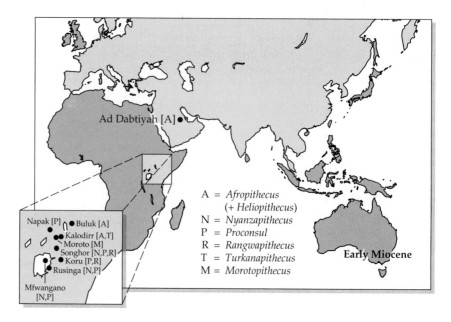

FIGURE 5–17   Map of the Old World showing the sites that have produced ape remains dating to the early Miocene. Note that these earliest apes were concentrated in Africa.

TABLE 5–1   *A List of Fossil Ape Genera*[a]

GENUS	AGE AND LOCATION
Afropithecus	Early–?mid Miocene (Africa, Saudi Arabia)
Dendropithecus	Early Miocene (Africa)
Dionysopithecus	?Early Miocene (Asia)
Dryopithecus[b]	Mid–late Miocene (Europe)
Gigantopithecus	Late Miocene–Pleistocene (Asia)
Kenyapithecus	Mid Miocene (Africa)
Laccopithecus	Late Miocene (Asia)
Limnopithecus	Early Miocene (Africa)
Lufengpithecus	Late Miocene (Asia)
Micropithecus	Early Miocene (Africa)
Morotopithecus	Early Miocene (Africa)
Nyanzapithecus	Early–mid Miocene (Africa)
Oreopithecus	Late Miocene (Europe)
Otavipithecus	Mid Miocene (Africa)
Pliopithecus	Mid–late Miocene (Europe)
Proconsul	Early Miocene (Africa)
Rangwapithecus	Early Miocene (Africa)
Sivapithecus[b,c]	Mid–late Miocene (Africa, Asia, Europe)
Turkanapithecus	Early Miocene (Africa)

[a] With the exceptions of *Otavipithecus*, *Morotopithecus*, and *Kenyapithecus*, all information from G. Conroy, *Primate Evolution*, W. W. Norton, 1990.

[b] *Rudapithecus* (Figure 5–20) is lumped with *Dryopithecus* by some authors and with *Sivapithecus* by others.

[c] Includes *Ouranopithecus* and the Pasalar fossils from Figure 5–20, and also *Ramapithecus* and *Ankarapithecus*.

Box 5-2

NAMING PROBLEMS AND FOSSIL HOMINOIDS

What makes an ape an ape? Or in slightly more stylish form, what is the essence of apeness? Answering this question is easy if we think only of living apes: Apes are big primates with distinctive five-cusped molar teeth (Figure 3–17), relatively large brains, and no tail. Furthermore, their locomotor patterns are distinctly forelimb-dominated; in the trees they often hang or swing about by their arms, and as adaptations for this sort of movement they have short, stiff backs, long arms, and shoulder and elbow joints that allow a wide range of movement. So far, so good. But as this chapter shows, the suite of features that characterizes modern apes was not present in all early hominoids—and this creates a terminology problem.

The very earliest catarrhines, such as the Oligocene primate *Aegyptopithecus*, showed a mixture of primitive traits that were sorted out differently in the evolutionary lineages leading to today's monkeys and apes. These early catarrhines are described as *generalized* because they combined certain apelike dental features (including five-cusped molars) with a monkeylike, tail-equipped body that was adapted for arboreal quadrupedalism rather than forelimb suspension. By about 20 mya, the Old World monkeys had emerged as a distinct evolutionary family that retained the old pattern of arboreal quadrupedalism and combined it with new dental specializations such as four-cusped, bilophodont molars (Figure 3–17). The emergence of the dentally distinct Old World monkeys left a group of catarrhine "remainders," all of which were characterized by old-style five-cusped (Y-5) molars, but which were wonderfully diverse in their postcranial anatomies. All of these Y-5 species are classified within the superfamily Hominoidea and a few—including *Morotopithecus*, *Dryopithecus*, and *Oreopithecus*, which possessed bodies adapted for suspensory locomotion—are clearly apes in the modern sense of the word. (As indicated in the text, these genera—particularly *Morotopithecus*—were separated in space and time, suggesting that forelimb-dominated locomotion may have evolved independently more than once among the hominoids. But that's another story.)

But what about the others? What evolutionary sense can we make of—and specifically, what should we call—creatures such as *Proconsul* whose dental and cranial traits earned them a place among the hominoids, but whose bodies looked like that of a monkey (albeit without the tail)?

Taking those questions in order, since all living apes show forelimb-dominated locomotion and human anatomy indicates descent from a swinging-and-hanging ancestor, it is clear that at some point the monkeylike hominoids disappeared entirely, leaving the superfamily to be represented exclusively by suspensory creatures. When and why this happened are both unknown at present and researchers anxiously are seeking new fossils to settle these issues. As to what we should call the Y-5 "nonswingers," at present there is no good term. Harvard's David Pilbeam prefers the accurate, but awkward, label "hominoids of archaic aspect," while the authors of this book have opted for "dental apes." It's an open question, however, and we invite your input on the matter. What name would you give to those monkeylike hominoids? You can e-mail your suggestions, as well as other comments about the book, to the following address: jimloy@uri.edu.

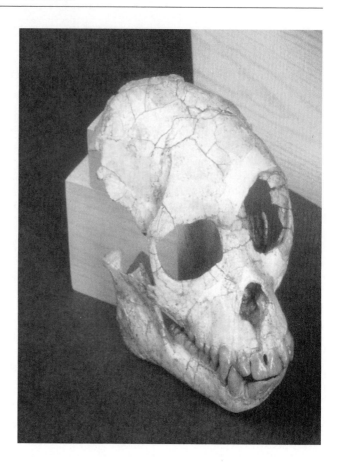

FIGURE 5–18   The skull of *Proconsul* is a typical ape skull. It combines a low cranial vault, projecting muzzle, and large anterior teeth.

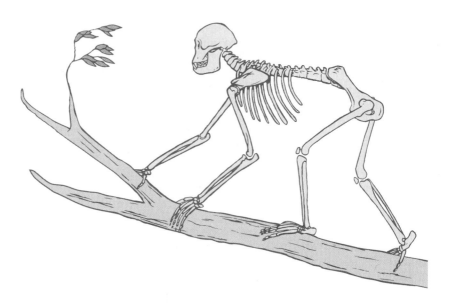

FIGURE 5–19   Reconstructed skeleton of *Proconsul*. Note the slender torso, the monkeylike limb proportions, and the lack of a tail.

and they ranged from monkey-sized creatures to animals as large as modern chimpanzees. As shown by the genus names in Figure 5–17 and Table 5–1, these early hominoids were a diverse lot, and their evolutionary relationships are not at all clear. Indeed, they were so diverse that many genera (e.g., *Proconsul*) resembled modern apes only in their dental and cranial traits (a fact that brings the proper use of the label "ape" into question; see Box 5–2). From the neck down, *Proconsul* and several others had more anatomical similarities to monkeys than to today's chimpanzees, orangutans, and gorillas. A few Miocene genera, however—particularly *Morotopithecus*, **Oreopithecus**, and **Dryopithecus**—had evolved adaptations for suspensory postures and locomotion, and thus looked like modern apes both above and below the neck (that is, cranially, dentally, *and* postcranially). David Pilbeam of Harvard University refers to the first category of creatures (e.g., *Proconsul*) as "hominoids of archaic aspect," and the second as "hominoids of modern aspect." We prefer the shorter terms "dental apes" and "suspensory apes" (see Box 5–2).

Dental apes, in the form of *Proconsul*, show up right at the very beginning of hominoid history, some 17 to 20 million years ago (Figure 5–20). As represented by

Oreopithecus and *Dryopithecus* ape genera from the mid-to-late *Miocene* of Europe.

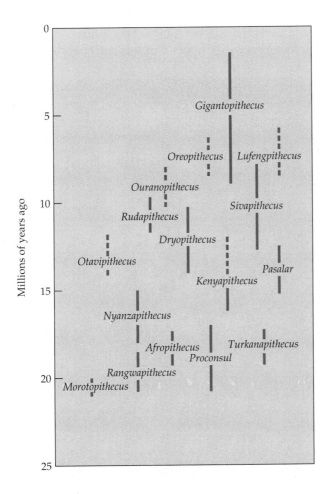

FIGURE 5–20   Various fossil ape genera are shown here along with their time ranges (solid lines denote well-known ranges; dashed lines indicate probable ranges).

Sivapithecus a genus of *Miocene apes* that include *Ramapithecus;* probably ancestral to the *orangutan.*

Sivapithecus, Lufengpithecus, and others, the dental apes continued until the late stages of the Miocene (Figure 5–20) and they are known from Africa, Asia, and Europe. The well-known African genus *Proconsul* (Figures 5–18 and 5–19) serves as a good example of these archaic hominoids. As expected from a catarrhine, *Proconsul's* protruding muzzle showed a dental formula of 2123/2123. In addition, it had projecting and pointed canine teeth, upper canines that sheared against the lower anterior premolars, and postcanine toothrows that were generally parallel. Other features worth mentioning are *Proconsul's* strongly receding forehead and low-vaulted braincase. Despite its apelike teeth and skull, however, *Proconsul* showed few similarities to modern apes from the neck down. As summarized in Table 3–4 and illustrated in Figure 5–16, modern apes have a broad chest, a short lower back, no tail, and shoulders and arms modified for forelimb-dominated locomotion (arm-hanging and arm-swinging). Although *Proconsul* did lack a tail, the similarities stop there. In contrast to modern apes, *Proconsul* had a long, flexible spine; a narrow torso; and monkeylike limb proportions (Figure 5–19). Judging from its postcranial remains, *Proconsul* was a rather generalized quadruped, certainly not an animal adapted for forelimb-dominated arboreal movement.

As regards the postcranially modern apes, it was thought until quite recently that adaptations for forelimb-dominated locomotion (arm-hanging and arm-swinging) were very late developments in hominoid evolution. For example, *Sivapithecus,* from the mid-to-late Miocene (Figures 5–20 and 5–21), shows elbow joints appar-

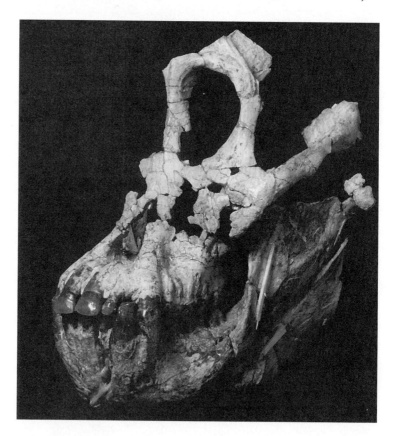

FIGURE 5–21   This *Sivapithecus indicus* skull was found in northeast Pakistan by David Pilbeam and his research team from Harvard. The skull had a bite mark in it, indicating that a hyena must have carried it to the spot where the head and the jaw were found within 2 feet (0.6 millimeters) of each other.

ently adapted for arboreal suspension, but the rest of its skeleton suggests quadrupedal walking. The oldest known full-fledged hanger-and-swinger was thought to be *Oreopithecus bambolii*, which inhabited Europe around 8 million years ago (Figure 5–22). This unique hominoid had a short trunk and a broad thorax, long arms and short legs, and elbow joints like those of living apes. Unfortunately, the evolutionary relationships of *Oreopithecus* are extremely obscure. It seems most likely that the line leading to *Oreopithecus* diverged from the main hominoid lineage fairly early, and therefore it is not directly ancestral to modern apes.

The discoveries of two new suspensory apes have pushed the advent of forelimb-dominated locomotion far back in hominoid history. First, in 1996, Spanish paleontologists Salvador Moyá-Solà and Meike Köhler published evidence that the European species *Dryopithecus laietanus* was an upright climber and swinger 9.5 million years ago. Fossils from the Spanish site of Can Llobateres revealed that, like modern apes, *D. laietanus* showed a short back, broad thorax, dorsally positioned shoulder blades, long arms and short legs, and large hands with long, powerful fingers (Figure 5–23). Clearly indicative of suspensory locomotion, these traits have convinced Moyá-Solà and Köhler that *Dryopithecus* is closely related to modern apes (Figure 5–24). The second new find, however, is much older than Can Llobateres and thus even more exciting. In April 1997, a team of researchers headed by Daniel Gebo of Northern Illinois University announced evidence of an upright climber and brachiator dating to 20.6 million years of age. Named *Morotopithecus bishopi* and recovered from a site in northeastern Uganda (Figure 5–17), this ancient hominoid showed a short, stiff back, broadening of the thorax, and modifications of the shoulder that allowed "climbing, a slow to moderate speed of brachiation, . . . quadrupedalism, and . . . an arm-hanging posture." Its discoverers suspect that *Morotopithecus*, which was quite large at about 100 pounds (45 kilograms), is not directly ancestral to modern hominoids, but rather represents a sister taxon that split off early from the lineage of living apes (Figure 5–24).

FIGURE 5–22 Skeleton and reconstructed habitual posture of *Oreopithecus*, an enigmatic ape from the late Miocene of Europe.

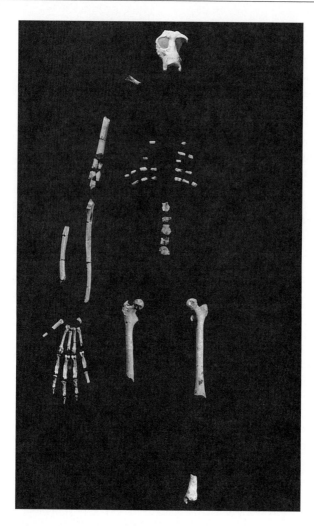

FIGURE 5–23   The skeleton of *Dryopithecus laietanus* from Can Llobateres (Spain). Note the long arm, large hand, and long, powerful fingers. All of these traits suggest forelimb-dominated, suspensory locomotion.

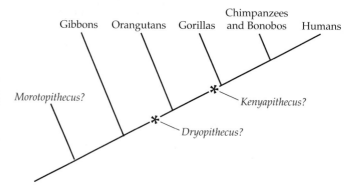

FIGURE 5–24   This branching diagram shows the possible placement of *Morotopithecus*, *Dryopithecus*, and *Kenyapithecus* on the evolutionary tree of hominoids. The diagram has no time scale.

Gibbons   Orangutans   Gorillas   Chimpanzees and Bonobos   Humans

Morotopithecus?

Kenyapithecus?

Dryopithecus?

In sum, the evidence from *Oreopithecus*, *Dryopithecus*, and *Morotopithecus*, in combination with that from the dental apes, indicates that hominoids have experimented with a variety of locomotor adaptations throughout the superfamily's long history. Most fossil species opted for *pronograde* locomotion (monkeylike quadrupedalism with the spine horizontal), but a few showed *orthograde* (spine upright) suspensory patterns similar to today's arm-hanging and arm-swinging apes. Exactly when and why the pronograde hominoids went extinct, leaving only orthograde locomotors among the living apes, is unknown.

After their evolutionary origin in Africa, the apes began to spread out. By the mid-Miocene, they had migrated into Eurasia, where they were spread from Spain to Turkey. The recently discovered species called *Otavipithecus namibiensis* shows that meanwhile, back in Africa, apes were living in the southern part of that continent as well as in their old East African haunts. Adaptive radiations occurred in both Africa and Eurasia, as well as continued geographic spread, and by the late Miocene there was a tremendous diversity of apes distributed across the Old World as far east as China. Most of the Miocene apes were moderate to large in body size, although some, such as the 660 pound (300 kilogram) *Gigantopithecus*, were enormous. The favorite habitat of the Miocene apes was dense woods and forests, and their primary foods varied from leaves (e.g., *Oreopithecus*) to fruits to mixed diets including tough, hard items requiring powerful chewing (e.g., *Sivapithecus* and *Gigantopithecus*). As one might expect, enamel thickness on their grinding teeth (molars and premolars) was as variable as their diets (all living apes have thin molar enamel, with the exception of the orangutan, which shows an "intermediate" thickness).

Ape diversity declined strongly in the very late Miocene in association with global climatic changes, principally continental cooling and drying. Forests shrank in size as open habitats expanded. We know that the ancestors of the modern large-bodied apes and hominids were diverging at this time, but we can draw few firm conclusions about evolutionary relationships. The orangutan lineage probably diverged between 13 and 16 mya, and it seems that the fossil genus *Sivapithecus* (now understood to include *Ramapithecus*, a genus once thought to be an ancestor of hominids) may be an evolutionary ancestor of the Asian great ape (Figure 5–25). Unfortunately the evolutionary histories of the African apes, chimpanzees, bonobos, and gorillas—humans' closest living primate kin—are very poorly known at present. One new and interesting suggestion is that *Kenyapithecus*, a 14-million-year-old hominoid from East Africa, is "the best, most likely ancestor of humans, chimps, [bonobos,] and gorillas" (see Figure 5–24). Monte McCrossin of Southern Illinois University recently floated this possibility based on new fossils he and his colleague Brenda Benefit discovered on Maboko Island in Lake Victoria. Citing cranial, dental, and postcranial features, McCrossin not only links *Kenyapithecus* with humans and the living African apes, but also identifies *Kenyapithecus africanus* as the first semiterrestrial hominoid, a species "caught in the act of undergoing the transition from life in the trees to life on the ground." If this is true, further study of *Kenyapithecus* promises to yield great insight into the habitat transition thought to have been critical for the later evolution of hominids.

In any event, we know that the African habitat was strongly affected some 8 million years ago by earth movements that produced the Rift Valley running down the eastern side of the continent (see Figure 6–1). Because of changes in air circulation and rainfall, the area west of the Rift remained humid and forested, while to the east a drier climate produced open savannas. Biomolecular studies suggest that the gorilla lineage may have branched off around the time the Rift Valley was formed, with hominids separating from the chimpanzee-bonobo lineage shortly thereafter. It appears that humans' last ape ancestors lived in Africa (as Darwin

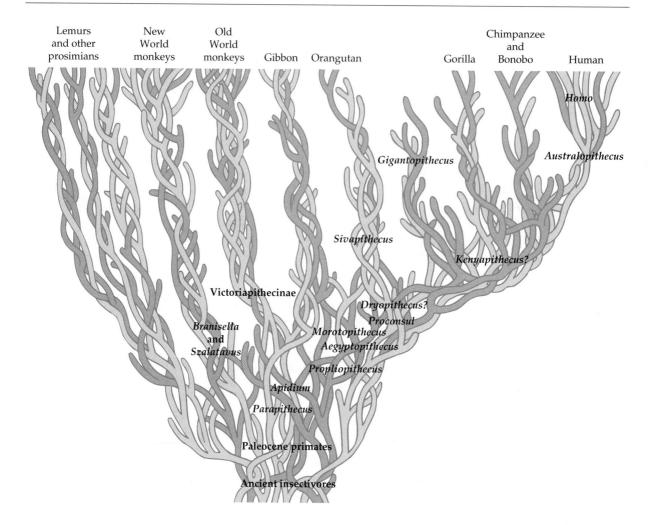

FIGURE 5–25 Evolutionary trees, or dendrograms, are always greatly oversimplified and in certain ways inaccurate, but they nevertheless give a good indication of the relative ages and phylogenetic relationships of the species shown. The multiplicity of lines indicates that any evolving lineage contains an unknown number of divergent populations that may or may not be different species. Many such populations become extinct. The chart is highly speculative.

Pliocene the geologic epoch extending from 5 to 1.6 million years B.P.

predicted) during the late Miocene, some 5 to 7 mya (Table 4–1b). But precisely what those apes were, what they looked like, and how they behaved remains to be discovered. But big changes were afoot: by early in the succeeding **Pliocene** epoch, unequivocal hominids had evolved.

Apes to Hominids: The Anatomical Criteria

We are now poised to review the fossil record of the human family, the family Hominidae. Indeed, most of the remainder of this book is devoted to that purpose. Before surveying the hominid remains, however, it is important to set out very clearly the minimum criteria for including a fossil species in that category. As reviewed in Chapter 3, living hominids (modern humans) are distinguished by several traits, including short, incisorlike canine teeth (Figure 5–26); skulls with flat faces and huge brains (Figure 5–27); fully opposable thumbs that give us a fine pre-

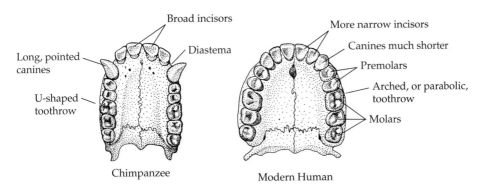

FIGURE 5–26   The dentition of the upper jaw of an ape (a chimpanzee) and a human is compared. Notice the distinct shape of the dental arcade, as well as the ape's large canines and diastemata.

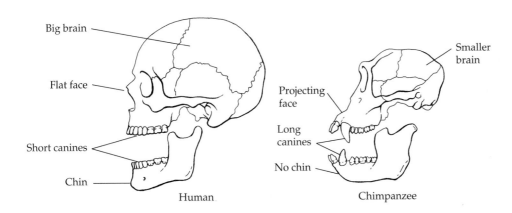

FIGURE 5–27   The ape and human skulls are quite distinct. The chimpanzee has a large jaw with large canines, especially in the male skull shown here. In humans, the teeth are smaller, and the canines generally project no farther than the other teeth. Humans also show a distinct chin, whereas apes do not. The enlarged braincase of humans brings about a more vertical alignment of the face and jaws. The scale is approximately one-fifth actual size.

cision grip; and numerous adaptations of the back, hips, legs, and feet that facilitate bipedal locomotion. Of these traits, only two—the first to evolve—are useful markers of the earliest hominids: reduced canine length and adaptations for bipedalism. But even these two are not equally useful. Some of the late Miocene apes (*Ouranopithecus*, for example) had relatively short canines, while those of some early hominids were relatively long in comparison to those of later members of the human family. Therefore, in the final analysis only evidence of habitual bipedalism unmistakably marks a fossil species as hominid.

Modern apes are long-armed and short-legged arborealists. They climb, swing, or hang about in the trees using forelimb-dominated movements, and when they come to the ground they walk quadrupedally. As adaptations for these locomotor patterns, apes have evolved (or retained) a distinct suite of postcranial traits. They

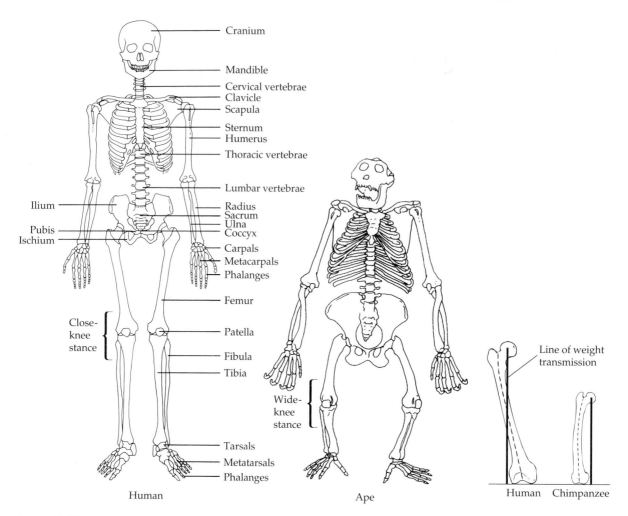

FIGURE 5–28   Humans (left) have evolved a close-knee stance, while bipedal apes (center) show a wide-knee posture. Postural and locomotor differences are reflected in the ape's lack of an angled femoral shaft in contrast to humans, who have one (right).

Wide-knee stance standing with the feet and knees about as far apart as the hip joints.

Iliac blade the broad portion of the *ilium*, one of the bones of the pelvis.

Anterior inferior iliac spine a projection from the *ilium* that serves as an attachment point for certain thigh muscles and also the *iliofemoral ligament*.

Ischium one of the bones of the pelvis

Sacrum the part of the vertebral column that articulates with the pelvis and forms the dorsal portion of the pelvic girdle.

have short, stiff, straight backs; tall, narrow pelvic bones similar to those of monkeys; widely spaced knees and feet (a **wide-knee stance**; Figure 5–28); and divergent big toes capable of grasping branches during climbing. Specifically with regard to the pelvis, the following distinctive anatomical traits can be identified in apes (Figure 5–29): (1) the **iliac blade** is tall and narrow and shows no sign of forward curvature into a "pelvic bowl"; (2) the **anterior inferior iliac spine** is very small and undeveloped; (3) the shaft of the **ischium** lies essentially in a straight line with the main portion of the ilium; and (4) the **sacrum** (the wedge of fused vertebrae that articulates with the pelvic bones) is relatively narrow. Additionally, with regard to the femur, or thighbone, the ape's wide-knee stance results in the lack of an angled shaft at the knee (Figure 5–28).

Equipped with this set of anatomical features, apes are capable only of energetically expensive and (somewhat) unstable bipedalism. A bipedal ape stands in a bent-hip, bent-knee posture with its center of gravity high above and anterior to the hip joints (Figure 5–30). This semi-upright posture is needed to produce an

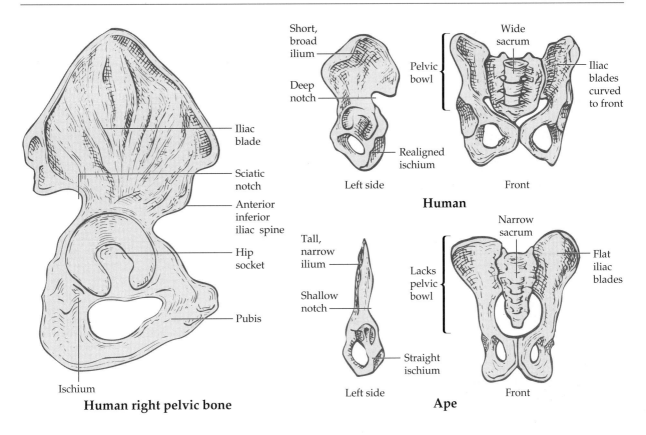

FIGURE 5–29   The right pelvic bone of a human (left) has a broad iliac blade, a deep sciatic notch, and a large anterior inferior iliac spine. The two pelvic bones plus the sacrum form a distinct pelvic bowl in humans (top right), while the iliac blades of an ape show no bowl-like curvature (bottom right). Drawings on right are not to scale. See also Figure 7–13 for photographs of ape and human pelvic bowls.

angle between the ischium and the femur—an angle that allows the **hamstring muscles** to extend (retract) the thigh—but it is maintained only with considerable muscular effort. When an ape walks, it takes short steps (the knee never passes behind the hip joints) and it balances by swaying its trunk to one side as the opposite leg is swinging forward (Figure 5–31). This "waddle-and-teeter" bipedalism is the best an ape can do, given its anatomy, but it is a most imperfect means of locomotion.

In contrast to apes, the human pelvis (Figure 5–29) features (1) a short iliac blade that has been widened and bent posteriorly (as shown by the deep **sciatic notch**); (2) anterior curvature and lateral flaring of the iliac blades to produce a bowl-shaped pelvic girdle; (3) strong enlargement of the anterior inferior iliac spine; (4) realignment of the ischium relative to the ilium; and (5) a wide sacrum. These evolutionary modifications went a long way toward perfecting bipedal walking. In conjunction with the development of a **lumbar curve** in the back, posterior expansion and bending of the iliac blades brought the human trunk over the hip joints and allowed straightening of the legs, while lowering the center of gravity to a point within the pelvic bowl (Figure 5–30). This greatly increased the energy efficiency of bipedalism and reduced its instability. The evolution of a pelvic bowl with broad, flaring walls allowed the lesser gluteal muscles (**gluteus medius** and **gluteus minimus**) to function as powerful lateral stabilizers of the trunk during

Hamstrings muscles of the hips and the back of the thigh; thigh extensors.

Sciatic notch a deep indentation of the *dorsal* edge of the hominid *ilium*.

Lumbar curve forward curvature of the vertebral column in the lower back that helps bring the hominid trunk over the hip joints.

Gluteus medius and gluteus minimus muscles of the hip; lateral stabilizers of the pelvis in modern humans.

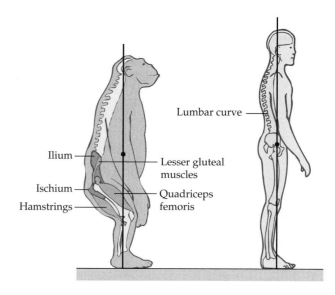

FIGURE 5–30   A bipedal ape (left) stands with its feet wide apart and with a bent-hip, bent-knee posture. The ape's center of gravity (see dot) is located high above and anterior to the hip joints. In contrast, a bipedal human (right) has its feet close together, and the center of gravity is located within the pelvic girdle.

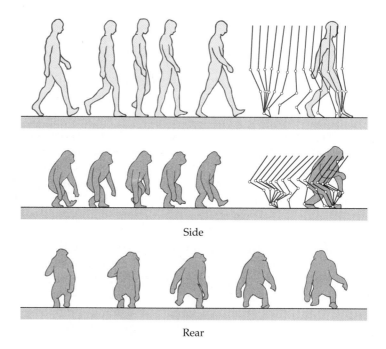

Side

Rear

FIGURE 5–31   Side views of bipedalism in humans and apes reveal that the human knee extends backward past the hips with each step, producing a long stride. In contrast, the ape waddles forward with short steps. A rear view shows how a bipedal ape teeters from side to side in order to balance its weight over the fixed leg.

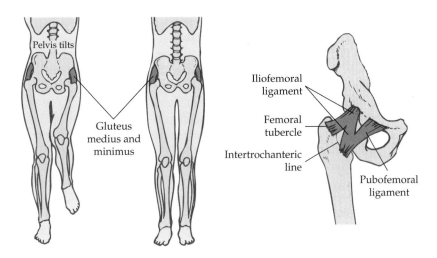

FIGURE 5–32 (Left) The lesser gluteal muscles of humans (gluteus medius and gluteus minimus) provide lateral stabilization of the pelvis over the fixed leg during bipedalism. (Right) A front view of the pelvis and the femur also shows the position of humans' iliofemoral ligament.

walking (no more teetering to balance the body and free the swing leg; Figure 5–32). Expansion of the anterior inferior iliac spine facilitated pulling the thigh forward (flexion) and also provided space for humans' large **iliofemoral ligament**, an anatomical feature that stabilizes the trunk against backward movement at the hips (Figure 5–32). And finally, the realignment of the ischium relative to the ilium resulted in an angle between the ischium and the femur that allows the thigh-extending hamstrings to work well with the body fully upright. This last change, in turn, allowed humans to take nice long strides on knees that swing back past the hips (no more waddling; Figure 5–31).

Two other changes in humans' postcranial anatomy deserve to be mentioned. We evolved a **close-knee stance** that pulled our feet nearer the body's midline, making lateral balancing of the trunk much easier than in wide-kneed apes and producing an angled femoral shaft (Figure 5–28). Additionally, we evolved nondivergent and nonprehensile big toes that function to propel our bodies forward during bipedal movement.

The pelvic anatomies of living apes and humans reveal two ends of an evolutionary continuum. We can expect the pelvic remains of early hominids to be intermediate between these extremes, with the very first members of our family resembling apes more than people. But the primary criterion for classifying a fossil species as hominid is clear: evidence of habitual bipedal movement. This criterion should be kept firmly in mind as we review the evidence of the beginnings of the hominid family in the next few chapters.

Iliofemoral ligament ligament that prevents backward movement of the trunk at the human hip.

Close-knee stance standing with the feet and knees closer together than the hip joints.

SUMMARY

As currently known, the fossil record indicates that the primate order originated about 60 million years ago (during the late Paleocene epoch) in Africa. This date is an approximation, however, based on very incomplete evidence, and future discoveries are likely to push the actual point of origin several million years back in time. Despite the uncertainty on dates, the earliest primates can be classified confidently as prosimians—not enormously different from today's lemurs, lorises, and tarsiers. By perhaps 45 to 50 mya, the ancient prosimians had given rise to the first anthropoids, although whether this occurred in Africa or Asia is hotly debated. By the Eocene-Oligocene boundary (35 million B.P.) the anthropoids were well established. Too primitive to be classified as either monkeys or apes, the early anthropoids nonetheless had such distinctive features of higher primates as bony eye sockets and fused frontal bones. The Oligocene epoch saw anthropoids differentiate into catarrhines and platyrrhines, and by 20 mya (the early Miocene), the first hominoids (apes) had evolved in Africa. Two distinct types of early apes can be identified: dental apes and suspensory apes. Dental apes resembled living hominoids (chimpanzees, etc.) in many dental and cranial traits, but they had monkey-like bodies and moved through the trees in a pronograde, quadrupedal fashion. In contrast, as their name implies, suspensory apes from the Miocene not only showed dental and cranial similarities to modern species, but also possessed postcranial adaptations for orthograde, forelimb-dominated locomotion (arm-hanging and arm-swinging). Finally, during the very late Miocene epoch, the Hominidae—the human family—evolved from an as yet undiscovered African ape ancestor. Marked primarily by distinctive adaptations for bipedal locomotion, the first hominids began the evolutionary journey that would culminate in modern humans.

POSTSCRIPT

To knuckle-walk or not to knuckle-walk? That is (sort of) the question that anthropologists have struggled with for years. More accurately, the question is whether or not hominids descended from knuckle-walking apes, as opposed to orthograde swingers-and-hangers. Supporters of a knuckle-walking ancestry for hominids point out that all three living African apes (gorillas, chimpanzees, and bonobos) show this type of locomotion, with only the fourth member of the African hominoid clade—humans—lacking it. Therefore, the argument goes, it seems clear that knuckle-walking must have evolved just once, sometime before the divergence of the gorilla lineage about 8 to 10 million years ago (see Table 4–1b), and that only humans have departed from the ancestral way of getting around. This is certainly the most parsimonious (least complicated) hypothesis since it involves the lowest number of locomotor innovations: knuckle-walking evolves once and bipedalism evolves once. Furthermore, says supporter David Begun of the University of Toronto, humans show subtle anatomical hints of a knuckle-walking past. For example, along with the African apes, humans show the early fusion of certain wrist bones (possibly for stability), as well as enlarged phalanges of the fingers (Figure 5–28). Begun thinks the simplest explanation is that humans descended from knuckle-walking ancestors.

Opponents to the hypothesis, however, raise several good points in counterargument. First, they tend to brush aside the admittedly equivocal pro-knuckle-walking anatomical evidence or offer different functional explanations for ape-human similarities. Second, they point out that there is no convincing evidence that any of the Miocene hominoids were knuckle-walkers. (True, but see below.) Finally, and more telling, preliminary analyses of the oldest known hominid fossils fail to show evidence of knuckle-walking (more on this in Chapter 7). The most reasonable scenario, according to this camp, is that the common ancestor of chimps, bonobos, and humans—who lived well after the divergence of gorillas—was a generalized swinger-and-hanger, that knuckle-walking evolved independently twice (among gorillas and in the genus *Pan*), and that bipedalism evolved once (although whether this occurred in the trees or on the ground is unclear). It's a somewhat more complicated theory, with three locomotor innovations, but it has the advantage of squaring with the fossil record and it agrees with the genetic evidence of humans' extreme closeness to the chimpanzee-bonobo clade.

All of which brings us to the latest piece of information to be brought to bear on this argument. Modern knuckle-walking apes can all be described as "semiterrestrial," spending considerable time both aloft and on the ground. Significantly, the antiquity of such semiterrestriality recently took a long step into the past thanks to the work of fossil hunters Monte McCrossin and Brenda Benefit. Based on fossils found on Maboko Island, McCrossin and Benefit suggest that semiterrestrial hominoid life began in the woodlands of East Africa about 14 million years ago and featured a species called *Kenyapithecus africanus* (originally named by Louis Leakey in 1967). The benefit to *Kenyapithecus* of coming down to the ground may have been a feast of hard fruit and nuts, but the significance of the find for humans is the probability that our ape ancestors were already on the ground when they evolved habitual bipedalism, not still hanging about in the trees. But was *Kenyapithecus* a knuckle-walker? Its total postcranial morphology says no, although tantalizing hints—such as modification of the third metacarpal (Figure 5–28) to prevent that finger from bending toward the back of the hand—suggest that some changes in that direction may have been underway. (This and other features have convinced McCrossin and Benefit that *Kenyapithecus* is the ancestor of the African apes and humans.) So, are we descended from knuckle-walkers? The jury is still out on that question, so stay tuned for future fossil discoveries.

REVIEW QUESTIONS

1. The Plesiadapiformes were once included among the primates. What aspects of plesiadapiform anatomy now convince many anthropologists that these creatures were *not* members of our order?
2. When and where did the suborder of the anthropoids arise? Describe the fossil evidence of the appearance of anthropoids.
3. Compare fossil apes with living apes with regard to postcranial anatomy and locomotor behavior.
4. What do we know about the age, location, identity, and behavior of humans' last ape ancestor?
5. Describe hominids' anatomical adaptations for habitual bipedalism.

SUGGESTED FURTHER READING

Aiello, L., and C. Dean. *An Introduction to Human Evolutionary Anatomy*. Academic Press, 1990.

Ciochon, R., and J. Fleagle. *Primate Evolution and Human Origins*. Benjamin/Cummings, 1986.

Conroy, G. C. *Primate Evolution*. W. W. Norton, 1990.

———*Reconstructing Human Origins*. W. W. Norton, 1997.

Coppens, Y. "East Side Story: The Origin of Humankind." *Scientific American*, 270, 1994.

Gebo, D. L. "Climbing, Brachiation, and Terrestrial Quadrupedalism: Historical Precursors of Hominid Bipedalism." *American Journal of Physical Anthropology*, 101, 1996.

Kay, R. F., C. Ross, and B. A. Williams. "Anthropoid Origins." *Science*, 275, 1997.

Larson, S. G. "Parallel Evolution in the Hominoid Trunk and Forelimb." *Evolutionary Anthropology*, 6, 1998.

Lovejoy, O. "Evolution of Human Walking." *Scientific American*, 259, 1988.

Martin, R. D. *Primate Origins and Evolution: A Phylogenetic Reconstruction*. Chapman & Hall, 1990.

McCrossin, M. L. "Bridging the Gap: Connecting the Origin of Bipedalism in Pliocene Hominidae With the Advent of Semi-Terrestrial Adaptations Among African Miocene Hominoidea." *Journal of Human Evolution*, 32, 1997.

Napier, J. R. "The Antiquity of Human Walking." *Scientific American*, 216, 1967.

Pilbeam, D. "Genetic and Morphological Records of the Hominoidea and Hominid Origins: A Synthesis." *Molecular Phylogenetics and Evolution*, 5, 1996.

INTERNET RESOURCES

PREHISTORIC CULTURES

http://www.d.umn.edu/cla/faculty/troufs/anth1602/

(Maintained by Professor Tim Roufs at the University of Minnesota at Duluth, this web site was constructed for a course that uses *Humankind Emerging* as its main text. Search the site until you find the information about fossil primates. You will probably want to revisit the Prehistoric Cultures site regularly to explore the links listed there.)

PRIMATE INFO NET—PRIMATE EVOLUTION

http://www.primate.wisc.edu/pin/evolution.html

(Links to sites concerning primate and human evolution.)

SIUC RESEARCH SURVEY: COMMON ANCESTORS

http://www.siu.edu/worda/persp/f97/survey.html

(Paleoanthropologist Brenda Benefit is profiled. She discusses her 1994 discovery of a *Victoriapithecus* skull in Kenya.)

USEFUL SEARCH TERMS:

bipedal locomotion
fossil primates
fossil apes
hominid evolution
human anatomy

Chapter 5 Timeline

	YEARS B.P.	FOSSIL RECORD	PRIMATES
Cro-Magnon, Neandertal, and *Homo erectus*	Pleistocene ◆		*Homo*
CENOZOIC	2 million —	Early *Homo*	
Early prosimians	Pliocene ◆	*Australopithecus* and *Paranthropus* *Ardipithecus*	
65 million	5 million —	Earliest hominids?	Australopithecines
Basic insectivores			
		Sivapithecus in Asia and Europe	
MESOZOIC	Miocene ◆	*Kenyapithecus* in Africa	
		Morotopithecus and *Proconsul* in Africa	
First mammals			Apes
225 million			
	25 million —		
	Oligocene ◆		Catarrhines and Platyrrhines
	35 million —	*Propliopithecus* and *Aegyptopithecus* at Fayum	
		Oligopithecines in Africa	
		Amphipithecus and *Pondaugia* in Burma *Siamopithecus* in Thailand	
PALEOZOIC			Early prosimians
	Eocene ◆	*Eosimias* in China	
		Algeripithecus in Algeria	
First vertebrates			
	58 million —		First primates
	Paleocene ◆	*Altiatlasius* in Morocco	
570 million			
PRECAMBRIAN	65 million —		

BACK BEYOND THE APES

The time scale of primate evolution is immense. The first part of the 60 million years of primate history was the age of the prosimians, which occupied much of the Old and New Worlds. By 20 million years ago the apes were established in Africa, and for this reason we too find our origin on this continent. By about 15 million years ago the apes had spread into Eurasia.

THE TRANSVAAL HOMINIDS

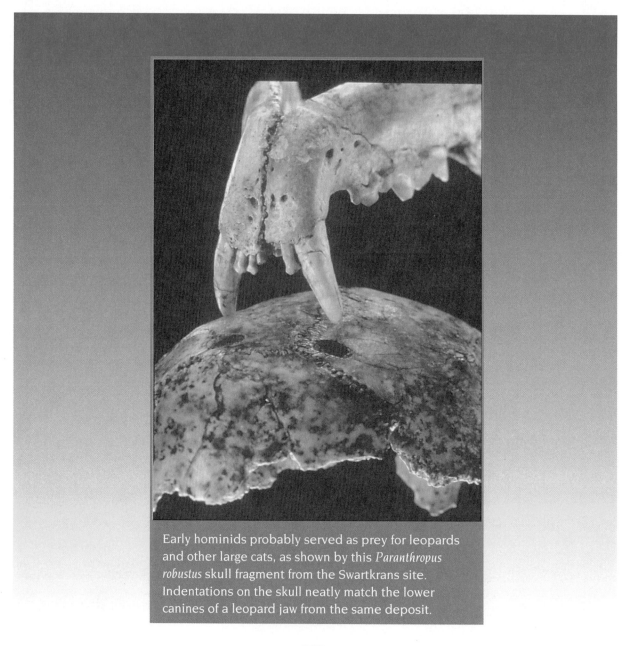

Early hominids probably served as prey for leopards and other large cats, as shown by this *Paranthropus robustus* skull fragment from the Swartkrans site. Indentations on the skull neatly match the lower canines of a leopard jaw from the same deposit.

I*n each great region of the world the living mammals are closely related to the extinct species of the same region. It is, therefore, probable that Africa was formerly inhabited by extinct apes closely allied to the gorilla and chimpanzee; and as these two species are now man's nearest allies, it is somewhat more probable that our early progenitors lived on the African continent than elsewhere.*

CHARLES DARWIN, 1809–1882. *The Descent of Man.*

OVERVIEW

The human family—the family Hominidae—branched off from ape stock some 5 to 7 million years ago. All members of that family, living and fossil, are referred to as *hominids*, and all hominids can be placed in one of two subfamilies: Australopithecinae (containing the genera *Ardipithecus*, *Australopithecus*, and *Paranthropus*) and Homininae (containing the genus *Homo*). The australopithecine subfamily was the earliest to evolve, and the first fossil evidence of these ancient bipeds was discovered in South Africa by Raymond Dart in 1924. Dart named his discovery *Australopithecus africanus* and claimed that it was intermediate between modern apes and humans. Dart's claims were largely dismissed by the scientific community until additional, and more complete, australopithecine materials were discovered by Robert Broom in the 1930s. Included in the new finds were the fossils of a more rugged species of australopithecine equipped with massive grinding teeth. Broom named this new creature *Paranthropus robustus*. Today the hominid status of the australopithecines is firmly established, and it is known that they roamed South Africa from more than 3 million years B.P. to just a million years ago. Although the issue is controversial, it appears possible that certain of the South African australopithecines may have manufactured stone tools.

 ## Mini-Timeline

DATE OR AGE	FOSSIL DISCOVERIES OR EVOLUTIONARY EVENTS
(A) DATE (YEARS A.D.)	
1995	"Little Foot" described from Sterkfontein
1965–1966	Brain, Tobias work at Swartkrans, Sterkfontein
1950	Le Gros Clark classifies australopithecines as hominids
1938	Broom discovers first *Paranthropus*
1924	Dart discovers first *Australopithecus*
(B) AGE (MILLION YEARS B.P.)	
2.0–1.0	*Paranthropus robustus* inhabits South Africa
3.5?–2.5	*Australopithecus africanus* inhabits South Africa

THE SCIENCE OF PALEOANTHROPOLOGY

Paleoanthropology the study of the fossil and cultural remains and other evidence of humans' extinct ancestors.

At long last, after warming up with discussions of Darwin's theories, genetics, primate behavior, and prehominid fossils, we are ready to address our main topics of interest: **paleoanthropology** and the evidence of human evolution. Although our review of the hominid fossil record will begin in 1924 in the limestone quarries of South Africa, the science of paleoanthropology can be traced back to the mid-nineteenth century. As will be described in a later chapter, Neandertal fossils were discovered in Germany as early as 1856, and just a few years later T. H. Huxley published *Evidence as to Man's Place in Nature* (1863; see Chapter 1). Huxley's book combined a discussion of the Neandertal remains with a thorough anatomical comparison of humans and apes. Many modern workers trace the formal origin of the science of paleoanthropology to Huxley's publication.

Modern paleoanthropology is a very complicated field of inquiry compared to its humble beginnings. Today the location, excavation, dating, analysis, and interpretation of hominid fossils requires the combined skills of a team of specialists (see Box 6–1). Sites are excavated with extreme care (Figure 6–1), and all fossils, artifacts, and other significant features are plotted on maps for further study. Geologists, paleontologists, and other scientists help to reconstruct the ancient landscape and ecosystem in detail. Laboratory analyses of fossils, and

FIGURE 6–1   Controlled excavations at the australopithecine site of Swartkrans, South Africa. The grid system is used for plotting artifacts and fossils.

Box 6-1

SPECIAL SKILLS TO STUDY FOSSIL SITES

In the Field

Paleoanthropologists	In charge of investigations from start to finish, they must pick the site, get permission to excavate, obtain financial support, hire the labor, and organize, plan, and supervise the work in progress. Finally, they must integrate the data collected by each of the specialists and publish their conclusions.
Geologists	Often assist in selecting the site. Their knowledge of the geologic history of the region is indispensible in determining the relative ages of fossils. Their study of the strata at the site determines the natural processes—deposition, volcanic action—that laid the strata down and the conditions under which fossilization took place.
Surveyors	Map the general region of the site and the site itself, plotting it in relation to natural landmarks and making a detailed record of its contours before they are obliterated by digging.
Draftspeople	Record the exact position of all fossils, tools, and other artifacts as excavated, marking their relationships to each other in both the horizontal and vertical planes.
Photographers	Document fossil remains and artifacts and their associations as they are uncovered, record work in progress and the use of special equipment, and provide overall views of the site as well as of personnel at work.

In the Laboratory

Petrologists	Identify and classify the rocks and minerals found around the site. They can determine the nature of rocks from which tools were made and identify stones that do not occur naturally in the area, which would indicate that the stones were imported by early humans.
Palynologists	Specialize in the study and identification of fossil plant pollen, which may shed light on early humankind's environment and diet and the climate at the time.
Pedologists	Experts on soil and their chemical composition, their findings round out the picture of the environment as it once was.
Geochemists	With geophysicists, conduct chemical and physical tests in the laboratory to determine the absolute age of material found at the site. They may also study the chemical composition of bones and artifacts.

In the Field and Laboratory

Preparators	At the site, preserve and protect fossils and artifacts with various hardening agents and make plaster casts for particularly fragile bones and other organic remains. In the laboratory, preparators clean and restore the specimens, making them ready for study by various specialists.
Paleontologists	Study the fossil animal remains found at the site. From the finds, they can learn much about the ecology and the eating habits of early humans.
Physical anthropologists	Specialists in the comparative anatomy of apes and humans, they evaluate remains found at the site and the evolutionary status of fossil hominids who lived there.
Taphonomists	Study the condition and arrangement of the fossils in relation to the deposits which carry them, to determine the origin and formation of the fossil assemblage.
Archaeologists	Study humankind's past material culture: tools of stone, bone, and wood; living sites, settlement patterns, and food remains; art and ritual.

the publication of results, may take several years after the original discoveries. The old days of publishing hasty descriptions and speculations about new fossils are (thankfully) just about gone. Such was not the case in 1924, however, when a young anatomist named Raymond Dart (1893–1988) found himself confronted with a remarkable South African fossil. Dart's discovery revealed the wonderful world of the most ancient hominids, the australopithecines (see Table 6–1), and it is to his story that we now turn.

DART'S DISCOVERY OF THE TAUNG SKULL (1924)

The importance of bipedalism cannot be overestimated. Bipedalism is much more than a mere rearing up and running about. As we have seen, apes and monkeys have all sorts of structural handicaps that hamper them in this respect; they stand with knees bent, unable to extend their legs fully, and they walk on the sides of their feet. They can move on two legs and sometimes do for short distances, but they are not made for it. Humans, however, cannot function properly in any other way. Somehow, somewhere, in the late Miocene or early Pliocene, the adaptations of bipedalism made their appearance in at least one kind of primate.

The first tangible evidence that a two-legged primate existed in the distant past came from an unexpected place, the Transvaal region of South Africa. Raymond Dart, professor of anatomy at the University of the Witwatersrand in Johannesburg, South Africa, encouraged his students to send him rock fragments that contained fossils. In 1924, a student brought him a fossil baboon skull that had come from a limestone quarry at a place named Taung, 200 miles (320 kilometers) from Johannesburg (see Figure 6–2). Hoping to obtain more fossils, particularly another baboon skull, Dart persuaded the quarry owner to save bone-bearing rocks, and in due course he was sent two boxes of broken rock containing fossils.

Dart found nothing of great interest in the first box, but his eye hit on something very strange in the second. On the top of the heap lay not a skull, but the next best thing to it: an oddly shaped rounded piece of rock that appeared to be the mold of the inside of a skull. Scarcely allowing himself to think what this might mean, Dart went through the rest of the box and found another piece of rock with a curved depression into which this mold fitted: part of the skull itself. In this second rock Dart could dimly perceive the outline of a broken piece of skull and the back of a lower jaw. He was looking from the rear at the inside of something's, or somebody's, head.

Endocast a fossilized cast of the interior of a skull; may reveal much about brain size and shape.

An **endocast** (a fossilized cast of the interior of a skull) of any species of primate would have been a notable discovery, but one look at this antique fragment sent Dart's mind racing. Here was no fossil baboon. The animal's brain capacity appeared to be three times larger than an ancient baboon's, and perhaps even larger than a modern adult chimpanzee's. The exciting thought struck Dart that he might be holding in his hands the "missing link" between ape and human.

Dart's first problem was to free the rest of the strange skull from the surrounding stone. Working with a hammer, chisels, and a sharpened knitting needle, he "pecked, scraped, and levered" bits of stone from the front of the skull and the eye sockets. After days of painstaking dissection, an incredible face began to emerge. Rather than the long projecting jaw and large canine teeth that clearly identify both existing and fossil baboons, this face had the relatively smaller jaw and shorter face of an ape; yet it was not overhung by the low brow of an ape, but

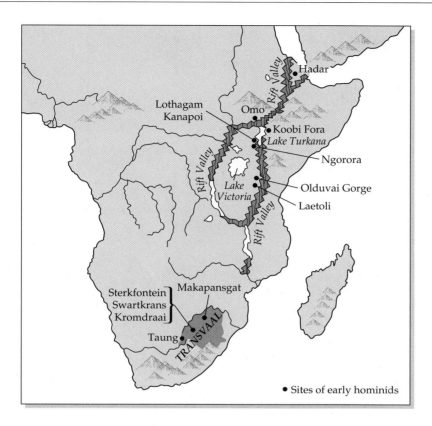

FIGURE 6–2 The earliest knowledge of australopithecines came from the Transvaal in South Africa. At a number of sites in this area, fossils were preserved in caves and hollows in the dolomite bedrock. Although their absolute age is not accurately known, they are broadly dated between 3.5 and 1 million years B.P.

surmounted by a forehead. From then on, Dart lay awake nights "in a fever of thoughts" about what kind of ape might have lived long ago on that grassy plateau.

Apes lived in tropical forests, but according to the prevailing wisdom there had been no such forests in South Africa for more than 100 million years. While ice advanced and retreated over much of the earth, and while mountains rose along the continental coasts, South Africa was believed to have always remained a dry, relatively undisturbed veld, much as it is today. Throughout prehistory the nearest natural habitat of apes was more than 2,000 miles (3,200 kilometers) north of Taung. Could some different kind of ape have found a way to adapt itself to life in an arid, open land?

The Evidence and Dart's Interpretation

Dart continued his exacting labor with the baffling fossil until, on the seventy-third day of work, the stone parted and he saw before him the face and most of the skull of a child now thought to have died at three to four years of age (Figure 6–3). It had a full set of milk teeth; the permanent molars were just beginning to erupt; and the canines, like those of humans, were quite small. After Dart studied his find

FIGURE 6–3   In 1924, Raymond Dart startled the anthropological world by his discovery of a small fossil skull from a quarry at Taung in South Africa. (The height of the skull and jaw is about 5 inches or 13 centimeters.) The following year he named the Taung specimen *Australopithecus africanus* and boldly declared it to be a human ancestor. His claim was derided, but finds made many years later proved that his fossil was indeed hominid.

Foramen magnum large opening in the cranial base, through which the spinal cord passes to the brain.

more carefully, he realized that the set of the skull suggested that the child had walked upright. One thing that made him feel sure he was dealing with a true bipedal creature was the position of the **foramen magnum**, the large hole through which the spinal cord passes into the skull on its way to the brain. In apes and monkeys the foramen magnum is near the back of the skull, reflecting the sloping position of the spinal column in quadrupedal posture. But in the Taung skull it faced almost directly downward (Figure 6–4): the Taung child had carried its head over its spine like a sphere balanced on the top of a pole. Whatever verdict the scientific establishment would eventually pass on the Taung child, Dart was certain that the creature had stood erect.

All previous discoveries of human predecessors were then thought to be authentic, if early, human beings, including Neandertal man and Java man (Chapter 10). All are now classified as *Homo* despite certain primitive features. The child's face before Dart seemed the reverse: an ape with human features. It could not possibly be a human. It was too primitive, too small-brained. A prehu-

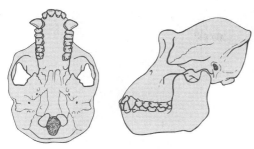

Female gorilla

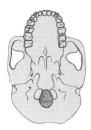
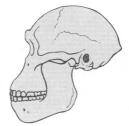

Australopithecus africanus

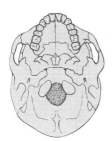
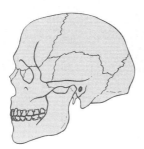

Homo sapiens

FIGURE 6–4 Improvement in the balance of the head during human evolution has involved movement of the **occipital condyles** and the associated foramen magnum (shown stippled) forward. (The occipital condyles are the bearing surfaces of the skull on the uppermost vertebra—the atlas; the foramen magnum is the hole in the base of the skull through which the spinal cord passes.) In this important characteristic of the skull base, *Australopithecus* is intermediate between apes (here, a gorilla [top] is illustrated) and modern humans (bottom). Scale is approximately one-fifth actual size.

Occipital Condyles pads of bone on the base of the skull that articulate with the uppermost vertebra.

man, then, a link with the ape past? Taking a deep breath, Dart announced to the world in 1925 that he had found a human ancestor that was not yet human. He gave it the formidable name of ***Australopithecus africanus*** (from *australis,* "southern," and *pithekos,* "ape"): African southern ape.

Because he was so confident of the significance of his find, Dart publicized his momentous news in record time. Less than four months after the skull had come into his hands, he wrote a full scientific report for the February 7, 1925, issue of the British scientific journal *Nature.* His report included the provocative statement, "The specimen is of importance because it exhibits an extinct race of apes intermediate between living anthropoids and man . . . a creature well advanced beyond modern anthropoids in just those characters, facial and cerebral, which are to be anticipated in an extinct link between man and his simian ancestor." That day, in South Africa and around the world, the headlines proclaimed that the missing link had been found. It was also the first link in a long chain of discoveries that would establish Africa as the place of origin of humankind.

Australopithecus africanus gracile australopithecine *species* that inhabited South Africa 3.5–2.5 mya.

FIGURE 6–5   Robert Broom was a passionate fossil hunter and distinguished paleontologist. He kept working until his death at age 85.

Dart's Claims Dismissed

Dart's report was intensely interesting to a number of scientists in Europe, not so much for the human attributes he claimed for the Taung creature as for the inexplicable presence of an ape so far south. The general conclusion was that this was a young specimen of an ancient chimpanzeelike or gorillalike species, but how it had wandered where no ape had ever before been known to go was extremely puzzling. As a result, Dart's claims about the Taung child had to endure a long period of skepticism.

This suspicion may seem strange. After all, anthropologists spend their lives looking for increasingly primitive, ever more apelike fossils. Why are they so reluctant to recognize one when it turns up? There are numerous reasons. For one, there are many false alarms. If this book were to catalog all the mistaken claims about hominid fossils made by laity and experts alike, it would have to be far longer than it is. At the time that Dart discovered the Taung skull, the fraudulent

Piltdown skull (Chapter 10) represented the generally held concept of our early ancestors. It suggested that early humans already had large brains but still had ape-like faces—a concept that satisfies modern human vanity, with its emphasis on the special quality of the human intellect. Dart's fossil was not so agreeable. It suggested the opposite; that face and teeth began to become recognizably human while the brain was still very small. And so anthropologists and anatomists were cautious, even prejudiced, and attacks on Dart were not long in coming. Dart's child, several critics suggested, was only "the distorted skull of a chimpanzee." There may also have been jealousy that some remote colonial professor, rather than a distinguished European, had made what was surely to become the greatest discovery of the age. Taung became something of a byword; it was ridiculed in songs and on music hall stages.

Despite the criticism, Dart was encouraged by a warm congratulatory letter from Robert Broom (1866–1951), a Scottish physician who had hunted fossils, particularly fossils of mammal-like reptiles, in many parts of South Africa (see Figure 6–5). Two weeks after the letter arrived, Broom himself appeared at Dart's laboratory. He spent a weekend studying the Taung child intensively and became convinced that, as "a connecting link between the higher apes and one of the lowest human types," it was the most important fossil discovered up to that time. He said so firmly in an article in *Nature*. After the first flare-up of attention, however, Dart's child was either forgotten or dismissed by most scientists. Nonetheless, Dart and Broom continued to study the skull.

Dentition of Taung

For his part, Dart worked away at the skull almost daily for more than four years. In 1929, he succeeded in separating the upper and lower jaws, which had been cemented together in a rock-hard mass of breccia (a mixture of sand, soil, and pebbles cemented by lime) that enclosed them. For the first time, he could examine the entire pattern of the teeth and get a good look at their grinding surfaces.

What he found strengthened his case that the fossil was neither an ape nor a baboon. In apes, as we have seen (Chapter 5), the front teeth are large, because they are used for threat and for tearing up the tough vegetable matter that forms much of an ape's diet. Ape canines, in particular, are so large that there must be spaces (diastemata) between the teeth of the upper jaw to accommodate the lower canines when the jaw is closed (Figure 6–6). At the same time, apes' jaws are relatively longer than humans' jaws, and heavier, too, and the muscles needed to move them are more massive. The Taung child, although a young individual and therefore lacking typical adult characters, could be judged to be distinctly more humanlike than apelike in all these characteristics. Its nicely curved jaw was shorter than a young ape's and more lightly made. Its canines and incisors were relatively small and set closely together. In fact, though the molars were larger than is now normal, most of the teeth could have belonged to a child of today. (Figure 6–7).

In the minds of Dart and Broom, any lingering doubts about the hominid nature of the creature vanished; but skeptics, they suspected, would take more convincing. What was needed was an adult skull, and also some legs or pelvic bones, to support the claim of erect posture that the position of the foramen magnum suggested. Broom was determined to find this evidence, but it was not until the 1930s that he was free to begin a serious search.

Mandible

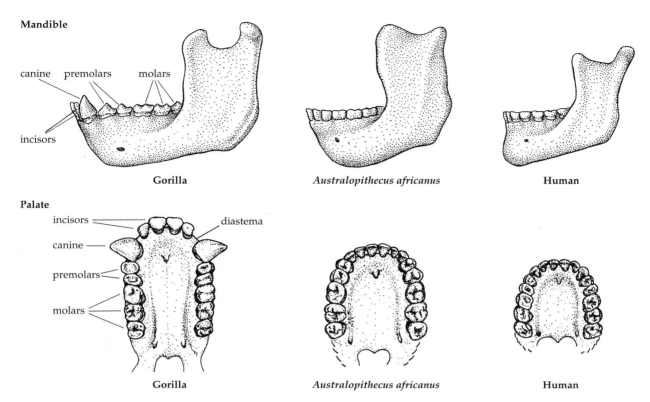

Gorilla   *Australopithecus africanus*   **Human**

FIGURE 6–6   These drawings show a lateral view of the mandibles (lower jaws) and a full view of the palates (upper jaws) of a gorilla, an adult *Australopithecus africanus*, and a modern human. The striking difference in the size and form of the canine teeth is clear, and in the gorilla palate we can see the gaps or diastemata, into which the lower canines fit on each side. The difference in the shape of the dental arcade in ape and hominid is also striking. The lateral view also shows distinct tooth wear: the ape teeth are used to crush and tear; the hominid teeth are used to crush and grind, which causes the typical flat wear of the hominid dentition. The drawings are not to scale.

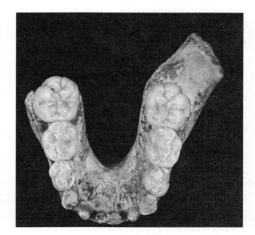

FIGURE 6–7   Lower dentition of the Taung child (*Australopithecus africanus*). The largest teeth are the first permanent molars.

DISCOVERIES OF ROBERT BROOM

The way was opened when Broom became curator of vertebrate paleontology at the Transvaal Museum in Pretoria. For the next year and a half, he was occupied with digging out, describing, and naming forty-four new fossil species of reptiles. He also unearthed a baboon jaw that at first appeared to be *Australopithecus*. It was not, but the publicity it engendered led two of Dart's students to tell Broom about some small skulls they had found in a quarry at Sterkfontein, a village not far from Pretoria (Figure 6–2).

A Skull from Sterkfontein (1936)

Ever since the first mining camps were opened during the South African gold rush of 1886, the people of the Sterkfontein area had been picking up fossilized remains of baboons, monkeys, and perhaps, unknowingly, hominids. By some extraordinary quirk of fate, the limeworks at Sterkfontein had even issued a little guidebook: "Come to Sterkfontein and Find the Missing Link." When Broom first visited the quarry, the manager, who had worked at Taung and knew about the *Australopithecus* child's skull, promised Broom that he would keep a sharp lookout for anything resembling the skull of a hominid.

When Broom returned on August 7, 1936, the manager asked, "Is this what you're after?" and handed him two-thirds of a superb brain cast, which had been blasted out only that morning. Broom anxiously dug into the debris to find the skull that had served as the mold. Though he worked until dark, he found nothing. The next day, as he sorted the piles of breccia, he recovered not only both sides of the upper jaw, but also fragments of the braincase. When the fragments were pieced together, Broom had parts of the skull of an adult *Australopithecus*.

Paranthropus robustus at Kromdraai

For three years, Broom, now in his seventies, continued to visit his fossil gold mine. One June day in 1938, the quarry manager met Broom and handed him an upper jaw with one molar in place. He had obtained it from a schoolboy who lived on a farm at Kromdraai, less than a mile away. Broom found the boy, who responded to Broom's first questions by pulling out of his pocket "four of the most wonderful teeth ever seen in the world's history." The boy also gave Broom a piece of a lower jaw. During the next two days, Broom and the boy sifted earth and found a number of scraps of bone and teeth. When the pieces were put together, Broom had most of another skull, though this one was different: the face was flatter than that of the Sterkfontein *Australopithecus*, the jaw was heavier, and, though the incisors and canines were still small, the molars were larger and less human.

When the newest findings were published, the situation seemed even more confused. The Kromdraai adult differed so markedly from both the Taung child and the Sterkfontein adult that it appeared increasingly likely to Broom that there were two species of early hominids in South Africa: the smaller, more slender "gracile" type with smaller molars that Dart had named *Australopithecus africanus*, and the heavy-jawed "robust" Kromdraai type with extremely large molars. Broom established a new genus and species for the Kromdraai type: **Paranthropus robustus**, or "robust near-man."

Broom's action in setting up a new genus for the Kromdraai fossils did not sit well with his paleontological colleagues, who thought he was going too far. Despite

Paranthropus robustus robust australopithecine *species* that lived in South Africa 2.0–1.0 mya; also known as *Australopithecus robustus.*

the apparent differences between the Kromdraai and Sterkfontein hominids in body size, muscularity, and dental proportions, many scientists thought the new genus was uncalled for. "Of course the critics did not know the whole of the facts," said Broom. "When one has jealous opponents one does not let them know everything." What he had not disclosed was that the fossils of animals found with the Kromdraai fossil were less archaic than the ones excavated with *Australopithecus africanus* and thus represented a different period. Fossil horses abounded at Kromdraai; none apparently occurred at Sterkfontein, only 1 mile (1.6 kilometers) away. Many other fossil animal species were not shared by the two sites. Also, the breccia itself in which the Kromdraai creature lay seemed to be of a different age from that which had held *Australopithecus africanus*. If the sites were occupied at various times—from several million to a half million years ago—then each might well have sustained a different species of hominid. Broom came to the conclusion that some of his *P. robustus* finds were as much as a million years younger than the Sterkfontein fossils—and this is still considered a more or less correct interpretation. (In 1977, Elizabeth Vrba, now at Yale University, suggested a date of 2.0 million years B.P. for Kromdraai based on an updated faunal analysis.) Today, the controversy over generic names—*Australopithecus* versus *Paranthropus*—continues unabated. For a variety of reasons (see the Postscript at the chapter's end), we agree with Broom's original naming system and (as shown in Table 6–1) recognize three genera of the earliest hominids: **Paranthropus** (including *P. robustus* and two species from East Africa, *P. boisei* and *P. aethiopicus*), **Australopithecus** (including *A. africanus* from South Africa; two East African forms, *A. afarensis* and *A. anamensis*; and, provisionally, one North-Central African species, *A. bahrelghazali*), and **Ardipithecus** (listed provisionally and including the species *A. ramidus*). Members of all three genera can be referred to as australopithecines. (Species designations within the genus *Homo* are not shown in Table 6–1. The taxonomy of this genus is controversial at present, as will be explained in later chapters.)

    Broom continued to search, and in due course he had more robust fossils to work with, having struck a rich find in a cave at Swartkrans (Figures 6–8 and 6–9)

Paranthropus a *genus* of the family Hominidae, subfamily Australopithecinae; contains three *species*: *P. robustus*, *P. boisei*, and *P. aethiopicus*.

Australopithecus a *genus* of the family Hominidae, subfamily Australopithecinae; contains four *species*: *A. afarensis*, *A. africanus*, *A. anamensis*, and *A. bahrelghazali* (provisional).

Ardipithecus ramidus provisionally, a new *genus* and *species* of the family Hominidae, subfamily Australopithecinae; known from East Africa and dating 4.4 mya.

TABLE 6-1   *Hominid Taxonomy*

FAMILY HOMINIDAE (COMMON NAME: HOMINIDS)

Subfamily Australopithecinae (Common name: australopithecines)[a]

Genus *Ardipithecus*	Species	*Ardipithecus ramidus* (provisional)
Genus *Australopithecus*	Species	*Australopithecus afarensis*
		Australopithecus africanus
		Australopithecus anamensis
		Australopithecus bahrelghazali (provisional)
Genus *Paranthropus*	Species	*Paranthropus aethiopicus*
		Paranthropus boisei
		Paranthropus robustus

Subfamily Homininae (Common name: hominines)

Genus *Homo*	Species	(Paleoanthropologists recognize between three and seven species of hominines. The taxonomic controversies will be discussed in later chapters.)

[a] A possible ninth species of australopithecine was announced while this book was in press. See the end of Chapter 7.

FIGURE 6–8 The almost perfect jaw of *Paranthropus robustus* found at Swartkrans. Note the huge molars and premolars and the diminutive front teeth that characterize the robust genus. This photograph is approximately three-quarters actual size.

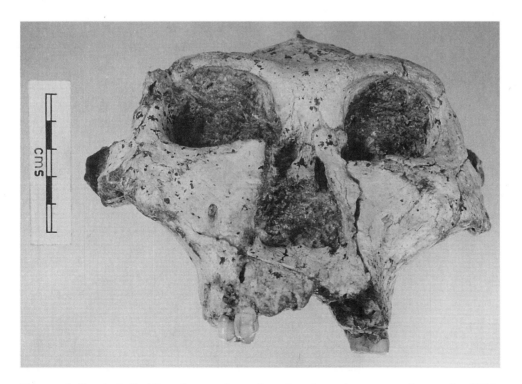

FIGURE 6–9 A skull of *Paranthropus robustus* from Swartkrans (museum catalog number SK48). Note the broad face, the large zygomatic arches, and the sagittal crest atop the skull.

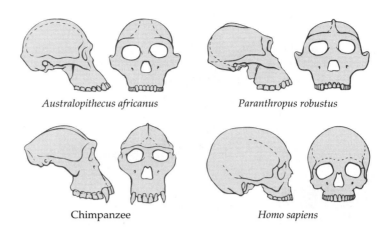

Australopithecus africanus   *Paranthropus robustus*

Chimpanzee   *Homo sapiens*

FIGURE 6–10   The skulls of two australopithecine species are here compared with those of a chimpanzee and a modern human. Notice the absence of the sagittal crest in *A. africanus* and its presence in *Paranthropus*. The large ape canine is not found in either australopithecine species. In the human specimen, notice the increase in the relative size of the braincase and the relatively smaller jaws. The pictures are not drawn to the same scale.

Sagittal crest a ridge of bone running front to rear along the midline of the skull; serves to attach certain jaw muscles. A *sagittal keel* is a slight elevation of the bone in the same location.

just across the valley from Sterkfontein. But the more new robust material he found, the more puzzled he became. Of the two types of hominid, *Paranthropus robustus*, the larger and more recent, seemed somehow the more primitive. Although a million years closer to us, it was not more humanlike, nor was it more apelike (Figure 6–10). Its jaws and molars were massive, less like those of modern humans than were the jaws and molars of *A. africanus*. The *Paranthropus* grinding teeth were huge in proportion to the size of the front teeth, for the canines were very small. Also, on its skull *P. robustus* had a bony ridge or crest, called a **sagittal crest**, to anchor large jaw muscles. These characteristics suggested that the creature was a vegetarian, and chewed up large quantities of tough vegetable food, as a gorilla does today.

Could the younger, robust type be the human ancestor? That just did not make sense. How could a less human hominid occur so much later than a more human one? Assigning *P. robustus* a role in human ancestry raised awkward problems. For one thing, an animal does not get specialized jaw equipment—a heavy jaw, oversized grinding teeth, and a bony ridge on its skull—overnight. It could be assumed that *P. robustus* had been following an evolutionary course toward a vegetarian life for a long time. Therefore the most reasonable expectation would be that the creature would continue to do so. Evolution does not work capriciously and rarely fast. It would be much more logical to assume that, since humans were known to have eaten all sorts of things (to be omnivores) for at least three-quarters of a million years, they probably had done so for a much longer time.

Age of *Australopithecus africanus*

Broom set out to calculate the age of *Australopithecus africanus*, a task that was not easy. Accurate dating was difficult because of the way the fossils were obtained and, more important, because of the unique geologic structure of the area. Most South African finds were made in lime-cemented breccia that had filled in ancient caves. This material had to be removed from quarries by blasting, which, of course, destroyed the stratigraphic pattern. In addition, because of the distinctive geology of South Africa, with no volcanic activity to deposit datable layers of ash, whatever stratigraphic clues could be discovered could not be matched with better known and better dated layers in other parts of the world. About the best Broom could do was to carefully examine the animal fossils associated with the *Australopithecus* remains. To Broom's frustration, not only were all the large mammals extinct, but they also were not known in any other place; there was nothing he could compare them with. The very fact of their extinction suggested, however, that they must have been at least a million years old, possibly much older. Making a bold guess, Broom announced that *Australopithecus africanus* was probably 2 million years old, of the Pliocene epoch.

His choice of 2 million years turned out to be more extraordinarily shrewd than it was shaky. For the moment, however, his announcement was greeted by the scientific community with derision. What bothered other scientists who examined the fossils or read about them was not the jaws but the rest of the head. They could not believe that a human ancestor with a brain scarcely bigger than a chimpanzee's had been running around on two legs in South Africa 2 million years ago.

As this creature was estimated to be more than twice as old as any other known hominid, it did not seem remarkable to Dart or Broom that this peculiar mixture of ape and human characteristics should exist in a fossil. Two million years, they reasoned, might bring one pretty close to a common ancestor for humans and apes. That ancestor could well display a confusing and unexpected mingling of characteristics.

World War II came and went, and still *Australopithecus* was scarcely recognized in the scientific world. This was partly because Dart was an anatomist and all but unknown to the paleoanthropological establishment, all of whose brightest stars were in the United States, England, France, and Germany; it was also partly because the brains of the South African fossil creatures just were not big enough to satisfy other scientists prejudiced by the Piltdown skull (see Chapter 10). Perhaps *Australopithecus* was simply an aberrant chimpanzee.

Further Discoveries at Sterkfontein

Meanwhile, fossil evidence continued to accumulate. In 1947, soon after the end of the war, Broom resumed working at Sterkfontein. One day a blast in some unpromising cave debris revealed the first of a series of important discoveries. When the smoke cleared, the upper half of a perfect skull (Figure 6–11) sparkled brilliantly in the sunlight. Lime crystals encrusting its inner surface caught and reflected the light like diamonds. The lower half of the skull lay embedded in a block of stone that had broken away. The glittering skull was believed to be that of an adult female. Her jaw protruded and her forehead was low, but to the trained eye there was an unmistakable quality of humanness about her. Her cranial capacity was 485 cubic centimeters (see Box 6–2). Her discovery was followed by other important finds (Figures 6–12 and 6–13): first, a male jaw with an intact canine tooth worn level with the other teeth, as human canines are, and then, in August 1947, a nearly perfect female pelvis. This was, after the skull, the most important discovery. There was no doubt that it had belonged to a creature that had walked and run upright, much as we do.

When Broom's Sterkfontein pelvis was reconstructed (Figure 6–14), it suggested a near-modern type of terrestrial bipedalism. Its short, broad iliac blades

---

Box 6-2

CHARACTERISTICS OF THE SOUTH AFRICAN AUSTRALOPITHECINAE[a]

TRAIT	*AUSTRALOPITHECUS AFRICANUS*	*PARANTHROPUS ROBUSTUS*
Height	F: 3.8 ft (115 cm) M: 4.5 ft (138 cm) (F is 83% of M)	F: 3.6 ft (110 cm) M: 4.3 ft (132 cm) (F is 83% of M)
Weight	F: 55–66 lb (25–30 kg) M: 90–132 lb (41–60 kg) (F about 54% of M)	F: 71–88 lb (32–40 kg) M: 88–176 lb (40–80 kg) (F about 60% of M)
Brain size (sexes combined)	454 cc mean (405–515 cc range)[b]	530 cc mean (range unknown)
Cranium	**Prognathic** face; lacks sagittal crest; low, flat forehead; low-vaulted braincase; lacks flexure (arching) of cranial base[c]	Face is wide, flattish, and "dished"; sagittal crest; low, flat forehead; low-vaulted braincase; some flexure (arching) of cranial base[c]
Dentition	Parabolic toothrow; short, incisor-like canines; no diastemata; lower P3s have two cusps; smaller grinding teeth than *P. robustus*	Parabolic toothrow; short, incisor-like canines; small anterior teeth; no diastemata; lower P3s have two or more cusps; very large grinding teeth
Diet	Mostly fruits and leaves; also, possibly grasses, sedges, some meat	Harder, tougher items than *A. africanus* (more nuts? gritty tubers?); some meat?
Limbs	Longer and larger arms and shorter legs than modern humans; apelike tibia; grasping big toes	Longer arms and shorter legs than modern humans; humanlike (non-grasping) big toes
Pelvis	Short, broad ilia; pelvic bowl nearly complete; short ischial shafts realigned in modern manner; pelvis wide between hip joints	Short, broad ilia; weak iliofemoral ligaments (?); shortening of ischial shaft (?); pelvis wide between hip joints
Locomotion	Bipedalism (probably primitive) and arboreal climbing	Bipedalism (more primitive than modern human walking?)
Known dates (million years B.P.)	3.5(?)–2.5	2.0–1.0

[a] Mean values for height, weight, and brain size are sometimes based on small samples and may change with additional fossil discoveries. For additional technical details and diagnostic traits, see Appendix III.

[b] The brain size of Sterkfontein fossil 505 is controversial. It is taken here as 515 cubic centimeters.

[c] A fully flexed (arched) cranial base suggests the presence of the throat anatomy that allows modern speech (see Chapter 13).

Prognathic having the lower face and jaws projecting in front of the upper parts of the face.

testified to a low center of gravity and formed a nearly complete pelvic bowl. Furthermore, the ischial shafts were relatively short and realigned with the ilia in a modern manner, while the anterior inferior iliac spines were enlarged. In all, the pelvis seemed to provide perfect confirmation of Dart's original claim: that *Australopithecus africanus* was an upright inhabitant of the South African savanna.

This interpretation of *A. africanus*, as an exclusively bipedal and terrestrial and rather humanlike species, held sway for half a century. Today, however, thanks to

FIGURE 6–11   This magnificent skull of *Australopithecus africanus* was found at Sterkfontein by Robert Broom in 1947. Although the teeth and jawbone are missing, the skull is otherwise complete and undistorted—a rare find. The photograph is approximately one-half actual size.

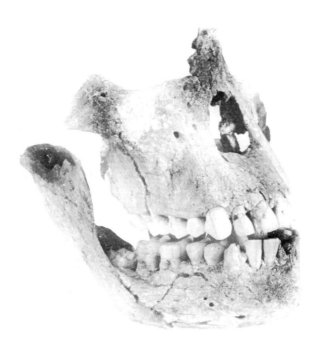

FIGURE 6–12   These beautifully preserved jaws were found at Sterkfontein by John Robinson, Broom's successor as curator at the Transvaal museum. This specimen has unusually large canine teeth for *Australopithecus africanus*.

FIGURE 6–13   The skeletal remains of *Australopithecus africanus* found by Robert Broom at Sterkfontein. These bones are believed to have belonged to a female, no more than 4 feet 3 inches (1.3 meters) tall. The pelvic bones were of exceptional importance in proving that *Australopithecus* was bipedal, as Dart had claimed in 1925. The photograph is approximately one-quarter actual size.

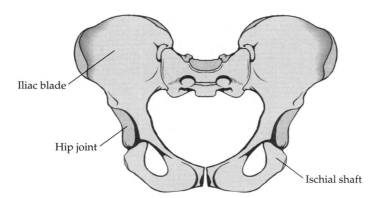

Iliac blade

Hip joint

Ischial shaft

FIGURE 6–14   The restored pelvic girdle of *Australopithecus africanus* from Sterkfontein. The wide pelvis has short, broad iliac blades; forwardly curved ilia producing a nearly complete pelvic bowl; and short ischial shafts that have been realigned in the modern manner. It is clearly the pelvis of a biped. Not drawn to scale.

new fossils from Sterkfontein, many paleoanthropologists think this view is probably too simplistic. First, in 1995 Ronald Clark and Phillip Tobias of the University of the Witwatersrand announced the discovery of four articulating (connecting to one another) foot bones from Sterkfontein that may be 3.5 million years old (Figure 6–15). Dubbed "Little Foot" and attributed to an early member of *Australopithecus africanus*, these bones show adaptations for bipedalism at the rear of the foot and the clear presence of an apelike, grasping big toe at the front. (It should be noted that although it is assigned to *A. africanus* here, the extreme age of Little Foot leaves open the possibility that it is from an older and more primitive species.) Second, a year later (1996) Lee Berger and Tobias described a 2.7-million-year-old *A. africanus* tibia (shin bone; see Figure 5–28) from Sterkfontein that shows evidence of apelike mobility at the knee joint. And third, in 1998 Henry McHenry and Berger described new postcranial fossils from Sterkfontein that suggest *A. africanus* may have had much larger forelimbs relative to the size of their hindlimbs than in modern humans—i.e., distinctly apelike body proportions. Together, the new fossils suggest to their South African discoverers that *A. africanus*, while bipedal, was also equipped for arboreal, climbing activities. In other words, this species probably was at home both on the ground

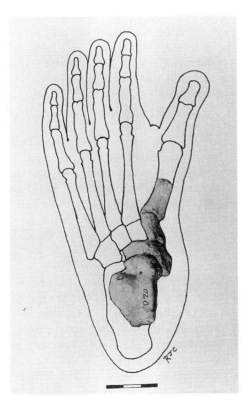

FIGURE 6–15   This drawing shows the reconstructed foot of *Australopithecus africanus* found at Sterkfontein. "Little Foot," as the fossil is called by its discoverers, displays adaptations for bipedalism at the rear of the foot and adaptations for climbing—primarily the grasping big toe—at the front. The fossil may be as much as 3.5 million years old. Figure is approximately one-half actual size.

(where it moved bipedally) and in the trees (where it used its opposable big toes for climbing). Interestingly, the 1996 paper also cited new evidence that in the distant past Sterkfontein may have been somewhat wooded, rather than strictly open grassland—an adjustment to the reconstructed habitat that agrees nicely with the new picture of *A. africanus* locomotion.

Finally, many of these details of locomotor anatomy may be verified by an exciting new fossil from Sterkfontein announced just as this book went to press. In December 1998, at a news conference in Johannesburg, Ronald Clarke described the discovery of a nearly complete *Australopithecus* skeleton from deep in the Sterkfontein cave. The skeleton represents the rest of the individual named Little Foot in 1995, and once it has been excavated and analyzed, it promises to reveal a wealth of new information about the biology and behavior of these early hominids. All of these new discoveries from Sterkfontein reflect the dynamic nature of paleoanthropological research.

Assessing *Australopithecus* and *Paranthropus*

These new discoveries are getting us ahead of our story, however, and it is important to remember that in the late 1940s, despite the australopithecines' humanlike traits, most scientists were still reluctant to admit them to the family Hominidae. This changed in 1950 thanks to the efforts of the British anatomist Wilfrid Le Gros Clark. By 1949, the remains of more than thirty gracile and robust individuals had been recovered from the South African caves, and Le Gros Clark, professor of anatomy at Oxford University, undertook an impartial, definitive study. He studied the South African fossils and compared them in every detail of shape and structure with a series of skulls and skeletons of modern apes. His verdict was unqualified:

> It is evident that in some respects they [the australopithecines] were definitely ape-like creatures, with small brains and large jaws. But in the details of the construction of the skull, in their dental morphology, and in their limb bones, the simian features are combined with a number of characters in which they differ from recent or fossil apes and at the same time approximate quite markedly to the *Hominidae*. All those who have had the opportunity of examining the original material are agreed on these hominid characters: the real issue to be decided is the question of their evolutionary and taxonomic significance.

By the mid-1950s, a total of five sites had yielded several dozens of individuals of both *Australopithecus africanus* and *Paranthropus robustus*. The growing fossil record confirmed Broom and his assistant, J. T. Robinson, in their certainty that they were dealing with two quite different creatures. Furthermore, another South African, C. K. Brain, had made detailed studies of the sediments at the various sites, and his findings had begun to produce more evidence of the relative age of the two types. The smaller, *A. africanus*, specimens were invariably more ancient, and at the site of Makapansgat, which Dart had excavated in 1947, they seemed to evolve toward somewhat larger forms. By contrast, the robust type was always of more recent date. It seemed that throughout its known existence it had evolved little, or not at all.

FOSSILS AND ARTIFACTS

Which, if either, of the two South African fossil types had led to humans still remained an unanswered question. If stone tools could be found associated with either type, some light might be shed on the matter.

Australopithecus at Makapansgat

At first, Dart and Broom were preoccupied with the fossils. The australopithecines were such ancient and controversial characters that for a number of years after their discovery the argument was less over whether they were or were not tool users than over whether they were or were not apes. In 1947, after eighteen years of concentrating on his work in anatomy at the University of Witwatersrand, Dart returned to the search for "dawn man." He analyzed thousands of fossilized animal bones associated with further remains of gracile *Australopithecus* that had been found in cave deposits 200 miles (320 kilometers) to the north of Sterkfontein, at Makapansgat (Figure 6–16). He called the collection an **osteodontokeratic culture** (meaning a culture of bone, tooth, and horn). His arguments, though ingenious, were not widely accepted. Today it seems clear that these extensive deposits were not of tools but of bones collected and gnawed by carnivores or, surprisingly, by porcupines (which are vegetarian rodents). The study of the origin and formation of assemblages of fossils such as these is termed **taphonomy**. It is, as we shall see, a branch of paleontology which has proved of immense value in understanding prehistoric environments and early hominid behavior (see Box 6–1).

Osteodontokeratic culture the culture of bone, tooth, and horn tools hypothesized by Raymond Dart for *A. africanus*; now largely dismissed.

Taphonomy scientific study of the conditions under which objects are preserved as fossils.

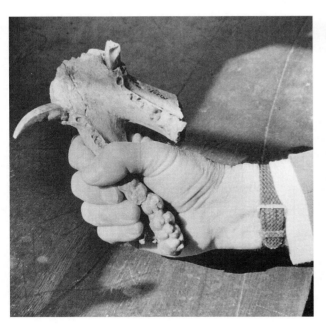 

FIGURE 6–16 Raymond Dart firmly believed that *Australopithecus africanus* used animal bones as a wide variety of tools. He demonstrated a pick (left) and a scraper (right).

Broom sought other clues, other cultural objects essential to hominid status. For years, he and his colleagues hunted for stone tools that might be associated with either the robust or the smaller, gracile hominids. For years they found none. Then, in 1953, two years after Broom's death, some simple pebble tools were discovered on a terrace in the Vaal valley, which had been formed during what was thought to be the same dry period in which the hominids had lived; the tools were fist-sized pieces of stone from which a few chips had been removed. At the time it seemed impossible to most archaeologists that they could have been made by the australopithecines, whose brains were no larger than that of a modern ape, and so the question of tools continued to haunt paleoanthropologists.

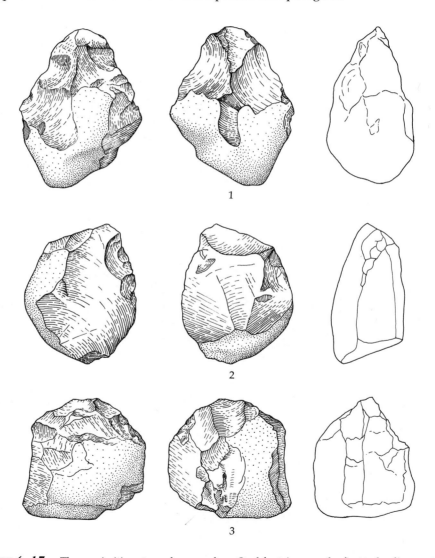

FIGURE 6–17 These primitive stone choppers from Sterkfontein were the first to be discovered in association with hominid remains in South Africa. Recent research has shown that they were associated not with *Australopithecus africanus*, but with *Homo habilis*, and are from a higher level of the cave deposits. *Homo habilis* is discussed in Chapter 8 and this type of simple stone tool is discussed in Chapter 9. The drawings are approximately 40 percent natural size.

Pebble Tools at Sterkfontein

But in 1957, once again new evidence was discovered. Working close by the cave at Sterkfontein that was yielding a gratifying supply of *A. africanus* remains, Broom's successor, J. T. Robinson, and an archaeologist, Revil Mason, dug into a layer of red-brown breccia and found several hominid teeth and nearly 300 pebble tools. To the untrained eye, the objects would have looked like naturally fractured stone, but close examination showed that chips had been flaked off two sides; the head of the stone was left round (Figure 6–17). A hammer stone held in the hand and guided by understanding had shaped the pebbles to cut, scrape, and crush. Not only their shape and the fact that they had been worked indicated that these were tools, but their location also did. The Sterkfontein cave is near the top of a hill where stones of that kind do not occur naturally, but such stones are common in the valley about half a mile (0.8 kilometers) away. Because stones do not climb hills unaided, they must have been carried to the site of the cave.

For many years the situation was extremely unclear. The breccia that had yielded the teeth and tools combination (a layer called Member 5; see Figure 6–18) was believed to be somewhat younger than that which had produced

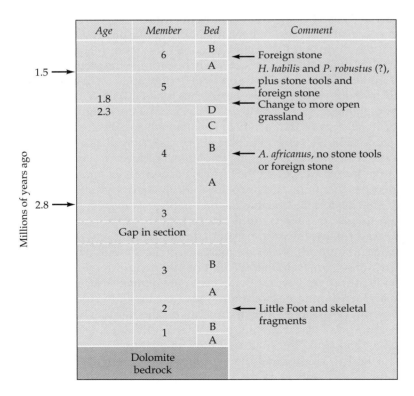

FIGURE 6–18   This diagram shows the various strata (identified as "members") at the Sterkfontein site. Note the extreme age of Member 2, which contained Little Foot. Most *Australopithecus africanus* fossils come from Member 4, while stone and bone tools, fossils of *Homo habilis*, and possibly the remains of *Paranthropus*, have been found in Member 5.

Sterkfontein's wealth of *A. africanus* remains. Furthermore, the Member 5 teeth were too few and too fragmentary to permit their assignment to a particular hominid species, and intriguingly, three of the teeth seemed quite robust (belonging to *Paranthropus*?). Since 1966, however, the mystery has cleared a little, thanks to the painstaking efforts of Phillip Tobias and Alun Hughes. Their work has established a recent age for Member 5 (now dated from between 1.8 and 1.5 million years ago; Figure 6–18), proving at least that the tools were not the work of *Australopithecus africanus*. Furthermore, Tobias and Hughes found, in addition to more stone tools, a fragmentary skull that is much more advanced than any australopithecine and that has been assigned to **Homo habilis** (see Chapter 8 for a full description of this hominine species). Thus it now seems quite certain that stone-tool-making hominids did not inhabit the Sterkfontein cave until almost a million years after the time of *A. africanus*. New dates suggest that the *Australopithecus*-bearing strata at Sterkfontein range from 3.5 (?) to 2.5 million years B.P., while the Member 5 deposits containing early *Homo*, stone tools (two bone fragments possibly used for digging were found as well), and, possibly, *Paranthropus*, date from around 1.8 to 1.5 million years ago.

Homo habilis one of the two *species* of "early Homo"; inhabited South and East Africa 2.0 to 1.6 million years ago, and perhaps as early as 2.3 million years ago.

ADDITIONAL FINDS AT SWARTKRANS

Robert Broom's early work on the hominids from Swartkrans has been continued by a succession of other researchers: first, John Robinson; then C. K. Brain (from the Transvaal Museum) and Elizabeth Vrba; and most recently, Randall Susman (from the State University of New York). Slowly but surely, the picture of hominid life at Swartkrans is taking shape. To begin with, it now appears that *Paranthropus robustus* lived in the Swartkrans area between 1.8 and 1.0 mya (note that this period overlaps the time range of Member 5 at Sterkfontein; see Figure 6–18). Second, the deposits at Swartkrans that produce *Paranthropus* fossils also consistently contain simple stone tools (flakes and pebble choppers), as well as a few bone fragments that may have been used as digging implements. Third, deposits dating around 1.0 mya *may* contain evidence—in the form of burned stones and bones—of extremely early fire use by hominids. (Many paleoanthropologists are skeptical about this evidence, preferring to conclude that the fires at Swartkrans were natural in origin and that even the *use* of such natural blazes by very early hominids has yet to be proved.) And finally, Swartkrans strata dating 1.8 to 1.5 mya have also produced the remains of a species of *Homo*—most researchers would say **Homo erectus**, but others are not so sure (see Chapter 10 for a full description of *H. erectus*). This last bit of evidence proves beyond doubt that *Paranthropus robustus* was contemporaneous with early hominines for quite some time in South Africa.

Homo erectus hominid *species* that inhabited much of the Old World between 1.9(?) million and at least 300,000 years B.P.; successor to "early *Homo*."

But what conclusions can we draw about the various hominid remains and artifacts found at Swartkrans? Of particular importance, which hominid species was making and using the stone and bone tools found there: *P. robustus* or *Homo erectus* (or both)? Traditionally, most paleoanthropologists have attributed the Swartkrans implements to *Homo*, but new analyses by SUNY's Randall Susman suggest that the old view may be in error. Susman has focused his attention primarily on the teeth and postcranial remains of *P. robustus* and his conclusions are quite interesting. First, judging by this species' massive teeth and jaws, there is still little doubt that we are dealing mainly with australopithecine vegetarians. The size of the teeth and the kind of wear that they exhibit make it clear that *P. robustus* ate mostly tough, hard to chew food items (nuts, roots, seeds), possibly supplemented by a bit of meat. Second, the foot bones of *Paranthropus* show that the big toe was incapable of apelike grasping—a finding that seems to rule out extensive arboreal climbing. Indeed, the entire foot is rather humanlike (with minor differences), suggesting a kind of terrestrial bipedalism not too different from our own. Third, according to Susman, the bones of the *P. robustus* hand reveal that this hominid had a fully opposable thumb and was capable of a precision grip. In other words, there is no anatomical reason why *Paranthropus robustus* could not have made and used simple tools—and Susman believes this is exactly what those creatures did. As his last point of proof, Susman notes that identifying *P. robustus* as the toolmaker is supported by the fact that there are twenty times as many individuals from that species represented at Swartkrans as there are *Homo* individuals. To him, it is more parsimonious to attribute the tools to the more populous species rather than to the minority type.

And so, in light of these new discoveries about the anatomical potential of *P. robustus*, we must recognize the very real possibility, or even likelihood, that this species was a tool user and possibly even a toolmaker. The wear on the Swartkrans bone tools suggests that they may have been used for digging, a finding that matches our ideas of the sorts of food *P. robustus* was seeking as part of its life on the ground. The stone flakes and choppers might have helped *Paranthropus* obtain and/or process both plant and animal foods (see Chapter 9), although more research is needed on this point. In any event, these new findings are fascinating, and although we may never know for sure whether *P. robustus* made and used tools, our knowledge of chimpanzee technology—combined with the growing body of information on australopithecine anatomy—make it clear that these early hominids had that potential, whether or not it was used and developed.

COMMENTS ON AUSTRALOPITHECINE PHYLOGENY

Thus far, we have said nothing about the possible evolutionary relationships between the South African australopithecines. There are some anatomical indications that *Australopithecus africanus* was ancestral to *Paranthropus robustus*, and such an arrangement agrees with the relative ages of the two species. Other bits of evidence, however, suggest that *A. africanus* was on the evolutionary line that led to hominines and was not ancestral to *Paranthropus*. For its part, *Paranthropus robustus*—along with its entire genus—seems to have gone extinct about a million years ago without leaving any descendants. Further evidence on this point, as well as additional details about the overall pattern of hominid evolution, will be presented in later chapters (see especially Figure 7–24).

SUMMARY

In 1924, Raymond Dart named a new primate genus and species—*Australopithecus africanus*—based on his study of a child's skull from Taung. Dart's claims, that the new species was bipedal and that it stood halfway between apes and humans, were dismissed by most of his colleagues. He did make one important convert, however, and that was Robert Broom, who immediately began to search the dolomite caves of the Transvaal and soon found more australopithecine remains, including those of a different species with massive teeth—*Paranthropus robustus*. In 1949, Wilfrid Le Gros Clark of Oxford University assessed the australopithecine finds, which by then included pelvic bones and other postcranial remains, and pronounced them hominid and bipedal.

In the three-quarters of a century since the australopithecines were first identified, extensive excavations in South Africa have established several facts (see Box 6–2). *Australopithecus africanus* was present in the region from about 3.5 to 2.5 million years B.P. This species was definitely bipedal when on the ground, but probably continued to engage in arboreal climbing as well. There are few, if any, indications that *A. africanus* was a toolmaker. The second type of South African australopithecine, *Paranthropus robustus*, has emerged as more habitually terrestrial than *A. africanus* and as a possible tool user and toolmaker. *P. robustus* apparently lived in the region from 2.0 to 1.0 mya. While *A. africanus* may have been ancestral to later, more modern hominids, it now seems certain that *Paranthropus robustus* was destined to become extinct without descendants.

POSTSCRIPT

How many genera of australopithecines inhabited southern Africa in the late Pliocene and the early Pleistocene? Could all of the South African fossils be accommodated within *Australopithecus*, or is a second genus—*Paranthropus*—needed for the robust forms? The question is not an easy one, and both options have loyal and vocal supporters. The basic issues are as follows.

When Raymond Dart and Robert Broom described and named their newly discovered hominids during the first half of this century, they followed a grand paleontological tradition of emphasizing the differences between fossils rather than their commonalities, and they created a plethora of new species and genus labels. The Taung child was christened *Australopithecus africanus*. Gracile fossils from Sterkfontein were first named *Australopithecus transvaalensis* and later *Plesianthropus transvaalensis*, while similar bones from Makapansgat became *Australopithecus prometheus*. The larger, big-toothed hominids from Kromdraai were called *Paranthropus robustus*, but equally robust specimens from Swartkrans were dubbed *Paranthropus crassidens*. By mid-century, at least three genera and five species of australopithecines had been suggested for southern Africa.

More recently, the original "splitting" of the South African fossils into numerous taxa has been countered by a trend toward "lumping" them into a minimal number of species and genera. Arguing that all of the South African australopithecines represent a single evolutionary grade of organization, and emphasizing the anatomical features they have in common, paleoanthropologists of the last few decades have tended to recognize only one genus (*Australopithecus*) and two species (*A. africanus* and *A. robustus*). Acknowledging diversity within unity, however, the two species were often described as representing a "gracile lineage" and a "robust lineage."

Within just the past few years, the argument for splitting the lineages into separate genera has been renewed with vigor. Much of this argument is based on the results of modern cladistic analyses that show, in the words of paleoanthropologist F. E. Grine, "that the 'robust' australopithecines [from both South and East Africa] form a monophyletic clade [indicating] the validity (and the necessity) of the generic name *Paranthropus*." (In this case, a monophyletic clade is a group of species marked by shared derived traits and containing only species more closely related to each other than to any species outside the clade.) Harvard professor emeritus of anthropology William Howells agrees with the revival of *Paranthropus*, noting that the anatomical differences between gracile and robust australopithecines at least equal those between living chimpanzees and gorillas, which are classified in separate genera (*Pan* and *Gorilla*). Numerous other authors, including British scientists Bernard Wood, Christopher Dean, and Christopher Stringer, and American researchers Leslie Aiello, B. Holly Smith, and Randall Susman, are also using the two-genus scheme.

We find the arguments convincing that the South and East African robusts form a monophyletic clade and that anatomically they are significantly different from the gracile forms, particularly in their facial features and enlarged postcanine teeth (see Appendix III). Therefore in this book we have adopted the two-genus classification for the australopithecines. But do we consider the matter settled? Not by a long shot. Most paleoanthropologists—particularly in the United States—still use (prefer?) the more conservative one-genus classification. One can only hope that additional fossil finds and new analyses will settle the issue definitively.

REVIEW QUESTIONS

1. In 1925, Raymond Dart claimed that *Australopithecus africanus* was an evolutionary link between apes and people. Why was his claim rejected by most of his anthropological and anatomical colleagues?
2. Describe the anatomical and behavioral differences between the two South African australopithecine genera, and between each one and modern humans.
3. Should the South African australopithecines be placed in a single genus or two genera? What are the arguments on each side of the question?
4. Traditionally, most anthropologists have concluded that the South African australopithecines did *not* make or use tools. Review the modern evidence, and evaluate the strength of that conclusion.

SUGGESTED FURTHER READING

Aiello, L., and C. Dean. *An Introduction to Human Evolutionary Anatomy*. Academic Press, 1990.

Broom, R. *Finding the Missing Link*. Watts, 1950.

Clarke, R. J., and P. V. Tobias. "Sterkfontein Member 2 Foot Bones of the Oldest South African Hominid." *Science*, 269, 1995.

Conroy, G. C. *Reconstructing Human Origins*. W. W. Norton, 1997.

Dart, R. *Adventures with the Missing Link*. Viking Press, 1959.

Grine, F. E. "Australopithecine Taxonomy and Phylogeny: Historical Background and Recent Interpretation," in R. L. Ciochon and J. G. Fleagle, eds., *The Human Evolution Source Book*, Prentice Hall, 1993.

Le Gros Clark, W. E. *The Antecedents of Man*. Edinburgh University Press, 1959.

———*Man-Apes or Ape-Man?* Holt, Rinehart & Winston, 1967.

Susman, R. L. "Fossil Evidence for Early Hominid Tool Use." *Science*, 265, 1994.

Tattersall, I. *The Fossil Trail*. Oxford University Press, 1995.

INTERNET RESOURCES

ORIGINS OF HUMANKIND
http://www.pro-am.com/origins
  (Information on australopithecine evolution and also new items on human origins.)

STERKFONTEIN CAVES
http://www.wits.ac.za/wits/fac/med/sterkf.html
  (Descriptions of several of the South African australopithecine discoveries.)

THE TALK.ORIGINS ARCHIVE: FOSSIL HOMINIDS
http://www.talkorigins.org/faqs/fossil-hominids.html
  (Discussions of australopithecine and other hominid fossils, particularly from an evolution vs. creationism perspective.)

USEFUL SEARCH TERMS:
  australopithecines
  Australopithecus africanus
  Paranthropus (or Australopithecus) robustus
  Raymond Dart
  South African fossil hominids

Chapter 6 Timeline

HOLOCENE	YEARS A.D.	DISCOVERIES
10,000	1998 — 1995 —	*Australopithecus* skeleton found at Sterkfontein Little Foot discovered at Sterkfontein
CENOZOIC	1988 —	Susman's assessment of *Paranthropus robustus*
	1977 —	Vrba starts work at Kromdraai
Proconsul		
Apidium, Parapithecus, Aegyptopithecus, and Propliopithecus	1966 — 1965 —	Tobias starts work at Sterkfontein Brain starts work at Swartkrans
Amphipithecus	1957 —	Robinson and Mason find tools at Sterkfontein
Eosimias	1950 — 1948 — 1947 —	Definitive assessments by Le Gros Clark published *Paranthropus* found at Swartkrans *Australopithecus africanus* skull and pelvis found at Sterkfontein; Dart discovers *Australopithecus* at Makapansgat
Early prosimians	1938 — 1936 —	*Paranthropus robustus* discovered by Broom at Kromdraai Broom's first adult *Australopithecus* found at Sterkfontein
65 million	1925 — 1924 —	Dart's publication on *Australopithecus africanus* Dart discovers *Australopithecus africanus* from Taung

	YEARS B.P.	FOSSIL RECORD	
		· ·	Later *Homo* species ·
	Pleistocene ◆		*Homo erectus/ergaster* ·
	2 million —	*Paranthropus robustus* at Kromdraai and Swartkrans with *Homo*	*Homo* and *Paranthropus robustus*
MESOZOIC	Pliocene ◆	*Australopithecus africanus* at Sterkfontein and Makapansgat	*Australopithecus africanus*
	5 million —	? Origin of bipedalism	
		· ·	· ·
First mammals	Miocene ◆		Ancient apes
		Sivapithecus in Europe and in Asia	
	10 million —		
225 million			
PALEOZOIC	15 million —	*Kenyapithecus* in Africa	

THE TRANSVAAL HOMINIDS

The history of discoveries in South Africa is a fascinating story still unfolding (top right). The age of the fossils (bottom right) is still a matter of some uncertainty, although luminescence dating and other procedures have clarified the situation a good deal.

EAST AFRICA:
THE AUSTRALOPITHECINE FOSSILS

Mary and Louis Leakey were a productive paleoanthropological team for many decades in East Africa.

Ex *Africa semper aliquid novi. ("Africa always has something new.")*
PLINY THE ELDER, 23–79. *Natural History*, Book VIII.

OVERVIEW

Hominid fossils have been discovered not only in South Africa, but at numerous locations in East, Northeast, and North-Central Africa as well. Sites centered on the Rift Valley have produced the remains of three australopithecine genera (*Ardipithecus, Australopithecus,* and *Paranthropus*) and six species. Although specialists disagree somewhat on species and genus names and the assignment of particular fossils, the following list of australopithecines from the **Plio-Pleistocene** of East Africa (broadly defined) seems reasonable: *Ardipithecus ramidus* (possibly the oldest biped); *Australopithecus anamensis*; *Australopithecus afarensis* (including the "Lucy" fossil); *Australopithecus bahrelghazali* (a new and provisional species from Chad); *Paranthropus aethiopicus* (the oldest member of the robust lineage); and *Paranthropus boisei*. (See also the announcement of yet another australopithecine species at the end of this chapter.) All of the australopithecines appear to have walked upright, but with their ape-sized brains, they almost certainly lacked speech and language. Questions about australopithecine material culture remain open, although there is no conclusive evidence for tool use or toolmaking by these hominids in East Africa. A consensus reconstruction of australopithecine phylogeny suggests that *Ardipithecus* may have given rise to *Australopithecus*; *Australopithecus*, in turn, gave rise to both *Homo* and *Paranthropus* (specialists disagree about the exact ancestor-descendant relationships in both cases); and *Paranthropus* then went extinct without descendants some 1.0 million years ago. Important topics in Chapter 7 include the various australopithecine species and

Plio-Pleistocene a combination of the last two epochs of the Cenozoic era; the *Pliocene* lasted from 5 to 1.6 million years B.P. and the *Pleistocene* from 1.6 million to 10,000 years B.P.

 Mini-Timeline

DATE OR AGE	FOSSIL DISCOVERIES OR EVOLUTIONARY EVENTS
(A) DATE (YEARS A.D.)	
1995	*Australopithecus anamensis* and *Aust. bahrelghazali* discovered
1994	*Ardipithecus ramidus* announced (originally, *Australopithecus*)
1978	*Australopithecus afarensis* announced
1968	*Paranthropus aethiopicus* named (originally, *Australopithecus*)
1959	*Paranthropus boisei* discovered at Olduvai Gorge (originally named *Zinjanthropus*)
(B) AGE (MILLION YEARS B.P.)	
2.3–1.3	*P. boisei* inhabits East Africa
2.7–2.3	*P. aethiopicus* inhabits East Africa
3.5–3.0	*A. bahrelghazali* inhabits North-Central Africa
4.2–2.5	*A. afarensis* inhabits East Africa
4.2–3.9	*A. anamensis* inhabits East Africa
4.4	*Ardipithecus ramidus* inhabits Northeast Africa
5.6	Lothagam fossil (oldest known hominid remains)

their characteristics; the first fossil evidence of habitual bipedalism; the selection pressures (including habitat type) that resulted in bipedalism; problems involved in the recognition and naming of extinct species; the varying lifestyles of the australopithecines; and the ancestor-descendant relationships binding the australopithecines to one another and to the genus *Homo*.

SEPARATING AUSTRALOPITHECINES AND HOMININES IN EAST AFRICA

As detailed in Chapter 6, the Plio-Pleistocene hominids from South Africa can be neatly arranged into just a few species: two australopithecines, *Australopithecus africanus* and *Paranthropus robustus*; and two hominines, *Homo habilis* and (probably) *Homo erectus*. In comparison, the fossil hominids from East Africa (including here the recent discoveries from Chad in the North-Central part of the continent) are overwhelming in their species diversity. In all, East Africa may have yielded the remains of as many as six australopithecine species representing three genera (but see the end of the chapter), and four species of pre-*sapiens* hominines. Given this diversity, we will use this chapter to describe first the australopithecine material, reserving the East African hominines for Chapter 8. Within each hominid subfamily, in accordance with our historical approach to the story of human origins, the

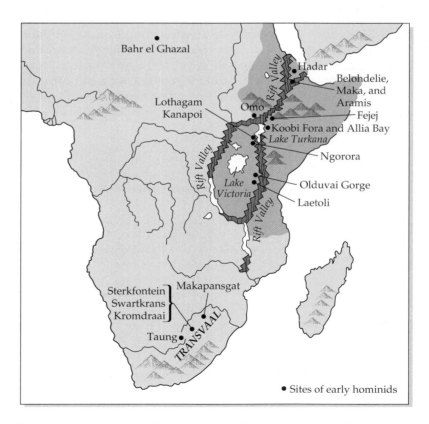

FIGURE 7–1   Southern, Eastern, and North-Central Africa, showing some of the many sites in which australopithecine fossils have been discovered.

various species will be presented initially in the chronological order of their discovery. The probable evolutionary relationships among the East African hominid species, including those between the subfamilies, will be discussed at the end of this and the following chapter.

DISCOVERIES AT OLDUVAI

The questions that archaeologists were trying to answer in South Africa's Transvaal—whether the early hominids made tools and where the first stone tool industries occurred—brought the attention of anthropologists to another part of the continent. During the 1950s, distinguished archaeologists Louis Leakey (1903–1972) and Mary Leakey (1913–1996) were finding the remains of an extensive pebble-tool industry 2,000 miles (3,200 kilometers) north of the Transvaal grasslands in a dry river canyon in northern Tanzania (Figure 7–1). That canyon, called Olduvai Gorge, was destined to play a major role in our knowledge of humankind's evolution.

Olduvai Gorge is an abrupt rent in the earth, some 25 miles (40 kilometers) long and 300 feet (90 meters) deep. Like a miniature Grand Canyon, its sides display different strata laid bare by the cutting of an ancient river (Figure 7–2). A German entomologist named Wilhelm Kattwinkel found the gorge in 1911 when he almost fell into its depths as he broke through some bush on the edge. A hasty exploration showed the place to be a rich source of animal fossils. Some of the fossils that Kattwinkel took back to Berlin were so unusual that an expedition, headed by Hans Reck, was sent out in 1913 to explore further. Its investigations were ended by World War I, and after the war Reck was unable to raise funds to resume operations.

FIGURE 7–2   Olduvai Gorge is a remarkable landform as well as a fossil gold mine. In this photograph the layers of sedimentary rock are obvious.

Eventually he wrote to Louis Leakey, then the young curator of the Coryndon Memorial Museum at Nairobi, Kenya, urging him to take over, but Leakey had to wait until 1931 before he could raise the money for an expedition to Olduvai.

One season spent exploring the gorge was enough to convince Leakey that Olduvai was a site "such as no other in the world." He found pebble tools in his first year there, long before they were discovered in South Africa, and no doubt he wondered if they could have been made by a creature similar to *Australopithecus*. For years, Leakey searched the clearly stacked strata of the gorge in vain, unable to find the maker of the tools. As money and transport permitted, Leakey returned to the gorge, along with his wife Mary and their sons. From each of the four principal beds that overlie one another from the river bottom to the surface of the plain some 300 feet (90 meters) above, the Leakeys eventually recovered an enormous number of animal fossils. They identified and classified more than a hundred species, most of them extinct and some unknown to science until the Leakeys discovered them.

FIGURE 7–3   A distinguished archaeologist, Mary Leakey worked at numerous African sites, including Olduvai and Laetoli, until her retirement in 1984.

FIGURE 7–4 Louis Leakey was somewhat eccentric, and a passionate, brilliant man. Here he is examining some of his important and numerous discoveries with his son, Richard.

Discovery of *Paranthropus boisei* (1959)

For twenty-eight years the Leakeys (Figures 7–3 and 7–4) were engaged in one of the most persistent and unrewarding efforts in the history of anthropology. Olduvai was far from the museum at Nairobi where Louis Leakey worked, and they could seldom spend more than a few weeks a year at the gorge. The trip was expensive, and in the early years it took several days to get to Olduvai on the very rough road from Nairobi. The gorge was stiflingly hot, and water had to be hauled from a spring 35 miles (55 kilometers) away. It was not until the 1950s that the Leakeys were able to begin extensive excavation at Olduvai, and until July 17, 1959, all they knew was that they were the possessors of a small collection of what they believed to be the oldest implements ever seen, collectively called the **Oldowan tool industry**.

On July 17, Louis Leakey awakened with a fever and a headache. His wife insisted that he remain in camp. But the work season was drawing to an end, and the day could not be lost, so Mary Leakey drove to the point where the party was working. As she walked slowly along the hillside of Bed I, the lowest layer of the gorge, a piece of bone exposed by recent erosion caught her eye. She recognized it as a piece of skull. Searching higher along the slope, she suddenly saw two big teeth, brown-black and almost iridescent, just appearing from the eroding hill. She marked the spot with a small piece of stone and sped back to camp.

Louis heard the car racing up the road and sprang up in alarm, thinking that his wife had been bitten by a snake. But as the car stopped, he heard Mary shout, "I've got him!" The "him," she felt sure, was a hominid fossil—the early human they had been seeking for so many years. Louis's fever and headache forgotten, he jumped in the car, and the couple drove back as fast as they could.

Oldowan tool industry earliest known stone-tool culture, dating 2.5 million years into the past and first made by early *Homo*. The products were very crude stone *choppers* and *flakes*.

The Leakeys went to work with camel's hair brushes and dental picks. The palate to which the teeth were affixed came into view, and then fragments of a skull emerged. In order not to lose a single precious scrap, the couple removed and sieved tons of scree (fine rock debris) from the slope below the find. At the end of nineteen days they had about 400 fragments.

While undertaking the delicate task of assembling the bits and pieces, the Leakeys continued to excavate the site. Not only had they discovered the oldest hominid skull found to that time in eastern and central Africa, but they had also unearthed what appeared to be a campsite of this ancient creature. Scattered on what had been the margins of an ancient lake were many tools made of flaked stone and pebbles, along with waste chips. Lying about, too, were the fossil bones of animals: complete remains of rats, mice, frogs, lizards, birds, snakes, tortoises, and some young pigs, and parts of small antelopes. But there were no remains of large animals. Nearly all these bones were broken, but the near-human skull and tibia and fibula (the two bones of the lower part of the leg) that appeared at the same site were not. It seemed to the Leakeys that the hominid had killed the other animals.

Sagittal suture the line of union joining the two main side bones of the braincase.

The skull that took shape from the fragments uncovered at the campsite was that of a nearly mature male (Figure 7–5). That the wisdom teeth were unworn and that the suture joining the two halves of the skull, the **sagittal suture**, had not yet closed indicated that it was a young adult. In brain size and in general appearance, the young male broadly resembled *Paranthropus robustus* of the south. The molars were extraordinarily large and heavy, but detailed study confirmed that they were, in their structure, undoubtedly hominid teeth. The skull had the characteristic massive face and teeth and rugged low cranium of *P. robustus* but was even larger and more specialized. These differences led Louis Leakey to set up a new genus for what he believed was the earliest tool user, and he named it ***Zinjanthropus boisei***. (*Zinj* means "Eastern Africa" in Arabic; *boisei* honored Charles Boise, who had helped to finance the Leakeys' search for early humans.) Today the skull is classified as ***Paranthropus boisei***. The skull is so much more heavily built than that of *P. robustus* that it is often described as *superrobust*.

Zinjanthropus boisei original name for the australopithecine *species* now called *Paranthropus boisei*.

Paranthropus boisei robust australopithecine *species* that lived in East Africa 2.3 to 1.3 million years ago; also known as *Australopithecus boisei*.

Age of *P. boisei*

Fortunately, the approximate age of the Leakeys' fossil could be determined because it had been found sandwiched between layers of volcanic ash. Geologists extracted minerals containing potassium from the volcanic ash covering *P. boisei* and also from an older volcanic bed that underlaid the site. When they analyzed these layers by the then-new method of potassium-argon dating, they were able to fix the startling age of about 1.75 million years, an age repeatedly confirmed by later potassium-argon tests. This dating of the fossil was extraordinary in itself, and it also had a valuable side effect: suddenly, Broom's original claim of an age of 2 million years for the early South African hominid *Australopithecus africanus* changed from being a wild guess to being an inspired deduction.

But several important questions remained unanswered, despite firm information about the antiquity of the *P. boisei* fossils from Olduvai. Chief among those questions was whether or not *Paranthropus* was responsible for the Bed I flake and chopper tools. Initially, the Leakeys thought that was probably the case, but later changed their minds following the recovery of hominine remains ("early *Homo*"; see Chapter 8) from the same rock layer. Today, most paleoanthropologists agree with the Leakeys' second thoughts and attribute the Bed I tools to hominines with

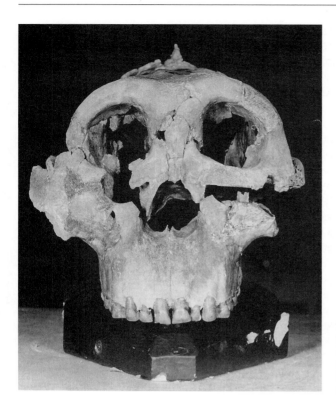

FIGURE 7–5   *Zinjanthropus*, the immense skull found by Mary Leakey at Olduvai in 1959. It is now classified as *Paranthropus boisei*. This photograph is approximately 45 percent actual size.

larger brains than that of *Paranthropus* (more on this in a later section). Nonetheless, if Randall Susman is proved right that *P. robustus* made the stone tools at Swartkrans (Chapter 6), it will be difficult to argue that *P. boisei* completely lacked the wherewithal to make and use similar implements. This issue of precisely who did, and who did not, make the first stone tools continues to dog paleoanthropologists working in Africa. It is hoped that further research will clarify the situation.

In any event, by the mid-1960s the hominid fossil record in Africa was already becoming complex. South Africa had produced the remains of two genera of australopithecines—*Australopithecus* and *Paranthropus*—as well as fossils of early hominines. For its part, East Africa had yielded evidence of *Paranthropus* coexisting with "early *Homo*" fully 1.75 million years ago. And somebody, or several fossil somebodies, in both parts of the continent had made those ancient stone tools. One mystery after another. It was time to break new ground in search of new evidence.

THE SEARCH MOVES NORTH INTO KENYA AND ETHIOPIA

The only ways to clear up the mystery were to find more fossils, to date more precisely the ones that had been unearthed, and to dig deeper into time. Toward those ends, an ambitious international expedition was organized in 1967 to look for hominid remains in Ethiopia. The expedition was under the direction of Yves Coppens and Camille Arambourg from France and the American anthropologist

F. Clark Howell. Its destination was a remote spot in the southern part of the valley of the Omo River, just north of Lake Turkana (Figures 7–1 and 7–6). Though one of the most desolate places anywhere south of the Sahara and one of the hottest, the area had several attractions. For one thing, it had been visited thirty-five years before by Arambourg, who had found it rich in animal fossils. For another, it bore a striking resemblance to Olduvai. It, too, is part of the Rift Valley geological complex, a giant crack in the earth that, running north and south through Africa, once was marked by chains of lakes and rivers and now is edged by towering escarpments. Much of the Rift Valley is dry now; its lakes are shrunken, some of its cliffs worn away, and its stones baked in the sun. There is no river at all today in Olduvai Gorge, except during flash floods, although the gorge was made by a river. At Omo, as at Olduvai, deep-cut riverbeds speak of ancient days and long-vanished landscapes. The Omo River still runs down from the Ethiopian highlands and empties into Lake Turkana, just over the border in northern Kenya. Lake Turkana itself has grown and shrunk twice at least in the past 4 million years. Today it is still a sizable lake 185 miles (300 kilometers) long. The brutal, arid lands around it are largely unexplored.

The Rift Valley is an unstable area on the earth's surface where the earth's crust is still moving. It has long been a center of volcanic activity and is pockmarked by cones and craters. Because of neighboring volcanic activity, Olduvai has invaluable layers of datable volcanic ash; so does Omo. Both places supported more life in the past than they do now. Laced with rivers, much greener, carrying a far larger animal population than they do today, each provided the lush water-edge environments, gallery forests, and woodland savannas, that the early hominids are believed to have preferred.

But Omo is also different from Olduvai, and the differences are what made it particularly appealing to the 1967 expedition. At Olduvai, the most accurate and useful pages of the volcanic timetable are crowded into an 800,000-year period that is not quite 2 million years old and are contained in layers not totalling much more

FIGURE 7–6   This aerial view of the Omo Valley in southern Ethiopia shows uplifted fossil-bearing deposits of the Shungura formation. The harder layers of rock are the datable volcanic tuffs.

than 100 feet (30 meters) thick (see Figure 5–3 and Table 9–1). At Omo the strata being investigated are more than 2,000 feet (600 meters) thick and span a far longer period of time. Moreover, they contain a great many layers of volcanic ash at varying intervals, some of them only 100,000 years apart, some more widely spaced, and each datable by chronometric methods. Together, scientists can use these layers of ash to step backward into time and into the earth, determining an approximate date at each step.

One does not have to dig at Omo to go deeper into time. The strata have been heaved up in the past and now lie at an angle to the earth's surface. One need only walk along to find successively older layers revealing themselves.

The Omo story begins a little over 4 million years ago and continues to about 1.5 million years B.P. This date conveniently overlaps with the fossil deposits at Olduvai, which begin about 1.9 million years B.P., so that the two sites, between them, give us an almost unbroken story for 4 million years.

Omo Hominids (1967–1974)

In this area of great promise, Arambourg, with Coppens, picked the spot he had worked before and knew to be productive. A second group, under Clark Howell's direction, went a short distance up the Omo River to tap a previously unexplored area. A third group, headed by the Leakeys' son Richard, picked another untapped spot, farther north and across the river from Howell. As it turned out, Richard Leakey's choice was the only one that proved somewhat unfruitful. He found plenty of fossil material there, but the strata were not old enough to be of interest to the expedition. He decided to dissociate himself from the project and returned home to Kenya to do some prospecting.

The other members of the expedition persevered where they were. Immediately they began recovering extinct animal fossils of extraordinary richness and variety. The great number of dated layers at Omo made it possible to trace the evolutionary changes that had taken place in some eighty species of mammals: six genera and eight species of extinct pigs laid their secrets bare in the strata; twenty-two kinds of antelope were discovered; and several extinct saber-toothed cats. Altogether, more than 150 species of fossil animals were found at Omo. These discoveries were so varied and told such a clear story that matching fossils from other places with those from Omo became a distinct possibility (faunal correlation; see Appendix II).

In addition to all the useful animal fossils found at Omo, traces of hominids began to appear. The French group first found a robust jaw that they felt was sufficiently different from known material to warrant a new name: ***Australopithecus aethiopicus***. Both parties found teeth, eventually more than 200 of them; then came other jaw fragments, parts of two skulls, and several arm and leg bones. It was a spectacular haul and an enormously significant one, for several reasons. First is the age of the oldest specimens, more than twenty teeth: 3.0 million years. These ancient teeth are almost certainly those of a small gracile australopithecine whose identity was not clarified until years later (see section on *A. afarensis*). Also of significance was the fact that remains of this small hominid were found along with superrobust fossils similar to, but much older than, *P. boisei* found at Olduvai. Furthermore, robust specimens continued to turn up in various layers, dating right up to 1.5 million years ago. *P. boisei* apparently lived at Omo for almost a million years.

Australopithecus aethiopicus original name for the robust australopithecine *species* now called *Paranthropus aethiopicus*.

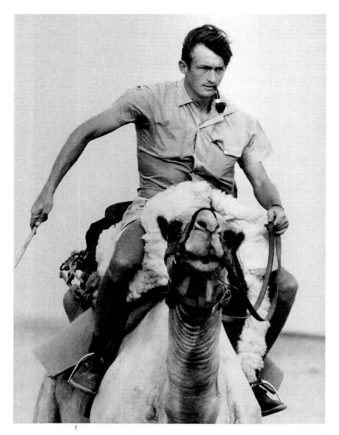

FIGURE 7–7 Richard Leakey's team had astounding success in finding fossil hominids in the desert regions east of Lake Turkana in Kenya.

Robust Hominids at Koobi Fora (1969–1976)

Meanwhile, Richard Leakey flew south in a helicopter, across the border into Kenya and along the eastern shore of Lake Turkana, previously called Lake Rudolf (Figures 7–1 and 7–7). Here, Leakey spotted some likely sites from the air and landed to find what has turned out to be one of the richest mines of hominid fossils in the world.

The results of work near Lake Turkana carried out by a large group of scientists directed by Richard Leakey and Glynn Isaac (1937–1985) of the University of California at Berkeley were sensational. At the sites east of the lake, named Ileret and Koobi Fora, they discovered three superb skulls, more than two dozen mandibles or parts of mandibles, some arm- and leg-bone fragments, and isolated teeth, amounting to more than 100 specimens in all. Much of this material is of the superrobust *P. boisei* type and dates from about 2 to 1.3 million years ago (Figure 7–8). When these East Turkana fossils are combined with the Omo finds, there is enough material in the way of young and old individuals, both males and females, and enough variation in dentition, for the outlines of a variable population of the superrobust *Paranthropus boisei* to begin to reveal itself.

Having a population to study instead of an individual fossil is extremely important. No two people today are exactly alike; no two australopithecines were, either. For that reason, drawing conclusions from a single fossil is risky.

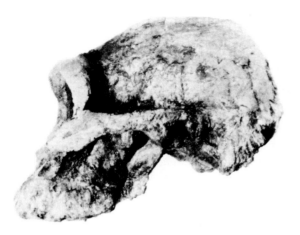

FIGURE 7-8 This skull (museum number KNM-ER 406) of *Paranthropus boisei*, found by Richard Leakey at Koobi Fora, is similar in many ways to that found by his mother at Olduvai (Figure 7–5). This photograph is approximately 30 percent actual size.

Measurements can be taken of a single fossil, and theories can be built up as a result of those measurements, but this information may be misleading because the fossil may not be typical. Only when a large number of specimens is available can variations be taken into account (Box 7–1). If visitors from outer space were to describe and name *Homo sapiens* by examining one skeleton—for example, that of a short, heavy-boned Eskimo—they certainly might be excused if they thought they had another species when they discovered a second skeleton, of a 6.5 feet (2 meters), slender-boned Watusi tribesman from central Africa.

That is why the *P. boisei* population that is emerging is so valuable. It begins to indicate some of the limits of variability beyond which no members of the species went. Any creature that does exceed those limits significantly can be presumed to be something else. And those limits are now well enough defined to make it quite clear that the gracile *Australopithecus* specimens *are* something else; doubt about the distinctiveness of the two lineages has now evaporated.

P. boisei, on the other hand, is quite similar to the robust types of South Africa, which also exist in sufficient numbers to constitute a variable population with limits of its own. Like *P. robustus* (Figure 6–9), *P. boisei* had a bony crest along the top of its skull, but its crest is more pronounced, for the anchoring of even bigger muscles to work a more massive jaw containing larger molars. This complex of features indicates a life adapted to eating large amounts of coarse, tough vegetable matter. It is the same adaptation as *P. robustus*, but larger and more highly evolved (Box 7–2).

Because on further analysis the known differences between *P. robustus* and *P. boisei* have proved to be almost entirely differences in size (particularly tooth size), some workers today consider both groups to be geographical subspecies of the single species *P. robustus*. Whether the remains in fact represent one or two distinct contemporary biological species is something that can be finally determined only when a great deal more fossil evidence is available. For our discussion, it is convenient to continue to distinguish them as separate species.

Box 7-1

DETERMINING THE CHARACTERISTICS OF A PREVIOUSLY UNKNOWN FOSSIL SPECIES

Drawing conclusions about extinct species from their fossil remains is a tricky business. Individual specimens are sure to vary and it is rare indeed for a single fossil to display the full suite of traits typical of its species. Furthermore, each species' set of defining parameters is actually a mix of discrete characteristics (e.g., its dental formula or the presence of a toothcomb) and characteristics that are continuous in their distribution (e.g., body weight, brain size, enamel thickness). While a species' set of discrete diagnostic traits may be made clear by only a few fossil specimens, establishing mean values and ranges for continuous traits obviously requires the recovery of a sample population. The following example uses the continuous trait of cranial capacity in an imaginary species of apes to show how calculated parameters change as a population of fossil specimens grows. Note the fluctuations in mean brain size and range of cranial volume as additional skulls are added to the set of known fossils.

A. THE FOSSILS:

From left to right, skulls are shown in the order of their discovery and with their brain sizes in cubic centimeters (drawings after Le Gros Clark, *The Antecedents of Man*, Edinburgh University Press, 1959).

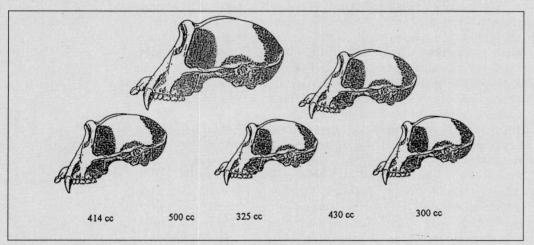

414 cc   500 cc   325 cc   430 cc   300 cc

B. SAMPLE POPULATIONS AND CALCULATIONS OF BRAIN SIZE:

SPECIMENS IN SAMPLE	MEAN CRANIAL CAPACITY	CHANGE VS. PREVIOUS MEAN
Skull 1	414 cc (range incalculable)	—
Skulls 1 & 2	457 cc (range 414–500 cc)	+ 10.4%
Skulls 1–3	413 cc (range 325–500 cc)	– 9.6%
Skulls 1–4	417 cc (range 325–500 cc)	+ 1.0%
Skulls 1–5	394 cc (range 300–500 cc)	– 5.5%

Note: Lest this made-up example seem unrealistic in the small size of its specimen population, compare the numbers of adult skulls with measurable cranial capacities known in 1996 from the South African australopithecines: A*ustralopithecus africanus,* 11; *Paranthropus robustus,* 8 (data from Wolpoff, 1996). Small sample size remains a problem for virtually all extinct hominid species and each new discovery has the potential to alter previous lists of defining characteristics.

Box 7-2		

CHARACTERISTICS OF THE EAST AFRICAN ROBUST AUSTRALOPITHECINAE[a]

TRAIT	*PARANTHROPUS BOISEI*	*PARANTHROPUS AETHIOPICUS*
Height	F: 4.1 ft (124 cm) M: 4.5 ft (137 cm) (F is 90% of M)	Unknown
Weight	F: 75–88 lb (34–40 kg) M: 108–176 lb (49–80 kg) (F is 57% of M)	Unknown
Brain size (sexes combined)	487 cc mean (410–530 cc range)	410 cc mean (range unknown)
Cranium	Tall, broad, "dished" face; sagittal crest; low forehead; low-vaulted braincase; some flexure of cranial base	"Dished" face; sagittal crest; low forehead; low-vaulted braincase (compared to *P. boisei*: unflexed cranial base; shallow jaw joint; extreme facial prognathism; parietal bones flared strongly at the mastoid)
Dentition	Parabolic toothrow; small incisors and canines; huge grinding teeth; lower P3s often have 3+ cusps	Grinding teeth appear to be as large as those of *P. boisei*
Diet	Hard, tough, fibrous vegetable foods; some meat	Unknown
Limbs	Longer arms and shorter legs than modern humans	Unknown
Pelvis	Short, broad ilia; short ischial shafts (?); pelvis wide between hip joints	Unknown
Locomotion	Bipedalism (primitive?)	Bipedalism (assumed)
Known dates (million years B.P.)	2.3–1.3	2.7–2.3

[a]Mean values, or range of values, for anatomical measurements may change with additional fossil discoveries. For additional technical details and diagnostic traits, see Appendix III.

A New Robust Australopithecine from West Turkana (1985)

In 1985 the number of robust australopithecine species increased by one because of discoveries made at the sites of Lomekwi and Kangatukuseo on the west side of Lake Turkana. From deposits dating about 2.6 million years of age, the excavating team, headed by Alan Walker and Richard Leakey, recovered a nearly toothless cranium (museum catalog number KNM-WT 17000, dubbed the Black Skull because of its coloration) and a partial mandible. Although much larger, the mandible is otherwise similar to a jaw found years earlier by French scientists at

Omo and named *Australopithecus aethiopicus*. The west Turkana cranium is massively built and quite prognathic (Figure 7–9). It features a low forehead and a small braincase (410 cc) and is topped by a sagittal crest that would have anchored large jaw muscles. The zygomatic arches flare widely to the side, and the face is somewhat "dished" (concave) in appearance. The few measurable teeth and tooth roots indicate that the grinding teeth were as large as those of *Paranthropus boisei*.

Naming the west Turkana skull and jaw has proved difficult. In many ways the fossils resemble *P. boisei*, and indeed, many paleoanthropologists view them as early remains of that species. But in other ways, such as the Black Skull's facial prognathism, its unflexed cranial base, and particulars of the jaw joint, the material differs from other robust forms (see Appendix III) while resembling the early gracile species *Australopithecus afarensis* (to be discussed shortly). Despite its similarities to *A. afarensis*, however, most workers agree that the west Turkana skull and jaw belong within the robust clade. Following the arguments given at the end of

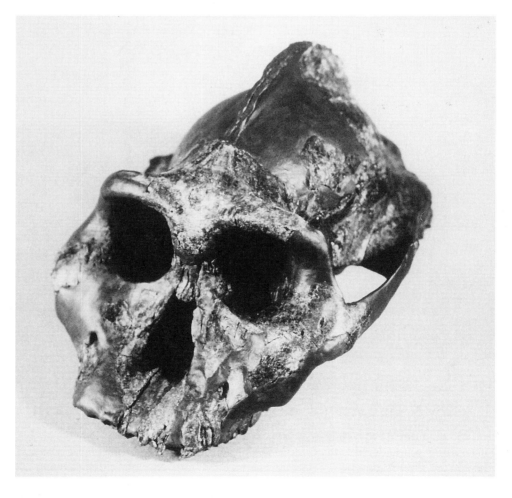

FIGURE 7–9   The Black Skull (museum number KNM-WT 17000) represents a new variety of australopithecine, *Paranthropus aethiopicus*. Although a member of the robust australopithecine clade, it resembles *Australopithecus afarensis* in several traits. Photograph is about 60 percent actual size.

Chapter 6, we agree with F. E. Grine, Bernard Wood, and others in classifying these fossils as a new species, ***Paranthropus aethiopicus***—a third variety of robust australopithecine (see Box 7–2). The *A. aethiopicus* jaw discovered earlier at Omo is also included here and thus renamed *Paranthropus*.

Paranthropus aethiopicus robust australopithecine *species* that inhabited East Africa 2.7 to 2.3 mya.

Obviously, the limited fossil material known to date allows only an incomplete picture of *Paranthropus aethiopicus*. Many more specimens, especially of the post-cranial skeleton, must be described for us to understand the species' adaptations, including its diet and locomotion. Interestingly, some new information about *P. aethiopicus* has been gained recently, not from new field work but rather from the continuing analysis of fossils (mainly teeth) collected in the 1960s and 1970s by Clark Howell's Omo team. (The fact that fossils recovered up to thirty years ago are just now being described shows how much longer laboratory analysis often takes compared to field collection.) First, the dental remains from Omo extend the time range for *P. aethiopicus* an additional 100,000 years into the past, back to 2.7 mya. *P. aethiopicus* was in residence at Omo until about 2.3 million years ago, by which time it had apparently given rise to *P. boisei*. Second, and importantly, comparisons of the teeth of *Paranthropus aethiopicus* from Omo with those of *P. robustus* from South Africa suggest an ancestor-descendant relationship between these two species as well. It thus appears entirely possible that *P. aethiopicus* was ancestral to all later members of the *Paranthropus* clade.

This brings us up to date for the story of robust australopithecine discoveries (further comments about their lifestyles will be made in a later section). A great deal remains to be said, however, about East African gracile australopithecines (genus *Australopithecus*) and their forebears, and for that account we must move north of Omo and Turkana to the Ethiopian badlands.

Discoveries at Hadar (1973–1976)

Five hundred miles (800 kilometers) to the northeast of Lake Turkana, near the Awash River in northern Ethiopia, at a barren and arid place called Hadar (Figures 7–1 and 7–10), extraordinary discoveries have given gracile australopithecines an extremely early date. At Hadar, an international expedition led by Maurice Taieb and Yves Coppens from France and Don Johanson from the United States made several extremely important fossil finds. The story began in 1973, when, during the first season at Hadar, Johanson found a hominid knee joint washed out of a slope. This discovery in itself would not have been so remarkable if the geologists and paleontologists had not assigned it a date of about 3 mya. Furthermore, an examination of its anatomy proved conclusively that the creature to whom the knee belonged had a close-knee stance and walked erect (Figure 7–11). Here was evidence of habitual bipedalism far older than anything known before. Hadar suddenly became the most intriguing prehistoric site on earth.

Johanson and his group returned to Hadar in the fall of 1974, and on November 30 he and his student Tom Gray made a short detour to look in a particular gully that had intrigued him. In it, the two men discovered one of the most remarkable finds in all paleoanthropology: the partial skeleton of a hominid about 3 million years of age. Given the name Lucy, the skeleton (from locality 288), which was 40 percent complete, represented a very small gracile *Australopithecus* (Figure 7–10). Although the knee joint and the pelvis again carry the marks of habitual bipedalism, the skull is primitive, as are other features of the skeleton, which is somewhat more apelike than that of *A. africanus* from South Africa.

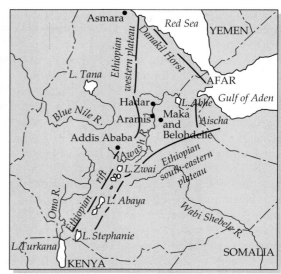

FIGURE 7–10   Important hominid remains have been recovered from the extensive stratified deposits at Hadar (right) in the Afar region of Ethiopia. At this site, Donald C. Johanson (at the bottom center) and his team discovered the bones of a skeleton in 1974. After three and a half weeks of mapping, collecting, and sieving, the bones were gathered into one of the most nearly complete early hominids yet found (bottom row, right photograph). "Lucy," as the skeleton is called, lived by a lake about 3 million years ago; she was only 3.5 to 4 feet (about 1.1 meters) tall and died when she was in her early twenties. Based on this and other discoveries, Johanson and his colleagues named a new species, *Australopithecus afarensis*. Also found in this region was a complete palate, dated at around 3.8 million years. In the bottom left photograph it is compared with a cast of a *Homo erectus* palate (right) that is less than 1 million years old. Their similarities suggest that the Afar palate is ancestral to *Homo*.

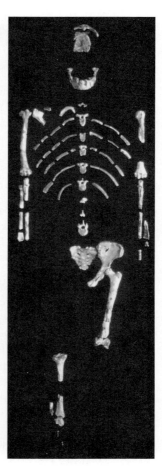

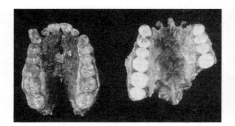

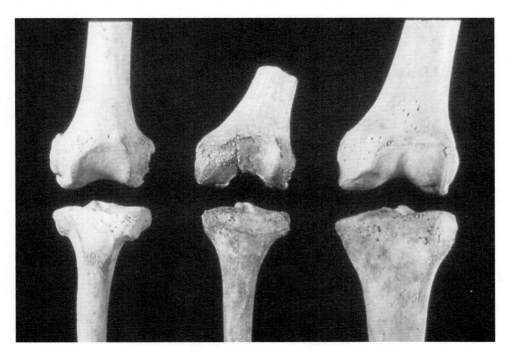

FIGURE 7–11   The interpretation of the *Australopithecus afarensis* knee bones can be understood from this figure. The critical character is the plane of the condyles of the knee joint in relation to the shaft of the femur. The frontal photograph of left knees shows that in the ape (left) the alignment is such that the leg is straight when the knee is extended. In humans (right) and in *A. afarensis* (middle), the alignment is such that the leg is angled at the knee. This is partially a product of the broadening of the pelvis (top drawings). The lower drawings show that the bearing surfaces of the knee condyles are broadened in bipedal species as an adaptation to the greater weight transmitted through the knee.

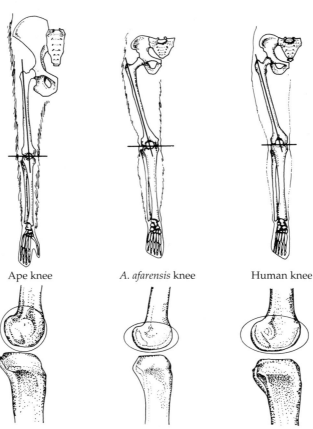

Ape knee   *A. afarensis* knee   Human knee

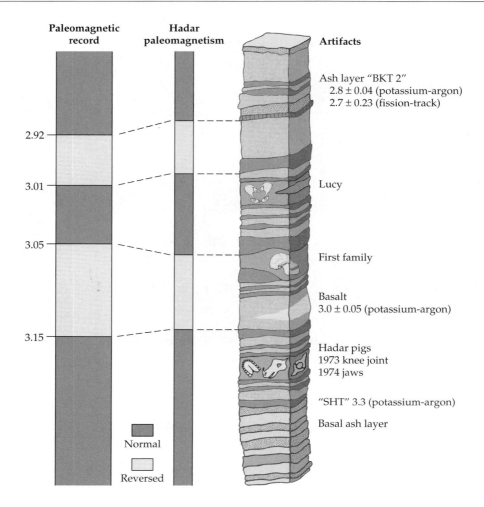

Paleomagnetic
record

Hadar
paleomagnetism

Artifacts

Ash layer "BKT 2"
2.8 ± 0.04 (potassium-argon)
2.7 ± 0.23 (fission-track)

2.92

3.01

Lucy

3.05

First family

Basalt
3.0 ± 0.05 (potassium-argon)

3.15

Hadar pigs
1973 knee joint
1974 jaws

"SHT" 3.3 (potassium-argon)

Basal ash layer

Normal

Reversed

FIGURE 7–12   Stratigraphic column at Hadar showing chronometric dates in million years B.P. and probable paleomagnetic match.

The 1975 season brought further remarkable discoveries. At a single site (locality 333), one of Johanson's team, Mike Bush, found further hominid fossils, this time a mixed collection of some 200 teeth and bone fragments, representing at least thirteen individuals, including males, females, and at least four children. The strange thing about this precious haul was that the hominid bones were all associated and from a single level, not mixed with animal bones as such fossils usually are. They have been called the "first family."

The final field season of 1976 was concerned mainly with stratigraphy and dating. Researchers now believe that this group of fossils probably falls into the time range 2.8 to 3.3 mya (Figure 7–12). The potassium-argon dates in this section agree with fission-track dates and have been cross-checked by the chemical signatures of the tuffs, while the fauna (in particular, the pig fossils) from the section also support the dates. Figure 7–12 also shows how the paleomagnetism of the section conforms to the paleomagnetic record. In summary, the site is quite well dated, although further dates from below the fossil-bearing strata would help sandwich the lower collection of fossils.

BOX 7-3

CHARACTERISTICS OF *AUSTRALOPITHECUS AFARENSIS*[a]

TRAIT	*AUSTRALOPITHECUS AFARENSIS*
Height	F: 3.3–3.4 ft (100–105 cm) M: 5.0 ft (151 cm) (F is 68% of M)
Weight	F: 66 lb (30 kg) M: 99–154 lb (45–70 kg) (F is 52% of M)
Brain size (sexes combined)	433 cc mean (400–500 cc range)
Cranium	Prognathic face; low, flat forehead; low-vaulted braincase; large brows; unflexed cranial base
Dentition	U-shaped toothrow; relatively large anterior teeth (incisors and canines); moderately large molars; canines that project somewhat; upper jaw diastemata; lower P3s at least semisectorial
Diet	Fruit and other plant foods; some meat (?)
Limbs	Long arms relative to legs; curved finger and toe bones (adaptations for arboreal movement?); close-knee stance
Pelvis	Short, broad iliac blades; incomplete pelvic bowl; weak iliofemoral ligament; ischial shaft relatively shorter than in apes, but not yet realigned in modern fashion; pelvis wide between hip joints
Locomotion	Bipedalism (probably primitive) and possibly arboreal climbing
Known dates (million years B.P.)	4.2–2.5

[a] Mean values, and ranges of values, for anatomical measurements may change with additional fossil discoveries. For additional technical details and diagnostic traits, see Appendix III.

The fossils from Hadar were described by Johanson and his associates. The characteristics of the group caused Johanson, Coppens, and Tim White to recognize a new, earlier, and very primitive species of *Australopithecus*: **A. afarensis**. The characteristics of this species are described below and summarized in Box 7-3.

But before describing the traits of *Australopithecus afarensis*, it may be useful to review quickly the anatomical expectations that we have of the first hominids. The biochemical and fossil data together indicate that the Hominidae diverged from the chimpanzee-bonobo lineage quite recently—probably only 5 to 7 million years ago. Given this recent evolutionary descent from ape ancestors, we expect the oldest members of the human family to show a clear mixture of ape traits and human traits. Apes have small brains, big canines, and bodies (particularly arms, hands, and feet) adapted for arboreal movement. In contrast, modern humans have huge brains, small canines, and bodies (particularly pelvic girdles, legs, and feet) specialized for bipedal locomotion. If we are correct in concluding that modern humans are descended—via the australopithecines—from a long-extinct

Australopithecus afarensis gracile australopithecine *species* that inhabited East Africa from 4.2 to 2.5 mya.

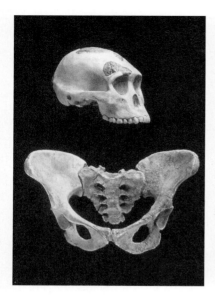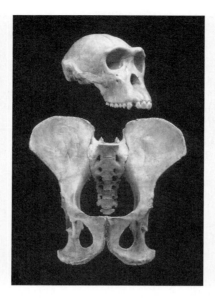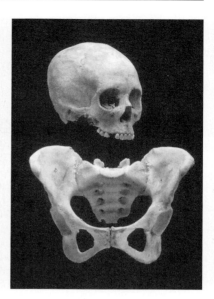

FIGURE 7–13   The restored pelvic girdle of *A. afarensis* (left) compared with that of a modern human (right) and a chimpanzee (center). Note the shorter, broader ilia and more bowl-like pelvis of *A. afarensis* compared to that of the ape. Also visible are the deep sciatic notches and extreme pelvic width (hip joint to hip joint) of *A. afarensis*. A typical skull for each species is shown with the corresponding pelvis.

species of ape, then our early australopithecine ancestors should be strongly intermediate between the two evolutionary grades.

The body size of *Australopithecus afarensis* varied considerably both within a sex and between sexes (sexual dimorphism), so that females, like Lucy, may have been just over 3 feet (about 1 meter) tall, while large males may have been as much as 5 feet (1.5 meters) tall. Weight probably varied from 66 to as much as 154 pounds (30 to 70 kilograms). The individuals, though small, were powerfully built: the bones were thick for their size and carried markings suggesting that they had been well muscled. As we have seen, the evidence of the knee joint makes it clear that, like all other hominids, they were habitually bipedal. Indeed, the likelihood that *A. afarensis* was more committed to a terrestrial way of life than South Africa's *A. africanus* is suggested by the fact that Lucy and her kin possessed humanlike, nonopposable (nongrasping) big toes. As described in Chapter 6, the big toes of *A. africanus* were divergent digits probably used for climbing, at least if Little Foot is properly assigned to that taxon. In the upper body, however, even *A. afarensis* may show signs of continuing arboreality, including relatively longer arms and shorter legs than those of modern humans, rather apelike wrist bones, and curved fingers (another apelike trait). In rebuttal, researchers who believe that *Australopithecus afarensis* was essentially fully terrestrial note that these creatures had short fingers (those of apes are long) and that the retention of some apelike traits is predictable in early hominids such as Lucy that recently evolved from ape ancestors.

The pelvis of *A. afarensis* shows unmistakable adaptations for habitual bipedalism (Figure 7–13). First, the iliac blades are short and broad, and deep sciatic notches indicate the extent of backward expansion and bending. Thus the center of gravity of *A. afarensis* was considerably lower than that of an ape, and as a consequence, bipedal balancing was much more stable and energy-efficient. Second, the iliac blades of *A. afarensis* are curved toward the front of the body, producing a partial pelvic bowl. Third, the anterior inferior iliac spines are well

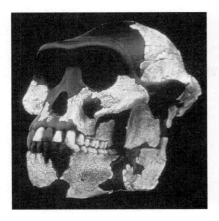 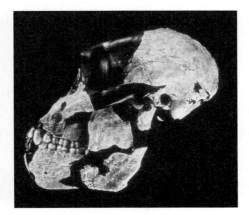

FIGURE 7–14   Composite reconstruction based on *A. afarensis* fossil skull fragments found at Hadar. Reconstruction by Tim White and William Kimbel. The photographs are approximately 25 percent actual size. See also the new *A. afarensis* skull shown in the color essay on fossil hominids.

developed and mark the upper attachment of powerful **rectus femoris** muscles that flexed the *A. afarensis* thigh and extended the lower leg during bipedal walking. And finally, the ischial shaft is relatively short compared to the shaft of an ape. In combination with these humanlike features, however, there are clear pelvic indications that the evolutionary transformation was not complete and that *A. afarensis* probably did not show fully modern bipedal locomotion. These indications include the incomplete pelvic bowl, the lack of modern realignment of the ischial shafts, the extreme width (hip joint to hip joint) of the pelvic girdle, and evidence that the iliofemoral ligaments may have been small and weak. This combination of derived and primitive traits has convinced some anthropologists and anatomists that *Australopithecus afarensis* showed a distinctively different and more primitive kind of bipedalism than modern humans, perhaps one with apelike balancing mechanisms and more twisting of the trunk.

> **Rectus femoris** one of the muscles that flexes the hominid thigh.

The skull bones of *Australopithecus afarensis* reveal a rather primitive mixture of traits (Figure 7–14; see also the color essay on fossil hominids). The face was prognathic, the forehead receded strongly from behind large brows, and the braincase was low-vaulted—a distinctly apelike cranium indeed. Furthermore, *A. afarensis*'s average cranial capacity of 433 cubic centimeters (range 400–500 cc) was only slightly larger than that of a chimpanzee (383 cubic centimeters mean).

Finally, the *A. afarensis* dentition is of great importance: it is apelike in many respects. In particular, the upper canine is somewhat pointed, with a large root, and is reminiscent of that of an ape; it also shows noticeable sexual dimorphism (Figure 7–15). The lower canines are associated with small diastemata in the upper jaw. At the same time, the first lower premolar (P3) is also remarkable in lacking or having only a small internal (lingual) secondary cusp; yet the tooth is not truly apelike, for the apes have no second cusp, but only one single large one. It is, as Johanson says, a tooth in transition. This feature and the form of the canines serve to separate the group from the gracile South African *A. africanus*. The molar teeth show the kind of wear we associate with modern humans, with an indication of the grinding of grit-laden foods. In some specimens, the canines show beginning wear from the apex. Finally, the shape of the toothrow is more apelike than human, as is the profile of the face (Figure 7–14).

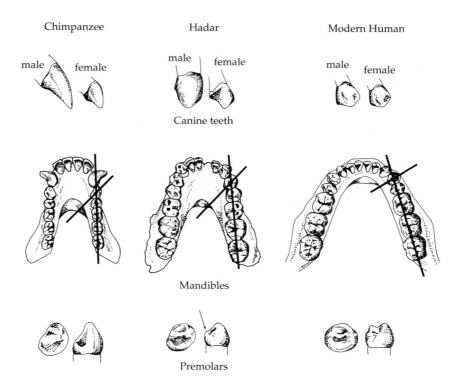

FIGURE 7–15   Comparison of Hadar (*A. afarensis*) with chimpanzee and modern human dentitions. At the top, a comparison of the male and female upper canines of each species. Notice the pointed ape canines and the blunt human teeth, together with the considerable sexual dimorphism in the ape and Hadar teeth. Below this, the three mandibles are illustrated. Notice the intermediate traits of the Hadar mandible. The lines show the alignment of the first lower premolar in relation to the molar series as a whole. At the bottom, a typical first lower premolar is illustrated. The ape premolar is one-cusped; the human premolar two-cusped. The Hadar premolar illustrated has a small lingual cusp (arrow) and is intermediate in form.

Altogether, the *A. afarensis* fossils show a remarkable set of traits that place them squarely in the family Hominidae, yet reveal many similarities to apes. Two and a half decades' work has made *A. afarensis* one of the best known of all fossil hominid species.

The species *A. afarensis* includes more than the Hadar fossils (see Table 7–1 and Figure 7–1). In addition, there are recently reported 4-million-year-old remains from Allia Bay, east Turkana, equally ancient Ethiopian fossils from Middle Awash sites such as Maka and Belohdelie, and 4.2-million-year-old specimens from Fejej in the Omo River basin. Although the extremely old (5.6 million years B.P.) mandibular fragment from Lothagam, Kenya, has been assigned to *A. afarensis* by some workers, specialists disagree on that classification and we believe this particular fossil should be put in suspension *pro tem* (see Box 7–4). Finally, among the most important *A. afarensis* fossils are the remains from a remarkable site in northern Kenya called Laetoli.

Discoveries at Laetoli (1974–1977) and the Awash (1981)

In 1974, Mary Leakey returned to Laetoli, a site south of Olduvai (Figure 7–1). The site was first visited by the Leakeys in 1935 and later by the German prehistorian

---

Box 7-4

WHAT TO MAKE OF THE LOTHAGAM JAW?

In 1967, paleoanthropologist Bryan Patterson led a fossil-hunting expedition to northern Kenya. At a location called Lothagam, just southwest of Lake Turkana, Patterson and his team hit pay dirt and unknowingly kicked off a controversy that has lasted thirty years. In this case, pay dirt consisted of a rather scrappy mandibular fragment, broken off in front of the first molar and preserving that tooth along with the roots of lower molars M2 and M3. Not much to look at, maybe, but the Lothagam jaw was wonderfully old. A battery of different dating procedures indicated that the fossil was probably in the neighborhood of 5.6 million years of age—perhaps the oldest known hominid fossil yet discovered.

But that is a big "perhaps," and therein lies the problem. Lothagam is so old and so fragmentary that it is very difficult to classify accurately. Patterson and his coworkers originally assigned it to *A. africanus* (yes, that's right, they thought it was possible that *A. africanus* had also lived in East Africa). Other workers have concluded that it is an ape jaw, and still others maintain that it is too fragmentary to be given a name at all. Finally, the latest analyses by Andrew Hill and A. Kramer have identified several traits shared by the Lothagam fossil and *Australopithecus afarensis*, and those researchers are comfortable assigning the specimen to that species.

If one follows Hill and Kramer, however, and assigns Lothagam to *A. afarensis*, it has the effect of expanding that species' time range back to 5.6 mya and placing it at the very base of the hominid evolutionary tree. Such a placement may be justified, but, as detailed in a later section, recent discoveries have produced a more morphologically suitable (that is, more apelike) candidate for that basal position, *Ardipithecus ramidus* (see Box 7–7 and Figure 7–24). *Ardipithecus* appears to be the perfect ancestor for *A. afarensis* except for the fact that assigning the Lothagam jaw to the latter species would preclude such an arrangement because of the two species' relative ages.

A temporary solution to this confusing situation is suggested by recent analyses showing that Lothagam broadly matches both *Ardipithecus* and *Australopithecus afarensis* in its anatomy. That being the case, many anthropologists—including the authors of this book—believe that Lothagam should be put in suspension until we have further information about its classification. In other words, since no one can classify the Kenyan jaw with any confidence, it seems best simply to work around it as we interpret the australopithecines' evolutionary relationships. Suspending Lothagam leaves the advent of *A. afarensis* at 4.2 million years B.P. (Box 7–3)—comfortably later than *Ardipithecus*—and enables us to ground hominids' evolutionary tree in the most apelike ancestor available (Figure 7–24).

L. Kohl-Larsen. Louis Leakey collected some fossils of Pliocene monkeys, which included some loose teeth, among them a canine tooth. This tooth has recently been reexamined and has turned out to be very similar to those of the species *Australopithecus afarensis*; it is of great interest because its discovery actually predated all the discoveries of Robert Broom in South Africa (Chapter 6). It was in fact the first evidence of an adult *Australopithecus* that was ever recovered.

In 1939, Kohl-Larsen collected a hominid upper jaw fragment with two teeth, which was called *Meganthropus africanus*. We now believe that these finds also belong, with the Hadar fossils, to the species *A. afarensis*.

TABLE 7-1   *A Partial Record of Australopithecine Fossils*

SPECIES	SOUTH AFRICAN SITES	AGE (MILLION YEARS)[a]	EAST AFRICAN SITES	AGE (MILLION YEARS)[b]
Ardipithecus ramidus			Aramis	4.4
Australopithecus anamensis			Allia Bay	3.9
			Kanapoi	4.2–3.9
Australopithecus bahrelghazali			Bahr el Ghazal (Chad)	3.5–3.0
Australopithecus afarensis			Omo	3.0–2.5
			Hadar	3.3–2.8
			Laetoli	3.8–3.6
			Maka/Belohdelie	4.0–3.4
			Allia Bay	4.0
			Fejej	4.2–4.0
Australopithecus africanus	Taung	2.8–2.6		
	Makapansgat	3.0–2.5		
	Sterkfontein	3.5?–2.5		
Paranthropus aethiopicus			Omo, Lomekwi, and Kangatukuseo	2.7–2.3
Paranthropus boisei			Peninj	1.5
			Olduvai	1.8
			Koobi Fora	2.0–1.3
			Omo	2.3–1.5
Paranthropus robustus	Swartkrans	1.8–1.0		
	Kromdraai	2.0–1.8		

[a]Dates attributed to South African sites often are based not on chronometric procedures, but on comparative analyses of fauna. Nonetheless, these dates probably do bracket the times of existence of the various fossil species.
[b]Most of the dates for sites in East and North-Central Africa are based on chronometric procedures and are therefore quite accurate.

When Mary Leakey returned to the site she collected more than twenty fragmentary hominid jaws from eroding Pliocene strata in this area (Figure 7–16). They represented eight adults and three children, and they were conveniently sandwiched between two volcanic ash strata dated 3.6 and 3.75 million years B.P. They have a striking affinity with the Hadar fossils, and it is claimed by Johanson and White that they belong to the same species; indeed, these workers selected one of the Laetoli jaws as the **type specimen** of the species *Australopithecus afarensis*. Some workers, however, believe, for several reasons, that the Laetoli finds may form a taxon (or taxa) distinct from the Hadar fossils. First of all, the Laetoli fossils carry some unique traits, and they have features in common with *A. africanus* and with *Homo habilis* from nearby Olduvai Gorge, though they are much older than either. Second, some researchers, such as anthropologist Sigrid Hartwig-Scherer, are troubled by the extreme degree of sexual dimorphism in body weight attributed to *A. afarensis*. Were there really two species, rather than one species with very large males and very small females? And third, the Hadar and Laetoli sites are just over 1,000 miles (1,600 kilometers) apart—a considerable distance for combining fossil assemblages to produce a single new species.

While many of these issues have yet to be settled, new discoveries and analyses have provided some light. Regarding the issue of sexual dimorphism in body size, recent fossil discoveries at the Ethiopian site of Maka (just south of Hadar)

Type specimen the *fossil* specimen that serves as the basis for identifying all other individuals in a *species;* usually the original specimen to be found.

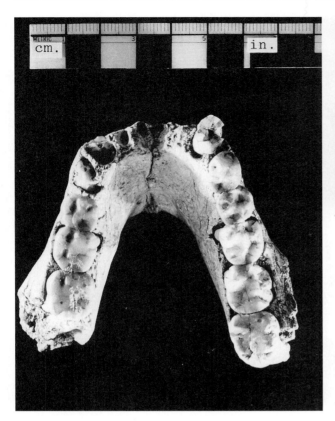

FIGURE 7–16 This hominid jaw from Laetoli was discovered in 1974 and is dated about 3.7 million years B.P. It has been selected as the type specimen of *Australopithecus afarensis*. The left photograph shows the relatively large but damaged canine tooth in the top right-hand corner. The right photograph shows the jaw from the right-hand side.

have shown that a single *A. afarensis* site can produce the same amount of intraspecific variation in tooth and body size as the combined Hadar-Laetoli assemblage. Furthermore, statistical analyses have shown that the degree of size dimorphism found in *A. afarensis* does not exceed that displayed by gorillas and orangutans. It seems entirely possible, therefore, that the original interpretation of (relatively) huge *A. afarensis* males and much smaller females was correct. And this is an important point, because it may well give us a critical clue about the mating system of these early hominids (as discussed in a later section).

Similarly, the problem of combining the Hadar and Laetoli samples into one, extremely widespread species has been eliminated by the discovery of new *A. afarensis* sites in-between. Fejej (Ethiopia) and Allia Bay (east of Lake Turkana, Kenya) fall almost exactly halfway between Hadar and Laetoli (Figure 7–1), and the demonstration of *A. afarensis* material from these localities should put an end to geographical qualms about the species' validity. For now, most anthropologists (including the authors of this book) are following Johanson and White and treating *Australopithecus afarensis* as a single, widespread, and anatomically variable species.

Paul Abell, a geochemist working at Laetoli, made another discovery that was, if possible, more remarkable than the fossil finds. Sandwiched in layers of volcanic ash were the preserved footprints of a whole range of animals, including elephants, rhinoceroses, many types of antelope, three kinds of giraffe, a saber-toothed cat, and many other species, all now extinct. One of these other species was a hominid: clearly impressed in the ash layer, hominid tracks cover a distance of more than 150 feet (45 meters). Portions of the tracks are slightly eroded, but several intact prints

FIGURE 7–17   The Laetoli site has produced a unique record of the footprints of animals dated from about 3.6 million years B.P. The footprints of a large proportion of the fossil species are present, including those of *Australopithecus afarensis* as shown in this picture and the photograph opening Chapter 9.

are preserved (Figure 7–17). The pattern and form of the footprints are like those made in soft sand by modern humans and suggest (like the other evidence) an evolved bipedalism. The smaller and larger footprints (on the basis of modern people's foot size) suggest a stature ranging from about 4 to 5 feet (1.2 to 1.5 meters). This discovery is a most remarkable one, and it is unique in paleontology for the number of mammalian species represented: a large proportion of the Laetoli Pliocene fauna have left their imprint. Above all, it is quite clear that *Australopithecus afarensis* was walking very nearly like a human about 4 million years ago—and perhaps earlier.

Interestingly, as we have shown, adopting bipedalism apparently did not require forsaking the trees completely—at least not initially. *A. afarensis* and *A. africanus* (and perhaps even the *Paranthropus* forms) show anatomical evidence of both the derived trait of terrestrial bipedalism and the continuation of some arboreal climbing and suspension. Indeed, australopithecine bipedalism has been described as "facultative" (optional, dependent on conditions), as opposed to the "obligatory" bipedalism of modern humans. And while the australopithecines' hips and legs were evolving relatively quickly in response to conditions favoring bipedalism, other parts of their anatomy were lagging behind. For example, new evidence from CT (computed tomography) images of australopithecine skulls has revealed that these early hominids had **semicircular canal** morphologies like those of apes, not of modern humans. This means that, although routinely bipedal, the australopithecines were not yet perfectly adapted to upright balance and coordination. As is so often the case with evolution, natural selection moved the early hominids toward full bipedalism through a mosaic of adaptive changes.

Semicircular canals fluid-filled canals of the inner ear that control balance and coordination.

THE PACE OF DISCOVERY QUICKENS AT CENTURY'S END

Paleoanthropology, like most sciences, tends to make progress in fits and starts. At times, long intervals elapse between major discoveries such as the identification of a new species or, even more significant, a new genus. At other times, however, fabulous new fossils seem to fall out of the sky in clusters, with each year bringing the announcement of some previously unknown hominid type. The 1990s has been a decade of the latter sort and thus a very exciting time for paleoanthropologists. Between 1994 and 1996, three new species and one new genus were added to the family Hominidae (see also the announcement at the chapter's end). The following sections tell the stories of those discoveries, after which we will attempt to synthesize the australopithecines' lifestyles and evolutionary relationships.

Australopithecus anamensis from Northern Kenya (1995)

The Leakey family has been blessed with two generations of talented fossil hunters. First, of course, there were Louis and Mary, whose pioneering work at Olduvai Gorge was described early in this chapter. Their rich paleontological legacy was carried on by sons Jonathan and Richard, and also by Richard's wife, Meave. And it is Meave Leakey, now the head of the division of paleontology at the National Museums of Kenya, who has made the latest headlines with her announcement (along with colleagues Craig Feibel, Ian McDougall, and Alan Walker) of a new, and very ancient, australopithecine from the Kenyan sites of Kanapoi and Allia Bay. The new hominid type, named ***Australopithecus anamensis***, clearly is one of, if not *the* oldest species of *Australopithecus* yet discovered. This claim is supported by Ar^{40}/AR^{39} dates of 4.2 to 3.9 mya—a range of dates that places *A. anamensis* father back in time than all but the most ancient noncontroversial fossils of *A. afarensis* (Table 7–1).

Australopithecus anamensis a new *species* of australopithecines from East Africa and dated 4.2 to 3.9 mya.

FIGURE 7–18 Paleoanthropologist Alan Walker sits in the midst of the bone bed at Allia Bay that produced fossils of *Australopithecus anamensis*.

Box 7-5

CHARACTERISTICS OF *AUSTRALOPITHECUS ANAMENSIS*[a]

TRAIT	*AUSTRALOPITHECUS ANAMENSIS*
Height	Unknown
Weight[b]	104–121 lb (47–55 kg)
Brain size	Unknown
Cranium	Mandibular symphysis slopes strongly down and back, suggesting facial prognathism; external acoustic meatus (ear canal) is small and apelike in outline
Dentition	U-shaped toothrows; all canines have long, robust roots; lower canines are larger than those of *A. afarensis*; lower P3 is very asymmetrical, with a centrally positioned and blunt main cusp (semisectorial?); thick molar enamel
Diet	Fruit and foliage; thick enamel suggests a diet including some hard items
Limbs	Elbow anatomy seems to rule out knuckle-walking; condyles of tibia differ from those of apes in both size and shape; top of tibia shows extra spongy bone for shock absorption; bottom of tibia shows extra bony buttressing at ankle
Pelvis	Unknown
Locomotion	Bipedalism (probably primitive; unknown whether accompanied by arboreal climbing)
Known dates (million years B.P.)	4.2–3.9

[a] Values for anatomical measurements may change with additional fossil discoveries. For additional technical details and diagnostic traits, see Appendix III.
[b] Weight estimated for one (presumably male) individual.

The remains of *A. anamensis* have been gathered from river deposits at Allia Bay and lakeside deposits at Kanapoi (the two sites lie some 90 miles [145 kilometers] apart and on opposite sides of Lake Turkana; see Figure 7–1). The Allia Bay fossils occur as a "bone bed," and each fragment was rolled and weathered as it was swept into position by a precursor of the modern Omo River (Figure 7–18). Among the Allia Bay fossils one finds aquatic animals (fish, crocodiles, and hippopotamuses), as well as the bones of leaf-eating monkeys and woodland antelopes—remains that collectively suggest a gallery forest habitat along the river. In contrast, the Kanapoi site probably combined "dry, possibly open, wooded or bushland conditions [with] a wide gallery forest." The remains of kudus, impalas, hyaenas, and a semi-terrestrial monkey called *Parapapio* (an early ancestor of today's baboons) confirm the somewhat more open conditions at Kanapoi. Meave Leakey and her team believe that the early hominids who lived at the two sites utilized a wide range of habitats.

So what sort of hominid was *Australopithecus anamensis*? As one might expect this far back in time, it was a bipedal species that still showed a goodly number of apelike traits throughout its body (Box 7–5). The list of fossils recovered thus far

---

Box 7-6

CHARACTERISTICS OF *AUSTRALOPITHECUS BAHRELGHAZALI*[a]

TRAIT	*AUSTRALOPITHECUS BAHRELGHAZALI* (PROVISIONAL)
Height, weight, and brain size	Unknown
Cranium	Mandibular symphysis shows a unique outline, particularly on the lingual (internal) surface
Dentition	Short, pointed lower canines; bicuspid (nonsectorial) lower P3s (this implies short upper canines); three-rooted lower premolars; premolar enamel thicker than in *Ardipithecus*, but thin compared to other australopithecines
Diet	Few hard items in the diet? Mostly fruit and foliage?
Limbs and pelvis	Unknown
Locomotion	Bipedalism (assumed)
Known dates (million years B.P.)	3.5–3.0

[a] For additional technical details and diagnostic traits, see Appendix III.

---

the symphysis back to the last premolar). Included in the jaw are all of the canines and premolars, and one lateral incisor. As indicated in Box 7–6 (and also in Appendix III), very little can be concluded about the anatomy and adaptations of this hominid because of the limited sample of fossils. *Australopithecus bahrelghazali* had short, but pointed, canines; bicuspid (nonsectorial) lower P3s; and a unique outline of the mandibular symphysis. Furthermore, it differed from other *Australopithecus* and *Paranthropus* species in its three-rooted lower premolars (theirs were two-rooted) and its thinner premolar enamel. Collectively, these traits support at least the provisional listing of *A. bahrelghazali* as a new australopithecine species, even though it may prove to be a geographical race of *A. afarensis*, with which it is approximately contemporary (Table 7–1).

Like many of the other australopithecine species, *A. bahrelghazali* apparently inhabited a lakeside environment that included both gallery forest and wooded savanna with open grassy patches. Furthermore, judging from its thin enamel, this early species apparently subsisted rather exclusively on soft foods—undoubtedly mostly fruits, foliage, and vegetables.

For now, that's about all we can say about *Australopithecus bahrelghazali*. Its main claim to fame is its extreme western location and, in fact, future discoveries may prove that it was named prematurely. Nonetheless, its relatively thin tooth enamel is worth remembering because it may help us make sense of the last species to be described in this chapter, *Ardipithecus ramidus*.

Oldest Hominid (?) Found at Aramis, Ethiopia (1992–1994)

Between 1992 and 1993, an international team of paleoanthropologists, including American Tim White, Gen Suwa of the University of Tokyo, and Berhane Asfaw of

FIGURE 7–21   (Left) Partial mandible of *Ardipithecus ramidus* from Aramis, Ethiopia. (Right) The upper arm bone of *A. ramidus* held here by paleoanthropologist Alemayehu Asfaw. Both photos © 1994 Tim D. White\Brill Atlanta.

the Ethiopian Ministry of Culture and Sports Affairs, focused its collecting efforts on early Pliocene deposits at the Aramis site in the middle of Ethiopia's Awash River drainage system (Figures 7–1 and 7–10). Suwa made the first Aramis discovery in mid-December 1992 when a glint of sunlight from a fossilized molar tooth caught his eye while he was surface hunting. "I knew immediately that it was a hominid," he said later, "and because we had found other ancient animals that morning, I knew it was one of the oldest hominid teeth ever found." That tooth proved to be just the beginning of a rich fossil find, and over the 1992 and 1993 field seasons, Suwa and his colleagues collected a total of seventeen fossil specimens, all of which date back to about 4.4 million years B.P. Among the ancient remains were several teeth, a partial mandible (Figure 7–21), some skull fragments, and a few arm bones (including the rare discovery of all three bones from the left arm of a single individual).

After extensive analysis of the Aramis fossils—and comparisons with living and fossil apes, modern humans, and several extinct hominid varieties—White, Suwa, and Asfaw concluded that they had discovered not only a new species of primitive hominid, but an entirely new genus! Selecting a genus name based on the word for "ground" (*ardi*) in the local Afar language and a species name based on the Afar word for "root" (*-ramid*), the researchers dubbed the new find *Ardipithecus ramidus* in May 1995. (Actually, there was one false start. The new fossil was announced as *Australopithecus ramidus* in September 1994. Over the next few months, the researchers had second thoughts and they changed the name in May 1995. At present, paleoanthropologists are split over what to call the Aramis fossils. We believe it is convenient to use the new genus name and have done so throughout this book, although the species name identifies the taxon adequately and is sufficient.)

The most important anatomical features of *Ardipithecus ramidus* can be summarized as follows (see also Box 7–7): canines shorter and more incisiform than those of apes, but less incisiform and larger (relative to the postcanine teeth) than those of *A. afarensis*; lower anterior premolars (P3s) lacking the honing facet (sectorial functioning) characteristic of apes; enamel on canines and molars that is thin compared to that of *A. afarensis* but approximates the condition in chimpanzees; similar to other australopithecines, but in contrast to apes, a forwardly placed foramen magnum; and, finally, a shape of the head of the humerus (upper arm bone) and the anatomy of the elbow joint resembling that of later hominids, not of apes. One additional characteristic that strongly differentiates *A. ramidus* from *A. afarensis* is the extremely apelike anatomy of the lower first deciduous molar found at Aramis.

White et al. believe that the Aramis fossils show enough derived features to be safely included in the hominid family. They point particularly to hominidlike modifications in the canine and lower P3 complex, the positioning of the foramen magnum, and the elbow anatomy. To its discoverers, *A. ramidus* fulfills virtually all the theoretical expectations of a species just this side of the ape-hominid split.

It is much too soon to report a consensus among paleoanthropologists regarding *Ardipithecus ramidus*. The few opinions that have been offered so far, however, show that there are both supporters and critics. Bernard Wood agrees enthusiastically

---

Box 7-7

CHARACTERISTICS OF *ARDIPITHECUS RAMIDUS*[a]

TRAIT	*ARDIPITHECUS RAMIDUS* (PROVISIONAL)
Height	At least 3.3 ft (100 cm; upper height limit and sexual dimorphism unknown)
Weight	At least 66 lb (30 kg; upper weight limit and sexual dimorphism unknown)
Brain size	Unknown
Cranium	Forwardly positioned foramen magnum; small occipital condyles; very flat surface of jaw joint
Dentition	Canines shorter and more incisiform than those of apes, but less incisiform and larger (relative to the postcanine teeth) than those of *A. afarensis*; lower anterior premolars (P3s) lacking evidence of sectorial functioning; thin enamel on canines and molars; apelike anatomy of lower first deciduous molar
Diet	Unknown (thin molar enamel may rule out "hard object feeder")
Limbs	Arm bones showing a mosaic of hominid and ape traits; elliptical shape of the head of the humerus and the anatomy of the elbow joint resembling those of later hominids; pelvic and lower limb anatomy unknown
Locomotion	Bipedalism? (classification tentative; knuckle-walking can be ruled out)
Known dates (million years B.P.)	4.4

[a] For additional technical details and diagnostic traits, see Appendix III.

with a hominid classification, saying that White et al. "present compelling fossil evidence that they have found the oldest hominid species yet." Wood is less than fully convinced, however, that the Aramis material represents the common ancestor of all later hominids. While conceding that this is the most likely phyletic position for the new fossils, he points out that certain features argue for exclusive ancestry of the *Paranthropus* clade only.

Chris Stringer of the British Museum (Natural History) affirms the importance of the Aramis discoveries, saying they "seem to take us closer to a common ancestor [of apes and hominids]." He is bothered, however, by the thin enamel on the Aramis teeth. Thin enamel is characteristic of the African apes, while all early hominids known prior to 1994 showed thick enamel. Two discoveries, however, suggest that enamel thickness may not be as useful a diagnostic tool as we once thought. First, of course, there is *A. ramidus* itself: more than likely a biped, judging from the placement of its foramen magnum, and sporting thin-enameled teeth. And second, there is the new fossil from Bahr el Ghazal in Chad, with enamel that seems to be thicker than that of *Ardipithecus*, but thin for a member of the genus *Australopithecus*. It seems likely that enamel thickness may no longer distinguish hominids from apes with certainty, and therefore we must look to other features as we try to figure out the proper classification and evolutionary relationships of creatures such as *Ardipithecus*.

Finally, Andrew Hill of Yale University voiced a problem that may have occurred to some readers when he said, "I would be happier if we *knew* [*A. ramidus*] was a biped" (emphasis added). As noted in Chapter 5, habitual bipedalism is *the* primary criterion for inclusion in the family Hominidae. And while certain features of the Aramis fossils (e.g., anterior placement of the foramen magnum) are quite *suggestive* of bipedalism, even White et al. admit that, given the current state of knowledge, "Bipedality . . . remains to be demonstrated." Nonetheless, according to White, the fossils analyzed and described thus far at least allow certain locomotor patterns, such as knuckle-walking, to be ruled out.

Therefore, it seems that the final resolution of questions about *Ardipithecus*'s locomotion—and, by extension, its inclusion in the hominid family—turns on the description of additional fossils, particularly parts of the postcranial skeleton. By an extraordinary stroke of luck, precisely such material was recovered during the 1994 field season at Aramis, including 45 percent of an adult individual. The new fossils include pieces from the skull, arms, vertebral column, pelvis, and legs. That's the good news. The bad news is that in order for these new specimens to reveal their secrets about *A. ramidus*, they must first be extracted from blocks of stone, reconstructed, and then thoroughly analyzed; a lengthy process that will take many months or even years to complete. Nonetheless, paleoanthropologists take some comfort from the fact that more information about *Ardipithecus* is at least in the offing.

If *Ardipithecus* does prove to have been a biped—and the oldest known biped, at that—it could yield important information about the environmental conditions that originally selected for this distinctly hominid way of getting around. As discussed in the next section and in greater detail in Chapter 9, it has long been thought that bipedalism began as an adaptation to life on the African savanna—the implication being that the earliest hominids changed quickly from their ape ancestors' forest-based existence to terrestrial life in an environment of broad grasslands dotted with occasional trees. In stark contrast to this theory, however, geologists working at Aramis have reconstructed the environment of *Ardipithecus* as relatively flat, closed woodland due to the occurrence of preserved wood and seeds, as well as the bones of woodland antelopes and colobine (leaf-eating) monkeys. The origin of bipedalism in the forest? Such a notion stands conventional anthropological wisdom on its head, but, as the following section shows, the australopithecine evidence suggests that it may be time to take the possibility seriously.

LIFESTYLES OF THE AUSTRALOPITHECINES

So much for the nuts and bolts of the australopithecine fossil record. Along with Chapter 6, this chapter so far has been concerned with presenting the details about the discoveries, locations, ages, and anatomies of the eight species of australopithecines (see Table 6–1 for a taxonomic refresher). They come from a variety of sites in South, East, and North-Central Africa and cover a combined time range of 5.6 to 1.0 mya (Figures 7–1 and 7–22; Table 7–1). But now it's time to put some flesh on those dry bones and to make a few educated speculations about how the various early hominids lived. The anatomical and archaeological evidence provides a good basis for such speculations, of course, but in addition, paleoanthropologists routinely apply models developed from the socioecology and behavior of nonhuman primates (especially the apes) and from modern humans who still live by hunting and gathering (see the Postscript to Chapter 11). It is important to keep in mind, however, that all reconstructions of australopithecine

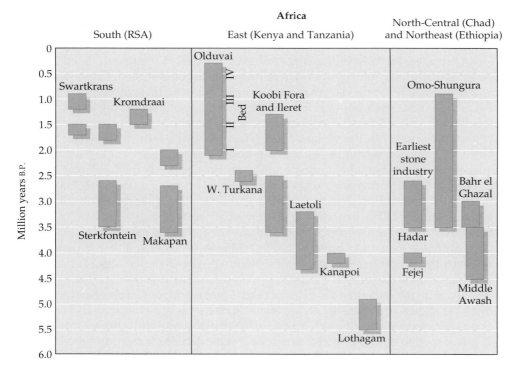

FIGURE 7–22 The approximate time spans of some of the deposits mentioned in the text. The South African dates are generally less reliable than those for East Africa and Ethiopia. The South African deposits usually represent a short time span that falls somewhere in the range of the time indicated. The East African and Ethiopian deposits are deep, and the range indicated is that actually represented by the deposits: fossils are found at many levels.

life ways are *hypotheses*, and as such they require further scrutiny and scientific testing. Some will eventually be accepted as proved facts; others will be rejected in favor of alternative interpretations.

We have three genera to deal with, and the first—*Ardipithecus*—will take hardly any time at all given its limited fossil record. *A. ramidus* appears to have inhabited East Africa's closed woodland environment and within that environment it probably survived on a standard hominoid diet of ripe fruit, leaves, insects, and—if its tastes were like those of modern chimpanzees—the occasional small animal. Certainly, judging from its thin dental enamel, *Ardipithecus* does not appear to have eaten very many things that were hard to open or tough to chew. The few fossils of *A. ramidus* described to date suggest that it moved bipedally throughout its habitat. Whether or not it still climbed about in the trees is unclear, although this seems likely given *Ardipithecus*'s recent descent from ape stock. Equally unclear is exactly what *Ardipithecus* was doing as it stood and moved in an upright posture. A clue on this point, however, comes from evidence that the Aramis habitat was not quite as closed as the label "closed woodland" implies. Along with the remains of forest creatures, the Aramis deposits contain the bones of such open-country animals as giraffes and rhinos. This suggests the presence at Aramis of (extensive?) grassy spaces and raises the possibility that *Ardipithecus* was moving bipedally across open country from one wooded food patch to another. Other possibilities, judging from observations of modern chimpanzees, are that *A. ramidus* might have stood bipedally to threaten other animals, to carry or brandish various objects, or to see over long distances. And that's really about all we can say about the oldest known hominid until more fossils are described. Species of the genera *Australopithecus* and *Paranthropus* make much better subjects for our evolutionary speculations.

Australopithecus is represented by four species: *A. afarensis*, *A. anamensis*, *A. africanus*, and *A. bahrelghazali*. These members of the so-called gracile lineage of australopithecines ranged from modern South Africa to Ethiopia and west to Chad. All of the gracile australopithecines used a mixed bag of habitats, including gallery forests at the edge of rivers and lakes and wooded savanna with open grassy patches. Within those habitats, the various species were mainly terrestrial bipeds, although both of the best known types—*A. afarensis* and *A. africanus*—appear to have retained adaptations for arboreal climbing (shown in their upper bodies and feet, respectively). Furthermore, given the grasping big toes of some (i.e., the Little Foot specimen), and the wide pelvises of all the gracile forms, it seems likely that their bipedalism was rather primitive and somewhat apelike, with some twisting of the trunk as the lead leg swung forward and with different balancing mechanisms. As with *Ardipithecus*, exactly how the *Australopithecus* species used their bipedalism is unclear; threatening, carrying things, making long-distance observations, and moving between dispersed food patches all remain as possibilities. Interestingly, there is no direct evidence that *Australopithecus* stood and moved erect so it could use tools. As shown in Table 7–2, none of these species has been found in direct association with stone tools, although their use of perishable tools (like the termite-fishing sticks of modern chimpanzees) cannot be discounted. With regard to food, and as judged by their moderately sized molars, the gracile australopithecines seem to have depended primarily on a soft diet of ripe fruit and foliage. Additionally, based on studies of the carbon (C^{13}) content of teeth from Makapansgat, it has been suggested recently that *Australopithecus africanus* (at least) ate grasses and sedges, or alternately, insects and small mammals that had eaten C^{13}-enriched plants. Such insectivory and small scale meat-eating, of course, has been seen in modern chimpanzees and bonobos. Finally, except for *A. bahrelghazali*, the *Australopithecus* species all showed thick dental enamel, suggesting that they were also beginning to eat some harder foods.

With regard to reproduction, the moderate to extreme sexual dimorphism in body size shown by *A. africanus* and *A. afarensis* suggests to some paleoanthropologists that these early hominids had polygynous mating systems characterized by fairly high levels of male-male breeding competition that favored increased male size. This suggestion has not gone unchallenged, however, and other workers remain skeptical that mating systems can be inferred accurately from the size differences between australopithecine females and males. A second possibility, and one that agrees with behavioral data from living hominoids (see Table 4–4), is that the australopithecines were promiscuous. At present, neither mating pattern can be proved nor conclusively rejected.

Turning now to the robust lineage, we find that *P. aethiopicus, P. boisei,* and *P. robustus* also used a variety of habitats; *P. robustus* was adapted to the open grasslands of South Africa (Figure 7–23), while to the north *P. boisei* seems to have preferred well-watered sites such as the gallery forests along rivers. The massive grinding teeth of the robusts suggest that, in contrast to their gracile cousins, they ate large amounts of predominantly tough, fibrous, and/or gritty vegetable foods. That the robusts' vegetable diet may have been supplemented by eating some amount of meat has recently been indicated by the strontium-to-calcium ratio in their bones. Tool use by the robust australopithecines is problematic. They overlapped in time and space with the earliest stone tools (Oldowan choppers and flakes), but because nowhere are they found *exclusively* associated with such tools (Table 7–2), they are often regarded as "nontechnological." Nonetheless, Randall Susman's argument that *Paranthropus robustus* made some or all of the tools at Swartkrans is plausible and, though lacking strong proof, should be given due consideration. At the very least, as with the other australopithecines, chimpanzee-type toolmaking should have been well within the capabilities of *Paranthropus*.

TABLE 7-2 *Associations Between Australopithecine Fossils and Tools*

Species and Site	Found in Association with Stone Tools?	Found in *Sole* Association with Stone Tools?
Ardipithecus ramidus		
Aramis	No	—
Australopithecus afarensis		
Hadar and elsewhere	No	—
Australopithecus anamensis		
Kanapoi and Allia Bay	No	—
Australopithecus africanus		
Sterkfontein and elsewhere	No	—
Paranthropus aethiopicus		
Omo and elsewhere	No	—
Paranthropus boisei		
Olduvai Gorge	Yes	No (*Homo habilis* also present)
Elsewhere	No	—
Paranthropus robustus		
Swartkrans	Yes	No (*Homo erectus?* also present)

FIGURE 7–23   Reconstruction of a group of robust australopithecines (*Paranthropus robustus*) foraging on the South African grasslands. The use of a digging stick is conjectural.

The *Paranthropus* species were all habitual bipeds, although some workers question whether or not they were fully modern in their locomotion. The robusts' long arms and short legs may reflect the continuation of arboreal activities, although this is difficult to determine with certainty (their limb proportions could also simply be the result of recent ape ancestry). And finally, the moderate to marked sexual dimorphism in body size found in the *Paranthropus* species may indicate polygyny, but, as noted above, other mating systems such as promiscuity cannot be ruled out, and social group type is also unclear.

Only two points remain to be covered. First, could the australopithecines talk? The most likely answer here is no. Judging from the smallness of their brains, the apelike proportions of their mouths and throats (see Chapter 13), and their (apparently) primitive lifestyle, it seems safe to conclude that all of the australopithecine species lacked speech and language. Which is not to say they couldn't communicate with one another. After all, nonlinguistic monkeys and apes have complex systems of nonverbal sounds, gestures, postures, and facial expressions that allow the transmission of information about emotions, intentions, and many other things (this is discussed in detail in Chapter 13). Furthermore, as a hominid subfamily, the australopithecines were around for a long time and they spread over much of the African continent: a record of temporal and geographic success that argues for good communication skills, but not necessarily for speech and language.

And, as the last topic in this section, what does the combined evidence from the australopithecines reveal about the origin of hominid bipedalism? Unfortunately, despite the recent spate of fossil discoveries, this question is still very difficult to answer with certainty. Part of the problem is the fact that the early hominids' home ranges included numerous *ecotones*, areas where two or more ecological zones met. Ecotone living allows a species to take advantage of many different environmental opportunities, but the mixed habitat makes it very difficult to tease apart the selective pressures responsible for particular adaptations. In the case of the australo-pithecines—whose environment, as we have seen, included gallery forest, woodland, and some savanna—bipedalism could have evolved as an adaptation for travel and foraging in the trees, on the forest (or closed-woodland) floor, or on the available open grassland. Each of these possibilities must be treated as a hypothesis and tested against the available evidence.

First, it seems reasonable to reject the notion of arboreal bipedalism despite the fact that arm-hangers and swingers already have the body in an orthograde posture. If Monte McCrossin and Brenda Benefit are right about the phylogeny and adaptations of *Kenyapithecus* (see Chapter 5), then our ape ancestors were on the ground for a long time before certain of them evolved habitual bipedalism.

The second hypothesis—that bipedalism evolved as an adaptation for movement across forest and woodland floors—must be taken more seriously (particularly if *Ardipithecus* proves to be a biped), but it's not at all clear why upright locomotion would have been more useful under those conditions than conventional quadrupedalism (the likelihood, mentioned in Chapter 5, that hominids are descended from knuckle-walking quadrupeds is reduced significantly by the elbow anatomy of *Ardipithecus*). Still, bipedalism as a forest/woodland adaptation cannot be rejected out of hand; the idea deserves further study and it has numerous supporters.

Finally, the third, and traditional, hypothesis—that upright walking began on the African grasslands—also remains a viable idea, especially in light of the grassy spaces apparently available at sites such as Aramis (home of *Ardipithecus*) and Kanapoi (home of *A. anamensis*). It seems entirely possible that bipedalism could have arisen as a speedy, energy-efficient, and cool (referring here to body temperature) means of moving across grassy spaces from one food patch to the next (see Chapter 9).

And so, does the combined evidence disprove the old notion that hominid bipedalism began when our ancestors left the trees and came down to live on the African savanna? The answer, unsatisfactory as it may be to some people, can only be "yes and no." For now, this is as good an answer as any to this interesting and important question. Additional fossil discoveries are needed to resolve the controversy. In the meantime, we must turn our attention to the evolutionary relationships that bind the australopithecine species to one another, as well as to the genus *Homo*.

EVOLUTIONARY MODELS OF THE SUBFAMILY AUSTRALOPITHECINAE

The phylogenetic relations among the australopithecines, as well as the evolutionary connections between that subfamily and the hominines (the genus *Homo*), rank near the top of the list of controversial topics in paleoanthropology. Using different methodologies and emphasizing different aspects of the fossils, researchers have come up with a wide variety of evolutionary trees for the earliest hominids. We have tried to illustrate some of that variety in Figure 7–24, where we present three phylogenetic schemes recently published by prominent workers. It is important to note that Figure 7–24 is not drawn to strict scale, and particularly that no attempt has been made to plot accurately the divergence dates for the various species. Within the figure, relatively certain relationships are shown by solid lines; merely possible relationships are shown by dotted lines. Furthermore, the new species *Australopithecus bahrelghazali* has been added to each diagram, but it is shown

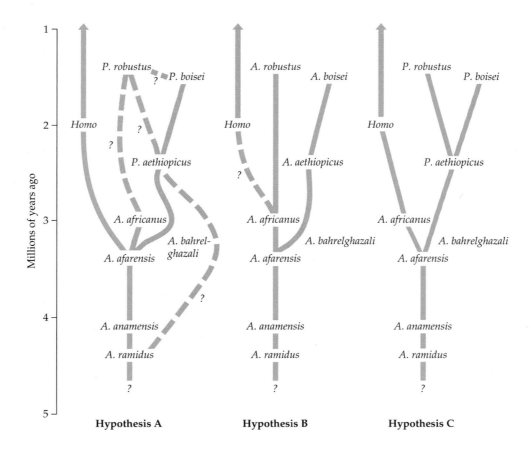

Figure 7–24   Three evolutionary trees for hominids. The various australopithecine species are identified individually, while the hominines are lumped into a single *Homo* lineage for simplicity (later chapters will expand on hominine phylogeny). Solid lines show ancestor-descendant relationships that seem conclusive to the particular researcher(s); dotted lines show questionable relationships. Hypothesis A is from Wood (1994), hypothesis B is from Leakey and Walker (1997), and hypothesis C is from Tattersall (1995). Although its evolutionary connections are unknown, *A. bahrelghazali* has been added to each hypothesis for completeness. See the text for full explanations.

separated as an indication that we do not understand its evolutionary connections as yet. Finally, the hominine branch of the tree is shown in extremely streamlined form. Hominine complexity—and there's plenty of it—will be discussed in detail beginning in the next chapter.

Hypothesis A was published by Bernard Wood in 1994. In his view, *Ardipithecus* was ancestral to all later hominids, *A. anamensis* was ancestral to *A. afarensis*, and *A. afarensis* in turn gave rise to *Homo*. *Paranthropus* is shown as a dead-end genus, possibly with multiple origins (i.e., not as a monophyletic clade): *P. aethiopicus* is descended from *A. afarensis* (or possibly from *Ardipithecus*) and *P. robustus* is possibly descended from *A. africanus*. *Australopithecus africanus* is shown as a descendant of *A. afarensis*, but the South African form is given no direct link at all with *Homo*.

Hypothesis B is the product of Meave Leakey and Alan Walker. From *Ardipithecus* through *A. afarensis*, the scheme is similar to the first hypothesis, but at that point the two phylogenies begin to differ. First of all, Leakey and Walker agree that *A. africanus* was the descendant of *A. afarensis*, but, in contrast to Wood, they believe the South African species might have been ancestral to *Homo*. Furthermore, Leakey and Walker classify all of the robust forms as members of the genus *Australopithecus* rather than *Paranthropus* (i.e., *A. robustus*, *A. boisei*, *A. aethiopicus*) and they too reject the theory that the three species constitute a monophyletic clade. Agreeing partially with Wood, they see *aethiopicus* as most likely descended from *A. afarensis*, and *robustus* definitely descended from *A. africanus* (all three evolutionary trees conclude that *boisei* descended from *aethiopicus*).

The third hypothesis, by Ian Tattersall, has a straightforward tree trunk in agreement with the other models (*Ardipithecus* through *A. afarensis*). It then differs from Wood and Leakey/Walker by arranging the three *Paranthropus* species in a monophyletic clade and by hypothesizing a clear-cut (as opposed to possible) ancestor-descendant link between *A. africanus* and *Homo*.

Which (if any) of these phylogenies is correct? Only time and further research will tell. The hominid fossil record has only begun to be discovered (witness the recent rush of new species) and thus our "family trees" must be flexible enough to accept new evolutionary relatives and revised positions for old ones. A few broad conclusions can be drawn, however, despite the confusion. First, the fossil and molecular data agree that the family Hominidae has been separated from the African apes for 5 million years or more (Box 4–1). Second, as a genus, *Australopithecus* preceded and was ancestral to both *Paranthropus* and *Homo*. And third, the *Paranthropus* forms were not on the direct evolutionary line to modern humans; indeed, the last representatives of that lineage went extinct about 1 million years ago without leaving any descendants.

LATE-BREAKING NEWS FROM THE FIELD

In April 1999, just as this book was going to press, a new hominid species from Ethiopia's Middle Awash region was announced. Named *Australopithecus garhi* by its discoverers, the species dates from 2.5 million years ago and may represent a link between *A. afarensis* and early *Homo*. A full description and interpretation of this new australopithecine must await comparative study—and the ninth edition of this book—but its naming caps a decade of exciting fossil discoveries.

SUMMARY

Since the discovery of *Zinjanthropus* (now *Paranthropus boisei*) at Olduvai Gorge in 1959, East Africa has produced the remains of a variety of Plio-Pleistocene hominids that collectively have established that continent as the birthplace of the human family. At present, the oldest of the East African species is *Ardipithecus ramidus* dating from 4.4 million years ago. Although its bipedalism (and therefore, its hominid status) requires further confirmation, *A. ramidus* seems a good candidate for the base of the hominid evolutionary tree (Figure 7–24). The genus *Australopithecus* was present in East Africa some 200,000 years later in the form of *A. anamensis* and *Australopithecus afarensis*. Finally, recently discovered fossils from Chad, dubbed *Australopithecus bahrelghazali*, have shown that the subfamily Australopithecinae had expanded its geographic range to 1,500 miles (2,5000 kilometers) west of the Rift Valley by 3.5 to 3.0 million years ago.

Sometime before its disappearance around 2.5 million years ago, the genus *Australopithecus* gave rise to two very different genera of descendants: *Homo* (the first hominines) and *Paranthropus* (a lineage characterized by enlargement of the grinding teeth, apparently an adaptation for a hard and tough diet). Many paleoanthropologists believe the three *Paranthropus* species constituted a monophyletic clade, the last member of which died without descendants about a million years ago, leaving *Homo* as the sole surviving hominid genus.

Collectively, the australopithecines (*Ardipithecus, Australopithecus*, and *Paranthropus*; see Table 6–1) inhabited a mixed environment that included gallery forest, woodland, and open grassland. Precisely why they evolved habitual bipedalism remains a mystery, although numerous hypotheses have been formulated on this issue. Recently, the traditional theory that upright walking began as an adaptation for life on the open savanna has come under intense criticism from researchers who prefer a forest/woodland origin. The australopithecines possessed ape-sized brains and apelike vocal tracts, and probably lacked speech and language. Conclusive evidence that they produced material culture (tools) is lacking at present, but indirect evidence to that effect is accumulating.

POSTSCRIPT

As shown in Tables 6–1 and 7–1, the subfamily of the australopithecines is now believed to have contained quite a variety of hominid types. Splitters and lumpers (see the Postscript to Chapter 6) will always disagree about taxonomic designations, but for this book we have settled on a three-genus and eight-species division of the australopithecines. Do we expect that this taxonomy will stand the test of time? Not on your life. Thanks to the continuing discoveries of new forms and the reanalysis of old ones, australopithecine taxonomy (indeed, the taxonomy of all hominids) will always be in a state of flux. A particular set of species and genus names is useful only so long as it provides a reasonable picture of the diversity and relationships of fossil populations, and as our information base and fossil collections increase, adding new names and changing old ones is inevitable. Robert Broom's *Paranthropus crassidens* from Swartkrans is now called *P. robustus*; the Leakeys' *Zinjanthropus boisei* is now *Paranthropus boisei*; the genus name *Ardipithecus* was coined in 1995 to accommodate the Aramis fossils. Just recently, in fact, the increase in new taxon names has been dramatic. Thanks to growing numbers of paleoanthropologists, improved search techniques, and long, hot hours fossil hunting, three species and one genus were announced in the two-year period of 1994–1995: *Ardipithecus ramidus, Australopithecus anamensis,* and *Australopithecus bahrelghazali.* And, just as we go to press, *Australopithecus garhi* has been named.

Why do we bother to point this out? Mainly because we hope to recruit some of the best and brightest readers of this book into the exciting and dynamic field of paleoanthropology. The constant flow of new discoveries, new laboratory procedures, new theories and controversies (e.g., forest versus savanna development of bipedalism), etc., bears witness to the fact that there is still much work to do and much to learn before we will truly understand the origin of humankind. Without a doubt, the next several decades are going to be exciting ones for paleoanthropologists. And so, although we can't promise a life quite as romantic and adventuresome as Indiana Jones's, if you have a flair for science, a willingness to work hard in the fossil fields and/or the laboratory, and an interest in foreign travel, you just might want to consider a career spent solving the greatest whodunit of all time: the mystery of human origins.

REVIEW QUESTIONS

1. What are the grounds for classifying the species *aethiopicus, boisei,* and *robustus* within the single genus *Paranthropus*? What do these species have in common? How do they differ from one another, from *Australopithecus*, and from *Ardipithecus*?

2. Summarize and compare the evidence for bipedalism in *Ardipithecus ramidus, Australopithecus anamensis,* and *Australopithecus afarensis.*

3. Discuss the forest versus savanna theories for the evolution of bipedalism. Which scenario do you find most convincing and why?

4. Does the East African evidence provide any clarification concerning the questions of tool using and toolmaking by *Paranthropus*?

5. Describe the lifestyles of the three australopithecine genera (*Ardipithecus, Australopithecus, Paranthropus*). Be sure to include information about habitat, locomotion (i.e., the variety, if any, of locomotor patterns), diet, and material culture.

6. Describe the main points of australopithecine phylogeny. In particular, what were the evolutionary fates of the three genera?

7. Why is it so difficult for paleoanthropologists to determine how many hominid species and genera they have discovered and how they relate to one another evolutionarily? Discuss the challenges of recognizing species in the fossil record.

SUGGESTED FURTHER READING

Aiello, L., and C. Dean. *An Introduction to Human Evolutionary Anatomy.* Academic Press, 1990.

Brunet, B., et al. "The First Australopithecine 2,500 Kilometres West of the Rift Valley (Chad)." *Nature*, 378, 1995.

Conroy, G. C. *Reconstructing Human Origins.* W. W. Norton, 1997.

Howells, W. *Getting Here.* Compass Press, 1993.

Johanson, D. C., and B. Edgar. *From Lucy to Language.* Simon & Schuster, 1996.

————, and T. D. White. "A Systematic Assessment of Early African Hominids." *Science*, 203, 1979.

Leakey, Mary D. *Olduvai Gorge*, vol. 3. Cambridge University Press, 1971.

Leakey, Meave, et al. "New Four-Million-Year-Old Hominid Species from Kanapoi and Allia Bay, Kenya." *Nature*, 376, 1995.

Tattersall, I. *The Fossil Trail*. Oxford University Press, 1995.

White, T. D., G. Suwa, and B. Asfaw. "*Australopithecus ramidus*, A New Species of Early Hominid from Aramis, Ethiopia." *Nature*, 371, 1994 (also 375, 1995).

INTERNET RESOURCES

AMNH ANTHRO BULLETIN
http://www.amnh.org/enews/anthro.html
(Information on AMNH anthropology and evolution exhibits. Includes a phylogenetic tree of hominids with skulls that can be examined in 3-D.)

ORIGINS OF HUMANKIND—GENERAL TOPICS
http://www.pro-am.com/origins/research/general.htm
(Articles by various contributors about the East African australopithecines. Also links to other websites.)

THE TALK.ORIGINS ARCHIVE—FOSSIL HOMINIDS
http://www.talkorigins.org/faqs/fossil-hominids.html
(Click on "Hominid Species" under the table of contents for descriptions of the East African australopithecines and other hominid varieties.)

ANTHROPOLOGY RESOURCES ON THE INTERNET
http://home.worldnet.fr/clist/Anthro/index.html
(A list of links to sites containing information about fossil hominids, as well as site addresses for museums, anthropology departments, etc. Very useful. After selecting "frames" or "no frames," click on "Physical Anthropology.")

USEFUL SEARCH TERMS:
Ardipithecus
australopithecines
Australopithecus
fossil hominids
Leakey (Louis, Mary, Richard)
Olduvai Gorge
Paranthropus

Chapter 7 Timeline

HOLOCENE	YEARS A.D.	DISCOVERIES

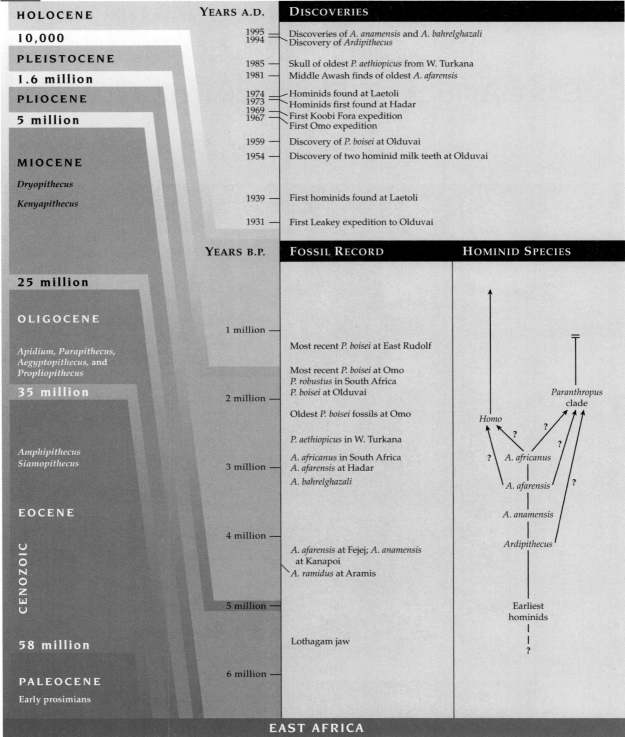

HOLOCENE		
10,000	1995	Discoveries of *A. anamensis* and *A. bahrelghazali*
	1994	Discovery of *Ardipithecus*
PLEISTOCENE		
1.6 million	1985	Skull of oldest *P. aethiopicus* from W. Turkana
	1981	Middle Awash finds of oldest *A. afarensis*
PLIOCENE	1974	Hominids found at Laetoli
	1973	Hominids first found at Hadar
5 million	1969	First Koobi Fora expedition
	1967	First Omo expedition
	1959	Discovery of *P. boisei* at Olduvai
	1954	Discovery of two hominid milk teeth at Olduvai
MIOCENE		
Dryopithecus		
Kenyapithecus	1939	First hominids found at Laetoli
	1931	First Leakey expedition to Olduvai

	YEARS B.P.	FOSSIL RECORD	HOMINID SPECIES
25 million			
OLIGOCENE	1 million		
Apidium, Parapithecus, Aegyptopithecus, and *Propliopithecus*		Most recent *P. boisei* at East Rudolf	
35 million	2 million	Most recent *P. boisei* at Omo *P. robustus* in South Africa *P. boisei* at Olduvai Oldest *P. boisei* fossils at Omo	
Amphipithecus *Siamopithecus*	3 million	*P. aethiopicus* in W. Turkana *A. africanus* in South Africa *A. afarensis* at Hadar *A. bahrelghazali*	
EOCENE			
	4 million		
		A. afarensis at Fejej; *A. anamensis* at Kanapoi *A. ramidus* at Aramis	
	5 million		
58 million		Lothagam jaw	Earliest hominids
PALEOCENE	6 million		
Early prosimians			

EAST AFRICA

The story of discoveries in Northeast, North-Central, and East Africa is as exciting as that of South Africa and new discoveries are reported every year. Dating of fossil deposits is far more secure in these areas than in South Africa because there has been much volcanic activity since the early Miocene and chronometric dating is therefore possible. Many of the deposits, moreover, are very thick and span a considerable time range.

8

EAST AFRICA: THE ADVENT OF *HOMO*

An artist's conception of how early *Homo* might have looked while chipping an Oldowan tool some 2 million years ago.

Intelligence . . . is the faculty of making artificial objects . . .
                    HENRI BERGSON, 1859–1941, *L'Evolution Creatrice*

More brain, O Lord, more brain!
                    GEORGE MEREDITH, 1828–1909, *Modern Love*

OVERVIEW

Between 4.4 and about 2.5 million years B.P., the hominid family was represented in Africa first by *Ardipithecus* and then by *Australopithecus*. Around 2.5 million years ago, for reasons that are not well understood, the Hominidae experienced a burst of extinction and speciation that led to the loss of *Australopithecus* and the addition of *Paranthropus* and *Homo*. Two species of the earliest hominines can be identified: *Homo habilis* (2.3 to 1.6 million years B.P.) and *Homo rudolfensis* (2.4 to 1.6 million years B.P.). Both were terrestrial bipeds (although not necessarily walking exactly like modern humans) and both had significantly larger brains than their australopithecine forebears. Furthermore, one or both of these "early *Homo*" species apparently made Oldowan stone tools—a development that paleoanthropologists believe signals increased meat in the diet. Early *Homo* spread from Northeast to South Africa and survived until 1.6 mya. By 1.8 mya, at the latest, early *Homo* (most likely, *Homo habilis*) had given rise to *Homo erectus*.

FIRST EVIDENCE OF THE HOMININES

As described in Chapters 6 and 7, the beginning of the hominid story is concerned exclusively with tales of the australopithecines. Represented more or less sequentially by the genera *Ardipithecus*, *Australopithecus*, and *Paranthropus*, the subfamily Australopithecinae enjoyed at least 3 million years of existence in Africa without

 Mini-Timeline

DATE OR AGE	FOSSIL DISCOVERIES OR EVOLUTIONARY EVENTS
(A) DATE (YEARS A.D.)	
1997	2.5-million-year-old Oldowan tools found at Gona
1994	*Homo habilis* (?) found associated with Oldowan tools at Kada Hadar
1960	Discovery of first *Homo habilis* fossils at Olduvai Gorge
(B) AGE (MILLION YEARS B.P.)	
1.0–1.3	*Paranthropus* goes extinct
1.8	Oldest definite *Homo erectus* fossils
2.3?–1.6	*Homo habilis* inhabits first East, then South Africa
2.4–1.6	*Homo rudolfensis* inhabits East Africa

TABLE 8-1   *Hominid Taxonomy*

Subfamily Australopithecinae (see Table 6–1 for species names)

    Genera
        Ardipithecus
        Australopithecus
        Paranthropus

Subfamily Homininae (Common name: hominines)

Genus *Homo*	Species	
		Homo rudolfensis
		Homo habilis
		Homo erectus
		Homo heidelbergensis
		Homo neanderthalensis
		Homo sapiens

competition from more advanced hominid types (roughly 5.6 to 2.4 million years B.P.). Then, about two and a half million years ago, a critical (for us) evolutionary development took place: one of the australopithecine species gave rise by clado-genesis to a different sort of creature, one that was bigger brained than its ancestors and definitely produced material culture. Paleoanthropologists classify these new creatures as *Homo*, the first representatives of the subfamily Homininae (Table 8–1), and this chapter is devoted to the story of their discoveries, adaptations, and accomplishments.

The Discovery of *Homo habilis* (1960–1964)

You will recall from Chapter 7 that in 1959 Mary and Louis Leakey hit paleontological pay dirt in Bed I of Olduvai Gorge. That was the year they discovered the skull of *Zinjanthropus* (now *Paranthropus*) *boisei*, a creature that they suspected was responsible for the numerous Oldowan stone choppers and flakes also found at the site. Their suspicions were short-lived, however, because just the next year a better candidate for the office of stone toolmaker showed up: a hominid with a much bigger brain than *Zinjanthropus*.

Early in 1960, the Leakeys' son, Jonathan, uncovered some teeth and bone fragments of a second Bed I hominid. Though found at broadly the same stratigraphic level as *Paranthropus* (*Zinjanthropus*) *boisei* and not far away, Louis Leakey realized the bones represented a creature far closer to modern humans than *P. boisei*, with its huge molars and sagittal crest. Nicknamed "Jonny's Child," after its discoverer and the fact that it was only ten to twelve years old at death, the new fossil showed much smaller grinding teeth and relatively larger front teeth than *Zinjanthropus*, as well as a larger braincase. By 1964, a thorough analysis of Jonny's Child, plus the discovery of additional and confirming specimens, convinced Leakey and his co-workers that the Bed I toolmaker was not *P. boisei*, but a previously unknown species that they named *Homo habilis* ("handy man").

TABLE 8-2 *A Partial Record of Early* **Homo** *Fossil Sites*

SPECIES	SOUTH AFRICAN SITES	AGE (MILLION YEARS)[a]	EAST AFRICAN SITES	AGE (MILLION YEARS)
Homo habilis	Sterkfontein	2.0–1.8	Olduvai Gorge	1.9–1.6
			Omo and Koobi Fora	2.0–1.8
			Hadar (?)	2.3
Homo rudolfensis			Omo and Koobi Fora	2.0–1.6
			Uraha (Malawi)	2.4

[a] As noted in Table 7–1, the East African sites are dated more accurately than those from South Africa.

Homo habilis remains have now been recovered from Olduvai Gorge, from Omo in extreme southwest Ethiopia (Figure 7–1), and from Koobi Fora in Kenya (Table 8–2). In addition, a recently discovered maxilla (upper jaw) from Hadar may well turn out to be *Homo habilis*. The known time range for the species currently stands at 2.0 to 1.6 million years B.P. (this extends back to 2.3 million years ago if the Hadar jaw is included). Among the most important specimens discovered thus far is a partial foot from Olduvai (OH 8; the toe bones and part of the heel are missing; see Figure 8–1), a very fragmented skull from the same locality (OH 24; Figure 8–2), and a much more complete skull from Koobi Fora that dates 1.9 million years of age (KNM-ER 1813; see Figure 8–3 and also the hominid color photo essay). Finally, in the mid-1980s, Donald Johanson and Tim White worked at Olduvai Gorge for four seasons and recovered a fragmentary skeleton that has

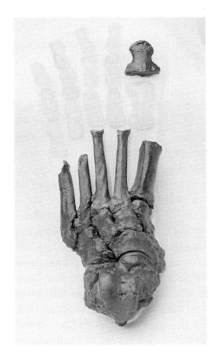

FIGURE 8–1 The *Homo habilis* foot from Olduvai Gorge (OH 8). Almost all of the toe bones (phalanges) are missing, as is part of the heel. Photograph is just over 50 percent actual size.

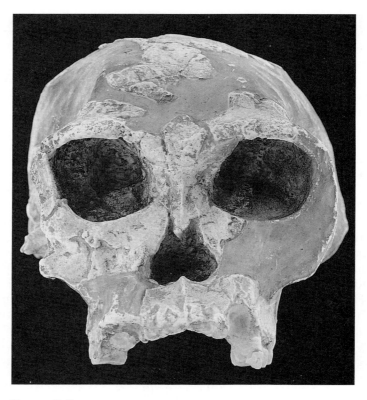

FIGURE 8–2   Cranium of *Homo habilis* (OH 24), approximately 1.8 million years old. Photograph is approximately 80 percent actual size.

been attributed to *Homo habilis* (OH 62). This find is particularly important because it provides critical information about body size, limb proportions, and other aspects of the postcranial anatomy of this species.

The taxonomic validity of *Homo habilis* is now widely accepted, although this was not the case initially, as described below. Indeed, over the years so much variable fossil material was attributed to *Homo habilis* that many scientists started to believe that it had come to contain specimens from more than one species. Splitting the *H. habilis* bone collection led to the recent naming of a second early hominine, **Homo rudolfensis** (more on this in a later section). Together, the two species are commonly referred to as "early *Homo*." In any event, the main characteristics of *Homo habilis* (as adjusted after the removal of the *H. rudolfensis* material) are summarized in Box 8–1. Comparisons with Boxes 6–2 and 7–3 show that *Homo habilis* had much in common with South Africa's *Australopithecus africanus* and East Africa's *A. afarensis*. For example, body size was very similar in the three species, all showed rather apelike limb proportions (relatively long arms and short legs), and all showed some indication of continuing arboreal activity (the OH 8 foot may have had a partially divergent, grasping big toe). The dentition of *Homo habilis* was much more modern than that of *A. afarensis*, but only marginally more so than that of *A. africanus*. It is immediately clear that the main factor differentiating *Homo habilis* from the australopithecines was brain size. With an average of 612 cubic cen-

Homo rudolfensis one of the two *species* of "early *Homo*"; inhabited East Africa 2.4 to 1.6 million years ago.

Box 8-1

CHARACTERISTICS OF *HOMO HABILIS*[a]

TRAIT	*HOMO HABILIS*
Height	F: 3.3 ft (100 cm) M: ?
Weight	F: 71 lb (32 kg) M: 82 lb (37 kg) (F about 86% of M)
Brain size	612 cc mean (509–674 cc range)
Cranium	Somewhat prognathic face; incipient brow ridge; fore-shortened palate; no sagittal crest; rounded mandibular base
Dentition	Narrower lower grinding teeth than in *Homo rudolfensis*; mostly single-rooted lower premolars
Limbs	Longer arms and shorter legs than modern humans; feet retaining adaptations for climbing
Locomotion	Bipedalism (probably almost modern, but with a few remaining apelike characteristics)
Known dates (million years B.P.)	2.0–1.6 (2.3–1.6 if Hadar jaw is included)

[a] Mean values for anatomical measurements may change with additional fossil discoveries. For additional technical details and diagnostic traits, see Appendix III.

timeters, *Homo habilis* had a bigger brain than apes and the various australopithecines, but a much smaller brain than modern people or the well-established hominine ***Homo erectus*** (Table 8–3). But what do these differences say about taxonomy? Specifically, do the brain size data help us decide whether *habilis* is a hominine or an australopithecine?

Homo erectus hominid species that inhabited much of the Old World between 1.9(?) million and at least 300,000 years B.P.; successor to "early *Homo*."

Classifying *Homo habilis*

Homo habilis earned neither name nor credentials easily. A few anthropologists preferred to identify it as an advanced type of the gracile *A. africanus* not deserving *Homo* status at all. Some still identify it in this way. Its qualifications as a distinct species have been in question from the day it was named.

Should it be called *Homo habilis* or *Australopithecus habilis*? Compared to the certified human beings of the genus *Homo* that came after, it seems scarcely human; compared to the more primitive types that preceded, its human credentials suddenly improve. This disconcerting shift of perspective always occurs when the eye runs down a series of fossils that are related to one another through direct descent. The differences among them are often differences in degree—not in kind—and obviously become more pronounced as one takes one's examples from more widely separated time zones. The more obvious characteristics of *Homo* are comparative: an increasingly large brain, a higher forehead, a "more delicate" jaw, and longer legs. But in a continuous series, where does one draw the line?

TABLE 8-3   *Cranial Capacities for Apes and Certain Hominid Species*

SPECIES	RANGE OF CRANIAL CAPACITY (CC)	AVERAGE CRANIAL CAPACITY (CC)
Chimpanzees	282–500	383
Gorillas	340–752	505
Ardipithecus ramidus	Unknown	Unknown
Australopithecus afarensis	400–500	433
Australopithecus africanus	405–515	454
Paranthropus robustus	Unknown	530
Paranthropus boisei	410–530	487
Paranthropus aethiopicus	Unknown	410
Homo habilis	509–674	612
Homo rudolfensis	752–810	781
Homo erectus	750–1,251	994
Modern humans	1,000–2,000	1,330

Note: Measurements of cranial capacity are always given in cubic centimeters (cc; a cubic centimeter equals about 0.06 in^3); the size of the brain itself is usually somewhat smaller because the cranial cavity also contains other structures. The above figures are approximate: for the two African apes, they are based on rather small samples; and in the case of the fossil groups, the samples are extremely small and may prove to be misleading. Furthermore, a recent study by Conroy, et. al. (1998), suggests that cranial capacities measured using traditional techniques may well be inflated compared to those done with modern CT scans and computer imaging. For modern humans, rare extremes exceeding even the approximate range given above have been found; the average figure is based on a limited number of samples. Slight variations in these figures will be found in other authors' works.

As a general rule, and within an order, species of animals with larger brains are more intelligent than those with smaller brains, but this does not hold among species of different body sizes. The significance of brain size is considered in Chapter 13. Within a species, variations in brain size are not believed to be related to intelligence among normal individuals. Data from Walker et al. (1987), Tobias (1985), Aiello and Dean (1990), and Brown et al. (1993). Fossils are attributed to *Homo habilis* and *Homo rudolfensis* following Wood (1992). West Turkana fossil KNM-WT 17000 is classified as *P. aethiopicus*.

The Question of Brain Size

The question of brain size continues to arise, but it is conceivably the wrong question. Since all creatures are bundles of characteristics, many of which may be evolving at different rates, drawing a line that is based on these characteristics always causes trouble. Early in this century, the British anatomist Arthur Keith chose to draw the line marking the appearance of humanity where the brain capacity touched 750 cubic centimeters. Anything below that, according to Keith, was not human; anything above it was. (Most modern people have brains in the 1,200 to 1,600 cubic centimeter range, although smaller and larger brains regularly occur; see Table 8–3). More recently, Wilfrid Le Gros Clark put the minimum at 700 cc. Clark's choice, unlike Keith's, was not arbitrary; it reflected the state of the fossil record at the time it was made: No accepted "human" skulls were known to exist with cranial capacities of less than 700 cc. Implicit in this situation, of course, was the possibility that an apparently human specimen with a slightly smaller brain might be discovered any day.

Homo habilis laid this problem right on the scientists' doorstep. The great difficulty in deciding whether it was human lay in the fact that the so-called type specimen, the first one to be found and named *Homo habilis* by the Leakeys, had a brain capacity estimated to be about 657 cubic centimeters—just under Clark's limit. Since then, five other *H. habilis* skulls have been measured by two experts: Phillip Tobias and Ralph Holloway. They came up with surprisingly uniform figures for these skulls. They range in capacity from 509 to 674 cc and average about 612 cc.

Too small-brained for a human? Perhaps, but probably too large-brained for a typical gracile *Australopithecus*, whose mean cranial capacity was only about 450 cc.

What is the meaning of brain size? How significant is the steady increase in cranial capacity that we find in human evolution? Large brains are found in large animals generally, and the brains of elephants and whales are very much larger than those of humans. As a general rule, among mammals brain size can best be interpreted when it is related to body size, and a doubling of body size during the evolution of a lineage usually results in a considerable increase in brain size (see Chapter 13). When we look at the figures in Table 8–3, therefore, we should consider the size of the animal itself. For example, the stature of *A. afarensis* varied from 3.3 to 5 feet (1 to 1.5 meters) tall, while that of modern humans varies from approximately 4.5 to over 6 feet (1.4 to 1.8 meters). The difference in relative brain size is therefore not quite as great as the table might suggest. It should not be forgotten, however, that many human populations—of pygmies, for example—fall into the range of stature for *A. afarensis* and yet have brains in the region of 1,200 to 1,350 cubic centimeters; three times as large. A consideration of stature is therefore not going to alter very seriously the significance of the figures for the Hominidae listed in Table 8–3.

As it turned out, Leakey and his colleagues didn't confront any of the hard questions about the meaning of brain size when they named *Homo habilis* in 1964. In the end, in order to get Jonny's Child and his ilk into *Homo*, they simply redefined our genus by lowering its "cerebral Rubicon." Down from Arthur Keith's 750 cc and Le Gros Clark's 700 cc, Leakey and his team proposed a lower limit of 600 cc for the absolute brain size of any specimen to be included in *Homo*. With the bar reset within its reach, *habilis* vaulted promptly into the genus *Homo* and it has been there ever since. In fact, *Homo habilis*'s staying power as a hominine has been impressive. Although there was grumbling initially, most researchers now accept *H. habilis* as a valid species. As discussed below, however, the same is not necessarily true of the other type of early *Homo*, *H. rudolfensis*.

Evidence of *Homo* at Koobi Fora

Early in the work at Koobi Fora (early 1970s), it became clear that the Lake Turkana region contained fossils of hominids other than robust australopithecines. Over time, a number of specimens were recovered of larger-brained, gracile creatures that did not fit well into either *Australopithecus* or *Paranthropus*. One of the finest fossils carries the museum number KNM-ER 1470, and it is an almost complete cranium and face, but with the skull base and jaw missing (Figure 8–3). ER 1470 combines a large face with strongly built zygomatic arches and relatively large molar teeth (much smaller than in *Paranthropus*, however). The skull is relatively lightly built, and the braincase is considerably larger than any australopithecine's at 775 cubic centimeters.

As the search for fossils continued at Koobi Fora, several other specimens of relatively large-brained hominids were discovered, including the splendid skull labeled ER-1813 (Figure 8–3). But what to call the nonaustralopithecines from Koobi Fora? Initially, they were lumped with similar specimens from Olduvai Gorge and classified as *Homo habilis*. This is still the position taken by South African anthropologist Phillip Tobias, who prefers a single-species interpretation of all early *Homo* material. Other workers disagree. Briton Bernard Wood and American G. P. Rightmire have both argued that there is too much variation in the combined Olduvai and Koobi Fora assemblage to be contained in a single species—even a species with marked sexual dimorphism in body size. It now seems increasingly

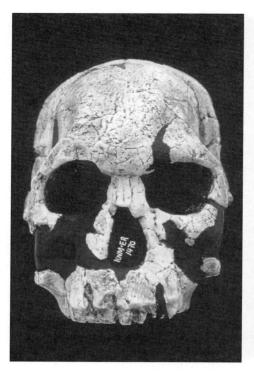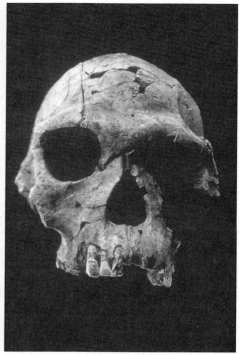

FIGURE 8–3 *Homo rudolfensis* (KNM-ER 1470; left) compared with *Homo habilis* (KNM-ER 1813; right). Note the differences in size of braincase and brows between the two early *Homo* species. See also the color essay on fossil hominids. Both photos are about 45 percent actual size.

likely that *Homo habilis*, was traditionally defined, probably contained at least two species. Wood has proposed the following solution to the problem (a solution that we have adopted for this textbook): Retain the name *Homo habilis* for the Olduvai material and some of the fossils from Omo and Koobi Fora (including ER-1813), and classify ER-1470 and certain other Omo, Uraha, and Koobi Fora specimens as belonging to a new species, *Homo rudolfensis*.

If the early *Homo* fossils from Olduvai and Koobi Fora are sorted in this way, interesting differences appear between the two resulting species (compare Boxes 8–1 and 8–2). *Homo habilis* (as now narrowly defined) has the more primitive-looking skull, with some prognathism, an incipient brow ridge, and a much smaller brain (although brain size is increased by about one-third over the australo-pithecine average). Additionally, the postcranial anatomy of the newly defined *Homo habilis* includes small body size, australopithecine-like limb proportions (Figure 8–4) and adaptations of the feet for climbing—features that suggest the continuation of arboreal activities in addition to terrestrial bipedalism. On the progressive side, however, the teeth of *Homo habilis* seem more like those of later hominids than do the teeth of *Homo rudolfensis*. For its part, *Homo rudolfensis* has a larger body, a flatter face and a larger brain than *H. habilis* (showing about a two-thirds increase in brain size over the australopithecine average), but these are combined with broad grinding teeth that remind one of *Paranthropus*. And while the limb proportions of *Homo rudolfensis* are currently unknown, certain features of the foot and the thigh are quite similar to those of later *Homo* species. The few pelvic remains of early *Homo* suggest that these hominids showed an almost modern form of bipedalism, but with a few remaining apelike characteristics.

These two species of early *Homo* overlapped temporally for 400,000 years or more (Table 8–2), and, at least at Koobi Fora, they overlapped geographically as

FIGURE 8–4   *Homo habilis* as reconstructed primarily from the Olduvai Gorge fossil OH 62, discovered in 1986. Note the relatively long arms and short legs of this species of early *Homo*.

well. *Homo rudolfensis* was apparently the first to evolve and may have been strictly an East African form. Recent discoveries at the Uraha site west of Lake Malawi have set the earliest date for *Homo rudolfensis* at about 2.4 mya. *Homo habilis* (as newly defined) ranged from Koobi Fora and Omo (and perhaps Hadar) in the north to Sterkfontein in the south (Chapter 6). But what were the lifestyles of the early *Homo* species like, and which one (if either) gave rise to more advanced hominines? It is to these questions that we now turn our attention.

EARLY HOMININE LIFESTYLES

In light of the fact that both species of early *Homo* are thought to be immediate descendants of *Australopithecus*, it should come as no surprise that paleoanthropologists think they lived a rather australopithecine-like lifestyle, albeit with one or two significant differences. Like the australopithecines, early *Homo* utilized a mixed bag of habitats including lake floodplains, gallery forests, woodlands, and savanna. Their primary locomotor adaptation to that mosaic environment was clearly terrestrial bipedalism, although certain primitive anatomical features suggest a few remaining apelike characteristics in their walking and the continuation of some amount of arboreal climbing. In particular, primitive features of the feet of *Homo habilis* (for example, a somewhat divergent big toe) have convinced some researchers that this hominid had a distinctly nonmodern gait: others are not so sure. Furthermore, while the postcranial remains attributed to *H. rudolfensis* look a bit more like those of modern humans, in several cases the species classification has been questioned. In all, considerably more material is needed before we can say for sure how early *Homo* moved and precisely what sort of habitats these hominids favored.

Unfortunately, we must be satisfied with equally fuzzy conclusions about the social groups, mating patterns, and communication skills of early *Homo*. Judging from body weight estimates, *H. habilis* and *H. rudolfensis* were less sexually dimorphic in size than the australopithecines (compare Boxes 8–1 and 8–2 with Boxes 6–2, 7–2, and 7–3). This suggests that they also were less likely to have had polygynous mating systems, but more precise conclusions are impossible at present. Whether early *Homo* moved about the African landscape in family groups or troops is equally unclear, although it does seem safe to rule out orangutanlike solitary ranging, given the predator pressure the first hominines must have faced. Finally, larger brains no doubt meant more complex communication skills than those of the australopithecines, but speech and language still seem to have been beyond the capabilities of early *Homo*. This conclusion is supported by evidence that they probably retained apelike proportions of the vocal tract (including an unflexed cranial base; see Chapter 13), and also by the simple nature of the Oldowan stone tools that they are assumed to have made.

The Oldowan stone tools bring us to the evidence that most researchers believe provides the best behavioral dividing line between the first hominines and the australopithecines: early *Homo* (one or both forms) is thought to have made and used stone tools on a regular basis, while the evidence for such behavior by the australopithecines is not conclusive (see Chapters 6 and 7, and especially Table 7–2).

Box 8-2

CHARACTERISTICS OF *HOMO RUDOLFENSIS*[a]

TRAIT	*HOMO RUDOLFENSIS*
Height (sexes combined)	4.9 ft (150 cm) (?)
Weight	F: 112 lb (51 kg) M: 132 lb (60 kg) (F about 85% of M)
Brain size (sexes combined)	781 cc mean (752–810 cc range)
Cranium	Flat face; no brow ridge; large palate; no sagittal crest; everted mandibular base
Dentition	Broader lower grinding teeth than *Homo habilis*; multirooted lower premolars
Limbs	Limb proportions unknown; feet more like those of later humans than was true for *H. habilis*
Locomotion	Bipedalism probably almost modern, but with a few remaining apelike characteristics
Known dates (million years B.P.)	2.4–1.6

[a] Mean values for anatomical measurements may change with additional fossil discoveries. For additional technical details and diagnostic traits, see Appendix III.

The oldest known stone tools have been recovered from the site of Gona, in the Hadar region of Ethiopia, and they are dated at 2.5 million years of age (see Figure 7–22). Consisting of simple cores, whole flakes, and flaking debris, the Gona assemblage is a clear example of the Oldowan tool industry identified by the Leakeys many years ago at Olduvai Gorge. At Gona, sharp flakes were struck off cores and then used as cutting implements, while the cores themselves apparently were used as hammerstones and multipurpose pounders (this can be detected from the way the cores are pitted and battered). Other ancient Oldowan assemblages have come from Omo (2.4 to 2.3 mya), the Semliki River Valley in the western Rift (2.3 mya), and, of course, Olduvai Gorge (1.9 to 1.7 mya). Admittedly, absolutely conclusive proof that the various Oldowan assemblages were made by early *Homo* is still lacking, but one recent discovery was very nearly the "smoking gun" that archaeologists are seeking. At the Kada Hadar site in Ethiopia, an upper jaw of early *Homo* (most likely *H. habilis*) was found "closely associated" with 2.3 million-year-old Oldowan tools. Pending the discovery of a skeleton with tool in hand, we find this sort of sole association of early *Homo* with Oldowan tools to be convincing, and so for the remainder of this discussion (and this book) we treat the first hominines as stone toolmakers without further qualifying remarks.

The question of what early *Homo* was doing with Oldowan tools remains unanswered, however, but a hint comes from Kada Hadar where a piece of bovid (cattlelike animals of the mammalian family Bovidae) shoulder blade was found bearing what appears to be a cut mark from a stone tool. As discussed in detail in Chapter 9, most paleoanthropologists conclude that Oldowan tools signal an increased reliance on meat in the early hominines' diet, although whether that meat was the result of scavenging or active hunting is unclear. The Oldowan flakes were probably used for butchering carcasses, while the cores were used to batter open bones so the marrow could be consumed. Beyond that, only one other statement concerning the diet of early *Homo* is possible. The relatively larger, multi-rooted grinding teeth of *Homo rudolfensis* suggest that members of that species ate more tough and hard food items (nuts, roots, seeds, etc.) than *Homo habilis*.

EARLY HOMININE PHYLOGENIES

One last topic remains before we close this relatively short chapter, and that is the evolutionary relationships of the two early *Homo* species. As described in Chapter 7 and diagrammed in Figure 7–24, the first hominines are thought to have descended from either *Australopithecus afarensis* or *Australopithecus africanus*. (But see the new information on *Australopithecus garhi* at the end of Chapter 7.) Teasing out the origins of *Homo habilis* versus *Homo rudolfensis* in any greater detail is impossible at this time. Equally difficult is determining which early *Homo* type (if either) gave rise to the next hominine species, *Homo erectus*. Ian Tattersall, of the American Museum of Natural History, is willing to venture an opinion, however, and he opts for *Homo habilis* as modern humans' direct ancestor. According to Tattersall, *Homo rudolfensis* "had some specializations [derived anatomical traits] which make it less likely than the smaller-brained and more primitive-limbed *Homo habilis* to have given rise to later humans." And in a very recent study, Daniel Lieberman of Rutgers University, along with his colleagues Bernard Wood and David Pilbeam, agree with Tattersall that *H. habilis* seems to be more closely linked to *Homo erectus* than does *H. rudolfensis*.

SUMMARY

Around two and a half million years ago, for reasons that are not well understood (but see the Postscript to Chapter 9), the African family Hominidae experienced a significant evolutionary shake-up (see Figure 7–24): the last representatives of *Australopithecus* died out and two new genera appeared, *Paranthropus* and *Homo*—the latter marking a new evolutionary grade for hominids. Shortly after its evolutionary appearance, *Homo* was present in at least two forms, *H. habilis* and *H. rudolfensis*, both bipeds (although apparently not fully modern in that locomotor pattern) and one or both making Oldowan stone tools. With significantly larger brains than the australopithecines, the two early *Homo* species were undoubtedly somewhat smarter than their predecessors (which would have facilitated toolmaking; see Chapter 9) and probably had more complex communication systems, although it seems unlikely that they had speech and language. Stone tool manufacture and use probably points to more meat in the early hominines' diet, but anthropologists are undecided about how additional meat was obtained (scavenging or active hunting?). In any event, along with the *Paranthropus* forms (with which early *Homo* had a long temporal overlap and even spatial overlap at some sites), the first hominines haunted the gallery forests, woodlands, and savannas of both East and South Africa for very nearly a million years. And, although the early *Homo* species were not quite at the point where most anthropologists are comfortable calling them human (admittedly, this is a matter of taste; there are no established criteria for the use of that term), one of them (probably *H. habilis*) gave rise to a species that clearly deserves that label: *Homo erectus*.

POSTSCRIPT

In the savannas and woodlands of Africa, the australopithecines rode the crest of hominid evolution for more than 3 million years. The robust lineage (*Paranthropus*)—with its enormous grinding teeth and demanding diet—passed into extinction without issue about a million years ago. In contrast, the gracile lineage (*Australopithecus*) was much luckier. It almost certainly gave rise near the end of the Pliocene to more humanlike hominids of the genus *Homo*. Many of the genes we carry about today were inherited from gracile australopithecine forebears.

But how do scientists decide that early *Homo*—*H. habilis* and *H. rudolfensis*—were members of our genus and not simply advanced australopithecines? What derived traits do these species share with later varieties of *Homo* that mark the genus boundary? As it turns out, this is not an easy question, and the answer has become more complex as the fossil record around the Plio-Pleistocene dividing line has become better known. One trait stands out above all others, of course, and that is *Homo*'s increased brain size. A convenient (but arbitrary) dividing line appears to be about 600 cubic centimeters: *Homo* is above that figure and the australopithecines below. In addition, thanks to modern cladistic analyses, we can expand the defining criteria for *Homo* using the following list (traits 2 to 9 are taken from B. Wood, 1992). Compared to the australopithecines, *Homo* shows the following:

1. larger brain (roughly 600 cubic centimeters and up)
2. thicker bones of the braincase

3. reduced postorbital constriction (narrowing of the skull at the temples)
4. occipital bone that makes an increased contribution to the cranial sagittal arc length
5. higher cranial vault
6. foramen magnum farther forward
7. flatter lower face
8. narrowed tooth crowns (especially the lower premolars)
9. shorter molar toothrow

One final trait is ineligible for inclusion in anatomical lists but cannot be dissociated from our image of *Homo*, and that is culture. Modern humans and our immediate ancestors, *Homo erectus*, are characterized by dependence on a cultural lifestyle. The widely accepted view that the hominids labeled early *Homo* made the Oldowan stone tools to a simple but recognizable pattern suggests to many anthropologists that these hominids had taken the first steps toward a cultural way of life and therefore, in addition to their anatomical distinctions, deserve to be included in our genus.

REVIEW QUESTIONS

1. Describe the anatomical traits of *Homo habilis* and *Homo rudolfensis*. How do these species of early *Homo* differ physically from their *Australopithecus* ancestors?
2. Describe the behavioral traits (group type, mating system, diet, material culture) of early *Homo*. Compare these traits with similar information for *Australopithecus* and *Paranthropus*.
3. Discuss the problem of identifying the maker(s) of the various Oldowan tool assemblages. What sort of evidence do you think is needed before a conclusive identification can be made?
4. Describe the possible evolutionary relations of the early *Homo* species. Which australopithecine type(s) do you think gave rise to them, and which early hominine variety do you think gave rise to *Homo erectus*?
5. Discuss whether or not the earliest hominines (or even the australopithecines) should be called "humans." What criteria would you establish for the use of this term?

SUGGESTED FURTHER READING

Bromage, T. G., F. Schrenk, and F. W. Zonneveld. "Paleoanthropology of the Malawi Rift: An Early Hominid Mandible From the Chiwondo Beds, Northern Malawi." *Journal of Human Evolution*, 28, 1995.

Johanson, D. C., and B. Edgar. *From Lucy to Language*. Simon & Schuster, 1996.

Kimbel, W. H., et al. "Late Pliocene *Homo* and Oldowan Tools From the Hadar Formation (Kada Hadar Member), Ethiopia." *Journal of Human Evolution*, 31, 1996.

Lieberman, D. E., B. A. Wood, and D. R. Pilbeam. "Homoplasy and Early *Homo*: An Analysis of the Evolutionary Relationships of *H. habilis sensu stricto* and *H. rudolfensis*." *Journal of Human Evolution*, 30, 1996.

Schrenk, F., et al. "Oldest *Homo* and Pliocene Biogeography of the Malawi Rift." *Nature*, 365, 1993.

Semaw, S., et al. "2.5-Million-Year-Old Stone Tools From Gona, Ethiopia." *Nature*, 385, 1997.

Tattersall, I. *The Fossil Trail*. Oxford University Press, 1995.

Wood, B. "Origin and Evolution of the Genus *Homo*." *Nature*, 355, 1992.

INTERNET RESOURCES

INSTITUTE OF HUMAN ORIGINS

http://www.asu.edu/clas/iho/
> (Description of the recent discovery of early *Homo* associated with stone tools. Also information about IHO activities and publications.)

ORIGINS OF HUMANKIND—GENERAL TOPICS

http://www.pro-am.com/origins/research/general.htm
> (Listed under earlier chapters, the Origins of Humankind website also provides information about the early hominines [*Homo habilis*] and their Oldowan stone tools, as well as news items on the latest discoveries.)

USEFUL SEARCH TERMS:

> *fossil hominids*
> *Homo habilis*
> *Oldowan tools*
> *stone tools*

Chapter 8 Timeline

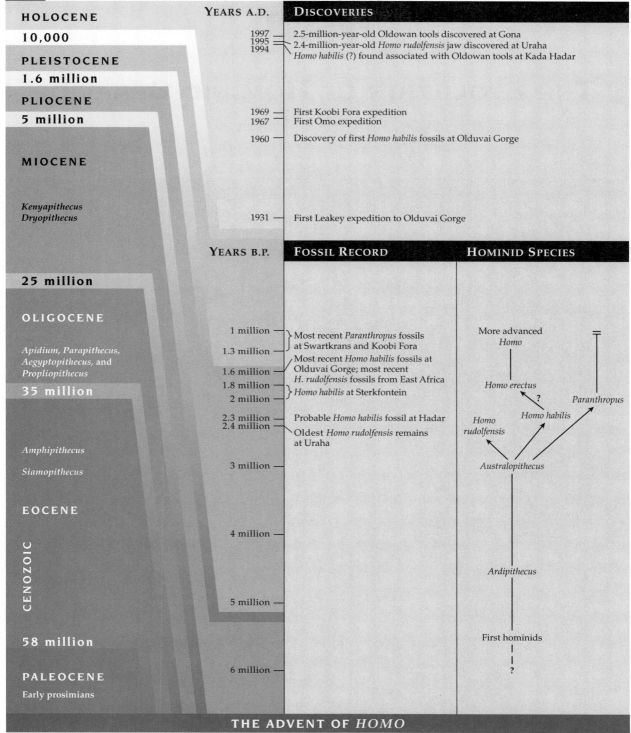

HOLOCENE	
10,000	
PLEISTOCENE	
1.6 million	
PLIOCENE	
5 million	
MIOCENE	
Kenyapithecus *Dryopithecus*	
25 million	
OLIGOCENE	
Apidium, Parapithecus, Aegyptopithecus, and *Propliopithecus*	
35 million	
Amphipithecus	
Siamopithecus	
EOCENE	
CENOZOIC	
58 million	
PALEOCENE	
Early prosimians	

YEARS A.D.

DISCOVERIES

1997 — 2.5-million-year-old Oldowan tools discovered at Gona
1995 — 2.4-million-year-old *Homo rudolfensis* jaw discovered at Uraha
1994 — *Homo habilis* (?) found associated with Oldowan tools at Kada Hadar

1969 — First Koobi Fora expedition
1967 — First Omo expedition

1960 — Discovery of first *Homo habilis* fossils at Olduvai Gorge

1931 — First Leakey expedition to Olduvai Gorge

YEARS B.P.

FOSSIL RECORD

HOMINID SPECIES

1 million — Most recent *Paranthropus* fossils at Swartkrans and Koobi Fora
1.3 million — Most recent *Homo habilis* fossils at Olduvai Gorge; most recent *H. rudolfensis* fossils from East Africa
1.6 million —
1.8 million — *Homo habilis* at Sterkfontein
2 million —

2.3 million — Probable *Homo habilis* fossil at Hadar
2.4 million — Oldest *Homo rudolfensis* remains at Uraha

3 million —

More advanced *Homo*

Homo erectus
?
Homo rudolfensis   *Homo habilis*   *Paranthropus*

Australopithecus

4 million —

Ardipithecus

5 million —

First hominids
|
?

6 million —

THE ADVENT OF *HOMO*

The earliest hominines (members of the genus *Homo*) have been recovered from sites in Northeast and East Africa. At least one variety of early *Homo*—*H. habilis*—also inhabited South Africa around 2 million years ago.

Chapter 9

THE EVOLUTION OF HOMINID BEHAVIOR

Footprints from Laetoli, Tanzania, dated at 3.6 million years old attest to the bipedalism of *Australopithecus afarensis*.

As unto the bow the cord is,
So unto the man is woman;
Though she bends him, she obeys him,
Though she draws him, yet she follows;
Useless each without the other!
HENRY WADSWORTH LONGFELLOW, 1807–1882. *The Song of Hiawatha, x.*

OVERVIEW

Working with fossils and artifacts, and with information about the behavior of modern humans and nonhuman primates, anthropologists attempt to reconstruct the evolution of hominids' lifestyles. This chapter describes the current state of such reconstructions and focuses on three primary topics: the selection pressures that favored the evolution of bipedalism; the nature and use of early stone tools; and the likely socioecology of early hominids. With regard to the first topic, several hypotheses are reviewed, including those linking bipedalism with tool and weapon use, energy efficiency, body temperature regulation, life in variable habitats, and reproductive success. Furthermore, the secondary links between bipedalism and childbirth patterns, and bipedalism and canine tooth morphology are described. The bipedalism sections are followed by a discussion of the nature and probable use of Oldowan choppers and flakes. The chapter ends with current reconstructions of early hominids' ranging and subsistence patterns. Important topics include bipedalism and the various selection pressures that may have favored its evolution; childbirth patterns and canine tooth morphology and how they may be linked to bipedalism; the nature and use of Oldowan tools; and the diets, food procurement patterns, and ranging patterns of early hominids.

HOMINID CHARACTERISTICS

As we have seen, hominids are characterized by a rather distinctive set of evolving traits including habitual bipedalism, canine reduction (shortening and blunting), brain enlargement, speech and language, and technology (i.e., the development of material culture, especially tools). While the fossil record makes it clear that these traits evolved individually and in a mosaic fashion rather than as a monolithic unit—bipedalism and canine reduction appearing early; brain enlargement, speech and language, and complex tools later—it is nonetheless true that they were intricately interrelated and variously set limits on, or facilitated the development of, one another. Since the mid-nineteenth century speculations of Charles Darwin and Ernst Haeckel, scientists have theorized about the course of hominid evolution, developing sometimes elaborate scenarios about the environmental conditions that selected for our package of traits and the sequence of trait development. Furthermore, since early in this century, it has been common practice to explain the most basic hominid traits (particularly bipedalism) as adaptations for terrestrial life on the African savanna. Recent discoveries have challenged this point of view, however, and the evidence from Aramis, Kanapoi, and elsewhere now has some paleoanthropologists theorizing that hominid evolution probably began in more wooded circumstances. But whether on the savanna or in the woodland, the specifics of hominid origins and the development of our distinctive traits still remain speculative and it is to certain of these evolutionary scenarios that we now turn our attention. We will focus primarily on hypotheses about the advent of bipedalism, canine reduction, and stone tool technology. Discussions of the evolution of human society and our enlarged brains (including the linguistic communication those brains allow) are reserved for Chapters 12 and 13, respectively. Before we begin, however, a cautionary note is in order. Some of the ideas we present below will seem almost self-evidently true; others will seem more outlandish. It is important, however, to remember that all of these evolutionary speculations are in fact *hypotheses*, useful for stimulating thought and research, but each requiring further scrutiny. Simply sounding plausible does not make an evolutionary explanation true. Only extensive testing will enable paleoanthropologists to reject some of the following ideas and to give increased credence to others.

BIPEDAL LOCOMOTION

In the Beginning

Our survey of the fossil record thus far has demonstrated that hominids diverged from apes sometime between 5.6 and 7 million years ago. Although the exact identity of our ape forebears remains to be discovered, our own postcranial anatomy— and more especially, that of the australopithecines and early hominines—provides clear evidence that those ancestral apes were arboreal creatures that engaged in arm-swinging and hanging, as well as quadrupedal climbing. If modern chimpanzees and bonobos are accurate models, our ape ancestors were rather generalized in their locomotion, their food tastes, and their pattern of habitat use. Ready to eat a variety of foods, capable of moving about in or across a variety of habitats, and living in or near the mosaic environment of the forest-woodland-savanna ecotone, our ape ancestors lived in a world full of opportunities—they could go in any of several directions.

Imagine hominids' ape ancestor confronting the following ecological possibilities. If in one part of this ape's range there are large forests and an abundance of fig trees, there will be little reason for the animal not to stay in the trees and become increasingly specialized as a fruit eater. In another part of the range or at another time, however, the environment might be somewhat different: fewer fig trees, but an abundance of seeds, berries, tubers, insects, and other food on the ground. Such a situation may have existed about 5 to 7 million years ago. At that time tropical forest extended through a good part of Central Africa as it does today. Of course, there also existed a comparably large amount of forest edge and open woodland, with opportunities for tree-dwellers to descend to the ground and eat the berries, roots, insects, and other food that abounded in the open. Such a place, where multiple ecological zones meet presents new opportunities for survival, for if an animal adapts to the mixed habitat, it can exploit the food found in several zones. Advanced apelike creatures thronged the late Miocene and early Pliocene forests, probably as a number of species, some of which must have lived on the forest edge. Like a good many monkeys and apes today, some of these creatures (among them our ancestors) undoubtedly came to the ground when opportunities for feeding presented themselves.

Opportunity and aptitude went together. No one decision by one ape or one group of apes had any evolutionary meaning whatsoever. But in places that, century after century, provided a better living on the ground for apes able to exploit it, the animals best adapted to living and feeding on the ground were the ones that spent the most time there and whose descendants became still better adapted to that environment and lifestyle.

The apes were not forced out of the trees. It is true that during the Pliocene the forests dried up and shrank somewhat, subtracting several million square miles of living space from the possible ranges of tree-dwelling apes. But the process was so gradual that at no time could it have affected the evolving habits of individual animals, and the extent of the forest-edge ecotone was not greatly altered. Variations of climate from one year to the next were all that concerned the animals. If a river goes dry and the trees along it die, the animals that formerly thrived there simply move away, taking their various ways of living with them. They do not abandon living in trees because some trees disappear; they simply find other trees.

Tool Use and Bipedalism

In his *Descent of Man*, Charles Darwin wrote, "The free use of arms and hands, partly the cause and partly the result of man's erect position, appears to have led in an indirect manner to other modifications of structure. . . . As they gradually acquired the habit of using stones, clubs or other weapons, they would use their jaws and teeth less and less. In this case the jaws, together with the teeth, would become reduced in size." Thus Darwin believed that bipedalism led to tool and weapon use and then to smaller jaws and teeth.

In contrast, the American anthropologist Sherwood Washburn suggested that tool using might have preceded walking on two legs; more than that, it probably helped to develop walking. He pointed out that apes, unlike monkeys, were characteristically upright even before they left the trees. Whereas monkeys ran along branches on all fours or jumped about in them, apes climbed hand over hand. They swung from branches, sat upright in them, and sometimes even stood on them. Their arms were well articulated for reaching in all directions, and the important, interrelated development of stereoscopic eyesight, a larger brain, and improved manual dexterity had already evolved. Apes, in short, had the physical equipment and dawning brain potential to use their hands in new and useful ways. That certain of them did so is suggested by the knowledge that chimpanzees, humans' nearest relatives, are simple tool users today. As we have seen, they throw stones and sticks as weapons. They use sticks, rocks, and handfuls of leaves for digging, cracking nuts, wiping themselves, and sopping up water.

Like Darwin, many authors have believed that hominids were bipedal from the time they first stepped away from the trees, and that it was this characteristic that gave them the opportunity to become tool users and toolmakers. If hominids found it technologically advantageous to walk on two legs from the beginning, the argument goes on, then, to make it easier for them to get about in that way, natural selection would inevitably improve their pelvis, leg bones, foot bones, and muscles.

But how much confidence can we have in the tools-and-bipedalism scenario? As we have seen from the fossils of *Australopithecus anamensis*, habitual bipedalism can be demonstrated clearly from about 4.2 mya (the evidence of earlier bipedalism by *A. ramidus* is too weak to be considered here). With their (presumably) ape-sized brains and hands at least as dexterous as those of modern apes, it seems possible that there was some degree of tool use by *A. anamensis*. Modern chimps, however, show us not only that apes can be tool users, but also that it's possible to be an occasional tool user and remain a quadruped. Therefore, chimp-type tool use might or might not have been sufficient to select for habitual bipedalism in the protohominids. A follow-up question then becomes: What about stone tool manufacture and use? Here the answer seems easier: because the appearance of *A. anamensis* predates the oldest stone tools by at least 1.7 million years, stone tool technology can be confidently ruled out as the stimulus for bipedalism in that species. In summary, the tools-and-bipedalism question remains something of a riddle. However, because the earliest hominids do not appear to have exceeded a chimpanzee level of technology, Washburn's argument that tool use was the trigger for locomotor change remains unconvincing.

Energy Efficiency and Bipedalism

There are several other theories about the origin of hominid bipedalism, including the notion that it was favored by selection because it was more energy-efficient than the terrestrial quadrupedalism of our last ape ancestor. The energy efficiency of different locomotor patterns is usually measured by standardized oxygen consumption. Modern humans show the greatest energy efficiency when they are walking at a moderate pace; indeed, our walking bipedalism is slightly more efficient than an average mammal's ambling along quadrupedally at the same speed. (We are not very efficient runners, however, using about twice as much energy as a running quadrupedal mammal of the same body size. This fact suggests that, if energy efficiency played a role, bipedalism probably evolved to allow us to walk, not run.)

But, of course, hominids descended not from an "average quadrupedal mammal," but from a quadrupedal ape, and so comparisons with living apes should provide even more specific clues to the evolution of our bipedalism. Energy studies of chimpanzees have shown that these apes consume oxygen at the same rate whether they are moving bipedally or quadrupedally. Regardless of how they are moving, however, chimps' energy efficiency compares poorly with that of other (equivalently sized) quadrupeds; in fact, chimps use about 150 percent more energy. Therefore, since bipedal humans have a slight energy edge on the average nonprimate quadruped, there is no doubt that human walking is *significantly* more efficient than chimpanzee quadrupedalism.

Results such as these have convinced several paleoanthropologists that selection for energy-efficient walking was probably an important factor in the evolution of hominid bipedalism, the main idea being that our ancestors were moving long distances each day as they traveled between widely separated food sources. But is there anything about our efficient ambling that identifies it as a savanna adaptation rather than an adaptation to the forest-woodland-savanna ecotone? Not really. Both the mixed-habitat ecotone and the open savanna by itself were probably characterized by patchily distributed food sources, some occurring on the ground and some in the trees (groves of trees commonly dot the African plains). As long as the distances between food patches were equivalent, upright walking would have had the same energy advantages whether the early hominids were moving through the woods or across the grasslands between food sources. Primatologist Lynne Isbell and her colleague Truman Young have argued that, faced with Miocene-Pliocene forest shrinkage and patchy food distribution, the earliest hominids had to evolve either energy-efficient locomotor abilities or smaller group sizes. Smaller groups (with fewer mouths to feed and thus a reduced need for travel to find the necessary

THE FACES OF PHYSICAL ANTHROPOLOGY AND ARCHAEOLOGY

The modern study of human origins is being conducted by men and women from a variety of backgrounds and cultures and with a wide range of research interests. Many of these scientists search field sites around the world for our ancestors' fossil remains or their artifacts; others conduct sophisticated laboratory analyses of those fossils and artifacts; and still others study the anatomical and behavioral links between humans and the other primates. Despite their research diversity, all of these specialists are dedicated to the common goals of illuminating humans' evolutionary history and understanding our species' place in nature. Several present-day anthropological researchers are pictured in the text, but, in addition, the following profiles and color photographs are designed to help you put a face on the modern scientific enterprises of physical anthropology and archaeology. ∎

Paleoanthropologist Dean Falk is a Professor at the University of Albany (SUNY) and earned her Ph.D. at the University of Michigan. Her research interests include hominid brain evolution (see her Radiator Theory in Chapter 13) and the application of advanced medical imaging technology to problems in that area. Here Dr. Falk is shown holding a stereolithographically-modeled copy of a skull from Petralona, Greece. The model (prepared by Horst Seidler of the University of Vienna and based on CAT scans of the original fossil) reveals features not visible on the actual specimen. (Photo by Mark Schmidt, University at Albany.)

John Mitani is an Associate Professor of anthropology at the University of Michigan. His Ph.D. is from the University of California at Davis. Professor Mitani has studied the behavior of gibbons, orangutans, gorillas, bonobos, and chimpanzees in the field, and much of his recent work has been focused on primates' vocal communication. Here he is shown following an adult male chimpanzee in the Mahale Mountains National Park, Tanzania. (Photograph personal property of John Mitani.)

Carol Ward is one of an increasing number of women active in recovering and analyzing the fossils that document human evolution. With a Ph.D. from The Johns Hopkins University, Dr. Ward holds a joint Assistant Professorship in the departments of anthropology and pathology/anatomical sciences at the University of Missouri. Most recently, she has contributed to the analysis of the *Australopithecus anamensis* remains and helped to study the Nariokotome *Homo erectus* skeleton. Here she is shown sieving excavated material for tiny fossil fragments. (Photograph personal property of Carol Ward.)

Archaeologist D. Bruce Dickson is a Professor of anthropology at Texas A&M University and holds a Ph.D. from the University of Arizona. In addition to being an expert on the Upper Paleolithic of Europe, he has spent several years excavating Stone Age sites in East Africa. Here he is shown examining a test trench at the Shurmai Rockshelter site in Kenya's Lakipia District. (Photograph personal property of D. Bruce Dickson.)

Primatologist Lynne Isbell holds a Ph.D. in animal behavior from the University of California at Davis. Currently an Assistant Professor of anthropology at that same university, Dr. Isbell specializes in the study of primate behavioral ecology, and in the application of nonhuman primate data to problems in hominid evolution. Here she is shown observing an adult male patas monkey (*Erythrocebus patas*) in Kenya. (Photograph personal property of Lynne Isbell.)

Ethiopian researcher Berhane Asfaw received his Ph.D. from the University of California, Berkeley. A former Director of the National Museum of Ethiopia, Dr. Asfaw currently manages the Rift Valley Research Service, a private paleoanthropological organization. Shown here in the East African fossil fields, Dr. Asfaw has participated in the discoveries of numerous hominid specimens, including the remains of *Ardipithecus ramidus*. (Photo by and courtesy of T. White, 1995.)

Paleoanthropologist Bernard Campbell received his Ph.D. from Cambridge University. He has taught at that institution, Harvard University, and the University of California at Los Angeles, and has conducted field work in South and East Africa and in Iran. Although retired from active teaching, Professor Campbell continues to publish widely on the evolution of human behavior and its ecological setting. Professor Campbell originally developed the text *Humankind Emerging* and guided it through six editions. (Photograph personal property of Bernard Campbell.)

James Loy (shown here with his wife Kent and two orphaned patas monkeys being hand-reared) is a Professor of anthropology at the University of Rhode Island. After earning a Ph.D. from Northwestern University, Professor Loy conducted research on the sexual behavior of Old World monkeys for over twenty years. He joined the publication team of *Humankind Emerging* with its seventh edition. (Photograph personal property of James Loy.)

food) would have been at a disadvantage in intergroup competition, however, and our ancestors opted for energy-efficient movement. Bipedalism allowed them to maintain large group size, move rapidly and with minimal energy expenditure between distant food patches, and then drive away rival foragers once they got there.

Not everyone is convinced, however, including Karen Steudel of the University of Wisconsin. Steudel argues that the earliest hominid bipeds—with their apelike bodies, lateral swaying, and inability to fully extend the leg past the hip—would not have been particularly energy-efficient (certainly not nearly as efficient as modern humans). She can see natural selection improving efficiency once the transition to routine bipedalism had been made, but she rejects the notion that efficiency triggered that transition.

And so it goes. It seems fair to say that presently anthropologists are split on the question of energy efficiency as a selection pressure for the evolution of hominid bipedalism. Even if proponents of the efficiency model prove to be right, however, it is possible that other factors may also have been at work selecting for upright walking, including the need for body temperature regulation.

Body Temperature and Bipedalism

Certain hypotheses explaining the evolution of hominid bipedalism are more dependent than others on the traditional view that it occurred on the sun-drenched African savanna. One recent and very interesting savanna-based scenario is the product of British physiologist Peter Wheeler, who has delved into the connection between body temperature and bipedalism. As anyone who has walked across the African plains knows, one of the most formidable problems facing a diurnal primate living on the savanna is regulating its body temperature. Overexposure to the rays of the equatorial sun can build up a dangerous heat load, and thus we might expect that savanna-dwelling early hominids evolved mechanisms to prevent excessive heat buildup and/or to rapidly dissipate body heat once it had accumulated. Wheeler has looked into this problem, and he is convinced that the solution may provide clues to the evolution of bipedalism.

Two key variables affect the accumulation of heat from direct solar radiation: the amount of body surface a creature has exposed to the sun's rays and the intensity (or heat) of those rays. Using scale models of australopithecines in various postures (Figure 9–1), Wheeler found that, when the sun is near the horizon or about 45 degrees above it (thus emitting cool to moderately warm rays), quadrupeds and bipeds have similar amounts of body surface exposed and accumulate equivalent heat loads. However, at noon, when the sun is directly overhead and its rays are the most intense, the heat load buildup of a biped is 60 percent less than that of a quadruped because of the biped's minimal surface exposure.

Wheeler has also calculated that bipedalism would aid in the dissipation of any body heat that did manage to accumulate. Bipeds are farther from the hot ground surface than are quadrupeds, and thus a biped's skin contacts cooler and faster-moving air currents; this contact aids in heat loss through convection. Such convectional cooling would, of course, be enhanced by the loss of thick body hair; the loss would allow an essentially naked surface to be held aloft in the cool breezes. Thus the temperature regulation model may help to explain the reduction of human body hair. Wheeler believes that early hominids might have increased their convectional heat loss by as much as one-third by adopting bipedalism.

Quadruped

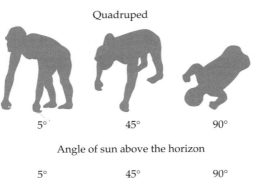

5°   45°   90°

Angle of sun above the horizon

5°   45°   90°

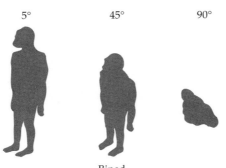

Biped

FIGURE 9–1   Models of hypothetical early hominids show how much body surface is exposed to direct solar radiation by quadrupeds (top) versus bipeds (bottom). From left to right, the sun is low on the horizon, 45 degrees above the horizon, and directly overhead. Note the small amount of body surface exposed by a biped at midday.

The combination of lower heat buildup and easy heat dissipation could have reduced the early hominids' dependence on shade and allowed them to remain active throughout much of the equatorial day and at relatively high temperatures. Furthermore, if heat loss could be accomplished mainly through convectional cooling, rather than by evaporative cooling through sweating, hominids' dependence on water would have been lowered. Wheeler has suggested that early bipeds may have required some 40 percent less water each day than a quadrupedal ape living under the same conditions. If true, this would have freed the early hominids to range widely across the savanna as they foraged.

Now clearly, Wheeler's beautiful theory must somehow deal with the ugly fact that many of the australopithecine sites seem to have been extensively wooded, including such key sites as Aramis (home of *Ardipithecus*; Chapter 7), Allia Bay (one of the sites that has produced *Australopithecus anamensis*; Chapter 7), and perhaps even Sterkfontein (home of *A. africanus*; Chapter 6). Nonetheless, Wheeler's faith in his hypothesis has yet to be shaken. He argues that some of the sites that have produced the oldest conclusive evidence for bipedalism—such as Kanapoi with its *A. anamensis* remains—were open enough for his model to have worked. He says, "We have to be careful about what we call savanna. Most savanna is a range of habitats, including bushland and quite dense trees. My arguments for bipedalism being a thermoregulatory adaptation would still apply, unless there was continuous shade cover, as in a closed-canopy forest. Nobody is saying that about [*Australopithecus*] *anamensis*." Wheeler's ideas are provocative and, given the right environmental setting, persuasive. Only time and further discoveries will tell if they are right, however.

Habitat Variability/Instability and Bipedalism

In a recent book entitled *Humanity's Descent*, Rick Potts of the Smithsonian Institution has proposed yet another habitat-related scenario for the evolution of bipedalism. In Potts's view, late Miocene-early Pliocene times in Africa were marked not only by habitat diversity (i.e., mixed habitats or ecotones, as discussed earlier), but also by dramatic habitat instability. According to Potts, environmental cycles (hotter/colder, wetter/dryer) and their accompanying habitat shifts (more/less forest, woodland, savanna) occurred much more often than tradition-ally portrayed and the resulting long-term instability selected for behavioral and anatomical flexibility and generality among the early hominids. He says, "[T]he benefits of walking erect are found in mobility itself. The distinctive two-leggedness of the early australopiths . . . afforded a certain flexibility of movement. Its success resided in the opportunities it gave to adjust locomotor style to changing land-scapes." Noting that the australopithecines' terrestrial walking can only be under-stood in the context of their concurrent arboreal adaptations, Potts argues that these early hominids evolved a mixed locomotor package that gave them access to the best of both worlds. The australopithecines were thus "liberated from the trees" and "unindentured to the ground." It remained for later hominid species, espe-cially *Homo erectus* (see Chapter 10), to make a full commitment to terrestrial life and leave the trees for good.

Reproduction and Bipedalism

Tool use, energy efficiency, temperature regulation, and habitat variability—these are only four of the many explanations that have been offered for bipedalism. Other hypotheses, less popular than those already presented, include the possibil-ities that bipedalism evolved to allow long-distance surveillance for predators or that bipedal displays fostered social control in early hominid groups. One thing is clear: regardless of what selection pressure(s) led to habitual bipedalism, evolution worked through the enhanced reproductive success of those individuals that were best suited for upright movement. American anthropologist Owen Lovejoy has emphasized the direct effects of bipedalism on hominids' reproductive efficiency. His hypothesis, which is both fascinating and controversial, links bipedalism with the evolution of several unique features of human reproduction (Figure 9–2).

As mentioned briefly in Chapter 4, the reproductive behavior of modern humans differs significantly from that of other primates. Two major changes dis-tinguish humans from the apes: the loss of estrus and strong paternal investment in children. Humans have continued the trend, first seen clearly among the apes, of relaxed hormonal control of sexual behavior. In our species, the ancient estrus cycle of sexual behavior has nearly, if not completely, disappeared. Sex can and does occur throughout the menstrual cycle, and ovulation (the optimal time for conception) is now hidden from both women and men. These changes, and par-ticularly the concealment of ovulation, make it difficult for both sexes to determine the paternity of offspring. Only within exclusive sexual relationships can one be sure that the male mate is the father of the female's children. This is critically important, since kin selection theory predicts that males will invest time, energy, and resources only in youngsters carrying their genes.

Lovejoy, who flatly rejects the energy-efficiency and body-temperature models of bipedalism, focuses his attention on behavior with direct, positive effects on the

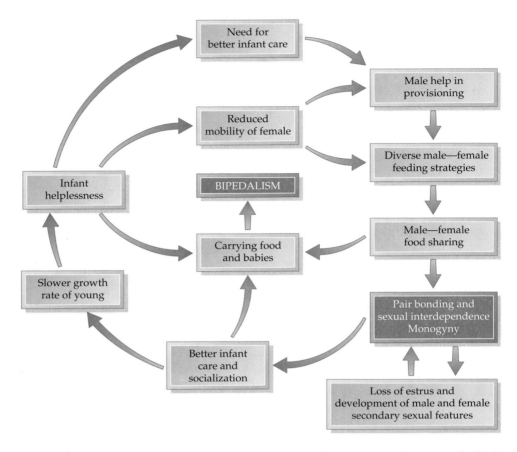

FIGURE 9–2   Pliocene adaptations of early hominids according to Lovejoy, drawn as a feedback system.

production and rearing of offspring. Arguing that a primary difference between humans and apes is our greater birthrate (that is, shorter interbirth intervals), he suggests that among the earliest hominids (*A. ramidus*? *A. anamensis*?) some males began to provide for females and young regularly. Such provisioning—locating, collecting, and furnishing food—would have reduced both the amount of parental investment required from females (they would not have been solely responsible for finding food for themselves and their babies) and the mortality risks of females and young (they would not have been ranging as far for food, and thus their risk of predation would be lower). The energy saved by provisioned females would then have been turned into increased reproduction; that is, they could give birth at shorter intervals while staying healthy. But where does bipedalism come in? Lovejoy argues that effective provisioning would have required bipedal locomotion so that males' hands were free to carry food.

So far, so good. Bipedal, provisioning males would have been favored by natural selection over nonprovisioning, quadrupedal males. But of course, this would have occurred only if males were actually investing in their own young, and thus Lovejoy speculates that provisioning males must have had a high degree of paternity certainty. He envisions such certainty as being the result of the evolution of monogamous "pair-bonded" nuclear families. Males provisioned only their female mate and her young, and because of the adults' **pair bond** (reinforced by the frequent copulation required for conception now that ovulation was hidden), females remained sexually faithful to their mates during the males' foraging trips.

Lovejoy's scenario, although ingeniously tying together locomotion, reproduction, and family structure, has come under intense criticism. First, it seems male-biased in its explanation of the evolution of bipedalism. As outlined, females' contribution to bipedalism amounted to little more than moving upright while manually carrying helpless infants and mating with bipedal males (both sexes would ultimately have become upright through shared genes for anatomical adaptations to bipedalism). Second, in the days before extensive hominid carnivory and the invention of carrying devices (i.e., perhaps among *A. ramidus*, *A. anamensis*, or *A. afarensis*), it is difficult to imagine males hand-carrying enough high-nutrient food to their mates to affect birthrates. Third, the extreme degree of sexual dimorphism in body size that seems to characterize the australopithecines argues in favor of some form of polygynous mating system, not monogamy (or more properly, monogyny; remember, however, that the polygyny interpretation has been challenged, see Chapter 7). Furthermore, monogamy isn't even characteristic of living humans, who have been described—taking all modern societies into consideration—as "mildly polygynous" (some 85 percent of modern societies allow polygamy). And finally, we agree with anthropologist and sociobiologist Donald Symons that there seems to be no good evidence whatsoever that an evolved pair bond characterizes modern humans. Humans form social and sexual relationships of varying duration, but there is little evidence that we have been shaped by evolution to form long-lasting, exclusive pair bonds. And if modern people lack long-lasting or permanent pair bonds, there is no basis for attributing them to early hominids. For all of these reasons, we have little confidence in the Lovejoy hypothesis.

And so at present there are a number of evolutionary scenarios that attempt to account for the appearance of habitual bipedalism. The earliest speculations were devised with savanna-dwelling hominids in mind, but recent discoveries have forced paleoanthropologists to start thinking in terms of woodland-dwellers or (more likely) mixed-habitat-dwellers as the first bipeds. It is worth repeating that these explanations are working hypotheses, none of which has been falsified unequivocally, and that they all have interesting and attractive features. Indeed, because each hypothesis may hold a grain of truth, it seems reasonable and probable that some *combination* of selection pressures, rather than a single evolutionary factor, led to erect walking. Additional speculative research and new fossil finds may someday help us to solve the riddle of bipedalism.

The Relationship of Bipedalism to Other Hominid Traits: Birth Pattern

While habitual bipedalism is *the* most distinctive hominid trait, there are others that are almost as diagnostic. Some are anatomical traits, such as short, incisorlike canine teeth and (among *Homo*) big brains. Others are social attributes, such as an evolutionary tendency toward increasingly complex interpersonal relationships and societies. How is bipedalism linked to these important secondary traits? Dealing with the social category, American anthropologist Wenda Trevathan and others have speculated on the possible effects of bipedalism on childbirth and, by extension, on hominid sociality. As shown in the preceding chapters, the evolution

Pair bond psychological relationship between mates; thought to be marked by sexual faithfulness.

Birth canal the passage
through the mother's pelvis
by means of which infants
are born.

of bipedalism involved a good deal of remodeling of the hominid pelvis. In particular, the shape of the **birth canal** changed from the ape's long oval, becoming quite wide transversely (from side to side) but shallow sagittally (from front to back) in *Australopithecus* (Figure 9–3). Later, in *Homo*, the canal regained a relatively long sagittal dimension—particularly at the exit, or outlet—producing a more rounded shape (Figure 9–3). A modern human baby, with its large skull, negotiates the birth canal by entering with the head oriented transversely. It then rotates 90 degrees into a sagittal position before exiting the canal facing the sacrum, that is, with its back toward the mother's face. A human mother is therefore in a bad position to assist in delivery, since her infant is exiting "down and back," away from her helping hands. Furthermore, pulling an emerging human infant up toward the mother's breast would bend it against the normal flexion of its body and would possibly result in injury. Interestingly, the human delivery pattern is very different from that of nonhuman primates, in which there is no fetal rotation (babies are sagittally oriented throughout birth) and newborns exit the canal face-to-face with their mothers. In this pattern, mother monkeys and apes routinely assist in delivery by reaching down and pulling emerging infants up and toward their chests in a curve that matches the normal flexion of the babies' bodies.

Trevathan has speculated that, at some point in human evolution, with the introduction of fetal rotation and down-and-back delivery, hominid mothers would have benefited significantly from the assistance of "birth attendants," and thus the behavior of seeking companionship at birth would have been selected for. In turn, seeking and giving assistance at births is viewed as contributing to the development of empathy, communication, and cooperation among the evolving hominids, that is, to the evolution of social relationships. Although speculative, this

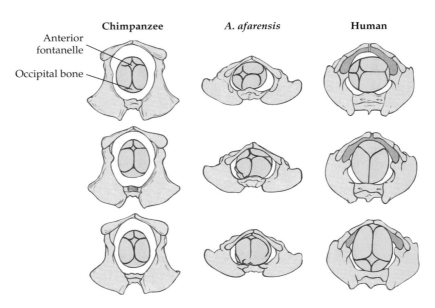

FIGURE 9–3   Three views of the fit between the fetal head and the birth canal in chimpanzees (left), *Australopithecus afarensis* (center), and modern humans (right). The top view shows the orientation of the fetal head at the entrance (inlet) to the birth canal; the middle view is at midcanal; the bottom view is at the exit (outlet). Fetal head size in *Australopithecus* is speculative and controversial.

all seems logical enough, but a major problem involves determining when the "human birth pattern"—possibly including the first birth attendants—originated. Trevathan thinks this might have occurred early, perhaps among the australopithecines. Other researchers, however, think that australopithecine births were as fast and trouble-free as those of living apes and argue that down-and-back human deliveries, with big-brained babies twisting and turning through a constricted birth canal, are probably the result of strong brain expansion within the genus *Homo*. If the latter view is correct, and it seems most probable, the human birth pattern is probably not much more than 2 million years old. Further insights into this interesting issue must await the discovery of additional pertinent fossils.

Bipedalism and Canine Reduction

Discussing the connection between bipedalism and canine anatomy, Sherwood Washburn, champion of the theory that tool use preceded and possibly stimulated bipedalism, called attention to the fact that the australopithecines had relatively small canine teeth that would have been of little value in aggression or defense. In contrast, in all other large, ground-dwelling primates—chimpanzees, gorillas, and, particularly, baboons—the male's canines are enormous teeth, true fangs. Among their uses are self-defense against both conspecifics and the large and dangerous predators to which ground-dwelling primates are exposed. As part of his scenario for early hominid evolution, Washburn argued that the loss of large canines must have been balanced by some other means of self-defense, namely, the use of various objects as weapons.

As noted at the beginning of this chapter, the hypothesis that tool use triggered bipedalism remains to be falsified completely, but the evidence in favor of the proposition is unconvincing. In that case, are there other explanations of canine reduction? If it was not related to tool use, what caused it? Clifford Jolly of New York University suggested an answer to that question. Jolly proposed that the evolution of hominids was marked by a shift from ape-type frugivory to a diet that included a significantly higher proportion of small, hard objects, such as seeds, nuts, and tubers. Such tough, hard to chew items would presumably have been plentiful in the forest-woodland-savanna habitat to which the early (and newly terrestrial) hominids were adapting. The evolutionary scenario proposed by Jolly became known as the *seed-eating hypothesis*.

Jolly's hypothesis of hominid canine reduction was based on two types of evidence. First, he presented comparative data from savanna baboons and gelada monkeys that suggested the presence of shorter canines in the more seed-dependent geladas. And second, Jolly argued that long, interlocking canines (such as those shown by apes) limit the range of movement of the lower jaw during chewing (particularly side-to-side grinding movements), and thus long canines would have been *selected against* as early hominids adopted a small-object diet. Finally, according to Jolly, the need for an upright posture during small-object harvesting could have selected for habitual bipedalism. And so, in contrast to Washburn's theories, the seed-eating hypothesis explains the primary hominid characteristics as being the results of a dietary change. In this scenario, tool use followed diet-induced dental and postural changes, rather than serving as the primary trigger for hominization.

Jolly's theory has been received with a mixture of support and disagreement. A very recent discovery that tends to weaken his model is the evidence that *Ardipithecus ramidus*—claimed by its discoverers to be the oldest hominid and to show some anatomical signs of bipedalism—had thin enamel on its canines and molars. As Tim White and his colleagues noted, the thin enamel of *A. ramidus* is hard to reconcile with a "hard-object" diet.

One of Jolly's most vigorous critics is American anthropologist Leonard Greenfield, who believes that flawed assumptions about dental mechanics underlie the seed-eating model. Greenfield has suggested as a substitute his *dual-selection hypothesis*. This model proposes that two forms of selection shaped canine tooth anatomy: selection for use as a weapon and selection for incisorlike functions. These selective forces tended to move canine anatomy in mutually exclusive directions and therefore can be viewed as competing with one another. If the weapon-use function prevailed, the canines would be long, fanglike teeth, but if incisorlike selection was stronger, the canines would be short and would have broader cutting edges. Finally, and of major importance, the dual-selection hypothesis assumes that, if selection for weapon-use functions diminished, canines would *automatically* shift toward an incisorlike anatomy.

Greenfield's model is interesting and may have some merit, but even if it proves to be correct and applicable to hominids, it leaves a critical question unanswered: Did the canines of early hominids get shorter and broader because they were no longer needed as weapons or because they were *strongly* needed as additional incisorlike teeth? And (to get back to Washburn), if selection for use of the canines as weapons diminished among the first hominids, was it because some sort of biodegradable implements were being used instead? The dual-selection hypothesis may help paleoanthropologists to answer at least the initial question, but first it must win acceptance among researchers, and initial reactions suggest that some find it wanting. Writing in 1995, J. M. Plavcan and Jay Kelley summed up the situation with regard to hominids' dental changes as follows: "At this point . . . we are aware of no hypothesis that satisfactorily explains canine reduction . . ." One can only hope that future discoveries and ideas will bring clarity to this problem of dental hominization.

This brief review has touched on some of the current explanations (or lack of them) for the main hominid adaptations. Clearly, definitive answers to "how" and "why" questions about the evolution of bipedalism, short canines, and numerous other traits of the human lineage await the efforts of future researchers. There seems little doubt, however, that once hominids had some of the major behavioral and anatomical cards on the table, particularly bipedalism and simple technology, a complex **positive feedback** system could have developed. One such feedback system is shown in Figure 9–4. As explained in earlier sections of this chapter, certain loops in this system are questionable; others, such as those connecting the triangle of technology (toolmaking), subsistence, and intelligence (brain size), were almost certainly of great importance, at least once *Homo* had evolved. While studying Figure 9–4, however, one must keep in mind that this and all speculation-based feedback models are primarily heuristic devices. The danger inherent in model building is that one may begin to have too much trust in the model as a representation of the real world. Most of the feedback loops shown in the figure await rigorous testing (See Box 9–1).

Positive feedback process in which a positive change in one component of a system brings about changes in other components, which in turn bring about further positive changes in the first component.

EARLY TECHNOLOGY

The origin of tools in human evolution must have occurred through trial and error. The nearest we can come to reconstructing that process is to remind ourselves that

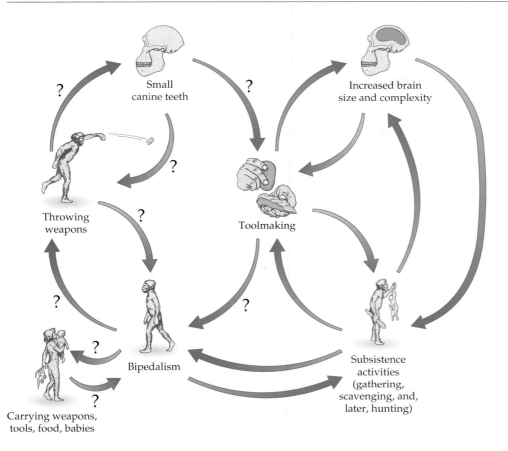

FIGURE 9–4 Numerous feedback systems occur in nature and are often interlocking. Negative feedback maintains stability, and positive feedback brings about major adaptive changes that constitute evolution. Shown here in simplified form is a positive feedback system that may have been important in hominid evolution.

there may have been a time when our ancestors could do with fewer tools than chimpanzees can use today. They must have worked their way up from a similar (but not necessarily identical) limited capacity to shape something for a purpose; for example, a grass stem for poking into a termite mound, a chewed-up mouthful of leaves to serve as a sponge, a stick or branch as something to be brandished in an effort to intimidate, or a rock to throw.

A group of not-too-large apes will seem more formidable standing erect because they appear larger; in fact, the erect posture is sometimes used by nonhuman primates as a gesture of threat. The brandishing of sticks or branches enhances that effect and may have been enough, on occasion, to swing the balance to the hominids in a set-to with hyenas over the possession of a kill. The earliest use of objects by our ancestors, probably then ground-dwelling scavengers and gatherers, may have received its strongest impetus from its value in threat displays against competing species. For an immensely long time, the found object was the only type of implement, picked up and then thrown away when its immediate use was over. But there must have come a stage at which early hominids began to recognize more and more clearly the usefulness of certain objects and, as a result, tended to

CURRENT ISSUE: *Still Lots to Do*

This chapter's discussions, about how and why hominids became bipeds and acquired short canines, reveals both the variety of our evolutionary scenarios and the depths of our residual ignorance. Paleoanthropologists have many hypotheses that explain the events of human evolution, but virtually all of these hypotheses require further refinement and testing before they can be considered proved in a scientific sense. For example, Washburn's weapons hypothesis, Jolly's seed-eating hypothesis, and Greenfield's dual-selection hypothesis all address the problem of canine reduction among hominids. Each explanation has something to recommend it, but each also has weaknesses or is somehow incomplete.

We draw attention to this cloud of anthropological ignorance in order to point out its silver lining of future opportunities. As noted in an earlier Current Issue item, there are still lots of hominid fossils out there to be found and the pace of discovery is picking up. But in addition to work in the fossil fields, there are many theoretical breakthroughs still to be made, increasingly sophisticated analyses to be done, and new approaches devised for solving old problems. For example, as we write

these words, the anthropological world is agog with the news that DNA taken from ancient Neandertal bones reveals that these people were genetically distinct and so can be considered a separate species from *Homo sapiens*. This sort of application of advanced genetics techniques to problems in the fossil record is unprecedented and it promises further surprises as it becomes widely used. Additionally, new information and procedures in physiology, anatomy, and growth; chronometric dating; archaeology (especially lithic analysis); and primatology (to name just a few fields) are all successfully being brought to bear on problems of human evolution.

The point is this: Students often ask about the opportunities for careers in anthropology. While we have no crystal ball to tell us about tomorrow's job market, we can say with certainty that there is much exciting work left to do in paleoanthropology. If that field seems to be the right choice for you, talk to your professor or academic advisor for more information or contact the American Association of Physical Anthropologists (the AAPA Internet site is listed at the end of this chapter). ▪

hang onto them longer, finally carrying them around much of the time. The great abundance of wood, and the fact that it is softer and easier to work than stone, suggests that the earliest hominids may have used wood a great deal, probably for digging. They may also have used the horns and long bones of some of the larger animals. But the great triumph of our ancestors as creators of culture came much later and is seen most clearly in the legacy they have left us of worked stone. All the oldest surviving artifacts are implements for cutting and chopping, not weapons. We can therefore recognize a clear succession: tool use, tool modification, and tool-making.

Earliest Stone Industry: The Oldowan

The magnet that drew Louis and Mary Leakey back to Olduvai Gorge year after year was the large numbers of extremely primitive stone implements. Mary Leakey made the study of these objects her special province. Her first monograph on the

TABLE 9–1 *Stratified Beds and Fossils at Olduvai Gorge*

APPROXIMATE AGE (YEARS)	BED	FOSSILS AND INDUSTRY
620,000–100,000	Upper beds	*Homo sapiens*
840,000–620,000	Bed IV	Fossils of *Homo erectus* Late Acheulean hand axes and cleavers
1.2 million–840,000	Bed III	No fossils Few artifacts
1.7–1.2 million	Bed II	*Homo erectus* and early Acheulean tools *Homo habilis* and Oldowan tools
2.2–1.7 million	Bed I	*Paranthropus boisei* and *Homo habilis* Oldowan choppers
2.2 million	Volcanic lava	

Note: The ages of the upper beds are still rather uncertain. Bed I fossil sites date 1.9–1.7 mya.

stone culture at Olduvai covers material taken from the gorge's lowest strata, known as Beds I and II, and a time period that extends from 1.2 to 2.2 million years ago (Table 9–1).

Certain details of the lives of the creatures who lived at Olduvai so long ago have been reconstructed from the hundreds of thousands of bits of material that they left behind—some stone, some bone; some large, some extremely small. No one of these things, alone, would mean much, but when all are analyzed and fitted together like a gigantic three-dimensional jigsaw puzzle, patterns begin to emerge that speak across the gulf of time.

Mary Leakey found that there were two stoneworking traditions at Olduvai. One, the **Acheulean industry**, appears first in Bed II and will be discussed in Chapter 11. The other, the Oldowan, is the older and more primitive and occurs throughout Bed I, as well as at other early African sites (see Chapters 6, 7, and 8). Its signature implements are what anthropologists for a long time called *pebble tools*, but what Mary Leakey preferred to call **choppers**. The word *pebble* suggests something quite small, and her term was an improvement, for many of the chopping tools at Olduvai are of hen's-egg size or larger, some of them 3 or 4 inches (8 to 10 centimeters) across. In addition to the choppers, Oldowan sites typically contain numerous stone flakes.

An Oldowan chopper (Figure 9–5) is about the most basic stone implement one can possibly imagine could be recognized on its own by archaeologists. (Even simpler tools, however, such as unmodified cobbles that were used as hammer stones, can often be recognized when they occur in association with a recognizable archaeological assemblage.) The chopper was, typically, made from a cobble, a stone that had been worn smooth by sand and water action. The stone selected was often that of a close-grained, hard, smooth-textured material such as quartz, flint, or chert. Many cobbles at Olduvai are of hardened lava that flowed out of the volcanoes in the region.

Acheulean industry stone tool tradition that first appeared about 1.7 to 1.4 mya in Africa and originated with *Homo erectus*.

Choppers small, generally ovoid stones with a few *flakes* removed to produce a partial cutting edge.

FIGURE 9–5   An Oldowan chopper was usually made by striking some flakes from a rounded cobble to give a cutting edge. It is one of the simplest stone implements. Scale is approximately twice actual size.

Oval or pear-shaped, and small enough to fit comfortably in the hand, such a water-rounded stone could be gripped firmly without hurting the palm. What an early toolmaker had to do to turn it into a tool was simply to smash one end down hard on a nearby boulder, or to balance it on the boulder and give it a good whack with another rock. A large chip would fly off. Another whack would knock off a second chip next to the first, leaving a jagged edge or perhaps a point on one end of the stone. There are large choppers and small ones. The tool was presumably held as one would hold a rock while banging downward, with a direct hammering or chopping motion. The small chips knocked off during the manufacture of choppers are known as **flakes**. Sharper than choppers, they often may have been more useful than the core. They undoubtedly became dull very quickly, however, for although stone is hard, its edges break easily.

Flakes sharp-edged fragments struck from a stone; the flake may then be used as a cutting tool.

But how were the Oldowan choppers and flakes used? What do they tell us about the lifestyle of their makers? American archaeologists Kathy Schick and Nicholas Toth have made an in-depth study of these questions, and their discoveries are revealing. In order to extract the maximum information from the ancient stone implements, Schick and Toth have used a combination of traditional and

FIGURE 9–6   Marks on the surfaces of fossil bones, such as those from Olduvai Gorge (left), can be produced in several ways. A study of fossil bones with the scanning electron microscope reveals whether such marks were made by hominids using stone tools. These marks typically contain white parallel striations in the bottom of the groove, as seen on modern bones that have been experimentally cut with stone tools (right). They are easily distinguished from the marks made by the teeth of carnivores.

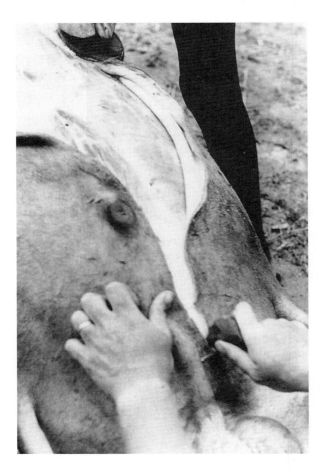

FIGURE 9–7   Archaeologists experimentally skinning a wildebeest (that died of natural causes) with a lava flake. Simple, sharp flakes were found to be excellent tools for skinning, defleshing, and dismembering animal carcasses.

innovative techniques. Of course, they have followed traditional archaeological procedures and studied the occurrence and distribution of Oldowan tools at the various African sites, and they have also studied the fossil bone assemblages associated with the tools. In addition, they have conducted numerous field experiments using newly made flakes and choppers to butcher animals that have died naturally and to smash animal long bones for marrow. Finally, they have utilized data from electron microscope studies of cut marks on fossil bones (Figure 9–6) and **microwear** on tool surfaces (the microwear pattern of chips, pits, and polish can provide excellent clues as to how a tool was used).

Based on all of their various analyses, Schick and Toth have concluded that the principal reason for the emergence of stone-tool technology among hominids was for quick and efficient butchering of animal carcasses before eating them on the spot or carrying them elsewhere for later consumption. Flakes were found to be excellent implements for skinning, defleshing, and dismembering animal carcasses (Figure 9–7)—even better than choppers, so often thought of as the premier Oldowan tools (indeed, many choppers may be nothing more than **débitage**, or waste cores left after flake manufacture). Using simple flake tools, Schick and Toth were able to skin even an elephant with its inch-thick hide! Choppers were useful for dismembering carcasses and, along with unmodified cobbles, for bone breaking (Figure 9–8). One should not conclude that Oldowan tools were used only for meat processing, however; microwear analyses have identified tools used for cutting soft plants and others used to work wood; hammer stones were no doubt used to crush

Microwear the microscopic pattern of scratches, pits, and polish produced during the use of a stone tool.

Débitage debris produced during stone tool manufacture.

FIGURE 9–8 The use of a stone chopper and an anvil to crack a limb bone in order to expose the marrow.

nuts; and the use, if any, of **manuports** (unmodified stones brought from elsewhere to the site by hominids) is unknown. Nonetheless, based on their work, Schick and Toth believe that the primary message of the oldest stone tools is a significant increase in meat eating by early hominids.

Because progress in the early Stone Age was slow, the beginnings of the Oldowan tool industry were probably far older than would be indicated even by the Gona site, which dates tools at about 2.5 million years B.P. (Chapter 8). But how much older no one yet has the slightest idea. After 2.5 million B.P., toolmaking and hominid evolution went hand in hand, but the earliest steps are unknown.

As we go back in time, we depend more and more on the ability of archaeologists to identify stone tools reliably; that is, to distinguish between them and naturally occurring rocks. There is no sure way of identifying individual primitive artifacts occurring alone, but if one or more of the following conditions is satisfied, the ancient presence of hominid toolmakers can usually be safely inferred:

> **Manuports** unmodified stones that could not have occurred naturally in an archaeological site and must have been carried there; how manuports were used is unknown.

1. The tools occur on an ancient land surface in reasonable numbers and conform to a regular and recognizable pattern.
2. The tools are made of a kind of stone that is not present locally and that therefore must have been brought there. The evidence of transport of materials is a very important feature of many stone-tool assemblages. The possibility of their arriving in position as a result of being washed by a river or glacier must be ruled out.
3. The tools are associated with bone fragments showing cut marks.
4. The tools occur with other signs of human habitation (e.g., with hearths or the foundations of a shelter).
5. The tools are of such sophisticated manufacture that they could not possibly have been generated naturally.
6. We can expect tools to be made of a rock suitable for bashing or cutting bones or flesh (i.e., not a soft sandstone), usually flint (also called *chert*). Primitive tools might be made of a number of kinds of hard rocks, but the materials from which advanced tools could be made are very much more limited in number.

Given that hominines and australopithecines were contemporary in Africa for 1.4 million years, and given that their remains occasionally occur together at sites that also include stone tools, it is sometimes extremely difficult to know for certain who made the Oldowan tools. In the past, most researchers have attributed stone tools from mixed-species sites to the larger-brained hominines (early *Homo*). To a great extent, this continues to be done although (as noted in Chapter 6) some paleoanthropologists such as Randall Susman have begun to question this practice, arguing that if australopithecine remains are more abundant at a particular site than hominine remains, then the australopithecines were probably responsible for any tools that are found. (Remember that Susman believes *Paranthropus* had both the anatomical and intellectual capacities for making stone tools.) Of course, a third possibility—that *both* the early hominines and certain australopithecines were toolmakers—must be considered as well. (Numerous additional questions about mixed-species sites are beyond our ability to answer at this time. Did one species scavenge off the food supplies of the other? Did one species prey on the other?)

In any event, in the final analysis Mary and Louis Leakey were quite certain they knew who had made the 1.8-million-year-old tools from Bed I at Olduvai Gorge: Jonny's Child, the hominid type whose brain so greatly exceeded that of the other candidate for toolmaker, *Paranthropus* (*Zinjanthropus*) *boisei*. And it was primarily these two factors—brain size and stone tool culture—that ultimately led the Leakeys to christen Jonny's Child, and its ilk, *Homo habilis*.

Occupation Levels at Olduvai Gorge

During their decades of work at Olduvai Gorge, Mary and Louis Leakey and their sons and co-workers laid bare numerous ancient hominid sites (Table 9–1). Sometimes the sites were simply spots where the bones of one or more hominid species were discovered. Often, however, hominid remains were found in association with concentrations of animal fossils, stone tools, and debris. In some places it appeared that the bones and stones had been gently covered without much disturbance by blown dust, encroaching vegetation, rising water, and mud. Other sites, however, revealed signs of disturbance by water and wind. Although many of the sites were originally called **occupation levels**, suggesting that the hominids found there actually camped on the spot, we are now wary of jumping to that conclusion. Only after a team of experts—archaeologists, geologists, paleontologists, paleoanthropologists, and taphonomists—has thoroughly studied a site can its true nature be understood.

> **Occupation level** land surface occupied by prehistoric *hominids.*

The oldest sites at Olduvai come from Bed I and date between 1.9 and 1.7 million years old (Table 9–1). Sites at this level have produced Oldowan stone tools in abundance and also (sometimes at the same location) fossils of both the robust australopithecine *Paranthropus boisei* and an ancient representative of our own genus, *Homo habilis*. For many anthropologists, Olduvai Gorge is particularly fascinating because of what we think it tells us about the lifestyle of the latter species. As explained earlier, when the bones of early *Homo* and *Paranthropus* are found together in association with stone tools and other artifacts, all tools and artifacts traditionally have been *assumed* to have been made by *Homo*. This assumption is, however, only the first step in the tricky process of understanding the Olduvai stone and bone assemblages. Other factors that make the interpretation of Bed I difficult include the extreme age and fragmentary nature of these sites from the dawn of culture and, most important, the simple inability to imagine how early *Homo* might have lived nearly 2 million years ago. What living analogues should we use? Should we assume that, although much smaller brained, *Homo habilis* behaved more or less like modern humans? Or should we envision *Homo habilis* as a sort of advanced ape? If we adopt the ape analogy, we risk underinterpreting the Olduvai sites. On the other hand, if we view *Homo habilis* as primitive, long-armed little humans, we risk overinterpretation. It is the latter error that some workers think we have been making for years.

> **Home base** camps where *hominid* groups gathered at evening for socializing, food sharing, and sleeping.

During the 1970s and early 1980s, many workers, including Mary Leakey and archaeologist Glynn Isaac, used an analogy from modern hunter-and-gather cultures to interpret the Bed I sites. They concluded that many of the sites were probably camps, often called **home bases**, where group members gathered at the end of the day to prepare and share food, to socialize, to make tools, and to sleep. The circular concentration of stones at the DK-I site (Figure 9–9) was interpreted as the remains of a shelter or windbreak similar to those still made by some African people (Figure 9–10). Other concentrations of bones and stones were thought to be the remains of living sites originally ringed by thorn hedges for defense against predators. Later, other humanlike elements were added to the mix, and early *Homo* was described as showing a sexual division of labor—females gathering plant foods and males hunting for meat—and some of the Olduvai occupation levels were interpreted as butchering sites (Figure 9–11).

FIGURE 9–9 This plan of an ancient land surface shows the distribution of bones and stones discovered at a site in Bed I of Olduvai Gorge by Louis and Mary Leakey. The dense concentration of rocks suggests to some the remains of a hut or a windbreak; to others it is merely broken lava rocks produced by the roots of an ancient tree. Stones are shown here in black; bones are outlined. Labels for objects other than bones and teeth identify stone tools using the scheme devised by Mary Leakey. Important implement types include choppers (CH), scrapers (SC), hammer stones (H), discoids (DC), heavily utilized material (UTH), and débitage (unmodified flakes, D).

Views on the lifestyle of early *Homo* began to change in the late 1970s, as many workers became convinced that these hominids had been overly humanized. Taphonomic studies by Pat Shipman and others began to show that early *Homo* shared the Olduvai sites with a variety of large carnivores, thus weakening the idea that these were the safe, social home bases originally envisioned. Furthermore,

FIGURE 9–10   This shelter of branches and grass, built by the Okombambi people of Namibia, is probably little different from those that may have been built far into the past. The evidence from Olduvai Gorge, Bed I, suggests to some a structure of this type (see Figure 9–9).

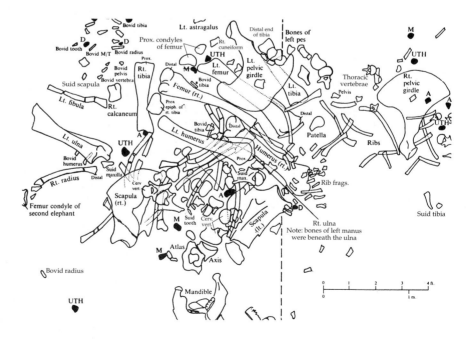

FIGURE 9–11   This plan shows part of the ancient occupation level of a possible butchery site in Bed I of Olduvai Gorge. Stone tools (solid black) are mixed in with almost the entire skeleton of an elephant, together with other food remains. Implement labels are as given in Figure 9–9, with the additional important occurrence of several manuports (unmodified rocks brought from another locality, M).

studies of the bone accumulations suggested that *Homo habilis* was mainly a scavenger—stealing from carnivore kills or using the carcasses of animals that had died naturally—and not a full-fledged hunter. Archaeologist Lewis Binford suggested that the Bed I sites were no more than "scavenging stations" where early *Homo* brought portions of large animal carcasses for consumption. Certain sites were regularly used because they allowed easy monitoring of the surrounding area for predators. Sleeping was done elsewhere, away from the remains of the day's meals, which would have attracted hyenas and other dangerous animals.

Rick Potts recently suggested that the Olduvai Bed I sites mainly represent places where raw and worked stone was cached for the handy processing of animal foods obtained nearby. Potts has proposed a resource transport hypothesis that he believes explains the primary subsistence innovation of early *Homo*. Potts believes that Oldowan toolmakers brought raw stone from sources several kilometers away and cached it at a number of locations within the group's territory or range (the original selection of a cache site may have been purely accidental and was very likely related to finding an available carcass on the spot). Stone tools could have been made at the cache sites for use elsewhere, but more frequently portions of carcasses were transported to the toolmaking site for processing. This idea is very similar to Binford's scavenging-station model, with the key addition of cached stone resources. Again, camping and sleeping at the food-processing sites is deemed unlikely by Potts because such locations would have attracted carnivores interested in leftover meat and bones. In this connection, Potts interprets the DK-I "windbreak" as merely a concentration of lava rocks broken up by the roots of an ancient tree, and not as the remains of a shelter at all. Also important is the fact that neither Binford's nor Potts's models necessarily include a sexual division of labor or food sharing (but neither do they preclude such behavior).

Most current interpretations of the subsistence, ranging, and tool-using patterns of early *Homo* are therefore much more conservative than they were just twenty years ago. Nonetheless, in a recent minor reversal of this conservative trend, Washington University anthropologists Lisa Rose and Fiona Marshall suggested that Plio-Pleistocene hominids at Olduvai and Koobi Fora probably *did* use certain spots as home bases. Rose and Marshall reason that foraging for meat (whether by scavenging or hunting) would have brought early hominids into contact with dangerous carnivores. However, rather than avoiding or fleeing from predators, it is speculated that the hominids might have cooperated to drive them away from kills and then, after the carcass had been transported to a home base (a regularly used site that also offered water, accommodations for safe sleeping, etc.), they would have cooperated once again to defend it against any carnivorous visitors. Thus, in the Rose and Marshall scenario, meat eating would have fostered increased sociality and home bases would "have become foci for a range of social, foraging, toolmaking, and carcass-processing activities [albeit with no implications for] a monogamous social organization or a well-defined sexual division of labor."

And so anthropologists continue to search for the best ways to interpret early hominids' behavior. Lacking good analogues for either the australopithecines or early *Homo*, some researchers prefer to view them as rather apelike, while others think of them as much more humanlike. Almost certainly the truth lies in-between. Although much more than advanced apes, both the australopithecines and early *Homo* no doubt were quite different from modern people with regard to their living arrangements, patterns of food procurement, and the sharing of food. As noted at the end of Chapter 8, few anthropologists are tempted to apply the term "human" either to the first hominids or the first hominines.

WHAT TRIGGERED BRAIN EXPANSION IN EARLY *HOMO*?

Before we end this chapter, it seems reasonable to ask whether the various interpretations of the lifestyles of early *Homo* provide any insights into their rather remarkable brain expansion compared to *Australopithecus*. Certainly, once bigger brains were in existence they would have allowed various other advances—increasingly sophisticated material culture and communication patterns, for example (see Figure 9–4)—but what might have triggered the evolution of bigger brains in the first place? Although fully aware that evolutionary speculations are risky and controversial endeavors, let's try our hand at one. Along with certain of our colleagues, we think the key elements in hominine brain expansion might have been group size, complex subsistence patterns, and the high nutritional value of meat. Anthropologist Robin Dunbar has produced good evidence that among the living primates there is a strong positive relationship between brain size and the size of a species' social groups. The implication is that the original function of big brains was to keep track of a complex network of social information: group-mates' identities, dominance relationships, alliances and friendships, grudges and debts. Remembering and manipulating social relationships and socially important information has clear effects on primates' chances of survival and reproduction, and there is every reason to believe that this was true among the early hominines just as it is today. Using an equation that related brain size to group size for primates, Dunbar plugged in *Homo habilis*'s brain size and came up with an estimated group size of eighty-two individuals for that species. (Dunbar notes that these are "cognitive groups," including individuals about whom one has social knowledge, but not necessarily with whom one lives on a daily basis.) So, if Dunbar is right, early *Homo* lived in a complex social environment within which a big brain would have been a great help in dealing with the soap opera of everyday life; that's evolutionary variable number one.

Variable number two involves subsistence and ranging patterns. Various studies have shown that among primates large brains also are correlated with diet. For example, omnivores are thought to have large brains partly because their lifestyle requires complex strategies for extracting high-quality foodstuffs. Similarly, primates with large home ranges (e.g., frugivores compared to folivores) seem to have bigger brains so they can handle a sophisticated "mental map" of their feeding area. The archaeological record supports both points for early *Homo*: the first hominines ate a complex, omnivorous diet including plant and animal products, and they apparently ranged over wide areas in the process of locating food and also raw stone for toolmaking. So far, so good, but can we connect the dots between group size and subsistence for early *Homo*? We think so, by linking Dunbar's line of reasoning with that of Rose and Marshall. If early *Homo* not only lived in groups but also actively scavenged for meat in groups, the hominines could have increased their odds for success by cooperatively driving predators away from kills and cooperatively defending kills against other hominids. Which brings us to evolutionary variable number three.

Big brains are metabolically expensive organs (it has been calculated that the modern human brain has a mass-specific metabolic rate nine times greater than the average mass-specific rate of the body as a whole) and meat is an energy-rich food. If the early hominines successfully increased their meat intake (and this is suggested by studies of Oldowan tools), this would have allowed brain expansion because the enhanced diet could nourish a larger brain. And so the links are as follows: big brains were selected for by pressures favoring increased social intelligence (group living) and subsistence intelligence (omnivory and wide ranging); group living facilitated cooperative scavenging (and possibly also small-scale hunting) and thus increased meat consumption; more meat in the diet allowed the expansion of metabolically expensive brains.

It is an interesting and plausible scenario, but like all such speculations it is only as good as rigorous tests prove it to be. Nonetheless, something happened around two and a half million years ago that propelled the early hominines beyond their australopithecine ancestors in both intelligence and material culture. But early *Homo* was also due to be outstripped by a descendant—*Homo erectus*, just after 2 million years B.P.

SUMMARY

The primary hallmark of hominids is bipedalism and yet, as this chapter has demonstrated, we have only an imperfect understanding of the selection pressures that produced our characteristic form of locomotion. Increased energy efficiency (compared to ape quadrupedalism), body temperature control, and adapting to variable and unstable habitats appear to be among the best explanations for the evolution of bipedalism, although there are several other suggestions that cannot be discounted entirely (such as freeing the hands for tool use and carrying things, and adopting an upright posture to harvest small food items). Furthermore, the connection between bipedalism and canine tooth reduction remains unclear. Undoubtedly, several variables—both anatomical and behavioral—were involved in a complex feedback system throughout hominid evolution.

As described in this chapter, our interpretations of early *Homo* are in a state of rapid change, and our understanding of the beginnings of a modern human way of life is incomplete. It now appears that anthropologists of the 1970s and 1980s were too eager to view early *Homo* as a food-sharing, shelter-building, hunter-and-gatherer who established base camps on the African plains and who might even have formed pair-bonded monogynous families. Recent analyses challenge several of these ideas. Although *Homo habilis* was clearly more of a meat eater than the australopithecines, we can have no confidence that these hominids hunted game any larger than that taken by chimpanzees. Indeed, all indications are that early *Homo* obtained most of its meat by scavenging on animals that had died of natural causes or from carnivore kills (some archaeologists, such as Lewis Binford, have suggested that hunting as a significant subsistence activity did not appear until the time of *Homo sapiens*; more on this in a later chapter). Likewise, we are speculating virtually without evidence if we attribute the beginnings of a sexual division of labor to early *Homo*. Certainly, at some point in hominid evolution, subsistence activities were partitioned sexually so that women mainly gathered plants and men hunted for animal foods. And it seems logical that the sexual division of labor was linked to the beginnings of significant food sharing. But we are outrunning our data if we confidently attribute these modern behaviors to early *Homo*, whose subsistence patterns may have been entirely unlike those of any living hominoid (anthropologist

Nancy Tanner believes that a female collective formed the core of early hominid social groups). And who made the Oldowan tools? Believers in the hunting-and-gathering sexual division of labor have traditionally said that males were the toolmakers, but we have no real proof of this, and indeed, there is evidence that some Oldowan tools were used to process soft plant foods—an activity traditionally viewed as females' work. If true, were females the primary Oldowan toolmakers? Some researchers think maybe so. And finally, shelter construction, monogyny, and pair bonds all seem to be much more the products of researchers' active imaginations than conclusions indicated by the data, although the idea that early hominines established base camps has recently been revived.

In summary, our present knowledge of early *Homo* (*H. habilis* and presumably *H. rudolfensis* as well) limits these hominids to the edge of culture and modern humanity. Further fossil discoveries and improved analytical techniques will yield new (and, very likely, unexpected) views of the early hominines, but for now, we must be content with a most imperfect picture of the first representatives of the genus *Homo*. In strong contrast, however, we can confidently describe the evolutionary descendants of early *Homo* as living a human lifestyle (i.e., a lifestyle broadly similar to that of modern people). And it is to these ancestors, *Homo erectus*, that we must now turn our attention.

POSTSCRIPT

In his classic work *On the Origin of Species*, Charles Darwin presented a model of continuous and gradual evolutionary change. In his descriptions of adaptation and speciation, Darwin put particular emphasis on the effects of intra- and interspecific competition (while also noting that organisms struggle with the physical environment) and repeatedly stated his belief that "Natura non facit saltum" ("Nature does not make jumps"). In Darwin's world—following the teachings of the geologist Charles Lyell—organic change was slow and stately.

In contrast to Darwinian slowness and uniformity, some researchers are beginning to present evidence for periods of accelerated tempo in evolution, including the evolution of hominids. A vigorous current supporter of this view is paleontologist Elisabeth Vrba of Yale University, who argues that life's history has been shaped by a process she calls "turnover pulse." According to Vrba, in response to dramatic (and, in the context of geological time, relatively rapid) change in the physical environment, entire communities of organisms may experience spurts (pulses) of speciation. And while these pulses do not involve any new or mysterious evolutionary processes, they are triggered primarily by environmental fluctuations that break up ecosystems long in equilibrium.

Vrba's work has identified two turnover pulse episodes with implications for hominid evolution: one about 5 mya near the Miocene-Pliocene boundary and a second in the late Pliocene about 2.5 mya. Both turnover pulse events were apparently triggered by drops in global temperatures and increased aridity on the continents—changes that, in turn, were due to continental drifting and altered global air and water circulation. In eastern and southern Africa, the cooling and drying trends resulted in the spread of grasslands and a reduction in bush and tree cover. Vrba has pointed out that the older cooling and drying event coincided with the first proliferation of African antelope species—whose presence clearly proclaimed savanna conditions—and fell *near* the evolutionary appearance of the australo-pithecines. In her view, therefore, the human family may have originated as part of a broad zoological response to shrinking woodlands and expanding grasslands.

Vrba's second cooling and drying episode—which saw global temperatures plunge some 10° to 20° F and the Sahara desert become established in northern Africa—occurred about 2.5 mya. That event witnessed the extinction of numerous older antelope species and the appearance of many modern genera, including several—like *Oryx*—that are strongly adapted to arid environments. Furthermore, many varieties of African animals, including early elephants, pigs, horses, bovids, and rhinos, showed dental changes that indicate an adaptation to diets with more tough and abrasive foodstuffs. And finally, as part of the 2.5-million-year B.P. turnover pulse, hominids experienced an adaptive radiation that resulted in the appearance of *Paranthropus* (with its huge grinding teeth) and early *Homo* (*H. habilis* and *H. rudolfensis*).

Vrba's turnover pulse hypothesis has attracted a good deal of attention and it is currently being evaluated and tested. To date, it has drawn both proponents and critics. Among the critics are Anna Behrensmeyer and several colleagues at the Smithsonian Institution. According to their analysis of mammalian taxa in the Lake Turkana region, the peak in speciation 2.5 million years ago proposed by Vrba "occurr[ed] over at least a million years and doesn't qualify as a pulse." Only time will tell whether Vrba's hypothesis will be accepted as a real evolutionary phenomenon, but in the meantime it is worth noting that it has much in common with the cladogenetic speciation model called **punctuated equilibrium**, which hypothesizes that most species experience lengthy periods of stasis (equilibrium) that are occasionally interrupted (punctuated) by rapid evolution and speciation by branching. Together, the punctuated equilibrium and turnover pulse hypotheses (assuming both are verified) could provide an important extension to evolutionary theories. Slow, steady Darwinian gradualism occurs under some ecological conditions, but when the physical environment shifts dramatically, individual species and entire communities of organisms may be thrown into pulses of accelerated speciation, extinction, and dispersal, as long-established ecosystems are disrupted. Clearly, hominids are not immune to such drastic changes. If Vrba is right, it is interesting to speculate on the contingent nature of hominid history and ponder where we might be if the late Pliocene pulse in East Africa had not occurred.

Punctuated equilibrium the hypothesis that most *species* have long periods of stasis, interrupted by episodes of rapid evolutionary change and speciation by branching.

REVIEW QUESTIONS

1. Review the evidence supporting the idea that tool use stimulated the beginnings of habitual bipedalism. If this hypothesis is true, what type and frequency of tool use do you think were involved?
2. Compare the various hypotheses about the origin of hominid bipedalism. Arrange the hypotheses in order from the most to the least likely, and then present evidence to support your ordering system.
3. Owen Lovejoy (and others) have argued that hominids evolved a pair bond and a tendency toward monogyny. Discuss the evidence for and against these propositions.

4. In the nineteenth century it was argued that "the brain led the way" in hominid evolution, that is that brain expansion and elaboration evolved early and other human traits (bipedalism, tool use, language, etc.) followed. Discuss the brain-first theory based on your knowledge of the sequence of appearance of distinctive hominid traits.

5. Describe the forms and functions of Oldowan tools. What do these tools suggest about the subsistence patterns of their makers? What conclusions can we reach about the sex(es) of their makers?

6. Which behavioral analogue do you prefer for interpreting the behavior of early *Homo*—chimpanzees or modern humans? Or should some combination of analogues be used? Explain your position.

7. What sort of group structure and mating pattern do you think characterized the australopithecines? What about early *Homo*? Present evidence to support your conclusions.

SUGGESTED FURTHER READING

Behrensmeyer, A. K., et al. "Late Pliocene Faunal Turnover in the Turkana Basin, Kenya and Ethiopia." *Science*, 278, 1997.

Jolly, C. "The Seed-Eaters." *Man*, 5, 1970.

Lovejoy, C. O. "Modeling Human Origins: Are We Sexy Because We're Smart, or Smart Because We're Sexy?" in D. T. Rasmussen, ed., *The Origin and Evolution of Humans and Humanness*. Jones & Bartlett, 1993.

Potts, R. *Humanity's Descent*. William Morrow, 1996.

Rose, L., and F. Marshall. "Meat Eating, Hominid Sociality, and Home Bases Revisited." *Current Anthropology*, 37, 1996.

Schick, K. D., and N. Toth. Making Silent Stones Speak. Simon & Schuster, 1993.

Tanner, N. M. *On Becoming Human.* Cambridge University Press, 1981.

Trevathan, W. *Human Birth: An Evolutionary Perspective.* Aldine de Gruyter, 1987.

Vrba, E. S. "Ecological and Adaptive Changes Associated with Early Hominid Evolution," in R. L. Ciochon and J. G. Fleagle, eds., *The Human Evolution Source Book*. Prentice Hall, 1993.

Wheeler, P. "Human Ancestors Walked Tall, Stayed Cool." *Natural History,* 102, 1993.

INTERNET RESOURCES

See the websites listed under Chapters 6, 7, and 8.

Chapter 10

DISCOVERING *HOMO ERECTUS*

Begun in the 1920s, excavations at the Chinese site of Zhoukoudian have produced the remains of some forty *Homo erectus* individuals, as well as thousands of stone tools.

*Then felt I like some watcher of the skies
When a new planet swims into his ken;
Or like stout Cortez, when with eagle eyes
He stared at the Pacific—and all his men
Looked at each other with a wild surmise—
Silent, upon a peak in Darien.*

JOHN KEATS, 1795–1821, "On First Looking into Chapman's Homer."

OVERVIEW

In 1887, a young Dutchman named Eugene Dubois (Figure 10–1) quit his job as a university professor and sailed to the East Indies in search of the "missing link." Incredibly, within four years he had accomplished his objective with the discovery of *Pithecanthropus erectus* in Java. Although Dubois's claim that ***Pithecanthropus*** was a "venerable ape-man" was greeted skeptically by the scientific community, it wasn't too many years before confirming fossils were unearthed in China and

Pithecanthropus the original *genus* name given by Eugene Dubois to fossil material from Java now classified as *H. erectus.*

FIGURE 10–1   An 1883 photograph shows Eugene Dubois (1858–1940) as a teacher in Amsterdam.

given the name ***Sinanthropus pekinensis.*** Today, *Pithecanthropus* and *Sinanthropus*, along with fossils from Africa and Europe, are classified as *Homo erectus*, an early-to-mid-Pleistocene species thought to be on the direct ancestral line to modern humans. This chapter tells the story of the various *Homo erectus* discoveries, including the 1984 find of a nearly complete skeleton at the west Turkana (Kenya) site of Nariokotome. Considerable attention is given to questions about the place of origin and subsequent migrations of *Homo erectus*—questions that cannot be answered conclusively at this time since we have about equally ancient fossils (1.9 to 1.8 million years old) from both ends of the species' geographic range (Africa and Southeast Asia). The anatomy of *Homo erectus* is described in some detail, and the evidence for language and speech in this species is reviewed. The chapter ends with a brief description of the probable evolutionary relationships of *Homo erectus*. Important topics and concepts in the chapter include the history of *Homo erectus* discoveries, the anatomical traits that define this species, evidence bearing on the question of language and speech, and evidence regarding the origin and spread of *H. erectus*.

One final introductory comment is in order before beginning the chapter. In several of the following sections, we have found it necessary to anticipate later evolutionary events and refer to ***Homo heidelbergensis***, a species that we suggest originated from *Homo erectus* stock some 800,000 to 600,000 years ago and later gave rise to both modern humans (*Homo sapiens*) and the Neandertals (now given their own species name, ***Homo neanderthalensis***). These are significant taxonomic changes from previous editions of this book in which we combined all "post–*Homo erectus* but premodern" hominids in the now-outmoded taxon "archaic *Homo sapiens*." Our rationale for this new taxonomic arrangement is presented fully in Chapter 14, along with complete descriptions of the various *Homo heidelbergensis* fossils and the Neandertal people. References made here to *H. heidelbergensis* result mainly from the half-million-year period of overlap between that species and late populations of *Homo erectus*, and paleoanthropologists' uncertainty over the classification of particular fossils and/or the species assignment of new behavior patterns.

Sinanthropus pekinensis the original name given by Davidson Black to ancient *fossils* from Zhoukoudian. These remains are now classified as *Homo erectus*.

Homo heidelbergensis successor to *Homo erectus*, first appearing about 800,000 to 600,000 years B.P.; ancestral to both *Homo sapiens* and the Neandertals.

Homo neanderthalensis a *species* of humans that inhabited Europe and the Middle East from about 300,000 to 30,000 B.P. Descended from *Homo heidelbergensis*, the species' common name is usually spelled Neandertal.

Mini-Timeline

DATE OR AGE	FOSSIL DISCOVERIES OR EVOLUTIONARY EVENTS
(A) DATE (YEARS A.D.)	
1996	Fossils from Ngandong and Sambungmacan are redated
1994	*Homo erectus* fossils from Sangiran and Modjokerto are redated
1984	Nariokotome *H. erectus* skeleton found
1929	First skull of *Sinanthropus* discovered
1891	Eugene Dubois discovers first *Pithecanthropus* fossils
(B) AGE (MILLION YEARS B.P.)	
1.8–1.6	*Homo erectus* at Dmanisi, Republic of Georgia
1.8–1.7	Oldest (?) Asian *H. erectus* fossils at Sangiran and Modjokerto
1.8	Oldest African *H. erectus* fossils at Koobi Fora
1.9	Hominids inhabit Longgupo Cave, China

EUGENE DUBOIS AND THE QUEST FOR THE MISSING LINK

In the mid-1800s, the Western world's interest was focused on the present and the future. It was an age of human progress and accomplishment, of prosperity, and of inventions that made life easier and more civilized: running water and lighted streets, iceboxes, sewing machines, elevated railways, lawnmowers, typewriters, and telephones. It is understandable, then, that the new theory about humankind's descent from prehistoric apes provoked doubt and opposition (see Chapter 1). In this atmosphere of progress and self-approval, the claim that humankind was merely an offshoot of an ape was rejected by much of the public and by many eminent scientists as well. No one had yet found any fossils proving a link between apes and humans. Most of those who doubted our primate origins did so not merely through acceptance of the Biblical account of creation, but also because for a long time there was no really convincing fossil evidence to support Darwin, Huxley, and other evolutionists.

Some scientists took the lack of any fossils of intermediate humanlike apes as proof that no such creatures had ever existed. At the other extreme, some of Darwin's early supporters rushed forward with fanciful pedigrees for humankind, making up in enthusiasm what they lacked in evidence. Even believers in human evolution were confused by the outpouring of rival experts' family trees for humankind, full of imaginary apish ancestors with scientific-sounding Greek and Latin names.

Eugene Dubois was born in Holland in 1858 and grew up in this atmosphere of often bitter debate over human origins. Although the Dubois family was conventional and religious, the home atmosphere was not one of narrow-minded provincial piety, and the boy's interest in science was encouraged. Dubois went to medical school and then, choosing academic life over medical practice, became an instructor in anatomy at the Royal Normal School in Amsterdam. He was fascinated by the many different family trees that were being published in both learned and popular journals and was much influenced by the work of Ernst Heinrich Haeckel, a German zoologist who had predicted in some detail what *should* be discovered about the course of human evolution (see Figure 10–2). For six years, Dubois delivered his lectures and gave no hint of the wild idea that was taking hold in him: to establish the human place in evolution and set the record straight once and for all, by finding a fossil of a primitive creature that was the clear forerunner of humans.

Dubois Begins Work in the East Indies

Dubois began to take up his vocation by going over all the clues he could find. One important clue was the first Neandertal fossil, which had been discovered in 1856, two years before Dubois was born (see Chapter 14). For many years, the Neandertal remains were the only trace of a nonmodern skeleton in the human closet. Dubois, a firm believer in evolution, considered the Neandertal fossils definitely human, and very ancient. To him, they suggested that the search for even more primitive creatures should be carried out in some region of limestone deposits and caves similar to the European habitat of the Neandertal, but they also suggested to him that Europe was not the place to look for a missing link. The creature that provided the evolutionary link between ape and human, Dubois rea-

THE MODERN THEORY OF THE DESCENT OF MAN.

FIGURE 10–2 Ernst Haeckel's work on the ancestry of humankind was one of the first attempts to deal with the specifics of evolution. Although his genealogical chart, which starts with a blob of protoplasm and ends with a Papuan, contains misconceptions and fictitious creatures, it is in some ways surprisingly accurate, considering the dearth of knowledge in his day. The animals illustrated were chosen as representatives of the taxonomic groups to which successive human ancestral species were believed to have belonged.

soned, must have lived long before the Neandertal, at a time when Europe was far too cold to permit its survival. The forebear he wanted to find must have lived in a tropical part of the world that had been untouched by the glaciers of the ice age.

Other clues as well pointed to the tropics. Darwin had suggested that our tree-dwelling progenitors lived in "some warm, forest-clad land"; Alfred Russel Wallace had also recommended that our forebears be sought in a tropical zone. Wallace had lived in Malaysia for eight years, and he had noticed that the islands of Sumatra and Borneo (Figure 10–3) are the home of both the gibbon, the most ancient living ape, and the orangutan, one of the most advanced species of ape. He wrote, "With what interest must every naturalist look forward to the time when the caves of the tropics be thoroughly examined, and the past history and earliest

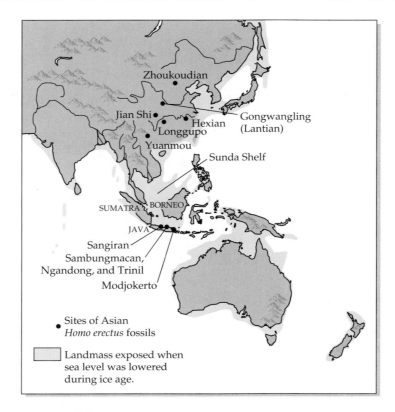

FIGURE 10-3   During glacial periods, when far more water was locked up in the polar and continental ice sheets than today, the world sea level fell. During the coldest periods, the maximum lowering of the sea appears to have been more than 330 feet (100 meters), which would have enlarged considerably the landmasses available for occupation by plant and animal life. Throughout the Pleistocene, the sea level fluctuated extensively.

appearance of the great man-like apes be at length made known." Wallace's curiosity about these islands and their caves proved contagious, and Dubois began to think seriously of going to the Dutch East Indies to explore the caves himself. The more he read about the geology and natural history of the region, the more convinced he became that the missing link would be discovered there. The islands once had been part of continental Asia; before the seas had inundated the lower land, turning the mountaintops into islands, animals could have wandered down freely from the north.

At age twenty-nine, Eugene Dubois set out to solve the mystery of human origins, to find the fossil of a creature with both apelike and humanlike traits that would prove the relationship between humans and apes. Dubois's planning focused on Sumatra, then under Dutch rule and therefore a practical place for a Dutch citizen to launch a paleontological expedition. In 1886, he told some of his colleagues at the University of Amsterdam that he had reason to believe he would solve the mystery of human origins. They tried to dissuade him, and one even politely suggested that Dubois was slightly mad. His requests for financial backing were turned down flatly by both philanthropists and government bureaucrats.

But Dubois was determined to get to Sumatra, and finally he was sent there by the Dutch East Indies Army, in which he enlisted as a doctor.

For the first two years in Sumatra, his investigations of a great many limestone caves and deposits yielded only teeth that were too recent to interest him; they belonged mainly to orangutans. In 1889, following the discovery by a mining engineer of a fossil skull at Wadjak, Java, Dubois persuaded the Dutch East Indies government to transfer him to that neighboring island for further paleontological investigations (Figure 10–3). The colonial government, showing new interest in his work, supplied him with a native crew of convict laborers and two Dutch officers to oversee them. With such backing, excavations began on a grand scale.

Beginning work in the Wadjak region, Dubois's crew had discovered a second—and similar—skull by September 1890. Both were modern in appearance and too recent to have belonged to a missing link. But the region was extraordinarily rich in fossils of many kinds, and Dubois set up several digging parties at different locations. By 1894, he had shipped to the Netherlands 400 cases of fossil bones, including specimens of many extinct and previously unknown animals.

At one site to the north, Dubois's foreman reported an unexpected problem. He had found that for many years natives of the area had been digging up fossils and selling them to Chinese merchants as **dragon bones** to be ground into powder for an ancient and popular Chinese medicine. The local fossil hunters, unwilling to give up a profitable business with the Chinese, would not sell any of their finds to Dubois's party. To make matters worse, the foreman soon discovered that his own workmen were stealing the fossils they unearthed and carrying them off to sell to the local traders. When called on for help, the colonial government issued an order outlawing the sale of any fossils to Chinese merchants in Java.

Dragon bones the ancient Chinese term for *fossils* of various sorts that were collected and ground into medicines.

Discovery of *Pithecanthropus* (1891)

To Dubois, the most promising site on the island seemed to be an exposed and stratified embankment along the Solo River, near the small village of Trinil in the center of Java (Figure 10–4). Here, in the months when the river was low, Dubois could survey a bank 45 feet (14 meters) high of ancient river deposits with clearly defined layers of fine volcanic debris and sandstone.

In a stratum about 4 feet (1.2 meters) thick just above the stream level, Dubois came upon a rich store of animal fossils: a stegodon, an extinct hippopotamus, a small deer, an antelope. Before he could pursue these interesting finds, the rains set in, and he had to abandon his excavations at the river until the following autumn. In August 1891, he and his crew set to work once more, digging down through the strata with hoes, hammers, and chisels—crude implements by later standards, but Dubois was one of the first scientists ever to attempt a systematic search for fossils. In September, he found his first recognizable fossil of a primitive primate: a single apelike tooth.

On first inspection, the fossil seemed to Dubois to be the wisdom tooth of an extinct giant chimpanzee. Later, comparing it with molars of other apes, he noticed a strange wrinkling of the crown, suggesting that it was, instead, the tooth of an orangutan. As Dubois mulled over the molar, the digging went on for another month. Then, only 3 feet (0.9 meters) to the side of where the tooth had been unearthed, and in the same layer, a workman discovered a heavy, brown rock that looked like a turtle's shell. After the earth was brushed away from the new find, it looked more like part of a skull. "The amazing thing had happened," wrote

FIGURE 10–4   At this bend in the Solo River at Trinil, Java, Dubois excavated the terraced bank where the Java fossils were found, at a depth of 48 feet (14.6 meters).

the English anatomist G. Elliot Smith years later. "Dubois had actually found the fossil his scientific imagination had visualized." Though he did not know it at the time, it was the evidence Dubois had crossed half the world to find.

The skull (Figure 10–5) was unlike any ever seen before. Clearly, it was too low and flat to be the cranium of a modern human. After detailed study of both the skullcap and the tooth, Dubois reported, "That both specimens came from a great manlike ape was at once clear." Despite his expert knowledge of anatomy, he found the skull peculiarly hard to place more precisely than that.

Shortly after these finds were made, the rains came, the river rose, and digging again had to be suspended until the following year. When digging resumed in 1892, Dubois cut a new excavation in the same deposit about 33 feet (10 meters) from where the strange cranium had been buried. There, ten months after the ape-like skull was found, he discovered another, even more surprising, primate fossil. This one (shown in Figure 10–6) was unmistakable. It was the left femur, or thighbone, of a primate that had walked erect! It resembled a human thighbone in almost every respect, except that it was heavier. Could the curious tooth, the problematic skull, and the unexpected thighbone all have belonged to the same individual? The implications were staggering.

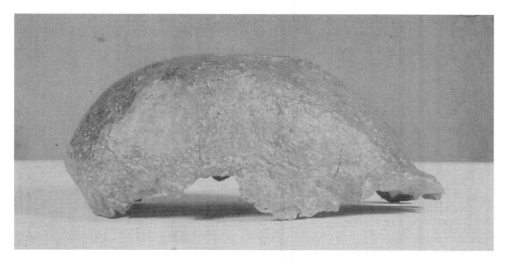

FIGURE 10–5   The skullcap of *Pithecanthropus erectus* was Dubois's greatest find. It was to be nearly forty years before another skull of this kind was found. Photograph is approximately 60 percent actual size.

FIGURE 10–6   The first femur that Dubois found appeared very modern and indicated an upright posture. The growth of bone on its inner surface near the top is an unusual pathological condition (probably myositis ossificans, an inflammatory disease of muscles that produce extra bony deposits) that is also found occasionally in modern humans but has no evolutionary significance. Photograph is just under 25 percent actual size.

Dubois measured and studied the apelike skull and the humanlike femur from Trinil and in 1892 announced that the skull and femur had belonged to the same creature, which he believed to have been an upright species of chimpanzee that he called *Anthropopithecus erectus*. In 1893, however, he changed his mind and the species' name. After further study of the femur, and after calculating that the fossil skullcap would have held a brain 2.4 times larger than that of an adult chimp, Dubois borrowed the name of Haeckel's hypothetical human ancestor and christened his fossil **Pithecanthropus erectus** (from the Greek *pithekos*, "ape," and *anthropos*, "man"). By appropriating this name for his Java find, Dubois boldly filed his claim to have found, as he cabled his friends in Europe, the "Missing Link of Darwin." He attributed it to a late Pliocene age.

Pithecanthropus the original *genus* name given by Eugene Dubois to fossil material from Java now classified as *H. erectus*.

The bones of *Pithecanthropus erectus* were one of the greatest fossil finds ever made, and even though he had only those few incomplete specimens, Dubois fully realized their importance. We now believe that *Pithecanthropus erectus* was actually an early human, a vital link in the chain of human evolution, not the half-ape Dubois had supposed it to be. We also now believe the Trinil skull to date from the middle Pleistocene—perhaps 800,000 to just over a million years B.P. (see Table 10–1).

TABLE 10–1 *A Partial Record of* **Homo erectus** *Fossils*

CONTINENT	SITE	AGE (YEARS B.P.)
Africa	Salé	300,000–200,000
	Sidi Abderrahman	300,000–200,000
	Thomas Quarries	350,000–240,000
	Lainyamok	600,000
	Ternifine	650,000–450,000
	Melka Kunture	900,000
	Olduvai Gorge	1.2 million–600,000
	Omo	1.4 million
	Nariokotome	1.5 million
	Swartkrans[a]	1.8–1.5 million
	Koobi Fora	1.8–1.6 million
Asia	Ngandong [Solo](?)[b]	46,000–27,000
	Sambungmacan(?)[b]	53,000–27,000
	Jian Shi	300,000–200,000
	Zhoukoudian	500,000–230,000
	Hexian	700,000–250,000
	Gongwangling [Lantian]	700,000
	Yuanmou	900,000–500,000
	Trinil	1.0–0.8 million
	Sangiran	1.7 million–500,000
	Modjokerto	1.8 million
	Longgupo[c]	1.9–1.7 million
Europe	Ceprano	700,000
	Dmanisi	1.8–1.6 million

[a] Some workers argue that the *Homo* fossils from Swartkrans do not fit easily into *H. erectus* and require their own species designation. We have opted to retain the traditional *H. erectus* classification, pending further information.

[b] Classifications for the Ngandong and Sambungmacan fossils are problematic. Some researchers assign them to *Homo erectus*, while others believe they belong in a more advanced species (perhaps *Homo heidlebergensis* or even *Homo sapiens*). They are included here provisionally, and their equivocal status is explained in the text and in Box 10–1.

[c] Although its discoverers claim the Longgupo Cave fossils may represent *H. habilis*, a more conservative view is that they are best assigned to early *Homo erectus*.

Java Controversy

Even before Dubois could show his discoveries to colleagues in Europe, his precious fossils became the focus of a raging scientific controversy that embroiled him throughout the rest of his life. His first cabled reports were met with skepticism. Some critics insisted that the fossil bones did not belong together at all and suggested that Dubois had simply made the mistake of mixing the skull and teeth of an ape with the thighbone of a human who had died nearby. One member of the Netherlands Zoological Society, writing in a Dutch newspaper in 1893, ridiculed Dubois's jigsaw-puzzle methods, asking whether more finds at the site in Java might not eventually lead to announcements of an even stranger creature: If another, more human, skull was discovered within 50 feet (15 meters) of the other bones, this unfriendly commentator queried, would this mean that *Pithecanthropus* had two skulls, one apelike and one humanlike?

To those unwilling to acknowledge any link with any form of anthropoid ancestor, *Pithecanthropus* was pure insult. Clergy hastened to assure their congregations that Adam, and not the crude half-ape–half-human brute unearthed in Java, was the true human ancestor. Dubois was denounced from pulpit and from podium, for scientists were almost as angry and as skeptical. The combination of apelike head and upright posture ran directly contrary to the belief that the development of a larger, better brain had come first in the separation of the human stock from earlier anthropoids. Scientists expected a being with a human head and an apelike body, not the reverse.

The arrival of the fossils themselves for close inspection did not settle the arguments. Only six weeks after Dubois reached Holland in 1895, he presented *Pithecanthropus* to the Third International Congress of Zoology at Leiden. Almost at once, a great quarrel broke out over where to place this Java "ape-human" in the scheme of evolution. Opinion seemed to harden along national lines: most German scientists believed that *Pithecanthropus* was an ape that had humanlike characteristics, while most English scientists thought it was a human that had apelike attributes. Only a few scientists were inclined to agree with Dubois that the fossils represented a transitional form, or "missing link," between apes and humans. Among those few supporting voices was the American paleontologist O. C. Marsh and the German evolutionist Ernst Haeckel, whose hypothetical *Pithecanthropus* had been given substance by Dubois.

Dubois gave his colleagues as much detailed knowledge of *Pithecanthropus* as he could. He exhibited the bones at scientific meetings throughout Europe, showed them to any scientists who wanted to examine them, and published detailed descriptions. He had to acquire the skills of a dentist, a photographer, and a sculptor. In order to make accurate brain casts, he spent weeks learning to use a fine dental drill, with which he could clean away minute stone particles inside the skullcap. He invented a special "stereorthoscope" camera, designed to photograph the fossils in various planes without distortion. For the public, he sculpted a life-sized reconstruction of *Pithecanthropus* (see Figure 10–7), ordering his son to pose for him during a school vacation. He patiently defended his claim for *Pithecanthropus*, carting the bones around in a battered suitcase, and seemed to develop an almost personal attachment to the fossil ancestor whose bones were a constant companion.

In spite of all Dubois's efforts, the attacks on *Pithecanthropus* continued. Dubois took them personally. Deeply hurt by the refusal of other scientists to accept his interpretation of the bones, he withdrew the remains of *Pithecanthropus* from the

FIGURE 10–7   Dubois's model of *Pithecanthropus* holds an antler.

public realm and refused to allow even scientific colleagues to examine them. He then turned his attention to research on brain evolution.

In 1920, Henry Fairfield Osborn, head of the American Museum of Natural History, appealed to the president of the Dutch Academy of Sciences to help persuade Dubois to once again make his fossils available for study. Soon afterward, in 1923, Dubois opened his strongboxes for Alés Hrdlička of the Smithsonian Institution and thereafter again exhibited *Pithecanthropus* at scientific meetings. He also released a cast of the *Pithecanthropus* skull that indicated a brain of about 850 cubic centimeters, well above the approximate range of 275 to 750 cc of the great apes and below the 1,000 to 2,000 cc range of modern humans.

Today there still remain some unanswered questions about Dubois's discovery. Do the bones really belong to the same creature? To suppose that two different primates—an unknown species of ape and an unknown species of human—had lived in Java at exactly the same time and had died within 35 feet (11 meters) of each other at Trinil seemed to Dubois far more improbable than to suppose that the various bones belonged to one creature with both apelike and human characteristics.

It now appears that Dubois was wrong about the association of the Trinil skull-cap and femur. Modern studies suggest that they were neither from the same individual nor from the same species. The skull is ancient and undoubtedly from the early human species now called *Homo erectus*, but the femur is probably younger by several hundred thousand years and belonged to *Homo sapiens*. Dubois was right, however, that his "venerable ape-man" was bipedal. Subsequent discoveries of *Homo erectus* postcranial material from sites such as Olduvai Gorge, Zhoukoudian, China (see Figure 10–3), and Nariokotome, Kenya (see Figure 10–17) have verified this point. As regards the Trinil molar tooth, Dubois's initial assessment—that it came from an orangutan—was, in fact, correct.

Because of the great controversy over whether *Pithecanthropus* was a human, an ape, or a true "missing link," Dubois's brilliant detective work in locating the fossils seemed only to add to the mystery of human origins instead of solving it. While anthropologists argued over the Java bones, Dubois withdrew into his home in Holland (his original fossils are still housed in Leiden). In the meantime, the controversy was being settled elsewhere.

TWENTIETH-CENTURY DISCOVERIES

Search for Human Fossils in China

The years following Dubois's discovery saw several important additions to the hominid fossil record: the Mauer mandible (now thought to be *Homo heidelbergensis*) was discovered near Heidelberg, Germany, in 1907; the fraudulent Piltdown remains were announced in England between 1912 and 1913 (see the Postscript to this chapter); and Dart's baby *Australopithecus africanus* from Taung was described in 1925. None of these finds, however, shed much light on Dubois's *Pithecanthropus erectus* fossils. That light came in 1927 with the discovery of more Asian "missing links" at the Chinese site of Zhoukoudian near Beijing (Peking).

The discovery of "Peking man" in 1927 involved a piece of scientific detective work almost as remarkable as Dubois's exploit in Java. This ancestor was added to the human family tree simply because a small band of scientists had gone to China determined to hunt it down. Even after Dubois's success in Java, the prospect of searching for a primitive human in China could appeal only to people prepared to spend their lives hunting for a needle in one haystack after another. But a Canadian physician, Davidson Black (1884–1934), was sure that he would unearth a human ancestor in China if only he looked long and hard enough. And so in 1919, when he was offered an appointment as professor of anatomy at Peking Union Medical College, which was being set up with funds from the Rockefeller Foundation, he eagerly accepted.

Black's conviction was based both on geologic evidence showing that the ancient climate and geography of China were quite suitable for primitive humans to exist there, and on the theory that patterns of evolution are closely related to climatic conditions. Also supporting his feeling was a single tantalizing piece of fossil evidence that some early primate had once inhabited China. In 1899, a German physician, K. A. Haberer, had chanced on an unusual fossil tooth among some "dragon bones" about to be ground up for medicine in a druggist's shop in Beijing. The tooth was among more than a hundred fossils the doctor had picked up in various Chinese drugstores and sent to paleontologist Max Schlosser. Schlosser identified the tooth as a "left upper third molar, either of a man or a hitherto unknown anthropoid ape" and predicted hopefully that further searching might turn up the skeleton of an early human.

Black's hopes of finding time for fossil hunting when he reached China were dissolved by an adviser from the Rockefeller Foundation, who warned him to concentrate on anatomy, not anthropology. It was not until 1921 that the search for early humans in China actually began. That year, a group led by John Gunnar Andersson, a Swedish geologist, began to dig at a site 25 miles (40 kilometers) southwest of Beijing, near the village of Zhoukoudian (see Figure 10–3). Excavations were proceeding at a rise called Chicken Bone Hill near an old limestone quarry, when Andersson was told by his workmen that much better fossils could be found on the other side of the village, at Dragon Bone Hill, beside another abandoned quarry.

The Chinese had been digging "dragon bones" out of this spot and others like it for hundreds of years, and no one will ever know how many powdered fossils passed harmlessly through the alimentary canals of dyspeptic Chinese. Whatever the losses may have been to paleoanthropology, some of the limestone caverns in the hillside were still richly packed with interesting material. There were bits of broken quartz among the limestone deposits around an ancient cliffside cave. The quartz would not naturally be associated with limestone, Andersson knew; it must have been brought there—perhaps by some toolmaking peoples of the past.

A great many fossils were dug out of the rock and shipped back to Sweden for study. Twenty different mammals were identified, many of them extinct species. But Andersson's toolmaker was not easily found. A likely tooth turned up, but it was then identified as the molar of an ape. Finally, in 1926, when one of Andersson's associates had given up and returned to Sweden and the digging had stopped, a closer study of this molar and another tooth found later suggested that they might indeed be human. The teeth were sent back to Andersson, who turned them over to Davidson Black for his expert appraisal. Preoccupied though Black was with medicine, he had never lost interest in the Zhoukoudian site. He was certain that the teeth came from a human of great antiquity, and he persuaded the Rockefeller Foundation to support a large-scale excavation of the site.

Sinanthropus Discovered (1927)

Work started up again at Dragon Bone Hill in 1927. At some remote time in the past, water had honeycombed the limestone of the hill with caves and fissures. The caves in turn had filled with the deposits of running water and with the debris of collapsing roofs. By the twentieth century, when modern quarrying had cut away one face of the hill, the former caves appeared only as fossil-bearing rock distinct from the limestone. Digging in this hard, compacted fill material proved difficult; blasting was often necessary. Just as much of a problem was the troubled political condition of China. Antiforeign riots were flaring, and bandits controlled the countryside around Beijing. For weeks at a time, the dig was isolated from the city. Nevertheless, work at the dig continued. On October 16, 1927, three days before the first season's work was to end, Birgir Böhlin, field supervisor, found another early human tooth. As he hurried to Beijing to take it to Black, soldiers stopped him several times, without suspecting that he carried a scientific treasure in his pocket.

Black studied the tooth exhaustively. Struck by its size and its cusp pattern, he became convinced that it was a very ancient human molar. Without waiting for any further proof, Black announced the discovery of a new genus and species of prehistoric human: *Sinanthropus pekinensis*, "Chinese man of Peking." Scientists were startled, and although Black traveled around the world to let them examine for

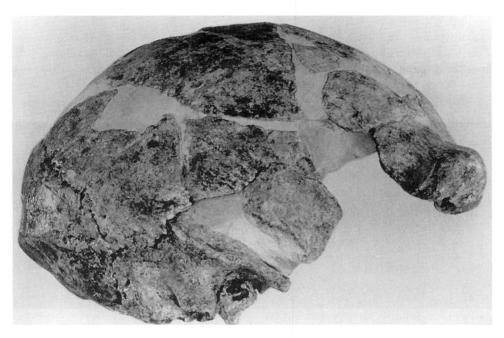

FIGURE 10–8   Although not the first to be discovered, this is one of several skullcaps of "Peking man" (*Homo erectus*) recovered from Zhoukoudian.

themselves the evidence (which he carried on a watch chain in his waistcoat pocket), many refused to recognize *Sinanthropus* as a legitimate ancestor on the evidence of only one tooth.

When Black returned to Beijing in 1928, his belief in the humanness of *Sinanthropus* was vindicated. His associates were waiting with fragments of a primitive human jaw they had dug out of the cave. And as tons of earth were excavated from the hillside and sifted for signs of fossil fragments, further teeth and several small fragments of human bone came to light.

Then, in 1929, Pei Wenzhong, a Chinese paleontologist working with Black, turned up the first skull of *Sinanthropus*. Work was about to be closed for the year when Pei opened up two caves at the extreme end of a fissure. On the floor of one was a large accumulation of debris. Pei brushed some of it away, and suddenly, partly surrounded by loose sand and partly embedded in travertine (a water-formed rock), there lay revealed the object of all the searching: a nearly complete skullcap (Figure 10–8). Even at first glance, Pei felt certain that it was a skullcap of *Sinanthropus*. After removing the skull and part of its stone bed from the cave, Pei carefully wrapped it up, set it in the basket of his bicycle, and pedaled the 25 miles (40 kilometers) to Black's laboratory in Beijing. Black showed Pei's discovery to Roy Chapman Andrews, an American scientist. "There it was, the skull of an individual who had lived half a million years ago," Andrews wrote. "It was one of the most important discoveries in the whole history of human evolution. He could not have been very impressive when he was alive, but dead and fossilized, he was awe-inspiring."

Black spent the next four months freeing the skullcap from the surrounding stone. When it was entirely clean he separated all the bones, made a cast of each one, and then reassembled the pieces. Black was now able to make a reliable estimate of the brain capacity of *Sinanthropus*. It came to about 1,000 cubic centimeters, marking its owner as definitely humanlike in this respect.

Intensive Work at Zhoukoudian

The news made headlines around the world. Excavations at Zhoukoudian were reorganized on a broader basis and went on for almost ten more years, finally taking on the proportions of a grand engineering project.

As work advanced, a whole hillside was sliced off, revealing deposits 160 feet (almost 50 millimeters) deep (Figure 10–9). They can be compared with an apartment building about sixteen stories tall, each story packed solid with blown-in debris combined with the abandoned rubbish of long-departed tenants. Layer on layer, the caves were filled through the ages with strata of clay, with soil carried in by the wind, with limestone drippings, with rock fallen from the ceiling—all sandwiching layers of human and animal debris. It is clear that large carnivores occupied the caves for long periods of time. Bones of extinct creatures such as the cave bear and a giant hyena, together with the remains of animals on which they preyed, occur at certain levels. At other levels it seems clear that human beings drove the carnivores out and took over the caves for themselves. At first, the animal and

FIGURE 10–9 The excavation of the cave filling at Zhoukoudian was a gigantic undertaking. Work continued at the site from 1927 to 1937.

human layers alternate fairly regularly, but toward the top, the evidence suggests that humans took over permanently.

A total of 1,873 workdays were devoted to dynamiting and removing some 706,000 cubic feet (20,000 cubic meters) of rock and earth and sorting through the debris for fossils. The findings constituted an encyclopedia of prehistory that has given us a great part of our knowledge of these people. By 1937, parts of more than forty men, women, and children had been unearthed; these fossils included five **calvariae** (skulls without faces or mandibles), nine fragmentary skulls, six facial fragments, fourteen lower jaws, 152 teeth, and numerous skeletal fragments.

Calvaria a braincase; i.e., a skull minus the facial skeleton and lower jaw (plural, calvariae).

Black organized the work, kept detailed records of all the finds, classified them, and made casts, drawings, and photographs of the heavy volume of material pouring into Beijing. Tragically, he did not live to savor the full bounty of Zhoukoudian. He died of a heart attack in 1934, but he had seen enough to realize the site's extraordinary significance.

The Rockefeller Foundation sought carefully for a successor and chose Franz Weidenreich (1873–1948), then a visiting professor of anatomy at the University of Chicago (Figure 10–10). Before the Nazis drove him from his native Germany, Weidenreich had completed important studies of the evolutionary changes in the pelvis and the foot that made possible our upright posture. His studies supported the contention of Darwin and Huxley that humankind is a descendant of some ancient anthropoid stock.

FIGURE 10–10   Franz Weidenreich (left, shown here with an unidentified colleague) succeeded Davidson Black at Peking Union Medical College in 1935 and pursued the excavations at Zhoukoudian with equal fervor.

Assessment of *Sinanthropus*

After Weidenreich's arrival at Zhoukoudian in 1935, only two more seasons of undisturbed digging could be carried out. Fighting between Chinese and Japanese guerrillas broke out nearby, and the archaeologists had to take refuge. With the approach of World War II, Weidenreich concentrated on making accurate drawings and casts of the skulls and published detailed photographs and descriptions of every important fossil. He began a classic series of studies of the fossils: *The Mandibles of Sinanthropus*, *The Dentition of Sinanthropus*, *The Extremity Bones of Sinanthropus*, and *The Skull of Sinanthropus*. All four supported Black's conclusion: *Sinanthropus* was not a link between apes and humans but an actual human, though a very primitive one. Weidenreich placed *Sinanthropus* solidly in the human lineage because members of the species undoubtedly could walk upright on two legs. "Apes, like man, have two hands and two feet, but man alone has acquired an upright position and the faculty of using his feet exclusively as locomotor instruments," said Weidenreich. "Unless all signs are deceiving, the claim may even be ventured that the change in locomotion and the corresponding alteration of the organization of the body are the essential specialization in the transformation of the prehuman form into the human form."

The teeth and dental arch of *Sinanthropus* testified further to human status. The canines were not the projecting fangs of the ape, and the dental arch was curved, not oblong. Still more evidence lay in the skull. Weidenreich arranged the skulls of a gorilla, *Sinanthropus*, and a modern human in a row, so that even a glance revealed their striking differences: the extremely low skull of the gorilla, the somewhat higher skull of *Sinanthropus*, and the rounded skull of a modern human (Figure 10–11). The low vault of the gorilla skull houses a brain averaging about 500 cubic centimeters; the higher dome of *Sinanthropus* held one of about 1,000 cc; and the high cranium of the modern human encloses a brain averaging about 1,330 cc. Because *Sinanthropus*'s brain was small compared to that of modern people, some scientists questioned the creature's human status. Weidenreich cautioned that brain size alone is no absolute determinant. One species of whale, he pointed out, has a brain approaching 10,000 cc, but this amounts to 0.04 ounces (1 gram) of brain for each 22 pounds (10,000 grams) of body weight, compared to our ratio of 0.04 ounces (1 gram) for every 1.6 ounces (45 grams) of weight. "Neither the absolute nor the relative size of the brain can be used to measure the degree of mental abil-

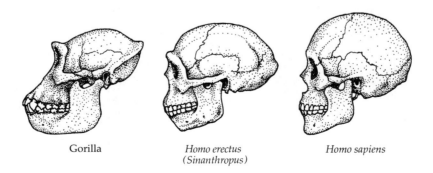

| Gorilla | *Homo erectus*
(*Sinanthropus*) | *Homo sapiens* |

FIGURE 10–11 Skulls of a female gorilla, *Sinanthropus*, and a modern Chinese (all equally reduced). Note the size and form of the braincase in relation to the jaws.

ity in animals or man," he added. "Cultural objects are the only guide as far as spiritual life is concerned. They may be fallacious guides too, but we are completely lost if these objects are missing."

Culture at Zhoukoudian

At Zhoukoudian cultural objects were not missing. The continuing excavations produced thousands of stone tools. Many were simple choppers with only a few chips removed, but they were made to a rough pattern. In the largest cave that was explored, 100,000 stone tools and fragments, most of quartz, were found. Some of them lay with charred bits of wood and bone. From this it was concluded that *Sinanthropus* had mastered the use of fire.

The bones and antlers of thousands of animals were present in the deposits. Nearly three-quarters of them belonged to deer; there were also bones of giant sheep, zebra, pigs, buffalo, rhinoceros, monkeys, bison, elephant, and even such river-dwellers as the otter. Among these were scattered the bones of predators; bear, hyena, wolves, fox, badger, leopard and other cats, and humans. All these bones came from species that are now extinct.

The possibility that some of the bones and antlers were shaped and used as tools was put forward by the distinguished French prehistorian Abbé Henri Breuil (Figure 10–12). His work has been cited by numerous authors, including Raymond Dart, who used it to support his thesis that there was a somewhat similar "osteodontokeratic" culture at Makapansgat, South Africa. However, as early as 1938 Pei had discussed the effects on bone of predators, rodents, water, soil chemistry, and so on. The fact is that, as Lewis Binford and C. K. Ho have pointed out, the evidence for a bone and horn industry at Zhoukoudian is not by any means conclusive; all the so-called tools of these materials could have been produced naturally, without any human activity. Interpretations of the Zhoukoudian cultural material will be discussed further in Chapter 11.

About 20 feet (6 meters) below the lowest outer threshold of the big cave, the expedition found what may have been *Sinanthropus*'s garbage dump, a stony amalgam of thousands of scraps of bone, stone chips, and hackberry seeds. All in all, by

FIGURE 10–12   Bone and antler fragments were found in abundance at Zhoukoudian. The photograph is approximately one-sixth actual size.

their handiwork as well as by their bodily structure, the specimens found in China indubitably established their right to a place in the human genus. Recent Chinese research places the human occupation of the cave between 230,000 and 500,000 years B.P.(Table 10–1).

Relationship of *Pithecanthropus* and *Sinanthropus*

Weidenreich's assessment corroborated Black's earlier conclusion that *Sinanthropus* was humanlike. In 1929, Black had compared his Zhoukoudian skull with Dubois's detailed description of *Pithecanthropus*. He concluded that the skulls were two specimens of the same type of creature. In each, the bones of the skull were thick, the forehead was low and sloping, and massive brow ridges jutted out over the eye sockets.

In 1931, on an upper terrace of the same Solo River whose banks had harbored the bones of Dubois's *Pithecanthropus*, fragments of eleven somewhat more recent skulls were excavated by Dutch geologists. This discovery encouraged G. H. R. von Koenigswald (1902–1983), a German paleontologist (Figure 10–13), to keep searching for more specimens of *Pithecanthropus*. Eventually, in 1937, in a region to the west called Sangiran, he found pieces of three more skulls, definitely human and definitely very old—and presumably remains of the genus *Pithecanthropus* that Dubois had named forty years before. When the most complete

FIGURE 10–13 G. H. R von Koenigswald worked in Java in the 1930s and managed to find more specimens of *Pithecanthropus*. He helped establish that *Sinanthropus* and *Pithecanthropus* were of the same genus.

skull was assembled, it scarcely could have been more like Dubois's fossil. "It was a little eerie," said von Koenigswald, "to come upon two skulls . . . which resembled each other as much as two eggs." In 1936, von Koenigswald had excavated a child's skull at Modjokerto, Java, which later proved to be that of a six-year-old *Pithecanthropus*.

In 1939, a historic meeting of *Sinanthropus* and *Pithecanthropus* took place in Weidenreich's laboratory, when von Koenigswald paid a visit and brought his Java fossils along to compare them with the Zhoukoudian finds. The two scientists concluded that *Pithecanthropus* and *Sinanthropus* were indeed close relations. "In its general form and size [the Peking man skull] agrees with the Java skull to such an extent that it identifies *Pithecanthropus* too, as true man, and a creature far above the stage of an ape," said Weidenreich, upsetting the judgment of Dubois that *Pithecanthropus* had come long before the first humans.

The assessment of von Koenigswald and Weidenreich was later corroborated by Wilfred Le Gros Clark. *Pithecanthropus*, Le Gros Clark said, appeared slightly more primitive, with a brain of about 900 cubic centimeters and a slightly heavier jaw. In addition, the animals associated with *Pithecanthropus* were a little older than those found at Zhoukoudian, and no tools were found with *Pithecanthropus*. Despite these differences, the two ancient beings were strikingly alike.

Von Koenigswald and Weidenreich had agreed that *Pithecanthropus* and *Sinanthropus* differed little more than "two different races of present mankind," and Le Gros Clark came to the same conclusion. He proposed dropping the *Sinanthropus* classification, which implied a separate genus, for it was doubtful that the two formed even separate species. He suggested that both should be identified as *Pithecanthropus* and distinguished only by their specific names, *Pithecanthropus erectus* for the Java finds and *Pithecanthropus pekinensis* for the Chinese discoveries.

The aging Eugene Dubois bitterly opposed Le Gros Clark's conclusion, continuing to insist that his own find was quite distinct from all others. But von Koenigswald and Weidenreich were little disturbed by his protests. More upsetting was the rumble of war.

Fate of the Java and Beijing Fossils

In Java, von Koenigswald knew that it was only a matter of time until the island would be seized. He quietly gave some of his most valuable fossils for safekeeping to a Swiss geologist and a Swedish journalist, neutrals in the conflict between Allies and Axis. (The journalist put the teeth in milk bottles and buried them one night in his garden.) When the Japanese occupied Java in 1942, they demanded that von Koenigswald give up his fossils. He surrendered a few, but he substituted plaster casts for some of the originals.

At the end of the war, von Koenigswald tracked down and reassembled all the fossils. "My happiness was complete," he said, "when I learned that my precious specimens had been saved. Large parts of my collections, many of my books, and all of my clothes had been stolen, but Early Man had survived the disaster." Von Koenigswald later exhibited *Pithecanthropus* in New York and then took the bones to the Netherlands and on to Frankfurt, Germany (many of the specimens have now been returned to Indonesia).

The Beijing fossils were not so fortunate as the Java fossils. By the autumn of 1941, the scientists working at Zhoukoudian were more immediately threatened than they had been before the war. After some debate about what to do with the fossils, the Chinese scientists appealed to the president of the Peking Union

FIGURE 10–14   The reconstruction of the skull and jaw of *Homo erectus* is based on numerous fossil finds. The general form of the face can also be reconstructed with reasonable accuracy, but we have little information on such important features as nostrils, lips, and hair.

Medical College to have the irreplaceable Beijing fossils taken to safety. It was arranged to send the collection to the United States. The boxes of fossils were entrusted to a detachment of U.S. Marines who were evacuating Beijing. The marines, with their baggage and the fossils, were scheduled to leave China on the steamship *President Harrison* on December 8.

But the rendezvous was never kept, for on December 7 Japanese bombs were dropped on Pearl Harbor, and total war came violently to the Pacific. The U.S. Marines and their precious cargo were captured by the invading Japanese, and somehow, in the chaos of war, the fossils of *Pithecanthropus pekinensis* were lost, never to reappear. Luckily, Weidenreich had overseen the preparation of a superb series of fossil casts, and these did survive. The casts, along with Weidenreich's excellent descriptions and photographs, preserve much information about the original Zhoukoudian fossils.

During the 1940s it became increasingly clear that *Pithecanthropus* showed strong anatomical resemblances to modern humans, *Homo sapiens*. As a result, in 1951, as part of a general taxonomic house cleaning, *Pithecanthropus*, in all of its Asian forms, was formally sunk into the single species *Homo erectus* (Figure 10–14). And no sooner had the new species been established than it proved to have some surprises up its sleeve. Discoveries over the following half century have shown that *Homo erectus* is much older than the initial 800,000-year estimate and was much more widely spread across the Old World.

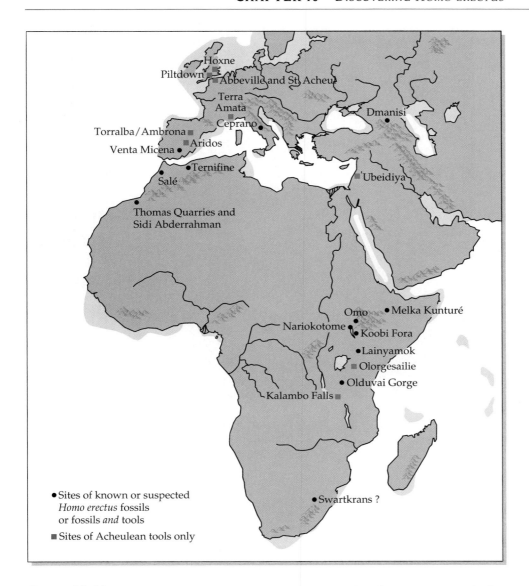

FIGURE 10–15   Since the earliest discoveries in East Asia, a number of sites in Europe and Africa have yielded fossil remains of *Homo erectus* and/or Acheulean tools. On this map, the coastline is shown as it might have been during a period of glaciation when the sea level fell. The site of the Piltdown "discovery" has been added, together with important archaeological sites mentioned in the text.

HOMO ERECTUS FOSSILS FROM AFRICA

Since the 1950s the continent of Africa has yielded numerous fossils of *Homo erectus* from a variety of locations (Figure 10–15 and Table 10–1). In 1954, *Homo erectus* mandibles dating 650,000 to 450,000 years B.P. were discovered at the northwest African site of Ternifine, Algeria. The next year another jaw was recovered from slightly younger deposits at the coastal Moroccan site of Sidi Abderrahman, and in 1971 cranial fragments of late *Homo erectus* also were reported from Salé, Morocco.

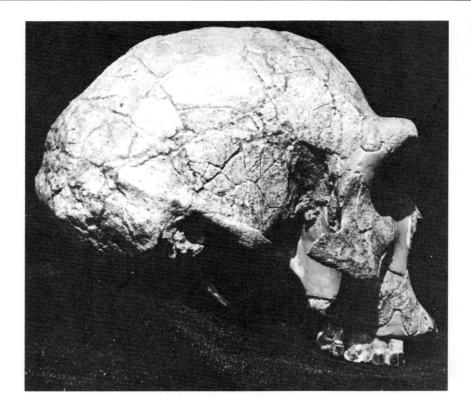

FIGURE 10–16   This skull from Koobi Fora in Kenya is one of the best-preserved skulls that belongs to the species *Homo erectus*. The present evidence suggests it may be 1.7 million years old. This photograph is approximately one-third actual size.

Fossils from South and East Africa have pushed the species farther and farther into the past. The Swartkrans site has produced remains dating between 1.8 and 1.5 million years of age that *may* represent *Homo erectus*. In 1960, Louis Leakey recovered undoubted *Homo erectus* remains (museum number OH9) dating 1.2 million years B.P. from Tanzania's Olduvai Gorge (since then, younger *H. erectus* fossils, circa 600,000 to 700,000 years of age, have also been found at Olduvai). Just north of Olduvai, the Kenyan site of Lainyamok has yielded *Homo erectus* teeth and limb bones dating around 600,000 years B.P., while the central Ethiopian site of Melka Kunturé has produced a cranial fragment that may go back 900,000 years. The distinction of producing the most ancient remains of East African *Homo erectus*, however, belongs to the Omo region of extreme southwestern Ethiopia and the east and west shores of Lake Turkana in Kenya. Relevant Omo fossils date to 1.4 million years ago, while discoveries in east Turkana's Koobi Fora region carry *Homo erectus* all the way back to 1.8 million years B.P. Among the Koobi Fora fossils is a superb skull, designated KNM ER-3733, whose owner boasted a cranial capacity of 850 cc some 1.7 mya (Figure 10–16).

But of all the African specimens, the *Homo erectus* boy from the west Turkana site of Nariokotome is perhaps the most exciting. Initially discovered in 1984 by the

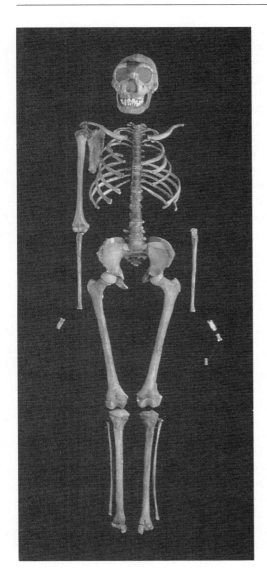

FIGURE 10–17   The most complete early hominid skeleton ever found was discovered at Nariokotome, west of Lake Turkana, Kenya, in 1984 and was excavated from sediments that are dated close to 1.5 million years ago. The skeleton, known as KNM-WT 15000, belongs to a twelve-year-old *Homo erectus* boy who would have grown into an adult more than 6 feet (1.8 meters) in height.

veteran fossil hunter Kamoya Kimeu, the specimen consists of a nearly complete skeleton (Figure 10–17) that lacks only the left humerus (upper arm bone), both radii (lower arm bones), and most of the bones of the hands and feet. Dated to 1.5 million years B.P., the Nariokotome boy was about twelve years old when he died (perhaps from the septicemia of a gum infection after the loss of a lower milk molar) and came to lie in a shallow swamp that was probably replenished seasonally by the floodwaters of the Omo River. After death, the body lay relatively undisturbed in the quiet water as it gradually decomposed. Small portions of the body were very likely eaten by scavenging catfish, and the skeleton was dispersed and damaged somewhat as large wading animals trampled and kicked the bones. Most of the skeleton, however, settled quietly into the mud and began the long wait until its discovery a million and a half years later.

The nearly complete nature of the Nariokotome skeleton has allowed detailed studies of *Homo erectus* anatomy never before possible. The boy was about 5.3 feet (160 centimeters) tall at death and would very likely have grown to be a big man of about 6.1 feet (185 centimeters) and 150 pounds (68 kilograms). His boyhood cranial capacity of 880 cc would probably have expanded to about 909 cc when he became an adult (68 percent of the modern human average). He had long arms and legs and a slender torso—bodily proportions identical to those of modern people who are adapted to hot, dry climates. His estimated adult pelvic dimensions, if characteristic of the species, suggest that *Homo erectus* newborns had relatively small brains (perhaps about 200 cc) and that, as in modern humans, rapid brain growth then continued for the first part of an infant's life. And finally, details of his thoracic (rib cage) vertebrae suggest that *Homo erectus* may have lacked the fine muscular control over breathing that is required for speech (more on this in a later section).

EVIDENCE OF *HOMO ERECTUS* IN EUROPE: MANY ARTIFACTS, FEW FOSSILS

As detailed in the next chapter, after about 1.5 mya, *Homo erectus* people in Africa, parts of Europe, and western Asia produced a new and distinctive type of stone tool industry called the Acheulean. In addition, *H. erectus* populations everywhere continued to make and use Oldowan flakes and choppers, and in eastern Asia these were their only stone implements. Both Acheulean and Oldowan sites attributed to *Homo erectus* have been excavated in Europe, but only a handful of *H. erectus* fossils have come from that continent. One of the most tantalizing specimens, a lower jaw discovered in 1991, comes from the Caucasus site of Dmanisi in extreme southeastern Europe (Figure 10–15). The find consists of a nearly complete mandible of a young adult who probably died at about 20 to 25 years of age. All of the lower teeth are preserved, although both rami (the vertical, posterior portions of the jaw that attach to the base of the cranium) are missing. The jaw is overwhelmingly *Homo erectus* in its anatomy, although it does show certain progressive tendencies such as the beginnings of a chin. Found in association with Oldowan type choppers and flakes, the Dmanisi jaw has been dated back to 1.8 to 1.6 mya and, along with a few other fossils, provides a strong challenge to the outdated theory that *Homo erectus* dispersed from Africa within the last million years (more on this below).

The single other European specimen of *Homo erectus* comes from the site of Ceprano, Italy, (Figure 10–15) and was discovered in 1994. This fossil is a calvaria with a sloping forehead, large brows, and a cranial capacity of 1185 cc. Estimated from geological studies to be about 700,000 years old, the Ceprano fossil (like the Dmanisi jaw) apparently was associated with an Oldowan-type chopper and flake tool assemblage.

Although these two are the only definite fossils of *Homo erectus* to come from Europe, we would be remiss if we ended this section without mentioning the exciting (and controversial) material from Venta Micena near Orce in southern Spain (see Figure 10–15). Dated by paleomagnetism and faunal studies to about 1.6 million years ago, Venta Micena has produced Oldowan tools, the remains of several immigrant animal species from nearby Africa (including hippos, ancestral zebras, and ancestral hyenas), and three bones—a skull fragment and two arm bones—that some workers attribute to *Homo* (species indeterminate, but probably *erectus*). If the latter remains prove to be human, they will represent the oldest western Europeans, but their hominid status has been challenged. None of the bones is distinctively human anatomically, and the cranial fragment in particular cannot be distinguished from that of a horse (genus *Equus*). On the other hand, immunospecificity studies of residual proteins recovered from the Venta Micena skull fragment have produced reactions characteristic of human, not horse, material. Unfortunately, these offsetting results leave the Venta Micena remains in taxonomic limbo at present. Nonetheless, the site is tremendously exciting because of its extreme age and undoubted stone tools. At 1.6 million years of age, Venta Micena is clearly the oldest hominid site in western Europe, matching Dmanisi in its antiquity. Furthermore, the Spanish material shows that the first documented human exodus from Africa occurred at both ends of the Mediterranean simultaneously (perhaps also in the center via Sicily?), rather than simply through the Middle East.

MORE FOSSILS AND SOME SURPRISING DATES FROM ASIA

World War II caused a temporary break in paleoanthropological activities in Asia, but during the second half of the twentieth century exploration resumed and more *Homo erectus* specimens were discovered. In China, intermittent work was resumed at Zhoukoudian during the 1950s and 1960s and new dental, cranial, and postcranial material was recovered. Additionally, Chinese workers found *Homo erectus* remains at several new sites including Gongwangling (where the finds included a partial skull with an estimated cranial capacity of about 780 cc), Yuanmou, and Hexian (Figure 10–3). The Hexian material, which is no older than 700,000 and perhaps as young as 250,000 years B.P. (Table 10–1), represents at least three *H. erectus* individuals and was discovered in 1980–1981. Finally, and most intriguing of all, excavations carried out between 1985 and 1988 at the Longgupo Cave site in Sichuan Province (Figure 10–3) may have produced the very oldest evidence of hominids in Asia. The Longgupo fossils include a partial mandible with the left P4 and M1 (Figure 10–18) and an upper incisor. Found in association with two apparent Oldowan tools, the teeth show similarities to both *Homo erectus* and *Homo habilis* and carry a paleomagnetic date of 1.9 to 1.7 million years ago. For simplification, and because of their early date and lack of diagnostic traits, we have chosen to treat the Longgupo fossils in this text as early *Homo erectus*. Nonetheless, some researchers (including the fossils' discoverers) think the teeth, and thus the first Asians, are best classified as a pre-*erectus* hominid type.

Java, too, has continued to produce *Homo erectus* fossils (some of them questionable, see below) since Indonesia's independence in 1945. Included in the new discoveries are clavariae and postcranial fossils from Ngandong (found between 1976–1980), a partial skull from Sambungmacan (1973), and an exceptionally complete cranium from Sangiran (found in 1993 and estimated to have a cranial capacity of 856 cc). The most exciting news from Java, however, is not about newly discovered fossils, but about the new and startling dates that have been determined for some long-known remains. First, to provide some background, until quite recently paleoanthropologists enjoyed widespread agreement on the origin and spread of *Homo erectus*. The consensus was that *H. erectus* had evolved in

FIGURE 10–18   The mandibular fragment from Longgupo Cave, Sichuan Province, China. The specimen resembles both *Homo habilis* and *Homo erectus*, and may be the oldest hominid fossil known from Asia.

Africa about 1.8 million years ago from early *Homo* stock (either *H. habilis* or *H. rudolfensis*) and then, about 1 mya, as a result of increased intelligence and cultural complexity, the species was able to expand its geographic range out of Africa and into Europe and Asia, reaching Java no later than 900,000 to 800,000 years B.P. It was a tidy scenario and one that seemed adequate for many years, but no more, thanks to new information. For starters, as mentioned earlier, a *Homo erectus* mandible dating 1.8 to 1.6 mya has now been reported from Dmanisi in the Republic of Georgia. Since its age may equal that of the oldest African *H. erectus* fossils, the Dmanisi jaw obviously muddies the question of where the species originated. But an even more dramatic challenge to the old scenario has come from Java, where a joint American-Indonesian research team has recently redated two of the classic *H. erectus* sites. Using an Ar^{40}/Ar^{39} dating technique, the team—headed by geochronologists Carl Swisher and Garniss Curtis—determined in 1994 that *Homo erectus* inhabited the Sangiran region more than 1.66 million years ago and the Modjokerto region as early as 1.81 million years B.P.! Thus it appears that *Homo erectus* may have inhabited extreme southeast Asia fully a million years earlier than traditionally believed. If these new dates are valid—and like all scientific findings, they require verification—then the evidence of *H. erectus* is equally old in Asia, Africa, and Europe, and traditional views on the species' place of origin and subsequent migrations may have to be revised substantially.

Careful readers will have realized that there's one more bit of evidence to be considered and that it too may weigh against the 1 million years ago migration scenario. If the discoverers of the Longgupo Cave hominid are correct in identifying their find as belonging to a pre-*erectus* species, it would go far toward proving that early *Homo* (*H. habilis*? *H. rudolfensis*?) was the first hominid type to spread out of African, not *H. erectus*. On the other hand, if a slightly older African *Homo erectus* specimen turns up in the future, enormous amounts of time probably aren't needed for the traditional Africa-to-Asia expansion. For example, an African origin for *H. erectus* at 2.0 million years ago, followed by a leisurely spread of 1 mile (1.6 kilometers) every ten years would have put hominids at Longgupo Cave and in Java 100,000 years later. In any event, only time and further discoveries will help to answer these questions. As things stand presently, none of the possible points of origin—Africa, Asia, or somewhere in-between—can be ruled out for *Homo erectus*.

Regardless of when and where they originated, however, *Homo erectus* people may have stayed around for a very long time. Carl Swisher and his team recently have been at it again, this time redating the Javanese sites of Ngandong and Sambungmacan (Table 10–1 and Figure 10–3). Based on chronometric dates taken from fossil water buffalo teeth collected at the two sites (the hominid fossils could not be dated directly without damaging them), the geochronologists estimated the age of Ngandong at 46,000 to 27,000 years B.P. and that of Sambungmacan at 53,000 to 27,000 B.P. Swisher and his colleagues concluded from these results that late *Homo erectus* may have overlapped in time with *Homo sapiens* in Southeast Asia, with the implication that local *H. erectus* populations probably were not ancestral to modern Asians (a possibility discussed further in Chapter 16). This is not the only possible interpretation of the Ngandong and Sambungmacan evidence, however, and in reality Swisher's dates have simply added to the considerable confusion that already surrounded these fossils.

The original confusion stemmed from the fact that both Ngandong and (to a lesser extent) Sambungmacan seem to be anatomically advanced compared to typical Asian *Homo erectus* specimens. For example, the Ngandong skulls show browridges without a central thickening, relatively broad frontal bones, lack of an extreme postorbital constriction, different proportions of the occipital bone, and a somewhat larger than average cranial capacity. For its part, Sambungmacan shows features of the frontal bone and forehead that resemble Ngandong and a brain size just about half way between Ngandong and typical Asian *H. erectus*. Although many paleoanthropologists join Swisher in deemphasizing the differences and including Ngandong and Sambungmacan in *Homo erectus*, other workers think the anatomical distinctions justify placing them in a different species—perhaps *Homo heidelbergensis* or *Homo sapiens* (albeit a somewhat primitive version). For the latter group of researchers, the new dates prove that the Ngandong and Sambungmacan people lived much too recently to have been *Homo erectus*, a species whose last undoubted populations died out between 300,000 and 200,000 years ago (Table 10–1). In summary, whether or not Ngandong and Sambungmacan should be included in *Homo erectus* probably cannot be decided on the current evidence. Therefore, to cover all possibilities, we have included both sites tentatively in the inventory of Table 10–1, and additionally, we have given them special treatment in our analysis of *H. erectus*'s anatomy.

THE ANATOMY OF *HOMO ERECTUS*

Fossils attributed to *Homo erectus* cover an enormous time span (1.9 million to at least 300,000 years B.P.) and an equally impressive geographic range (from South Africa to southeast Asia). As a consequence of its longevity and geographic spread, *Homo erectus* has been traditionally understood to display a good deal of anatomical variability (Figure 10–19).

Indeed, some researchers think there is too much variability to be contained within one species. They argue that the material classified as *H. erectus* should be

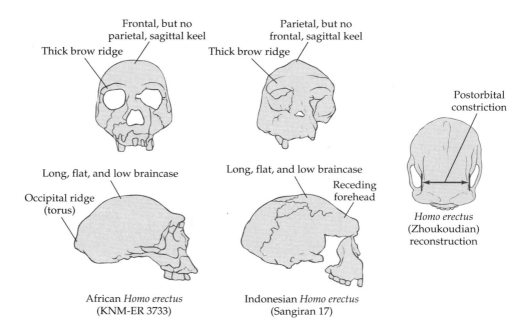

FIGURE 10–19   *Homo erectus* skulls from Africa (left) and Asia (center) are compared. Shared traits include the long, low-vaulted, and wide braincase, large brows, an angled occipital region, and an occipital ridge. Also, both African and Asian Home erectus skulls may show some sagittal keeling. A superior view of the skull of *H. erectus* (right) reveals a marked postorbital constriction (specimen from Zhoukoudian).

Homo ergaster species name given by some paleoanthropologists to certain African *fossils* regarded by most workers as early *Homo erectus*. The authors of this book side with the majority.

divided, retaining the name *Homo erectus* for the Asian fossils from Java and China, and classifying at least the early African remains from Lake Turkana (KNM ER-3733 and 3883, and the Nariokotome boy, KNM WT-15000) as a separate species called **Homo ergaster**. (Interestingly, certain later African fossils, such as Louis Leakey's 1.2-million-year-old skull from Olduvai Gorge, would be left in *H. erectus*.) Supporters of this scheme view *Homoergaster* as more closely related (and more likely to be ancestral) to modern humans than was Asian *Homo erectus*. Other scientists disagree with the proposed taxonomic split, however, and chief among the dissenters is G. Philip Rightmire, who has made *Homo erectus* something of a research specialty. Rightmire and like-minded paleoanthropologists conclude that there is insufficient anatomical difference to justify the recognition of two separate species, arguing that *Homo erectus*'s anatomical variability simply matched its geographic spread. The single-species group points out that many of the traits claimed to be distinctive, derived features of Asian *Homo erectus* can also be identified on

Sagittal keel a slightly raised ridge running down the center of a skull; smaller than a *sagittal crest*.

some of the early African specimens. For example, **sagittal keeling** of the frontal and/or parietal bones is common among the Asian fossils, but it is also present on KNM ER-3733 and 3883 from East Africa (Figure 10–19). At least for the moment, the authors of this book agree with the Rightmire camp and thus retain the traditional classification scheme and treat *Homo erectus* as one variable and widespread species. We hasten to add, however, that this taxonomy does not imply that the evolutionary descendants of *H. erectus* (i.e., *Homo heidelbergensis*, see below) were

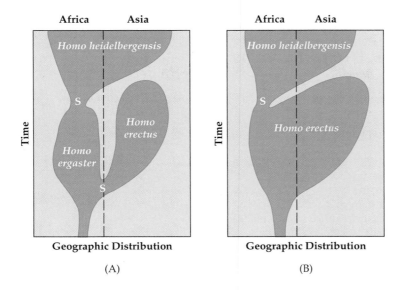

FIGURE 10–20 In phylogenetic scheme A, the African species *Homo ergaster* gives rise first to the Asian species *Homo erectus* and later to the worldwide species *Homo heidelbergensis*. This view is favored by Bernard Wood, Ian Tattersall, and others, and it would successfully explain why modern humans show few of the anatomical specializations of Asian *H. erectus*. Scheme A does require, however, splitting mid-Pleistocene hominids into two species. Phylogenetic scheme B, on the other hand, retains all mid-Pleistocene hominids in the single, widespread species *Homo erectus*. Stronger African than Asian resemblances for *Homo heidelbergensis* are then explained by that taxon's speciation event occurring in Africa. The authors of this text prefer scheme B, given the available evidence. The letter S marks a speciation event. (Figure modified from Harrison, 1993.)

equally related to the African and Asian populations of the ancestral species. As shown in Figure 10–20b, a speciation event located in Africa could have produced descendants who carried more African than Asian traits. With these taxonomic issues out of the way, we can proceed to the anatomy.

In many important ways, *Homo erectus* had reached anatomical modernity. On average, these people were as tall and as heavy as modern humans (compare Boxes 10–1 and 16–1; indeed, some researchers think *H. erectus* was slightly heavier than living people). They seem to have had a modern body build, with a distinct waist instead of the potbelly that probably characterized earlier hominids (see Figure 8–4; this finding has implications for the diet of *Homo erectus*, as discussed in Chapter 11). Furthermore, the limb proportions of *H. erectus* were similar to those of modern humans, in contrast to the long arms and short legs of early *Homo* (Box 8–1). There can be no doubt that *Homo erectus* stood and moved in a fully modern, upright fashion.

Despite their modern postcranial skeletons, however, *Homo erectus* individuals differed greatly from modern people in their brain size and cranial anatomy. Including Ngândong and Sambungmacan, she average brain size for *Homo erectus* was 994 cubic centimeters (range 750 to 1,251 cc; Box 10–1)—some 27 to 62 percent bigger than early *Homo*, but still only two-thirds the modern average. (Without the recent Javanese skulls, the *H. erectus* average drops to 937 cc [range 750 to 1,225 cc].) But because brain expansion in *Homo erectus* was matched by increased body size,

Box 10-1

CHARACTERISTICS OF *HOMO ERECTUS*[a]

TRAIT	*HOMO ERECTUS* (INCLUDING NGANDONG AND SAMBUNGMACAN)	*HOMO ERECTUS* (EXCLUDING NGANDONG AND SAMBUNGMACAN)[b]
Height (sexes combined)	4.8–6.1 ft (145–185 cm)	—
Weight (sexes combined)	123–128 lb mean (56–58 kg) (range up to 150 lb, or 68 kg)	—
Brain size (sexes combined)	994 cc mean (750–1,251 cc range)	937 cc mean (750–1,225 cc range)
Cranium	Long, low-vaulted (platycephalic) braincase, widest at the base; large brow ridges; some sagittal keeling common; thick skull bones; unflexed cranial base; **occipital torus**	—
Dentition	Both anterior and posterior teeth smaller than those of early *Homo*	—
Limbs	Relative arm and leg lengths within modern human range of variation	—
Locomotion	Bipedalism (fully modern)	—
Distribution	Africa, Asia, Europe	—
Known dates (years B.P.)	1.9 million to ca. 27,000	1.9 million to ca. 300,000

[a] For additional technical details and diagnostic traits, see Appendix III.
[b] Adjusted trait descriptions are given only as needed.

Occipital torus a ridge running side-to-side across the occipital bone.

Platycephalic a term describing a skull that is long, low-vaulted, and wide.

the species' relative brain size (brain size controlling for body weight) was not significantly greater than that of early *Homo* (see Chapter 13). Furthermore, the enlarged *H. erectus* brain was still encased in a primitive-looking container (Figures 10–16 and 10–19). The skull of *Homo erectus* was constructed of thick cranial bones, and it was long, low-vaulted, and widest at the base, a combination of traits labeled **platycephalic**.

The front of the cranium was topped with huge brow ridges, and behind those brows the skull showed a distinct postorbital constriction at the temples. Often, particularly in the Asian specimens, the top of the skull showed a distinct sagittal keel (the function of this feature, like many others, is unknown). And finally, at the back the skull of *Homo erectus* was ridged and angled sharply toward the cranial base (Figure 10–19), and the cranial base itself tended to be rather flat and unflexed, lacking the arched configuration characteristic of modern humans (see Chapter 13).

Several researchers have attempted to determine whether *Homo erectus* showed any significant evolutionary changes in anatomy during its long period of existence, and here again opinions differ. Milford Wolpoff of the University of Michigan has argued that brain size did show such an increase, but Rightmire and others disagree. In the latest statement on the subject, David Begun and Alan Walker present

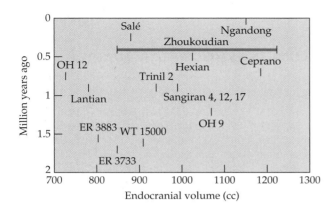

FIGURE 10–21 A comparison of brain sizes from African and Asian *Homo erectus* specimens (most, but not all mentioned in the text). Some researchers believe the fossils reveal little, if any, increase in brain size during the species' period of existence. Others disagree, but small sample sizes prevent a firm conclusion. (Figure modified from Begun and Walker, 1993.)

evidence that little, if any, expansion of the brain occurred from early to late *Homo erectus* (Figure 10–21). Similarly, Walker and various co-workers have argued that *Homo erectus* showed no significant temporal changes in stature, dental dimensions, or skull shape. The weight of the evidence at present seems to indicate that *Homo erectus* experienced a rather long period of anatomical stasis (see Box 10–2). Its characteristic anatomy remained essentially stable for more than a million years, and then disappeared only upon the evolution of *Homo heidelbergensis*.

Anatomical Evidence of Speech and Language

A crucial question that so far has defied our attempts at an answer concerns the beginnings of those uniquely human traits, speech and language (see Chapter 3 for definitions). The australopithecines all seemed too small-brained and behaviorally primitive to have had language and speech. Early representatives of *Homo* showed a strong increase in brain size and the beginnings of stone-tool technology, but most workers hesitate to regard them as linguistic creatures. But what about *Homo erectus*? Surely, with all we know about the anatomy of this species, we can draw some clear conclusions about its linguistic capacities.

Unfortunately, it seems that when it comes to elucidating speech and language evolution, additional anatomical knowledge has exacerbated rather than reduced the problem. Certainly *Homo erectus* had an absolutely larger brain than its evolutionary predecessors, but this only increases the likelihood rather than proving conclusively that they produced spoken language. An examination of the brain's so-called language areas (see Chapter 13) is also inconclusive. Although **Broca's area** in the inferior frontal lobe is well developed in *Homo erectus*, recent research on modern humans has shown that this cortical region supports both the hierarchical organization of grammar and the manual combination of objects, including tool use. Whether the manual coordination involved in tool manufacture and use or the production of hierarchically organized speech, or both, were associated with Broca's area development in *Homo erectus* is unknown. Furthermore, **Wernicke's area** in the temporal lobe appears to be extremely difficult to assess for most ancient skulls—including those of *Homo erectus*—because of distortion during fossilization. And finally, **hemispherical asymmetry** in the cerebrum—demonstrable in the Nariokotome boy and very likely associated in that specimen with right-handedness—cannot be trusted as a guide to language abilities since asymmetry

Broca's area part of the human *cerebral cortex* involved with the hierarchical organization of grammar and the manual combination of objects.

Wernicke's area part of the human *cerebral cortex* essential in comprehending and producing meaningful speech.

Hemispherical asymmetry the condition in which the two cerebral hemispheres differ in one or more dimensions. In most modern humans, the left hemisphere is somewhat larger than the right.

Box 10-2

WAS HOMINID EVOLUTION SMOOTH OR JUMPY?

One of the perennial questions that students ask about human evolution concerns its pattern and speed. Did new species of hominids originate through the slow accumulation of small-scale change in existing lineages, as suggested by traditional Darwinian theory? Or did hominids evolve by starts and stops, with each new species appearing quickly, then entering a long period of stasis (stability in genes and traits), and then finally perhaps giving rise rapidly to some descendant species? These two models of species development—respectively called *phyletic transformation* (gradualism) and *punctuated equilibrium*, and illustrated below—were described in earlier chapters (see Chapter 2 and the Postscript to Chapter 9), but the present discussion of *Homo erectus* provides a convenient occasion to revisit them because this particular species of early humans has been claimed to be a clear example of evolutionary stasis.

Although not everyone agrees, many anthropologists accept the argument that *Homo erectus* evolved quickly into its characteristic set of phenotypic traits about 1.9 to 1.8 million years ago and then experienced a lengthy period of anatomical stasis that finally ended with (was punctuated by) the cladogenetic appearance of *Homo heidelbergensis* about a million years later. *Homo erectus*'s more or less stable brain size, among other attributes, seems to support this interpretation, as does the apparently rapid appearance of *Homo heidelbergensis* with its bigger brain and more modern face and teeth (see Chapter 14).

A second claimed case of hominid punctuated equilibrium involves *Australopithecus afarensis*. After originating just prior to 4 million years ago, *A. afarensis* survived as a recognizable species (i.e., experienced evolutionary stasis) for perhaps 1.5 million years before giving rise to *Australopithecus africanus* and/or the first hominines (see Chapter 7).

Together, these cases provide impressive evidence that, at least occasionally and perhaps predominantly, hominid evolution has moved to the beat of punctuated equilibrium. Nonetheless, some paleoanthropologists argue vigorously that slow, steady phyletic transformation has also operated during certain stages of hominid prehistory, perhaps especially during the evolution of anatomically modern humans (see the regional-continuity theory in Chapter 16). As with so many issues, the jury is still out regarding the *prevailing* mode of speciation within the human family. Given the mixed bag of evidence, perhaps the most prudent position is to assume tentatively that both patterns—gradual and rapid speciation—have played some part in our evolutionary history.

We can conclude that rates of organic evolution are known to have varied widely. Periods of rapid evolutionary change at certain stages of mammalian evolution have long been recognized. There were doubtless variations in the rate of human evolution, and although a pattern is beginning to emerge, the exact form of that pattern is still unclear.

(continued)

(including left-hemisphere dominance for vocalizations) has been documented for monkeys and apes.

Two negative bits of anatomical evidence argue against spoken language in *Homo erectus*. First, although there is some variation among specimens, the cranial

Box 10-2   *(continued)*

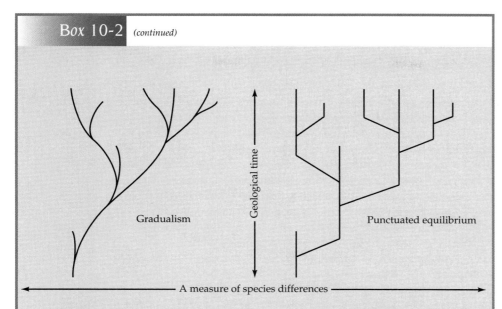

In a simplified model of phyletic gradualism (left), the continuous accumulation of small evolutionary changes is shown by smooth right and left curves of the lineage lines. In this model, species often are recognized arbitrarily as subdivisions of an evolving lineage. In contrast, the punctuated equilibrium model (right) shows species as "locked into" relatively stable phenotypes for long periods (shown by vertical lines). Genetic and phenotypic stasis is then interrupted periodically by rapid speciation events (angled lines). (Figure from Roger Lewin, *Human Evolution: An Illustrated Introduction*, 3rd ed., Blackwell Science, 1993. Reprinted by permission of Blackwell Science, Inc.)

base is generally flat and unflexed. As detailed in Chapter 13, this suggests a short pharynx and an inability to produce the full range of modern vowel sounds. Second, analyses of the vertebral canals of the Nariokotome boy have revealed dimensions similar to those of monkeys and apes in the thoracic (rib cage) region (Figure 10–22). In contrast, modern humans have enlarged canals in their thoracic vertebrae, possibly to accommodate increased nerve connections with the rib cage muscles that control this part of the breathing apparatus. The small thoracic canals found in *Homo erectus* suggest to Alan Walker and others that this species lacked the fine control of breathing that is essential for modern speech.

So, could *Homo erectus* talk? The best answer from anatomy is a rather unsatisfying "maybe." After a thorough review of the evidence, Walker thinks that speech and language probably appeared rather late in hominid evolution and that archaeology may be a better guide to these capacities than is anatomy. This is an important point to keep in mind when we examine the archaeological evidence gathered from *Homo erectus* sites (Chapter 11).

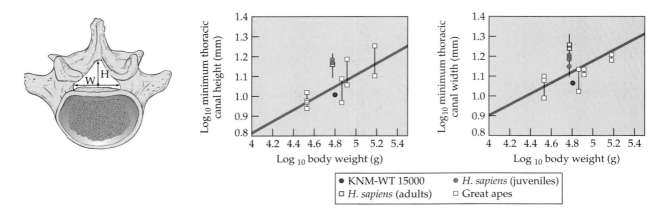

FIGURE 10–22   A representative human vertebra (left) showing the vertebral canal and how it can be measured. The Nariokotome boy (KNM-WT 15000) had smaller thoracic canal measurements than both adult and juvenile modern humans (center and right). The KNM-WT 15000 dimensions are roughly comparable to those of some apes.

EVOLUTIONARY RELATIONSHIPS OF *HOMO ERECTUS*

Our interpretation of the fossil evidence is that *Homo erectus* evolved from some form of early *Homo* around 1.9 million years B.P. As explained above, it is impossible at present to pinpoint the place of origin of *H. erectus*, although an East African homeland still seems most likely. Following its advent, *Homo erectus* spread across the face of the Old World—eventually occupying portions of Africa, Asia, and Europe—and survived until at least 300,000 years B.P. (and perhaps as late as 53,000 to 27,000 years B.P. if one includes Ngandong and Sambungmacan).

At some point in the mid-Pleistocene—roughly, sometime around 800,000 to 600,000 B.P., judging by fossils discovered in southern Europe and Africa—*Homo erectus* gave rise to a new and bigger-brained descendant that many paleoanthropologists call *Homo heidelbergensis* (note that some workers still interpret *Homo erectus* as evolving into "archaic *Homo sapiens*"; see this chapter's Overview and also Chapter 14). As shown in schematic form in Figure 10–20, this speciation event probably occurred in Africa. Undoubtedly more intelligent than their ancestors and with a more complex culture, *Homo heidelbergensis* lived on eventually to give rise to both modern humans and the Neandertals.

Those are the bare bones of the *Homo erectus* story. They appeared, they survived, they begat descendants, they became extinct. But many questions remain unanswered. What adaptations—cultural as well as biological—enabled them to survive for the better part of two million years? In order to understand *Homo erectus* more completely, we must now turn to the archaeological record.

SUMMARY

First discovered in Java in 1891, *Homo erectus* is now known from Asia, Africa, and Europe. Traditionally the species was thought to have originated in Africa slightly less than two million years ago and then to have spread to other parts of the Old

World. This interpretation has recently been called into question, however, by reports of very ancient fossils from the Republic of Georgia, China, and Java. Compared to its evolutionary predecessors, *Homo erectus* had achieved considerable modernity in its anatomy. These people were as tall and as heavy as modern humans, and they showed modern limb proportions. Average brain size had increased to more than 900 cubic centimeters, but these big brains were still contained in rather primitive-looking skulls that were long, low-vaulted, and widest at the base. Despite their large brains, however, there seems to be little anatomical evidence that *Homo erectus* had spoken language. Their unflexed cranial base suggests an inability to produce the full range of vowel sounds, and details of the thoracic vertebral canals may indicate that they lacked the breathing control needed for modern speech. *Homo erectus* survived for more than one and a half million years, and most populations seem to have gone extinct about 300,000 to 200,000 years ago. If one includes Ngandong and Sambungmacan as relict populations of the species, however, its final disappearance was as recent as 53,000 to 27,000 years B.P.

Some researchers believe that the anatomical variability of *Homo erectus* justifies splitting the taxon into two species: the name *Homo erectus* would be retained for specimens from Olduvai Gorge and Asia, while the name *Homo ergaster* would be introduced for early African specimens from the Lake Turkana region. We do not believe that such a step is warranted at present and thus have treated *Homo erectus* as a single, anatomically variable, widely spread species.

POSTSCRIPT

From the story of human evolution told thus far, one could get the impression that anthropologists' first reaction to new fossil finds is skepticism and rejection. Dubois's *Pithecanthropus* was taken by most experts at the turn of the century as either an incredibly apelike human or a somewhat humanlike ape; very few of Dubois's colleagues agreed with him that it was a creature intermediate between humans and apes. Similarly, Raymond Dart's claim in 1925 that *Australopithecus africanus* was an evolutionary relative of humans was widely rejected by the scientific community. Why were these apparently reasonable—and subsequently verified—claims so unsuccessful when they were first made? What kept anthropologists and anatomists from recognizing these fossils for what we now know them to be? The answers to those questions are actually rather complex. But if we limit our attention to the British scientific community, two primary explanations appear that together teach a lesson about how science should be conducted. First, neither *Pithecanthropus* nor *Australopithecus* fit the theoretical expectations of the senior English scientists, and second, after 1912 there was a much more acceptable candidate for the role of "missing link": **Piltdown man** (Figure 10–23).

To address the issues in order, Grafton Elliot Smith was a major force in British anatomy and anthropology in the first half of the twentieth century. He was an acknowledged expert on primate brains, and he believed strongly that in human evolution "the brain had led the way." In other words, Elliot Smith held the view that expansion and elaboration of the human brain had preceded all other major evolutionary events—particularly dental changes and bipedalism—and, indeed, had made them possible. The unexpected combination in Dubois's *Pithecanthropus* of fully developed bipedalism with a small (850 cc) brain did not sit well with Elliot Smith. And if *Pithecanthropus* was a bitter pill, *Australopithecus africanus*, with its

Piltdown man a "doctored" modern human skull and ape jaw "discovered" in 1911 and supposed to represent a very primitive human, *Eoanthropus dawsoni*, but exposed as a hoax in 1953.

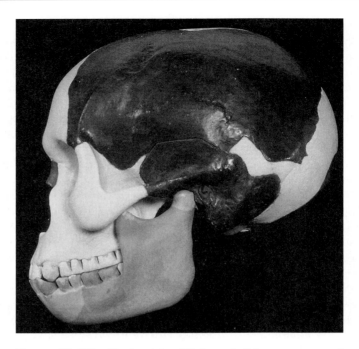

FIGURE 10–23　The fraudulent Piltdown skull, here reconstructed, led scientists astray for forty years in their understanding of human evolution. The black shaded area of the skull distinguishes the original fragments. The remainder is reconstruction.

ape-sized brain (about 405 cc for the Taung fossil), humanlike teeth, and Dart's claim of bipedalism, was a horror! For Elliot Smith, both fossils challenged a theoretical position that he had laboriously constructed and in which he was strongly invested, and not surprisingly, he greeted them with skepticism.

Furthermore, after 1912, agreeing that the brain had "led the way" was quite easy for British scientists because a wonderful fossil that matched their theoretical expectations to the letter had been discovered right on English soil: Piltdown man. The Piltdown fossils were brought to public attention by amateur archaeologist Charles Dawson and paleontologist Arthur Smith Woodward. Dawson had made the original discovery of apparently ancient skull fragments in a gravel pit near Piltdown Common in 1911. With Smith Woodward's help, additional remains were recovered in 1912, and in 1913 the Jesuit paleontologist Teilhard de Chardin retrieved a lower canine tooth from the Piltdown gravels. When the pieces were reconstructed, they produced a very large (almost 1,500 cc) and high-vaulted braincase with an apelike jaw and somewhat projecting lower canines. Elliot Smith's theories seemed to be verified: Piltdown man combined a modern-sized brain with a primitive dentition. Furthermore, it was thought that *Eoanthropus dawsoni* ("Dawson's dawn man"), as the Piltdown specimen had been officially dubbed, was quite old—probably Pliocene in age and fully as ancient as *Pithecanthropus*. And so Dubois's and Dart's fossils, with their theoretically unpopular mixtures of traits, were pushed aside in favor of Piltdown.

For forty years, Piltdown man influenced researchers' interpretations of human evolution. Unfortunately, with each new find, Piltdown became more and more of an oddity. The accumulating collection of australopithecine fossils and the remains from Zhoukoudian and elsewhere all seemed to proclaim that the legs and the teeth, not the brain, had led the way. Finally, in the early 1950s, scientists at Oxford University and the British Natural History Museum initiated a series of new analyses to test the unspeakable possibility that the Piltdown fossil was a fraud. To their dismay, the tests proved beyond a doubt that a hoax had been perpetrated. Bones had been stained and broken, and teeth had been filed flat in order to make it appear that the skull and the jaw belonged to the same ancient creature. In reality, an ape's jaw had been combined with a human skull, and the best scientific minds in the world had been hoodwinked!

Over the years, several people were held up as suspects by amateur sleuths bent on solving the Piltdown hoax. Many thought that Dawson, the original discoverer, was the joker; others believed Arthur Keith, Teilhard de Chardin, or even Elliot Smith himself to be the culprit. Only in May 1996 was the mystery finally solved. Based on materials found in an old trunk stored in a loft at the British Natural History Museum, it appears certain that the hoaxer was one Martin Hinton, museum curator of zoology at the time of the fraud. Hinton had the materials and the experience to pull off the hoax and he apparently had the motive—it seems he was angry at his boss Arthur Smith Woodward over money (specifically, how Hinton was to be paid for a cataloging project taken on during his vacation).

Ironically, over the years Piltdown has changed from an embarrassment to anthropology to a useful reminder not to become overly invested in a particular theory or to put unqualified trust in new discoveries that fit one's expectations. *Eoanthropus* now serves to remind us that science makes progress only through a healthy mix of hard work, insight, skepticism, data sharing, and careful verification or falsification of results. The scientific method is self-testing and self-correcting; it is the *only* route to reliable knowledge.

REVIEW QUESTIONS

1. Summarize the anatomical differences between *Homo erectus* and early *Homo*. How did *Homo erectus* differ anatomically from modern humans?
2. Discuss the reasoning that led Eugene Dubois to search for the "missing link" in Java. How do modern paleoanthropologists decide where to search for fossils?
3. There are few indications from anatomy—other than gross brain size—that *Homo erectus* had language. Discuss how a hominid species might have lived for nearly two million years and inhabited both tropical and temperate habitats *without* modern language.
4. Discuss the implications of Longgupo Cave, Dmanisi, and the redated Javanese fossils from Sangiran and Modjokerto for our interpretations of the origin and spread of *Homo erectus*.
5. Discuss the implications of the young ages (53,000 to 27,000 B.P.) recently calculated for the fossils from Ngandong and Sambungmacan. What do these dates suggest about the link between *H. erectus* and modern Asians?

SUGGESTED FURTHER READING

Jia, Lanpo, and Huang Weiwen. *The Story of Peking Man*. Oxford University Press, 1990.

Rightmire, G. P. *The Evolution of Homo erectus*. Cambridge University Press, 1990.

Spencer, F. *Piltdown: A Scientific Forgery*. Natural History Museum, London and Oxford University Press, 1990.

Swisher, C. C., et al. "Age of the Earliest Known Hominids in Java, Indonesia." *Science*, 263, 1994.

Swisher, C. C., et al. "Latest *Homo erectus* of Java: Potential Contemporaneity With *Homo sapiens* in Southeast Asia." *Science*, 274, 1996.

Theunissen, B. *Eugene Dubois and the Ape-man from Java*. Kluwer, 1989.

Walker, A., and R. Leakey, eds. *The Nariokotome Homo erectus Skeleton*. Harvard University Press, 1993.

INTERNET RESOURCES

In addition to the several paleoanthropology websites listed in earlier chapters, the following sites will prove useful for information about *Homo erectus* and other fossils mentioned in Chapter 10.

HOMINID EVOLUTION BIBLIOGRAPHY

http://www.ipfw.indiana.edu/east1/coon/web/hominid.htm

(This site contains a useful listing of scientific books and articles about *Homo erectus*.)

PILTDOWN: THE MAN THAT NEVER WAS

http://unmuseum.mus.pa.us/piltdown.htm

(Information about the Piltdown hoax and photos of several of the men involved.)

THE AFRICAN EMERGENCE AND EARLY ASIAN DISPERSALS OF THE GENUS *HOMO*

http://www.sigmaxi.org/amsci/articles/96articles/Larick.html

(An interesting and important paper about the ancient Asian fossils—including the Longgupo Cave remains—that have some paleoanthropologists questioning whether *Homo erectus* was the first hominid to expand its range out of Africa.)

THE FOSSIL EVIDENCE FOR HUMAN EVOLUTION IN CHINA

http://www.cruzio.com/~cscp/index.htm

(Maintained by anthropologist Dennis Etler, this website contains an extensive catalog of Chinese human fossils, useful photos and maps, and links to other interesting sites about evolution.)

USEFUL SEARCH TERMS:

Homo erectus
Pithecanthropus
Piltdown
Sinanthropus

Chapter 10 Timeline

	YEARS A.D.	DISCOVERIES
HOLOCENE	1994 —	*H. erectus* at Ceprano
10,000	1991 —	*H. erectus* at Dmanisi
PLEISTOCENE	1984 —	*H. erectus* skeleton found at Nariokotome, West Turkana
1.6 million	1975 —	*H. erectus* at Koobi Fora
Earliest Oldowan tools at Omo and Hadar		
PLIOCENE	1960 —	*H. erectus* at Olduvai
5 million	1955 —	*H. erectus* at Ternifine
	1953	Piltdown finds shown to be a hoax
Earliest australopithecines	1936 —	New finds in Java
	1929 —	First skull of *Sinanthropus*
	1921 —	Excavation begins at Zhoukoudian
10 million	1912 —	Piltdown finds revealed
	1894 —	Dubois's treatise on *Pithecanthropus*
	1891 —	Dubois discovers *Pithecanthropus* skull in Java

	YEARS B.P.	FOSSIL RECORD	HOMINIDS
15 million	53,000–27,000 —	Ngandong and Sambungmacan	*Homo heidelbergensis*
MIOCENE	600,000 —	*H. erectus* at Zhoukoudian (Beijing fossils) and at Ternifine	
Proconsul	1 million —	*H. erectus* at Trinil (Java)	*Homo erectus*
	1.4 million —	Olduvai *H. erectus*	
20 million	1.8 million — 1.9 million —	*H. erectus* at Koobi Fora and Modjokerto (Java); *P. robustus* in South Africa; *H. habilis* and *P. boisei* at Olduvai; gracile hominids and *P. boisei* at Koobi Fora	Early *Homo*
	2.2 million —	Hominids at Longgupo Cave	
	2.6 million —	*A. africanus* in South Africa	*Australopithecus africanus*
25 million	3 million —	*A. afarensis* at Hadar	*Australopithecus afarensis*
OLIGOCENE	3.7 million —	*A. afarensis* at Laetoli	*Australopithecus anamensis*
Apidium, Parapithecus, and *Aegyptopithecus*	4.2 million —	*A. anamensis* in Kenya	*Ardipithecus ramidus*
	4.4 million —	*A. ramidus* at Aramis	

(CENOZOIC)

DISCOVERING *HOMO ERECTUS*

Discoveries of *Homo erectus* have been made throughout the Old World since the first Java finds in 1891. *Homo erectus*'s predecessors, early *Homo*, were intermediates between the ancestral *Australopithecus* and themselves.

ENVIRONMENT AND TECHNOLOGY OF *HOMO ERECTUS*

These early Acheulean hand axes from Peninj, Tanzania, are made from large lava flakes.

Man *is a tool-making animal.*

BENJAMIN FRANKLIN, 1706–1790.

OVERVIEW

As currently known, the fossil record indicates that prior to the appearance of *Homo erectus*, hominids' geographic range was limited to Africa (the Longgupo Cave fossils are treated as early *Homo erectus* here). All that changed with the evolution of *H. erectus*, however, and by 1.8 million years B.P. these early humans were spread from Africa to extreme southeast Asia and were beginning a period of existence that would last until at least 300,000 years ago and possibly later. But what allowed such phenomenal geographic spread and species longevity? This chapter examines several cultural innovations and behavioral changes that might have contributed to the success of *H. erectus*: stone-knapping advances that resulted in Acheulean bifacial tools; the beginnings of shelter construction and the control and use of fire; and increased dependence on hunting. Important topics and concepts include Ice Age climatic conditions; the manufacture and use of Acheulean tools; artifactual evidence for *Homo erectus*'s presence in central and western Europe; the absence of Acheulean tools in the Far East and the possible use of bamboo tools in that area; evidence for the construction of shelters and the control and use of fire; and, finally, the anatomical and archaeological evidence for the appearance of hunting-and-gathering as a way of life.

HOMO ERECTUS: NEW QUESTIONS ABOUT AN OLD SPECIES

For more than a quarter of a century, the story of *Homo erectus*—including time and place of origin, cultural development, geographic spread, and role in human evolution—seemed straightforward. Anthropologists seemed to have many more answers about the species than questions (or, at least, many of the major problems appeared to have been solved). Now all of that has changed. With the recent

Mini-Timeline

AGE (YEARS B.P.)	FOSSIL DISCOVERIES OR EVOLUTIONARY EVENTS
400,000–300,000	First regular use of fire; oldest shelter construction
1.5 million	Nariokotome *Homo erectus* skeleton
1.7–1.4 million	First Acheulean tools (Africa); establishment of a hunting-and-gathering way of life
1.8 million	*Homo erectus* present in Africa, Java, and the Caucasus
1.9 million	Oldest known *Homo erectus*(?) from Longgupo Cave, China
2.5 million	Oldest Oldowan choppers and flakes

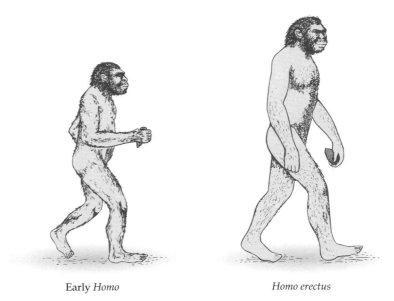

Early *Homo*   *Homo erectus*

FIGURE 11–1 Although imaginative, these reconstructions probably give a reasonable approximation of the posture and form of early *Homo* and *Homo erectus*. The main differences between them probably are in the size and proportions of the body and in the size of the brain.

announcements of *Homo erectus* fossils from the Caucasus and from Asia that are fully as old as African representatives of the species (and perhaps older in the latter case)—we face more questions than answers. Certainly *Homo erectus* can still claim the distinction of being the first hominid species known to exist outside Africa, and in our view, it still seems reasonable to assume an African origin for the species since all convincing pre–*H. erectus* hominid fossils are from that continent. Furthermore, *Homo erectus* enjoyed impressive longevity as a species and great geographic spread, lasting for nearly two million years and inhabiting the Old World from Southeast Asia to Europe and south to the tip of Africa. Nonetheless, many traditional scenarios about connections between cultural (particularly technological) developments and geographic spread must be reexamined. It is time to stop and take stock of what we know and don't know about these early humans and their lifeways, and it is to that end that this chapter is dedicated.

As described in Chapter 10, the anatomy of *Homo erectus* seems quite modern in many ways. For example, it appears that these early humans were about as tall and at least as heavy as people today, and that they had modern limb proportions (Figure 11–1). Additionally, judging from the skeleton of the Nariokotome boy, *Homo erectus* had a barrel-shaped thorax above a distinct waist. This body build, which also characterizes modern humans, contrasts strongly with the funnel-shaped rib cage of apes (compare the ape and human skeletons shown in Figure 5–28). The strong implication is that, like modern people, *Homo erectus* had a linear and relatively slender body shape, distinctly different from the potbellied bodies of apes and earlier hominids (the reconstructed thorax of *Australopithecus afarensis* is strongly funnel-shaped).

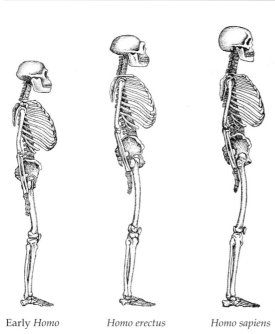

Early *Homo*   *Homo erectus*   *Homo sapiens*

FIGURE 11–2 The anatomy of *Homo erectus* was becoming very modern in most features and distinct from early *Homo*; the differences in the skull are the most striking. In addition, *Homo erectus* probably had longer legs and shorter arms than their ancestors. Stature is a very variable characteristic, and some living populations of *Homo sapiens* are smaller than the average *Homo erectus* and no bigger than the skeleton of early *Homo* shown here. The thorax of early *Homo* was probably more apelike (funnel-shaped) than that of *Homo erectus*, although it does not show clearly in this side view. The bones known from the right side of the body are colored.

Despite the similarities, however, there are also clear differences between *H. erectus* and modern people. First, *Homo erectus* possessed a brain that was only about two-thirds modern size, and, as we have seen, that brain was packaged in a rather primitive-looking skull. The thick-boned cranium of *Homo erectus* was long, low-vaulted, and wide at the base. Additionally, the face was more prognathic than that of modern humans, sticking out in front of the braincase rather than being tucked underneath the frontal portion of the cranium (Figure 11–2), and the cranial base was flat and unflexed. Studies of the surface anatomy of the *Homo erectus* brain, combined with other aspects of anatomy, fail to provide compelling evidence for spoken language, at least not complex modern language.

THE WORLD OF *HOMO ERECTUS*

What sort of world did these early people with their smallish brains and primitive skulls inhabit? Clearly, the answer to that question varies from one *Homo erectus* population to another, since the species lived a long time and was spread from the tropics to the cold-temperate zones. Traditionally, we might have said that they preceded and then overlapped the beginnings of the Ice Age. It is now known, however, that the Ice Age began much farther back in time and involved a more complex pattern of glacial advances and retreats than thought originally (Figure 11–3). The first important Plio-Pleistocene glaciation occurred around 2.4 million years ago, and there were additional important pulses on both sides of the 2.0-million-year B.P. mark. Granted, there was an intensification of the climatic swings in the mid-Pleistocene that resulted in a series of very strong glacial advances, but it

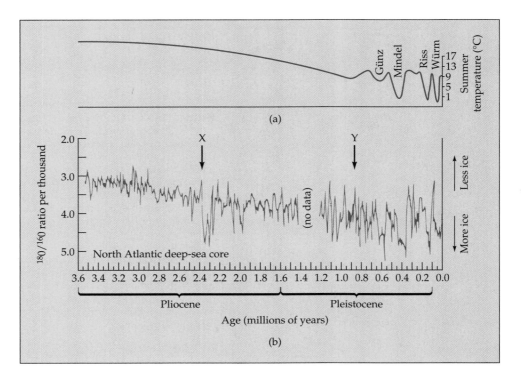

FIGURE 11–3   Plio-Pleistocene glacial and interglacial cycles now extend much farther into the past than originally believed based on evidence from the European Alps (a). Oxygen isotope measurements from deep-sea cores (b) show evidence for Northern Hemisphere glaciations starting about 2.4 million years ago (Point X) with an intensification following the mid-Pleistocene (Point Y).

is no longer accurate to describe the Ice Age simply in terms of the traditional four-stage Alpine glaciation series (Günz, Mindel, Riss, and Würm; indeed, some specialists have suggested that this outmoded terminology should be discarded entirely). During periods of glaciation, worldwide temperatures would have fallen significantly, and parts of the Northern Hemisphere would have been bitterly cold. Rainfall patterns would have been altered, probably producing more extensive grasslands in North Africa and other parts of the Old World. In addition, with so much water locked up in the glaciers, ocean levels would have dropped some 330 feet (100 meters) or more, exposing continental shelves and creating land bridges between locations now separated by the sea (Figures 10–3 and 10–15).

All these factors—temperature, rainfall, land bridges, and the distribution of grasslands and forests—would have affected hominids' abilities to spread beyond the continent of Africa. As noted earlier, we prefer the traditional assumption that *Homo erectus* was the first species to take advantage of the changing conditions and extend its geographic range. And starting with the following section on stone-tool technology, this chapter is dedicated to examining how cultural developments might have facilitated *Homo erectus*'s geographic expansion. Nonetheless, it is worth noting that environmental conditions that would have allowed geographic expansion probably also existed during the time period of early *Homo* (at about 2.4 and 2.0 million years B.P.; Figure 11–3), and a pre–*H. erectus* exodus from Africa cannot be disproved conclusively at present (see Chapter 10).

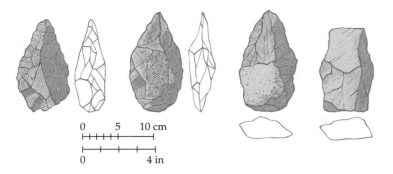

FIGURE 11–4   These early Acheulean artifacts are from Olduvai Gorge and date to approximately 1.5 million years B.P. From left to right, three hand axes (the right one is quite crude in its chipping) and a cleaver are shown. Note the cleaver's straight bit.

STONE TOOLS

As described in Chapter 9, stone-tool technology probably got its start with early *Homo*, and by the time *Homo erectus* appeared, Oldowan choppers and flake tools had been in use for at least half a million years. For another 100,000 to 400,000 years, Oldowan tools continued to be the top-of-the-line implements for early *Homo erectus* in Africa. The same may have been true in Asia, although the association of early Asian (i.e., Javanese) *Homo erectus* with stone tools of *any sort* remains questionable. In any event, between 1.7 to 1.4 million years B.P., Africa witnessed a significant advance in stone-tool technology: the development of the Acheulean industry of bifacially flaked tools and its premier implement, the **hand ax**. Named after a much later French site at St. Acheul, where hand axes were found in abundance, the Acheulean tool kit included not only bifacial hand axes, picks, and cleavers (Figure 11–4), but also an assortment of Oldowan-type choppers and flakes, suggesting that the more primitive implements continued to serve important functions.

> **Hand ax** a bifacially flaked stone implement that characterized the *Acheulean industry*.

In order to understand the nature of this advance in **lithic technology**, we need to take a closer look at how stone tools are made. First of all, not all stones are suitable for use in tool production. Rocks of a coarse, granular composition, such as granite, are almost useless for making chipped tools; they do not fracture along smooth, clean edges but tend to crumble. Certain other rocks, such as common feldspar, tend to break only along certain fracture lines and hence cannot be controlled by the toolmaker. The ideal stone from the point of view of the toolmaker is one of flint or chert: hard, tough, and of a smooth, fine-grained consistency. Stone of this type behaves somewhat like glass; it fractures rather than crumbles, and cone-shaped flakes can be knocked off it that are razor-sharp. Flint was the most common of the desirable tool stones in western Europe, and the typical Acheulean implement there was a flint hand ax. In Africa, Acheulean tools were often fashioned from large lava flakes.

> **Lithic technology** stone-tool technology.

Combining various kinds of stone with various ways of working them produces a surprising variety of results. The finer-grained the stone, the flatter and more leaflike the flakes that can be chipped loose from it. The size and shape of these flakes can be further controlled by how they are separated from the original stone. They may be knocked loose by a hammer or pried loose by a pointed stick or bone. The angle at which the hammer blow is struck can be changed to produce either a small, thick flake or a large, thin one. Also, different kinds of hammers produce different kinds of flakes. Relatively soft hammers of wood or bone produce one kind, hard stone hammers produce another, and a wooden point pressed against the edge of the stone will produce still a different kind. Even the way a tool is held while it is being made will affect the kind of flake that can be struck from it: when it is held in the hand, the results are not the same as when it is balanced on a rock.

Every toolmaker must have had a good deal of skill, based on necessity, on years of practice, and on an intimate knowledge of the nature of different stones. For each stone has its own qualities, which vary further depending on whether the stone is hot or cold, wet or dry. But the basic principles of toolmaking are fairly simple. If you decide to try it, you may be surprised at how hard a blow it takes to crack or flake a stone, but if you do it right, the stone will behave in a predictable way.

Core and Flake Tools

Core tool implement shaped from the core of a rock nodule.

Flake tool implement made from a flake struck from a larger stone.

Despite all the variations in techniques and materials, there are still only two basic categories of tools: **core tools** and **flake tools**. To make a core tool, take a lump of stone and knock chips from it until it has the desired size and shape; the core of stone that remains is the tool (Figures 11–5 and 11–6). A flake tool, as its name implies, typically is a chip struck from a core. It may be large or small, and its shape may vary, depending on the shape of the core from which it was struck. It may be used as it is, or it may itself be further flaked or chipped, somewhat in the manner of a core tool. In any event, the flake itself, and not the core from which it was struck, is the tool.

In the earliest days of toolmaking, flake tools were very simple. Whatever happened to fly off a core would be put to use if it had a sharp edge. In general, flakes were used as cutters, because their edges were sharper than the edges that could be produced on core choppers, which were more useful for heavy hacking. As time went on, more and more skills were developed in the manufacture of flakes, and eventually it became a much more sophisticated method of toolmaking than the simple core technique.

The Acheulean industry is noted for its use of a prepared core in the production of its characteristic implement, the biface, a tool whose cutting edge has been flaked more carefully on both sides to make it straighter and sharper than the primitive Oldowan chopper. This may seem like an awfully small improvement, but it was a fundamental one and made possible much more efficient tools. The purpose of the two-sided, or bifacial, technique was to change the shape of the core from essentially round to flattish, for only with a flat stone can one get a decent cutting edge. The first step in making an Acheulean hand ax was to rough out the core until it had somewhat the shape of a turtle shell, thickest in the middle and thinning to a coarse edge all around. This edge could then be trimmed with more delicate little scallops of flaking (Figure 11–7). The cutting surfaces thus produced were longer, straighter, and considerably keener than those of any Oldowan chopper.

FIGURE 11–5 Stone toolmaking is not simple; it requires skill and much practice. Most people, however, can learn how to make simple tools. These photographs show Francois Bordes making a chopping tool (bottom right).

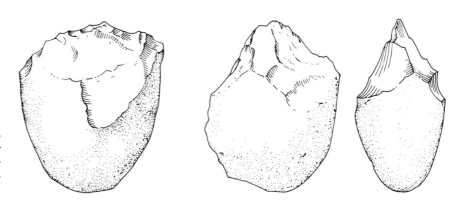

FIGURE 11–6 It is not difficult to see how a simple chopper (left) developed into a very primitive biface or hand ax (right). These tools are from Olduvai.

FIGURE 11–7   Making a hand ax is more difficult than making a chopping tool, as shown by these photographs of Francois Bordes. Having knocked the end off a large flint nodule, Bordes has prepared a striking platform (upper left). Using a hammer stone, he proceeds to strike off several large flakes, roughing out the general shape (upper center, upper right, and lower left). He then switches to an antler hammer, working both sides of the tool to thin out and retouch the edge (lower center). The final product, with long, straight, sharp edges (lower right), is one of the tools used for thousands of years by *Homo erectus* and *Homo heidelbergensis*.

One technological improvement that permitted the more controlled working required to shape an Acheulean hand ax was the gradual implementation, during the Acheulean period, of different kinds of hammers. In earlier times, it appears, the toolmaker knocked flakes from the stone core with another piece of stone. The hard shock of rock on rock tended to leave deep, irregular scars and wavy cutting edges. But a wood or bone hammer, being softer, gave its user much greater control over flaking. Such implements left shallower, cleaner scars on the core and produced sharper and straighter cutting edges. In time, the use of stone was pretty much restricted to the preliminary rough shaping of a hand ax, and all the fine work around the edges was done with wood , antler, and bone (Figure 11–7).

Acheulean hand axes were usually pear-shaped or pointed and were somewhat larger than chopping tools. Some have been recovered that were more than 2 feet (0.6 meters) long and weighed more than 25 pounds (11 kilograms). Obviously these were far too heavy and cumbersome to have been used for the kind of cutting and scraping that the smaller ones were designed for. One suggestion is that they may have been fitted to traps, set to fall and split the skulls of animals that triggered them.

Another type of implement that appears for the first time in the Acheulean industry is the **cleaver**. A cleaver had a straight cutting edge at one end and actually looked much more like a modern ax head than the pointed hand axes did. It was probably used for heavy chopping or for hacking through the joints of large animals (Figure 11–4).

As noted earlier, Acheulean tools originated in Africa between 1.7 and 1.4 million years ago. They were then produced continuously (along with a few Oldowan choppers and flakes) throughout *Homo erectus*'s long African residency and beyond, finally disappearing about 200,000 years B.P. Acheulean tools were being made in the Middle East by 1 mya, as shown at the site of 'Ubeidiya in Israel, and they were present in Europe as early as 500,000 to 780,000 years B.P. and in northeastern Pakistan by 400,000 to 730,000 years B.P. Several later sites in Africa and Europe show that the Acheulean tradition survived *Homo erectus* in some areas and was continued for a time by their descendants. Generally, Acheulean tools from sites clearly older than 400,000 to 500,000 years B.P. are attributed to *Homo erectus*, even in the absence of confirming fossils. At several important Acheulean sites, however, the toolmakers' species identity remains ambiguous because the sites lack hominid fossils and they date to a period when *Homo erectus* and *Homo heidelbergensis* overlapped in time. Examples of Acheulean assemblages that could have been produced by either late *H. erectus* or *Homo heidelbergensis* include Africa's Kalambo Falls; Torralba and Ambrona in Spain; Abbeville, St. Acheul, and Terra Amata in France; and Hoxne in England (Figure 10–15).

Wherever they are found, Acheulean hand axes and cleavers are generally interpreted as being implements for processing animal carcasses (Figure 11–8). True, the cleavers could have been used to chop and shape wood, but according to archaeologists Kathy Schick and Nicholas Toth, the wear pattern on cleaver bits is more suggestive of use on soft material, such as hides and meat. Schick and Toth believe that Acheulean tools represent an adaptation for "habitual and systematic butchery, [and] especially the dismembering of large animal carcasses," as *Homo erectus* experienced a strong dietary shift toward more meat consumption. Schick and Toth leave unanswered the question of whether meat was obtained primarily by scavenging or by hunting.

By now careful readers will have noticed that no sites in China or Southeast Asia are included in the inventory of Acheulean locales. In fact, there is strong evidence that Acheulean tools were never produced in much of the Far East. As first pointed out in 1948 by Hallam Movius (then of Harvard University), Acheulean sites are common in Africa, the Middle East, Europe, and much of western Asia, but they are strangely absent in far eastern and southeastern Asia. The line dividing the Old World into Acheulean and non-Acheulean regions became known as the **Movius line** (Figure 11–9). Hand-ax cultures flourished to the west and south of the line, but in the east, only choppers and flake tools were found (Figure 11–10). (Today we know the actual situation wasn't quite as clear as first described. There are a few examples of crude hand axes from sites in South Korea and China, but nothing that is clearly Acheulean. Also, there are some African and European sites contemporaneous with the Acheulean that produced only chopper and flake assemblages. Nonetheless, the Movius line remains a useful heuristic device for archaeologists.)

Cleaver an *Acheulean* stone implement with a straight cutting edge at one end; probably used for butchering animal carcasses.

Movius line The geographic dividing line between the Acheulean tradition in the West and non-Acheulean lithic traditions in eastern and southeastern Asia.

FIGURE 11–8   Held in the palm of the hand, an Acheulean hand ax would have been an excellent tool for dismembering and butchering animal carcasses.

But why were there no Acheulean hand-ax cultures in the eastern extremes of Asia? Traditionally this has been a hard question to answer, since researchers believed until quite recently that *Homo erectus*'s departure from Africa postdated the invention of Acheulean tools by some 400,000 years. If *Homo erectus* left Africa with Acheulean technology, why didn't the tradition arrive in eastern Asia? Was it discarded or forgotten along the way? The new dates from Java help solve this riddle somewhat, since they place *Homo erectus* in Southeast Asia at least 100,000 years *before* the earliest possible advent of the Acheulean in Africa. It thus appears that even if, as traditionally thought, *Homo erectus* turns out to be a native African species that spread to Asia, its initial migration certainly predated the development of Acheulean tools. Thus a chronological barrier might have prevented the introduction of Acheulean technology to eastern Asia.

Schick and Toth have listed several other explanations for the absence of the Acheulean tradition from eastern Asia. Perhaps it was due to a paucity of suitable

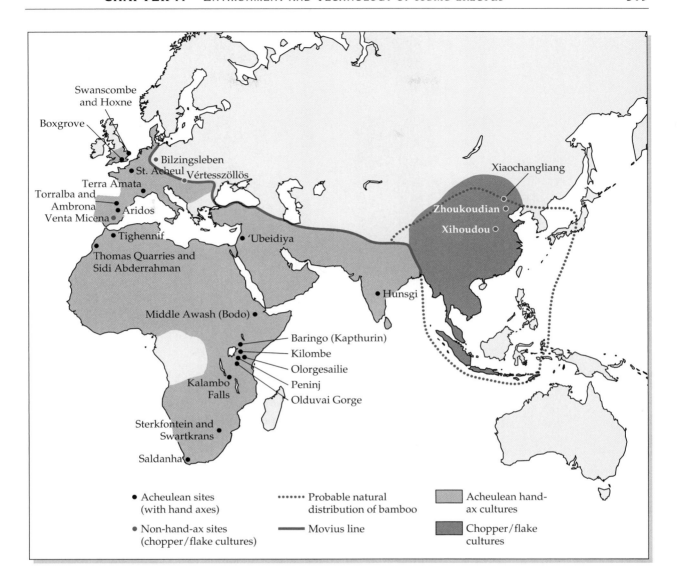

FIGURE 11–9   The "Movius line" divides the world of *Homo erectus* and its immediate descendants into Acheulean hand-ax cultures to the west and chopper-flake cultures to the east. Note that in the east and Southeast Asia the absence of hand-ax cultures coincides closely with the presence of bamboo.

raw stone; coarse quartz is common in the East, but fine-grained flints, cherts, and lavas are rare. This distribution of raw materials would lend itself to the production of Oldowan choppers, but not to bifacial hand axes requiring extensive chipping. Alternatively, the absence of the Acheulean tools may be related to different functional requirements in Asia compared to the West. If the Acheulean developed as an adaptation for meat processing by African hunters-and-gathers operating in open country, it may have been distinctly less useful in the closed and forested habitats of Asia, where large prey animals were probably less common and vegetable foods easier to harvest.

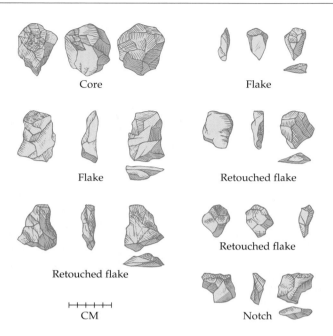

Core

Flake

Flake

Retouched flake

Retouched flake

Retouched flake

CM

Notch

FIGURE 11–10   Assemblages of choppers and flake tools such as these characterize the early Stone Age of east Asia.

Certainly the most intriguing of the explanations for the "missing Acheulean" is the suggestion by anthropologist Geoffrey Pope and others that, in far eastern and southeastern Asia, bamboo tools were used in place of stone implements to perform a variety of tasks. To quote Pope, "There are few useful tools that cannot be constructed from bamboo. Cooking and storage containers, knives, spears, heavy and light projectile points, elaborate traps, rope, fasteners [and] clothing . . . can be manufactured from bamboo." When a bamboo stalk is split, it produces razor-sharp "stick knives" that can be used to butcher animals or perform other hacking and scraping jobs. Such bamboo utensils are still used in some parts of the world today (Figure 11–11), and as Pope has pointed out, the natural distribution of bamboo coincides closely with those Asian areas that lack Acheulean tools (Figure 11–9). Pope's conclusions remind us that *Homo erectus* (like its ancestors) almost certainly used a variety of biodegradable tools (whether bamboo or some other material) of which we have no evidence. Such tools would always have been of great importance and their development could have been of as great value to the evolving hominids as was their stone industry.

We can conclude, therefore, that while the Acheulean tradition, with its hand axes and cleavers, was an important lithic advance by *Homo erectus* over older technologies, it constituted only one of several adaptive patterns used by the species. Clever and behaviorally flexible, *Homo erectus* was capable of adjusting its material culture to the local resources and functional requirements. Nonetheless, the Acheulean tradition clearly reflected significant cognitive progress by *Homo erectus* people over their evolutionary predecessors. As American anthropologist A. J. Jelinek remarked, Acheulean tools were the first "fully conceived implements whose final form is regularly patterned and in no way suggested by the shape or exterior texture of the stone from which they were made. This is certainly a significant step in conceptualization." Interestingly, once in existence, the Acheulean tradition showed very little overall change during perhaps 1.5 million years. Harvard's William Howells has referred to this lack of change as a "general stag-

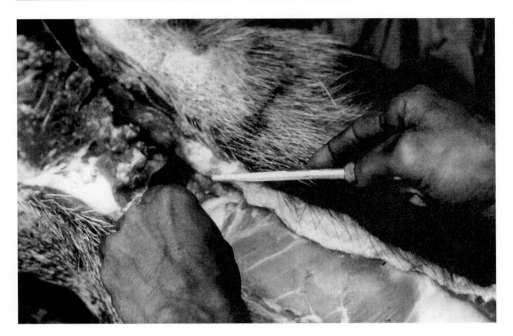

FIGURE 11–11   Split bamboo has razor-sharp edges and can be used as a "stick knife." Here a bamboo knife is used to butcher a pig in New Guinea.

nation" in material culture, and he has attributed it to a long period of stasis in intelligence and communication skills—a stasis that apparently was interrupted only by the evolution of *Homo heidelbergensis*.

SHELTER AND FIRE

As noted earlier, Plio-Pleistocene glaciations would have been associated with a variety of environmental changes including a strong drop in global temperatures. The cold would have been worst, of course, for populations living near the glaciers (as in Europe) or in the higher latitudes (as at Zhoukoudian). But what enabled *Homo erectus* to inhabit and thrive in so many parts of the Old World, including such environmentally challenging regions as northern China and periglacial Europe? True, from the beginning *Homo erectus* people were toolmakers, and as described in the last section, by no later than 1.4 million years ago their lithic technology had made a strong advance with the development of the Acheulean tradition. It is equally certain that *Homo erectus* would have gained some relief from the elements by seeking refuge in caves and rock shelters. But would this behavior have been enough? For years, scientists have searched for—and argued about—evidence that *Homo erectus* had gained additional control over its environment through the construction of shelters and the control and use of fire. The evidence is sparse and difficult to interpret, but a review of it should prove instructive.

Let's begin with the evidence for "domestic architectural features" (shelters and huts). At the site of Soleihac in southeastern France, *Homo erectus* apparently left a collection of choppers and flakes (no hand axes) a little more than 900,000 years ago. Also from Soleihac comes a rather mysterious line of basalt blocks 66 feet

(20 meters) long. It is difficult to know what to make of the line of stones. Are they all that's left of a shelter, or are they a natural feature of the site? Some researchers, such as paleoanthropologist Richard Klein, are clearly skeptical. According to Klein, "[The basalt line] may represent the oldest structural remnant in Europe, *if it is truly of human origin*" (italics added).

For the next, and considerably more impressive, evidence of shelter construction, we must jump forward a half million years to the 400,000 to 300,000-year-old French site of Terra Amata (located under the modern city of Nice). Excavated in the 1960s by Henry de Lumley, the site is claimed to have revealed evidence in the form of ancient postholes and concentrated artifacts of several huts measuring 20 to 49 feet (6 to 15 meters) long by 13 to 20 feet (4 to 6 meters) wide. De Lumley concluded that the hut roofs had been supported by two or more large posts, and that the walls were made of saplings and branches (Figure 11–12). He also estimated that each hut was large enough to hold up to fifteen people. Shelters very similar in size and construction to those envisioned by de Lumley have been documented among some modern hunter-and-gatherer groups (Figure 11–12).

In addition to the apparent remains of ancient shelters, Terra Amata also produced evidence of the control and use of fire. In the center of each reconstructed hut was a hearth, a fairly compact area of baked and discolored sand, and some hearths were ringed by a windscreen of stones, suggesting that the shelters were rather drafty (Figure 11–13). Little evidence was found for cooking food, although de Lumley believes that the Terra Amata people may have heated stones in order to boil food in wooden containers. Rather, the fires were apparently kept burning for warmth. Around one hearth there were impressions on the floor that were apparently made by animal skins, suggesting that the inhabitants slept by the fire at night.

The most problematic aspect of Terra Amata is not the archaeological evidence, however; rather, it is our inability to determine accurately the hominid species responsible for the site. Terra Amata has produced no fossil remains of its inhabitants that would allow their identification. Couple that fact with the young age of the site—perhaps 300,000 years B.P.—and it becomes clear that either late

FIGURE 11–12   The drawing at right reconstructs the kind of huts that Henry De Lumley excavated at Terra Amata in France. The hut has been cut away to show the method of construction. The exact form of the roof is uncertain, but this type of construction is common today in Africa, as can be seen in the photograph of a San hut in the northern Kalahari. The drawing shows some worked stones in the center. The oval of rocks and the central postholes were the main clues to the size and form of construction at Terra Amata.

FIGURE 11–13   On one of the Terra Amata hut floors, a windscreen of stones still shields a shallow hearth (left).

Homo erectus or *Homo heidelbergensis* might have been the builders and firemakers of Terra Amata.

In summary, there appears to be no convincing evidence that *Homo erectus* regularly constructed huts, windbreaks, or any other sort of shelter during the bulk of its long period of existence. Shelter construction apparently developed late in the species' life span, if at all, and therefore cannot be used as an explanation of *Homo erectus*'s capacity for geographic expansion (which was displayed very early). As Richard Klein noted, "The argument for *H. erectus* as builder remains hypothetical."

As it turns out, proving the use of fire by *Homo erectus* is almost equally problematic, although we have more evidence. The oldest evidence of fire use comes from Koobi Fora and other Kenyan sites and dates about 1.6 to 1.4 million years B.P. Some researchers, such as Randy Bellomo of the University of South Florida, believe that a strong case can be made for hominids (presumably *Homo erectus*) using controlled fire at this time for protection against predators and for heat and light. Other workers are not so sure. The problem is that the baked earth found at these sites could have been produced as easily by natural fires as by fires started— or at least controlled—by *Homo erectus*. Ash alone, or baked earth alone, does not necessarily prove hominid involvement. Something more must be present: other artifacts or some degree of spatial arrangement, such as the hearths at Terra Amata.

Better evidence of the use of fire comes from sites that date near the end of *Homo erectus*'s existence as a species. The French site of Menez-Dregan has produced evidence of a hearth dating 465,000 to 380,000 years B.P., but unfortunately the identity of the responsible hominids is unclear. Furthermore, from the 400,000-year-old sites of Torralba and Ambrona in Spain come animal bones (including those of elephants, horses, deer, and rhinos), as well as Acheulean tools and scattered bits of charcoal. Initial interpretations of the sites proposed that *Homo erectus* hunters had used fire to drive animals into marshy areas where they finished them off. Reanalysis of the sites in the 1980s, however, indicated that natural deaths of most of the animals (followed perhaps by hominid scavenging) and natural causes of the charcoal (e.g., brush fires) were more likely explanations than hominid activity.

At another 400,000-year-old site—Zhoukoudian, China, renowned as the home of "Peking man"—ash is (apparently) present in abundance, along with chopper and flake tools and the fossilized remains of late *Homo erectus*. Chinese workers and others have long claimed that, at Zhoukoudian, *Homo erectus* people kept fires burning more or less continuously to warm their cave homes, to keep away predators, and to cook their food. One typical illustration shows a *Homo erectus* woman feeding the fire as a man chips a stone tool and a second man hauls in a deer for dinner (Figure 11–14). But how accurate is this cozy domestic scene, even for late *Homo erectus*? While acknowledging some evidence of fire use at Zhoukoudian, archaeologist Lewis Binford and his co-workers have challenged the notion that fire played a regular or important role in the daily life of these early humans. Binford reexamined the evidence from Zhoukoudian and found that many of the extensive "ash" layers reported from the site may in fact be the results of the decalcification of massive organic deposits (including bird droppings, bat guano, and hyena feces) and not evidence of fire at all. Or, he suggested, if fires had occurred, they may have involved the accidental ignition of the organic material, which then slowly smoldered for some time. Binford found no evidence of hearths, nor any clear and recurring associations between ash, stone tools, and *Homo erectus* fossils. In other words, all the ingredients of the traditional cozy scene were present, but they were simply not connected. As for cooking food, Binford found some support for the practice, but precious little. A few burnt bones were recovered, including evidence of at least two episodes of roasting horses heads. Some other burnt bones, however, had clearly been dry (meatless) when burned, a fact suggesting that they may have been caught up in smoldering organic material. Binford and his colleagues concluded that *Homo erectus* shared the Zhoukoudian site with hyenas, and that hyena—not hominid—activity probably accounted for most of the accumulated materials in the cave.

FIGURE 11–14   This painting by English artist Maurice Wilson dates from 1950 and shows a typical "home-hearth-and hunting" interpretation of *Homo erectus*.

Finally, as described above, both the use and control of fire can be documented at the site of Terra Amata, but some doubt remains about whether *Homo erectus* or later people were responsible. In all, the evidence for the control and use of fire by *Homo erectus* is very slim, and what little there is occurs very late in the species' life span. The evidence at present suggests that fire was not the key to either the geographic spread or the success of these early humans.

SUBSISTENCE PATTERNS AND DIET

Early discoveries of *Homo erectus* fossils in association with stone tools and animal bones readily lent themselves to the interpretation of a hunting-and-gathering way of life—an interpretation that anthropologists eagerly embraced. The *Homo erectus* inhabitants of Zhoukoudian in China were described as deer hunters who consumed (cooked?) meals that combined venison with local plant products such as hackberries (Figure 11–14); at Torralba and Ambrona in Spain, the archaeological evidence—primarily the presence of Acheulean tools—was believed to indicate that *Homo erectus* hunters had systematically dispatched and butchered elephants on the spot, possibly after driving them into a marshy area by using fire; and in Africa, the Olorgesailie site was interpreted as showing that *Homo erectus* hunters occasionally preyed on fellow primates, including giant gelada baboons. All of these bits of data were then combined into an elaborate picture of the society and lifestyle of *Homo erectus* that generally tended to portray these Plio-Pleistocene hominids as an early version of modern human hunters-and-gatherers (see Chapter 12).

As we have seen, several of the original studies describing *Homo erectus* as a hunter-and-gatherer have come under intense criticism. For example, Lewis Binford and his colleagues have reexamined the material from the late–*H. erectus* site of Zhoukoudian and concluded that there is very little *conclusive* evidence of systematic hunting. Comparisons of the Zhoukoudian animal bones with faunal remains from both carnivore (especially hyena) dens and undoubted hunting sites (such as the 105,000-year-old European site of Combe Grenal) convinced Binford that the Chinese assemblage was primarily the result of animal activity rather than hunting-and-gathering. A few of the deer and horse bones at Zhoukoudian showed cut marks from stone tools that overlay gnaw marks by carnivores, suggesting that *Homo erectus* was not above scavenging parts of a carnivore kill. While acknowledging that *Homo erectus* certainly used the Zhoukoudian cave site, Binford and his co-workers were forced to conclude that at Zhoukoudian "all the positive evidence is consistent with what is believed to be evidence for hominid scavenging [and] there are *no positive indicators* of hunting in the available data" (italics in the original). In a similar fashion, archaeologist Richard Klein has shown that the bone and stone assemblages at Torralba and Ambrona fail to provide conclusive proof of *Homo erectus* hunting. Both sites could be nothing more than lakeside or streamside assemblages produced by regular animal use for feeding and drinking, predation by carnivores, and scavenging by Acheulean tool-producing people. At both sites, the archaeological evidence for scavenging by hominids is much more convincing than is that for actual hunting.

But do these reanalyses of some classic *Homo erectus* sites provide the last word on the question of hunting by these people? Must one conclude that hunting-and-gathering as a primary way of obtaining food appeared only at the level of *Homo heidelbergensis* and the Neandertals, where unequivocal proof can be presented at last? We think not. We believe that there are at least two sorts of evidence that show that *Homo erectus* people were consuming so much more meat than their evolutionary predecessors that hunting was almost certainly a regular subsistence pattern. First, there is the matter of their advance in stone-tool technology. As noted earlier, archaeologists Kathy Schick and Nicholas Toth, among others, have concluded that Acheulean hand axes and cleavers were used primarily for dismembering and butchering large animal carcasses. This conclusion is based on studies of the artifacts' design and wear patterns, as well as on experimental studies of how they could have been used most effectively. It appears, therefore, that the development of the Acheulean tradition is a clear indicator of a distinct shift toward greater reliance on meat by *Homo erectus*. The absence of Acheulean tools in eastern and southeastern Asia may well be related to the presence of fewer game animals in tropical forests than in open grasslands, although, as discussed above, other explanations may apply as well.

The second sort of evidence in favor of hunting by *Homo erectus* involves anatomy, specifically the size and shape of these early people. With regard to body size, Alan Walker has concluded that *Homo erectus* was a species of big individuals, comparable to the top 17 percent of modern human populations in height and within the modern range with regard to weight (possibly with a slightly higher average weight). Furthermore, Walker argues that early African *Homo erectus* differed little in body size from late Asian members of the species, implying a long period of anatomical stasis once an adaptive body build had evolved. Compared to early *Homo* (*H. habilis* and *H. rudolfensis*), *Homo erectus* showed an increase in body size of about one-third (compare Boxes 8–1, 8–2, and 10–1). To us, it seems difficult to explain an increase in body size of this magnitude simply as the result of increased scavenging activities.

As for *Homo erectus*'s body shape, two aspects concern us: the enormous enlargement of the brain and the coincidental reduction of the gastrointestinal tract. As noted in Chapter 10, *Homo erectus* (including Ngandong and Sambungmacan) showed a 27 to 62 percent increase in brain size compared to the two species of early *Homo*. Furthermore, as shown by analyses of the Nariokotome skeleton, *Homo erectus* was probably the first hominid type to show a barrel-shaped thorax and a distinct waist similar to modern human anatomy. Earlier species apparently possessed funnel-shaped rib cages and potbellies like living apes. This modification in the shape of the *H. erectus* thorax suggests significant reduction in the size of the gastrointestinal tract. Both brains and intestines are metabolically expensive organs: brains have a mass-specific (i.e., organ or part-specific) metabolic rate about 9 times higher than the average mass-specific rate for the body as a whole, and the splanchnic organs (intestines and liver together) have a mass-specific rate that is 9.8 times higher than the bodily average (Table 11–1). Researchers Leslie Aiello and Peter Wheeler believe there were only two ways to accommodate the increased energy demands of the big brain of *Homo erectus*: either raise the overall basal metabolism rate of the body or compensate for brain growth by reducing the size of some other metabolically expensive organ(s). All indications are that our forebears evolved down the second path. Modern humans show a standard basal metabolism rate for mammals our size, but we have much bigger brains and smaller gastrointestinal tracts than expected (Figure 11–15). Furthermore, the energetic savings realized by reducing the digestive system are approximately the same as the added costs of a larger brain. Beginning with *Homo erectus*, humans experienced an evolutionary trade-off of intestines for brains.

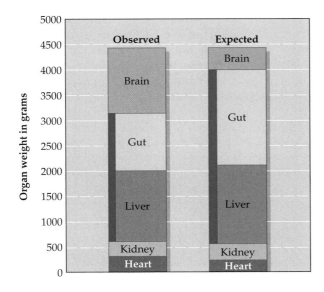

FIGURE 11–15 The right-hand column shows the organ weights predicted (expected) for a 143 pound (65 kilogram) human with typical primate organ sizes. The left-hand column shows the actual (observed) organ weights found in 65-kilogram modern people. The modern human brain is almost three times larger than expected, while the gut is 40 percent smaller. (Figure from Aiello and Wheeler, 1995; reprinted by permission of the University of Chicago Press.)

TABLE 11–1 *Mass-specific Organ Metabolic Rates in Humans*[a]

ORGAN	METABOLIC RATE IN W. KG^{-1} (WATTS PER KILOGRAM)
Brain	11.2
Heart	32.2
Kidney	23.3
Liver and gastrointestinal tract	12.2
Skeletal muscle	0.5
Lung	6.7
Skin	0.3

[a] Mass-specific organ metabolic rates are those for a 65 kilogram human male with a bodily basal metabolism rate (BMR) of 90.6 watts. The average mass-specific metabolic rate of the human body as a whole is 1.25 W. Kg^{-1}. (Data from Aschoff, et al. (1971), as reported by Aiello and Wheeler (1995); reprinted by permission of the University of Chicago Press.)

Reducing the digestive system has dietary implications, of course, which brings us back to the question of *Homo erectus*'s subsistence patterns. Animals that depend on poor quality (low energy) and hard to digest diets (folivores and, to a lesser extent, frugivores) consume large quantities of food and then process it slowly in their large stomachs and intestines. More carnivorous animals, on the other hand, eating higher quality (higher energy) and more digestible diets, need both less food and smaller digestive organs for its processing. We agree with Aiello and Wheeler that the anatomical evidence places *Homo erectus* in the latter group. By becoming active and effective hunters, *Homo erectus* people were able to tap into an extremely energy-rich food source. Their meat-intensive diet required less digestive effort than was true for earlier hominids—thus allowing organ gastrointestinal —and simultaneously provided plenty of energy for their expanding brains. As discussed in Chapter 9, several factors have been suggested as triggers for brain expansion among hominids, with the pressures for increased social intelligence and subsistence intelligence being high on the list. The evolution of a hunting-and-gathering lifestyle by *Homo erectus* would have simultaneously relaxed the metabolic constraints on brain growth and intensified the selective pressure for further expansion. In Leslie Aiello's words, "The surplus [energy] was used to feed our brains, which began to grow significantly at this time. It was a loop. We started to eat meat, got smarter, and thought of cleverer ways to obtain more meat, although learning to obtain other rich, but easily digestible foods, such as nuts, was probably also involved."

Therefore, in contrast to some of our colleagues, we believe that the archaeological and anatomical evidence converges on the conclusion that *Homo erectus* was a hunting-and-gathering species. These were not the first hominoid hunters, of course—occasional small-scale hunting is seen among nonhuman primates, especially chimpanzees, and cannot be conclusively denied to the australopithecines or early *Homo*—but it does appear that for *Homo erectus* active hunting took on unprecedented importance. In doing so, hunting may have had significant effects on material culture and society, as discussed in the next chapter.

SUMMARY

Homo erectus evolved sometime in the late Pliocene. If the new dates from Java and Longgupo prove to be valid, the species was spread from extreme southeastern Asia to eastern Africa by 1.8 million years ago. What enabled this phenomenal geographic spread? Was it increased intelligence? (See Box 11–1.) Certainly this must have played a part, as *Homo erectus* showed a significant jump in overall brain size compared to early Homo. But precisely how increased intelligence aided the species' spread and longevity is unclear. Was it spoken language? Maybe, but the indicators are mixed. *Homo erectus* probably had a large enough brain for language, but the proportions of its throat probably did not allow the modern range of vowel sounds, and it may not have had the fine control of breathing that modern speech requires. If these people produced spoken language, it probably was not as rich in sounds or as rapid and complex as that of modern humans.

But what of culture? Surely there were key cultural advances that set *Homo erectus* apart from early *Homo* and enabled its success. Again, the only possible answer is "maybe." Admittedly, this is not very satisfying, but for a couple of reasons it is the best we can do at present. First, we are limited primarily to statements about the *material culture* of *H. erectus*, that is, their tools and other artifacts. Social and behavioral traits, such as group composition, level of social organization, territoriality, and cooperation in (and/or division of) subsistence activities, do not fossilize and can only be inferred (see Chapter 12). And inferred cultural advances must be considered only as hypotheses for investigation, not as reliable explanations of other phenomena. Thus we can draw solid conclusions only about a greatly impoverished version of culture—but that's the nature of the archaeological data currently available.

Second, although the innovations in material culture are there, in most cases the timing is wrong, at least wrong in order for them to work as explanations of *Homo erectus*'s initial geographic spread. As summarized in Table 11–2, only one technological advance can be attributed undeniably to *Homo erectus*, and that is the early development of the Acheulean lithic tradition, with its bifacial tools, particularly hand axes and cleavers. As discussed above, this innovation in stone-tool technology probably signaled a shift from scavenging-and-gathering to hunting-

Box 11-1

HOMO ERECTUS: BUILDER OF BOATS?

As detailed in this chapter, the combination of factors that enabled *Homo erectus* people to spread from Africa to southern Europe and even as far as modern-day Indonesia remains unclear. Lithic innovations may have played a role, but the evidence is equivocal. Shelter construction and the regular use of fire probably came too late to have made a difference. A recent archaeological report, however, has suggested another technological breakthrough that might have fostered *H. erectus*'s geographic spread: boat building.

Just as the final revisions were being made to the current edition of this text, archaeologist Mike Norwood of the University of New England (New South Wales, Australia) and his co-workers announced the discovery of ancient chopper and flake tools from the east Indonesian island of Flores. Dated by the zircon fission-track technique to between 900,000 and 800,000 years B.P., the Flores tools seem almost certainly to have been the work of *Homo erectus* since they greatly predate the evolution of modern humans and since *Homo heidelbergensis* fossils have not been found in this part of

the world (see Chapters 14 and 16 for details). The most interesting aspect of the Flores tools, however, is related to the island's location. Because it is surrounded by deep-water straits, Flores seems unlikely to have been connected by a land bridge to the rest of Southeast Asia during the Pleistocene—not even at the peak of the various glaciations, when sea levels would have been dramatically lower than today. This means that whoever made the Flores stone tools had to cross about 12 miles (19 kilometers) of open water to colonize the island. Norwood and his colleagues thus conclude that mid-Pleistocene *Homo erectus* people in Indonesia were able to construct some sort of watercraft that were sufficiently reliable to take out on the open sea. *Homo erectus* as boat builder? The possibility has important implications for our interpretations of *Homo erectus*'s intelligence and communication (that is, linguistic) skills, and it could help to explain how the species moved so rapidly across certain portions of the Old World. Further evidence such as that from Flores is eagerly awaited.

and-gathering—an extremely important change in subsistence patterns that helped catapult *Homo erectus* to the top of the Plio-Pleistocene food chain and enabled the exploitation of energy and nutrient-rich animal products with an entirely new intensity. Other cultural innovations frequently attributed to *Homo erectus*, such as shelter construction and the control and use of fire, probably came so near the end of the species life span that many researchers feel they are better assigned to later humans, most likely *Homo heidelbergensis*. Unfortunately—at least for our understanding of the Old World wide spread of *Homo erectus*—even the appearance of Acheulean tools and hunting-and-gathering as a way of life postdate the traditionally hypothesized exodus from Africa. The very earliest dates given for Acheulean technology are 1.7 million years ago, and many archaeologists prefer 1.5 to 1.4 mya. Since *Homo erectus* people (or their ancestors?) *had* to have left Africa before 1.8 million years B.P., the conclusion seems inescapable that they did so as *scavengers* and gatherers, and with tools no more complex than Oldowan choppers and flakes. Their successful colonization of Eurasia is all the more impressive.

As noted by William Howells, *Homo erectus* was a very stable species once its basic adaptive niche had taken shape. After inventing Acheulean tools and

TABLE 11–2   *A Distribution of the Technological and Subsistence Innovations of* **Homo erectus** *to Early, Middle, and Late Stages of the Species' Span*[a]

STAGE	BRACKETING DATES (MILLION YEARS B.P.)	TECHNOLOGICAL OR SUBSISTENCE INNOVATION
Early *Homo erectus*	1.9–1.2	Acheulean industry (Oldowan continues as well). Hunting-and-gathering lifestyle likely (more meat).
Middle *Homo erectus*	1.2–0.6	No clear innovations. Acheulean continues west of Movius line, Oldowan to the east.
Late *Homo erectus*	0.6–0.03	Shelters (possibly). Control and use of fire (possibly).

[a] Stages were arbitrarily defined as approximately 600,000-year periods. Ngandong and Sambungmacan are excluded.

adopting a hunting-and-gathering lifestyle, *Homo erectus* showed little if any cultural change for well over a million years! In the next chapter, we will investigate further the behavioral and societal implications of hunting-and-gathering for these early humans.

POSTSCRIPT

For paleoanthropologists and archaeologists, interpreting the fossils and artifacts that they discover is both the bane of their existence and the spice of life. How can we ever know what prehistoric tools were used for or how the toolmakers organized and lived their lives? These are difficult questions precisely because there are few established principles regarding how interpretations of ancient bones and stones should be carried out. Some headway is surely being made and, as shown by the reanalyses of Zhoukoudian by Lewis Binford and of Torralba and Ambrona by Richard Klein, researchers are becoming increasingly cautious and conservative in their interpretations of prehistoric sites. Modern researchers are much less prone to hasty speculations than their predecessors were, preferring to force recovered bone and stone assemblages to *prove* the existence of particular behavioral patterns. Thus both Binford and Klein question the regular use of fire by *Homo erectus*. Nonetheless, guidelines for interpretations are few and far between, and therefore disagreements among specialists are legion. Consider the problem of analogue models.

Two sources of information are commonly used to interpret the behavior of prehistoric hominids: data from modern people still practicing hunting-and-gathering and data from nonhuman primates (usually apes; Figure 11–16). Conclusions about extinct hominid types are then reached by a process of triangulation; that is, nonmodern hominids are described as behaviorally intermediate between modern hunters-and-gatherers and apes, with humanlike traits predominating in relatively recent species and apelike traits predominating in very ancient hominid types. Thus *Homo erectus* has been described traditionally as a sort of primitive human, while the australopithecines have been interpreted as more like apes.

In principle, there is nothing wrong with this sort of triangulation. Problems arise, however, in determining which analogue model—modern hunters-and-gatherers or apes—is most appropriate in each case and (perhaps more important) because reliance on these two established models sometimes seems to limit our imagination and prevent us from considering the possibility of adaptive systems unlike those known in any living primate. Leaving some room for imaginative interpretations (always tentative and constructed as testable hypotheses) is quite important, since comparative information from apes is limited by the small number of living species and since comparative data from modern hunters-and-gatherers, almost all of whom live in marginal habitats, may not be representative of the past, when hunting-and-gathering people had access to richer environments. And finally, it must be remembered that arguing from living systems to systems that are extinct is a multistep process that involves data gathering at several levels, rather than a simple transference from the present to the past (Figure 11–17).

Now, with these heavyweight considerations in mind, let's take a look at a distinctly lightweight question: Did *Homo erectus* people make and use bolas? The bola is the throwing implement of the gauchos and other people of the Argentine pampas and consists of spherical stones tied together by leather thongs in groups

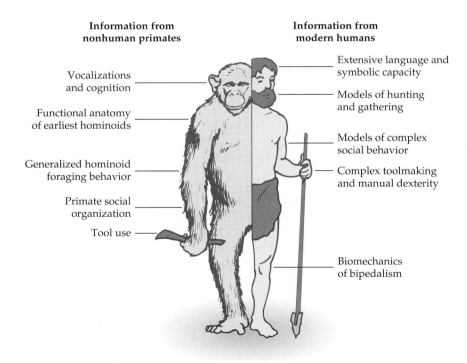

Information from nonhuman primates

Vocalizations and cognition

Functional anatomy of earliest hominoids

Generalized hominoid foraging behavior

Primate social organization

Tool use

Information from modern humans

Extensive language and symbolic capacity

Models of hunting and gathering

Models of complex social behavior

Complex toolmaking and manual dexterity

Biomechanics of bipedalism

FIGURE 11–16 This figure shows some of the sorts of information researchers can derive from nonhuman primates and living humans that aid in the interpretation of extinct hominids.

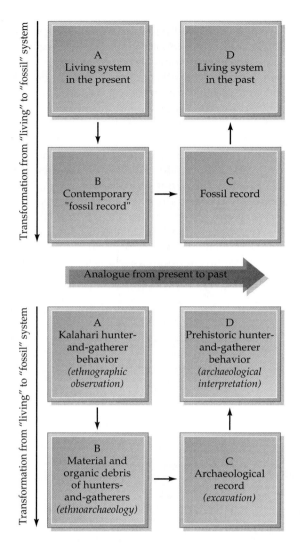

Transformation from "living" to "fossil" system

A
Living system
in the present

D
Living system
in the past

B
Contemporary
"fossil record"

C
Fossil record

Analogue from present to past

Transformation from "living" to "fossil" system

A
Kalahari hunter-
and-gatherer
behavior
(*ethnographic
observation*)

D
Prehistoric hunter-
and-gatherer
behavior
(*archaeological
interpretation*)

B
Material and
organic debris
of hunters-
and-gatherers
(*ethnoarchaeology*)

C
Archaeological
record
(*excavation*)

FIGURE 11–17 Making inferences using analogue models is a multistep process. The top set of boxes shows the route of inference making. The bottom set gives an example by ethnographic analogy.

of two or three. It is used by hunters to entangle and trip up game. Interestingly, *Homo erectus* sites regularly produce rounded, battered pieces of stone that are usually labeled simply as *spheroids*. However, because of the physical similarity between spheroids and modern bola stones, some anthropologists have made the simple transference from living people to the past and have concluded that *Homo erectus* hunters also used the bola. But how much confidence can we have in this conclusion? Very little, according to recent results from experimental archaeologists Kathy Schick and Nicholas Toth. After considerable rock pounding, Schick and Toth found that initially angular stones—particularly chunks of quartz—that were used as hammers for several hours always ended up with a spherical shape *"without any necessary intent or predetermination"* (italics in original). Since *Homo erectus* people presumably used hammer stones a lot—to shape other stones, smash bones for marrow, and so on—Schick and Toth believe it is best to regard *Homo erectus* spheroids simply as well-used hammers rather than as bola stones. The moral of this little story is clear: Analogies from the present to the past must be made with extreme care and, if at all possible, must be subject to testing.

REVIEW QUESTIONS

1. Describe the innovations in material culture attributed to *Homo erectus*. Which ones are we sure of, and which are we not? Where do these innovations fall within the species' time span?
2. Speculate about why *Homo erectus* apparently stagnated with regard to material culture. What anatomical or environmental factors might have contributed to this stasis?
3. There seems to be little direct evidence that *Homo erectus* could talk very well. If this is true, how do you think the species communicated? How would a lack of modern language have affected the species' potential for geographic spread?
4. How do you feel about referring to *Homo erectus* individuals as "people" and "early humans"? What criteria do you think must be met before a hominid is labeled a "human"?
5. Why have so few Acheulean hand axes been found in eastern and southeastern Asia? Give as many explanations as you can for their absence.
6. Describe the hypothesized relationships between brain size, digestive system size, and diet of *Homo erectus*. Discuss the various ways brain enlargement could be both the result of evolutionary pressures and the trigger for further evolution.

SUGGESTED FURTHER READING

Aiello, L., and P. Wheeler. "The Expensive-Tissue Hypothesis." *Current Anthropology*, 36, 1995.

Binford, L. R., and N. M. Stone. "Zhoukoudian: A Closer Look." *Current Anthropology*, 27, 1986.

de Lumley, H. "A Paleolithic Camp at Nice." *Scientific American*, 220, 1969.

Klein, R. *The Human Career*. University of Chicago Press, 1989.

Pope, G. G. "Bamboo and Human Evolution." *Natural History*, 98, 1989.

Schick, K., and N. Toth. *Making Silent Stones Speak*. Simon & Schuster, 1993.

INTERNET RESOURCES

STONE AGE HAND-AXES

http://www.abotech.com/articles/kowalski02.htm

   (This site includes an excellent set of hand ax photos. The accompanying text, however, contains several questionable statements and should be viewed with caution.)

   Other websites containing useful information about *Homo erectus* are given at the end of Chapter 10 and the reader is referred to that list.

USEFUL SEARCH TERMS:

   Acheulean
   Homo erectus
   Oldowan
   Tool industries

Chapter 11 Timeline

HOLOCENE	YEARS B.P.	FOSSILS AND BEHAVIORS	LITHIC AGES
10,000			Upper Paleolithic (40,000 B.P.)
	53,000–27,000 —	Ngandong and Sambungmacan fossils	
PLEISTOCENE	100,000 —		Middle Paleolithic (200,000 B.P.)
1.6 million	200,000 —		
	300,000 —	Regular use of fire; oldest shelters	
PLIOCENE	400,000 —	*H. erectus* at Zhoukoudian, China	Lower Paleolithic
5 million	500,000 —		
	600,000 —		
	700,000 —	*H. erectus* at Gongwangling (Lantian), China and Ceprano, Italy	
	800,000 —		
	900,000 —	*H. erectus* at Trinil, Java	
	1 million —		
	1.25 million —		
	1.4 million —		
	1.5 million —	Nariokotome boy	
	1.6 million —	Beginnings of Acheulean tradition and beginnings of hunting-and-gathering lifestyle	
	1.7 million —		
	1.8 million —	*H. erectus* in Africa, the Caucasus, and Java	
	1.9 million —	Hominids at Longgupo Cave, China	
	2 million —	Hominids spread out of Africa (?)	
MIOCENE		?	
	2.5 million —	Oldest Oldowan tools at Gona, Ethiopia	

Developing the Acheulean stone tool tradition seems to have been the primary technological innovation of *Homo erectus*.   Researchers disagree whether these early humans used fire and built shelters.

Chapter 12

HUNTING, GATHERING, AND THE EVOLUTION OF SOCIETY

The Yanomamo people of Brazil combine hunting-and-gathering with horticulture.

It *is far from easy to determine whether Nature has proved a kind parent to man or a merciless stepmother.*

PLINY THE ELDER, 23–79. *Natural History*, Book VII, 1.

OVERVIEW

As discussed in Chapter 11, we believe that hunting-and-gathering as a hominid way of life can be traced back in time to *Homo erectus*. To be sure, some components of hunting-and-gathering behavior almost certainly predate this species. Chimpanzees hunt, and other subsistence behaviors, such as scavenging, would have continued, but on a reduced scale. A good deal is known about hunting-and-gathering as it is (and was) practiced by modern people, thanks to studies done during historic times by anthropologists and others. Modern hunters-and-gatherers tend to show a distinctive cluster of anatomical, behavioral, and societal traits that accompany their trademark subsistence patterns. Among the accompanying traits are the development of relatively hairless skin and cooling by sweating; the sexual division of roles for subsistence (women gathering and men hunting) and for child care activities; the development of the family as a cultural unit; the formalization of outbreeding (exogamy); and the regular use of base camps.

It is usually impossible to pinpoint the appearance and full development of particular traits by time, place, and species. Taken as a whole, however, the cluster probably began to evolve among *Homo erectus*, experienced significant progress among *H. heidelbergensis* and *H. neanderthalensis*, and was developed fully by the time of *Homo sapiens*. We choose to discuss these (primarily social) adaptations at this point simply because the hunting-and-gathering life was introduced in the two preceding chapters, not because we think the trait cluster was particularly well formed among *Homo erectus* people. Important topics and concepts include evidence of hunting-and-gathering; the nutritional benefits of such a lifestyle; the various techniques used by human hunters; the evolution of female and male social (including parental) roles; the evolution of the family; the development of exogamy; the development of home bases; and evidence of aggression and possibly cannibalism by *Homo erectus*.

BEHAVIORAL SPECULATIONS

Humankind and human society are so closely interwoven that it makes no sense to talk of human evolution without considering human society. Indeed, our social life is the area in which our humanity is most strikingly expressed. That society evolved, as did humankind, is not in question. But because we are the bearers of symbolic culture, the evolution of human society is not another biological phenomenon such as the evolution of ant or bee society. Although human social evolution rides on the back of human biological evolution, the mechanism of change is different. The use of the word *evolution* is justified by reference to its original meaning: an "unfolding." The unfolding or development of human society, though it bears many resemblances to the evolution of organisms, was and is distinct, and the two should be not confused. Evidence for social evolution is provided by archaeologists, and in this chapter we consider some of that evidence in more detail.

Before we begin, however, we want to reinforce the caveat given in the Overview. We believe the anatomical and archaeological evidence indicates that *Homo erectus* people subsisted by hunting-and-gathering (remember that not all anthropologists agree with that assessment, some preferring to envision scavenging-and-gathering subsistence for *H. erectus*). Furthermore, using *Homo erectus* as a starting point, one can legitimately argue that at some point(s) during the past two million years, a behavioral package called the hunting-and-gathering lifestyle evolved. This lifestyle included numerous social changes (role differentiation, families, mating rules, etc.) that went a long way toward converting early humans into modern humans with regard to behavior. In this chapter, we speculate—sometimes rather freely—about the development of that lifestyle despite the fact that few, if any, of its aspects can be anchored in time, space, or by species. Certainly, it seems most unlikely that *Homo erectus* showed the full behavioral package, given their smallish brains (compared to modern people) and limited communication skills, but, as described below, they probably showed some of its components, with others evolving among their descendants. And so, with that understanding and without worrying too much about the links between particular behavioral innovations and particular species, let us review the evidence and formulate some hypotheses about how the hunting-and-gathering way of life evolved.

THE ARCHAEOLOGY OF THE HUNTERS

The interpretation of archaeological sites is not always as straightforward as it may appear. Many of the sites in Olduvai Gorge excavated by the Leakeys have probably been correctly interpreted; they include ancient land surfaces preserved more or less as they were left by early hominids. It often happens, however, that some movement occurs in such deposits, and in more extreme cases the archaeological remains may be washed out by heavy rains or river action and redeposited in another place. Such deposits are called **secondary sites**. In many instances, the stones and bones may be sorted by the moving waters of a river and deposited in very dense accumulations that have the superficial appearance of being the result of human activity.

Secondary sites archaeological sites in which the artifacts have been disturbed by natural forces and then redeposited.

The distinction between primary and secondary sites in archaeology is an important one. In the past, investigators have sometimes been misled into believing that bones or stone tools scattered on an ancient riverbank represented an original living floor. In many cases, microscopic analysis of the material is required, which will reveal if the bone or stone has been battered or "rolled" in the flowing river or still remains in an uneroded condition.

Such a site is Olorgesailie in southwestern Kenya, where for many years it was thought by some archaeologists that there was definite evidence of hunting and butchery. Here, at one site, in an area only 40 by 50 feet (12 by 15 meters), Glynn Isaac unearthed bones and teeth of at least fourteen adult and seventy-six juvenile monkeys of the now extinct species **Theropithecus oswaldi**. Mixed with them was more than a ton of Acheulean hand axes and cobbles (altogether 4,751 artifacts). The date is estimated at about 650,000 years B.P. It seemed to some that a massive organized slaughter had been conducted on the site, followed by a tremendous amount of butchery. A band of hominids—most likely *Homo erectus*, given the tools and the age—appeared to have ambushed and killed a big troop of these formidable

Theropithecus oswaldi an extinct species of gelada baboon.

animals (the baboon males were almost the size of the hunters). The density of bones and stone tools was most unusual.

Glynn Isaac, however, believed it most likely that the stone tools and bones had been washed down the river, sorted, concentrated, and deposited in distinct areas on its banks. Taphonomic studies have shown that such a hypothesis of secondary deposition is a probable explanation of these dense accumulations of material. The site contains an enormous hoard of heavy stone tools, and overall the evidence suggests that *Homo erectus* was systematically butchering the giant gelada monkeys and perhaps even hunting them, upstream of the actual site, and that this probably continued over a considerable period of time.

We must bear the difficulties of archaeological interpretation in mind as we turn to look at the evidence of the beginnings of systematic hunting by hominines.

Hunter's Diet

As discussed in Chapters 8 and 9, the archaeological evidence suggests that early *Homo* groups consumed a wide variety of animals, some of which they possibly caught, but many of which they scavenged. The picture changes with *Homo erectus*. Although they undoubtedly continued to rely heavily on plants for nourishment—as do practically all modern humans—they surely possessed both the intellect and the equipment necessary to assure themselves a more regular supply of meat.

Like all evolutionary change, this development was a slow matter of advantage and capacity reinforcing each other. Humans did not become hunters because some individuals decided they liked meat. Instead, creatures able to catch, eat, and digest meat were favored, at a particular time and place, in the competition for survival. Hunting makes available to humans far more food per square mile of the African savanna than plant life can provide. As vegetarians, humans can make use of only a limited number of the things that grow on the ground: mainly roots, nuts, fruits, berries, and some tender shoots. The most abundant plants—the grasses of the savanna and the leaves of the forest trees—contain a high proportion of cellulose, which cannot be digested by the human stomach. But the animals that live on the things that humans cannot digest may themselves be both edible and nourishing. Through hunting, previously inedible vegetation, converted to edible meat, became available as a rich food source for humans.

Hunting not only increased the amount of food available but also provided better food. Meat is a much more concentrated form of nourishment, a more efficient source of energy, than wild vegetables, fruits, and berries. Venison, for instance, yields 572 calories (calories measure the energy available in food) per 3.5 ounces (100 grams) of weight, whereas the same weight of most fruits and vegetables yields well under 100 calories. One medium-sized animal would have provided, in a compact, easily carried form, the same amount of energy as the results of a whole day's foraging for vegetables. (Nuts yield more calories than most meats and were undoubtedly a vital part of early humans' diet when and where nuts could be found, but nuts grow only in certain localities, and most of them are at least roughly seasonal, whereas game is widely available throughout the year.) Finally, the high protein content of meat is a very important dietary factor.

Another very important factor in the development of hunting and the evolution of *Homo erectus* is the seasonality of vegetable food in the temperate regions. In tropical savanna regions, with their biannual wet and dry seasons, the supply of vegetable foods is more or less continuous—barring a prolonged drought—as the success of the vegetarian savanna monkeys demonstrates. In northern temperate zones, however, there is a real dearth of vegetable foods after the nuts and berries have been consumed in the fall. In the winter and early spring, meat, we can suppose, may have been a major part of the diet of *Homo erectus* groups that had expanded into the temperate zones. Hunting was surely an essential adaptation for any groups that were to succeed in the cold winters of temperate Eurasia.

Skin Adaptation

One major physical change that had possibly occurred by the time of *Homo erectus* was adaptation of the skin. When hominids started diverging from the African apes, they probably were just as hairy as those animals are now. In time, their hair must have grown less dense and the sweat glands in their skin more numerous. By the time of *Homo erectus*, if not before, the skin probably had become relatively hairless and had developed a greater number of sweat glands (Figure 12–1). This change sharply differentiates humans from other primates. Today, our body hair is generally much shorter, finer, and sparse compared to apes, and over large areas of our bodies it is almost invisible. Conversely, we have from 2 to 5 million sweat glands, more than are found in any other primate and far more productive of sweat.

Scientists are not sure why this change in body hair took place, but it seems to have been connected with an increasing ability to sustain strenuous physical exertion. As we have seen, most meat-eating animals hunt at night. When hominids moved from the protective forests onto the open savanna and became *daytime* scavengers, hunters, and gatherers, they solved one problem—avoidance of nocturnal predators—but created a new one. They generated a great deal of body heat (metabolic heat), just at the time of day when the temperature of the air was high, so that the cooling effect of the air was low. To maintain a constant body temperature, essential to any mammal, a very efficient cooling mechanism was

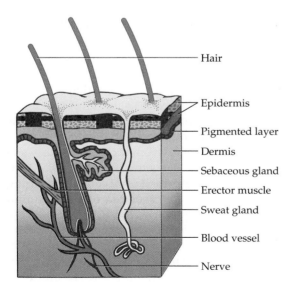

Hair

Epidermis

Pigmented layer

Dermis

Sebaceous gland

Erector muscle

Sweat gland

Blood vessel

Nerve

FIGURE 12–1   The skin is an organ of astonishing complexity. It is the barrier between the relatively closed system of a human body and its external environment; it is strong, elastic, waterproof, protective, and self-repairing. Beyond this, it serves as a sense organ, an excretory organ, a heat-control mechanism (involving hair and sweat glands), and the organ of individual identification. It responds to environmental stress, both directly (suntanning and healing) and indirectly (sweating).

required. A logical evolutionary adaptation to this biological need was the increased number of sweat glands, producing far more sweat per gland, and the reduction of hair cover. During heavy exertion or in hot weather, the sweat glands bathe the body in moisture. Evaporation of this moisture cools the surface of the skin and the blood just below it. Dense hair would inhibit evaporation and would get matted and clogged by dried sweat. Hence, the theory goes, the marked decrease in hair density.

There are, of course, other savanna animals that sweat heavily during strenuous exertion and yet retain a full coat of hair; zebras are an example. But their metabolic rate is noticeably lower than that of humans, and their dependence on grazing allows them to lead a much less active life. Strenuous exertion is rare and occurs mostly during the cooler night, when predators are active.

Sweating is not an unmitigated blessing to humans. As biologist William Montagna pointed out, sweating represents a major biological blunder in some ways, for it drains the body of enormous amounts of moisture, requiring fairly constant replenishment, and depletes the system of sodium and other essential elements. But higher primates all require regular supplies of drinking water, and so this requirement was nothing new. Sweating humans were certainly better equipped than their ape and monkey relatives to exert themselves for long periods in the tropical sunlight, and it can be assumed that the dramatic changes in the skin, however they occurred, made it possible for humans to engage successfully in their new way of life.

Hunting and Intelligence

It seems likely that many of the important physical adaptations that equipped humans for hunting had already been achieved by *Homo erectus*'s predecessors. What, then, made *Homo erectus* able to develop the art of hunting? The answer almost certainly lies in the enormous increase in the size and the adaptive capabilities of the brain. Hunting was more than a physical activity; it helped to create a new way of life, ultimately involving complex communication, culture, and improved social organization. Hunting became as much a matter of the mind as of the body.

We have seen that one indication of *Homo erectus*'s increasing mental ability is the refinement and improvement of their technology. Their stone tools and weapons were improvements over those of their predecessors, and they may also have had wooden spears, which would have made hunting safer and more effective. Even if they only jabbed with the spear rather than throwing it, they could still attack an animal without getting within immediate reach of its claws and teeth. And a spear embedded almost anywhere in an animal's body is likely to disable the animal; a stone, to be equally effective, must be thrown accurately to hit a vulnerable spot. The oldest evidence of wooden spears comes from the European sites of Schöningen, Germany, and Clacton, England, and dates to about 400,000 B.P. at both sites. The three Schöningen spears are truly impressive implements, ranging in length from 6 to 7.5 feet (1.8 to 2.3 meters) and sharpened at one end. Found along with numerous animal bones—mostly horse bones, many of which show signs of butchery by stone tools—the Schöningen spears are balanced like modern javelins and apparently designed for throwing, not jabbing. But once again, we must be very careful how we interpret the archaeological evidence. Neither Schöningen nor Clacton has produced any classifiable hominid fossils and both sites fall into the temporal overlap zone of *Homo erectus* and *Homo heidelbergensis* (similar to the site of Terra Amata; see Chapter 11). Thus, we cannot say for sure whether the first spear-makers were late *Homo erectus* people or their immediate descendants.

Perhaps as important as any improvement in weapons technology was a change in tactics. We can suppose that with a bigger brain *Homo erectus* had a greater attention and memory span. By being able to remember information from their own and their fellows' past experiences, they could amass knowledge of animal behavior, plan ahead, work out strategies, and roam farther afield than their forebears without getting lost. Furthermore, they could cooperate more subtly with other band members, increasing their chances of making a kill.

BEGINNINGS OF HUNTING

Homo erectus's success must have depended to a large extent on their guile and their understanding of animal behavior. If so, just how did they hunt? Some methods are perhaps documented in the remains found in excavated sites; others are suggested by examining hunting techniques employed in modern times by hunters-and-gatherers—by ethnographic analogy.

Homo erectus people were undoubtedly clever enough to have looked carefully for the weaknesses of the animals they hunted, big or small. African hares are quick but vulnerable, and they, too, must have figured as part of *Homo erectus*'s diet. How easily they can be caught by an intelligent (and agile) human was demonstrated by Louis Leakey, who ran them down and captured them with his bare hands. The technique is simple. The hunter, on spotting a hare, need only watch its long ears. When the hare is about to dodge, it lays its ears all the way back. Seeing this telltale sign, the hunter veers immediately either to the left or to the right, which gives a 50/50 chance of picking the way the hare is going to go. If the hunter has guessed correctly and is quick, the animal will be caught. If the hunter misses, the hare will usually run for cover and freeze there. The hunter, with the advantage of the primates' highly developed color vision, will see through the animal's camouflage and simply go over and pick up the prey.

Persistence Hunting

Early hunters may well have used a technique that anthropologist Grover S. Krantz has called **persistence hunting**. Development of this method, too, would have required insight into the behavior of animals, such as the tendency of antelopes and gazelles to move in an arc when trying to escape from a pursuer, giving the intelligent hunter the opportunity to cut them off. But the key to persistence hunting is persistence: never allowing the animal to rest, but keeping it constantly in motion until it grows so tired it can go no farther; when it slumps from exhaustion, it can be killed easily. The Tarahumara Indians of Mexico have been known to pursue a deer for as long as two days. Although the hunters may at times lose sight of their quarry, they never lose track of its spoor—hoofprints, droppings, and other signs of its passage—and relentlessly continue the pursuit until the deer collapses.

The possibility that *Homo erectus* and all later hominids might have practiced persistence hunting is supported by their anatomy. Their barrel-shaped rib cages would have allowed high levels of sustained activity. Specifically, ventilation of the lungs would have been enhanced by the ability to raise the upper part of the rib

persistence hunting hunting by chasing the prey until it stops, exhausted, when it can be killed.

cage (enlarging the thorax) when taking deep breaths. Furthermore, a distinct waist (rather than an apelike potbelly) would have allowed the early hunters' upper bodies to twist at the abdomen and their arms to swing freely—both traits that help to stabilize the upper body during bipedal running.

Stalking, Driving, and Ambush

The early hunters' arsenal of techniques almost certainly included stalking, driving, and ambush. Although these patterns sound rather complex—and thus, at first glance, probably beyond the capabilities of a simple communicator like *Homo erectus*—it must be remembered that in the Taï Forest groups of male chimpanzees have been observed to cooperate in driving monkeys through the trees, blocking their escape, and ambushing them for the kill (Chapter 4). Killing prey at close range was undoubtedly a risky business for early human hunters, but as noted above, it could have been done using throwing or jabbing spears, or simply by stoning cornered or immobilized animals to death. As described in Chapter 11, the Acheulean sites of Torralba and Ambrona (Spain) were originally interpreted as yielding evidence of *Homo erectus* hunters driving elephants into bogs, finishing them off, and then butchering them (Figure 12–2). More recent analyses, however, by Richard Klein and taphonomist Pat Shipman have shown that, while hominids (either *Homo erectus* or *Homo heidelbergensis*) used some of the carcasses at these sites (as shown by cut marks) and at a third elephant-butchering site called Aridos near Madrid, no conclusive evidence of actual hunting exists. The hominids may simply have been scavenging the remains of animals that had died naturally or had been killed by carnivores. Incontrovertible evidence of hunting by deliberately driving

FIGURE 12–2   Workers clear the floor of the Spanish site of Ambrona, where elephant bones (in the foreground) showing cut marks made by stone tools were found.

large and dangerous animals probably postdates *Homo erectus*. At the site of La Cotte de St. Brelade on the British Channel Island of Jersey, archaeologists have unearthed evidence of mammoth and rhinoceros drives dating from 240,000 to 125,000 years B.P. But at this date, the hunters were very likely representatives of *Homo heidelbergensis*.

Because they were hunters and gatherers (and occasional scavengers), it seems very probable that the nomadic lifestyle imposed on *Homo erectus* by their wandering and migratory prey must have affected them enormously. It forced them to cover new ground and exposed them to varied new experiences and sensations. All primates are curious, and doubtless *Homo erectus* explored the diverse features of their enlarging world with interest. They must have had to solve new problems, such as how to transport food and water as they moved from one hunting ground to the next. No direct evidence has been discovered so far to show that they had receptacles of any sort, but one can speculate that they might have used crude bags made of animal hides or perhaps containers made of wood, leaves, or even clay. Material for toolmaking was probably transported, at least in small quantities, and tools were often made at the butchery site. As *Homo erectus* and their descendants extended their range northward, the cooler climates could have stimulated the control and use of fire and the construction of clothing of some sort. Both these behaviors can be related to meat eating. The cold, harsh winters of the north deprived the early hunters of a year-round supply of vegetable food and put an even higher premium on meat. Clothing could have been made from the pelts of animals; impressions in the ground at Terra Amata and elsewhere suggest to some researchers that 300,000 to 400,000 years ago early humans were using animal skins as clothing and/or bedding.

NEW SOCIAL DEVELOPMENTS

As *Homo erectus*, *H. heidelbergensis*, and others adopted a hunting-and-gathering way of life, humans took a major step toward setting themselves apart from their animal ancestors and establishing the genus *Homo* as supreme among the creatures of the earth. The dependence on meat and the expansion into temperate regions of the Old World must have profoundly influenced human social organization.

The expansion into temperate zones was perhaps the high adventure of those million years or so during which *Homo erectus* people established themselves as nature's dominant species. Before the great expansion, their immediate ancestors had been evolving by the dictates of natural selection in much the same way as other animals had: adapting imperceptibly to their environment; depending on a generally benign habitat for food and warmth; and having very little awareness of the past or thought for the future. But when *Homo erectus* spread into the world's previously unpeopled regions, their relationship to natural selection began to alter. *Homo erectus* prevailed over the obstacles of new environments not because they developed new bodily equipment but because they had a better brain. At least by the time of late *Homo erectus*, they were meeting the challenges of changing conditions with solutions of their own making, rather than waiting until evolution created solutions for them. For the first time, hominids were taking an active part in their own adaptation and evolution. Humans' "cultural environment" was beginning to take shape.

The Evolution of Male and Female Roles

As discussed in Chapter 9, it is very difficult to speculate about the behavior and social relations of early *Homo* (*H. habilis* and *H. rudolfensis*) because of a paucity of information about anatomy and subsistence patterns, and because these hominids were probably on the fringe of humanness with regard to intelligence. But with *Homo erectus* it's an entirely different story. Thanks to the discovery of critical post-cranial material at Nariokotome and elsewhere, and because we believe these hominids were the first to live a hunting-and-gathering lifestyle, we can sketch a much more complete picture of their lives.

Let's begin with the implications of *Homo erectus*'s pattern of brain growth. Among modern humans, because of constraints on women's pelvic dimensions related to efficient bipedal locomotion, babies are born with brains that are only about 25 percent of adult size (in comparison, a chimpanzee infant has accomplished 45 percent of total brain growth at birth; see Box 12–1). As we all know, modern human babies are **altricial** or helpless at birth and completely dependent on adult care. Ours is a particular kind of helplessness, however, that is called **secondary altriciality** because it affects mainly the motor skills and not the senses. Although their sensory systems quickly become functional, modern babies' motor skills take a long time to develop. But our babies are accomplishing something vital during their period of motor helplessness: they are undergoing very rapid postnatal brain growth that will carry them to about 70 percent of adult brain size by one year of age. Thus, modern babies play catch-up in brain growth during their first year of life, but only at the cost of requiring full-time care. And, of course, since humans are mammals, the responsibility for the care and feeding of dependent infants falls primarily on their mothers, producing an immediate distinction between women and men that has had far-reaching effects on their respective roles in many cultures.

The pelvis of the *Homo erectus* boy from Nariokotome has been studied by Alan Walker and Christopher Ruff. From the adolescent's pelvis, Walker and Ruff have calculated the probable pelvic dimensions of *Homo erectus* adults and have concluded that this species resembled modern humans in producing secondarily altricial infants. Among *Homo erectus* people, infants' brains were probably about 22 percent of adult size at birth but grew rapidly (more than doubling in size) during the immediate postnatal period, when the infants were almost certainly totally dependent on adult care. The strong implication of this finding is that, as among modern humans, *Homo erectus* women were cast in the role of primary caretakers for extremely helpless infants and very likely experienced some behavioral limitations as a result.

As noted in the last chapter, the large size and modern body build of *Homo erectus* people and their development of effective butchering tools suggest to us that they were becoming increasingly dependent on meat as a dietary staple, and that they were obtaining animal resources primarily by hunting, although scavenging would have continued as well. Since *Homo erectus* women would have had the primary responsibility for slow-developing, dependent children, it seems likely that this species was the first to show a sexual division of subsistence activities—women doing *most* of the gathering and men doing *most* of the hunting (Figure 12–3). We are emphasizing the word "most" here because among modern hunters-and-gatherers the sexual division of subsistence activities is often less than clear-cut. Indeed, in a few living hunter-and-gatherer societies, women make a major contribution to the

Altricial the state of being born helpless and requiring parental care.

Secondary altriciality the phenomenon of an infant's motor skills requiring a lengthy period of postnatal development, as opposed to its sensory systems, which are functional at birth or soon after; characteristic of *H. erectus* and later hominids (see *altricial*).

BOX 12-1

CURRENT ISSUE: *Brains, Babies, and Bipedalism*

Human babies are born with heads much too large for their bodies. Far from being concerned about this anatomical mismatch, however, most people think it makes the top-heavy little rascals all the more attractive. Well, newborns with big heads may be cute, but they spell trouble for a significant number of human births and thus provide a good example of an evolutionary compromise between competing selection pressures. The following table contains data for apes and humans on the relative size of newborns' heads compared to the smallest dimension of mothers' birth canals (for apes, cranial breadth is given as a percentage of the width of the birth canal inlet [top of the canal]; for humans, cranial length, not breadth, is given as a percentage of inlet width since that is the dimension that squeezes through the inlet's transverse diameter; data from Rosenberg, 1992.).

SPECIES	INFANT HEAD AS PERCENTAGE OF PELVIC INLET WIDTH
Orangutans	73.1
Chimpanzees	72.4
Gorillas	64.4
Modern humans	101.8

The numbers show that baby apes' heads are considerably smaller than their mothers' birth canals. As a consequence, ape births tend to be quick (usually two hours or less) and difficult deliveries are unusual. In comparison, human babies have heads that are slightly longer than their mothers' birth canals are wide. Thus, human deliveries routinely take three to four times as long as those of apes and run a much higher risk of complications. One measure of the degree of difficulty of human births is the maternal mortality rate. According to Laurel Cobb (personal communication), an international consultant on maternal and child health, worldwide about 320 women die giving birth for every 100,000 new babies (40 percent of these deaths are due to obstructed labor or hemorrhage). In less developed countries, where medical care is often inadequate, as many as 900 maternal deaths per 100,000 live births can occur. Of the two figures, the second undoubtedly comes closer to measuring maternal mortality among *Homo sapiens* prior to the advent of effective medical care.

The evolutionary conflict noted above pitted the biomechanical requirements of bipedalism against the need for larger birth canals as brain size rose in the genus *Homo*. Compared to the australopithecines, modern humans show both bigger brains (two to three times larger among adults; Table 8–3) and more narrow pelvises (this made lateral balancing easier and bipedalism more energy efficient). Among the apes, and perhaps the australopithecines as well, nearly half of total brain growth occurs before birth, but for this pattern to have been continued among large-brained *Homo*, the birth canal needed to be enlarged. Lateral expansion (widening) of the pelvis was not mechanically feasible, however, because it would have required either increasing the mass of the lesser gluteal muscles or lengthening the neck of the femur (see Chapter 5 and Figure 5–32). Given these anatomical constraints and the continuing strong pressure for brain enlargement, natural selection fashioned the modern human compromise: match the newborn head to the maternal birth canal as closely as possible and reduce the prenatal percentage of total brain growth to about 25 percent. As described in this chapter, the latter change led to the phenomenon of secondary altriciality.

Pain and difficulty in childbirth are part of the human condition. Biblical literalists believe this was part of God's curse on Eve for her disobedience in the Garden of Eden. Evolutionary biologists, on the other hand, understand it as the result of natural selection generating a tightly balanced compromise between bipedal locomotion and prenatal brain development. Women in the process of giving birth undoubtedly are too busy with the task at hand to worry about which explanation is correct. ■

FIGURE 12–3   *Homo erectus* probably evolved a pattern of division of labor similar to that of these present-day !Kung San. While the men search for meat, the women gather and dig vegetable foods.

hunting effort, while in all such cultures, men may do some gathering of vegetable foods. There is nothing about their respective anatomies that strictly limits the sexes to different subsistence roles.

Together *Homo erectus* women and men no doubt made an effective economic team. Based on studies of modern hunters-and-gatherers, it can be estimated that vegetable foods gathered mostly by women made up 60 to 80 percent of the diet, the remaining 20 to 40 percent consisting of meat usually obtained by male hunters (Figure 12–4). Not only is it likely that gathering made the largest contribution to the *Homo erectus* diet, but it is important to note that it also represented an entirely new subsistence pattern for hominoids. Occasional hunting of small game followed by food sharing can be documented among apes, and it almost certainly characterized the australopithecines and early *Homo* as well. But gathering, along with the subsequent sharing of vegetable foods, was a novel and important development not found among apes. Undoubtedly, when *Homo erectus* women assumed the primary role as gatherers of vegetable foods, it had significant effects on social relations. Furthermore, gathering almost certainly provided important selection pressures for the development of material culture. Of primary importance would have been the invention of containers, such as animal skins, bark cloth, woven sacks or wooden bowls, that would have enabled the gatherers to bring home a substantial load each day. And finally, gathering, along with hunting, no doubt

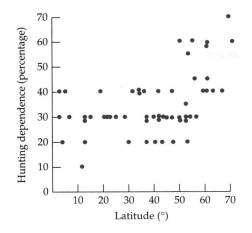

Figure 12-4 Among living hunters-and-gatherers, the percentage of food obtained through hunting varies strongly with latitude. In tropical and subtropical areas, hunting generally contributes 10 to 40 percent of the total food, while in higher latitudes (as among certain Eskimo groups) the bulk of the diet may come from meat.

contributed to the development of a migratory lifestyle, as *Homo erectus* bands moved seasonally within their home ranges or territories in search of fluctuating vegetable and animal resources.

Families and Bands

As mentioned above, a sexual division of subsistence activities strongly implies food sharing, and it seems quite safe to conclude that this practice existed among *Homo erectus* people. Women and men shared the fruits (often, literally) of their labors, and judging from their body size, the combined diet must have been quite nutritious. But with whom would these people have shared their food? Certainly mothers would have shared with their children, but what of sharing between men and women and between men and children? As suggested by Owen Lovejoy, it seems reasonable that adults would have shared frequently with their mates, and that women would have focused their sexual activity on supportive males. Men would then have been selected to share with the offspring of their mates since, presumably, these were also their own children in most cases. Combining a degree of paternity certainty with dietary interdependence might have been among the first steps toward the development of that human institution, the **family**, although whether that innovation took place among *Homo erectus* or later humans is unknown.

Family in human society, generally a unit marked by subsistence interdependence, sexual relationships among adults, and parent-offspring relationships.

    Homo erectus bands are thought to have had from 25 to more than 100 members (given their brain size, the "cognitive groups" of *Homo erectus* may have been 111 or more; see Chapter 9). Each band very likely moved within a large home range (or a territory, if it was defended). Among modern hunters-and-gatherers, population density ranges from one or less to about six persons per square mile (0.4 to 2.3 persons per square kilometer). Within the *Homo erectus* band, it seems likely that interdependence of males and females, of children and adults, and perhaps even of adult males was being intensified compared to that of earlier hominids. Some anthropologists think that increased male interdependence would have fostered male-male cooperation during hunting and thus increased the amount of meat coming into a band (Figure 12–5). Additionally, at some point in our hunting-and-

FIGURE 12–5   Two !Kung brothers and their wives go out in the morning to find food. The men carry springhare poles, bows, and quivers of arrows for hunting; the women, one carrying two children, will gather plant foods.

gathering past, people began to recognize and formalize relations between genetic kin. As discussed in Chapter 4, kinship affects the behavior and societies of non-human primates, although it is clearly not consciously or symbolically recognized. Monkeys and apes tend to behave altruistically toward kin more often than toward nonkin (such altruistic behavior may include food sharing) and to avoid close kin in mating. Thus food sharing by early hunters that went beyond the bounds of the immediate family was probably patterned by kin relations—and very likely the same was true of mate selection.

Incest Taboo

As family patterns developed among human hunters-and-gatherers, avoidance of inbreeding (sexual relations between closely related individuals) very likely became an established pattern. Inbreeding inhibitions have been found in several species of monkeys and apes. Among rhesus and Japanese macaques, for instance, there is apparently some sort of restraint against sex between mother and son; in chimpanzees this inhibition is usually extended to brother and sister, although in other ways the sex lives of chimpanzees are promiscuous. In modern humans an **incest** taboo is found in all societies (though a few societies have carefully defined exceptions). At some time during human evolution, then, the partial inhibition became a hard-and-fast taboo. It seems fair to suggest that such a development postdated *Homo erectus* given their apparently low level of speech and language. Perhaps it was not until the time of *Homo heidelbergensis* (or even later) that humans

Incest legally prohibited sexual relations between kin. How closely related individuals must be for mating to be considered incestuous differs from culture to culture.

grew more aware of kinship structures within the community and developed sanctions against sex within the family. Perhaps familiarity inhibited sexual interest. This change may have functioned to retain stability in the family and the broader social structure. Bonds within the family may certainly be threatened by incest, and development of bonding between descent groups (whenever they evolved) would have depended on extending the incest taboo to a widening group of kin. That extensive inbreeding can be genetically undesirable was surely not known to the early hunters, yet in this respect also a taboo would be an advantageous behavior pattern.

Exogamy

Ultimately, the early hunters-and-gatherers must have shown an increasing tendency to look around widely for mates until, eventually, they reached beyond their own band to select partners from neighboring groups. Among modern humans this practice is called **exogamy**, and it involves the exchange of marriage partners (incipient exogamy probably did not include formal marriages). The beginnings of exogamy may be rooted in the ancient primate pattern of one or both sexes emigrating from the natal group as young adults and thus avoiding close inbreeding (see Table 4–4). Among the early hunters, exogamous mating could also have promoted the development of blood ties between groups that would have encouraged intergroup harmony. If competition for game among neighboring bands was a potential problem at the time, this development could have been of great social importance. When bands with adjoining hunting ranges are related, sharing develops; when game and other foods become scarce, the bands can hunt freely over one another's ranges. By bringing in mates strange to the group, exogamy would have made family ties and band identity even more important. Rules of exogamy—which today cause individuals to marry outside their social group and may even specify the outside group into which they must marry—are characteristic of all existing traditional human societies and are undoubtedly an ancient custom, and certainly one of extraordinary importance.

> **Exogamy** among modern humans, the pattern of marrying (and mating) between individuals from different social groups.

Home Base

With the evolution of a sexual division of subsistence activities and child care, the early hunters-and-gatherers must also have shown another cultural development vital to society's growth: the home base. As discussed in Chapter 9, the presence of home bases in pre-*erectus* hominids is questionable, although a few researchers think they can detect evidence for their existence in the archaeological record. The advent of the hunting-and-gathering lifestyle, however—with males and females foraging separately and males ranging widely—would almost certainly have necessitated the creation of the home base. Here children could be looked after, women could stockpile the fruits of their gathering, and men could bring their supplies of meat after a day or two on the hunt.

As explained in Chapter 11, we think the lithic and anatomical evidence indicates a hunting-and-gathering lifestyle for *Homo erectus* and, therefore, we hypothesize that this species used home bases. Direct evidence of home bases is scanty, however, and currently limited to late *Homo erectus* times (e.g., Zhoukoudian and, possibly, Terra Amata; see Chapter 11). Further archaeological work on this problem is urgently needed.

Whenever they developed, once home bases existed they gave humans a new social blueprint and one unique among primates. For one thing, the existence of a home meant that the sick or infirm no longer faced abandonment along the way; they had a place where they could rest and mend in comparative safety. "For a wild primate," Sherwood Washburn and Irven DeVore noted, "a fatal sickness is one that separates it from the troop, but for man it is one from which he cannot recover even while protected and fed at the home base. . . . It is the home base that changes sprained ankles and fevers from fatal diseases to minor ailments."

Thus development of the home could have affected the normal life span. Still, only a few *Homo erectus* individuals are believed to have attained the age of forty, and anyone who survived to fifty would have reached a ripe old age indeed. Most died much earlier, as shown by the evidence from the cave at Zhoukoudian: 50 percent of the human bones found there belonged to children under fourteen.

For the long-range development of human society, the real importance of the home base was that it provided a medium for cultural growth. Within its safe circle could grow a fellowship, a self-awareness and trust, and a sense of community that was new on earth. There people could begin to learn more than simply how to survive; they could improve their tools and weapons, evolve complex linguistic skills, and look not only to the past but to the future.

INTRASPECIES AGGRESSION

Theories of Aggression

The home, for all it contributed to human growth, could also be involved in another, and much less desirable, hallmark of human society—one that some observers think they can trace to *Homo erectus*. That is humans' unhappy tendency to do violence to other humans.

Author Robert Ardrey hypothesized that people instinctively guard whatever territory they consider their own, such as that of a home base, and will defend it, violently if necessary, against all intruders. He suggested that an inborn drive for aggression carried over from animal forebears explains all humans' violent behavior, from wars to riots to throwing dishes in a domestic quarrel. Konrad Lorenz, an Austrian authority on animal behavior, argued that this innate drive will express itself in one way or another; if it is not channeled productively, in society's terms, it will burst out destructively—sooner or later, but inevitably.

Most anthropologists and ethnologists today disagree with Lorenz's and Ardrey's hypotheses. They believe that humans have no specific innate drive for aggression but merely the potential for this kind of behavior, and that this potential is shaped by society. When people are threatened or think they are threatened by another, their response may just as well be to flee the threat as to fight the provoker. All vertebrate animals are provided with a dual innate response to danger of "fight or flight." Thus all species have the possibility of peaceful coexistence. Among humans, culture and experience determine which response they make.

Aggression Among *Homo erectus*

The possibility of conflict within or between bands of *Homo erectus* cannot be entirely eliminated. Much that we know portrays *Homo erectus* as solid and industrious social humans, sharing the burdens of a primitive existence. Yet among the fossils unearthed on the cave floor at Zhoukoudian were human skulls that were faceless and had been opened at the base. This evidence can be explained in many ways; some archaeologists conclude that the first humans practiced cannibalism and ate the brains of the dead. Savage as this act is now considered, it does not necessarily make *Homo erectus* less human. In fact, it could be taken as evidence of a step toward modern humanity.

Among the tribal peoples that have been known to practice cannibalism in recent times, the act is nearly always carried out not for the sake of food, but as a ritual (Figure 12–6). The distinction between dietary and ritual cannibalism is important; it is extremely rare for people to eat other people merely for food.

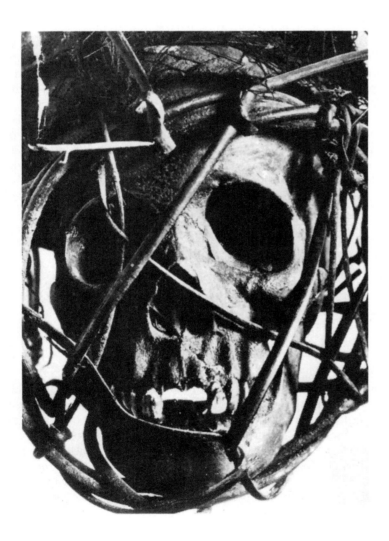

FIGURE 12–6   Bornean headhunters usually keep the skull of the man they have killed as a trophy. The base of the skull is always damaged; the foramen magnum has been enlarged and the brain removed. It is normally eaten, an example of ritual cannibalism.

Writing of twentieth-century headhunters, G. H. R. von Koenigswald explained, "The head hunter is not content merely to possess the skull, but opens it and takes out the brain, which he eats in order by this means to acquire the wisdom and skill of his foe." The very evidence suggesting that the first humans ate each other and each other's brains, then, may suggest that they had some spiritual notion that cannibalism could increase their powers.

On the other hand, some archaeologists, including Lewis Binford, have criticized this traditional interpretation of the deposits and human bones at Zhoukoudian. Binford points out that the bones of *H. erectus* are found in deposits that also contain a wide range of other bone fragments, together with remains of numerous predators, including the Chinese hyena. The removal of the faces of the human skulls and the destruction of the skull base are exactly what happens when gnawing predators or scavengers chew out the face of their prey. But earlier investigators also believed that the way in which the human long bones were broken at Zhoukoudian indicated cannibalism: the breaks were distinctive and even diagnostic of human activity. Yet it was already known as early as 1939 that hyenas chewed and split long bones in this way. So it seems clear that, while it is entirely possible that early humans occasionally practiced cannibalism, the archaeological evidence at this site is not irrefutable.

Whatever the correct explanation of the Zhoukoudian materials, conflicts between bands, if they occurred, must have been rare in an uncrowded world such as that of *Homo erectus*. No doubt true warfare was a later (and dubious) achievement that probably came after humans settled down on the land, became a more numerous species, and forged cultures that encouraged individual and group pride in possessions, territories, and beliefs, even as they fostered art, science, and literature.

These are today's problems, of course, and there is little reason to think they afflicted *Homo erectus*. They were confronting their own challenges and, with perseverance and imagination, solved them remarkably well. To their success, and that of their descendants, *Homo heidelbergensis*, we owe many of our flaws and triumphs.

SUMMARY

This chapter has described several anatomical, behavioral, and social developments that accompanied the hunting-and-gathering lifestyle: relatively hairless skin allowing the loss of body heat by sweating; a variety of new hunting techniques; intensification of the sexual division of child care (linked to the evolution of secondarily altricial infants); sexual division of subsistence activities (men hunting, women gathering); the family as a social unit; incest avoidance and, ultimately, exogamy; home bases; and interband aggression. Although we believe that this package of innovations began its evolution among *Homo erectus*, undoubtedly it was incomplete in many ways, given the relatively small brains and limited communication skills of those early people. *Homo heidelbergensis*—the immediate descendants of *H. erectus*—and later humans were probably responsible for many of the traits we attribute to hunters-and-gatherers. Collectively, the hunting-and-gathering package made an important contribution to the modernization of humankind.

POSTSCRIPT

A Chinese proverb says that a picture is worth a thousand words. The same can be true, of course, of a name, a descriptive term, or a slogan. All can conjure up entire gestalts, complex units composed of associated elements that collectively go far beyond the literal meaning of the name, term, or slogan. Take, for example, hunting-and-gathering.

As used in this chapter to describe the subsistence activities of *Homo erectus* people and their descendants, the term hunting-and-gathering simply identifies the two main ways we think these early humans obtained food. The term itself says nothing about amounts of food obtained by hunting versus gathering, or the identities of the hunters and the gatherers, or the value placed by the culture on hunted versus gathered food items. Read literally, the term says that early humans hunted some and gathered some. Period. But things are not so simple. In anthropological circles, hunting-and-gathering is a loaded label. Ever since the development during the mid-twentieth century of the "hunting hypothesis" (described by Matt Cartmill in *A View to a Death in the Morning*), the term hunting-and-gathering has carried a long train of implied elements, including sexual division of subsistence activities, with men hunting and women gathering; the greater value (either nutritional or symbolic) of meat over vegetable foods, with men thus making a more important dietary contribution than women; men as far-ranging providers and protectors and women as stay-at-home dependents; men as strong and aggressive and women as weak and passive; men as the creators and users of technology and women as nontechnological creatures; men as dominant and women as subordinate; and finally, men as the "movers and shakers" of human evolution, with women riding men's evolutionary coattails.

No wonder many researchers, and especially feminist anthropologists, fulminate against the term! In hindsight, the original hunting-and-gathering gestalt was strongly sex-biased in its overemphasis on men and its deemphasis on the role of women. It's time for some adjustments. First, as discussed in this chapter, although among living hunters-and-gatherers men do *most* of the hunting and women do *most* of the gathering, the subsistence activities of the sexes may overlap significantly, and in some cultures women hunt a good deal. Second, although there is much variation from culture to culture, meat obtained by hunting usually makes up a considerably smaller portion of the diet than plant foods obtained by gathering. Thus, if the term were intended as a literal description of dietary proportions, with the larger portion listed first, it should read "gathering-and-hunting" (many anthropologists prefer to use it this way). And furthermore, if one sex had to be identified as the primary dietary providers, it would be women. Third, the hunting-gathering dichotomy has few clear technological implications. Both forms of subsistence activities would have been enhanced by the use of implements: stone picks, digging sticks, and wooden or fabric containers for gathering; wooden spears and stone tools for killing animals; and stone or bamboo implements for butchering. Surely there were plenty of opportunities (and selection pressures) for both sexes to make technological contributions. And finally, it simply makes no sense to talk of one sex leading the way in evolution, with the other following in its wake. The physical traits and behavior (including subsistence behavior) of each sex have evolved *in the context of the opposite sex*. In other words, females have "enabled" males' traits, and males have "enabled" females' traits. It takes two to tango (or, in this case, evolve).

We have chosen to use the term hunting-and-gathering in its traditional form because we want to emphasize the increased importance of hunting among *Homo erectus* people and later humans. Our usage is certainly not intended to elevate or demean the cultural or evolutionary contributions of either sex. Over the last 2 million years, humans have become extremely omnivorous in their diet—gathering, scavenging, catching, killing (and long after *Homo erectus*, growing) a wide variety of foodstuffs. Because meat is harder to obtain than vegetable food, because it is rarer, more nutritious, and very tasty, it has probably always been more highly valued than vegetables, even though its total dietary contribution is less. Nonetheless, both women and men have contributed in important ways to change and expansion in the human diet, and in turn, dietary diversity has played a major role in the evolutionary success of humankind.

REVIEW QUESTIONS

1. Review the evidence regarding the question of whether *Homo erectus* people were hunters. What sort of archaeological or anatomical evidence is needed to settle the matter conclusively?
2. Explain how the production of secondarily altricial infants may have been linked to a sexual division of labor among *Homo erectus*. Can you envision a child care system that would not have restricted the ranging and activities of *Homo erectus* women?
3. If *Homo erectus* women gathered and men hunted, what are the implications about who made and used the various types of Acheulean tools?
4. What form do you think the first human families took? Monogynous? Polygynous? Review the factors that may have contributed to the evolution of the family.
5. Several complex social factors are discussed in this chapter including the interdependence of family members, incest avoidance, and exogamy. Discuss whether these traits could have developed among *Homo erectus* or if they are better attributed to later humans. Support your position with archaeological and/or anatomical evidence.
6. What is your view of the hunting-and-gathering lifestyle as described here? Is it still overblown and sex-biased, or does it seem to be a reasonable picture of early human subsistence and social life?

SUGGESTED FURTHER READING

Binford, L., and C. K. Ho. "Taphonomy at a Distance. Zhoukoudian, 'The Cave Home of Bejing Man'?" *Current Anthropology*, 26, 1985.

Cartmill, M. *A View to a Death in the Morning.* Harvard University Press, 1993.

Conroy, G. C. *Reconstructing Human Origins.* W. W. Norton, 1997.

Isaac, G. L. "The Diet of Early Man: Aspects of Archaeological Evidence from Lower and Middle Pleistocene Sites in Africa." *World Archaeology*, 2, 1971.

Thieme, H. "Lower Palaeolithic Hunting Spears From Germany." *Nature*, 385, 1997.

Trevathan, W. *Human Birth: An Evolutionary Perspective.* Aldine de Gruyter, 1987.

Walker, A., and C. Ruff. "The Reconstruction of the Pelvis," in A. Walker and R. Leakey, eds., *The Nariokotome Homo erectus Skeleton.* Harvard University Press, 1993.

INTERNET RESOURCES

SCIENCE NEWS ONLINE

http://www.sciencenews.org/sn_arc97/3_1_97/fob2.htm

(Further information on the 1997 discovery of 400,000-year-old wooden spears in Germany.)

Other websites containing information about *Homo erectus* and its culture can be found at the ends of Chapters 10 and 11. The reader is referred to those lists.

USEFUL SEARCH TERMS:

Homo erectus

Human evolution

Chapter 13

THE EVOLUTION OF LANGUAGE AND THE BRAIN

These naturally occurring endocasts from South Africa give a good idea of the topography of the australopithecine brain.

$\mathbf{H}$*e gave man speech, and speech created thought, Which is the measure of the universe.*
         PERCY BYSSHE SHELLEY, 1792–1822. Prometheus Unbound, II, IV, 72–73.

$\mathbf{S}$*peech was given to man to disguise his thoughts.*
         Attributed to CHARLES MAURICE DE TALLEYRAND, 1754–1838.

OVERVIEW

Of all of the various traits of living humans, spoken language appears to be unique. At first glance, language and speech seem to separate us rather cleanly from all other living organisms, and virtually all theories of human origins include spoken language as a key evolutionary milestone in our history. But how wide is the "language gap" between humans and other animals, when did it first appear, and how closely is it related to differences in brain anatomy? This chapter addresses these and other questions as it describes the anatomical specializations (brain size and organization, and throat and mouth anatomy) that enable humans to talk. The chapter also compares human language to the communication patterns of wild monkeys and apes, discusses apes' abilities to learn gestural and computer-based language systems in the laboratory, and reviews the hominid fossil record for evidence of the beginnings of spoken language. The chapter ends with a discussion of the archaeological evidence for the appearance of the fully integrated human mind. Important topics and concepts include early theories of language development; primate communication in the wild (including the production of vocal symbols); laboratory studies of apes' capacity for language; language areas of the human brain; contributions of the pharynx to speech; brain enlargement among primates and its implications for theories of mind and language; and, finally, the archaeological evidence for the evolution of the mind among hominids.

 Mini-Timeline

DATE (YEARS B.P.)	SPECIES AND RECONSTRUCTED COMMUNICATION
130,000 – present	*Homo sapiens*: modern speech and language; modern mind achieved
800,000 – 100,000(?)	*Homo heidelbergensis*: modern speech and language evolving, but not yet achieved; mind approaching modernity(?)
1.9 million (?)–300,000	*Homo erectus*: rudimentary speech and language (at best); primitive mind(?)
2.4–1.6 million	Early *Homo*: probably lacked speech and language; primitive mind(?)
5.6–1.0 million	Australopithecinae: almost certainly lacked speech and language; apelike mind (?)

WAYS OF COMMUNICATING

As the social life of humans grew more complex, the ability to communicate must also have developed. Spoken language, we can now see, was humankind's passport to a totally new level of social relationship, organization, and thought; it was the tool that allowed humans to vary expressions to meet changing conditions instead of being limited by less flexible patterns of communication, as other primates are.

Early Theories on the Origins of Speech

When did hominids begin to speak? How did they start? What did their first words sound like? Investigators have been seeking answers to these questions for thousands of years. In ancient Egypt, the pharaoh Psammetichus ordered two infants reared where they could hear no human voice. He hoped that when at last they spoke, uninfluenced by the sound of the Egyptian tongue, they would resort to their earliest ancestors' language, which confidently assumed lurked within them. One child finally uttered something that sounded like *bekos*, or "bread" in the language of Phrygia, an ancient nation of central Asia Minor. Phrygian, said Psammetichus triumphantly, was obviously humankind's original tongue.

Many centuries later, King James IV of Scotland tried a similar experiment with two babies. The result, he let it be known, was that his experimental subjects spoke passable Hebrew. This report must have pleased Biblical scholars of the day, for they had contended all along that Adam and Eve had conversed in Hebrew. A Swede of the late seventeenth century believed otherwise: he announced that in the Garden of Eden, God had used Swedish, Adam Danish, and the serpent French.

As time went on, all sorts of theories sprang up about the origins of speech. The eighteenth-century French philosopher Jean-Jacques Rousseau envisioned a group of tongue-tied human beings getting together and stammering out more-or-less overnight a language they could use. Why they felt the need for one, and how they had communicated with each other before they had invented the words to communicate with, Rousseau failed to mention. His contemporary, the German romantic historian Johann Gottfried Herder, also espoused the notion that language was humanmade, not God-instilled, as most people believed. Anything so illogical, so imperfect as language could hardly be attributed to a divinity, Herder argued. But he would have none of Rousseau's ideas, either. Instead, he saw language springing from the innermost nature of humans, in response to an impulse to speak. Just how language took shape Herder could not say, but he imagined that it had started when humans began imitating the sounds of the creatures around them, using eventually the imitative sounds as the words for the animals themselves. This theory, known today among those who disagree with it as the "bow-wow thesis," was followed by a number of others, similarly named and ridiculed, ranging from the whistle-and-grunt thesis to the ouch-ouch, which claimed that language had arisen from exclamations of pain, pleasure, fear, surprise, and so on.

Darwin's concept of human evolution provided a new way of approaching the problem of the origin of spoken language. Scientists are now beginning to develop numerous theories about how we came to speak. Studies of animals, particularly monkeys and apes, both in the laboratory and in the wild, have given us an understanding of the foundation on which language is based; they have shown that there is considerably more of the ape in talkative humans than most people think. Examination of that foundation is necessary, because understanding what communication was like before there were words helps make clear why and how spoken language evolved and emphasizes the tremendous biological and cultural changes that it made possible.

Communication Among Animals

Nonhuman vertebrates and insects have some intriguing ways of communicating. Honeybees perform a kind of dance on the honeycomb; the dance accurately transmits information about the direction, distance, and nature of a food source. Dogs and wolves use scents to communicate in addition to barks, howls, and growls; they also use a system of visual signals that includes not only facial expression and body movement but also the position of the tail.

Communications get more complex as the social organizations of animals do, and next to ourselves the nonhuman primates have the most intricate systems of all. Far from depending only on vocalizations, nonhuman primates seem to rely heavily on combinations of gestures, facial expressions, and postures as well as scents and sounds (Figure 13–1). They apparently are able to lend many shades of meaning to this body language vocabulary. Often they use sounds as a means of

FIGURE 13–1   Facial expression is one of the most important modes of nonverbal communication in both chimpanzees and people. The functions of such expressions in the two species are quite closely related.

FIGURE 13–2   A dominant male chimpanzee reassures a young male that is presenting his rump in appeasement. As a result, the younger male now feels able to turn and face his superior.

calling attention to their other signals. On some important occasions, however, only sounds will do. On discovering something good to eat, a monkey or ape will let out a cry of pleasure that brings the rest of the troop running; sensing danger, it will give a shriek that causes its companions to seek shelter frantically.

This wordless communication system serves the nonhuman primates extremely well. As social animals living in troops, they use it to keep in touch with one another at all times. More important, it allows individuals to display their feelings and to recognize at a glance the intentions and moods of others, enabling them to react appropriately. Many of the signals express the established hierarchy of dominance and submission within the group (see Figure 13–2). A subordinate male chimpanzee, seeing signs of aggression directed at him by a male of superior rank, backs up to the other and presents his rump in a gesture of appeasement—unless he intends to challenge the other male. Different signals, vocal and visual, help individuals stay in contact when moving through the community territory. Still other signals promote mating behavior or foster good mother-infant relations. A mother chimpanzee has been observed to calm her disturbed youngster simply by touching its fingers lightly with hers (Figure 13–3). So complex and so delicate is this language of gesture in the chimpanzee that it cannot be said to be less evolved than our own. It serves to maintain an extremely complex social system.

Yet for all its complexity, and however well suited it may be to the chimpanzees' needs, such a communication system falls far short of humans' spoken language. As far as is known, nonhuman primates in the wild are limited in the ways they can refer to specific things in their environment and cannot communicate thought through the complex phonetic codes called words that are used by humans. Nor do they seem able to refer easily to the past or future with the aid of their signals. For them, what is out of sight is usually out of mind. The signal system narrowly circumscribes what can be communicated, and vocalizations and facial expressions are under limited voluntary control, at best.

This is not to say that the nonhuman primates' vocal signals are entirely unspecific. Some apes indicate the desirability of the food they are eating by the intensity of their food calls. During normal feeding, chimpanzees emit food grunts,

FIGURE 13–3   Among chimpanzees, as among humans, physical contact is a most important means of communication between individuals. Even a touch is reassuring. This photograph is of wild chimpanzees in Tanzania.

but for a favorite food they give the more excited food bark. They still cannot say "banana," of course, but they communicate something more than simply "food." Even more specialized is the danger-call system of the African vervet monkeys, which have three alarm calls for three kinds of predator and a fourth for baboons. The vervets use a chitter for snakes (Figure 13–4), a chirp for ground-dwelling carnivores, and a *r-raup* sound to warn of birds of prey. When tape recordings of their alarm calls are played back to them, a chirp is enough to send the vervets scrambling to the tips of branches, well out of reach of ground animals, whereas a *r-raup* launches them from the trees into the thickets below, where predatory birds cannot get at them. As the young mature, they are able to make finer distinctions between the different alarm calls. A cry of "Watch out—eagle!" is beyond their capabilities, but it is also beyond their needs. They do not have to know whether it is an eagle or a hawk diving on them; what matters is that they get the message that the danger is from above, so that they can flee in the right direction.

Young vervets sometimes make mistakes in giving alarm calls, and as they grow up they improve their performance. The calls can also be adapted and modified for different circumstances. This evidence suggests that the alarm calls are learned or are reinforced by learning rather than being simply innate.

In addition to vervets' predator-specific alarm calls, some other species of nonhuman primates are also capable of conveying specific environmental information

FIGURE 13–4   Vervets (*Cercopithecus aethiops*) are here photographed responding to the presence of a python. The appropriate snake alarm call caused the monkeys to run to the nearby acacia trees.

by using vocalizations. For example, rhesus macaques have five acoustically different scream vocalizations that they can give when threatened or attacked. These screams are essentially recruitment devices (cries for help), and primatologists Sarah and Harold Gouzoules and Peter Marler have found that the particular scream an animal gives depends on the identity of its opponent (kin or nonkin, dominant or subordinate) and the severity of the fight. Group mates are clearly able to screen the various calls for help, and their responses match the caller's level of danger.

Distinct alarm calls like those of vervet monkeys or foe-specific screams like rhesus monkeys' may be more widespread than we know. However, based on current knowledge the vocalizations which are most typical of the higher primates, such as grunts and barks, and which have been well studied in a number of species, especially chimpanzees, are quite distinct and do not indicate a particular feature of the environment so much as an inner state of excitement.

Limbic and Nonlimbic Communication

In their function, as well as in their causation, the vocal and visual signals used by nonhuman primates can be divided into two kinds. The majority of these signals, probably most of the vocal signals, as we have seen, express inner emotional and physiological states and are under only limited voluntary control. They allow all members of the troop to monitor the emotional status of all other members. All signals of this sort are generated mainly by a group of structures in the brain known collectively as the **limbic system** (the "emotional brain"). These signals come from below the level of conscious awareness, just as the human scream is generated. (We will take a closer look at the limbic system later in this chapter.)

In contrast to these signals, some gestures appear to communicate conscious will or intent. A chimpanzee holds out its hand as a gesture of submissive greeting or raises it in threat. A young baboon anxiously presents to a superior male, backing rump first toward him. A mother chimpanzee uses her hand to beckon to her infant or repel its approach. These conscious gestures, which are normal, voluntary movements, have taken on a role in communication. Because of the intentions and wishes they symbolize, they fall into a category very different from the expressions of emotion we have considered above. They are generated not by the limbic system but by the higher centers of the brain, just as human language is. It is for this reason that chimpanzees are excellent gestural mimics and, as we shall see, can learn sign language.

Ronald Myers and his colleagues at the University of California have clearly demonstrated the dichotomy. In humans, both the face and the voice are activated by two quite distinct brain mechanisms: the limbic system and the cortex. In the rhesus monkey, Myers and his colleagues have shown that the vocal apparatus and facial musculature typically are activated by the limbic system alone and are poorly accessible to voluntary control by the motor cortex of the brain (labeled *motor output* in Figure 13–14).

Both kinds of communication are seen in our own behavior. We, too, have a repertory of wordless signals that universally express emotions: a person has only to smile to demonstrate friendly intentions; clenched fists and jaws, scowls, and frowns are unmistakable signs of anger or disappointment; and the laugh, the cry, and the scream are direct expressions of inner psychological and physiological states. Humans even have acquired an involuntary signal other primates do not have: the blush, over which most people have little or no control, but which sends a clear message about what is going on inside the brain. And when humans are most excited, they often show it by speechlessness. Such basic signals are in a different category from the many other body motions humans use, such as shaking and nodding the head, shrugging the shoulders, and clapping the hands; these are really abbreviated substitutes for spoken language and vary in meaning from one place to another. Nonverbal communication is still an essential component in modern human relationships (see Figure 13–1).

In this context, the observations made of vervet monkeys by Robert Seyfarth and Dorothy Cheney are of the greatest interest. Alarm calls, which appear to benefit kin (kin selection) as well as the alarmist itself (as a result of reciprocal altruism) are made by many social species of birds and mammals. Among primates, vervets have received the most detailed study. It is clear that their calls, described above, refer to objects in the vervets' environment and are not merely expressions of emotion (no support for the "ouch-ouch" hypothesis). Thus they are described as *semantic* rather than *affective*: they are words, not vocalized emotions. The sounds are arbitrary and do not resemble in any way the objects to which they refer (no support for the "bow-wow" hypothesis). However, it must be added that there is certainly an affective component of emphasis, such as volume, length, or rate of delivery, just as there is in human language.

Limbic system the emotional brain; a group of structures in the brain important in regulating such behavior as eating, drinking, aggression, sexual activity, and expressions of emotion. Proportionately smaller in humans than in other primates, it operates below the level of consciousness.

To students of language evolution the vervets are fascinating. The research suggests that vervets have evolved the ability to use vocalizations which are not generated by the limbic system but which are probably learned and therefore generated in the cortex. These symbols, as we may correctly call them, have many of the characteristics of human language and show us that the higher primates do have the capability of developing such symbols, which indicate how language may have first made its appearance in our own evolution. It remains to be seen whether the great apes also carry such intimations of linguistic ability.

Signals generated by the limbic system are less important to humans than they are to other animals, for they make up a smaller part of humans' total communication system. Much of the information necessary for social interaction among humans is conveyed vocally; a blind human can communicate satisfactorily. But deafness from birth probably has a greater impact on communication; because babies born deaf cannot hear and imitate spoken words, they can learn to speak only with great difficulty. Fortunately they can use sign language—a real language, although nonvocal.

Nature of Language

Spoken language provides a magnificently efficient and versatile means of communication. It is a complex system of chains of symbols to which meanings have been assigned by cultural convention. The number of meanings that can be so assigned is, in practice, infinite. Its coded series of sounds conveys conscious thought at least ten times faster than any other method of signaling can—faster than hand signs, moving pictures, or even other kinds of vocalizations. Through language, humans can step outside themselves and give things and people names, reflect about others and themselves, and refer to the past and the future. Most important of all, language gives people the capacity to share their thoughts. As Sherwood Washburn and Shirley Strum wrote, "It is the communication of thought, rather than thought itself, that is unique to man, makes human cultures possible, that is the primary factor in separating man and beast." Discussion, complex bargaining, and democratic processes became a possibility for the first time.

Whenever spoken language evolved—and, as noted in earlier chapters, its full development probably postdated *Homo erectus*, despite that species' worldwide spread—it was the new and extraordinarily efficient means by which humans acquired and passed on from one generation to the next the flexible network of learned, rather than genetically inherited, behavior patterns and the knowledge that allowed them to alter their environment and adapt to new ones. Once language had evolved, culture had a symbolic form that changed its whole nature. From this point in human evolution, culture and its medium—language—were necessary for survival.

ABILITY TO SPEAK

Though it has long been clear that this watershed in evolution occurred largely because of the ability to use words to communicate symbolic meaning, it was not at all clear until recently why humans alone, and not their intelligent close relatives among the apes, are capable of speech. After all, apes have much of the vocal apparatus—lips, a tongue, and a larynx or voice box with vocal cords—that humans have.

Talking Apes?

An eighteenth-century French physician and philosopher Julien Offroy de la Mettrie imagined that apes were on about the same intellectual level as retarded humans and that all they needed to turn them into "perfect little gentlemen" was speech training. Not until early in the twentieth century, however, were any scientific attempts made to teach apes to talk. One couple worked with a chimpanzee called Viki, and only after six years of the most painstaking effort on their part and a great deal of frustration on hers did she manage to say, on cue, what sounded like "Mama," "Papa," "up," and "cup." It was clear that, although accomplished gestural mimics, chimpanzees cannot mimic vocally, as humans can.

A more recent experiment made by Beatrice and Robert Gardner produced a more startling result. A chimpanzee named Washoe learned by age five to understand more than 350 hand signals of the standard American Sign Language (ASL) of the deaf, and to use at least 150 of them correctly (see Figure 13–5). With these, she learned to name things and express her wants and needs by using those names. Another chimpanzee, Sarah, learned to communicate with her keepers by selecting

FIGURE 13–5 One of the most impressive projects for teaching a chimpanzee sign language was run by Columbia University psychologist Herbert Terrace. In this photograph, his subject, Nim Chimpsky, is signing "give" to his teacher and companion, Laura Petitto. Nim gained a firm command of about 125 signs, understood many more, and produced thousands of combinations of two or more signs.

from a number of plastic signs that carried particular meanings, which she placed on a magnetic board. A third chimpanzee, Lana, learned to communicate by pressing buttons on a computer keyboard. A gorilla, Koko, trained in ASL, by Penny Patterson of Stanford, has learned a vocabulary of more than 350 hand signals and understands many more. Others are teaching the orangutan. Constant training by humans enables these apes to associate visual symbols not only with concrete objects, but also with such abstracts as adjectives, verbs, and even prepositions. With these symbols it is claimed that they can construct simple sentences, which they use to express their desires. It is said that they can also lie, abuse their trainers, and invent new expressions. Examples of the latter include "water bird" for swan (Washoe) and "white tiger" for zebra and "eye hat" for mask (Koko). Koko has also combined signs to make entirely new words.

But of all the ape subjects used thus far in language studies, perhaps the most accomplished is Kanzi, a male bonobo under observation at Georgia State University. Psychobiologist Sue Savage-Rumbaugh has worked with Kanzi since his infancy. Kanzi showed early an outstanding—and spontaneous—ability to master the meaning of lexigrams (word symbols or icons) on a computer keyboard, and after learning a number of lexigrams, he began to combine them to produce the occasional multiword message (such as "Matata group room tickle," in which he requested that his mother, Matata, be allowed to join in a tickling session in the group room). But even more impressive, as a youngster Kanzi began to comprehend a certain amount of spoken English, and by age five he was able to respond correctly to Savage-Rumbaugh's spoken requests and directives (Kanzi has even shown the ability to respond appropriately to some novel sentences *the first time he heard them*). Furthermore, it appears that as part of his spontaneous development of speech comprehension, Kanzi may have picked up a bit of English **syntax**. According to Savage-Rumbaugh, Kanzi's lexigram-encoded messages to his human companions often have "a primitive English word order."

It is difficult to know precisely what to make of the linguistic feats of Kanzi and the other ape language subjects. Clearly these apes have a certain capacity for symbol comprehension and use, but their best efforts still do not exceed those of a two- to three-year-old human child. These studies show that, with exposure to humans (and usually after considerable instruction), apes can learn symbols and use a symbolic means of communication, but in all cases they produce messages only by gesture or icon manipulation, and not by means of their vocal apparatus. Furthermore, their messages show only a very rudimentary syntactic structure (at best) and no development of phrases or other linguistic subunits. Nonetheless, Kanzi, Koko, Lana, Washoe, and the others have certainly narrowed the "language gap" between apes and humans. As Kathleen Gibson of the University of Texas and other researchers have argued, these results strongly suggest that a *quantitative* rather than *qualitative* gap in communication capacities separates humans from their ape relations. It remains true, however, that ape language certainly does not amount to human language in the complete sense, and most importantly, it is never expressed as speech.

Syntax the rules of structure in *language*.

The Pharynx

A clear boundary between apes and humans becomes obvious when one considers means of language transmission. Spoken language requires equipment, both physical and mental, that apes and monkeys simply do not have (see Figure 13–6). The adult human tongue, for example, is thicker than that of monkeys and apes, and

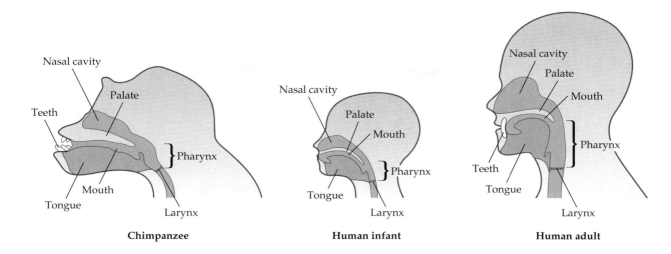

FIGURE 13–6   Insights into the speaking ability of early hominids have come from comparisons of the vocal apparatus of modern human adults and babies with that of a chimpanzee. To form words, sounds must be modulated by the pharynx, which lies above the larynx. The human newborn baby resembles the chimpanzee with its high larynx and short pharynx. By the age of three, the child's larynx has descended from the level of the fourth cervical vertebra to that of the seventh, and the long human pharynx is complete.

unlike theirs, it bends in a sharp angle into the throat. In addition, the human **larynx,** with its vocal cords, lies farther down the throat than the ape larynx. The part of the throat above the larynx, the **pharynx,** is proportionately much longer in humans than in any other primates.

The pharynx serves as a combined opening for the windpipe (trachea), which goes to the lungs, and the gullet (esophagus), which leads to the stomach. The anchor for the base of the tongue, it also plays a fundamental part in producing speech, and this is where the longer human pharynx becomes important. It is the pharynx that modifies the sounds made by the vocal cords and gives them the varying tones that language requires. To provide this control, the muscles of the pharynx walls and the base of the tongue move continuously during speech, constantly and precisely varying the dimensions of the pharynx; the greatest width of the pharynx is at least ten times its narrowest. These dimensional changes produce much the same effect on sounds that an organ achieves with its dozens of pipes of different lengths and diameters, each making a particular tone. The pharynx is extremely important to speech; it is quite possible to speak intelligibly without the larynx or the tip of the tongue as long as the pharynx and the base of the tongue are intact.

Monkeys and apes, lacking the human vocal equipment, vary the shape of only their mouths when they vocalize; there is practically no movement of the pharynx, the musculature of which is rudimentary. The oral cavity of the mouth is large, and the tongue is incapable of forming the consonants of speech. They can produce only a limited number of distinct sounds—ten to fifteen in most cases—and because of limitations of the brain's cortex, they cannot combine them at will to form words.

The same limitation restricts the vocalization of human babies, who at birth are unable to make the vowel sounds typical of human speech. For at least six weeks a baby's tongue remains immobile during its cries. It rests almost entirely within

Larynx the voice box; the organ in the throat containing the vocal cords, important in human *speech* production.

Pharynx the throat, above the *larynx*.

the mouth, as in nonhuman primates, and the larynx sits high in the throat. This arrangement permits babies as well as all other primates to swallow and breathe at the same time without danger of choking. By the time babies reach the babbling stage, at around three months, the base of the tongue and the larynx have begun to descend into the throat, enlarging the pharyngeal region. Not until this development is complete during the third year are humans physically equipped to make all of the speech sounds that distinguish them from their simian relatives.

Centers of Vocal Communication: The Cerebral Cortex

Cerebral cortex gray, wrinkled, outer layer of the brain; largely responsible for memory and, in humans, reasoned behavior and abstract thought. (Also referred to as the *neocortex*.)

Other equally important reasons why humans can talk and the nonhuman primates cannot have to do with the brain. When people use their voices to communicate, they are doing more than making noise. They are codifying thought and transmitting it to others in a string of connected sounds. The coding begins in the **cerebral cortex**, the convoluted outer layer of the brain. The cortex (or neocortex) has three primary areas and several lesser areas of importance in speech production (Figure 13–7). All primary areas typically occur on one cerebral hemisphere only, usually described as the dominant hemisphere, because speech is so important in human life. The dominant hemisphere is the left hemisphere in about 95 percent of right-handed people and 70 percent of left-handers. But speech production is not an entirely asymmetrical matter. The nondominant hemisphere does play some part in speech, influencing such things as rhythm, emphasis, and intonation.

One of the cortical regions long thought to be of primary importance in speech production is called Broca's area and is located in the inferior frontal lobe of the dominant hemisphere. Traditionally, Broca's area has been understood as the region that sends codes for the succession of phonemes (speech sounds) to an adjacent part of the brain (the motor cortex, just anterior to the central sulcus; Figure 13–7) that controls the muscles of the face, jaw, tongue, pharynx, and larynx; thus it helps set the speech apparatus in operation. Damage in the vicinity of Broca's

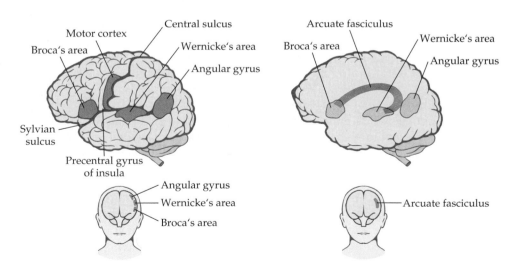

FIGURE 13–7   Areas of the brain cortex (surface layer) involved in speech production are shown in the left drawing. The drawing at the right shows the arcuate fasciculus, which links Wernicke's to Broca's areas deep within the brain. Wernicke's area and the angular gyrus are also involved in the decoding of speech.

area has been linked to a form of aphasia (loss or impairment of speech) in which articulation is slow and labored. While much of this traditional view may still be correct, recent work has raised questions about precisely how Broca's area is involved in speech. In this work, researchers using PET (positron emission tomography) technology have measured the patterns of cranial blood flow in normal, conscious humans involved in language and speech tasks and other activities. The PET results have convinced some workers that much of Broca's area is involved either with the hierarchical organization of manual object combination or with higher-level coordination of oral movements and that only part of the area is involved specifically in speech. This idea is supported by evidence that lesions limited strictly to Broca's area frequently fail to produce full-blown Broca's aphasia. The PET studies have found other areas more directly related to speech just anterior to Broca's area or deep within the Sylvian sulcus (Figure 13–7; the latter areas do not show on the surface of the cerebral cortex). Furthermore, new studies of stroke patients have turned up yet a third cortical area that contributes to the coordination of speech articulation. Patients with damage to the left precentral gyrus of the insula (Figure 13–7) commonly have trouble with misarticulations such as "catastrophe, patastrofee . . . katasrifrobee." It seems that humans' dominant frontal lobe contains several articulatory centers.

Enlarged Broca's areas occasionally turn up on hominid endocasts, but because of the PET and other studies, some researchers are beginning to distrust such evidence as a clear sign of speech in our extinct forebears. But do not count out Broca's area quite yet. The importance of that cortical region for speech was revived by a 1997 study showing that late bilinguals (persons who acquire conversational fluency in a second language as young adults) actually develop within Broca's area a second center of activation specifically for the new language. In contrast, persons who acquire bilingual fluency during childhood have a single center of activation that serves both of their languages. Overall, the various studies suggest that Broca's area is indeed important for speech, but that it is not alone in determining word production.

The second primary region is Wernicke's area, located farther back in the dominant hemisphere, in the temporal lobe; it is vital to the process of comprehension. Damage to Wernicke's area usually produces another form of aphasia: speech that is fluent but meaningless. A bundle of nerve fibers (the arcuate fasciculus) transmits signals from Wernicke's area to Broca's, making possible the vocal repetition of a heard and memorized word.

The third primary region, adjacent to Wernicke's area, is the **angular gyrus**. It occupies a key position at the juncture of the portions of the cerebral cortex connected with vision, hearing, and touch—the parts of the brain that receive detailed information from the world outside the body. Linked to these sensory receivers by bundles of nerve fibers, the angular gyrus operates as a kind of connecting station, permitting one type of incoming signal to be associated with others. For example, the angular gyrus makes it possible for the brain to link a visual stimulus produced by the sight of a cup with the auditory stimulus produced by a voice saying "cup" and with the tactile stimulus produced when the hand picks up the cup. The importance of these associations is clear when we think of the way children learn the words for things: when children ask, "what's that?" and are told by their parents, they match the image of the seen object with the sound of the spoken word and thus absorb the name for the object, automatically filing the sound for that association in their memory bank. This process of association and memorization is the first and most basic step in the acquisition of language.

Angular gyrus part of the human *cerebral cortex* that allows information received from different senses to be associated.

It is important to note, however, that the human brain is an elaboration on an older pattern found in many nonhuman primates. Anthropologist Dean Falk of the State University of New York àt Albany has conducted numerous studies of the comparative anatomy of anthropoid brains, and she has this to say: "There are frontal lobe and temporal/parietal regions in the brains of monkeys and apes that appear to be in (somewhat) similar positions and to have similar arrangements of cells as Broca's and Wernicke's areas do in [modern] human brains. There is also some evidence that the left hemisphere differentially processes socially meaningful vocalizations in nonhuman higher primates. It therefore appears that . . . human language areas are an elaboration on the basic primate pattern" (an elaboration that Falk limits to the genus *Homo*). Kathleen Gibson is in basic agreement with Falk's elaboration theory and argues that human language is the result of quantitative increases in brain size and information-processing capacities, not the appearance of entirely new cortical areas.

Limbic System

And so the brains of monkeys and apes are broadly similar to humans' brains but are significantly less developed in some important areas. An ape's angular gyrus is small, and there is limited association between information signals coming from different senses. Apparently, incoming signals are routed mainly to another part of the brain altogether: the limbic system (see Figure 13–8). All mammals, including humans, have this evolutionarily ancient region lying near the core of the brain, a kind of netherworld of neurological activity. Among other things, it activates the physical responses that go with hunger, fear, rage, and sexual activity, and it triggers the feelings that accompany these responses (Figure 13–9). If a monkey sees a predator, the visual signal feeds into the limbic system and produces a physical reaction—the sounding of the danger call with its accompanying facial expression, perhaps—and also makes the animal feel fear. Similarly, sexual signals sent out by a female chimpanzee go to the limbic system of a male, causing him to feel sexually stimulated and prompting a sexual response. Humans are no different.

In other words, information channeled to the limbic system from the outside produces an instantaneous, unthinking, adaptive response. As anthropologist Jane

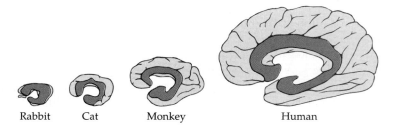

Rabbit   Cat   Monkey   Human

FIGURE 13–8   These drawings of the brain in partial section show the relative size of the limbic regions in different species (dark shading, approximately to scale). The limbic system is the "emotional brain" in all mammals, including humans. It is connected with the expression and decoding of much of the nonverbal communication that plays such a big part in the social life of mammals. Though still large and important in humans, it is no longer the largest component of the brain, as it is in other mammals. The limbic system lies beneath the neocortex, which is distinctive of mammals and reaches its greatest development among primates.

FIGURE 13–9   Chimpanzees have a complex repertoire of facial expressions, as varied as our own. Most facial expressions are components of the multimodal communication system generated by the limbic system.

Lancaster writes, the limbic system "makes the animal want to do what it has to do to survive and reproduce."

As we have seen, among the responses that are directed largely by the limbic system are facial expressions and vocal signals—cries of fear or pleasure, for example—that are quite distinct from language. That communication through signals like these is controlled by this part of the brain can be demonstrated by laboratory experiment. When electrodes are planted in the limbic system and related structures of a monkey, and its brain is stimulated electrically, the animal responds with its repertory of cries, even though the situations that normally stimulate those sounds (aggressive behavior by a dominant animal, food, enemies) are not present. Furthermore, other monkeys of the same species in the laboratory react to these sounds (by cringing, searching for food, taking an alert stance) just as though they were bona fide signals. Similar experiments have been performed on human subjects during brain surgery, and they react in a similar way. When certain parts of the human limbic system are stimulated, the patient responds with sounds.

The sounds produced through the limbic system in both ape and human are not the sounds of speech. In apes, both vocal and facial expressions are largely under limbic, not voluntary, control. They reflect emotion, not volition. This suggests that primate vocalization did not evolve into spoken language, which is clearly a volitional act. Instead, language is an entirely novel development in our evolution. For that distinctive emblem of humanness it was necessary for other parts of the brain, specifically the angular gyrus, Wernicke's area, and Broca's and neighboring areas of the cortex, to develop fully. It was through this development and the evolution of the speech apparatus that emerging humans began to speak and to leave the inarticulate apes far behind.

In the cortex evolved the means of producing complex vocal sounds that could be used to communicate intent, will, and desire, as could the gestures discussed earlier used by nonhuman primates. Spoken language is a learned symbolic communicatory system that is cortical in origin. It can be used to refer to all kinds of objects, processes, and concepts, and indeed it is practically unlimited in its value to human society. It was certainly one of the most important developments in human evolution, because it made possible our extraordinary cultural adaptations.

EVOLUTION OF SPEECH

It is obviously impossible to pinpoint when hominids began to use language: the development of speech and other human characteristics was infinitely gradual. The process may have begun when they started making and using tools. If early hominids at first depended on gestures to communicate, such hand signals would no doubt have eventually become inadequate; the hominids might literally have had their hands full, carrying tools or food. Thus the ability to use sounds voluntarily to attract attention and to make meaning clear would have proved a great advantage.

But for the process of naming things to start, the vocal apparatus had to be modified, and the brain had to evolve. This development must have taken hundreds of thousands of years. Some small mutations may have enabled *Australopithecus* to make a few voluntary sounds, providing an edge in the competition for survival. The ability to signal one another through a more extensive repertory of phonemes would have been a definite advantage to the australopithecines' descendants. And then, as the number of phonemes grew, brain development could have permitted more precise differentiation between them and new combinations of them, so that primitive words may have taken shape. All the while, the brain and the vocal apparatus would have been involved in a feedback relationship with each other, changes in one fostering development of the other: the success of the cortex in forming a rudimentary sound code would have affected the vocal apparatus, and this, in turn, would have helped enlarge the speech centers of the brain, and so on, until the rudiments of speech appeared. Then hominids were ready to begin combining a few separate sounds, or words, representing specific elements of terrain, the hunt, the family, and seasonal changes, into simple combinations that conveyed a great deal of information.

Phonation: Flexing the Cranial Base

What this first speech sounded like depended on how far the dual development of vocal apparatus and cortical brain equipment had progressed. Linguist Philip Lieberman's analysis of the character of modern speech emphasizes the importance of the human vocal equipment. He points out that the pharynx is essential for producing the vowel sounds *a* ("ah"), *i* ("ee"), and *u* ("oo"), which are crucial to all modern languages, from English to Kirghiz. Virtually all meaningful segments of human speech contain one or more of these sounds. Combining these vowel sounds with a wide assortment of consonants, the human vocal apparatus not only can produce an infinite number of variations but also, and more important, can connect them with great rapidity in the coded series of sounds that is spoken language.

This involves the putting together of separate phonetic segments into a sound that can be understood as one word. A person saying *bat*, for instance, does not articulate the fragments of sound represented by the letters *b*, *a*, and *t* but combines these elements into one syllable. This ability to combine sounds gives the voice the ability to put together and transmit more than 30 phonetic segments a second.

The key to human phonation lies in the position of the larynx. As we have seen, during modern human growth the pharynx lengthens and the larynx descends in the neck, so that by the age of three the low larynx separates humans from all other primates. Edmund S. Crelin and Jeffrey Laitman have shown that this movement is associated with the appearance of flexion in the base of the skull (the basicranium). A skull with a flat base is associated with a high larynx, and this is found in all nonhuman primates and in newborn human babies. In contrast, a flexed cranial base is found in all modern humans after the early years of life and is associated with a low larynx. Researchers have examined the cranial base of various hominid fossils and report that the flexion in *Australopithecus* was the same as that of extant apes. Similarly, although there is some variation, the cranial base in *Homo erectus* is essentially unflexed. Thus the crucial restructuring of the upper respiratory tract may not have begun until after *H. erectus*. Full basicranial flexion similar to that seen in modern humans is first found among certain specimens of *Homo heidelbergensis* some 400,000 to 300,000 years ago (Figure 13–10).

Articulation: Oral Cavity Dimensions and Tongue Innervation

But basicranial flexion is not the end of the story, as other studies have shown. The pharyngeal cavity and the larynx together generate the vowel sounds, but it is the tongue and lips that produce articulation of these sounds by interspersing the vowels with consonants. Research by Linda Duchin of the University of Washington, Seattle, has shown how very different the tongue musculature and oral cavity of the chimpanzee are from those of humans. The production of consonants has not been reported in chimpanzee vocalizations, evidently because the palate and the mandible create a much longer oral cavity than in humans, and the muscles that support and move the tongue (its extrinsic muscles) lie in slightly different places and are set at different angles than those of humans. The **hyoid** bone, to which some of these muscles are attached, lies in a different position in apes: higher and farther back than in humans. Altogether, these differences mean that control of the tongue in apes is less efficient than in humans. Furthermore, because of the larger oral cavity in apes, the tongue cannot reach all the necessary contact points needed to create consonants during phonation. In humans, the position of the anchorage of the tongue muscles and the smaller oral cavity mean that the tongue can move very rapidly from point to point in the mouth to create the fast-changing consonants of speech. Notice the extraordinary speed and accuracy of your tongue movements during speech. No wonder slow and slurred speech is one of the first signs of inebriation!

Measurements of the oral cavities of *Homo erectus* and Neandertal fossil skulls fall close to or into the human range and distinguish them clearly from the chimpanzee. This would appear to imply that these fossil hominids may have had some potential for articulate speech. Interestingly, these suggestive findings have been reinforced recently by the research of Richard Kay, Matt Cartmill, and Michelle Balow on the anatomy of the **hypoglossal canal** in hominoids. This canal carries the

Hyoid a bone of the throat positioned just above the *larynx* and just below the *mandible*. The hyoid provides attachment for one of the muscles of the tongue and for certain muscles of the front of the neck.

Hypoglossal canal an opening in the occipital bone just anterior to the occipital condyle; allows the passage of the hypoglossal nerve to the tongue musculature.

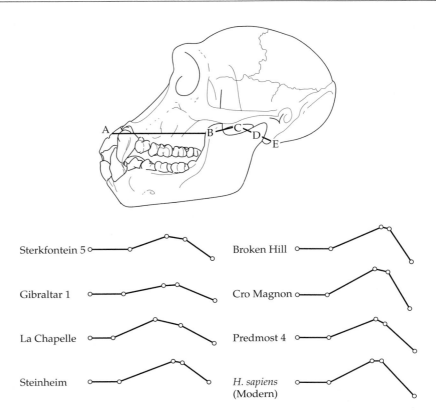

FIGURE 13–10   Cranial base profiles from fossil hominids and modern humans document the recent development of full basicranial flexion and modern throat proportions. As shown here on the skull of a female chimpanzee (top), profiles are measured by connecting five midline points: A, prosthion (most anterior point on the alveolar process—toothbearing ridge—of the upper jaw); B, staphylion (near the posterior edge of the hard palate); C, hormion (near the posterior edge of the vomer, one of the internal bones of the face); D, sphenobasion (a point on the sphenoid/occipital articulation); E, basion (midpoint of the anterior margin of the foramen magnum). At the bottom of the figure, cranial base profiles are shown for an australopithecine (Sterkfontein 5), two Neandertals (Gibraltar and La Chapelle), two *Homo heidelbergensis* specimens (Steinheim and Broken Hill [=Kabwe]), two fossil *Homo sapiens* (Cro-Magnon and Predmost 4), and modern humans. (Figure modified from J. Laitman, R. Heimbuch, and E. Crelin, "The Basicranium of Fossil Hominids as an Indicator of Their Upper Respiratory Systems." *American Journal of Physical Anthropology*, 51, 1979. Copyright © 1979, John Wiley and Sons, Inc. Reprinted by permission of Wiley-Liss, Inc., a subsidiary of John Wiley and Sons, Inc.)

nerve to the muscles of the tongue, and Kay et al. think canal size was probably correlated closely with tongue coordination and the capacity for speech. Their comparisons of canal cross-sectional areas in modern African apes, living humans, and several fossil hominids produced some fascinating results. Specimens of *Australopithecus africanus*, and possibly *Homo habilis*, were found to be similar to apes with regard to hypoglossal canal size, and both early hominid types had significantly smaller canals than modern humans. In contrast, the hypoglossal canals of Neandertal and *Homo heidelbergensis* people had reached modern size, suggesting that modern vocal capacities may have begun in the middle Pleistocene, well before the appearance of *Homo sapiens*. (This question is discussed more fully in the next chapter.)

Speech is therefore a product of both phonation (made possible by a low larynx and an adjustable pharynx) and articulation (made possible by an efficiently controlled tongue in a small oral cavity). Phonation and articulation are unique to humans and arose as a result of changes in the balance of the head on the vertebral column and the reduction of the jaws.

While this research is by no means conclusive, it does give us some useful insight into the evolution of the speech apparatus and thus into the evolution of speech.

The Importance of Rudimentary Speech

While all of these various considerations are enlightening, they still fail to tell us precisely when and in which hominid species language first evolved. Perhaps we will never have conclusive answers to those questions. Nonetheless, as we wrestle with these issues, it is important to keep in mind that spoken language need not have been fully developed in order to be useful to ancestral hominids. Even extremely rudimentary speech would have allowed *Homo erectus* people, for example, to communicate a great deal about themselves and the world around them. It is necessary only to listen to very young children to see how effective language can be, even in its simplest form. Between the ages of eighteen and twenty-four months, only half a year or so after children first speak, they begin to use two-word sentences. The sentences are neither copies of grown-up speech nor reductions of it, but the children's own inventions, conforming to what would seem to be native, universal rules of grammar. They are made up of so-called "open words," words that can be said by themselves and still mean something (such as the nouns *blanket*, *milk*, and *baby*), and "pivot words," often prepositions, adjectives, or verbs (such as *on* and *hot*). At this age, children put words together to describe the world or to get people to act ("pajama on"), but they are not used to express emotion.

Only when the children are three or four do they begin to put feelings into words. Before then they rely, as nonhuman primates must, on the workings of the limbic system to call attention to their needs. Rather than say, "I'm angry," or "I'm afraid," they demonstrate physically how angry or afraid they are. They find temper tantrums, whimpering, or crying a much easier way to communicate; that is, they find emotions easier to express than to explain. As any parent knows, children have little difficulty in making themselves understood. Perhaps the early humans, speaking the simplest of sentences reinforced by gestures and hand signals, communicated just as well with some rudimentary version of human speech.

Whatever it sounded like, and at whatever age they began to use it, once our ancestors developed language it became a tool used in its own right—a tool to drive like a wedge into the environment, hurrying the split from nature that marked their development and foreshadowed ours. For the first time in human history, cultural evolution, because of speech, began to outpace biological evolution, as instinct and emotion were counterbalanced by symbol and custom.

THE BRAIN

Humans Among Mammals

For many researchers, the most striking evidence of the evolution of language is the increase in size of the hominid brain. Evidence of this increase is the expanding cranial capacity that we see in successive hominid fossil skulls. As we saw in Chapter 8, the cranial capacity trebled during the past 3 million years, certainly a very rapid rate of evolution. But to see this figure in perspective, we need to relate it to body size, for a simple increase in body size itself (accompanied by an appropriate increase in brain size) can occur rapidly in evolution and is not an unusual occurrence. To relate brain size to body size, we need to calculate how large a brain a typical ape would have if it were to have a body the same size as ours. The answer reveals that the present human brain is 3.1 times larger than we would expect in a primate of our build. It appears, then, that our brain's trebling in size occurred despite only a moderate increase in our body size. This is perhaps the most significant anatomical fact about the species *Homo sapiens*.

This characteristic is perhaps even more striking when we remember that monkeys and apes have the biggest brains in relation to body weight of any land animal. California psychiatrist Harry Jerison has introduced the **encephalization quotient (EQ)** to compare relative brain sizes. The EQ is calculated by relating the brain size of each species to the size expected for an average mammal of the same body weight. By definition, an average mammal has an EQ of 1.0. If the relative brain size is smaller than average, then the EQ has a value of less than 1.0; if the relative brain size is larger than average, then the EQ ranges above 1.0. Figure 13–11 very briefly summarizes Jerison's results. Insectivores and rodents are in one group, with EQs generally below 1.0. Ungulates (hoofed mammals), carnivores, and prosimians make a second group, with EQs slightly over 1.0. Monkeys and apes are quite distinct from these other groups, with EQs ranging between 1.0 and 5.0. Modern humans have an average EQ of about 7.2. Here again we see that humans are absolutely distinctive in the size of their brains.

Encephalization quotient (EQ) in mammals, a number expressing observed brain size in a particular species relative to expected brain size calculated from body weight.

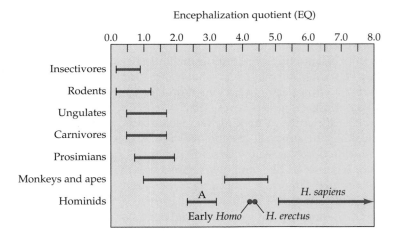

FIGURE 13–11   The encephalization quotient (EQ) is shown here for several groups of mammals including a number of hominids. For most groups, a range of EQ values is shown by a horizontal line; for two hominid species, small sample sizes allow only EQ means (shown by dots). The upper range of values for monkeys and apes is generated by certain small and distinctive New World monkeys. Hominid types include the australopithecines (A), early *Homo*, *Homo erectus*, and *Homo sapiens*. The EQ range for modern humans extends to a high value of about 10.6. Average EQ for modern people is about 7.2. (Data from H. J. Jerison, *Evolution of the Brain and Intelligence*, Academic Press, 1973.)

TABLE 13–1 *Ratio of Weight of Brain to Weight of Body in Certain Mammals*

MAMMALS	BRAIN-BODY RATIO
New World, squirrel monkey	1:12
New World, tamarin	1:19
Porpoise (dolphin)	1:38
Higher primates	
Humankind	1:45
Australopithecus afarensis (estimated)	1:100
Old World monkey (Macaca)	1:170
Gorilla	1:200
Elephant	1:600
Sperm whale	1:10,000

If we relate brain weight to body weight and generate a simple ratio, we get further remarkable results (Table 13–1). Here, surprisingly, humans do not fall at the top of the list; the highest positions are occupied by two small New World monkeys. It was in fact these monkeys that generated the largest EQ values for monkeys and apes in Figure 13–11. This anomalous state of affairs can be understood as a product of a higher primate with relatively small body size, for another fact of brain development is that small animals in any particular order have relatively larger brains than large species. For the same reason, large animals (within any particular order) have relatively smaller brains. Thus, as Table 13–1 shows, elephants and whales have the largest brains of any living animals (of about 4,000 cubic centimeters and 6,000 cubic centimeters, respectively), but nonetheless have relatively small brains within their respective orders. The most surprising figure in Table 13–1 is that for the porpoise. Although good data on the brain and body sizes of porpoises are very limited, it does appear that this group of marine animals has exceptionally large brains, and this ratio is particularly striking in the smaller species. The dolphin brain is famed not only for its size but for the extent of its convolutions, which implies a relatively immense neocortex. The explanation for this remarkable looking brain is still one of the great mysteries of modern biology.

If primate brains are relatively large, we may then ask if the proportions of the different parts separate them from those of other orders of mammals. We have seen (Figure 13–8) that the development of the neocortex is distinctive in mammals and especially in primates, a characteristic that becomes clear in dissection and measurement. The jackal, a large-brained carnivore, has a brain of about 2 ounces (64 grams), the same size as that of the macaque monkey. In the jackal, the cerebral hemispheres form 60 percent of the brain, but in the monkey they constitute 78 percent of the brain.

Within the order Primates, however, the story is different. It has been claimed that the human brain is preeminent and unusual in the development of the neocortex, especially the prefrontal and association areas. According to British psychologist Richard Passingham, however, the evidence for these detailed claims is still flimsy, and they cannot be substantiated at present. He demonstrates convincingly, though, that in the human brain the relative proportions of the main subdivisions of the brain, including the neocortex, do indeed differ from those which might be expected in monkeys and apes of similar body weight (Figure 13–12). He points out, however, that the human difference is in fact predictable from higher

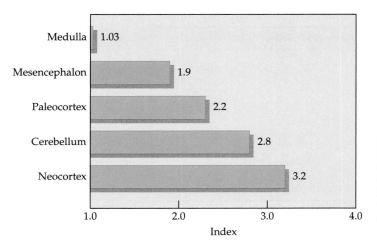

FIGURE 13–12   Indices comparing the size of parts of the human brain with values predicted for a primate of the same body weight. The index is the actual value of the part in humans divided by the predicted value. Notice that not only the neocortex but other parts, particularly the cerebellum, show considerable development. Certain of the parts are labeled in Figure 13–14.

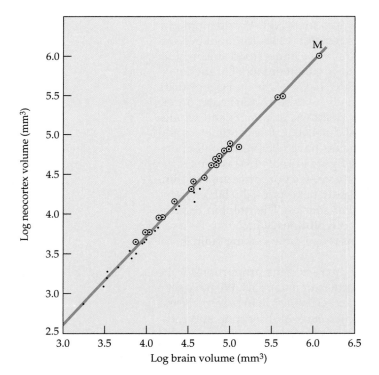

FIGURE 13–13   When we plot the volume of the neocortex (in cubic millimeters) as a function of the volume of the brain, we find that the relationship is the same throughout the primates. The slope of the line is steeper than 45 degrees because the neocortex is relatively larger in larger brains by a constant proportion: dot, prosimians; circled dot, monkeys and apes; M, humans.

primate data if the brain proportions are related to brain size and not body size (Figure 13–13). We have known for some time that the functional areas of the brains of apes and humans are comparable (Figure 13–14); now we can conclude from evidence currently available that the human brain is in most ways a standard higher primate brain that has simply been increased in size by a factor of 3.1. No new structures appear to have been introduced at this gross level of measurement.

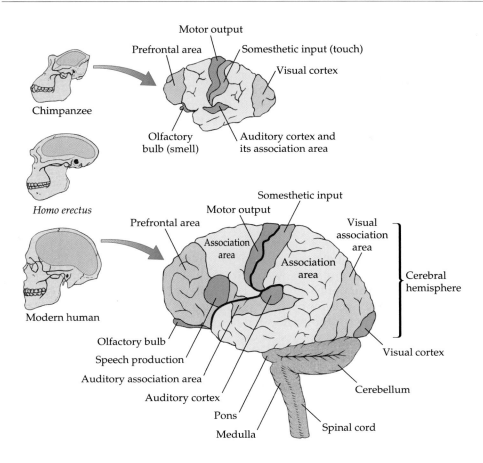

FIGURE 13–14 Comparison of ape and human brains shows that the human brain is not only bigger but more deeply folded. The form of the brain of *Homo erectus* can be guessed at only by the shape and size of the endocranial cast.

When we come to consider the more detailed structure of the neocortex, of the neurons, and of their interconnecting pathways, however, we may be forgiven for expecting something distinctively human and we are not disappointed. Ralph Holloway of Columbia University summarizes the evidence that human brains have larger and more complex neurons (individual brain cells) and many more interconnections among them than other primate brains. He shows, too, that the brain cells are less densely packed than in other primates, for while the number of neurons has remained the same, thickness of the neocortex has increased dramatically.

We can therefore conclude that the unique human potential has been made possible by our large brain. Expansion of a standard primate brain has provided us with behavioral possibilities undreamed of in other, even closely related, species. This brain, absolutely as well as relatively large, with its absolutely large number of neurons (about 10^{10}) and its unbelievably large number of dendritic interconnections (about 10^{12}), gives us the human potential for making tools, talking, planning, dreaming of the future, and creating an entirely new environment for ourselves. The primate laws of relative brain growth have been followed closely in most respects, with the most important exception being the brain-body ratio. That factor of 3.1 has lifted humans far above their animal cousins into a new order of organic life.

The size of the brain, therefore, crudely measured in cubic centimeters, tells us something very profound about human nature. Our brain is not so much different from other brains as it is bigger. We are not a unique evolutionary experiment, but a superprimate. Quantitative changes in the evolving hominid brain, however, produced extraordinary qualitative changes in behavior.

Group Size, Brain Size, Language, and Radiators

An interesting theory that links encephalization and language to increasing group size has been presented by Leslie Aiello and Robin Dunbar. As noted in Chapter 9, Dunbar and others have shown that among the primates brain size is correlated positively with group size, suggesting selection for social intelligence (Figure 13–15). Larger social groups mean more relationships to coordinate, a task that monkeys and apes usually accomplish by grooming one another. Total daily grooming time therefore also shows positive correlations with both brain size and group size, and can amount to 20 percent of the day before it begins to compromise the animals' time budgets for other activities such as feeding, resting, and travel.

Aiello and Dunbar hypothesize that hominid evolution was characterized by pressure for ever-larger groups because bigger groups would have meant increased protection against predators and other dangers, as well as an improved ability to compete successfully against other hominid groups for food and space. They further suspect that as hominid groups continued to grow, they eventually reached the size where grooming was no longer viable as the main way of coordinating and servicing the expanding number of social relationships. At about the point where 25 to 30 percent of the day would have been needed for enough phys-

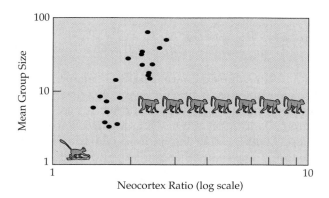

FIGURE 13–15   When relative neocortex size (the Neocortex Ratio) is plotted against mean group size for nonhuman primates, a strong positive correlation is revealed. As shown by the icons, the prosimians' values are clustered in the lower left portion of the chart. All of the highest values are from monkey and ape species. (Figure modified from R. I. M. Dunbar, "The Social Brain Hypothesis." *Evolutionary Anthropology*, 6, 1998. Copyright © 1998, John Wiley and Sons, Inc. Reprinted by permission of Wiley-Liss, Inc., a subsidiary of John Wiley and Sons, Inc.)

ical grooming to ensure group cohesion, time budget constraints should have selected for some other form of social lubrication. Aiello and Dunbar conclude that language evolved as that social lubricant; a form of vocal grooming that facilitated the maintenance of large groups. Based on their calculations of the relationship between relative neocortex size and group size, Aiello and Dunbar suggest that the critical language-inducing group size was reached by the middle Pleistocene (about 250,000 years B.P.) and thus language with significant social information content had its first effects among *Homo heidelbergensis* (albeit after a gradual evolutionary development). This conclusion is in agreement with the data on cranial base flexion, as noted earlier in this chapter.

Brain growth and language obviously carried enormous survival and reproductive benefits for our hominid ancestors, and Aiello and Dunbar may be correct in concluding that pressure for larger groups was the driving factor behind these related developments. Nonetheless, it may have been a simple and early change in the brain's cooling system that made them possible. Paleoneurologist Dean Falk has developed what she calls the radiator theory of brain evolution. According to Falk, in response to their evolving bipedalism, the australopithecines developed new means of draining blood from their (elevated) braincases. *Paranthropus* (and, in Falk's opinion, the Hadar hominids as well) evolved a system in which an enlarged occipital-marginal (O/M) sinus delivered blood to the vertebral plexus at the base of the skull (Figure 13–16). This system worked well enough as long as the brain was not overheated and remained relatively small, and thus Falk concludes that the robust australopithecines probably lived mainly in forests rather than on the savanna, and that their potential for brain growth was limited. In contrast to the robust (plus Hadar) hominids, however, Falk describes the gracile australopithecines and their *Homo* descendants as evolving a "radiator" system that allowed both savanna living *and* continued expansion of the brain. The graciles' radiators worked like this. Instead of an enlarged O/M sinus, they evolved a two-way system of emissary veins that passed through the bones of the skull via small openings called foramina (Figure 13–16). The emissary veins were capable of draining blood *from* the braincase to the vertebral plexus when the individual was at or below normal body temperature, and of pumping blood *into* the braincase when the individual was overheated. This two-way system allowed evaporation-cooled blood from the skin to be shunted to overheated brains in hominids who were working up a sweat during their gathering and scavenging (and later, hunting) on the tropical savanna. And the radiator system was wonderfully modifiable. Over time, the gracile australopithecine-*Homo* lineage evolved more and more emissary veins that allowed better and better temperature regulation. To quote Falk: "[The cranial radiator system] released thermal constraints that had previously kept brain size in check." Apparently, hominids' cranial radiators allowed them to combine diurnal exploitation of the tropical savanna with continued brain expansion. (It is worth noting, however, that this interesting theory has not gone unchallenged. In particular, Braga and Boesch [1997] have questioned Falk's conclusions. Further research by both supporters and opponents will be necessary before the ultimate fate of the radiator theory is known.)

Interestingly, according to the EQ data presented in Figure 13–11, brain expansion within the gracile australopithecine-*Homo* line was not smoothly continuous. Rather, after early *Homo*'s significant increase in relative brain size over that of the australopithecines, brain expansion seems to have entered a prolonged period of stasis. The Jerison EQ value for early *Homo* is 4.3; that for *Homo erectus* is about the

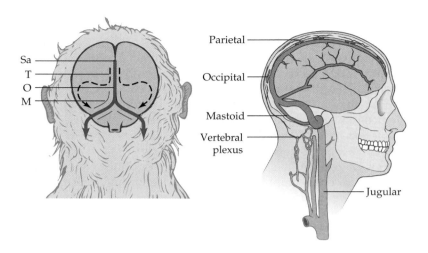

FIGURE 13–16   Blood flow from the cranium of a robust australopithecine is shown at left (rear view of skull). In addition to exiting the skull via the superior sagittal sinus (Sa), blood drained out through the enlarged occipital sinus (O) and marginal sinus (M). The transverse sinus (T) was of relatively little importance in these hominids. In contrast, in the gracile australopithecine/*Homo* lineage, a radiator network of emissary veins evolved for cranial drainage and brain cooling. The side view of a modern human skull at right shows the parietal, occipital, and mastoid emissary veins and their drainage target, the vertebral plexus.

same at 4.4. Thus it appears that *Homo erectus*'s increase in brain size was matched by a proportionate enlargement in body size, and that *Homo erectus* was no brainier, relatively speaking, than early *Homo* (*H. habilis* and *H. rudolfensis* considered collectively). The EQ stasis came to an end in post-*erectus* humans when a strong enlargement of the brain went unmatched by increased body size. This trend carried humans to the modern average EQ value of 7.2.

The Evolution of Mind

To close this chapter, we want to discuss briefly what many people would say is the most important result of humans' brain growth: the evolution of a theory of mind. According to psychologists David Premack and G. Woodruff, having a theory of mind involves being able to attribute beliefs, knowledge, and emotions to oneself and to others. In species that possess a theory of mind, individuals benefit by using these attributed mental states to manipulate others (for example, by sharing or denying information or through deception). Although more evidence is needed, it appears that by the time apes reach adolescence, they *may* possess something like a theory of mind, judging from examples of deception and from the fact that they seem to have some self-awareness. Monkeys, on the other hand, apparently lack such a theory completely (see Chapter 3). Precisely when during hominid evolution a theory of mind developed is unclear, but some psychologists, such as the Russian scientist L. Vygotskii, believe that modern people *learn* a theory of mind through the medium of language.

Recently, Steven Mithen of the University of Reading used the archaeological record to reconstruct the evolution of the human mind. His results, although speculative, are interesting and deserve our attention. Mithen assumes that hominids descended from ape ancestors with modular brains; that is, brains that were partitioned into separate functional domains (this idea is based on evidence of mental modularity in chimpanzees, see Figure 13–17). The three domains attributed to the ape-hominid common ancestor are General Intelligence (the center of trial-and-error and associative learning, responsible for foraging decisions, tool use, etc.), Social Intelligence (responsible for handling information about relationships with group mates), and Natural History Intelligence (responsible for information about the environment and essential resources). The three domains are viewed as complementary to one another, but they are hypothesized to have had few interconnections—a condition that prevented the flow of information and insights from one area to another. Mithen describes this as a Swiss-army-knife type of brain, with intelligence domains that functioned just as individually as the various blades, screwdrivers, scissors, and other tools in a modern Swiss army knife.

From the strictly modular brain of our last ape ancestor, Mithen then proceeds to reconstruct the brains of a series of hominid species leading to modern humans. In general, the various functional domains are interpreted as increasing in size and complexity during hominid evolution, but continuing to operate in a "stand alone" fashion (that is, to have few, if any, interconnections). At the level of early *Homo*, Mithen envisions the evolution of a new domain of Technical Intelligence (his evidence is the first stone tools). This particular domain is hypothesized to

FIGURE 13–17 As interpreted by Steven Mithen, the brain of a chimpanzee (and by implication, that of the ape/human common ancestor) contains(ed) three stand-alone functional domains: general intelligence, social intelligence, and natural history intelligence.

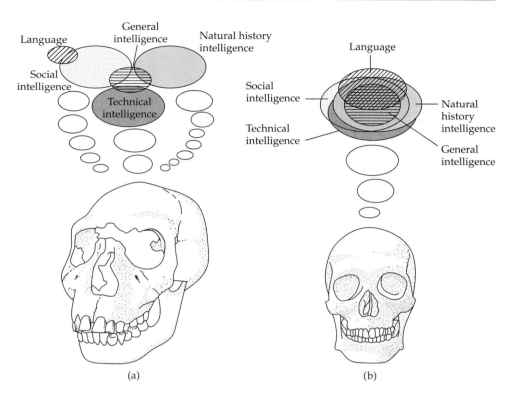

FIGURE 13–18   (a) By the time of *Homo erectus*, according to Steven Mithen, technical intelligence had evolved as well as a small language domain, and natural history intelligence had increased in size and complexity. Few interdomain connections are envisioned, however. (b) Only among *Homo sapiens* does Mithen recognize a modern mind with "full cognitive fluidity" (that is, numerous interdomain connections). Skulls not drawn to scale.

have grown rapidly in size, reaching a level of considerable importance among *Homo erectus* hunters-and-gatherers (Figure 13–18a). Also at the *Homo erectus* level, Mithen suggests that an incipient Language domain evolved as an offshoot of Social Intelligence. Despite these new functional areas, however, the evolving hominid brain, according to Mithen, was still essentially a Swiss-army-knife affair as recently as 200,000 years ago. Indeed, it is not until the appearance of *Homo sapiens* that Mithen finally recognizes evidence of extensive interdomain connections. Modern humans are interpreted as having brains with "full cognitive fluidity"—characterized by the free flow of information and ideas among the various intelligence domains—and, by implication, a complete theory of mind (Figure 13–18b).

Mithen's analysis is interesting, though far from fully convincing. As an attempt to reconstruct the brains and minds of our ancestors from the archaeological record, it has broken new ground. Nonetheless, like any new model, the follow-up studies it spawns may, or may not, support the original hypothesis. Only time will tell. Tracing the evolution of the human mind—one of the few features that sets our species apart from all other animals and a key element in our global domination—remains a formidable challenge.

SUMMARY

Language is perhaps the most remarkable and distinctive characteristic of humans. In its spoken form, it combines a variety of features: the arbitrary form of speech units (sounds, words) with regard to their referents, the combination of units following elaborate rules of syntax, the ability to refer to things not physically present and to the past and future, and the openness of the system to the invention of new units. *In their entirety*, these features differentiate us quite cleanly from the rest of the animal world, even though apes have been shown to possess rudimentary language capacities. Combined with culture, spoken language must have provided a strong stimulus to human evolution and contributed significantly to our modern way of life. It is this central importance of language that makes our inability to pinpoint its evolutionary beginnings so frustrating. But those beginnings are starting to take shape.

The evolution of language and speech apparently involved several interconnected anatomical developments. First, there was an increase in overall brain size (a development possibly driven by pressure for ever-larger social groups). This would have provided enlarged cortical areas for sensory input, association, memory, coding, and motor output. Second, there was the elaboration of the language-speech areas in the hominid cerebral cortex. Broca's area, Wernicke's area, and the angular gyrus are the three main cortical regions that have been implicated in language and speech production, although others have been identified as well. Third, before modern speech was possible, the proportions of the throat and the oral cavity had to change, and certain of these modifications—in particular, the lengthening of the pharynx—were related to flexure of the cranial base. And finally, fine control of breathing was perhaps achieved through increased innervation of the intercostal muscles of the rib cage.

Using these anatomical points, we can evaluate the likelihood of language and speech among the hominid species described thus far. First, beginning with the oldest members of the human family, the australopithecines appear to be very poor candidates for language and speech. Their brains were small (ape-sized) and showed little if any humanlike development of the language-speech areas. Furthermore, although the robust forms (*Paranthropus*) showed some flexure of the cranial base—and thus presumably some lengthening of the pharynx—this feature was absent in the gracile forms (*Australopithecus*). Second, early *Homo* appears to be a better candidate for language and speech, but the evidence is equivocal. Arguing against language and speech is evidence that *Homo habilis* and *Homo rudolfensis* possessed brains that were still only about one-half modern size and, in addition, apparently lacked cranial base flexure. Furthermore, the stone tools produced by early *Homo* are quite simple, and their reconstructed lifestyle seems to have been very different from that of modern humans. On the other hand, some researchers, such as South Africa's Phillip Tobias, believe that early *Homo* had significantly enlarged Broca's and Wernicke's areas, and therefore that a primitive spoken language might have been possible. On balance, it appears reasonable to deny language and speech to early *Homo* until more positive indicators are forthcoming.

With regard to *Homo erectus*, the question of language and speech is particularly difficult since they were much more like us—physically and behaviorally—than were any of the earlier hominids. But despite their large brains (including Ngandong and Sambungmacan, 75 percent of the modern average), which included some development in the speech-language cortical areas, it seems safest to conclude that *Homo erectus* people possessed, at best, an extremely rudimentary form of speech that fell short of a fully articulated language. We base this conclusion on the following considerations: their cranial bases generally lacked flexure, suggesting a short pharynx and a limited ability to produce speech sounds; analyses of the thoracic vertebrae suggest that innervation of the rib cage was insufficient for the fine control of breathing required by speech; cognitive group size was still relatively small; and finally, except for the invention of Acheulean stone tools, preserved remains suggest that the material culture of *Homo erectus* remained very simple until quite late in the species' existence.

Evidence for speech and language increases strongly at the level of *Homo heidelbergensis*. Certain fossils from this species showed the first full basicranial flexion (this trait was variable, however), brain size had increased significantly compared to *Homo erectus* (see Chapter 14), and cognitive group size may have reached a language-inducing level. These are powerful indicators that speech and language had begun, but we need more evidence—particularly archaeological evidence—before we can be secure in this conclusion. The probability remains that *Homo sapiens* is the only fully linguistic species the world has ever known.

Finally, researchers are developing new and exciting ways to probe the evolutionary development of the human brain and mind. Certain recent studies have suggested that our ancestors began with an assortment of stand-alone mental modules and from there evolved an interconnected, modern mind. This idea remains speculative, however, and much more work is needed in this area.

POSTSCRIPT

Although Alfred Russel Wallace shared with Charles Darwin a deep understanding of natural selection and of its potential in the evolutionary process, he had one major problem in coming to terms with human evolution. This difficulty still constitutes a stumbling block for many people seriously interested in the origin of humanity.

Wallace believed, with Darwin, that variation and natural selection were responsible for organic evolution, but he identified three points at which, he concluded, some other (spiritual or perhaps divine) factor had operated: (1) the origin of life, (2) the origin of consciousness, and (3) the origin of the modern human brain. It is with the third phenomenon that we are concerned here. Wallace could not see how the advanced moral and intellectual nature of humanity could possibly have evolved as a product of natural selection, and he took issue with Darwin over this problem. To restate his case in modern terms: How could our brain, extraordinarily capable in art, language, music, mathematics, science, and ethics, have evolved so long ago? How could this brain, originally evolved to hunt and gather, now design a computer or build a vehicle to travel to the moon? Wallace replied, "We can only find an adequate cause in the unseen universe of spirit." He is not the only one who has attributed the creation of the human mind to a divine hand.

Darwin's answer was first of all one of horror! "I hope you have not murdered too completely your own and my child," he wrote. His considered reply may be translated into modern terms: The ancient brain was in fact already adept at handling complex socialization, emotional expression, language, natural history, hunting techniques, and simple technology, together with much else besides. Such capabilities already required a large and complex brain which, like a computer (though vastly more complex), can be turned to different uses depending on the program installed. A computer originally bought as a word processor can also be used for a vast array of other functions if correctly programmed. The hard-wiring is almost infinitely versatile if the design is appropriate. Referring to the human brain, Stephen Jay Gould has written that "the additional capacities are ineluctable consequences of structural design, not necessarily direct adaptations." Our large brains were selected in evolution for flexibility and intelligence, but they contain "a terrifying array of additional capacities including, I suspect, most of what makes us human." This is a profound comment on the nature of humankind.

For Alfred Russel Wallace, a divine touch was necessary for the production of the human brain. Charles Darwin, in contrast, was convinced by his studies of the continuities of animal and human behavior that the human brain was not a special and unique gift from God, but, no less miraculous, an astounding product of variation and natural selection.

REVIEW QUESTIONS

1. Compare the communication systems of modern humans and animals. How are animals limited in their communication compared to people? What similarities, if any, do animals' communication systems show to humans' language and speech?
2. Discuss the connections between the evolution of language and humans' theory of mind.
3. How do the following cortical areas affect speech and language among modern humans: Broca's area, Wernicke's area, the angular gyrus, the precentral gyrus of the insula, and the limbic system?
4. Compare the brains of apes and modern humans with regard to absolute size, EQ, and the development of the language-speech areas.
5. Describe the Aiello and Dunbar theory that language development was triggered by the increasing size of human groups. What evidence do they have for group sizes among extinct hominids?
6. Discuss the evidence (anatomical and archaeological) for and against the presence of language and speech in the various fossil hominid species. When do *you* think linguistic communication evolved and under what circumstances?
7. Using Steven Mithen's modularity model, compare the organization of a chimpanzee's brain with that of a modern human. Describe the sequence of changes that may have converted the ape brain into one with full cognitive fluidity.

SUGGESTED FURTHER READING

Aiello, L., and R. I. M. Dunbar. "Neocortex Size, Group Size, and the Evolution of Language." *Current Anthropology*, 34, 1993.

Cheney, D. L., and R. Seyfarth. *How Monkeys See the World*. University of Chicago Press, 1990.

Deacon, T. W. *The Symbolic Species: The Co-Evolution of Language and the Brain*. W. W. Norton, 1997.

Falk, D. *Braindance*. Henry Holt, 1992.

Laitman, J., and R. C. Heimbuch. "The Basicranium of Plio-Pleistocene Hominids as an Indicator of Their Upper Respiratory Systems." *American Journal of Physical Anthropology*, 59, 1982.

Mithen, S. *The Prehistory of the Mind*. Thames and Hudson, 1996.

Savage-Rumbaugh, S., and R. Lewin. *Kanzi: The Ape at the Brink of the Human Mind*. Wiley, 1994.

Tobias, P. *The Brain in Hominid Evolution*. Columbia University Press, 1971.

INTERNET RESOURCES

EVOLUTION AND PSYCHOLOGY: LINKS

http://watarts.uwaterloo.ca/~acheyne/pce.html
> (A useful site providing links to information on brain evolution, the evolution of signs and language, and the evolution of consciousness.)

LANGUAGE RESEARCH CENTER

http://www.gsu.edu/~wwwlrc
> (Maintained by the Language Research Center at Georgia State University, this site contains useful information about ape language studies. Profiles of the various animal subjects, including Kanzi, are also available.)

ORIGINS OF HUMANKIND: ARTICLES: BRAIN

http://www.pro-am.com/origins/research/general_1.htm
> (A short article describing Dean Falk's "radiator theory" of brain cooling and evolution.)

THINKING ABOUT THINKING

http://humanitas.ucsb.edu/users/steen/Abstracts/Gardner_on_Mithen.html
> (An interesting review by psychologist Howard Gardner of Steven Mithen's book *The Prehistory of the Mind*.)

USEFUL SEARCH TERMS:
> *ape language*
> *brain evolution*
> *encephalization*
> *hominid brains*

Chapter 13 Timeline

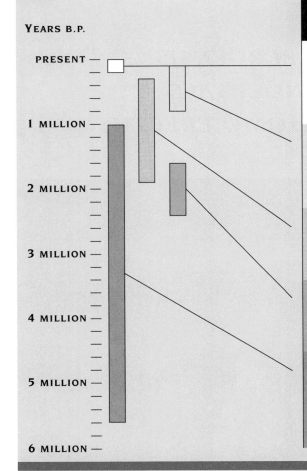

YEARS B.P.

PRESENT

1 MILLION

2 MILLION

3 MILLION

4 MILLION

5 MILLION

6 MILLION

SPECIES AND RECONSTRUCTED COMMUNICATION AND BRAIN ORGANIZATION

Homo sapiens: ca. 200,000 to 130,000 B.P. to present; hunting and gathering and, later, domestication of plants and animals; complex material culture; 1330 cc average brain; flexed cranial base and long pharynx; speech begins at 1–1.5 years; fully linguistic, allowing rapid and complex communication; full modern mind.

Homo heidelbergensis: 800,000 to 100,000 B.P.; hunting and gathering; bifacial tools of several styles; material culture increasing in complexity; average brain size over 1200 cc; first evidence of full basicranial flexion; group size may have been language-inducing and complex language possibly was developing; mind approaching modernity (?).

Homo erectus: 1.9 million to 300,000 B.P.; hunting and gathering; Acheulean bifacial tools and (probably, but late) fire, shelters; 994 cc average brain; flat cranial base and short pharynx; lacked fine control of breathing; probably lacked complex language and speech; primitive mind (?).

Early *Homo:* 2.4 to 1.6 million B.P.; scavenging and gathering; Oldowan choppers and flakes; 612–781 cc average brain; flat cranial base and short pharynx; probably lacked language and speech; primitive mind (?).

Australopithecus and *Paranthropus:* 5.6 to 1.0 million B.P.; gathering and scavenging(?); no conclusive evidence of tool manufacture or use; 410–530 cc average brain; flat cranial base and short pharynx (*Australopithecus*); some cranial base flexure and lengthening of the pharynx (*Paranthropus*); lacked significant enlargement of cortical speech and language areas; almost certainly lacked language and speech; apelike primitive mind (?).

As hominids' brains increased in size, so did the likelihood of linguistic communication. Anthropologists are confident of spoken language only among post-*erectus* species of *Homo*.

Chapter 14

HOMO HEIDELBERGENSIS AND THE NEANDERTALS: SUCCESSORS TO *HOMO ERECTUS*

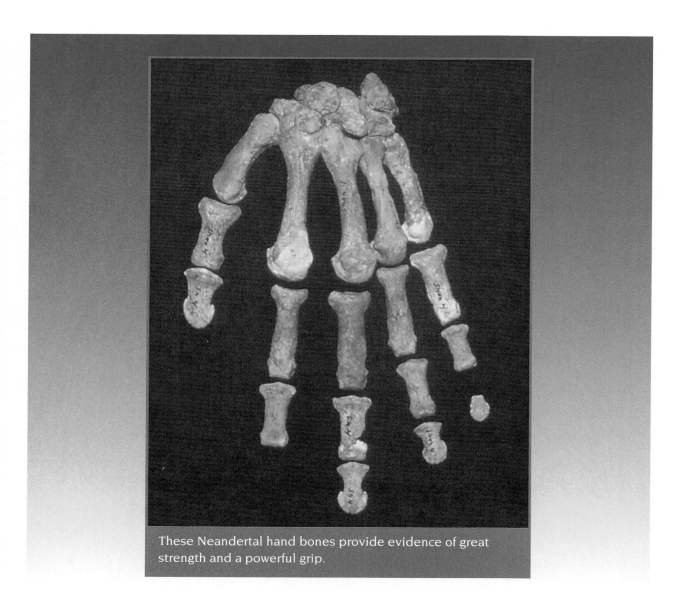

These Neandertal hand bones provide evidence of great strength and a powerful grip.

The savage . . . breathes only peace and liberty; he desires only to live and be free from labour.

JEAN-JACQUES ROUSSEAU, 1712–1778.
A Discourse on the Origin of Inequality.

And the life of man, solitary, poore, nasty, brutish, and short.
THOMAS HOBBES, 1588–1679. Leviathan, Pt. 1, Ch. 13.

OVERVIEW

Deciphering the hominid fossil record from the middle-to-late Pleistocene is quite difficult at present. The human types that came after *Homo erectus* were geographically widespread and anatomically variable, and as a consequence, workers disagree on the number of post-*erectus* species and their relations to one another. Although many paleoanthropologists currently recognize three such species— *Homo heidelbergensis*, **Homo neanderthalensis**, and *Homo sapiens*—no two experts agree on the exact allocation of fossils to these taxa and some researchers argue that additional post-*erectus* species should be recognized. Nonetheless, despite the confusion, a reasonable (but clearly provisional) interpretation of the later stages of hominid evolution has *Homo erectus* as the immediate ancestor of *H. heidelbergensis*, who, in turn, gave rise (at different times and in different places) to both the Neandertals (*H. neanderthalensis*) and modern *Homo sapiens*. The present chapter utilizes this evolutionary scheme as it describes the two premodern but post-*erectus* species, *Homo heidelbergensis* and the Neandertals. Following the chronological order of the species' discoveries, the Neandertals are discussed first, including a description of their long history of being misunderstood and bestialized. Important

Homo neanderthalensis a *species* of humans that inhabited Europe and the Middle East from about 300,000 to 30,000 B.P. Descended from *Homo heidelbergensis*, the species' common name is usually spelled Neandertal.

 Mini-Timeline

DATE OR AGE	FOSSIL DISCOVERIES OR EVOLUTIONARY EVENTS
(A) DATE (YEARS A.D.)	
1997	Genetic evidence suggests Neandertals were a distinct species
1976–1997	*H. heidelbergensis* and *H. neanderthalensis* fossils found at Atapuerca
1978	Dali skull discovered in northern China
1976	Bodo fossil found in Ethiopia
1921	Kabwe skull found in Zambia
1907	Mauer jaw (type specimen: *H. heidelbergensis*) found in Germany
1913	Boule's monograph on the La Chapelle Neandertal remains
1856–1848	Neandertal discoveries in Germany and Gibraltar
(B) AGE (YEARS B.P.)	
30,000	Approximate date of Neandertals' extinction
300,000	Oldest Neandertals at Sima de los Huesos (Atapuerca)
800,000	Oldest *Homo heidelbergensis* at Gran Dolina (Atapuerca)

topics and concepts in the chapter include the various fossil discoveries; the anatomy of *H. heidelbergensis* and *H. neanderthalensis*; Marcellin Boule's "misanalysis" of the Neandertals; recent genetic evidence that the Neandertals were a distinct species; and, finally, the evolutionary relationships connecting the post-*erectus* human types.

THE DESCENDANTS OF *HOMO ERECTUS*

Perhaps 800,000 years ago, a new species of humans split off from *Homo erectus*. This speciation event—which many investigators conclude occurred in Africa or western Eurasia—produced a larger-brained and smaller-jawed type of human classified here as *Homo heidelbergensis*. Subsequent migrations carried these still-premodern people throughout Africa, into Europe, and east as far as modern China. Within the confines of Europe, *H. heidelbergensis* gave rise to the even larger brained Neandertals around 300,000 years ago. And some 100,000 to 170,000 years later and back in Africa, a different *Homo heidelbergensis* population apparently evolved into anatomically modern people (*Homo sapiens*). Put thus, the outlines of mid-to-late Pleistocene human evolution seem simple. In reality, they are anything but clear. As described in this chapter, the three-part division of the successors of *Homo erectus*—into *Homo heidelbergensis*, *Homo neanderthalensis*, and *Homo sapiens*—is accepted by many, but not all, paleoanthropologists. The species names given to particular fossils are often controversial, origins and extinctions of individual species are generally hard to identify, and the possibility exists that additional species from this time period will be named in the future. Nonetheless, despite the remaining uncertainty, the evolutionary relationships described above serve well as a provisional framework for analyzing mid-to-late Pleistocene human remains. Problems with the framework will be pointed out as we go along. In the following section, we first turn our attention to the Neandertals because, although they are phylogenetically younger than *H. heidelbergensis*, they were discovered much earlier, at a time when Western science was just beginning to struggle with the possibility of human evolution.

FIRST VIEW OF NEANDERTALS

Of all the kinds of prehistoric peoples, certainly those who project the clearest image are the Neandertals. For many they are *the* Stone Age humans, shambling, beetle-browed louts who prowled the earth during the time of the glaciers. The Neandertals got such a poor reputation among the general public because they were grievously misjudged by the experts. Previously, many paleoanthropologists regarded Neandertals as a brutish breed that at best represented an insignificant side branch of the human family tree. Only recently has this misjudgment been remedied, and it now seems clear that they were members of a distinct and accomplished species. From perhaps as early as 300,000 years ago to about 30,000 years ago, they expanded the regions occupied by humans into arctic climates, devised ingenious stone tools to exploit nature, developed a relatively complex society, and possibly opened the door to the world of the supernatural. Clearly they were people of great achievements.

Why did the experts misjudge the Neandertals? Many reasons could be given: the scarcity of fossils, errors in reconstructing bone fragments, and other technical difficulties. But perhaps more important, these problems were compounded by an accident of timing. To tell the story of the Neandertals, we have to return again to the nineteenth century—to a time even before the publication of Darwin's *On the Origin of Species*, when almost no one believed that humankind had ever had a primitive ancestor.

The first fossil skull ever to be positively identified as belonging to an ancient human was that of a Neandertal. No one was prepared for the sight of a primitive-looking skeleton in the human closet, and when such a skeleton was found in 1856, it caught everyone off guard. Having nothing with which to compare the first Neandertal skull except the skull of a modern human, scientists of the time were struck more by the differences between the two than by their similarities. Today the reverse is true. Compared to their predecessors, *Homo erectus*, Neandertals showed considerable evolutionary advancement. They may have been a little shorter than the average modern European, and considerably heavier-featured, squatter, and more muscular than most, but with regard to brain size and some other features, they compare well to modern people.

First Discovery (1856)

The first Neandertal to be recognized as a primitive human was discovered in 1856, not far from the city of Düsseldorf, Germany, where a tributary stream of the Rhine flows through a steep-sided gorge known as the Neander Valley, *Neanderthal* in nineteenth-century German (see Figure 14–6). In 1856, the flanks of the gorge were being quarried for limestone. During the summer, workers blasted open a small cave about 60 feet (18 meters) above the stream. As they dug their pickaxes into the floor of the cave, they uncovered a number of ancient bones. But the quarriers were intent on limestone; they did not pay much attention to the bones, and most of what was probably a complete skeleton of a Neandertal was lost. Only the skullcap (Figure 14–1), ribs, part of the pelvis, and some limb bones were saved.

The owner of the quarry thought these fragments belonged to a bear, and he presented them to a local science teacher, J. K. Fuhlrott, who was known to be interested in such things. Fuhlrott had enough knowledge of anatomy to realize that the skeletal remains came not from a bear but from a most extraordinary human with thick limb bones and a heavy, slanted brow. The appearance of the bones suggested to Fuhlrott that they were fossilized and thus very ancient. Furthermore, their primitive characteristics hinted at an entirely unknown variety of ancient humans.

Knowing that this judgment was bound to be disputed, Fuhlrott called in Hermann Schaffhausen, professor of anatomy at the University of Bonn. Schaffhausen agreed that the bones represented one of the "most ancient races of man." He had in mind, however, an age of no more than a few thousand years; the fossil fragments could have come, he suggested, from some barbarian who had lived in northern Europe before the Celtic and Germanic tribes arrived.

Missing Links in the Chain of Being

Schaffhausen can hardly be criticized for missing the truth about the bones from the Neander Valley: the scientific community of 1856 did not realize that humankind had been on earth for a substantial length of time, and no respectable scientist believed that people had ever existed in any form other than that of the modern human. Such a notion would have been directly contrary to the belief in Genesis and in what was known as the Chain of Being, a grandly conceived hierarchy of all

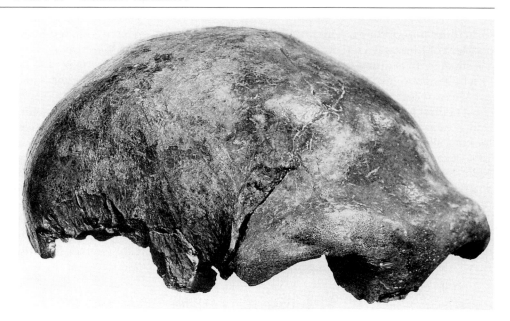

FIGURE 14–1   The skullcap from the Neander Valley is possibly the most famous fossil discovery ever made. Following its discovery in 1856, it was thought by many to be the skull of some pathological idiot. Today we know that it belonged to an early, but by no means excessively primitive, variety of humans. This photograph is just over one-half actual size.

living things. The separate links of the Chain of Being were thought by most scientists to have been fixed forever at the Creation; species never changed and certainly never evolved from the lowlier forms.

As we have seen (Chapter 1), this orderly scheme still held in 1856, but it was being shaken both by changing ideas about the age of the earth and by the appearance of animal bones unlike those of any living creature, suggesting to some dissenting thinkers that the Chain of Being did not tell the full story of life. But extinct animals were not the only threat to the established scheme. Records exist of a few primitive-looking human fossils that were found as early as the year 1700, and many finds probably went unrecorded before (and after) that. Remains that are now also known to be Neandertal had been uncovered in Belgium in 1829 and on the north face of Gibraltar in 1848. Unlike the bones from the Neander Valley, however, these finds received no publicity, and science was not forced to grapple with their significance. But when Darwin's *On the Origin of Species* was published in 1859, the way was open to the recognition of fossilized human ancestors of not completely human form.

Homo neanderthalensis?

Experts familiar with human skeletons and skull structure could see some very peculiar things about this Neandertal skull (see Figure 14–1). It was clearly human-like, yet it had strongly developed eyebrow ridges and a retreating forehead, and it was much flatter on top and more bulging in the back than is typical of the skull of a modern human. At the time, it was easier to regard the skull as a deformed specimen of a modern human skull than to accept the possibility that human ancestors actually looked like that. That opinion of the skull—that its owner had been a not very ancient pathological idiot—prevailed for many years.

Darwin heard about these remarkable bones but never investigated them. However, his friend and supporter Thomas H. Huxley undertook a thorough study of the unprecedented skull. In the condition in which it had been discovered, Huxley determined that the cranium could hold 63 cubic inches (1,030 cubic centimeters) of water; complete, it would have contained 75 cubic inches (1,230 cubic centimeters), which is not far from the average cranial volume of many modern people. Therefore the brain must have been of modern size, too, and the limb bones, though on the bulky side, Huxley found to be "quite those of an European of middle stature."

"Under whatever aspect we view this cranium," wrote Huxley in 1863, "we meet with ape-like characteristics, stamping it as the most pithecoid [apelike] of human crania yet discovered." In view of the large cranial capacity, however, Huxley did not see Neandertal as an ancestral form. He wrote, "In no sense can the Neanderthal bones be regarded as the remains of a human being intermediate between men and apes." Noting that the fossils were more nearly allied to the apes than these creatures are to monkeys and prosimians, he concluded that they were human. "In still older strata," Huxley wondered, "do the fossilized bones of an Ape more anthropoid, or a Man more pithecoid, than any yet known await the researches of some unborn palaeontologist?"

Meanwhile, a second skull had been brought to England from the Natural History Society collections in Gibralter, where it had been discovered in a cave in 1848. When it was exhibited at the meetings of the British Association for the Advancement of Science in 1864, it was seen quite clearly to be a second example of a human with the hitherto unique but recognizable shape of the Neandertal skull.

William King, professor of anatomy at Queen's College in Galway, Ireland, accepted the German fossil as an extinct form of humanity. In 1864, King suggested that the specimen be placed in a separate species, *Homo neanderthalensis*. In giving the fossil the genus name *Homo*, King was acknowledging a general similarity to humankind, but he believed that he could not add the species name for modern humans, *sapiens*, because, as he wrote, "The Neanderthal skull is so eminently simian . . . I am constrained to believe that the thoughts and desires which once dwelt within it never soared beyond those of the brute."

King's taxonomic assessment was closer to being correct than anyone else's, but he changed his thinking when he heard what the German pathologist Rudolf Virchow had to say. In a closely reasoned paper, Virchow stated that the man from the Neander Valley was not ancient at all, but a modern man who had suffered from **rickets** in childhood and arthritis in old age; at some time during his life, he had also received several stupendous blows on the head. This pronouncement, coming from a highly respected source, effectively silenced all further speculation.

Rickets pathological condition involving curvature of the bones; caused by insufficient vitamin D.

How could authorities such as Rudolph Virchow conclude that the Neandertal bones were modern? The incompleteness of the fossil was one factor: because the skull lacked a face and a jaw, it was hard to tell what the original owner had looked like. Also, no one could say for certain that the Neandertal bones were really old, for no stone tools or bones of extinct animals had accompanied the fossil, and no reliable methods of dating existed. Without proof of great age, it was thought best to err on the side of caution and presume a date not too remote from the present. It would not be fair to indict the cautious scientists of the day for inclining toward the safest position. Those who accepted the theories of Darwin were open-minded by any standard, but it took a large measure of intellectual courage to surrender the accepted wisdom of centuries for Darwin's brave new world of evolution.

The Darwinians, to their great credit, were actively interested in discovering a primitive human ancestor from the moment *On the Origin of Species* appeared. But they had no way of knowing where to look. Huxley, a bold and brilliant man, believed that there was little hope of finding fossils that would reveal human evolutionary history. Some of the evolutionists did not even think that it was necessary to peer into the past. They believed that the present offered examples of humans who were intermediate between the evolutionists themselves and some primitive ancestral form. One presumed authority pointed to mental institutions: "I do not hesitate to uphold . . . that microcephali and born idiots present as perfect a series from man to ape as may be wished for." Although such surmises received only slight approval, they do suggest one reason for failure to understand the evolutionary significance of Neandertal. Scientists evidently did not expect evolutionary intermediates to turn up in a cave, and so they never really gave the evidence a fair chance.

As soon as Virchow had announced that the odd appearance of the bones from the Neander Valley was the result of disease rather than antiquity, the fossil ceased to disturb anatomists. They simply forgot about it. Prehistorians, however, were still very interested in finding an ancient fossil ancestor of *Homo sapiens*—as long as the fossil looked like a modern human; anything that resembled an animal ancestor, or an ape or a monkey, would surely be rejected automatically.

Discoveries at Spy (1886)

In 1886, additional primitive-looking fossils appeared. A cave near a town called Spy in Belgium (see Figure 14–6) yielded two skeletons. One skull, probably from a female, was reminiscent of the original fossil from the Neander Valley, although the cranium was higher and the forehead somewhat less slanted. The other skull was virtually identical to the German find (see Figure 14–2). Coincidence? Yes, said Rudolf Virchow, dismissing the Spy skeletons as further diseased specimens of modern humans. But this explanation began to sound hollow. Not only was such a coincidence of pathological deformity most unlikely, but these fossils were

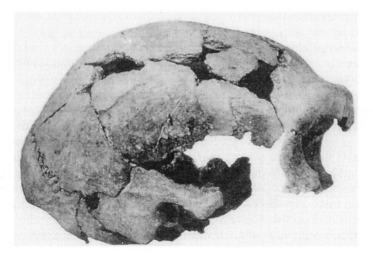

FIGURE 14–2   The skull of Spy I, though incomplete, shows clearly the long head and the large brow ridges typical of Neandertals. This photograph is approximately 40 percent actual size.

definitely very old: along with them were found primitive stone tools and remains of extinct animals. Most scientists were obliged to admit that an archaic people, distinct from modern humans, had indeed lived in Europe during some bygone era.

The fossil skeletons found at Spy lacked some parts, but they were complete enough to serve as models for a rough sketch of the Neandertals. These people were short and thickset. Their heads were long and low, with large brow ridges. Their faces were massive and protruding, with a heavy jaw but a receding chin. Could these have been our ancestors? Nearly all scientists said no. They were willing to give Neandertal a place on the human family tree, but not on any branch shared by modern humanity. Some authorities believed that the Neandertals might represent an offshoot from the main evolutionary line; if they were related to humans at all, they were poor and distant relatives.

By this time the initial shocked reaction to Darwin's theory of evolution was over, and the disturbing idea that humans had been around for tens or hundreds of thousands of years was becoming accepted. The fossils from Spy indicated that the Neandertals were ancient people, not modern ones deformed by disease. And Dubois's discovery of small-brained *Pithecanthropus* (Chapter 10) helped put the Neandertals in perspective. Although most experts were not yet willing to trace our lineage through a Neandertal stage of evolution, their belief that humankind could never have looked so primitive as Neandertal was being recognized as perhaps a subjective feeling, and thus open to debate. At this time, when the riddle of human ancestry was already confusing, new evidence appeared that further complicated the problem.

La Chapelle-aux-Saints (1908) and Other Finds

In the first decade of the twentieth century, archaeologists were at work in the Dordogne region of southwestern France (see Figure 14–6 and 16–2). From the 1860s on, countless stone tools had been found in southwestern France, proof that the Dordogne had been a population center in ancient times. Beginning in 1908, a magnificent series of Neandertal fossils was also discovered. One of the first fossils to turn up was the skeleton of an old man in a cave near the village of La Chapelle-aux-Saints (Figure 14–3). A nearby cave at Le Moustier, from which quantities of stone implements had been excavated earlier, yielded the skeleton of a Neandertal youth. A rock shelter at La Ferrassie produced adult male and female Neandertals and later the remains of several children (see Figure 14–4). Another rock shelter at La Quina held parts of several Neandertal skeletons.

The great value of this material was its completeness. The bones from Spy had given a rough portrait of the Neandertal people, but as long as the fossil record remained essentially fragmentary, venturesome scholars could leap to extremes and see them as either *Homo sapiens* or very apelike. The wealth of skeletal material from southwestern France now seemed to promise enough data to set the most vivid anthropological imagination to rest. Now scientists would be able to reconstruct what a Neandertal looked like and study the physical resemblances—or lack of them—between Neandertals and modern humans.

Boule's Reconstruction (1911–1913)

The man from La Chapelle-aux-Saints was selected for a detailed reconstruction of what was thought to be a typical Neandertal. The task of rebuilding the skeleton

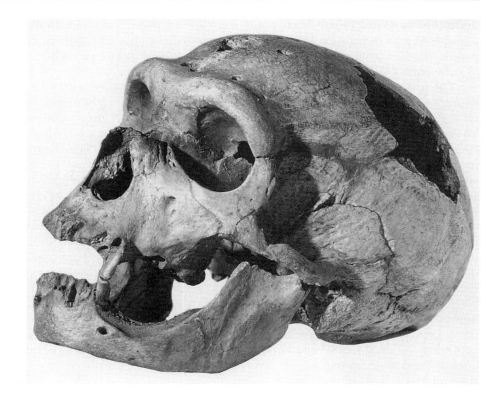

FIGURE 14–3   The skull of the old man of La Chapelle-aux-Saints shows he lost many teeth during life. He was less than 5 feet (1.5 meters) tall and bent by arthritis, but he had a large cranial capacity of about 1,625 cubic centimeters. The average modern human capacity is 1,330 cc. The photograph is approximately 45 percent actual size.

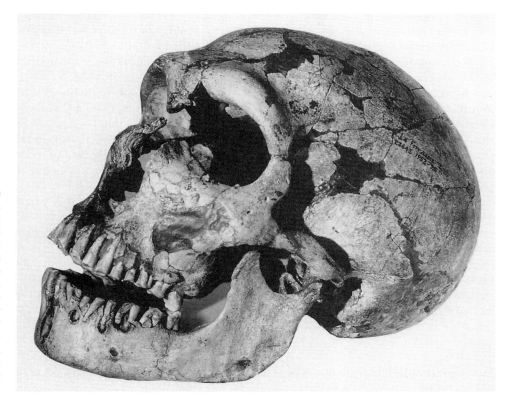

FIGURE 14–4   The male skeleton from La Ferrassie, buried with five others, had an even larger cranial capacity than La Chappelle: 1,689 cubic centimeters. His front teeth show a rare type of extreme wear that is found today among some Eskimo tribes and other hunting people. It may have been caused by chewing animal skins to soften them for clothing. This photograph is just over 40 percent actual size.

FIGURE 14–5   Marcellin Boule made a series of errors when he reconstructed the skeleton from La Chapelle-aux-Saints and so implied that all Neandertal people walked with stooping gait and bent knees.

fell to a French paleontologist named Marcellin Boule, of the French National Museum of Natural History. On this project, Boule had an unusually fine set of bones to work with. The materials were well preserved, and although some of the bones were broken, everything of importance was available except some teeth and vertebrae. Despite the completeness and good condition of the bones, Boule proceeded to commit an astonishing series of errors—and they were not corrected for decades. Boule's mistakes—due in equal parts to his theoretical leanings, his habit of ignoring important work by others when it suited him, and the fact that human paleontology was in its infancy—combined to make the reconstructed skeleton appear quite apelike from head to toe (see Figure 14–5). He mistakenly arranged the foot bones so that the big toe diverged from the other toes like an opposable thumb, which implied that Neandertals walked on the outer part of their feet, like apes. Boule's interpretation of the knee joint was equally incorrect: he declared that Neandertals could not fully extend their legs, a fact that would have resulted in the bent-knee gait that observers could readily see the skeleton would adopt if it could walk. In every respect, the posture of Boule's reconstruction seemed nonhuman. Unfortunately, photographs of Boule's reconstruction appeared in many textbooks during the first half of the twentieth century.

The most devastating conclusion of Boule's study was on the intelligence of the man from La Chapelle-aux-Saints. Boule ignored the fossil's large cranial capacity. He looked only at the long, low skull—and perceived severe mental retardation. He cited the interior of the skull as support for this judgment; measuring the space behind the retreating forehead, the paleontologist determined to his satisfaction that there was not much room for the frontal portion of the brain, which was then thought (incorrectly) to be the center of higher intelligence. And so Boule ranked the fossil man's brainpower somewhere between that of apes and modern humans, but closer to that of the apes.

Boule wrote disparagingly of the "brutish appearance of this muscular and clumsy body, and of the heavy-jawed skull that declares the predominance of a purely vegetative or bestial kind over the functions of the mind. . . . What a contrast with the men of the next period, the men who had a more elegant body, a finer head, an upright and spacious brow, and who were the first to merit the glorious title of *Homo sapiens!*" Boule was willing to grant the Neandertals the honor of the genus *Homo*, but he relegated them to *Homo neanderthalensis*—in his view a separate, aberrant species that had died out long ago.

Marcellin Boule was a man of excellent reputation and formidable diligence, virtues that made his errors all the more serious. Between 1911 and 1913, he published his conclusions in three exhaustive volumes. Packed with detail and ringing with confidence, these monographs had tremendous influence on scientists and the public alike. Although a few prehistorians stuck to their view that Neandertals were respectable ancestors of modern humans, practically everyone now believed that such a lineage had been proved impossible.

The sheer force of Boule's work was not the only reason for its acceptance. Some circumstantial evidence pointed toward an evolutionary gap between the Neandertals and the later **Cro-Magnons,** those "elegant men of the next period" to whom Boule referred, who by this time were acknowledged to be the immediate ancestors of present-day Europeans. (The Cro-Magnons are discussed in Chapters 16 and 17.) Even if the Neandertals were not quite as debased as Boule supposed, they definitely looked different from the anatomically modern Cro-Magnons, and no one had come across a fossil that indicated an evolutionary transition between the two. Without an intermediate fossil, it was only prudent to assume that the Cro-Magnons derived from stock that had been occupying Europe or some other part of the world during or possibly before the era of the Neandertals, thus granting the Neandertals no significance in human evolution.

Archaeologists believed that there was no cultural connection between the Neandertal and the Cro-Magnon peoples. The stone tools of the Cro-Magnons seemed markedly more sophisticated than Neandertal implements. And when archaeologists dug down through successive layers in caves, they sometimes found sterile layers between the Neandertal deposits and the deposits left by Cro-Magnons, indicating that no one had occupied the cave for a time. These layers containing no sign of human occupation were interpreted as proof that the Neandertals had become extinct without having given rise to their successors in western Europe.

For the better part of the twentieth century, the classification of the Neandertals and their place in hominid evolution was in dispute. Some paleoanthropologists have preferred to follow William King's lead of 1864 and give them a separate species designation, *Homo neanderthalensis*. Others have opted to include the Neandertals within *Homo sapiens*, but as a distinct subspecies, *H. sapiens neanderthalensis*. As a result of this uncertainty, there has been continuing controversy about whether or not the Neandertals made a genetic contribution to modern people. As detailed in a later section, many of these problems recently have been clarified by the extraction and analysis of Neandertal DNA. This genetic research suggests strongly that the Neandertals did belong to a different species from modern people and thus it is unlikely that we carry many (if any) of their genes. Furthermore, there is evidence that the Neandertal species is much older than anyone ever expected, having split off from the line leading to modern humans some three hundred thousand years ago. But, *Homo sapiens* or not, archaeological studies and fossil discoveries made since Boule's day have shown that the

Cro-Magnon anatomically modern humans living in Europe between 40,000 and 10,000 years ago.

Neandertals were a very capable and successful species that spread widely across Europe and western Asia. It is to those discoveries and studies that we now turn our attention.

NEANDERTALS IN EUROPE AND BEYOND

Marcellin Boule had depicted the Neandertals as creatures that might have had a hard time surviving, much less thriving, in the world. But if geographic range is any measure of success, these "uncouth and repellent" people seem to have done quite well. As shown in Figure 14–6, Neandertal remains and artifacts have been recovered from the western extremes of Europe (from Gibraltar and possibly Pontnewydd in Wales), throughout the bulk of that continent, and to the east as far as Israel, Iraq, and Uzbekistan (Teshik-Tash is one of the easternmost sites). In fact, the world of the Neandertals was quite extensive, covering an area some 4,000 miles (6,400 kilometers) east to west and 1,500 miles (2,400 kilometers) north to south. The fossil record shows that they inhabited that world for some 270,000 years and biomolecular estimates may increase that figure to as much as 500,000 years (discussed in a later section). Furthermore, the archaeological record shows that the Neandertals' culture was rich and included a number of modern traits, at least in incipient form (see Chapter 15). They were very much like us in many ways, but quite different in others. Table 14–1 lists several of the more important Neandertal sites, along with their ages.

TABLE 14-1   *A Partial Record of Neandertal Sites*

GEOGRAPHIC AREA	SITE	AGE (YEARS B.P.)
Europe	Zafarraya	30,000–27,000
	St. Césaire	36,000–32,000
	Le Moustier	41,000
	La Chapelle-aux-Saints	47,000
	Gibraltar	50,000
	Monte Circeo	52,000
	La Quina	64,000
	Spy	68,000
	La Ferrassie	70,000
	Neander Valley	100,000–30,000
	Krapina	100,000
	Fontechevade	115,000
	Saccopastore	120,000
	Biache-St.-Vaast	180,000–130,000
	Ehringsdorf	225,000
	Pontnewydd[a]	225,000
	Atapuerca (Sima de los Huesos)	300,000
Middle East and Western Asia	Amud	41,000
	Kebara	64,000–60,000
	Shanidar	70,000–50,000
	Teshik-Tash	75,000–30,000(?)
	Tabūn	110,000

[a] The Pontnewydd specimens are linked to the Neandertal lineage only by shared dental traits.

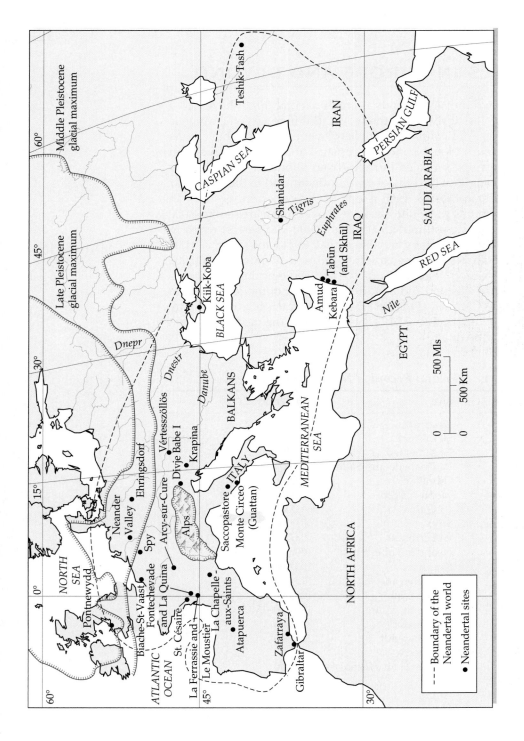

FIGURE 14–6 The Neandertals' world extended over Europe, the Middle East, and portions of western Asia. Only a few of the known Neandertal sites are shown. (After Annick Peterson from *In Search of the Neanderthals* by Christopher Stringer and Clive Gamble. © 1993 Christopher Stringer and Clive Gamble. Reprinted by permission of the publishers, Thames and Hudson.)

Discoveries from Israel

During the early 1930s, a joint Anglo-American expedition was looking for fossils in what is now Israel, then called Palestine. The expedition had extraordinary good luck in two caves on the slopes of Mount Carmel, overlooking the Mediterranean near Haifa (see Figure 14–6). The first find, at Mugharet et-Tabūn (Cave of the Oven), was a female skeleton, definitely Neandertal-like but possessing a skull slightly higher-domed than usual and with a more vertical forehead. A second Mount Carmel site, Mugharet es-Skhūl (Cave of the Kids), yielded remains of ten individuals. Some resembled Neandertals in a few features, others looked more advanced, and one approached the appearance of modern humans (Figure 14–7). This last individual displayed only a trace of the Neandertal brow ridge, but the forehead was steeper, the jaw more delicate, the chin more pronounced, and the shape of the cranium distinctly modern. Today we have further important discoveries from Israel: undoubted Neandertal skeletons from Amud (north of the Sea of Galilee; see the color essay on fossil hominids) and Kebara, and several more of the modern-looking skeletons from Qafzeh (south of Nazareth). The variation exhibited is striking. The sites from this region appear to span a period from about 120,000 to 40,000 years B.P.

The initial impression left by the Skhūl and Qafzeh people was that they occupied an evolutionary middle ground between the Neandertals and modern humans. They were certainly extremely variable in form. Some paleoanthropologists concluded that these fossils were hybrids: products of interbreeding between

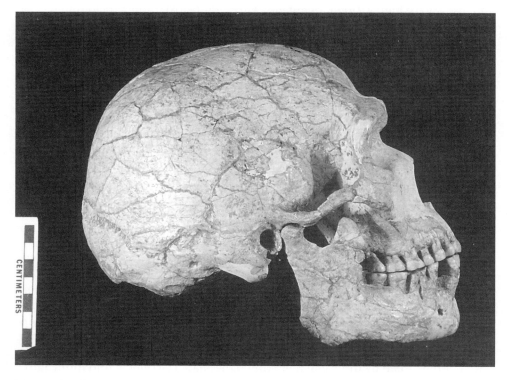

FIGURE 14–7   Shown here is the skull of an early *Homo sapiens* fossil from the cave of Skhūl on the slopes of Mount Carmel. This skull shows several modern features, including a chin and a relatively steep forehead. The photograph is about 45 percent actual size.

Neandertals and modern-type people. Louis Leakey even suggested that any mating between Neandertals and people of modern type might well have produced sterile offspring, like a mule born of a horse and a donkey. Today, both the Skhūl and Qafzeh specimens are classified as early representatives of *Homo sapiens*, albeit with a good deal of anatomical diversity.

The latest dates for the Middle Eastern cave-dwellers are surprising and have necessitated considerable revision in our understanding of human occupation in that region. Although scientists originally believed that more modern-looking people lived only after the Neandertals, new dates based on uranium analyses, thermoluminescence, and electron spin resonance indicate that Neandertals and early moderns may have been approximate contemporaries in the Middle East for thousands of years. The Neandertal remains from Tabūn are now known to date to approximately 110,000 years B.P., while the early moderns from Qafzeh and Skhūl date to 120,000 to 90,000 and 100,000 to 80,000 years B.P., respectively. Neandertals continued to use the region until at least 41,000 years ago, based on the dates from Amud, but by 37,000 years ago modern people were probably back in exclusive possession of the Middle East.

Other Mid-Eastern/Western Asian sites are worth mentioning before we return to Europe for the alpha and omega of the Neandertal specimens. First, the site of Shanidar in the Zagros Mountains of Iraq (Figure 14–6) yielded several Neandertal skeletons during excavations carried out between 1951 and 1960 (Shanidar is discussed in Chapter 15 in connection with Neandertal burial practices). Dated about 50,000 years B.P. or a little earlier, the Shanidar skeletons show fully developed and typical Neandertal traits (see the next section on anatomy), and also a very high incident of antemortem (pre-death) trauma including broken ribs, scalp wounds, apparent stab wounds, and degenerative joint disease. As paleoanthropologist Glenn Conroy of Washington University remarked, the "Neandertals clearly had a tough time of it" as they hunted and gathered and perhaps also fought with one another (see Chapter 15). Second, the easternmost Neandertal remains showed up in 1938 during work at the cave site of Teshik-Tash located in the Bajsun-Tau Mountains of Uzbekistan, about 78 miles (125 kilometers) south of Samarkand (Figure 14–6). At this rugged, high-altitude site, a nine-year-old Neandertal boy was found buried, and it appeared that some care had been given to the interment.

Oldest and Youngest Neandertals Found in Spain

For the most exciting recent fossil finds of Neandertals, however, we return to Europe and to the country of Spain. Here researchers have uncovered evidence not only of the very oldest members of the Neandertal lineage, but also what may have been the final survivors. The most ancient material comes from the site of the Sima de los Huesos (Pit of Bones) in the Sierra de Atapuerca, some 150 miles (250 kilometers) due north of Madrid. In the Sima de los Huesos, the remains of more than thirty-two early humans have been found deep in a cave, scattered about a small chamber at the bottom of a narrow shaft 40 feet (13 meters) deep. Intermingled with the bones of bears and other animals, the human remains in the Pit of Bones apparently accumulated as people living near the cave's mouth disposed of their dead by dumping them down the shaft. Carrying a minimum age of 200,000 B.P., but probably closer to 300,000 years old, the Sima de los Huesos fossils share many traits with *Homo erectus* and other features with modern *Homo*

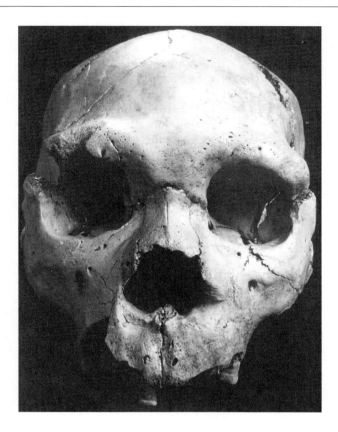

FIGURE 14–8   This skull from the Spanish site of Sima de los Huesos in the Sierra de Atapuerca displays several evolving Neandertal traits, including large brows and midfacial prognathism. Cranial capacity was 1,125 cubic centimeters. Photograph is about 55 percent actual size.

sapiens. The majority of their anatomical characteristics, however—including the shape of the brows, projection of the face, and the shape of the back of the braincase (see Figure 14–8)—are shared with undoubted Neandertals, and thus they are classified here as the oldest known members of that lineage.

The Neandertals seem to have made their evolutionary exit about 270,000 years later in the same region that witnessed their origin. The southern Spanish cave site of Zafarraya (Figure 14–6) has produced typical Neandertal stone tools (Mousterian tools; see Chapter 15) dating to 27,000 years B.P. From slightly older deposits (30,000 B.P.?) at the same site have come Neandertal fossils. It seems quite likely that the Zafarraya population was one of the last to become extinct as the Neandertals disappeared from the face of the earth.

NEANDERTAL ANATOMY

As noted earlier, Marcellin Boule's misanalysis of the La Chapelle-aux-Saints Neandertal skeleton misled anthropologists for quite some time. We now have a much more accurate picture of Neandertal anatomy thanks to a careful restudy of that specimen and to the discovery of several additional fossils. A La Chapelle restudy conducted in 1957 by William Strauss and A. J. E. Cave found that Boule had seriously underestimated the deforming effects of arthritis in the La Chapelle fossil—a condition that had affected the shape of the skeleton's vertebrae and jaw—and also that he had improperly reconstructed the feet and other parts of the body. Contrary to Boule's descriptions, the restudy showed that the Neandertal from La Chapelle-aux-Saints did not have prehensile big toes, apelike neck vertebrae, or an apelike pelvis. All in all, Strauss and Cave found their Neandertal subject to be quite modern in shape. They wrote, "If he could be reincarnated and placed in a New York subway—provided that he were bathed, shaved and dressed in modern clothing—it is doubtful whether he would attract any more attention than some of its other denizens."

Several of the more important anatomical features of the Neandertals are summarized in Box 14–1. As shown there, they were well within the range of modern body size (height and weight), although on average they were shorter and considerably more stocky than most living people. The Neandertals were built to withstand the extreme cold of the European Ice Ages (see Chapter 15). Their broad bodies and relatively short limbs helped to conserve heat in accordance with Bergmann's and Allen's rules (discussed in Chapter 18; see Figures 14–9 and 14–10). They were also built for strength, with thick limb bones, broad shoulder blades that anchored powerful arm muscles, and massive hands (see the chapter opener illustration). Atop their ruggedly built bodies, the Neandertals carried large and distinctive heads. Their skulls showed a long and rather low-vaulted braincase; midfacial prognathism; cheekbones that were swept back rather than laterally flaring; a large nose; large brow ridges; and variability in the degree of cranial base flexure (see Figures 14–2, 14–3, 14–4, and 14–8). Additionally, the Neandertal occipital bone at the back of the skull tended to protrude somewhat and featured a characteristic depression or pit for the attachment of neck muscles, the **suprainiac fossa**. And within their big skulls, the Neandertals possessed equally large brains. Average brain size calculated over their entire 300,000 to 30,000 B.P. time period is 1,410 cubic centimeters—some

Suprainiac fossa a characteristic depression on the occipital bone of *Neandertals*.

Box 14-1

CHARACTERISTICS OF THE NEANDERTALS[a]

TRAIT	*HOMO NEANDERTHALENSIS*
Height (sexes combined)	4.9–5.6 ft (150–170 cm)
Weight (sexes combined)	110–143 lb (50–65 kg)
Brain size (sexes combined)	1,410 cc mean (1,125–1,750 cc range)
Cranium	Occipital depression (*suprainiac fossa*); occipital torus; large nose; midfacial prognathism; variability in degree of cranial base flexure; modern hyoid bone
Dentition	Large incisors: gap behind lower M3
Limbs	Robust, stocky physique as adaptation to cold; short legs; powerful hands
Locomotion	Bipedalism
Distribution	Middle East, Europe, Western Asia
Known dates (thousand yrs)	300,000–30,000 years B.P.

[a] Mean values for anatomical measurements may change with the addition of new fossil discoveries. For additional technical details and diagnostic traits, see Appendix III.

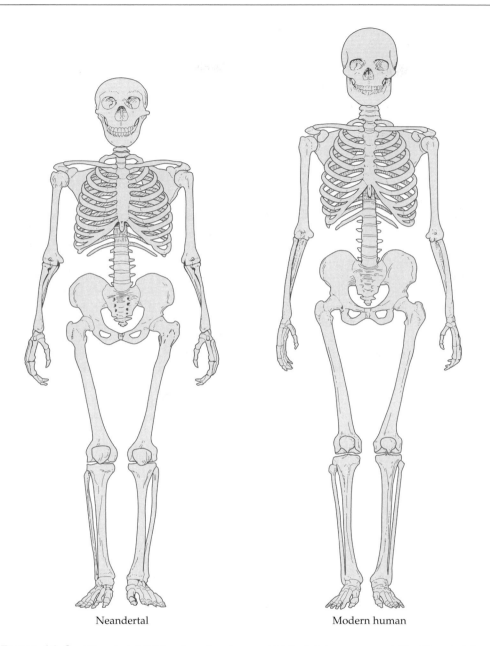

Neandertal   Modern human

Figure 14–9 Neandertal (left) and modern human (right) skeletons compared. The Neandertals possessed a shorter, more robust body, with a broad chest and powerful arms and hands. Note also the interspecific differences in brow size and height of the cranial vault. (From *The Last Neanderthal* by Ian Tattersall. Westview Press, 1999.)

6 percent more than modern humans' average size (1,330 cubic centimeters) and 10 percent more than that of the Neandertals' immediate ancestors, *Homo heidelbergensis*. Furthermore, brain size seems to have increased from early to late Neandertal times. Pre-classic Neandertals from the period of 300,000 to 100,000 B.P. showed an average cranial capacity of 1,275 cubic centimeters, while so-called classic

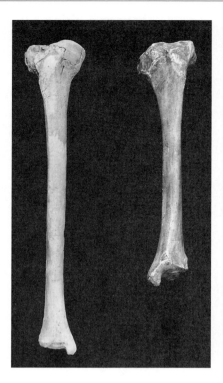

FIGURE 14–10   The short and strong tibia (shinbone) on the near left is from the Neandertal site of Spy. It is noticeably different from the less robust, longer, non-European tibia on the far left, which is from Skhūl. The plaster cast of a Neandertal footprint from an Italian cave suggests a broad, short foot. Both photographs are approximately one-fifth of actual size.

Neandertals (90,000 to 30,000 B.P.) showed an average of 1,519 cubic centimeters—a 19 percent intraspecific increase in brain size.

The Neandertals' jaws and teeth also had certain distinctive features (see Figures 14–3 and 14–4). The mandible usually lacked a chin, although some individuals showed incipient development of this trait. Midfacial prognathism resulted in the lower toothrow being moved forward, producing a characteristic space between the last molar and the **ramus** of the mandible (the **retromolar gap**). Finally, many Neandertal fossils show extreme wear of the front teeth (Figure 14–11), a feature thought to reflect the use of the teeth as tools (Figure 14–12).

In summary, the Neandertals were smallish, but powerful and rugged people who thrived for some 270,000 years in Europe and certain adjacent areas. Although the latest studies show that they probably were not us—that is, not *Homo sapiens*—but rather a distinct species, *Homo neanderthalensis*, they were a remarkable offshoot of hominid evolution and produced a complex culture (described in Chapter 15). Interpretations of the Neandertals' evolutionary origin and ultimate extinction will be presented in a later section, but first we must return to the mid-Pleistocene and take a look at the Neandertals' probable ancestor (and ours as well), *Homo heidelbergensis*.

Ramus the vertical portion of the *mandible*; as opposed to the mandibular body, which bears the teeth.

Retromolar gap the space between the M3 and the mandibular *ramus*; characteristic of *Neandertals*.

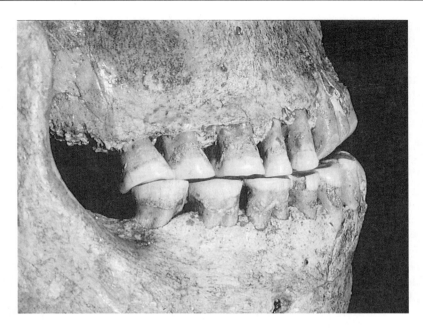

FIGURE 14–11   Lateral view of the dentition of a Neandertal from Shanidar, Iraq. The retromolar gap is obvious at the left and strong wear can be seen on the upper front teeth (right).

FIGURE 14–12   American Museum of Natural History reconstruction of a classic Neandertal group. Note how the woman in the center is anchoring an animal skin with her teeth as she scrapes it with a stone tool. Such use of the teeth would have caused the wear seen in Figure 14–11.

SPECIATION IN THE MIDDLE PLEISTOCENE: *HOMO HEIDELBERGENSIS*

As noted at the start of this chapter, fully a half million years before the appearance of the Neandertals there was another, and extremely important, hominid speciation event. By about 800,000 B.P., humans who were larger-brained and smaller-jawed than *Homo erectus* had evolved in Africa or western Eurasia. It was not long at all before similar humans were living in modern-day Spain, Germany, and England, and by perhaps 600,000 years ago they could be found in eastern Asia as well (see Figure 14–13 and Table 14–2). These various populations are grouped here into the species *Homo heidelbergensis*—a taxon thought by many researchers to be ancestral (at different times and in different places) both to the Neandertals and to *Homo sapiens*.

African Fossils

In 1921, some laborers mining lead and zinc ore in Zambia (previously Northern Rhodesia), thousands of miles from Europe, uncovered a skull and other human bones that somewhat resembled Neandertals. The fossil fragments came from a cave in a knoll called Broken Hill, which rose above plateau country just north of the Zambesi River, at a place called Kabwe (see Figure 14–13). The presence of stone tools and extinct animal bones indicated considerable age, and indeed the skull is currently dated at 250,000 to 130,000 years B.P.

The fossil human from Kabwe had a large, heavy skull (1,285 cubic centimeters) and a receding forehead like the European Neandertals. The heavy bar of bone over the eyes was even more pronounced than any yet seen. But there were also anatomical differences: the limb bones were straighter and more slender than those of the European Neandertals.

The newly discovered fossil (Figure 14–14) was called *Rhodesian Man*. Where did it fit into human evolution? Its age initially was uncertain. Some scholars,

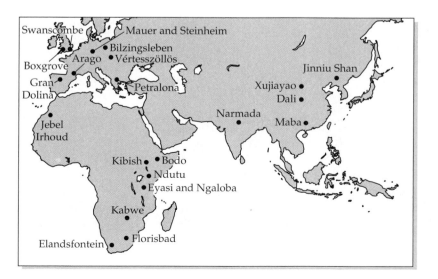

Figure 14–13   Fossils of *Homo heidelbergensis* have been found in Africa, Asia, and Europe. This map shows only a sample of all known sites.

TABLE 14-2 *A Partial Record of* **Homo heidelbergensis** *Sites*

Geographic Area	Site	Age (Years B.P.)
Africa	Singa (Sudan)	97,000
	Jebel Irhoud	125,000–90,000
	Eyasi	130,000–35,000(?)
	Omo Kibish 2	130,000(?)
	Ngaloba (LH18)	150,000–125,000
	Kabwe	250,000–130,000
	Florisbad	260,000
	Elandsfontein	350,000–130,000
	Ndutu	400,000–200,000
	Bodo	600,000
Asia	Xujiayao	125,000–100,000
	Narmada	150,000
	Maba	150,000
	Dali	300,000–200,000
	Jinniu Shan	300,000–200,000
	Diring Yuriakh(?)	300,000
	Yunxian	600,000(?)
Europe	Vértesszöllös	210,000
	Steinheim	250,000
	Swanscombe	250,000
	Bilzingsleben	340,000–230,000
	Petralona	400,000–200,000
	Arago	400,000
	Boxgrove	500,000
	Mauer	700,000–400,000
	Atapuerca (Gran Dolina, TD6)	800,000

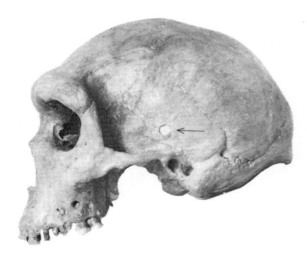

Figure 14–14 *Homo heidelbergensis* people somewhat similar to the European Neandertals flourished during the same period in Africa. This skull from Kabwe, in Zambia, is exceptionally powerfully built. The hole in the temporal bone (arrow) was probably caused during life by a small tumor. This photograph is approximately 40 percent actual size.

echoing Virchow, proclaimed that the Rhodesian fossil was from a modern-day mortal deformed by disease. A British expert entrusted with the job of describing the bones for his fellow scientists went to the opposite extreme. Following Boule's example, he declared that the formation of the pelvis "leaves no doubt that the gait of Rhodesian Man was simian, and that he walked with a stoop." He considered the creature "nearer to the Chimpanzee and Gorilla than was Neandertal Man." We now know that this analysis was completely erroneous.

Since then further discoveries have followed: a cranium found in 1953 at Elandsfontein, South Africa, on an open site near Saldanha Bay has turned out to be very similar to the Kabwe skull, though less complete. It is probably of about the same age, though it may be older, possibly dating to 350,000 years B.P. In 1973, a crushed human skull was found near Lake Ndutu in Tanzania, which has turned out to be of the same general type but may be even older (400,000 to 200,000 years B.P.)

Finally, a cranium found in 1976 at Bodo, Ethiopia, carried the African fossil record of *Homo heidelbergensis* all the way back to 600,000 years B.P. (Figure 14–15 and Table 14–2). Although discovered in association with Acheulean artifacts, the Bodo fossil has a much larger cranial capacity (1,300 cubic centimeters) than expected for *Homo erectus* and also shows a more modern skull shape. In particular, Bodo shares a number of facial traits with the Kabwe skull and with more modern humans.

Asian Fossils

Asia too has contributed its share of apparent *Homo heidelbergensis* remains, some quite ancient. Examples include the fossil from the Narmada Valley, near

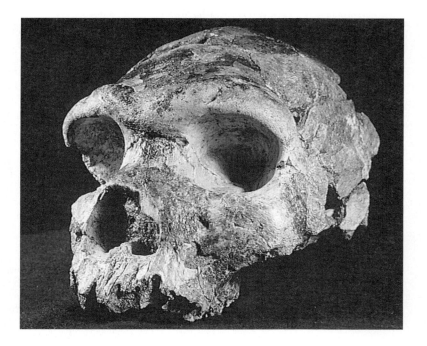

FIGURE 14–15   The Bodo cranium is the oldest African *Homo heidelbergensis*, dating to 600,000 years B.P. Skull is about 70 percent actual size.

Hoshangabad in central India, where Indian paleontologist Arun Sonakia made the first discovery of a Pleistocene hominid from the subcontinent. In 1982, Sonakia unearthed a heavy skullcap (without a jaw) from alluvial river deposits of the late Middle Pleistocene epoch—probably in the region of 150,000 years B.P. The skull is heavily built and reminiscent of the Beijing *Homo erectus* fossils; it also bears some resemblances to European forms. Though it still remains to be described in detail, it seems best classified as *Homo heidelbergensis*. It is associated with hand axes, cleavers, and scrapers of quartzite, together with some small flint artifacts. Its considerable importance lies in the way it links Europe and China both geographically and anatomically.

China itself has produced several fossils of *Homo heidelbergensis*, including some with impressively early dates (see Table 14–2 and Figure 14–13). From the site of Dali in north China, a nearly complete skull dating 300,000 to 200,000 years B.P. was discovered in 1978. The Dali fossil resembles *Homo erectus* in its long, low, thick-walled cranium and large brow ridges, but it seems more modern in the higher placement of maximum cranial width and reduced postorbital constriction. Furthermore, the midfacial dimensions of the Dali fossil seem most similar to the *H. heidelbergensis* specimens from Steinheim, Arago, and Jebel Irhoud. With a cranial capacity of 1,120 cubic centimeters, Dali seems best classified as Chinese *Homo heidelbergensis*, at least tentatively. Similar classification appears appropriate for fossil remains from the sites of Xujiayao (125,000 to 100,000 years B.P.), Maba (150,000 years B.P.), Jinniu Shan, and possibly Yunxian. The Jinniu Shan site has yielded a probable *Homo heidelbergensis* skull with an impressive cranial capacity of 1,390 cubic centimeters that dates from about 300,000 to 200,000 years ago. Yunxian has produced two crania that are even older—possibly as much as 600,000 years of age according to recent paleomagnetic work—but whose mixture of "*erectus*-like" and more modern traits makes them hard to classify. The Yunxian skulls are tentatively included in *Homo heidelbergensis* pending further information.

And finally, there is new and tantalizing archaeological evidence suggesting that the geographic range of *Homo heidelbergensis* may have extended as far as northern Siberia. In 1982, stone choppers and flakes were discovered by Russian archaeologists at the site of Diring Yuriakh, located on the Lena River south of the town of Yakutsk, some 1,500 miles (2,400 kilometers) north of Beijing, China, and 300 miles (480 kilometers) south of the Arctic Circle. No human fossils were found with the stone tools, but their thermoluminescence date of 300,000 years B.P. is comparable to the ages of the Jinniu Shan and Dali fossils (Table 14–2), suggesting that the Siberian implements were probably made by *Homo heidelbergensis*. (Although late *Homo erectus* was probably still alive in Asia 300,000 years ago [see Table 10–1], it seems unlikely that this species produced the Diring Yuriakh tools as it probably had not achieved the level of cultural sophistication necessary to survive the bitter Siberian winters.)

Homo heidelbergensis Remains From Europe

Several European sites have produced fossils of *Homo heidelbergensis*, including the oldest known remains of that taxon. To begin with a discovery made in 1907, quarry workers found a primitive-looking mandible at the site of Mauer near Heidelberg, Germany (Figure 14–13). This fossil was the first to carry the name *H. heidelbergensis* (given to it by the paleontologist Otto Schoetensack) and it has become the type specimen for the species. The Mauer jaw is between 700,000 and 400,000 years old and shows similarities both to its *Homo erectus* ancestors (in its overall robustness) and to *Homo sapiens* (in its molar size). Interestingly, it shows few traits that anticipate the Neandertals except for certain details of the teeth.

Other interesting fossils were discovered in the mid-1930s in Thames River gravel deposits near the English village of Swanscombe (Figure 14–13). At that site a human skull was unearthed that was dated to approximately 250,000 years B.P. using geologic information and faunal correlation. The partial skull consists only of three bones: both parietals and the occipital—the face is missing (Figure 14–16). Its fragmentary condition makes the Swanscombe skull difficult to classify and therefore the fossil is somewhat controversial (see below).

A very similar skull—this time with a face—was discovered at Steinheim, Germany, in 1933. Approximately the same age as Swanscombe (Table 14–2), the Steinheim fossil has a braincase that is more or less similar to the English specimen and that held a 1,100 cubic centimeter brain. The Steinheim skull also shows rather heavy brows and a low forehead (Figure 14–16). Unfortunately, like Swanscombe, the Steinheim fossil is hard to classify, despite its more complete nature. Both fossils are anatomically intermediate between *Homo erectus* and modern humans, and neither is clearly a Neandertal. As a temporary measure, Steinheim and Swanscombe are treated here as representatives of *Homo heidelbergensis*, although it is possible that they were actually early members of the Neandertal lineage along with the people from the Sima de los Huesos (Atapuerca).

The oldest hominid fossil known from England was excavated in 1993 at the site of Boxgrove in West Sussex (Figure 14–13). The fossil is a fragment of a massive left tibia, or shinbone, and is between 524,000 and 478,000 years old (roughly the same age as Mauer). Analyses of the bone suggest assignment to *Homo heidelbergensis*. Besides being the earliest evidence of hominid occupancy of the British Isles, the Boxgrove tibia is exciting because it is accompanied by Acheulean stone tools. As noted in Chapter 11, a critical absence of hominid fossils leaves the identity of the toolmakers uncertain at several Acheulean sites in Europe; particularly sites that fall within the period of *Homo erectus–Homo heidelbergensis* overlap. At Boxgrove, however, it seems likely that a half million years ago the latter people made and used Acheulean tools, and this discovery will no doubt have implications for interpreting other sites.

In 1960, the Greek site of Petralona (Figure 14–13) produced a large-brained (1,230 cubic centimeters) skull that may be *Homo heidelbergensis*. Dating approximately to 400,000 to 200,000 years B.P., the Petralona skull shares some features

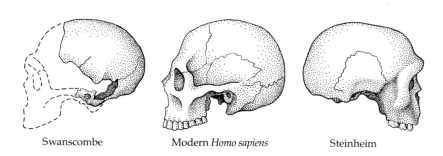

Swanscombe   Modern *Homo sapiens*   Steinheim

FIGURE 14–16   The Swanscombe and Steinheim skulls compared with the skull of a modern human being. The form of the back of the skull is quite comparable; the differences lie in the face. Drawing is just under 25 percent actual size.

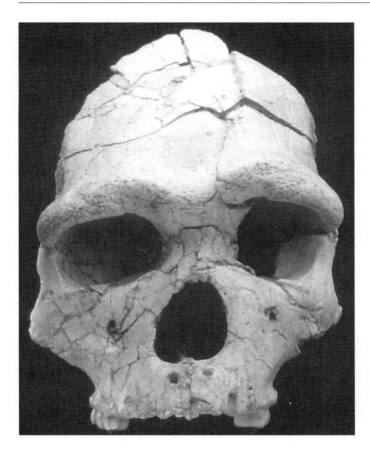

FIGURE 14–17 The skull from Arago is much more robust than those from Swanscombe and Steinheim. Photograph is approximately 60 percent actual size.

with its *Homo erectus* ancestors and others with the more modern specimen from Kabwe in Africa. Certain features of the Petralona face and braincase suggest links to the later Neandertals. Also resembling *Homo erectus* to some extent, but with a projected brain size that is too large and a date (210,000 years B.P.) that is too late, are some scrappy dental and cranial remains from Vértesszöllös in Hungary (Figure 14–13).

In 1971, a new discovery was made of fossil humans from approximately 400,000 years B.P. Henry and Marie-Antoinette de Lumley excavated a cave at Arago near Tautavel in the Pyrenees (see Figure 14–13). Along with stone implements, the de Lumleys found the partial skull of a man about twenty years old (see Figure 14–17) and two partial jaws of other individuals. The man had a forward-jutting face, heavy brow ridges, a slanting forehead, and a braincase somewhat smaller than the modern average. The two jaws were massive and somewhat resembled the Mauer jaw of much greater antiquity; they seemed well suited to chewing coarse food. Altogether classified here as *Homo heidelbergensis*, the fragments appear to be more primitive in form—that is, closer to *Homo erectus*—than Swanscombe and Steinheim.

But of all the European specimens we are classifying here as *Homo heidelbergensis*, perhaps none is as remarkable as those from the Gran Dolina site in Spain's Atapuerca mountains (Figure 14–13). Located just a short distance from the Sima de los Huesos, the Gran Dolina cave site has produced the oldest known human fossils from Europe. From a deep level called the Aurora stratum, or TD6, researchers at Gran Dolina have recovered human fossils dated by paleomagnetism to more than 780,000 years of age (converted here to 800,000 B.P. for convenience). Found in association with a pre-Acheulean chopper-and-flake tool assemblage, the TD6 fossils show smaller jaws and teeth than *Homo erectus*, a cranial capacity of more than 1,000 cubic centimeters, separated brow ridges, and in at least one specimen—a juvenile designated ATD6-69—modern-looking midfacial features. Indeed, the facial features of ATD6-69, along with certain other cranial and dental traits, have convinced the Spanish team excavating the site that the TD6 materials constitute a new species of premodern humans. In May 1997, they named that species **Homo antecessor**. Initial reactions to the new species designation are mixed, however, and many anthropologists prefer to keep the TD6 fossils in *Homo heidelbergensis*, at least for the time being. The argument to reject *H. antecessor* as a valid taxon revolves mainly around the danger of assuming that one juvenile's modern midfacial features accurately reflect the general condition of its population. (Were adults' faces equally modern?) For the time being, the authors of this text agree that a conservative approach is best and we lump the TD6 fossils into *Homo heidelbergensis*. Exciting things are happening at Gran Dolina, however, and further discoveries there could justify future modifications of our taxonomic scheme.

In summary, discoveries from Africa, Asia, and Europe indicate that by 800,000 to 600,000 years ago *Homo erectus* had given rise to a more modern human type, *Homo heidelbergensis*. The precise location of that transition is unclear at present, but Africa or western Eurasia seems most likely. After spreading widely across the Old World, *H. heidelbergensis* lasted until perhaps 100,000 years B.P., and maybe even later (Table 14–2). Following a description of the anatomy of *Homo heidelbergensis*, we will take a look at the probable evolutionary relationships of this species and the Neandertals.

Homo antecessor proposed new *species* name for certain fossils from the site of Gran Dolina, Spain; taxon not recognized in this book.

THE ANATOMY OF *HOMO HEIDELBERGENSIS*

Compared to their *Homo erectus* ancestors, *Homo heidelbergensis* people had made progress toward modernity in several points of anatomy (see Box 14–2 and Figure 14–18). Perhaps the most significant advance was in their brain size, which now averaged 1,283 cubic centimeters—almost a 30 percent increase over the most inclusive *Homo erectus* average (compare Box 10–1). Increased brain size was accompanied by a rise in the height of the cranial vault (the bones of which were still generally quite thick), while brow size, facial prognathism, and tooth sizes all showed declines. Brows also showed a change in shape from the straight, shelf-like structures of *Homo erectus* to curved prominences above the separate eye sockets. Most *Homo heidelbergensis* individuals (e.g., Mauer and Arago) continued to lack a distinct chin, but some specimens do show incipient development of this feature. Equally variable is the degree of flexure of the cranial base (an important indicator of how the vocal apparatus was configured), with some specimens (e.g., Kabwe) approaching the modern condition. Finally, *Homo heidelbergensis* faces were sometimes quite broad, with rather large noses (e.g., Bodo and Kabwe).

Few conclusions can be drawn about the postcranial skeleton of *Homo heidelbergensis* because of a paucity of relevant fossils. It seems likely that these people were essentially modern in their overall height and weight, but there are some tantalizing hints that they might have been much more powerfully built than modern humans. For example, the fragmentary tibia from Boxgrove, England, has very large midshaft dimensions (approximating the condition in Neandertals) and thick

Box 14-2

CHARACTERISTICS OF *HOMO HEIDELBERGENSIS*[a]

TRAIT	*HOMO HEIDELBERGENSIS*
Height (sexes combined)	Essentially modern? 4.9–6.1 ft (150–185 cm)?
Weight (sexes combined)	Essentially modern? 110–165 lb (50–75 kg)?
Brain size (sexes combined)	1,283 cc mean (1,100–1,450 cc range)
Cranium	Compared to *Homo erectus*: smaller and separated brows; higher cranial vault; less prognathic face; incipient chin on some specimens; variability in degree of cranial base flexure
Dentition	Similar to *Homo erectus*, but with smaller teeth overall
Limbs	Modern arm and leg proportions; massive construction suggests a powerful body
Locomotion	Bipedalism
Distribution	Africa, Asia, Europe
Known dates	800,000–100,000(?) years B.P.

[a] Mean values for anatomical measurements may change with the addition of new fossil discoveries. For additional technical details and diagnostic traits, see Appendix III.

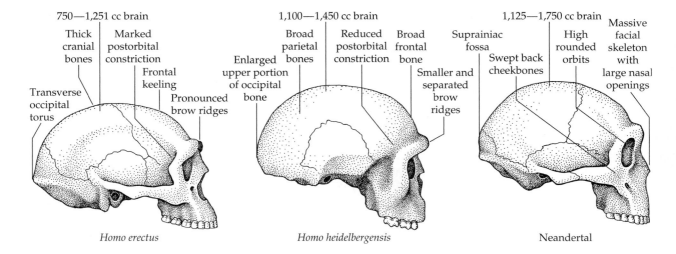

Homo erectus   Homo heidelbergensis   Neandertal

FIGURE 14–18 Compared to *Homo erectus*, *Homo heidelbergensis*—represented here by the Steinheim fossil—and the Neandertals showed much larger brains and more modern cranial anatomies. Nonetheless, the latter two species also retained such primitive traits as relatively large brows. Several distinctive traits are listed for each species, and others are given in Appendix III. The drawings are about one-quarter actual size.

walls. Similarly robust femoral and tibial fragments were found at Kabwe. Modern humans have apparently experienced a significant reduction in bodily robustness compared to their *H. heidelbergensis* forebears.

Not surprisingly, given the species' wide range and the likelihood of inter-population differences in adaptations, *Homo heidelbergensis* shows not only temporal but geographic variability. Nonetheless, there appears to be enough internal consistency to consider it a valid taxon, at least until further discoveries that might prove the case to be otherwise.

EVOLUTIONARY RELATIONSHIPS IN THE MID-TO-LATE PLEISTOCENE

Deciphering the evolutionary connections of mid-to-late Pleistocene humans was facilitated recently by genetic analyses suggesting strongly that the Neandertals were a distinct and dead-end species. Prior to this genetic breakthrough, the Neandertals' classification and their place in hominid evolution—including whether or not they were ancestral to modern people—had been matters of chronic dispute among anthropologists (standard anatomical and archaeological studies had proved unable to decide the issues). In July 1997, it was announced that a team of German and American scientists had succeeded in extracting mitochondrial DNA (**mtDNA**) from the original (1856) Neandertal fossil and comparing it with mtDNA from modern humans (see Chapters 2 and 16 for more on mtDNA). The procedures the team followed were ingenious and they involved some of the latest genetic techniques. After determining that the fossil (which dates to between 100,000 and 30,000 years B.P.) contained sufficient DNA for analysis, the researchers extracted genetic material from an arm bone and then cloned it using the **polymerase chain reaction** (PCR). This procedure involves heating DNA to separate the two intertwined strands (see Chapter 2) and then using a particular enzyme, DNA polymerase, to induce the replication of each strand's missing partner. PCR enables researchers to make an infinite number of copies of small amounts of DNA, and in the case at hand it allowed the ultimate assembly of a mitochondrial DNA sequence 379 base pairs in length. When the Neandertal sequence was compared with modern human mtDNA samples, an average of 27 differences (substitutions) was found, with modern Africans, Europeans, Asians, Native Americans, and Australian/Oceanic people being equally distant from the Neandertal sample. In contrast, variation among those same modern populations was found to average only about 8 substitutions for this particular mtDNA sequence. Finally, the differences between humans and Neandertals were found to be half as great as those between humans and chimpanzees (which show an average of 55 substitutions) for the cloned sequence.

Clearly, these genetics data need to be confirmed by studies of other specimens, but assuming that they will be validated, how can the mtDNA differences best be explained? Without doubt, the simplest tentative interpretation is that the Neandertals belonged to a distinct species that deserves its own designation (*Homo neanderthalensis*), that their evolutionary line separated long ago from that leading to modern humans (lengthy separation would allow the accumulation of numerous mtDNA differences), and that little or no interbreeding occurred between the two evolutionary lineages (more on this in Chapter 16). It now seems likely that the old view of the Neandertals as a geographic race of "archaic *Homo sapiens*" should be discarded. An estimate of the date of the evolutionary origin of the Neandertals

mtDNA genetic material found in the *mitochondria* of cells.

Polymerase chain reaction known as the PCR, this is a technique for making an infinite number of copies of a *DNA* molecule from a single precursor.

can be derived from the magnitude of the mtDNA differences and it suggests separation about 690,000 to 550,000 years ago—roughly twice as early as the fossil evidence suggests. If these figures prove to be valid, they show that molecular divergence between populations begins long before anatomical divergence can be recognized. In summary, the anatomical, archaeological, and molecular data now seem to converge on the conclusion that the Neandertals were a distinct species for hundreds of thousands of years. They seem to have been a sister species to modern humans (*Homo sapiens*), not a part of that species or its ancestor.

With the Neandertal question apparently resolved, interpreting the rest of mid-to-late Pleistocene human evolution might seem simple, but in fact that is not the case. Many researchers prefer the scheme illustrated in Figure 14–19A, in which *Homo erectus* (or, for some, *H. ergaster*; see Chapter 10) gave rise to *Homo heidelbergensis* (probably in Africa or southwest Asia), who in turn was ancestral (at different times and probably in different places) to both the Neandertals and *Homo sapiens*. Proponents of this view include Bernard Wood, Ian Tattersall, Donald Johanson, Philip Rightmire, and Christopher Stringer, among others, and, as a tentative explanation, we are inclined to accept it as well. An alternative scheme, suggested by the Spanish discoverers of the Atapuerca fossils, is shown in Figure 14–19B. Here a newly named species, *Homo antecessor*, represented by the

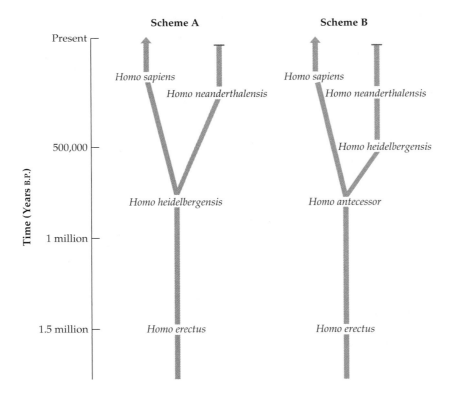

FIGURE 14–19   Two alternative schemes for mid-to-late Pleistocene human evolution are shown. (A) Here *Homo erectus* gives rise to *H. heidelbergensis*, who is the common ancestor of modern humans and the Neandertals. (B) Alternately, *Homo erectus* gives rise to *Homo antecessor*, who is the common ancestor of modern humans and *H. heidelbergensis*, with the latter being ancestral to the Neandertals. The authors of this text favor phylogeny A, although the evidence for neither scheme is conclusive.

800,000-year-old Gran Dolina specimens, is shown arising in Africa from *Homo erectus* (for some, *H. ergaster*). *Homo antecessor* then serves as the common ancestor of *Homo heidelbergensis* (who ultimately gave rise to the Neandertals) and *Homo sapiens* (modern humans). The basis of this alternative point of view is the claim that *Homo antecessor*, who shares numerous traits with both *H. heidelbergensis* and *H. sapiens*, is in fact more like modern humans than is the more recent species, *H. heidelbergensis*. Investigators such as Leslie Aiello of University College London, who views *Homo heidelbergensis* as a "wastebasket taxon" characterized by more than its share of variation, welcome the naming of *Homo antecessor*. In contrast, many other researchers, such as Fred Smith of Northern Illinois University and Philip Rightmire, argue that the Gran Dolina material is insufficient evidence for a new species.

At present, the most straightforward view of mid-to-late Pleistocene human evolution is probably scheme A. As always, the picture may be changed significantly by future discoveries. For now, however, let us turn our attention to the cultural advances of *Homo heidelbergensis* and the Neandertals. As the next chapter will show, both species were beginning to act like modern people in many ways.

SUMMARY

At least two, and possibly more, species of archaic (premodern) humans existed during the mid-to-late Pleistocene. The most straightforward evolutionary reconstruction views *Homo erectus* as giving rise to *Homo heidelbergensis* around 800,000 to 600,000 years ago. Bigger-brained and smaller-jawed than their ancestors, *Homo heidelbergensis* people then spread from their (probable) African homeland to inhabit portions of Europe and Asia as far east as modern China. *Homo heidelbergensis*, in turn, apparently gave rise to the Neandertals—a powerfully built variety of archaic people centered in Europe and western Asia—about 300,000 years ago or earlier. The Neandertals went extinct without descendants about 30,000 years B.P., despite the fact that they were rugged people with the largest average brain size recorded for any hominid species. In contrast, the other species that descended from *H. heidelbergensis*, namely modern humans (*Homo sapiens*), has not only survived but thrived since its evolutionary appearance between 200,000 and 130,000 years ago.

Regardless of their increased brain sizes, both *H. heidelbergensis* and the Neandertals characteristically showed a set of rather primitive skull traits: large brows, some facial prognathism, relatively low-vaulted skulls, and little development of the chin. Flexure of the cranial base was variable, with some specimens reaching the modern human condition—a development that suggests concomitant improvements in linguistic skills (see the Postscript to this chapter).

Although many questions remain unanswered with regard to human evolution in the aftermath of *Homo erectus*, certain long-standing problems are yielding to continued investigation. Of particular importance, recent studies involving the extraction and analysis of Neandertal mtDNA support the view that these people constituted a distinct species and that they probably made little, if any, genetic contribution to *Homo sapiens*.

POSTSCRIPT

Following their origin from *Homo erectus* stock some 800,000 to 600,000 years ago, *Homo heidelbergensis* people fairly quickly replaced their evolutionary ancestors as the dominant human form throughout the entire Old World. Subsequently, after their own origin, the Neandertals (*Homo neanderthalensis*) took control of Europe and portions of western Asia from about 200,000 to 40,000 years B.P. Clearly, these ancient people were quite capable hunters-and-gatherers with cultures sophisticated enough for them to exploit not only tropical and temperate habitats, but in the case of the Neandertals, rigorous periglacial environments as well. But many issues remain undecided, and chief among them are the now-familiar questions concerning speech and language. Did *Homo heidelbergensis* people and/or the Neandertals have language, and could they talk?

The answer on both counts and for both species appears to be "yes." All post-*erectus* and premodern people had essentially modern-sized brains (see Boxes 14–1 and 14–2) and (presumably) strong development of the speech-language areas of the cerebral hemispheres. Additionally, both *Homo heidelbergensis* and the Neandertals have produced a few specimens with modern or near-modern configurations of the cranial base and vocal tract (examples include Kabwe and Steinheim for the first species and Saccopastore for the second). Finally, as will be discussed in Chapter 15, these same people showed numerous cultural advances over their *Homo erectus* predecessors. Based on this combination of anatomical and archaeological evidence, most anthropologists concede linguistic abilities to mid-to-late Pleistocene humans. Specialists start to quibble, however, when they discuss *degrees* of linguistic sophistication. For example, some adult Neandertal skulls such as La Chapelle-aux-Saints show little flexion of the basicranium, suggesting a primitive vocal tract. Based on this and other bits of evidence, British researchers Chris Stringer and Clive Gamble conclude that this species may have had "a rudimentary form of language, but that it was probably simple in construction and restricted in its range of expression." Other experts, however, including Dean Falk, argue that Neandertal cultural complexity strongly implies fully modern speech.

In an extensive review of the evidence for the evolution of speech and language, paleoanthropologist Lynn Schepartz of the University of Michigan argued that language has a long history within the genus *Homo*. She concluded that virtually all species after *Homo erectus* had language and were talking, although some populations (some species?) were perhaps better at it than others. Schepartz makes an important point in her review when she notes that modern people (anthropologists included) have a strong tendency to be "linguicentric," that is, to view speech and language not only as variables that separate us from all other living species, but also as traits that therefore must have separated anatomically modern humans from all fossil predecessors. If we can no longer uniquely define ourselves as toolmakers or hunters, perhaps we can hold the line at "Humans the Talkers"! But, of course, such "lines in the sand" have a way of eroding with new discoveries (studies of chimpanzees forced the abandonment of labels such as Man the Toolmaker and Man the Hunter), and thus, as Schepartz correctly points out, such centristic approaches should be rigorously avoided if we are ever to attain a true understanding of hominid evolution. It is important to remember that language capability probably evolved slowly like most biological traits and that in evolving lineages, sharp lines of demarcation are impossible to draw.

REVIEW QUESTIONS

1. Summarize the anatomical differences between *Homo heidelbergensis* and *Homo neanderthalensis*. How did each of these species differ from *Homo erectus*?
2. Since the original Neandertal discovery in 1856, these robust humans have been variously classified as pathological specimens of modern *Homo sapiens*, a distinctive regional variety of "archaic" *Homo sapiens*, or members of an entirely separate species, *Homo neanderthalensis*. Explain the reasoning behind these different points of view and describe the latest findings on the taxonomy of the Neandertals.
3. The role of *Homo heidelbergensis* in human evolution during the mid-to-late Pleistocene is a matter of current controversy. Describe the various possibilities, being sure to consider the newly suggested species, *Homo antecessor*.
4. The Sierra de Atapuerca sites of Sima de los Huesos and the Gran Dolina have recently produced a wealth of mid-to-late Pleistocene hominid fossils. Describe the fossil evidence from those sites and explain its implications for the peopling of Europe.

SUGGESTED FURTHER READING

Arsuaga, J., et al. "The Sima de los Huesos Crania (Sierra de Atapuerca, Spain). A Comparative Study." *Journal of Human Evolution*, 33, 1997.

Bermudez de Castro, J. M., et al. "A Hominid From the Lower Pleistocene of Atapuerca, Spain: Possible Ancestor to Neandertals and Modern Humans." *Science*, 276, 1997.

Carbonell, E., et al. "Lower Pleistocene Hominids and Artifacts From Atapuerca-TD6 (Spain)." *Science*, 269, 1995.

Krings, M., et al. "Neandertal DNA Sequences and the Origin of Modern Humans." *Cell*, 90, 1997.

Pitts, M., and M. Roberts. *Fairweather Eden*. Fromm International, 1998.

Rightmire, G. P. "The Human Cranium From Bodo, Ethiopia: Evidence for Speciation in the Middle Pleistocene?" *Journal of Human Evolution*, 31, 1996.

Stringer, C., and C. Gamble. *In Search of the Neandertals*. Thames and Hudson, 1993.

Tattersall, I. *The Fossil Trail*. Oxford University Press, 1995.

Trinkaus, E., and P. Shipman. *The Neandertals*. Knopf, 1993.

INTERNET RESOURCES

ARCHAEOLOGICAL EXCAVATIONS AT BOXGROVE
http://www.ucl.ac.uk/boxgrove/
> (In 1993 a 500,000-year-old *Homo heidelbergensis* tibia was found at this English site. Details of the fossil and the location are given here.)

GRUPO DE PALEONTOLOGÍA HUMANA UNIVERSIDAD COMPLUTENSE (UCM)
http://atapuerca.geo.ucm.es/
> (This beautifully illustrated website describes the excavations conducted since 1978 in the Sierra de Atapuerca in northern Spain. Remains from the Atapuerca digs have been variously classified as *Homo heidelbergensis*, *Homo neanderthalensis*, and *Homo antecessor*.)

ORIGINS OF HUMANKIND: HUMAN ORIGINS NEWS
http://www.pro-am.com/origins/news/article24.html
> (A transcript of the CNN news report concerning the 1997 analysis of Neandertal mitochondrial DNA.)

THE ARAGO CAVE

http://www.culture.fr/culture/arcnat/tautavel/en/index.htm

(This website contains some nice illustrations and useful information about the Arago *Homo heidelbergensis* discovery. It is written for a precollege audience, however.)

THE FOSSIL EVIDENCE FOR HUMAN EVOLUTION IN CHINA

http://www.cruzio.com/~cscp/index.htm

(Along with material on older hominid specimens, this website contains information on likely Chinese *Homo heidelbergensis* fossils from Dali, Maba, and elsewhere.)

USEFUL SEARCH TERMS:

Homo heidelbergensis
Homo neanderthalensis
Neandertal (or Neanderthal)

Chapter 14 Timeline

HOLOCENE		YEARS A.D.	DISCOVERIES		PUBLICATIONS
10,000					
100,000	"Classic" Neandertals; also Skhūl, Qafzeh, Maba	1992 — Atapuerca Neandertals		1997 —	Neandertal mtDNA report
200,000	Swanscombe, Steinheim, Kabwe, and Dali				
250,000					
300,000	Sima de los Huesos	1976 — At Bodo			
350,000	Elandsfontein				
400,000	Petralona	1971 — At Arago			
500,000	Mauer	1965 — At Hortus		1964 —	Swanscombe report
		1961 — At Amud			
600,000	Bodo	1957 — At Shanidar		1957 —	La Chapelle reconsidered by Strauss and Cave
PLEISTOCENE					
800,000	Gran Dolina				
1 million	*Paranthropus* extinct	1939 — At Monte Circeo		1939 —	Full publication of finds at Tabūn and Skhūl
		1938 — At Teshik-Tash			
		1935 — First Swanscombe discoveries			
		1933 — First Qafzeh discoveries; at Steinheim			
		1931 — At Skhūl, and Tabūn			
		1926 — Gibraltar child		1928 —	Monograph on Rhodesian finds
		1924 — At Kiik-Koba			
		1921 — At Kabwe (Broken Hill)			
		1914 — At Ehringsdorf		1913 —	Boule's monograph on La Chapelle finds
	Earliest Acheulean tools	1909 — At La Ferrassie			
1.6 million		1908 — At La Chapelle, Le Moustier, and La Quina			
	H. habilis at Olduvai				
	H. erectus in Africa, the Caucasus, and Java				
		1886 — At Spy			
2 million					
PLIOCENE				1864 —	King creates species *Homo neanderthalensis*
				1863 —	Huxley's report on the Neandertal skullcap
	H. rudolfensis			1859 —	Darwin's *On the Origin of Species*
		1856 — In Neander Valley			
2.5 million	Earliest Oldowan tools				
		1848 — In Gibraltar			

DISCOVERY OF *HOMO HEIDELBERGENSIS* AND THE NEANDERTALS

Chapter 15

HOMO HEIDELBERGENSIS AND THE NEANDERTALS: CULTURE AND ENVIRONMENTS

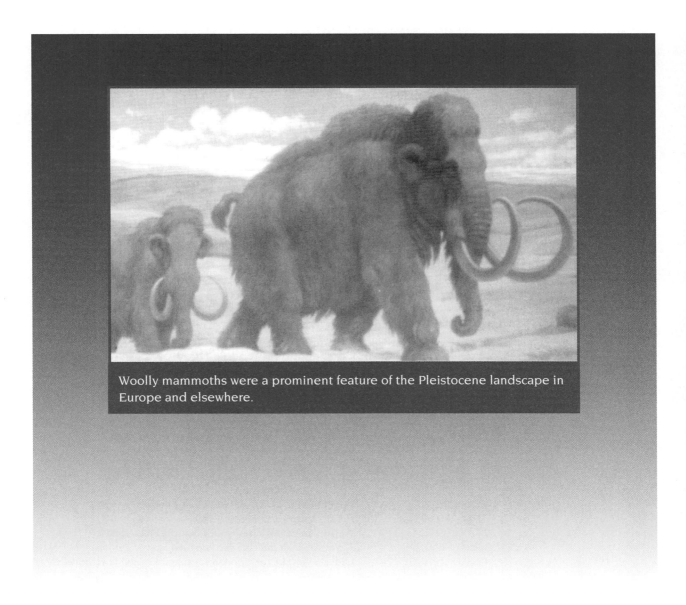

Woolly mammoths were a prominent feature of the Pleistocene landscape in Europe and elsewhere.

> **M**an is no more than a reed, the weakest in nature. But he is a thinking reed.
>
> Blaise Pascal, 1623–1662. Pensées, VI, 347.

OVERVIEW

Homo heidelbergensis and the Neandertals (henceforth collectively referred to as "archaic humans") differed from their *Homo erectus* forebears in a number of significant ways. Not only were they considerably brainier, but in addition—and perhaps as a consequence—they showed a number of important cultural advances. This chapter describes the cultural innovations that allowed these archaic people to inhabit not only the hospitable tropics and subtropics of the Old World, but also the considerably more challenging periglacial northern regions. Important topics and concepts in the chapter include lithic innovations, such as the Levallois and disk-core techniques, and the beginnings of blade technology; the challenges—biological and cultural—imposed by periglacial conditions; the intelligence of archaic humans; cultural variation among archaic populations; evidence of rituals, art, and burial practices; and evidence of violence—possibly including cannibalism—among archaic people.

RANGE AND ADAPTATIONS OF MID-TO-LATE PLEISTOCENE HUMANS

Two hundred and fifty thousand years ago the archaic human population (including both *Homo heidelbergensis* and the Neandertals) was probably less than 3 million. But this unimpressive total is deceptive, for even then humankind occupied far more of the earth's surface than any other mammalian species. Most of Europe was then woodland, frequently interrupted by lush meadows, with temperatures so warm that water buffalo thrived in central Germany and monkeys chattered in dense woodlands along the northern Mediterranean coast. Most of Asia was less hospitable, and archaic human bands apparently generally avoided the heartland

 Mini-Timeline

Date (Years B.P.)	Evolutionary Events or Cultural Developments
30,000	Last known Neandertals in southern Spain
34,000	Carved bone and ivory ornaments among late Neandertals
50,000	Shanidar flower burial
82,000–43,000	Bone flutes possibly carved by Neandertals
90,000–30,000	Period of the classic Neandertals
250,000	Approximate beginning of the Middle Paleolithic
300,000–200,000	Levallois flaking technique invented
400,000	Oldest evidence for wooden spears (attributed to *H. heidelbergensis*)

and far north of that continent because of harsh winters and/or dry, blistering summers. (Note, however, the evidence of archaic humans at Diring Yuriakh in Siberia some 300,000 years ago; see Chapter 14.) But human groups were scattered around the entire southern perimeter of Asia, from the Middle East to Java and northward into central China. In all probability the most densely populated continent was Africa. This sprawling landmass may have contained more people than the rest of the world put together.

The sorts of lands settled by these various people reveal much about their ability to deal with nature. They almost invariably lived in grasslands, savannas, or partially wooded country. There was a very good reason for this preference: These regions supported the herds of grazing animals that provided much of the meat in the human diet. Even though vegetable foods probably still provided the bulk of a group's diet, wherever animals were lacking, humans stayed away. The unoccupied areas included the deserts, the rain forests, and the dense evergreen woods of the north—a very substantial portion of the earth's surface. A few herbivorous animal species did exist in the forests of north and south, but they tended to wander alone or in small groups, for the scantiness of forage and the difficulty of moving through the thick growth of a forest made herd life impractical. To find and kill solitary browsers and grazers was so difficult at this stage of human development that it seems probable human groups usually were not attracted to these regions.

Another environment that resisted human invasion for a long time was the **tundra** of the far north. Here, obtaining meat was not the problem. Enormous herds of reindeer, bison, and other large, vulnerable animals found ready forage in the mosses, lichens, grasses, and shrubs of the nearly treeless tundra country. Archaic people, however, would have had difficulty coping with the extreme cold of the region. Consequently, archaic humans stuck primarily to the same lands that had supported their *Homo erectus* ancestors: the savannas and open thorn woodlands of the tropics and the grasslands and open deciduous woodlands found in the temperate latitudes.

Tundra treeless, low-vegetation arctic or subarctic plain, swampy in summer, with permanently frozen soil just beneath the surface.

The adaptations shown by *Homo heidelbergensis* people to these various environments will be described separately from those of the Neandertals. As the following sections will show, because of unevenness in the archaeological record, we can say much less about our actual ancestors—*H. heidelbergensis*—than about our Neandertal cousins. Nonetheless, enough evidence exists to demonstrate that both species showed significant cultural progress compared to *Homo erectus*.

CULTURAL DEVELOPMENTS AMONG *HOMO HEIDELBERGENSIS*

Lithic Technology

The stone tool industries of *Homo heidelbergensis* bridge the gap between the Lower Paleolithic (characterized by Oldowan choppers and flakes and Acheulean hand axes) and the next lithic stage, the **Middle Paleolithic**. Recognized mainly by declining numbers of hand axes and the invention of the **Levallois technique** for the production of prepared flakes (see Box 15–1), the Middle Paleolithic is reckoned by many archaeologists to have begun around 250,000 years ago and lasted until about 35,000 years B.P. As expected, given the postulated descent of *Homo heidelbergensis* from *H. erectus*, the oldest tool kits known for the younger species tend to continue the Acheulean hand axe tradition (Table 15–1). For example, the Bodo skull from

Middle Paleolithic a period of stone tool manufacture in the Old World (mainly Europe, Africa, and western Asia) that lasted from about 250,000 to 35,000 years B.P.

Levallois technique stone-knapping method in which a core is shaped to allow a *flake* of predetermined size and shape to be detached; originated at least 250,000 years B.P.

Box 15-1

INVENTION OF THE LEVALLOIS TECHNIQUE

A significant advance in stone tool technology occurred at the start of the Middle Paleolithic and presumably can be attributed to *Homo heidelbergensis*. Prior to that time, early *Homo* and *H. erectus* toolmakers had produced flake tools by simply banging away at a large core with a hammer stone. The resulting flakes were unpredictable in their sizes and shapes, but they served well enough as butchering implements. Some 300,000 to 250,000 years ago, however, some particularly ingenious stone-knappers developed a sophisticated new technique for making flake tools. Called the Levallois technique after the Parisian suburb where such tools were first discovered by archaeologists, the procedure involves carefully preparing a stone core and then producing a finished implement with a single blow (see Figure 15–1). First, a nodule of flint or other stone is chipped around the sides and on the top. This produces a prepared

core that looks something like a tortoise and removes all (or most) of the nodule's original surface. Then the prepared core is given a well-aimed blow at a point on one end. This detaches a flake of predetermined size and shape, with long, sharp cutting edges. Much less wasteful of raw material than earlier flaking methods, the Levallois technique also represents a remarkable insight into the potential of stone, for no tool is visible until the very end of the process (in contrast, in the making of a hand axe, the tool gradually and reassuringly takes shape as the stone-knapper works). The oldest known Levallois flakes are from the La Cotte site on the English Channel island of Jersey and date to 238,000 years B.P. The actual invention of the technique is thought to have taken place in Africa by at least 250,000 years B.P., and possibly as early as 300,000 years ago.

(continued)

TABLE 15-1   *A Partial Record of* **Homo heidelbergensis** *Lithic Cultures*

GEOGRAPHIC AREA	SITE/FOSSIL	AGE (YEARS B.P.)	TOOL KIT
Africa	Jebel Irhoud	125,000–90,000	Mousterian , Levallois-flaked tools
	Eyasi	130,000–35,000(?)	Acheulean tools (probable)
	Kabwe	250,000–130,000	Sangoan tools
	Elandsfontein	350,000–130,000	Acheulean tools (probable)
	Ndutu	400,000–200,000	Acheulean tools
	Bodo	600,000	Acheulean tools
Asia	Xujiayao (China)	125,000–100,000	Flake tools (no hand axes)
	Narmada (India)	150,000	Late Acheulean tools
	Dali (China)	300,000–200,000	Flake tools (no hand axes)
Europe	Vértessöllös	210,000	Flake tools, choppers (no hand axes)
	Swanscombe	250,000	Flakes, choppers and Acheulean tools
	Bilzingsleben	340,000–230,000	Flake tools (no hand axes)
	Arago	400,000	Late Acheulean, including small flake tools
	Boxgrove	500,000	Early Acheulean hand axes
	Gran Dolina	800,000	Flake tools, choppers (no hand axes)

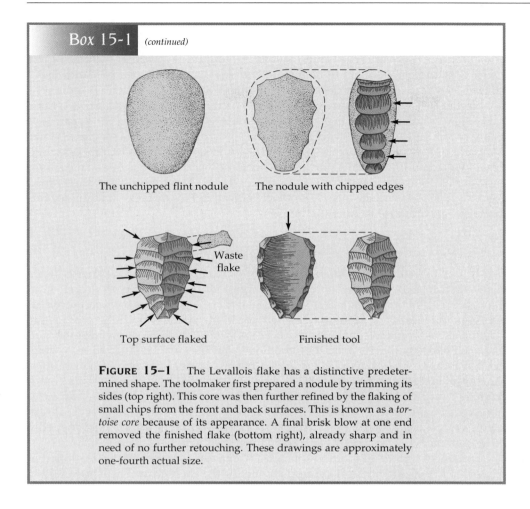

The unchipped flint nodule   The nodule with chipped edges

Waste flake

Top surface flaked   Finished tool

FIGURE 15–1 The Levallois flake has a distinctive predetermined shape. The toolmaker first prepared a nodule by trimming its sides (top right). This core was then further refined by the flaking of small chips from the front and back surfaces. This is known as a *tortoise core* because of its appearance. A final brisk blow at one end removed the finished flake (bottom right), already sharp and in need of no further retouching. These drawings are approximately one-fourth actual size.

Ethiopia—which dates to 600,000 years B.P.—was found in association with Acheulean hand axes and cleavers. The same is true for other early African fossils such as Ndutu and Elandsfontein, as well as remains from the 500,000-to-400,000-year-old European sites of Boxgrove (England) and Arago (France). The easternmost Acheulean assemblage that can be attributed to *Homo heidelbergensis* comes from Narmada in India and dates to 150,000 years B.P. Interestingly, the absolutely oldest fossil remains of *Homo heidelbergensis*, those 800,000-year-old bones from Gran Dolina in the Atapuerca mountains, are not accompanied by Acheulean tools, but rather by a flake-and-chopper assemblage that lacks hand axes.

A second feature of the Middle Paleolithic industries produced by *Homo heidelbergensis* is their diversity. This is not unexpected, of course, given the wide geographic spread of *H. heidelbergensis* and the fact that *Homo erectus*'s tool kits also showed regional distinctions (see Chapter 11). As shown in Table 15–1, *Homo heidelbergensis* people in eastern Asia continued the local tradition of producing nondescript flake tools and pebble choppers (implements that may have been used in combination with bamboo tools; see Chapter 11). The Levallois technique apparently never spread to that part of the Old World. In contrast, African and western Asian Middle Paleolithic assemblages included Levallois flake tools and a variety of implements including scrapers, choppers, and **denticulates**. In East and Central

Denticulates stone implements made with toothed or notched edges.

Sangoan *Middle Paleolithic tool industry from East and Central Africa; associated with Homo heidelbergensis.*

Africa, *Homo heidelbergensis* people made stone tools attributed to the **Sangoan industry**. The Kabwe fossil, dated to 250,000 to 130,000 years B.P., was found in association with several such implements. Although the Sangoan included some hand axes and scrapers, its most distinctive tools were long, narrow, and heavy stone picks that may have been used for woodworking by archaic populations adapted to forested environments. But perhaps the most intriguing African lithic assemblage of all is that from Jebel Irhoud in Morocco (Figure 14–13). Here, *Homo heidelbergensis* people produced a stone tool industry that has been classified as *Mousterian* (this tool culture is described fully in later sections). Complete with Levallois-flaked implements, the Jebel Irhoud tool assemblage is unusual because Mousterian tools are almost always associated with Neandertals, but the human remains from this site show no Neandertal affinities. No good explanation for this archaeological puzzle is known at present.

Nonlithic Artifacts

In addition to their stone tools, *Homo heidelbergensis* people left a few other artifacts that help archaeologists decipher their adaptations. For example, as described in Chapter 12, 400,000-year-old wooden spears were recently recovered at Schöningen, Germany (a similarly aged spear fragment was discovered at the Clacton site in England some years ago). Made of spruce, six to seven feet long, and balanced like a modern javelin, the Schöningen spears were designed for throwing, not close-range jabbing, and they would have required a strong-armed hunter. Further evidence that *Homo heidelbergensis* hunters used such implements comes from the 500,000-year-old Boxgrove (England) site, where researchers found a rhinoceros scapula with a circular hole in it—a hole precisely like that expected from a thrown spear. It appears that *Homo heidelbergensis* hunters were tough, ruggedly built humans who were ready to take on even the most dangerous game.

Evidence of other adaptations of *H. heidelbergensis* people is sparse. As noted in Chapter 11, they may have been responsible for the shelters and hearths found at Terra Amata, and the likelihood that *H. heidelbergensis* people controlled and used fire is strengthened by the report of a possible hearth at Schöningen and by ash deposits at the 210,000-year-old Vértesszöllös site. With regard to clothing, it seems most unlikely that humans would have been able to inhabit the cold northern regions of Europe 500,000 to 250,000 years ago without at least the rudiments of bodily coverings, but conclusive evidence has yet to be discovered. Finally, at present we simply have no information about any belief systems, burial practices, or artistic products of *Homo heidelbergensis*. For mid-to-late Pleistocene evidence on those topics, we must leave *Homo heidelbergensis* and turn to a better known species, the Neandertals. And in turning to the Neandertals, we also leave behind the tropics and subtropics of the Old World, where some fortunate archaic populations inhabited fairly hospitable environments. The Neandertals' world belonged primarily to the higher Eurasian latitudes, where at times the environment became as inhospitable as hominids have ever known.

THE PENULTIMATE PLEISTOCENE GLACIAL CYCLE

Just after 200,000 years ago, the weather in the Northern Hemisphere began to grow colder. Glades and meadows in the deciduous woodlands of Europe broadened at an imperceptible rate; the tangled, lush woodlands along the Mediterranean gradually withered; and the expanses of spruce and fir in eastern Europe slowly yielded to the expanding steppe, or grassy plain. Similar changes occurred in China and North America. The increasing cold did not necessarily mean that the basic patterns of human life were about to change. Because the archaic humans' way of life was nomadic to begin with, they had simply to follow wherever the herd animals led or perhaps adopt a different mix of hunting, scavenging, and gathering. But certainly the pressure to develop a different material culture was felt by groups that had formerly had no pressing need for fire, clothing, or artificial shelter. These groups now had to develop skills in cold-weather survival.

Snow was falling in the mountain ranges of the world, more snow than could melt during the summer. Year by year it piled up, filling deep valleys and compacting into ice. The stupendous weight of the ice caused its lower layers to behave like very thick putty, sliding outward from the valleys as the ever-accumulating snow pressed down from above. Inching through the mountain ranges, the great fingers of ice plucked boulders from cliffsides and used them like a giant's scouring powder to grind the once-green land down to bedrock. In the summer, torrents of meltwater carried the debris of sand and rock dust out in front of the advancing ice, where it was later picked up by winds and blown across the continents in great yellowish-brown clouds. And still the snow continued to fall, until in some places the ice sheets grew more than a mile thick, burying the mountains and causing the very crust of the earth to sag under the load. At their fullest extent, the great sheets of ice called glaciers covered more than 30 percent of the world's land surface, compared to a mere 10 percent today. North America was covered by ice from the Arctic regions to a point south of today's Great Lakes. Continental ice sheets existed in the mountains and highlands of central Asia, and along the extreme southern tip of South America. Europe was almost entirely icebound. The surrounding ocean and seas offered a limitless source of moisture for snow, which fed separate glaciers that spread outward from the Alps and the Scandinavian ranges to cover vast stretches of the continent (see Figure 14–6).

This glacial age, which lasted from about 186,000 to 128,000 years ago, was one of the worst climatic traumata in the 5-billion-year history of the earth. Although many similar glaciations are believed to have occurred during the last 700,000 years (Figure 15–2), and some undoubtedly affected such early European arrivals

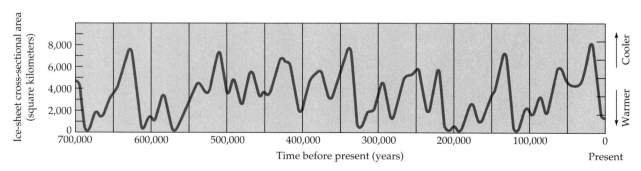

FIGURE 15–2 The Pleistocene ice ages most probably were caused by periodic variations in the geometry of the earth's orbit, and such variations as are believed to have occurred concur with evidence from other sources (oxygen isotope analysis of deep-sea cores). From these data it has proved possible to calculate the cross-sectional area of ice sheets at any time during the past 700,000 years. As we see in this chart, the main peaks of cold weather occurred approximately every 100,000 years, but many other cold oscillations came between these peaks.

as the *Homo heidelbergensis* people of Mauer, Boxgrove, and Bilzingsleben (see Figure 14–13 and Table 14–2), the glaciation of 186,000 to 128,000 years ago was the first ice age to try the endurance of *Homo neanderthalensis*. The Neandertals were to survive 60,000 years of bitter cold, interspersed with mild spells, before the northern part of the earth warmed up again—for a time.

Changes Around the World

The effect of the climatic changes was enormous. During the cold periods, the wind patterns of the world were disrupted. Rainfall increased in some places and diminished in others. Patterns of vegetation were greatly altered. Many animal species died out or evolved new, cold-adapted forms, such as the cave bear and the woolly rhinoceros in northern latitudes.

During some particularly severe phases of the glaciation 186,000 to 128,000 years ago, what is now England and other parts of northern Europe, which had been so pleasant a few thousand years earlier, became so bitterly cold that midsummer temperatures were often below freezing. The temperate woodlands of central and western Europe were transformed into tundra or steppe. As far south as the shores of the Mediterranean, trees gradually died and were eventually replaced by grassland. Few hominid fossils are known from Europe during the coldest phases of this glaciation, and it seems likely the climate was too cold for humans.

What happened in Africa is less clear. In some places, reduced temperatures were apparently accompanied by greater rainfall, allowing trees or grass to grow on formerly barren parts of the Sahara and the Kalahari. Woodland may have increased at the expense of savanna. At the same time, changing wind patterns had a drying effect on the dense Congo rain forest, causing it to give way in parts to open woodland or grassland. Thus, while Europe was becoming less habitable, Africa was probably becoming more so, favoring an expansion of people through much of that continent.

The land resources available to human groups during the glaciation also were increased by a worldwide lowering of sea levels. So much water became locked up in the huge ice sheets that the level of the oceans dropped by as much as 330 feet (100 meters), exposing to the elements large areas of the continental shelves, those shallow submarine plains that reach outward from the continental margins, in some places for hundreds of miles, before dropping off steeply to the ocean floor far below. The baring of formerly submerged land gave humans access to millions of square miles of new territory, and there is no doubt that they took advantage of this dividend of the ice ages. Each year, bands of people and their game must have wandered farther into newly drained land.

Stimulus to Intelligence and Ingenuity

During the 60,000 years of glaciation, surviving inhabitants of the northern latitudes suffered enormous hardships. These hardships may have had a stimulating influence on intelligence, cultural inventiveness, and subsistence creativity.

Recently, at Lazaret, near Terra Amata in southernmost France (see Figure 10–15), Henry and Marie-Antoinette de Lumley made a spectacular find that seems to reflect that inventiveness and creativity: remnants of shelters that had been constructed *inside* a cave. These simple shelters, dating to about 125,000 years ago, were tents, probably consisting of animal hides anchored by stones around the perimeter. Perhaps the Neandertal or *Homo heidelbergensis* hunters who occupied the cave from time to time set up the tents to give their families some privacy or to keep off water that dripped from the ceiling. But the weather must have been a consideration, too. The entrances of the tents faced away from the cave mouth, a fact suggesting that the winds blew cold and hard even at this spot close to the Mediterranean.

Finally, around 128,000 years ago, the long glacial agony began to taper off, and another period of relative warmth began. It was to last almost 60,000 years. Glaciers shrank back into their mountain fastnesses, the seas rose, and northern latitudes all across the world once again became an inviting place for humans. By 90,000 years ago, the "classic" stage of the western European Neandertals had begun.

Neandertal Cranial Capacity and Intelligence

The classic Neandertals had evolved gradually, we assume, from people such as those from the Atapuercan site of the Sima de los Huesos. As described in Chapter 14, the classics were characterized by a set of cold-adapted traits that served their ancestors well throughout the glaciation 186,000 to 128,000 years ago and benefited the descendants during the final Pleistocene glacial period. The classic Neandertal body was stocky and had short limbs; the jaw was massive and chinless; the face was out-thrust; and the skull was still low, with a sloping brow. But the volume of the braincase equaled or exceeded that of present-day humans.

In fact, from the limited sample available from this period, it seems that the mean size of the classic Neandertal brain (some 1,519 cubic centimeters) was significantly larger than the modern human average (1,330 cubic centimeters). This size has long presented paleoanthropologists with a puzzle, for the meaning of this figure is hard to determine. We know that brain size is related broadly to body size (Chapter 13), and it seems that the most likely explanation is that the large brain was a product of the powerful bodies of those people, whose postcranial adaptations can to some extent be compared with those of today's Eskimo. Whatever the reason, there is no justification in supposing that the Neandertal people lacked intelligence compared with ourselves, though that is not to say that their brains were necessarily entirely similar to our own (see Box 15–2).

Perhaps the best way to assess the powers of the Neandertal brain is to find out how Neandertal people dealt with the world. Anthropologists who study their stone technologies detect evidence of quickening intelligence everywhere. As described more fully in a later section, the old tradition of hand axes persisted, but it was becoming ever more varied. The double-edged hand axes now came in many sizes and shapes, often so symmetrical and painstakingly trimmed that esthetic impulses seem to have guided their makers. When people made small hand axes for roughing out spears or notched flakes to strip the bark off spear shafts, they made them just right, taking care to shape the implements for maximum efficiency at their intended work (Figure 15–4). In general, increased lithic complexity characterized the Neandertals' tool assemblages.

Box 15-2

CURRENT ISSUE: *Brainy Neandertals*

Every now and then, one will read in the press or hear in conversation the term Neandertal used in a derogatory fashion, implying stupidity and backwardness, for example, "What are you, some kind of Neandertal?!" Indeed, not too long ago even competent anthropologists occasionally referred to the Neandertals as "those poor, dumb brutes." Nowadays things have changed, however, and new discoveries suggest that the Neandertals were neither dumb nor brutes. During their classic phase, the Neandertals' brains averaged 1,519 cubic centimeters—a 14 percent increase over the modern average of 1,330 cc. Although differently shaped than ours (see Figure 15–3), the Neandertal brain may have been nearly—if not equally—as capable, and undoubtedly provided them with a high level of intelligence. Witness the fact that the Neandertals lived by their wits through some of the worst climatic conditions ever experienced by humans and also showed several important cultural advances (discussed in later sections of this chapter).

Of course, raw brain size alone isn't the whole story, as shown by evidence from modern humans. In our species, size differences beyond a minimum threshold (about 1,000 cubic centimeters) show little, if any, correlation with intelligence. To give just one example, Leo Tolstoy and Anatole France—both great nineteenth-century writers and high achievers—had brains of 2,000 and 1,100 cc, respectively. Furthermore, as discussed in Chapter 13, *Homo sapiens* has probably experienced important structural changes in the brain compared to our evolutionary ancestors and (in the case of the Neandertals) collateral relatives.

In any event, this Current Issue item is intended to keep you from "misspeaking" the next time you decide to lob an evolutionary slur at someone (not a practice that we encourage, by the way). Unless you are referring to their big brows, projecting face, or retromolar gap, we suggest that you refrain from labeling your adversaries as Neandertals. The term also connotes a very large brain, which may not be the implication you want to convey. ∎

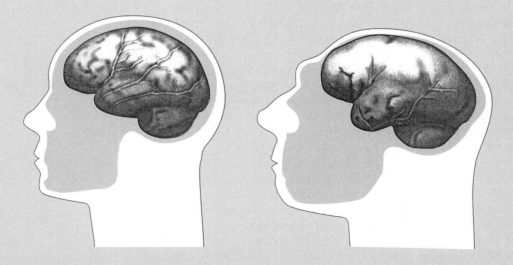

FIGURE 15–3   The brains of classic Neandertals (right) exceeded those of modern humans (left) in size. The Neandertal brain was simply packed into a longer and lower braincase. (From *The Last Neandertal* by Ian Tattersall. Westview Press, 1999.)

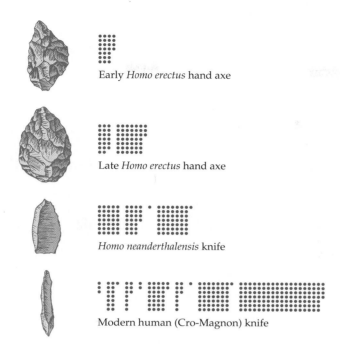

Early *Homo erectus* hand axe

Late *Homo erectus* hand axe

Homo neanderthalensis knife

Modern human (Cro-Magnon) knife

FIGURE 15–4 Steady progress in the manufacture of tools is traced in this diagram, which shows how increasing numbers of blows (dots) and of different steps (clusters of dots) in toolmaking led to finer tools and the more efficient use of the raw material. The most primitive tool required 25 blows and one step; the latest and most sophisticated took 251 blows and 9 complex steps. The first and second tools shown represent the Acheulean toolmaking techniques of *Homo erectus;* they were rough-hewn from single pieces of flint. The third was made by the Mousterian technique, which involved chipping a flake from a core and then modifying the flake. The bottom tool, a knife so sharp that one edge had to be dulled to permit grasping, was shaped by the more intricate Aurignacian technique of the Cro-Magnons (see Chapter 16).

THE ICE SHEETS RETURN

After a respite of warmer weather between 128,000 and 71,000 years ago, the glaciers once again began to grow (Figures 15–2 and 15–5). This last major glacial cycle of the Pleistocene produced cold weather that lasted until about 13,000 years ago, but it was not overly severe at first. Initially it brought snowy winters and cool, rainy summers. Nevertheless, open grassland spread, and formerly wooded portions of Germany and northern France were transformed into tundra or a forest-tundra mixture where open areas of moss and lichens alternated with groups of trees.

During preceding ice ages, the archaic human bands had pulled back from such uncongenial lands. Now, in the summer at least, the northern populations stayed, subsisting on the herds of reindeer, woolly rhinoceros, and mammoth (see Figure 15–6 and the chapter title page). They had to be creative scavengers and hunters, for tundra country offered little vegetable food to tide them over on lean days. Evidence from Russia shows that settlements extended right up to the Arctic Ocean northwest of the Ural mountains. Here there are indications of huts or windbreaks built with mammoth tusks and skins, warmed by small fires, together with remains of polar bears, which evidently were hunted. No doubt the death toll was

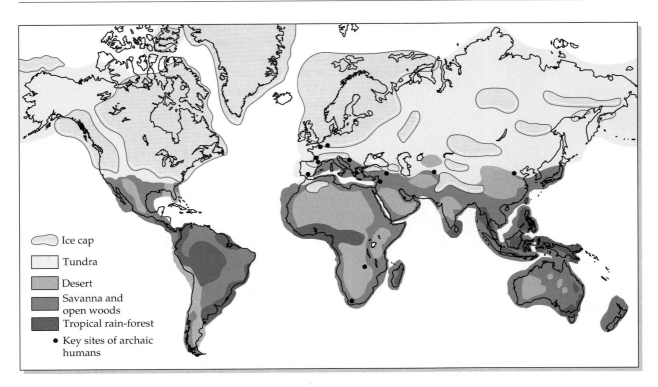

FIGURE 15–5 This map gives an idea of the climate and vegetation of the world at the first peak of the last glaciation, about 70,000 years ago.

high on the northernmost frontier, and bands remained small and scattered. Away from the frigid border of the ice sheets, populations were denser.

To understand the extent to which these populations depended on cultural adaptations, we must remember that hominids are biologically adapted to a tropical climate. Hominids had evolved an efficient system of perspiration to prevent overheating in the tropics, but lacked a counterbalancing system effective against overcooling. Such changes require a long time to evolve. Archaic humans did not have to wait for such evolutionary changes to cope with the cold, however: they were intelligent enough to deal with the problem without depending on biological evolution. They generated extra heat with well-controlled fires, almost certainly put on hide clothes, and either took shelter in caves or, where there were no caves, constructed their own shelters.

Sunlight and Skin Color

One noteworthy physical change that very likely coincided with humans' expansion into northern lands was associated with the use of clothing and with the scarcity of sunlight during winter in the higher latitudes. Their skin probably got lighter. There is no certain evidence, but it seems likely that the australopithecines, and early, tropical *Homo* as well, had been quite dark-skinned. In equatorial regions, dark brown skin has an advantage. Overexposure to ultraviolet (UV) rays of the tropical sun is harmful to skin, and many experts believe that as the hominid

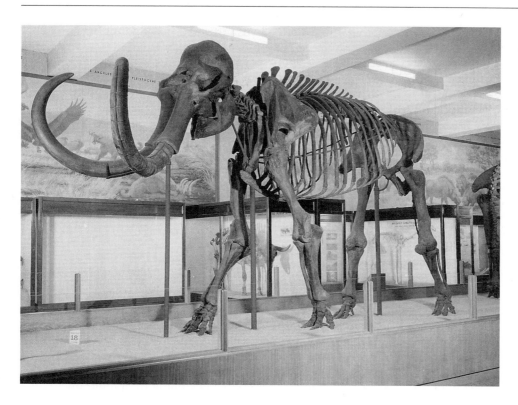

FIGURE 15–6   The eight-ton woolly mammoth (12 feet, or 3.7 meters tall) was ideally suited to the rigors of Ice-Age Europe. Shaggy hair and a layer of fat insulated it from the cold, and its ears were small to reduce heat loss. The woolly mammoth disappeared about 10,000 years ago, possibly being unable to adapt to the increasingly temperate climate of its last home, the grazing grounds in Siberia and North America. Complete animals, with muscles and skin intact, have been found in frozen ground in Siberia.

skin became less hairy and more exposed, the melanocytes (the cells that produce the skin-darkening pigment melanin) compensated by producing extra pigment, which blocked the ultraviolet rays. This UV blockage could have prevented potentially lethal skin cancers.

But the presence of a screen of pigment also inhibits the beneficial UV-induced synthesis of vitamin D in the skin. This decrease of vitamin production is not a serious problem in the tropics, where there is so much sunlight that enough of the essential vitamin is made anyway. When people settled permanently in regions with less sunlight, however, they did not produce enough vitamin D; pigment was no longer a protection but a drawback. This problem was exacerbated by the onset of the cold. Animal hides worn against the cold decreased the amount of sunlight that could fall on the skin. If the human of the north was to get enough vitamin D, any skin exposed would have to be able to absorb light and synthesize vitamin D extremely rapidly. In these conditions, a level of pigmentation that could further the contribution of vitamin D to the body's chemistry was better for survival, and lighter skin evolved. In this way we can account for the evolution of light-skinned humans in northern latitudes. Skin color is simply an evolutionary response to the intensity of UV light in different geographic regions and the extent of clothing required.

The significance of vitamin D in the lives of archaic populations was probably considerable. Today we know that humans can obtain the vitamin only from milk and fish oils, and so eating fish can substitute for exposure to sunlight. Further, we have learned that deficiency in the vitamin causes the bone-bending disease rickets. It is no surprise, therefore, that we find many skeletons of early northern peoples, especially children, showing direct evidence of a deficiency in the vitamin. And it is equally unsurprising that, among the first modern people who followed them in these icy regions, and whom we know to have had fishing tackle, the incidence of the disease is greatly reduced. The importance of sunlight to the survival of archaic human inhabitants in northern lands, and the limitations that it placed on their further expansion, cannot be exaggerated.

CULTURAL DEVELOPMENTS AMONG THE NEANDERTALS

Lithic Technology

The Neandertals' ability to survive and spread throughout the northern latitudes must have been due, at least in part, to cultural advances, and chief among these were new stone-knapping techniques and a variety of new tools. Early in the final glacial cycle, they invented a new stoneworking method that brought about the permanent ascendancy of the versatile tools made from flakes over those made by shaping a heavy core. Fine flake tools had now been made for a long time by the Levallois technique (see Box 15–1), but the new method was far more productive. Stone-tool remains indicate that at this period people began to trim a nodule of stone around the edges to make a disk-shaped core; then, aiming hammer blows toward the center of the disk, they repeatedly rapped at its edges, knocking off flake after flake until the core was almost entirely used up. Finally, the unfinished flakes were further trimmed so that they had edges for work on wood, carcasses, or hides (Figure 15–7).

Disk-core technique *Neandertal* stone-knapping method in which a core is trimmed to disk shape and numerous *flakes* are then chipped off; the flakes are then generally retouched.

The great virtue of the new **disk-core technique** was twofold. It permitted the production of large numbers of usable flakes with little effort, and because flakes can be retouched easily so that they have a shape or an edge, the new technique ushered in an era of specialization in tools. Neandertal tool kits were far more versatile than those of earlier peoples. Francois Bordes, a French archaeologist who was at one time the world's foremost expert on Neandertal stonecrafting, listed more than sixty distinct types of cutting, scraping, piercing, and gouging tools. No one band of Neandertals used all these implements, but the kit of a given band nonetheless contained a great many special purpose tools, such as saw-toothed implements and stone knives with one blunt edge that enabled the user to apply pressure more firmly. Different tool kits were probably prepared for different needs. New weapons may also have been made at this time. Spears probably were improved when pointed flakes were attached to long pieces of wood by being wedged into the wood or tied with thongs. With such an arsenal of tools, the Neandertals could tap natural resources as never before. Confirming this point, recent archaeological and taphonomic studies conducted in the Middle East by American researchers Curtis Marean, Soo Yeun Kim, and John Shea confirm that the Neandertals were active and vigorous hunters (as opposed to mainly scavenging for meat) and that in that area they regularly preyed on herd-dwelling species such as dromedaries, wild horses, and ibexes.

FIGURE 15–7   The disk (top left) is all that remains of what started as a much larger core. Refinements in the initial shaping of the core, and in the way it was struck, permitted the toolmaker to flake the core until it was almost all used up. Such technical mastery could then turn the flakes into tools such as the double-edged scraper (upper right) and the thin-bladed point (lower right), both shown in full view and (lower left) in profile. The photographs are approximately 40 percent actual size.

Everywhere north of the Sahara and eastward as far as Teshik-Tash, retouched flakes became the preeminent tools (see Figure 15–8). The tools made within this broad area are collectively placed in the **Mousterian industry** (see Figure 15–9), after the French site of Le Moustier, where such tools were first found in the 1860s. The makers of this wide-ranging culture were usually Neandertals, but in the Middle East, Mousterian tools have also been found in association with early anatomically modern people, and at Jebel Irhoud in Morocco they were made by *Homo heidelbergensis*.

One Middle Eastern Neandertal site in particular also provides a fascinating preview of the lithic advances that came to characterize the **Upper Paleolithic** period (40,000 to 10,000 years B.P.) in much of the Old World. As discussed in Chapter 16, **blade tools**—razor-sharp slivers of stone defined as being at least twice as long as they are wide—are generally recognized as the primary new stone tool type of the Upper Paleolithic. Amazingly versatile tools, whether used unmodified or given a distinctive shape by further flaking, blades made their first appearance in the cultural sequence of the Israeli site of Tabūn more than 90,000 years ago. At Tabūn the blade assemblages are overlaid by thick Mousterian deposits, however, and because both anatomically modern humans (*Homo sapiens*) and the Neandertals were using the Middle East at this point in time, we cannot be sure exactly which species of humans made the ancient blades. In any event, they were the archaeological version of a flash in the pan and, with the exception of one or two other brief appearances (e.g., at Klasies River Mouth in South Africa around 70,000 to 50,000 years B.P.; see Figure 16–1), blade tools remained absent from humans' tool kits until the true beginning of the Upper Paleolithic.

Mousterian industry a *Middle Paleolithic* tool industry from Europe and the Middle East; primarily associated with the *Neandertals*.

Upper Paleolithic a period of stone tool manufacture in the Old World that lasted from about 40,000 to 10,000 years B.P.; associated primarily with anatomically modern humans.

Blade tools slender, razor-sharp *flake* tools that are at least twice as long as they are wide.

The abundance and variety of scrapers in the Neandertals' tool kits confirms our suspicions that these people must have spent enormous amounts of time preparing animal hides for use as loose-fitting clothing and possibly in the construction of shelters (Figure 14–12). Furthermore, we can assume that the geographically widespread Neandertals—and *Homo heidelbergensis* people as well—were clever enough to modify their resource use to fit the locally available raw materials (e.g., in treeless areas, use of bone in place of wood for various purposes) and were always alert to the value of local specialties. A good example of the latter sort of flexibility comes from the sun-baked Negev region of Israel where ostrich eggshells have been unearthed along with Mousterian tools. The strong implication is that Neandertal people used the locally available eggshells as water containers, thus enabling a band to survive a journey across the parched hills from one water hole to another.

Hunting Rituals and Magic

Discovery after discovery has suggested that the Neandertals probably started some of the activities and beliefs that are considered most characteristic of humankind. They possibly attempted to control their own destiny—particularly their success in hunting—through magical rites. They buried their dead (at least occasionally) and may have conceived of a life after death. They may even have

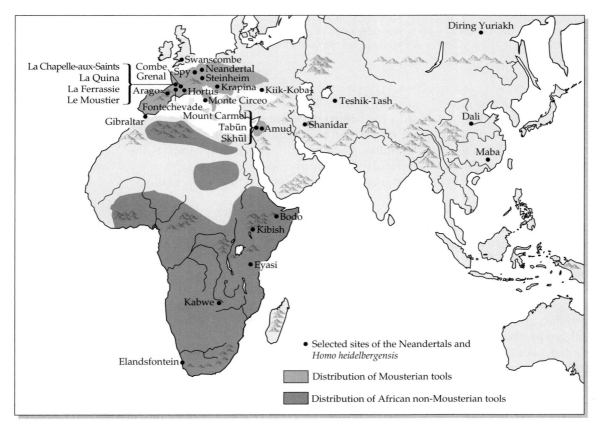

FIGURE 15–8   Archaic humans were widely dispersed throughout the Old World and they adapted to a wide variety of ecological zones.

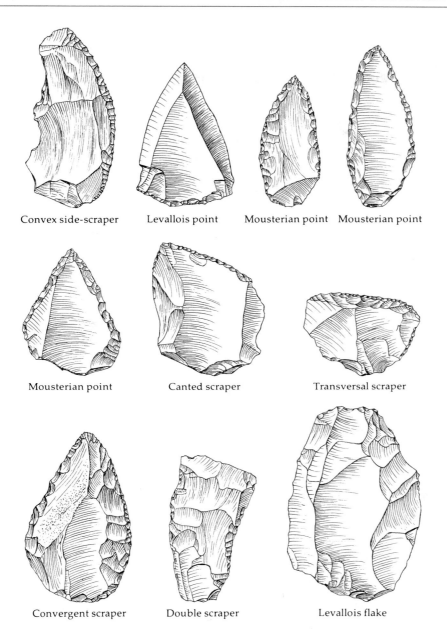

Convex side-scraper   Levallois point   Mousterian point   Mousterian point

Mousterian point   Canted scraper   Transversal scraper

Convergent scraper   Double scraper   Levallois flake

FIGURE 15–9   Flint tools of the typical Mousterian. The points are carefully worked and retouching is expertly done, usually on two sides. Drawings are approximately one-half actual size.

taken (albeit late in their existence) the first hesitant steps into the realm of art. And they cared for aged and handicapped individuals. In fact, it seems that the Neandertals may have been among the first people to display nearly the complete spectrum of behavior that constitutes modern human nature. Whether they exceeded contemporary *Homo heidelbergensis* populations in behavioral modernity remains an open question because of unevenness in the archaeological record. Further evidence on this point is urgently needed.

To begin at the top of the list, it seems logical that the Neandertals, like modern hunters-and-gatherers, must have had rites related to that most vital activity, hunting. The outcome of the hunt affected every individual. It was a matter of great importance that the supply of animals remain plentiful and that the hunters of the band enjoy good luck and safety in the hunt. But nothing in their world was guaranteed. Hunters could be injured. A long spell of bad weather could cut down on the catch. Animal herds might be destroyed by disease, changes in the predator population, or a host of other ecological factors. Mysterious forces operating beyond the horizon could interfere with or prevent animal migrations, causing herds to disappear.

Before this era, these various liabilities had probably been regarded as largely beyond human control. But the Neandertals may have attempted to manipulate the hidden forces of their universe that controlled success and failure in the hunt: they may have practiced hunting magic. One clue to their efforts comes from the Grotto della Basua (Cave of Witches) west of Genoa, Italy. In the depths of the cave, almost 1,500 feet (450 meters) from the entrance, Neandertal hunters threw pellets of clay at a stalagmite that to this day has a vaguely animal shape. The inconvenient location of the stalagmite rules out the possibility that this was merely a game or a kind of target practice. The fact that the Neandertal hunters went so far back into the farthest reaches of the cave to throw the pellets suggests that this activity had a magical meaning of some kind.

In 1970, Ralph Solecki discovered apparent evidence of a deer ceremony at a cave in Lebanon. Here, about 50,000 years ago, a fallow deer was dismembered, and the meat was placed on a bed of stones and sprinkled with **red ocher**. The natural pigment was almost certainly intended as a symbol of blood—the blood of the earth, in a sense. The rite seems to represent a ritualistic or magical attempt to control life and death in the deer kingdom.

Red ocher powdered mineral and earth mixture used as a red pigment.

The most famous example of what has been claimed to be Neandertal hunting magic is the so-called bear cult. It came to light when a German archaeologist, Emil Bächler, excavated the cave of Drachenloch between 1917 and 1923. Located 8,000 feet (2,400 meters) up in the Swiss Alps, this "lair of the dragons" tunnels deep into a mountainside. The front part of the cave, Bächler's work made clear, served as an occasional dwelling place for Neandertals. Farther back, Bächler found a cubical chest made of stones and measuring approximately 3.25 feet (1 meter) on a side. The top of the chest was covered by a massive slab of stone. Inside were seven bear skulls, all apparently arranged with their muzzles facing the cave entrance. Still deeper in the cave were six bear skulls, seemingly set in niches along the walls. The Drachenloch find is not unique. At Regourdou in southern France, a rectangular pit, covered by a flat stone weighing nearly a ton, held the bones of more than twenty bears (Figure 15–10).

The original owner of these bones is not in dispute. It was the cave bear, *Ursus spelaeus*, now extinct. A barrel-chested brute that outweighed the grizzly, the cave bear measured 9 feet (2.7 meters) from nose to tail. Swift, powerful, and unpredictable, cave bears competed with Neandertals for living quarters in caves. There is considerable dispute, however, over whether the Neandertals deliberately collected and stored cave bear bones (particularly skulls) for rituals of some sort. Supporters of the "bear cult" point to modern rites involving bears among several northerly hunting peoples. Certain Siberian tribes worship bears as the mythical first humans, and the Ainu people of northern Japan used to consider bears intermediaries between humans and the reigning spirits of the land. The Ainu sacrificed a bear annually in order to ensure good hunting for the coming year.

FIGURE 15–10 Fact or fancy? For some researchers, the discovery of bear skulls apparently stacked in a pit supports the idea that the cave bear was the center of a Neandertal cult.

But skeptics, such as Stanford University's Richard Klein, maintain that purely natural processes may account for the observed occurrence and arrangement of cave bear bones. In Klein's view, bears moving about inside their dens would naturally displace skulls and other bones into depressions in the floor or against the cave walls. Furthermore, rock slabs falling from cave ceilings could give the appearance of covering deliberately cached bones. Finally, and most important, none of the bear bones is associated with Neandertal artifacts, nor do the bones show any cut marks from stone tools. Thus, for Klein, any association between the bear bones and Neandertals is based strictly on circumstantial evidence.

What conclusion can we draw from these various bits of evidence? A stalagmite pellet-target, an ocher-stained deer carcass, and cave bear bones that may have been given special handling and storage—even collectively they provide only shaky support for ritualistic practices by archaic people. In sum, the evidence of a bear cult and other hunting rituals is tantalizing, but inconclusive. Additional discoveries are needed to settle the issue, and until they are forthcoming, the specialists will continue to disagree. The problem is complicated by the fact that the Neandertals and other archaics were so anatomically similar to modern people that we are sorely tempted to view them as like us behaviorally and psychologically as well. Good scientific practice, however, demands that we resist that temptation and not allow our speculations to outrun the available data. We must avoid both over-modernizing our archaic ancestors and interpreting their behavior as less developed than it really was.

Beginnings of Art and Music?

As will be explained in Chapter 17, one of the hallmarks of the Upper Paleolithic was a dramatic flowering of art—engravings, statuary, and magnificent cave paintings. A few tantalizing artifacts suggest that the Neandertals may have dabbled in art just before, and coincidental to, the arrival of modern humans, but they managed only a generally low level of accomplishment.

The Neandertals occasionally made use of such natural pigments as red or yellow ocher and black manganese. These occur at Neandertal sites in powder form and sometimes in pencil-shaped pieces that show signs of being rubbed on a soft surface, such as human skin or animal hides.

There is no sign of a representational engraving or statuary from this era, and only one or two perforated teeth that might have been used in a necklace, a very

FIGURE 15–11   This small stone from a Mousterian site at Tata in Hungary, dated 50,000 years B.P., carries an engraved cross. We do not know its significance, but the stone is one of the earliest possible examples of artistic or symbolic decoration. This photograph is approximately actual size.

common personal ornament among hunters, including later *Homo sapiens* people. There are a few indications, however, that the Neandertals were beginning to sense the visual possibilities of the materials around them. A cave at Tata in Hungary has yielded both a small engraved stone (Figure 15–11) and a piece of ivory that had been trimmed into an oval shape, polished, and then coated with ocher. At the cave of Péch de l'Azé in southern France, a Neandertal bored a hole in an animal bone; the bone may have been an amulet of sorts. Finally, from another French site, Arcy-sur-Cure (see Figure 14–6), dating about 34,000 years B.P., comes a carved bone pendant (Figure 15–12), some pierced animal teeth, and two fossils of marine

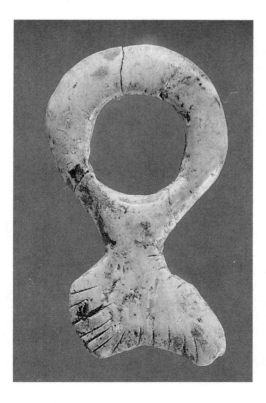

FIGURE 15–12   This carved bone pendant comes from the site of Arcy-sur-Cure (France). Dating to 34,000 years B.P., it is thought by some archaeologists to be the work of Neandertals who had been exposed to the culture of Upper Paleolithic *Homo sapiens*. Photograph not to scale.

animals that may be early examples of objets d'art. Overall, Neandertal material art is scanty and unimpressive, and certain late pieces—such as the Arcy-sur-Cure pendant—may be the result of Neandertal exposure to Upper Paleolithic people.

But if examples of material art are scanty, evidence of the performing arts—music, song, dance—was nonexistent for the Neandertals until just recently. In 1995, the Neandertal cave site of Divje Babe I in northwestern Slovenia (Figure 14–6) yielded a fragmentary cave bear bone that was perforated with four round holes, all nicely aligned and on one side. After making comparisons with similar Upper Paleolithic objects, the bone's discoverer, paleontologist Ivan Turk of the Slovenian Academy of Sciences, concluded that it is probably all that is left of a Neandertal flute. If Turk is correct (skeptics claim the "flute" is nothing more than a bone fragment with carnivore tooth punctures), the Divje Babe I artifact, dated to 82,000 to 43,000 years B.P., is not simply the oldest, but also the only, evidence for music making by the Neandertals. Commenting on the find, University of Washington paleoanthropologist Erik Trinkaus noted that the flute "reinforces the basic humanness of the Neandertals." The only comparable artifact, according to Trinkaus, is a similarly aged bone whistle or flute fragment from Libya made by archaic, but non-Neandertal, people (i.e., *Homo heidelbergensis*). And so, to whatever extent music is a measure of behavioral modernity, it seems possible that both varieties of pre-modern humans may have possessed it.

Death and Burial: The First Evidence

Of all the various indications of the humanlike behavior of the Neandertals, their practice of burying the dead is the best documented and easiest to interpret. Death is life's bitterest fact, the inescapable defeat at the end of the long struggle to survive and prosper, and humans are not the only creatures saddened by it. Many animals seem momentarily distraught when death claims one of their number; elephants, for instance, have been observed trying to revive a dying member of the herd, even attempting to get it back on its feet by lifting it with their tusks. But only people anticipate the event far in advance, acknowledging that it will inevitably occur, dreading it, refusing to accept it as conclusive, and taking some solace in belief in an afterlife. One mark pointing to this belief among archaic people is their occasional burial of the dead—not known from any earlier stage of human culture.

The Neandertals were not credited with deliberate meaningful burial of their dead until more than a half century after the species was discovered. The original Neandertal bones taken from the cave in the Neander Valley of Germany may have belonged to someone who was buried by members of the group, although no one suspected so when the bones were found in 1856. The two fossils discovered at Spy in Belgium in 1886 had indeed been buried; apparently fires had been lighted over the bodies, perhaps in an effort to counteract the chill of death. But no one had guessed in 1886 that Spy had been the scene of an ancient burial. Then, in 1908, the cave of La Chapelle-aux-Saints in France almost shouted its evidence of a Neandertal funeral rite. The excavators found an ancient hunter who had been laid out carefully in a shallow trench. A bison leg may have been placed on his chest, and the trench was filled with broken animal bones and flint tools. These various articles could have been interpreted as provisions for the world beyond the grave, for it was well known in the early 1900s that many modern cultures bury their dead with food, weapons, and other goods. But most experts failed to make the connection.

La Ferrassie (1912–1934)

The evidence continued to turn up. In 1912, two more Neandertal graves were found at the site of La Ferrassie, not far from the cave at La Chapelle. The diggers who carried out the excavation wrote:

> We have been able to recognize, at the base of the Mousterian layer, the existence of two small trenches measuring 70 centimeters wide by 30 centimeters in depth, very precisely cut in half-sphere form in the underlying red-yellowish loamy gravel, filled with a mixture of nearly equal parts of the black earth of the Mousterian fireplace above and of the underlying gravel. The existence of artificially dug graves was absolutely obvious. . . . This is, then, in the clearest way, proof of a funeral rite.

The excavation of the Ferrassie site took many years, and the complete results were not published until 1934. This rock shelter appears to have served as a family cemetery. Six Neandertal skeletons were eventually exhumed: a man, a woman, three children five to six years old, and an infant (see Figure 15–13). The most perplexing grave was located in the rear of the shelter. Here, in a gently sloping trench, the skeleton and the skull of a child were interred, separated by a distance of about 3 feet (0.9 meters). The skull was covered by a triangular limestone slab whose underside displayed a number of cup-shaped impressions, possibly symbolic markings of some sort. Why were the head and the rest of the body separated? One authority, the Abbé Jean Bouyssonie, a French prehistorian, has suggested that the child was killed and beheaded by a wild animal, and that the head was intentionally buried upslope from the body so that, in the afterlife, it might somehow find its way down the slope and rejoin the trunk. This is a pure guess, but there must have been some reason for the odd arrangement.

Middle Eastern and Asian Burials

Several non-European sites have yielded evidence that the Neandertal people buried their dead. Far to the east, on the Crimean peninsula that juts into the Black

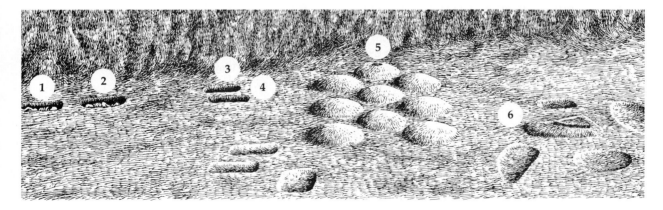

FIGURE 15–13   The care that Neandertals sometimes lavished on their dead is made clear at La Ferrassie, in France. Here archaeologists have discovered what may be a 70,000-year-old family cemetery, containing the skeletons of two adults and four children. The drawing here shows a site about 85 feet, or 26 meters, long. The presumed parents were buried head to head (at locations 1 and 2 in the drawing); two skeletons (3 and 4), possibly of their children, each about five years old, were neatly interred near their father's feet. The significance of the nine small mounds is not clear, but one contained the bones of a newborn infant and three beautiful flint tools (5). The triangular stone (6) covered the grave of a six-year-old child.

Sea, the graves of two individuals were found in a cave at Kiik-Koba in 1924 (see Figure 15–8). One trench held the remains of a one-year-old child resting on his side with his legs bent. This skeleton was in poor condition because later inhabitants of the cave had dug a pit for their fire directly over the grave and inadvertently disturbed the bones. Three feet (0.9 meters) away from the child was the grave of a man, also lying on his side with his legs tucked up. The body was oriented east to west—as were the Spy fossils and five out of six of the Ferrassie fossils. Possibly the orientation had something to do with the rising or setting sun.

Even farther to the east, at Teshik-Tash in Uzbekistan (Figure 15–8), the partial skeleton of a Neandertal boy was found in a shallow grave surrounded by several pairs of mountain goat horns. The horns may have served some ritual function, but this point is unclear, since goat horns are found throughout the Teshik-Tash deposit and not just in association with human remains.

Finally, perhaps the most amazing Neandertal burial of all was found in the Shanidar cave in Iraq (Figure 15–14). There Ralph Solecki dug down through compressed deposits to uncover a total of nine burials. At the back of the cave, in a layer estimated to be 50,000 years old, he found the grave of a hunter with a badly crushed skull. As a routine procedure, Solecki collected samples of the soil in and

FIGURE 15–14 Kurdish shepherds, shown here helping with the excavations at Shanidar, still use the cave to shelter themselves and their animals during the cold winters, much as their predecessors did thousands of years ago.

FIGURE 15–15   The skeleton known as Shanidar 4, which pollen tests suggest was buried with bunches of wild flowers related to hyacinths, daisies, and hollyhocks. The age is about 50,000 years.

around the grave (shown in Figure 15–15) and sent them to a laboratory at the Musée de l'Homme in France. There his colleague Arlette Leroi-Gourhan checked the pollen count, hoping it would provide useful information on the prevailing climate and vegetation.

What she found was completely unexpected. Pollen was present in the grave in unprecedented abundance. Even more astonishing, some of it appeared in clusters, and a few clusters had been preserved along with the parts of the flowers that had supported them. Leroi-Gourhan concluded that no birds or animals or wind could possibly have deposited the material in such a way in the recess of the cave. Masses of flowers may have been placed in the grave by the companions of the dead man. Leroi-Gourhan believes that the hunter was laid to rest on a woven bedding of pine boughs and flowers; more blossoms may very well have been strewn over his body.

Microscopic examination of the pollen indicated that it came from numerous species of bright-colored flowers, related to grape hyacinth, bachelor's button, hollyhock, and groundsel. Some of these plants are used in poultices and herbal remedies by contemporary peoples in Iraq. Perhaps the mourners, too, believed that the blossoms possessed medicinal properties and added them to the grave in an effort to restore the fallen hunter to health in the afterlife. On the other hand, the flowers may have been put there in the same spirit that moves people today to place flowers on graves and gravestones.

These are powerful images, suggesting as they do the beginnings of modern reactions to death. But not all researchers agree with Leroi-Gourhan's interpretation. Some prefer instead a completely naturalistic explanation for the pollen distribution patterns such as the action of burrowing animals. The case of the Shanidar flower burial remains somewhat problematic.

In sum, there is little doubt that archaic humans, and perhaps the Neandertals in particular, performed deliberate burials. But does this prove that they were the first hominids to ritually dispose of deceased group mates? Probably, but the case rests on negative evidence to some extent and is therefore inconclusive. Burial is only one of several types of funeral rite, but it is the one most likely to preserve remains for discovery by later archaeologists. Other funeral patterns, such as ritual exposure of the body to the elements, could have been practiced before the advent of burial customs, leaving no traces. Precisely when hominids began to respond ritually to death remains unclear.

Also still open to question are such issues as how frequently burials were performed by archaic humans, how elaborate they were, and what they tell us about these peoples' belief systems. Some researchers feel that the burials reflect archaic humans' belief in a spirit or soul that continued to exist after an individual's death. If true, then we can date the beginnings of religion from Neandertal times. In contrast, skeptics such as Chris Stringer and Clive Gamble suggest that the first burials were more akin to "corpse disposal" and may tell us little about spirituality. Once again, as with hunting ritual and art, there is abundant room for overmodernizing archaic humans, and only additional, well-controlled excavations will clarify the meaning of their burial practices.

The Old and the Handicapped

For many researchers another indication of the Neandertals' similarity to modern humans was their treatment of old or handicapped individuals. The man of La Chapelle-aux-Saints, for instance, was long past his prime when he died. His skeleton reveals that he had been bent over by arthritis and could not possibly have taken part in a hunt. Even the act of eating must have been difficult for him because he had lost all but two teeth. Had he lived at some earlier time, he might well have been abandoned to starve after his economic usefulness to the group was over. But the Neandertals evidently were not ruled by such stern logic. This man's companions unselfishly provided food, and they probably even softened it for him by partially chewing it.

Concern for the handicapped is suggested also by remains at Shanidar. Some of the bones found there belonged to a forty-year-old man who was probably killed by a rockfall. Study of his skeleton revealed that before his accidental death he had had the use of only one arm; his right arm and shoulder were poorly developed, probably because of an accident in childhood or a birth defect (Figure 15–16). Despite the major disability, he lived to a ripe age. His front teeth are unusually worn, the wear suggesting that he spent much of his time chewing animal hides to soften them for use as clothes or perhaps that he used his teeth in lieu of his arm to hold objects.

Evidence of Violence

The fact that the Neandertals and other early humans could find a place in their society for aged or handicapped individuals does not necessarily mean that they were always full of love for their fellow humans. It is impossible to know the reason for increased evidence of violence. Perhaps it was due to an increase in population coupled with dependence on inadequate technology to obtain resources. At

FIGURE 15–16
There is convincing evidence that the Neandertals cared for old or handicapped individuals. This painting by Richard Schlecht shows a youngster providing guidance and support for a crippled Neandertal at Shanidar.

many sites there is plentiful evidence of the darker side of human nature. A fossil of an early modern human found at Skhūl bears the traces of a fatal spear wound. The point of a wooden spear, long since decayed, had passed through the top of the man's thighbone and the socket of the hipbone, ending up inside the pelvic cavity.

Another ancient act of violence is recorded in the Shanidar Neandertal deposits. One of the ribs of the fossil of a hunter from the Iraq cave was deeply grooved by the point of a weapon, probably a wooden spear. The top had penetrated the man's chest and perhaps punctured a lung, but this hunter had somehow survived the wound, for the bone shows signs of healing. The original Neandertal man from Germany had also survived a grievous injury, although his recovery was incomplete: his left elbow bones were so misshapen that he could not have raised his hand to his mouth. Whether the damage was done by human or beast will never be known. There may be a hint, however; T. Dale Stewart points out that in the three specimens from Skhūl, Shanidar, and the Neander Valley, the injuries involved the left side of the body. This side would tend to be most easily injured in combat between right-handed opponents.

Evidence of Cannibalism?

That archaic people sometimes killed one another should surprise no one. Perhaps more surprising is the suggestion that they also occasionally ate one another.

Among the several reputed cases of cannibalism three stand out: Krapina, Hortus, and Monte Circeo. Let us examine each case individually.

The Krapina site in Slovenia was excavated in 1899 and revealed the remains of about twenty Neandertal people—men, women, and children—who lived some 100,000 to 50,000 years ago. Their skulls were in fragments, and their long bones were split, a condition suggesting that both brains and marrow had been consumed. Early investigators interpreted Krapina as a cannibal feast. Recent reanalyses, however, have brought that interpretation into question. While cut marks from stone tools are found on the Krapina bones, it is impossible to tell whether they indicate cannibalism or some sort of preburial preparation of corpses. Furthermore, bone fragmentation at the cave site could have been the result of roof falls, crushing during fossilization, and the use of dynamite during excavation. Although cannibalism remains a possibility, it is not a foregone conclusion.

At Hortus, a French site excavated in 1965, broken and scattered Neandertal remains were once again discovered. The remains were mixed with other animal bones and food refuse, and some researchers drew the conclusion that the ancient inhabitants of the site had made no distinction between human meat and that of bisons or reindeer. Once again, however, careful reanalysis has not supported the original interpretation. At Hortus, no stone cut marks are to be found on the Neandertal remains, nor can deliberate splitting of long bones be proved. In short, no evidence of cannibalism exists at this site.

Finally, at the 52,000-year-old site of Monte Circeo, Italy, the skull and jaw of a Neandertal man were discovered in 1939 (Figure 15–17). The find was determined

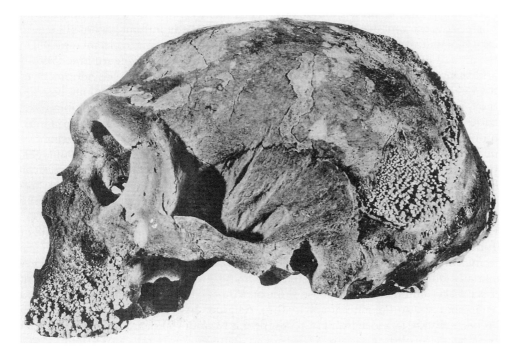

FIGURE 15–17 The skull from the cave at Monte Circeo was a classic Neandertal cranium and was mixed with other bones in a hyena den. Its base was broken open, but the opening showed the tooth marks of hyenas. In other respects the skull is very well preserved. Apart from the lower jaw, the rest of the skeleton has been destroyed. Photograph is just over one-half actual size.

to be evidence of ritual cannibalism because of the separation of the skull from its body, the fact that the foramen magnum had been greatly enlarged, and the apparent placement of the skull in a ring of stones. It was widely concluded that the original owner of the skull—a Neandertal man in his forties—had been killed by a blow to the head and that his brains had been extracted and eaten in some sort of ritual. As in the other cases, however, reanalysis of the Monte Circeo skull using modern techniques and information has told another story. It now appears clear that the Monte Circeo cave was a hyena den in Neandertal times and that the famous skull is all that is left of a hyena's meal. Indeed, close scrutiny reveals hyena gnaw marks at several places on the skull, including the enlarged basal opening, and stone cut marks are absent. As for the "ring of stone," it appears to have been a natural occurrence caused by a landslide.

It thus appears that we must be very careful about attributing cannibalistic behavior to archaic humans. While the evidence of intraspecific violence—including the use of deadly force—is undeniable, conclusive proof of the consumption of human flesh is lacking. Should such evidence ever be forthcoming, investigators will be faced with determining whether it constitutes proof of ritual cannibalism or dietary cannibalism (the latter being motivated by hunger alone). But for now, the argument is moot.

SUMMARY

Both *Homo heidelbergensis* and the Neandertals clearly surpassed their *Homo erectus* ancestors in lithic technology and cultural complexity. Indeed, their cultural accomplishments, in combination with a few key biological adaptations, allowed them to exploit a wide range of climatic zones, including challenging periglacial regions. In the area of lithic technology, the archaic humans showed an increase in tool types and stone-knapping techniques. Of primary importance was the development of the Levallois stone-knapping technique by *Homo heidelbergensis*. A similar, but distinct, innovation—disk-core flaking—involved rotating a stone core to obtain the correct angles for flakes to be detached. Levallois flakes were common in all archaic tool kits except for those in eastern Asia. Here *Homo heidelbergensis* people continued their traditional production of nondescript chopper-and-flake assemblages, possibly supplemented by bamboo tools. In contrast, African and European *Homo heidelbergensis* populations showed a continuation of the Acheulean hand axe tradition early on, and later produced Levallois-flaked tools. For their part, the Neandertals developed a varied tool culture called the Mousterian, which was widely spread across Europe and the Middle East. At the Israeli Neandertal site of Tabūn, a scattering of pre–Upper Paleolithic blade tools was also found.

Clear evidence exists that archaic people, especially the Neandertals, occasionally buried their dead. Questions remain, however, about the frequency of this practice and the elaborateness of the burial rites. Few conclusions can be drawn at present about the state of spirituality, religious beliefs, and rituals among the archaics. Evidence once thought to support a Neandertal bear cult is currently in considerable doubt. The same may be said about evidence for cannibalism. There is no doubt, however, that archaic people sometimes used deadly violence on one another.

Overall, both *Homo heidelbergensis* and the Neandertals (*Homo neanderthalensis*) showed considerable progress toward modernity compared to *Homo erectus*. And yet in some ways they were still hovering at the edges of what we today under-stand as human behavior and culture. One final transformation remained before fully modern people would walk the earth.

POSTSCRIPT

Humans are simultaneously fascinated and horrified by the thought of cannibal-ism. It's one of those "Ugh, that's awful . . . but please tell me more!" kinds of topics. We wince and grimace, but we read every gory detail about survival can-nibalism following a plane crash or the possibility of ritual cannibalism in cul-tures other than our own. We can't imagine being cannibals ourselves, but for some reason we are fascinated that others might be now or might have been in the past. That fascination has led to numerous allegations of cannibalism but to little universally accepted evidence for the practice either historically or prehistorically. But that situation may be changing.

Some scholars, such as American anthropologist William Arens, believe that cannibalism has rarely been practiced by humankind. In his 1979 book, *The Man-Eating Myth*, Arens concluded that "the available evidence does not permit the facile assumption that [cannibalism] was or has ever been a prevalent cultural fea-ture. It is more reasonable to conclude that the idea of the cannibalistic nature of others is a myth." These sentiments were echoed by British researcher Paul Bahn of Hull University: "There are no reliable first-hand witnesses of [cannibalism], and almost all [historical and ethnographic] reports are based on hearsay."

Contrary to the position taken by Arens and Bahn, however, many anthropol-ogists, historians, and others accept as true the descriptions by early Spaniards of large scale ritual sacrifice and cannibalism by the Aztecs and other native cultures in Mesoamerica. According to Fray Bernardino de Sahagún, a Franciscan friar who lived among the Aztecs in the mid-sixteenth century, ceremonies honoring deities such as the rain god Tlaloc and Xipe Totec (the war and fertility god) involved mas-sive sacrifices of adults and children, with the bodies being cooked and eaten after-ward. And, on the other side of the world, there are numerous accounts of cannibalism among the late nineteenth century rain forest Aborigines of northern Queensland, Australia. Furthermore, archaeologists are starting to provide hard—and hard to deny—evidence of cannibalism from around the world. For example, at the site of Fontbrégoua Cave in southeastern France, butchery marks and bone breakage patterns strongly suggest that anatomically modern agricultural people practiced a bit of cannibalism there some 6,000 years ago. (Whether it was ritual or starvation cannibalism is impossible to tell.) Going back a bit further in time (12,000 years B.P.), a good case can be made for cannibalism at Cheddar Gorge in Somerset, England. There, several individuals were beheaded, their bones were smashed to extract the marrow, and the flesh was apparently consumed. And finally, going all the way back to 800,000 years B.P., it seems possible that the *Homo heidelbergensis* people living in Spain's Atapuerca mountains may have butchered human carcasses and consumed the meat.

By far the best archaeological evidence for cannibalism, however, comes from the American Southwest. Working with Anasazi remains from the Four Corners area (where New Mexico, Arizona, Utah, and Colorado join), Christy Turner of Arizona State University and the late Jacqueline Turner developed a "minimal taphonomic signature" for determining whether cannibalism had occurred at a prehistoric site. As described in their 1999 book, *Man Corn*, before cannibalism can be accepted as probable, six features of perimortem (near death) bone damage have to be present: (1) extensive breakage, (2) cut marks, (3) anvil abrasions (marks made when bones scoot across an anvil as they are smashed), (4) burning, (5) pot polish (a characteristic polish that develops on the tips of bone fragments as they are cooked in a pottery vessel), and (6) many missing vertebrae (which have a tendency to be smashed to bits as the bones are being prepared for cooking). Using this conservative yardstick, the Turners documented cannibalism in several dozen sites attributable to the Chacoan Anasazi people and dating between 800 and 1100 years ago. (Interestingly, the neighboring Mogollon and Hohokam people did not show this behavior.) The Turners do not believe that Anasazi cannibalism was a response to starvation conditions, but rather that it was a combination of religious rituals and social control that was brought into the Southwest by immigrants from Mesoamerica. While other researchers may disagree with that last speculation, few will be able to find fault with the Turner's evidence for the violent killing and subsequent consumption of men, women, and children.

On balance, therefore, the evidence from history, ethnography, and archaeology suggests that cannibalism has occurred among recent people and also occurred among our evolutionary forebears. (This includes chimpanzees, who occasionally eat one another.) While its frequency of occurrence has yet to be determined, it seems safe to say that it has been neither universal nor rare. The circumstances of eating human flesh include (at least) dire emergencies, rituals, prolonged shortages of other food sources, and the use of cannibalism to terrorize and control enemy groups. It appears that cannibalism is an unpleasant, but all too real, component of human behavior.

REVIEW QUESTIONS

1. Describe the culture of *Homo heidelbergensis* people, especially their lithic technology and hunting implements. Can you detect any improvements over the material culture of *Homo erectus*?

2. Describe the culture of the Neandertals, including both its material and behavioral aspects. Argue for or against the notion that the Neandertals were behaviorally human in the modern sense.

3. Describe how the Neandertals treated their dead. Were they actually practicing burial rites, or simply corpse disposal? (Be sure to include the Sima de los Huesos Neandertals in your analysis.) Do you think the Neandertals' treatment of the dead reveals a developing spirituality?

4. From 1911 to 1913, Marcellin Boule described the Neandertals as "bestial" creatures who represented "an inferior type [of hominid] closer to the Apes than to any other human group." Based on your knowledge of Neandertal anatomy and culture, how would you respond to Boule?

SUGGESTED FURTHER READING

Bahn, P. G. "Cannibalism or Ritual Dismemberment?" in S. Jones, et al., eds. *The Cambridge Encyclopedia of Human Evolution*. Cambridge University Press, 1992.

Solecki, R. S. *Shanidar: The First Flower People*. Knopf, 1971.

Stringer, C., and C. Gamble. *In Search of the Neandertals*. Thames & Hudson, 1993.

Tattersall, I. *The Last Neanderthal*. Macmillan, 1995.

Turner, C. G., II, and J. A. Turner. *Man Corn.* University of Utah Press, 1999.

White, T. D. *Prehistoric Cannibalism at Mancos 5MTUMR-2346.* Princeton University Press, 1992.

Wilford, J. N. "Discovery of Flute Suggests Neandertal Caves Echoed With Music." *The New York Times*, October 29, 1996.

INTERNET RESOURCES

NEANDERTHAL NOTES

http://www.sciam.com/0997issue/0997scicit4.html

(Maintained by *Scientific American* magazine, this website describes the 1995 discovery of an apparent flute in association with Neandertal tools.)

Other websites relating to the Neandertals and *Homo heidelbergensis* are listed at the end of Chapter 14.

USEFUL SEARCH TERMS:

Homo heidelbergensis

Homo neanderthalensis

Neanderthal

Chapter 15 Timeline

HOLOCENE	**YEARS B.P.**
— 10,000	
UPPER PALEOLITHIC	
— 40,000	

FOSSILS AND ARTIFACTS

MIDDLE PALEOLITHIC

30,000 — Last Neandertals in Spain

St. Césaire
Le Moustier
La Chapelle
Shanidar flower burial

— 200,000
50,000 —

Shanidar fossils

Charred skulls at Hortus

Neandertal bone flutes

Homo erectus at Zhoukoudian
500,000

La Quina, La Ferrassie, Spy fossils

Teshik-Tash goat horn burial

Disk-core technique of toolmaking originated

Kiik-Koba burials

Skhūl, Qafzeh burials
Fontéchevade skull
100,000 — Tent shelters in caves at Lazaret
Tabūn
150,000 — Ngaloba, Narmada

200,000 — Ehringsdorf and Kabwe
Levallois technique originated
250,000 — Swanscombe, Steinheim, Dali fossils

1 million
Paranthropus extinct
300,000 — Sima de los Huesos fossils

LOWER PALEOLITHIC
350,000 — Yunxian

400,000 — Arago fossils; oldest wooden spears

450,000 —

500,000 — Boxgrove, Mauer

Acheulean industry originated
1.5 million
550,000 —

600,000 — Bodo

650,000 —

700,000 —

H. erectus in Africa, the Caucasus, and Java

750,000 —

1.8 million

800,000 — Gran Dolina

Mousterian Industry in Middle East and Europe

Acheulean Industry

HOMO HEIDELBERGENSIS AND NEANDERTAL ENVIRONMENTS AND CULTURE

The age of many of these specimens is still in doubt but the order of antiquity shown here is probably correct.

Chapter 16

THE FINAL TRANSFORMATION: THE EVOLUTION OF MODERN HUMANS

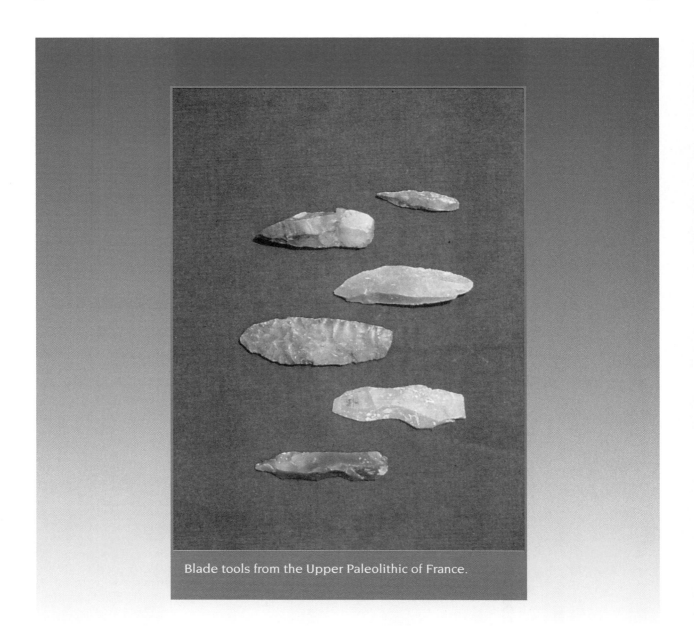

Blade tools from the Upper Paleolithic of France.

> **T**he troubles of our proud and angry dust are from eternity, and shall not
> fail. Bear them, we can, and if we can we must.
>
> **A. E. HOUSMAN,** 1859–1936. Last Poems, ix.

OVERVIEW

It appears that fully modern people (*Homo sapiens*) evolved from *Homo heidelbergensis* stock around 130,000 years ago, but the details—biological, cultural, and geographic—of that transformation are matters of considerable controversy. Two major evolutionary scenarios are currently being debated. The "regional-continuity" model holds that modern humans evolved more or less independently in several geographic regions, the species' unity being maintained by gene flow. In contrast, the "rapid-replacement" model holds that anatomically modern people evolved only once, most likely in Africa or the Middle East, and then spread quickly across the Old World, replacing all nonmodern hominids. This chapter discusses the evidence—cultural, anatomical, molecular, and fossil—supporting these competing evolutionary models. In addition, the spread of modern humans to the Americas and to Australia is described. Important topics and concepts in this chapter include the anatomy of fully modern people; the emergence of the Upper Paleolithic; fossil evidence supporting the regional-continuity and rapid-replacement models; the fate of the Neandertals in the transformation to modernity; genetic and chromosomal evidence of the geographic origin of modern people; and the colonization of the Americas and Australia.

EARLY DISCOVERIES OF ANATOMICALLY MODERN PEOPLE

In recent years prehistorians have begun to seek the origins of modern humankind in diverse parts of the globe: Africa, the Orient, and Australia. But the story of the discovery of early modern people begins in the Dordogne region of France (Figures 16–1 and 16–2), where archaeologists from many countries have excavated and analyzed and argued since 1868, when the first site was laid bare. This important

 Mini-Timeline

DATE (YEARS B.P.)	EVOLUTIONARY EVENTS OR CULTURAL DEVELOPMENTS
12,500	Native Americans at Monte Verde (Chile)
40,000–10,000	Upper Paleolithic in Europe
40,000–20,000	Possible time of first human migration into the Americas
55,000	Humans present in northern Australia
130,000	Oldest fossils of anatomically modern humans
200,000	Possible start of *Homo heidelbergensis-Homo sapiens* speciation event

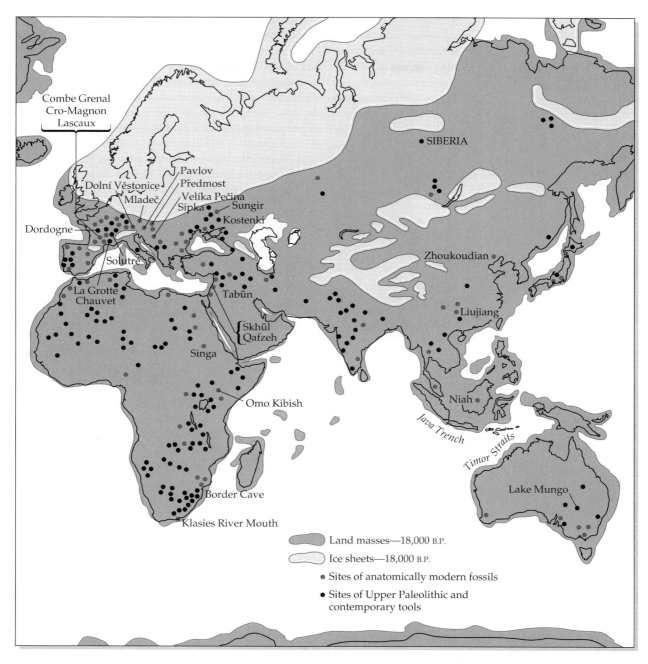

FIGURE 16–1   Anatomically modern fossils and related archaeological sites are today being discovered in many regions of the Old World. Humans of modern aspect lived in many places and varied environments and their population and technology rapidly developed.

discovery takes us back again to the nineteenth century, twelve years after the first Neandertal find, but still long before anyone really understood its implications or the full meaning of human evolution.

FIGURE 16–2   Many of the sites where humans are known to have lived about 30,000 years ago are in Europe, particularly in the Dordogne in southwestern France. The caves in which these people sheltered themselves from the ice age glaciers also protected and preserved their artifacts and bones for hundreds of centuries.

Discovery in the Dordogne (1868)

The first discovery of modern human fossils was made prosaically enough by a gang of railway workers cutting into a hillside just outside the village of Les Eyzies, France. They dug out the earth from an overhanging rock shelter in one of the many limestone cliffs that loom over the village, and with the dirt came bones and what looked like stone tools. Scientists summoned to the site soon uncovered the remains of at least four human skeletons: a middle-aged man, one or two younger men, a young woman, and a child two or three weeks old. The skeletons were similar to those of modern humans and were buried with flint tools and weapons, seashells pierced with holes, and animal teeth similarly perforated, probably to make ornaments.

The name of the rock shelter was Cro-Magnon, in garbled recognition of a local hermit called Magnon who had lived there. And so the name Cro-Magnon was affixed to these newfound humans. In the succeeding years, the name was broadened to include all anatomically modern people inhabiting Europe between about 40,000 and 10,000 years ago, during a period technically known as the Upper Paleolithic.

The limestone cliffs in the Dordogne region seem peculiarly adapted to human habitation (see Figure 16–3). These masses of rocks were formed more than 100 million years ago by the accumulation of tiny lime-containing animals on the floor of the shallow ocean that once covered most of Europe. The skeletons of these minute animals formed, in time, a building material that was to be immensely useful to humankind. Strong but water-soluble, the exposed lime of the Dordogne cliffs is honeycombed with rivers, streams, and waterfalls, which hollowed out ledges, shelters, and caves.

The entrance to one cave, Font-de-Gaume, halfway up a cliff that juts out into a little valley, effectively commanded the approach of animals, friends, or ene-

FIGURE 16–3   Excavation of a rock shelter in the Dordogne called Abri Pataud. A steel grid has been constructed to enable the excavator to plot the depth and position of every fragment of archaeological evidence. The overhanging limestone cliffs extend upward and outward.

mies. Surely, over tens of thousands of years, these cliffs positively affected the formation of human character in this region. In a sense, they provided a stage setting that enabled humans to see themselves as dominant creatures in their local environment. During the times when people lived there more or less permanently, the cliff dwellings must have enhanced their sense of identity and contributed to early stirrings of community pride. Here were their burial pits and the secret shrines where rituals of the hunt were performed. Here were the scenes of their mating and the birthplace of their children. The beauty of the area around Les Eyzies must have aroused strong attachments in the Cro-Magnon people, just as living humans have a special feeling for "home."

A more concrete advantage of the Dordogne region was the extraordinary natural riches it offered its prehistoric inhabitants. The Massif Central, a mountainous plateau that covers most of central France, begins about 50 miles (80 kilometers) east of Les Eyzies. Its high plains would have been a fruitful summer hunting ground that provided reindeer, horses, and bison in abundance. West of Les Eyzies, the coastal plain stretching toward the Atlantic was also good grazing ground. The Vézère River ran then in much the same course as it does now, providing water and, to the successors of those who learned to take advantage of it, a ready supply of fish. Many of the caves and shelters face south, offering warmth and protection from the cold winds of winter. Although many peoples around the world 30,000 to 20,000 years ago were probably nomadic, following game through seasonal migrations, it seems likely that the hunters who lived in this fortunate region were able to stay there for the greater part of the year.

Characteristics of Anatomically Modern People

In the years since the discovery of the fossils in France, the ancient skeletal remains of anatomically modern people have been turning up all over the world: in Hungary, Russia, the Middle East, North and South Africa, China and Southeast Asia, and even in Australia and North and South America (see Figure 16–1). Not all the fossils are complete, of course, and some are no more than fragments, but everywhere they are anatomically modern.

The bones of these fossils are frequently less massive than those of their predecessors. Further, their skulls are generally like the skulls of people living today, with a definite chin, a high forehead, a flexed cranial base, and a cranial capacity equal to that of modern humans (see Figure 16–4 and Box 16–1). Of particular importance, these people had the necessary physical equipment to construct complex and elaborate patterns of speech such as we ourselves use. The existing human languages are closely related and probably originated about 40,000 years B.P.

FATE OF THE ARCHAIC HUMANS

But what became of the Neandertals and other archaics who struggled so hard against the world around them to sustain their developing humanity? Some paleoanthropologists believe that many or all—including the European Neandertals—

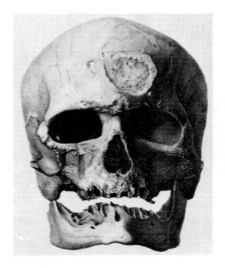
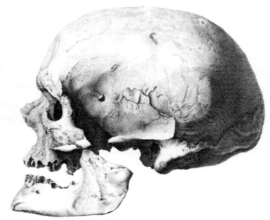

FIGURE 16–4 Nineteenth-century drawings of the fossilized skull from Cro-Magnon, France, the first of the very early specimens of modern *Homo sapiens* to be found. Notice the well-developed chin and the high forehead. The drawings are approximately one-third actual size.

Box 16-1

CHARACTERISTICS OF ANATOMICALLY MODERN PEOPLE (HOMO SAPIENS)[a]

TRAIT	HOMO SAPIENS
Height (sexes combined)	ca. 5 to 6 ft (140–185 cm)—extremely variable (F is 90%–95% of M)
Weight (sexes combined)	ca. 100 to 200 lb (40–70 kg)—extremely variable (F is 90%–95% of M)
Brain size (sexes combined)	1,330 cc mean (1,000–2,000 cc range)
Cranium	High-vaulted, globular skull with widest point high on the sides; small brows; high forehead; little facial prognathism; flexed cranial base
Dentition	On average, smaller front and rear teeth, and more lightly built jaws than *Homo erectus* and some archaics; definite chin
Limbs	Relatively long legs and short arms overall; body build that varies strongly with climatic conditions
Distribution	Africa, Asia, Europe, Australia, Americas
Known dates	ca. 130,000 years B.P. to present

[a] For additional technical details and diagnostic traits, see Appendix III.

evolved into modern humans. Many researchers, however, believe that most archaic populations became extinct and were replaced by modern people from elsewhere. Let us look at the archaeological and fossil evidence for these contrasting points of view.

Sequence of Tools

With regard to the Neandertals in particular, paleoanthropologists and archaeologists have long hoped that the tools they left behind would yield a clear picture of their passing. For awhile, this appeared to be possible. Only a few years ago textbooks cited the sequence of tool-bearing layers in caves and rock shelters in western Europe as proof that all Neandertals became extinct. It was thought that the tools made by Neandertals declined in number and quality as the end of their period neared; then no tools were made at all, the result being sterile layers with no sign of human habitation; then brand-new styles of tools abruptly began. This was interpreted as a clear sign of one people's becoming extinct and another's arriving on the scene.

Although an off-and-on sequence of tool-bearing strata—Neandertal layers fading into sterile layers followed by Cro-Magnon layers—is indeed found at some Neandertal sites, archaeologists have now discovered many exceptions. At some sites, successive layers show that toolmaking proficiency rose, rather than declined. Also, sterile layers do not always appear between layers containing Neandertal and Cro-Magnon tools; more often, there is no break, a fact indicating that occupation of the site was virtually continuous. Finally, the differences between Neandertal and Cro-Magnon tools do not necessarily indicate that one culture disappeared to be replaced by an unrelated one. The situation is clearly more complex than it was thought originally.

Flakes and Blades

As explained in Chapter 15, with few exceptions, the tools associated with archaic peoples all over the world are categorized as Middle Paleolithic. The word *Paleolithic* is derived from the Greek *palai* ("long ago") and *lithos* ("stone"). Middle Paleolithic is a broad term that covers Mousterian tools and also some Asian and African industries. (The Lower Paleolithic includes earlier stone industries such as the Oldowan and Acheulean.) The comparable term for tools associated *primarily* with anatomically modern people is Upper Paleolithic. Most Middle Paleolithic tools consist of flat flakes shaped and retouched to provide the desired working edge. Upper Paleolithic toolmakers produced flakes, too, but they specialized in a kind known as *blades*, which are essentially parallel-sided and at least twice as long as they are wide. This shift in the fundamental unit of the tool kit is marked enough so that many collections of Middle and Upper Paleolithic tools can be distinguished at a glance.

Blades are more economical to make than flakes because they yield more than five times as much cutting edge per pound of stone. Progress is also apparent in craftsmanship. Tools of the Upper Paleolithic are more finely made, requiring extremely precise chipping to produce the desired point, notch, or cutting edge. And there are many more kinds of special-purpose tools. Upper Paleolithic kits often include a high percentage of **burins**—chisel-like tools useful, as we shall see, for cutting bone, antler, and ivory.

Burin a chisel-like tool used to shape other materials, such as bone, antler, and wood; a tool for making tools.

Indeed, the use of nonlithic materials that could be shaped, such as bone, antler and ivory, is an important marker distinguishing Upper Paleolithic assemblages from earlier cultures. In addition, as detailed in Chapter 17, the Upper Paleolithic saw the true beginnings of art, the full development of elaborate burial rituals, the refinement of shelter construction and use of fire, and the development of extensive trade networks.

The details of the technological shift from the Middle Paleolithic to the Upper Paleolithic are hazy despite many years of diligent archaeological work. In Southeast Asia, blade industries began to appear in some areas around 30,000 to 20,000 years B.P. In contrast, prehistoric Australians apparently never reached the level of Upper Paleolithic stone technology. And it has become clear recently that, in Europe, western Asia (including the Middle East), and Africa, the transition was not as clean as once thought. For example, the Mousterian industry included some blade tools although, compared to those of succeeding Upper Paleolithic industries, the frequencies were quite low. Furthermore, in both the Middle East (at Tabūn) and South Africa (at Klasies River Mouth), cultural sequences have been discovered that show Upper Paleolithic blade assemblages alternating with Mousterian or other Middle Paleolithic industries. Some archaeologists now speak of the early and tentative appearance of "pre–Upper Paleolithic" technology between 70,000 and 50,000 years ago, 10,000 years or more before the traditional date for the start of the Upper Paleolithic.

Several other sites provide additional evidence against rigid associations of the Middle Paleolithic with archaic people only and the Upper Paleolithic solely with *Homo sapiens*. At Skhūl and Qafzeh in the Middle East, early anatomically modern (or near-modern) fossils were accompanied by Mousterian implements, while at the French sites of Arcy-sur-Cure and St. Césaire, undoubted Neandertal fossils (dating to 34,000 years B.P. at Arcy-sur-Cure) were found in association with an Upper Paleolithic industry called the **Chatelperronian**.

Aurignacian and Chatelperronian Industries

Known primarily from northern Spain and France, the **Aurignacian** and Chatelperronian industries marked the appearance of the Upper Paleolithic in Europe. Broadly contemporaneous, these cultural traditions shared an emphasis on blade technology, plus the appearance of well-made bone implements and objects of personal adornment such as beads and pendants. Despite their similarities, however, the Aurignacian and Chatelperronian industries appear to tell very different stories about the origins of the European Upper Paleolithic.

The Aurignacian industry (Figure 16–5), with its finely retouched blade tools, was so completely unlike any typical Middle Paleolithic style that it almost certainly was imported into western Europe, apparently from the east. Although the physical identity of the very earliest Aurignacians (circa 40,000 years B.P.) remains undetermined, by 30,000 years ago they were fully modern Cro-Magnons. At most European sites, the Aurignacian replaced the preceding Mousterian culture more or less abruptly, a fact suggesting to many anthropologists the rapid replacement of the Neandertals by fully modern humans.

In contrast, the Chatelperronian industry (Figure 16–6) seems to have been an indigenous development that originated in Spain and France from a variant of the Mousterian (the Mousterian of Acheulean tradition). In addition to sidescrapers, denticulates, and Mousterian points, the Chatelperronian included blades, burins, endscrapers, and numerous bone artifacts. As noted above, the Chatelperronian is associated with Neandertal remains at St. Césaire and Arcy-sur-Cure. The question is: Do these sites really reflect Neandertal involvement in the development of the European Upper Paleolithic, and, more important, do they provide evidence that the Neandertals evolved physically into modern people? Although there are sharp differences of opinion on the subject, many paleoanthropologists agree with Richard Klein that the Chatelperronian is best explained as being the result of traits diffusing from the Aurignacian into an otherwise Mousterian cultural context. In other words, the Chatelperronian probably reflects cultural diffusion from

Chatelperronian an *Upper Paleolithic* tool culture of western Europe, largely contemporaneous with the *Aurignacian* culture (40,000 to 27,000 years B.P.).

Aurignacian an *Upper Paleolithic*, mainly European, tool culture that existed from about 40,000 to 27,000 years ago.

 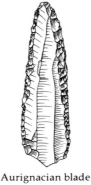 

Scraper   Aurignacian blade   Scraper

FIGURE 16–5   Typical Aurignacian tools of the Upper Paleolithic. The Aurignacian appears to have developed in the East, probably in western Asia. The most typical Aurignacian tool was the blade, much longer and narrower than any scraper. The Aurignacian retouching was very fine. The tools were made from a specially prepared core. The drawings are approximately one-half actual size.

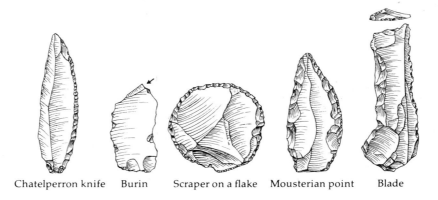

Chatelperron knife   Burin   Scraper on a flake   Mousterian point   Blade

FIGURE 16–6   Typical Chatelperronian tools of the Upper Paleolithic. This tradition began with strongly marked Mousterian features and included Mousterian points, flakes, and other tools (compare with Figure 15–9). Later tool kits contained a high proportion of burins and points. These drawings are approximately one-half actual size.

modern humans to Neandertals and need not imply any ancestor-descendant relationship between the two.

In summary, it appears safest at present to view the Upper Paleolithic as broadly starting in Europe, western Asia, and Africa about 40,000 years ago (thus overlapping briefly with the end of the Middle Paleolithic) and primarily as the result of cultural innovations by *Homo sapiens*. Klein and others think that the Upper Paleolithic transformation was the result of a "biologically based [advance] in human mental and cognitive capacity," that is, the achievement of full modernity of the human brain.

Fossil Record

Fossils should give us a more direct line of inquiry than tools into the fate of the archaic humans, provided enough could be found. With a complete series of fossils from all over the world dated from about 200,000 to 30,000 years ago, it should be easy to study the remains and tell what happened to the archaics. Regrettably, the trail of humanity through this period is not yet well enough marked by well-dated bones to provide a conclusive picture of the transition.

As detailed in a later section, the oldest known remains of anatomically modern humans (*Homo sapiens*) come from sub-Saharan Africa. Some specimens, such as Omo Kibish 1 and the remains from Klasies River Mouth, may date back to 130,000 years B.P. Additionally, moderns from around 100,000 years B.P. have been discovered at sites in the Middle East (e.g., Skhūl and Qafzeh in Israel).

The next oldest *Homo sapiens* fossils come from sites in Asia. A cave in south China, at Liujiang, has yielded anatomically modern remains dated at 67,000 years B.P., and from similar fossils found at a place called Salawuzu, we have a date of 50,000 to 37,000 years B.P. A skull from Niah in Sarawak on the island of Borneo carries an early (but questionable) date of 40,000 years B.P., but is supported by Australian evidence from two skeletons with a date of 25,000 years B.P., There is also impressive archaeological evidence from Australia going back beyond 40,000 years B.P.

FOSSIL HOMINIDS

Some 5 to 7 million years ago, the human family (Hominidae) appeared in Africa as the result of an evolutionary divergence from the ancestors of chimpanzees and bonobos. The earliest hominids are classified into three genera—*Ardipithecus, Australopithecus* and *Paranthropus*—and placed in their own subfamily, the Australopithecinae. All are collectively referred to as australopithecines. Predictably, the australopithecines retained a number of apelike features while showing the diagnostic hominid traits of bipedalism and canine reduction. More advanced hominids—belonging to the subfamily Homininae and its sole genus, *Homo*—evolved from australopithecine stock around 2.4 million years B.P. Members of the genus *Homo* are collectively called hominines and they are distinguished from the australopithecines by larger brains, smaller faces, and a cultural way of life. Furthermore, while the australopithecines' geographic range was limited to Africa, hominines spread worldwide into virtually all inhabitable areas. The following photographs survey some of the more important hominid fossils. ∎

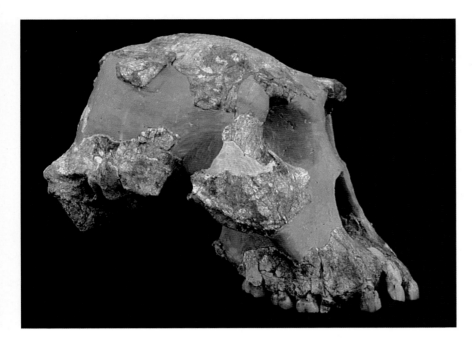

The reconstructed skull of one of the oldest australopithecine species, *Australopithecus afarensis*, is shown here. Combining a low-vaulted skull, an ape-sized brain, a prognathic face, and distinctive hominid bipedalism, *A. afarensis* inhabited East Africa from about 4.2 to 2.5 million years ago. The discovery of this skull of an adult male was announced in 1994.

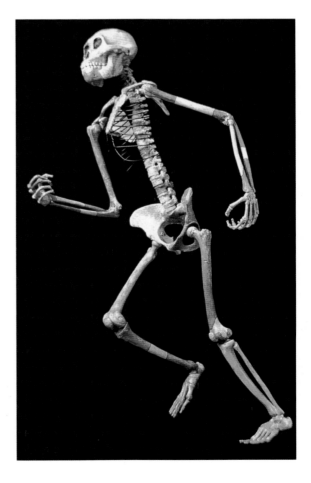

This reconstruction of a running *A. afarensis* individual was done by paleoanthropologist Owen Lovejoy. Although *A. afarensis* retained apelike limb proportions—long arms and short legs—its pelvis showed the short, broad iliac blades of a biped.

These figures from the American Museum of Natural History attempt to capture the appearance of *A. afarensis* in life. Limb proportions, degree of facial prognathism, and female-male size dimorphism are known from fossil material, but skin color, hair density, and the details of soft tissue anatomy are speculative.

Australopithecus africanus lived in South Africa between 3.5 and 2.5 million years B.P. Although its brain size was about the same as that of *A. afarensis* and the face was still markedly prognathic, the dentition of *A. africanus* was considerably more humanlike. This fossil is from the Sterkfontein site.

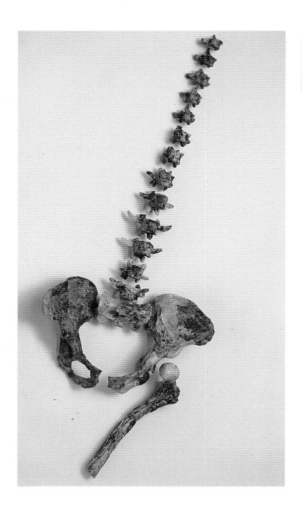

The pelvis of *Australopithecus africanus* was remarkably humanlike. Although still quite wide between the hip joints, it showed broad iliac blades and a nearly complete pelvic bowl. The pelvis, femur fragment, and vertebrae shown here are from Sterkfontein.

Three species of "robust" australopithecines of the genus *Paranthropus* inhabited East and/or South Africa from about 2.7 to 1.0 million years B.P. The genus is represented here by the massive skull of a male *P. boisei* from Olduvai Gorge, Tanzania. All of the *Paranthropus* species show remarkable enlargement of the grinding teeth, suggesting a diet of tough, chewy items.

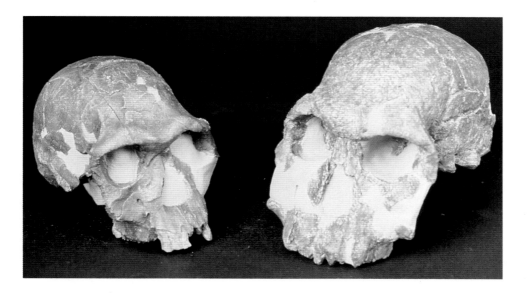

The first representatives of the genus *Homo* evolved in Africa over 2 million years ago. *Homo habilis* (at left, represented by KNM-ER 1813) inhabited both East and South Africa between 2.3 and 1.6 million years B.P., while *H. rudolfensis* (at right, represented by KNM-ER 1470) was strictly an East African species (2.4 to 1.6 million years B.P.). The two species are collectively called "early *Homo*." *Homo habilis* had a somewhat smaller brain, a more prognathic face, and narrower grinding teeth than *H. rudolfensis*.

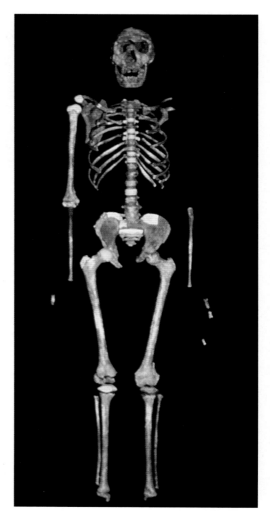

About 1.9 to 1.8 million years ago, *Homo erectus* evolved from some variety of early *Homo*. Represented here by the 1.5-million-year-old skeleton from Africa's Nariokotome site, *Homo erectus* people were tall and had modern limb proportions. Furthermore, they had brains that averaged almost 1000 cc in size. *Homo erectus* were found in Africa, Europe, and Asia, and their point of origin is currently a matter of some controversy.

The species *Homo heidelbergensis* dates back some 800,000 years into the past. It was characterized by larger brows, lower foreheads, and somewhat more prognathic faces than modern people. Shown here are skulls from two African sites. The Kabwe, or "Rhodesian Man," skull (left) may date to 250,000 years B.P., while the Bodo skull from Ethiopia (right) is 600,000 years old.

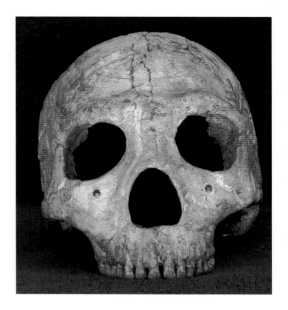

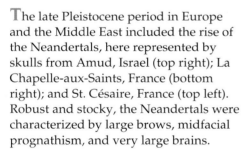

The late Pleistocene period in Europe and the Middle East included the rise of the Neandertals, here represented by skulls from Amud, Israel (top right); La Chapelle-aux-Saints, France (bottom right); and St. Césaire, France (top left). Robust and stocky, the Neandertals were characterized by large brows, midfacial prognathism, and very large brains.

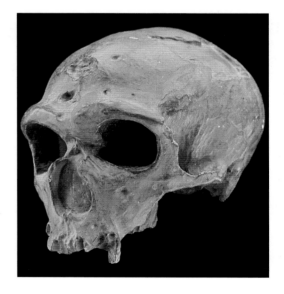

Anatomically modern humans (*Homo sapiens*) first appear in the fossil record about 130,000 years ago, apparently having evolved in Africa or the Middle East. A skull from the Moroccan site of Jebel Irhoud (right; 125,000 to 90,000 years B.P.) shows the larger brows and lower cranial vault of *Homo heidelbergensis*, while a skull from the Israeli site of Qafzeh (left; 120,000 to 90,000 years B.P.) is clearly modern.

Interestingly, in contrast to Africa and Asia, dates from Europe suggest that if that continent was involved in the archaic-to-modern transition it was little and late. Archaic people, in the form of the Neandertals, gave way to *Homo sapiens* between 40,000 and 30,000 years B.P. Judging from sites such as Zafarraya, Spain, and St. Césaire, France, the Neandertals held out the longest in western and southwestern Europe (see Table 14–1). Upper Paleolithic cultures, most of which can reasonably be assumed to indicate the presence of modern humans, date back some 10,000 years before the Neandertals' ultimate demise. Somewhat younger is the fossil evidence of European *Homo sapiens*, which dates back to slightly more than 30,000 years (e.g., at Velíka Pečina in Croatia). There is some possibility that barriers of glacial ice kept Europe out of the mainstream of the last stages of human evolution (Figure 16–1).

The main landmasses of the Old World were probably fully, if sparsely, populated at 200,000 years B.P. by archaic humans. But from about 130,000 years B.P. onward, and especially after 40,000 years B.P., we find increasing evidence of anatomically modern people more or less indistinguishable from the present populations of these lands. They were modern from head to toe, talented as artists, and skilled in a wide range of technology. We must now ask ourselves how, where, when, and why the transition was made.

The Regional-Continuity Model

All specialists agree that the transition of archaic humans into *Homo sapiens* involved elevation and rounding of the cranial vault (which produced a fairly steep forehead); full flexion of the cranial base; reduction of the brows; development of a distinct chin; and probably some decrease in the size of the face and teeth (see Box 16–1 and Figures 16–7 and 14–16). Average brain size may have gone up or down a bit, depending on whether one believes we evolved only from *Homo heidelbergensis* or from all archaics generally (see below), but such changes in volume were probably insignificant. Whether there were important advances in the internal organization of the brain/mind is another question, however, and some researchers, such as Richard Klein and Steve Mithen (see Chapter 13), believe that a fully modern brain—one with full cognitive fluidity, to use Mithen's terms—appeared only with the evolution of *Homo sapiens*. Despite general agreement on the biological modifications of modernity, however, paleoanthropologists have recently disagreed sharply on the specifics of *Homo sapiens*'s evolution. Two primary models (as well as several intermediate schemes) have been proposed.

The first model hypothesizes that modern humans evolved more or less simultaneously across the entire Old World from several ancestral populations. Dubbed the regional-continuity model, and illustrated in Figure 16–8 (top), this scheme envisions a broad-scale transformation of *Homo erectus* into modern humans via several, geographically varying, archaic populations. In other words, all or most archaic humans from around the Old World—including the Neandertals and the people we are calling *Homo heidelbergensis*—are hypothesized as having contributed to the modern gene pool. In order for this sort of transformation to work, its supporters propose that there was extensive gene flow among the various populations of *Homo erectus*, and later populations of archaic people (gene flow is shown as dashed lines in Figure 16–8). Africa is viewed as exchanging genes with Eurasia, which in turn shared alleles with East and Southeast Asia and Australia. Because of gene flow, regional-continuity supporters argue, new traits evolving in one region would have been carried inevitably to all other regions, and thus all of

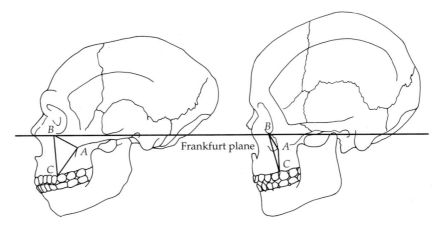

FIGURE 16–7 This comparison of a classic Neandertal (La Chapelle, left) and a modern human (right) provides an extreme example of the cranial differences between archaic people and *Homo sapiens*. The anatomical distance between modern humans and our actual ancestors, the *Homo heidelbergensis* people, was probably not quite so great (see Figure 14-16). The horizontal line called the Frankfurt plane, which passes through the lower margin of the orbit and the auditory meatus (ear hole), enables the skulls to be drawn in comparable orientation. Differences in the A-B-C triangles reflect the midfacial prognathism of the Neandertal compared to the nonprognathic modern face.

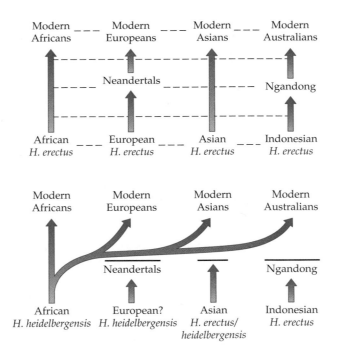

FIGURE 16–8 The hypothesis of regional continuity (top) proposes that *Homo erectus* people on each continent evolved through various archaic types into modern humans. In this model, intercontinental gene flow is shown by horizontal dashed lines. In contrast, the hypothesis of rapid replacement (bottom) envisions modern *Homo sapiens* evolving once—in Africa from *Homo heidelbergensis* ancestors—and then migrating throughout the Old World replacing their archaic predecessors. Note that details about the evolutionary connections between *Homo erectus*, *Homo heidelbergensis*, and the Neandertals are not shown in the bottom model, but can be found in Figure 14–19. Redrawn after C. B. Stringer and C. Gamble, 1993.

humanity would have evolved together from the level of *H. erectus* to full modernity. Let us examine some of the fossil evidence for this evolutionary model.

In the Middle East, an ancestral relationship between archaic and modern people seems possible, with the fossils from Zuttiyeh, Skhūl, and Qafzeh somewhat bridging the evolutionary gap. The oldest of these three sites is Zuttiyeh cave in Israel. In the mid-1920s, a distinctly archaic partial face plus frontal bone was found there (Figure 16–9) that has been dated to 350,000 to 250,000 years B.P. Unfortunately, the fragmentary nature of the Zuttiyeh fossil and its mosaic of traits allow numerous comparisons but very little certainty with regard to its phylogenetic connections. With its large brows (centrally thickened and thinning laterally), receding frontal, and gracile zygomatic bones, the Zuttiyeh face shows some similarities to the archaic skull from Steinheim, Germany (Table 14–2). Looking eastward, it has also been noted that Zuttiyeh's flat upper face and frontal contours resemble the *Homo erectus* population from Zhoukoudian, China. Finally, considering only possible Middle East connections, some workers think Zuttiyeh was ancestral to the Skhūl and Qafzeh people, while, in sharp contrast, others regard it as a member of the Neandertal lineage. For their parts, the Skhūl (100,000 to 80,000 years B.P.) and Qafzeh (120,000 to 90,000 years B.P.) fossils look somewhat transitional since each includes some primitive features, although on balance both fall within the modern category. For example, Skhūl 5 shows moderate brow ridge development (Figure 14–7), while Qafzeh 9 shows rather significant facial prognathism. Taken together, Zuttiyeh, Qafzeh, and Skhūl *may* document a gradual archaic-to-modern transition in the Middle East, but other interpretations also are possible.

In eastern Europe, although clear intermediates are missing, regional continuity has been postulated based on the fact that the most recent archaic specimens anticipate modern features, while the oldest true moderns appear rather primitive. In the latter category are the specimens from Mladeč and Předmost (both sites in Moravia) and Velíka Pečina (in Croatia; see Figure 16–1), all probably more than 30,000 years old and therefore among the oldest European *Homo sapiens* fossils, and all showing a mosaic of traits including some Neandertal-like features (e.g., thick cranial bones and large brow ridges among the Mladeč people). The possibility that the Neandertals were ancestral to modern Europeans has long been promoted by

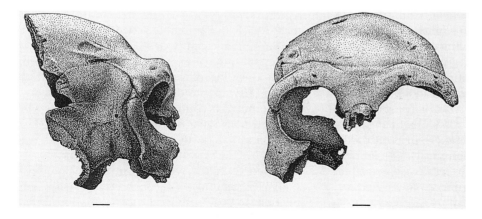

FIGURE 16–9   Side and front views of the fragmentary face from Zuttiyeh, Israel. Dated at 350,000 to 250,000 years B.P., this specimen is drawn slightly less than one-half actual size.

regional-continuity supporters (see Figure 16–8) and the fossils from eastern Europe appear to provide some support for this view. As discussed in Chapter 14, however, archaeological evidence from western Europe and the Middle East does not support this connection, and the same is true for the single comparison of Neandertal and *Homo sapiens* mtDNA.

Arguments for regional continuity in China are based on claims that certain dental and cranial traits show long histories of evolutionary occurrence in that area. In particular, evidence for a broad and flat face is claimed to link fossil and modern inhabitants of the Far East. The proposed continuity sequence in China views the archaic fossils from Dali, Jinniu Shan, Maba, and Xujiayao (all dated to 300,000 to 100,000 years B.P.) as evolutionary descendants of the Zhoukoudian *Homo erectus* people, and as the probable ancestors of modern populations such as that from Liujiang (67,000 years B.P.).

In the Indonesian/Australian region, a medley of cranial features has been used to argue that modern Australian Aborigines are descended from Javanese *Homo erectus* via intermediate populations such as Ngandong, Java, and (later) Willandra Lakes, Australia (same location as Lake Mungo in Figure 16–16). Among the traits claimed to show evolutionary continuity in this part of the Old World are well-developed brow ridges, a receding forehead, and facial prognathism. As explained in Chapter 10 and discussed further below, however, new evidence that the Ngandong fossils are quite young may bar them from a role as the Aborigines' ancestors. Furthermore, although regional-continuity proponents maintain that several anatomical traits link the late Pleistocene specimen from Willandra Lakes (WLH 50) with Ngandong on the one hand and modern Aborigines on the other, a 1998 analysis of eleven skull measurements offers differing evidence. In the new study, Chris Stringer has found WLH 50 to be no closer metrically to the Ngandong population than to a sample of African archaics (e.g., Jebel Irhoud, Ngaloba, Singa, Omo Kibish 2). Additionally, Stringer's study suggests that with regard to its modern traits, WLH 50 is somewhat closer to the Middle Eastern specimens from Skhūl and Qafzeh than it is to modern Australian Aborigines.

Finally, certain fossils in Africa from the period between 400,000 and 50,000 years B.P. may constitute an evolutionary series of humans from fully archaic to intermediate to anatomically modern (see Table 16–1). Very robust archaic skulls include the Kabwe fossil from Zambia and the Elandsfontein skull fragments from South Africa. These two skulls date to at least 130,000 years B.P., and may go back a quarter of a million years or more. Omo Kibish 2 and the Ngaloba fossil are more lightly built archaics from East Africa and both date around 130,000 years B.P. Additionally, the Ileret cranium from Kenya, recently dated to about 270,000 years B.P., has been described as showing anatomical traits that approach modernity. Lastly, the fossil remains of fully modern humans who lived 130,000 years B.P. have been recovered from the South African site of Klasies River Mouth on the Tsitsikama coast of Cape Province. Somewhat younger modern populations have been documented at Border Cave on the Swaziland border (see Figure 16–1) and elsewhere in South Africa, as well as at the north African site of Dar-es-Soltan (Table 16–1).

This overview of the fossil evidence for the regional-continuity model has been brief and selective, but it gives a general sense of the data base used by those researchers who argue for a broad-scale phyletic transformation of *Homo erectus* into modern humans via various archaic populations (an interpretation with interesting taxonomic implications; see Box 16–2). An extreme version of the regional-continuity model remains the minority opinion among present-day

TABLE 16–1   *Selected Human Fossils From Africa, Dated Between 400,000 and 50,000 Years B.P.*

SITE	ANATOMICAL TYPE	APPROXIMATE AGE	DATE OF DISCOVERY
Ndutu, Tanzania	Archaic[a]	400,000–200,000	1973
Elandsfontein, RSA[b]	Archaic	350,000–130,000	1953
Ileret, Kenya	Intermediate?	ca. 270,000	1992
Florisbad, RSA	Intermediate	260,000	1932
Kabwe, Zambia	Archaic	250,000–130,000	1921
Singa, Sudan	Intermediate	200,000–100,000	1924
Omo Kibish 2, Ethiopia	Archaic	ca. 130,000	1967
Ngaloba, Laetoli, Tanzania	Intermediate	ca. 130,000	1978
Omo Kibish 1, Ethiopia	Modern	ca. 130,000	1967
Klasies River Mouth, RSA	Modern	130,000–120,000	1972
Border Cave, RSA	Modern	85,000–50,000	1941
Die Kelders Cave, RSA	Modern	75,000–60,000	1976
Equus Cave, RSA	Modern	75,000–60,000	1985
Dar-es-Soltan, Cave 2, Morocco	Modern	70,000–50,000	1975

[a] Most of the archaic and intermediate fossils listed here are tentatively classified as *Homo heidelbergensis* (see Table 14–2).
[b] Republic of South Africa.

paleoanthropologists, however, for a variety of reasons. First, many researchers prefer to interpret hominid evolution—including its final stages and the appearance of modern humans—as primarily involving repeated cladogenetic (branching) speciation, not widespread phyletic change within a single variable species or a series of connected chronospecies (see Chapter 2). Second, even the experts disagree on the diagnostic usefulness of many of the traits claimed to show regional continuity. Third, there is a marked lack of simultaneity in the first appearances of modern humans in the different regions of the Old World. The very oldest modern fossils are from Africa (Table 16–1), whereas elsewhere moderns appear much later. Fourth, as detailed in the next section, there is a growing body of genetic and molecular evidence for our species' cladogenetic evolution in Africa or the Middle East, followed by widespread migration. Fifth and finally, two recent studies have weakened key elements in the regional-continuity argument. As noted in Chapter 14, mtDNA data collected from the original Neandertal specimen suggests that these people belonged to a distinct and dead-end species that made little, if any, contribution to modern humans' gene pool. These results, although requiring confirmation, reduce the likelihood of an evolutionary link between the Neandertals and modern Europeans (see Figure 16–8, top). Furthermore, the possibility that the Ngandong (Solo) population was ancestral to modern Australians (Figure 16–8, top) has been reduced by new studies showing that the Ngandong people lived so late in time (46,000 to 27,000 years B.P.; see Chapter 10) that they were in fact the contemporaries of anatomically modern Indonesians and Australians who had migrated into the region from elsewhere (see below).

At present, therefore, the hypothesis of regional-continuity across the entire Old World is an embattled, minority opinion, but one that certainly still has its supporters. We now turn our attention to an alternative hypothesis that is more popular among anthropologists as an explanation for the origin of modern humans: the rapid-replacement, or "out-of-Africa," model.

Box 16-2

CURRENT ISSUE: The Imprecise Art of Taxonomy

As described in Chapter 3, anthropology shares with the other life sciences a system of classifying and naming organisms called taxonomy. Following Linnaeus, every species is given a two-part name: genus first and species second (e.g., *Homo sapiens*). Such labels—and their referents—may vary somewhat among workers according to individual scientists' views on the correct grouping of living and/or fossil creatures. Indeed, because taxonomy is a combination of science and art, every taxonomic scheme—including the one used in this book—is somewhat idiosyncratic. Nonetheless, everyone has a stake in achieving sufficient taxonomic agreement for clear communication about the subjects and results of their research. Indeed, facilitating the flow of scholarly information is the primary raison d'être for taxonomy.

Paleoanthropologists are most interested, of course, in the taxonomy of fossil hominids. It follows, therefore, that among the most controversial—and, to opponents, alarming—side effects of the regional-continuity model are the naming problems it raises with regard to Pleistocene hominines. Regional-continuity proponents view the last stages of human evolution as a case of widescale phyletic transformation and, as discussed in Chapter 2, the boundaries between sequential species in an evolving lineage are not realities of nature but conveniences for human communication. Our minds work in such a way that we can deal with discrete categories or sets of verbal symbols, but are unable to communicate linguistically about continuously varying phenomena. However, it is no solution to lump species together, just to avoid having to define boundaries. The regional-continuity proponent Milford Wolpoff has proposed "sinking" *Homo erectus* and *H. heidelbergensis* into *Homo sapiens* so that there is no species boundary to be defined between them. Thus *Homo sapiens* would become a very long-lived and very variable species. But if we follow that course, one could argue that there is no reason to retain the *Homo habilis/Homo erectus* boundary either, since some scientists believe it is equally hard to define and equally artificial. Indeed, the whole system of artificial boundaries breaks down; if we destroy one, we may as well destroy them all. (Mathematical solutions to these sorts of problems have been proposed under the rubric Fuzzy Set Theory; see Willermet and Hill, 1997.) The best course of action at present is to stay with what is in practice a second-rate taxonomic system, but which is the best available currently. It must be said, however, that the system permits fairly successful communication among scientists, in spite of its drawbacks.

The tendency of the human mind to deal in sharply defined categories or sets is the cause of a much more serious version of this taxonomic problem, which overflows into the social and political scene. When we try to communicate about the living members of our species, we again find it necessary to categorize them, even though continuities exist between all the so-called racial groups (see Chapter 18). Whether we call certain Americans blacks and whites or African-Americans and European-Americans (for example), we still are using categories that, by their nature, obscure the truth. But this is the way our minds and our language work. Whatever euphemism we use to describe these groupings of *Homo sapiens*, we still hide the continuity which exists between people with pinkish-buff skin and those with brownish skin. Political correctness may change the terminology, but the terminology remains inaccurate, and always will be so.

So taxonomy presents us with an insoluble linguistic problem when we come to deal with aspects of the natural world. It is a problem that begins with communication about the evolutionary process of continuous change and variation, and—unless carefully monitored—can end in prejudice and racism. ∎

The Rapid-Replacement Model

Without doubt, one of the strongest pieces of evidence for the rapid-replacement model is the clear occurrence of anatomically modern humans in the adjacent regions of Africa and the Middle East long before they showed up in Europe, Asia, and Australia—a pattern that strongly implies a single, branching origin. As shown in Table 16–1, modern humans were apparently living in South and East Africa as early as 130,000 years ago. Relevant fossils come from Omo Kibish and the Klasies River Mouth. The archaic and transitional populations that were likely to have given rise to these early moderns have been discovered at Elandsfontein, Kabwe, Ngaloba, and Singa, and in North Africa at the Moroccan site of Jebel Irhoud. By 120,000 to 80,000 years ago, essentially modern people were inhabiting such Middle Eastern sites as Skhūl and Qafzeh.

In comparison, the appearance of anatomically modern humans outside Africa and the Middle East was much later. Cro-Magnon people first appeared in Europe sometime after 40,000 years ago and, as shown by the skull from Liujiang, anatomically modern humans were present in China by 67,000 years B.P. In addition, Niah Cave in Sarawak has produced modern fossils dating to 40,000 years B.P., just slightly older than the modern material from the Upper Cave at Zhoukoudian (about 25,000 years B.P.). And finally, there is evidence of the occupation of northern Australia—presumably by modern people—by 55,000 years B.P. A brief survey of the fossil record, therefore, can be interpreted as providing solid evidence in favor of an African–Middle Eastern birthplace for anatomically modern people.

Detailed comparative analyses of the known fossils also seem primarily to support the rapid-replacement model. For example, University of São Paulo anthropologist Marta Mirazon Lahr recently took a close look at the cranial traits claimed to reflect morphological continuity from *Homo erectus* to modern people in East Asia and Australia. She concluded that the features in question "are not exclusive to these regions, either spatially or temporally, and some occur at a higher incidence in other populations." Based on her studies, Lahr favors the hypothesis of a single African origin for modern humans. In a similar vein, American paleoanthropologist Diane Waddle has conducted a matrix correlation test of the regional-continuity and rapid-replacement models. Using more than 150 different cranial traits and measurements, Waddle calculated and compared overall "morphological distances" between groups of fossils arranged by region (West Europe, East Europe, Southwest Asia, Africa) and age (600,000 to 125,000, 125,000 to 32,000, and 32,000 to 8,000; all in years B.P.). Waddle ran her comparisons several times, varying the hypothetical place of initial appearance of modern humans and the amount and pattern of gene flow between regions. In the end, it was concluded that the study "support[ed] a single African and/or [Middle Eastern] origin for modern humans."

Finally, there are now several genetic or molecular studies that bear on the regional-continuity versus rapid-replacement question. For example, a team of researchers led by A. M. Bowcock of the University of Texas recently analyzed diversity in humans' polymorphic microsatellite alleles, reasoning that the oldest populations should show the greatest amount of genetic variation. (As a reminder, satellites are usually noncoding DNA sequences that accumulate at certain points on chromosomes; see Chapter 2). Using genetic information from 148 people representing fourteen indigenous populations and five continents, Bowcock et al. found that the "diversity of microsatellites is highest in Africa, which . . . supports the hypothesis of an African origin for [modern] humans." Similar results have come from studies of genetic variation in certain regions of the Y chromosome; variation that is inherited only through the male line. When diversity in the YAP (Y Alu polymorphism) region of that chromosome was examined, African populations were found to contain more variation than non-African groups, a finding that supports the idea that humans have been living in Africa longer than elsewhere. In fact, researchers estimate that the first man to show the pattern of Y chromosome mutations since inherited by all men worldwide—an individual dubbed our "African Adam"—lived around 185,000 years ago. Interestingly, however, the Y chromosome data also showed evidence of some Asian patterns occurring among modern Africans, rather than strictly the reverse. It appears, likely, therefore, that initial movements of early modern humans from Africa to Asia were probably followed at some later time(s) by back-migrations in the opposite direction.

The conclusion that the first anatomically modern Asians were migrants from Africa—rather than the results of an independent evolutionary origin *in situ*—recently gained strong support from a study of the genetic profiles of twenty-eight present-day Chinese populations. Chinese geneticist J. Y. Chu and colleagues used genetic information to work out the most likely ancestral migration routes into and throughout Asia. As they noted in a 1998 paper describing their work, "[I]t is now probably safe to conclude that modern humans originating in Africa constitute the majority of the current gene pool in East Asia."

Without doubt, however, the best known genetic studies probing the place and date of modern humans' origin are those focused on mitochondrial DNA (mtDNA). This work has attracted tremendous media attention to the possibility of an "African Eve," but it has also been something of a "two steps forward, one step backward" affair because of the initial publication of somewhat flawed results. Although some anthropologists have come to distrust the mtDNA studies, most believe the studies provide important information about recent human evolution. A closer look at this controversial research follows.

Analyses of mtDNA (Figure 16–10) were pioneered by the late Allan Wilson of the University of California, Berkeley, working with numerous colleagues. In the late 1980s, Wilson's research team set out to measure the variations in mtDNA in people from several living populations. Because mtDNA is found only in the cytoplasm of the cell and because sperm provides almost no cytoplasm to the fertilized egg, no mtDNA is inherited from the father (that is, fertilization involves the combination of only the *nuclear* DNA of egg and sperm). Thus the genetic codes carried by a cell's mtDNA come from the mother alone, and each of us carries the mtDNA that we inherited from our mother, her mother, our maternal great-grandmother, and so on along a single genealogical line. This is quite a different mode of inheritance from that of nuclear DNA, which comes from an expanding network of grandparents of both sexes. Our ancestral mtDNA lineage converges with that of others with whom we share female grandparents, to produce an expanding inverted tree of relationships (Figure 16–11). Using identifiable differences in the mtDNA of their subjects—differences which presumably accumulate through mutations at the rate of 2 to 4 percent per million years—the Wilson team attempted to construct a branching dendrogram or tree. Their results are shown in Figure 16–12, and they led Wilson and his co-workers to the following set of conclusions:

1. The mtDNA structure of the female common ancestor of all modern humanity was closer to that of most living Africans than to any other geographic group. Therefore the common female ancestor of modern human-

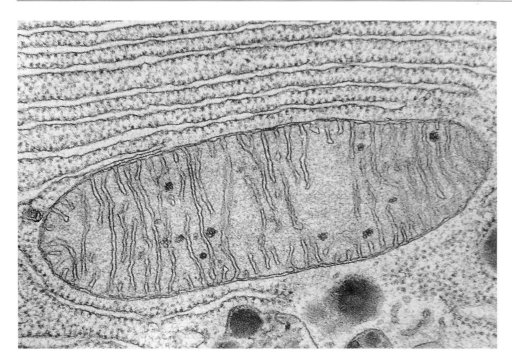

FIGURE 16–10 Mitochondria, like the oblong body in the center of this photograph, are apart from the nucleus, the only structures in the cells of vertebrates that carry DNA and synthesize proteins. Their special properties suggest strongly that they were originally free-living organisms that invaded the cells of other animals and adapted to a symbiotic existence within them.

ity was most probably a woman living in Africa. The media predictably named her Eve!

2. The amount of genetic change (0.6 percent) recorded between the most different individuals tested (calibrated on the basis of 5 million years B.P. for the chimpanzee-hominid split) suggests a period since that common ancestor lived of between 150,000 and 200,000 years or to take a rough mean, say, 175,000 years. This was roughly the time of late *Homo heidelbergensis* and just prior to the appearance of anatomically modern humans.

3. It follows that the population to which Eve belonged gave rise to all living humans through a process of successful diversification, adaptation, and expansion out of Africa and throughout the world. It does not mean that Eve was the only woman alive at that time, but that her female progeny alone gave rise to the existing human race. She was undoubtedly a member of an interbreeding population, but the female progeny of other individuals living at that time must have eventually died out.

4. It also follows that other populations of *Homo* that lived before about 250,000 years B.P. in places other than Africa (that is, European and Asian *Homo erectus* and archaic humans) did not contribute to the mtDNA of modern humankind unless there were very rapid migrations back into Africa before the critical date of origin. This reasoning suggests that living humans have no common female ancestors from among these early Eurasian groups, though we could in theory have male ancestors.

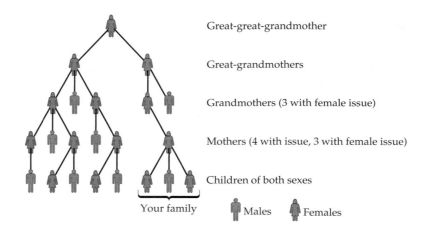

Great-great-grandmother

Great-grandmothers

Grandmothers (3 with female issue)

Mothers (4 with issue, 3 with female issue)

Children of both sexes

Your family

Males   Females

FIGURE 16–11   Mitochondrial DNA (mtDNA) is passed from one generation to another only through females in the cytoplasm of their egg cells. None is carried in the spermatozoa. If you trace your ancestry through your mother and your maternal female grandparents you will eventually find that you share a single great-great-grandmother with the entire human race. The hypothesis of Wilson and his colleagues suggests that this ancestor was an African who lived about 200,000 years ago. In this chart such an ancestry is set out for five generations.

These are broad and sweeping conclusions and, wrapped in the scientific sophistication of molecular studies, the mtDNA research initially seemed to provide proof positive of a common African ancestor for all living humans. But to survive in science, research results must withstand the challenges of skeptics, and here the mtDNA studies have not been entirely successful. Indeed, it now appears that the critics have uncovered serious flaws in the original mtDNA research. For one thing, the validity of these studies depends on the ability of modern computer programs to produce accurate ancestor-descendant trees, and skeptics have pointed out that the geographic identity of "Eve" is affected by such apparently simple things as the order in which individual subjects' mtDNA types are entered into the computer for analysis. Enter the data in one sequence, and the computer says "Eve" was African. Enter the same data in another sequence, and the computer may well put "Eve" in an entirely different location. Additionally, some critics have strongly challenged the selection of subjects for the original mtDNA studies, claiming that the researchers did not control adequately for recent (historic, as opposed to prehistoric) interbreeding between representatives of different geographic populations.

Problems such as these have led some anthropologists to dismiss the validity of mtDNA studies altogether. Nonetheless, in a recent review article on the subject, mtDNA researcher Mark Stoneking urged against throwing the baby out with the bathwater. While admitting that there were serious problems with the first mtDNA analyses, Stoneking maintained that "an African origin still appears to be the best explanation for the [original and other] mtDNA datasets." Stoneking also noted that a second measure of mtDNA variation—information on sequence changes by nucleotide bases (presumably a reliable indicator of accumulated mutations)—also points to African populations as the oldest on earth.

One other small but important piece of evidence from genetic studies tends to support the rapid-replacement model and argues against the regional-continuity

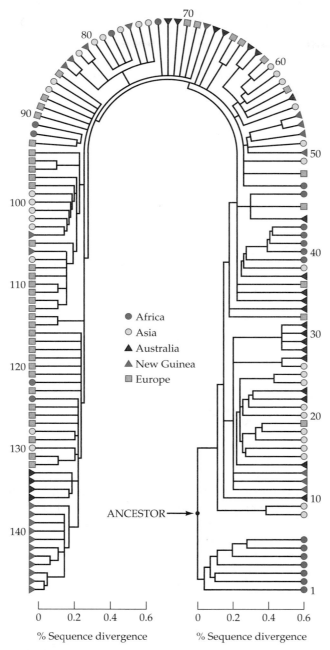

FIGURE 16–12 This diagram was prepared by Allan Wilson and co-workers to present the results of their mtDNA analysis. It would normally have been drawn unfolded, but in order to save space the "tree" has been folded around a point toward the top of the page. The hypothetical ancestor Eve is to the bottom right, and the distances between the branching points and the tips of the branches leading to 147 modern individuals reflect the percentage of the molecular sequence which has mutated. The geographic origin of the individual tested is shown in the key. It is of interest that the members of each geographic region fall into more than one group. The branching pattern within the African group suggests that the population there has been more or less constant since the time of Eve. Elsewhere the branching pattern suggests an expanding population—exactly as might be predicted. The African populations are more diverse mitochondrially, and this diversity suggested to the Wilson team that the population is older.

hypothesis. Genetic studies often allow estimates of humans' global population size at various points in the past, and they suggest that around the time when modern humans originated our ancestors numbered only between 5,000 and 10,000 individuals worldwide. These numbers are significant because they seem too small to allow the extensive gene flow required for the regional-continuity model to work (see Figure 16–8, top).

To summarize, the mtDNA controversy notwithstanding, the combined evidence currently favors the rapid-replacement hypothesis rather than the regional-continuity model. As diagramed in Figure 16–8 (bottom), anatomically modern people probably first evolved by branching speciation in Africa or the Middle East around 130,000 years ago and then spread throughout the world, replacing all of their archaic predecessors. Whether or not this was a rigid replacement with no interbreeding between moderns and archaics is difficult to say. The Neandertal mtDNA data suggest little, if any, interbreeding between moderns and Neandertals in Europe. On the other hand, other genetic data, plus the 1998 discovery in Portugal of a 24,500-year-old skeleton claimed to show both Neandertal and modern traits, suggest that some interbreeding did occur. This possibility tends to soften the scenario into more of a replacement-and-hybridization phenomenon. Overall, however, African genes and traits seem to have carried the day during humans' final evolutionary transformation and the genetic contributions by non-African, archaic people to the modern gene pool are likely to have been small. The message is clear: the biological core of every living person is overwhelmingly African.

THE BIOLOGICAL AND CULTURAL TRANSITION

Our discussion to this point has focused mostly on the who, when, and where aspects of humans' final evolutionary transition. We have not yet addressed what sorts of selection pressures could have produced the extensive remodeling of the human skull from the forms characteristic of *Homo erectus* and the archaics to that of living people. In the following section, we briefly examine a few hypotheses about the evolution of modern cranial and dental traits.

Among the most striking changes in the skull is a reduction in the masticatory apparatus. This seems to have begun toward the end of *Homo erectus* times—say, 0.8 million years ago—and reached its end about 70,000 years ago, with our present head shape. The masticatory apparatus includes both the jaws, the teeth, the associated musculature, and the supporting structures on the cranium to which the muscles are attached. Thus the skull responds in its shape to the stresses placed on it by the jaws, and these stresses are caused not just by the action of the jaw muscles, but also by the weight of the entire apparatus. Thus the heavy jaws of *Homo erectus* and later, archaic humans, were balanced by a relatively large occipital bone, which sometimes projected backward as a bunlike torus. Well-developed nuchal (neck) muscles held the head up and balanced the weight of the jaws.

A number of reasons for the reduction of the jaws and teeth among anatomically modern people have been proposed. The first and most obvious would seem to be that some changes had occurred in diet and food preparation that reduced the requirement for very powerful jaws, and it is significant that this change was accompanied by a marked development in technology—certainly toward the end of the period in question. Earlier developments may have occurred that are not recorded in the archaeological record. We can only guess that by grinding grain, chopping vegetation and meat, and eventually cooking food, early moderns reduced their need of heavy jaws.

Second, according to Loring Brace, the size of the front teeth in particular was a sort of "technological" adaptation for some archaic people. Brace thinks that archaics such as Neandertals regularly used their front teeth as a built-in tool, serving as pliers to hold one end of some material such as wood or hide so that one hand would be free to cut, scrape, or pierce the material with a stone implement (see Figure 14–12). This application is also inferred from examination of the wear on the incisor teeth and of their form, which is called *shovel-shaped*. This term implies that the incisors were strengthened on their inner borders in a way that gave them a curved and shovel-like shape. Patterns of wear on the incisors of some fossils suggest that the Neandertals softened animal hides by chewing them; people may also have twisted plant fibers or straightened wooden shafts with the aid of their teeth (see Figure 14–11).

As discussed earlier, the Neandertals apparently were not the direct ancestors of modern humans. Nonetheless, improvements in stone implements may also have affected our *Homo heidelbergensis* ancestors, allowing them to rely less and less on their front teeth as a built-in tool. This decreased reliance then possibly led to a gradual reduction in tooth and jaw size, which in turn permitted reduction in the face and other features of the skull, giving rise to people with heads like ours.

Pilbeam's Hypothesis

Many scientists believe that this hypothesis cannot account adequately for the transformation of *Homo erectus* and archaic humans into people of modern appearance, and they offer alternatives. David Pilbeam proposed another sort of evolutionary mechanism that may have contributed to the changes in the human skull. He suggested that the head gradually became more modern in form because of the evolution of the upper part of the throat into a pharynx capable of producing the full range of modern vocalizations. As we saw in Chapter 13, when, in modern human development, this essential part of the vocal tract starts to take on its final shape, the larynx moves down in the throat, and the base of the skull, which is rather flat at birth, takes on a concave arch. The pharyngeal space is thus formed in front of the topmost vertebra, and the arch in the base of the skull serves as a roof.

Pilbeam believes that the evolution of the pharynx's arched roof may have affected the overall structure of the human skull. As the arch formed, the base of the skull shortened (just as the ends of a piece of cloth that is lifted slightly in the middle pull together). If the starting point of this process were a long, low skull, the shortening of the skull base might have caused the facial region to pull inward from its formerly out-thrust position. With the face thus pulled in, the whole braincase would have had to become higher to contain the same amount of brain tissue. And as this shaping happened, the brow and the sides of the skull would have become more vertical. Thus the ancient, low-vaulted skull could have been transformed into a modern *Homo sapiens* skull. Archaic and modern skulls are, in effect, just different ways of packing the same quantity of brain tissue. The overall shape of the package is dictated primarily by only one of its dimensions—the length of the base of the skull—which is in turn related to the presence of a modern pharynx.

Recently, Pilbeam's hypothesis has received strong support from the work of Rutger's University anthropologist Daniel Lieberman. Using CT scans and radiographs of modern and fossil specimens, Lieberman has determined that a single evolutionary change—namely, shortening of the sphenoid bone in the cranial base—probably triggered the final steps in the modernization of the human skull. (To better understand the concept of sphenoid shortening, refer to Figure 13–10. Lessening sphenoid length would reduce the *horizontal* distance between points B and D.) Lieberman's data show that modern humans' sphenoids are significantly shorter than those of the Neandertals (our collateral relatives) and *Homo heidelbergensis* (our actual ancestors). Shorter sphenoids led to reduced facial prognathism and that, in turn, led to smaller brows, more vertical foreheads, and a more rounded skull shape.

Like Pilbeam, Lieberman links sphenoid shortening and the associated skull changes with the evolution of a modern vocal tract. It appears that speech was an incredibly important—indeed, formative—adaptation for *Homo sapiens*. This is not to say that the Neandertals, *Homo heidelbergensis*, or possibly even *Homo erectus* were completely incapable of speech. What we see in the evolution of anatomically modern people is the final, very significant, step. Natural selection may have worked at maximum speed to weed out the slow talkers and to foster better speaking ability. It is almost impossible today, tens of thousands of years later, to sense the powerful evolutionary pressures that may have been launched when this new element was introduced into the vocal tract. The development of a modern pharynx, with its enormous potential for communication, may very well explain a leap in physical and cultural evolution.

The Appearance of the Chin

Shortening the skull base, as described above, tucked the face and jaws of newly modern humans downward and backward into close proximity to the neck. This shift in position, although affecting a set of dwindling structures (teeth, jaws, and supporting facial bones), led to the evolution of that distinctive modern trait, the chin. Analyses of the mechanics of chewing have revealed how and why the chin was produced. During chewing, the mandible is subjected to bending and twisting stresses as the jaw muscles pull it backward and forward and from side to side. Furthermore, lateral grinding on the molars concentrates stress specifically at the **mandibular symphysis** (the midline of the lower jaw). Symphyseal stresses continue to be an issue for living people because, although we have small jaws and teeth, we can still generate powerful grinding by the molars. Typically, skeletal stresses like those on the mandible are counterbalanced by thickening the bone in question and in earlier hominids (as in nonhuman primates) lower jaw reinforcement usually involved internal thickening (Figure 16–13). This option was not open to modern humans, however, because tucking an internally buttressed mandible up against the neck could have threatened to constrict vital soft structures such as blood vessels, the windpipe, and the larynx. Given these anatomical constraints, natural selection found a compromise—the lower margin of our lightly buttressed symphysis was everted slightly (turned outwards). This simple modification produced an externally reinforced jaw that was adequately spaced from the neck and in the process gave us a chin.

Mandibular symphysis the midline connecting the right and left halves of the lower jaw.

Transition Completed

The most probable answer to our question of why modern head and jaw forms evolved is that all the factors that have been mentioned were at work: the pharynx certainly increased in length, and the jaws, teeth, and associated bony structures

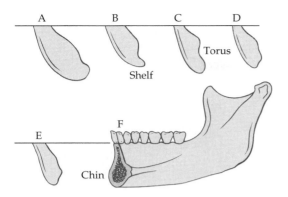

FIGURE 16–13 This figure shows cross-sections of the symphyseal region of several nonhuman primates and hominids: [A] gorilla, [B] chimpanzee, [C] *A. africanus*, [D and E] archaic *Homo*, and [F] modern human. For all drawings, the front of the jaw is to the left and the internal surface to the right. Note that internal buttressing can occur as a shelf of bone at the lower margin of the jaw and/or a mandibular torus higher on the symphysis.

were indeed reduced in size. The changes at the back of the skull were most probably no more than a product of the important new developments taking place at the front.

Much now is known of the period of transition, but much remains to be learned. Hardly any relevant fossil evidence is available from some crucial areas of the world: Arabia, at the crossroads of two continents; the endless reaches of Central Asia; and the subcontinent of India, rich in game and characterized by the sort of warm climate that early humans favored for millions of years.

Whenever and wherever it began, the evolutionary transition transformed humankind. By about 30,000 years ago the changes were largely complete, and the world was populated with people who looked like ourselves. People were living in larger bands than they ever had before. Cultures were branching and rebranching along countless idiosyncratic paths, like a plant that has lived long in the shade and is suddenly offered the full strength of the sun. Successful initiatives in technology or art or symbol making brought on more initiatives, and cultural change steadily accelerated.

A NEW BREED

Variability

Like people living today, the first modern people developed characteristic physical types from region to region, and possibly even from site to site within a region (Figure 16–14). Their diverse environments, climates, and food supplies account for some of the variations. Such physical characteristics as tallness and shortness, dark skin and light skin, straight hair and curly hair, had formed and would continue to evolve during the millennia when the human body had to accommodate itself to both heat and cold and to the variations of sunlight in different latitudes. The relatively short, thick body of the Eskimo, for instance, conserves heat better than the tall, thin bodies of some sub-Saharan Africans, which present a much greater area of skin to be cooled by the air. Similarly, thick, straight hair, in the opinion of some scholars, may help to maintain the temperature of the brain in cold climates, whereas tightly curled hair seems to be an adaptation to guard against hot tropical sunshine.

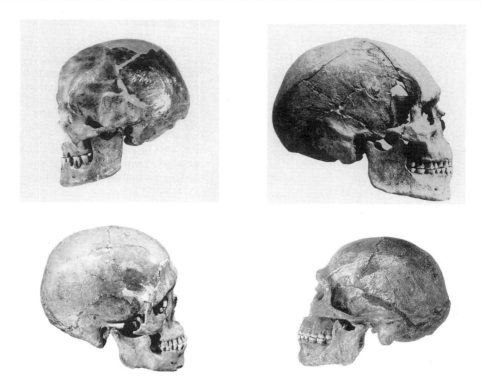

FIGURE 16–14   Four anatomically modern European skulls show some of the variation we would expect to find in a population the size of the one that occupied Europe. These are from Chancelade and Combe Capelle in France (top, left and right); from Grimaldi in Italy, near the border with France on the Mediterranean coast (bottom left); and from Předmost in Moravia (bottom right). All are dated at about 25,000 to 20,000 years B.P. These photographs are approximately one-fifth actual size.

Advantages of the Large Gene Pool

It is likely that by 20,000 years B.P. many of the physical changes wrought by the environment had largely reached their present state. That peoples varied in physical type from one location to another may be related as much to demography as to geography, for there was a great increase in numbers of people and a continued division of human populations into many fairly isolated groups. The gene pool grew with the expanding total population, but its division into small breeding populations still partially inhibited gene flow.

When the population of a species is relatively small, the genetic material available to it is relatively limited in scope, and trait variation may be similarly limited. But as the population increases, it also begins to vary more, simply because greater numbers provide more opportunities for variations to appear. When gene flow within a large population is limited, as it may have been at this period, the variations may become specialized, adapting to local environments according to the dictates of natural selection and perhaps the chance consequences of the founder effect (Chapter 2).

NEW LANDS

The first anatomically modern people lived through the last ice age. Warm and cold periods followed one another in close succession—close at least in geologic time. With each cold interlude the glaciers advanced and with each warm interlude they withdrew. Islands rose and fell and natural causeways and corridors appeared, making new traffic routes for the coming and going of humans. Along one of these ancient routes *Homo sapiens* moved northward from central or southern Asia into the chilly reaches of Siberia. From Siberia they migrated across the wide land bridge of Beringia—now covered by the Bering Sea—into the continent of North America and then south along the Pacific coast or possibly by way of an ice-free inland corridor (Figure 16–15). All indications are that *Homo sapiens* were the first humans to enter the Americas, but it may well have been a near thing. As noted in Chapter 14, stone tools from the Russian site of Diring Yuriakh suggest that *Homo heidelbergensis* people had advanced well into the depths of northeast Asia some 300,000 years ago. Judging from the available evidence, however, these archaic humans did not then proceed to cross the Beringia bridge.

The Americas

Exactly when humans first entered the Americas is still quite uncertain. It has been believed for many years that the oldest evidence for the first Americans did not predate 10,000 years B.P., and there was no sure evidence of tool traditions of very much greater antiquity. Today we have good evidence of stone spear points from North America, called *Clovis points*, back to 11,500 years B.P. These points were produced by big-game hunters who were most accomplished, as their butchery sites make clear. But radiocarbon dates are beginning to accumulate from much earlier times.

One important—but controversial—early date from the New World comes from Brazil, at Pedra Furada in the state of Piaui (Figure 16–15). Here the French archaeologists Niede Guidon and Georgette Delibrias excavated a cave site with remarkable results. They obtained a series of radiocarbon dates from well-stratified deposits, with hearths and a stone industry, which apparently take human occupation at the site back to more than 32,000 years B.P. There is even evidence of rock painting estimated at 17,000 years B.P. as spalls of paint that have fallen from the painted cave walls are present in the deposits. The Pedra Furada dates are still considered tentative by many archaeologists, but if confirmed, they will support other claims of early dates from South and Central America, such as Pikimachay (Peru) at 19,000 years B.P., the Alice Boer site (Brazil) at 14,200 years B.P., and the Caverna da Pedra Pintada site (Brazil) at 16,000 to 9,500 years B.P. Additionally, in Mexico the site of El Cedral may be older than 30,000 years B.P., and deposits at Hapacoya may date to 24,000 years ago. And finally, there is a site in Chile, Monte Verde, that has yielded a very reliable date of 12,500 years B.P. and evidence of at least semi-sedentary living.

The various extremely early dates from New World habitation sites are exciting, but difficult to interpret. A conservative view, based on the solid date of 12,500 years B.P. from Monte Verde, suggests an initial entry into North America by *at least* 20,000 years B.P., followed by movement farther south. An even earlier entry—perhaps 42,000 to 21,000 years ago—has been suggested by the results of

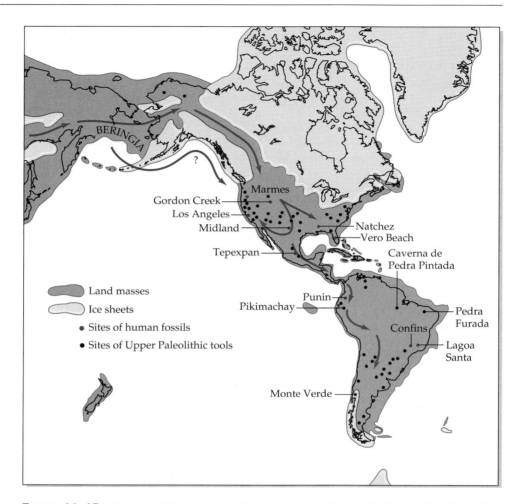

FIGURE 16–15   Much is still to be learned about the arrival of humankind in the New World. This map gives an idea of the migrants' most probable routes and of the extent of the landmass during the last glaciation. Carbon 14 and other dates from many sites suggest that humankind entered North America before 20,000 years B.P. and possibly as early as 40,000 years B.P.

genetic (mtDNA) studies. Greater precision in dating is needed, and the final answer may not be long in coming. The land bridge from Asia was open only intermittently, although migration by boat may have been possible at other times. Furthermore, current evidence suggests that both the inland corridor leading south through the Canadian Rockies and coastal routes were made impassable by the glaciers between 20,000 and 13,000 years B.P. And finally, although it seems clear that all immigrants were anatomically modern people (*Homo sapiens*), accumulating physical and archaeological evidence suggests that the New World was peopled by not one, but at least two or more, migratory waves.

Australia

Although the vast ice caps of the last glaciation locked up enough of the world's water to drop sea levels more than 330 feet (100 meters), adding great expanses of dry land to the continents, such extensions never joined Australia to the mainland of Southeast Asia. The subsidence of waters from the comparatively shallow Sunda Shelf united Borneo, Java, and Sumatra to the mainland of Southeast Asia and probably exposed enough small islands to make a good deal of island-hopping feasible. But between Australia and the shelf at the edge of the Asian mainland still remained the waters of the Timor Trough, 10,000 feet (3,050 meters) deep and 60 miles (97 kilometers) wide. How did humankind manage to get across it?

It was long assumed that humans did not reach this major island continent until the ancestors of the modern Aborigines migrated there by boat, probably from Southeast Asia, some 10,000 to 8,000 years ago. Then, in the 1930s, finds indicated an earlier human arrival, and in 1968 archaeologists digging near Lake Mungo in New South Wales discovered a 25,000-year-old skeleton of a woman, unmistakably modern in her anatomy, and artifacts dating back as far as 32,000 years B.P. (Figure 16–16).

A site from Arnhem Land in Australia's Northern Territory, called Malakunanja, has recently yielded artifacts and dates which stretch the evidence for human occupation back to 55,000 years B.P. The dating has been obtained by both C^{14} and thermoluminescence and for this reason is reasonably secure. Such an early date is supported by dates from northeast Papua New Guinea of 40,000 years B.P. and from southern Australia of 38,000 years B.P. Although there are no human remains from any of these sites, the evidence from artifacts makes it clear that humans were present in Australia at this early time. If the first Australians settled there as early as 55,000 years B.P., they would have had considerably greater problems than if they had arrived as late as 30,000 years B.P. during the last glaciation, as the sea level at 55,000 B.P. was only about 98 feet (30 meters) below its present levels, which means that far wider straits and far more ocean would have had to be crossed by watercraft than if sea levels had been lower. There was, however, a cold spell between 70,000 and 60,000 years ago, and during this time the sea level dropped 195 to 225 feet (60 to 70 meters). On the present evidence, this might have been the opportunity that made it possible for this historic human migration. Even if this was indeed the case, these early people must have crossed seas as wide as 250 miles (400 kilometers), an extraordinary undertaking. It is very hard to imagine either the means or the motivation for such a remarkable journey.

The earliest clear archaeological evidence of any form of watercraft dates from only 5,500 years ago. At this time the predynastic Egyptians depicted sailing boats in their rock carvings. The Chinese may well have developed the junk at an earlier date, but the evidence is lacking. And then there is the recent suggestion that Asian *Homo erectus* built watercraft some 0.9-0.8 million years ago (Chapter 11). In any event, excavations in Australia show that people from Southeast Asia must have mastered to a remarkable degree the arts of sea travel and navigation at an extremely early point in our prehistory. Was their craft simply a raft of bundled bamboo and reeds, meant for offshore fishing? Or was it perhaps a primitive version of the dugout canoe used today by Melanesians? Even more intriguing is the question of how the voyagers happened to journey to Australia. Were they carried there inadvertently by a wayward current or, according to one far-out speculation, by a massive tidal wave like the one that rolled out from the island of Krakatoa during a volcanic eruption there in the nineteenth century? Did they go to Australia purposefully, and if so, what drew them? We do not know.

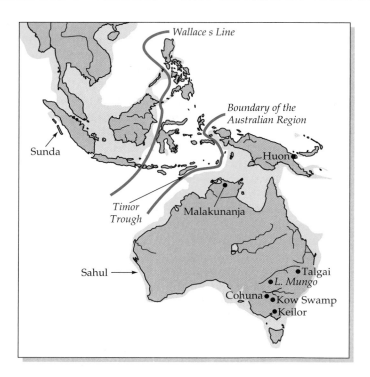

FIGURE 16–16   Map of Southeast Asia and part of Australasia showing the two ancient landmasses Sunda and Sahul, which were separated by the Timor Trough. The shaded area indicates the coastline that would be exposed by a drop in the sea level of 490 feet (150 meters). Wallace's Line represents the edge of the Sunda region. Important archaeological sites are marked with a dot, and those mentioned in the text are labeled. Adapted from J. P. White and J. F. O'Connell, *Science*, 203, 1979.

Diet and Hunting

Like the migrations of all the peoples who had gone before them, the movements of these people were probably activated by a search for food. In the means they used to achieve this end—in their implements, their techniques, their social organization, and their choice of habitation—they went far beyond what anyone had done before. Their diet included almost every sort of food the earth provided, and they became enormously adept at acquiring those foods. Indeed, in living off the land, and living well, they must have been far more successful than anyone before their time or since.

When early hominids developed their skills as hunters, they tapped a source of food energy unavailable to their mainly vegetarian predecessors. When they began to hunt migratory grazing animals and an occasional predatory animal whose territory extended beyond their own, their intake of food energy began to draw on a still wider range of resources. Thus, when territorial expansion took humans into the temperate zone, where grazing herd animals sometimes migrate between winter and summer feeding grounds, their food intake tapped nutritional energy from distant sources that were sometimes extremely different from the resources supplied by their own immediate environment. Cro-Magnons, harvesting the reindeer of the Dordogne region, were benefiting from the nutrients of the northern pastures and coastal plains where the reindeer herds did some of their grazing, but where people seldom, if ever, ventured. Anthropologists call this kind of long-distance food collection living on **unearned resources** (see Figure 16–17). Of all the ways in which organisms had adapted to and drawn sustenance from their environment (short of actually controlling it), this was the most sophisticated. Not until pastoralism and agriculture were developed did humans' exploitation of nature become more effective.

> **Unearned resources** resources that are outside a predator's range, but to which it nonetheless gains secondary access by consuming prey animals with larger ranges.

Modern archaeological techniques give us a glimpse of the variety and complexity of the ecological adaptations accomplished by the Upper Paleolithic people. In the next chapter we will look at the technology of these people in more detail, at their arts, and at what we know of their beliefs about the world in which they lived.

SUMMARY

The oldest fossils of anatomically modern people (*Homo sapiens*) date from about 130,000 years ago and come from Africa. Modern fossils that are only slightly younger have been found in the Middle East. The complete replacement of archaics by modern people took quite some time, however, and was not completed until perhaps 30,000 years B.P. Precisely how the evolutionary transition occurred is currently a matter of much debate among paleoanthropologists, but there seem to be two primary possibilities. The rapid-replacement hypothesis holds that modern people evolved once, by cladogenetic branching, in Africa and/or the Middle East. Once in existence, modern people spread all across the Old World, replacing archaic humans everywhere. This rapid-replacement model is well supported by the fossil record, and also by anatomical, genetic, and molecular studies. A second, and less likely, hypothesis holds that modern people evolved more or less simultaneously in several regions of the Old World. This model, dubbed the regional-continuity hypothesis, envisions broad-scale phyletic transformation of *Homo erectus* into archaic humans and then into *Homo sapiens*. As noted, the weight of the evidence strongly favors rapid replacement, but it is important to remember that some slight hybridization (gene leakage) between *Homo sapiens* migrants and indigenous archaics cannot be ruled out completely (perhaps as shown by the new skeleton from Portugal). Thus, some non-African, archaic populations may have contributed a bit to the *Homo sapiens* gene pool.

The physical changes from archaic people to modern humans involved mainly a remodeling of the cranium and the face. Skulls became more rounded and higher-vaulted; foreheads became more vertical; faces and teeth were reduced in average size; the chin was added; and, of particular importance, the cranial base became sharply flexed. The last change may well have allowed the full development of modern speech and may have facilitated rapid cultural progress.

Once anatomical modernity had been achieved, humans did not waste much time spreading to Australia and the Americas. Modern people were living in Australia some 55,000 years ago, and they may have entered the New World via the Bering Strait between 42,000 and 21,000 years B.P.

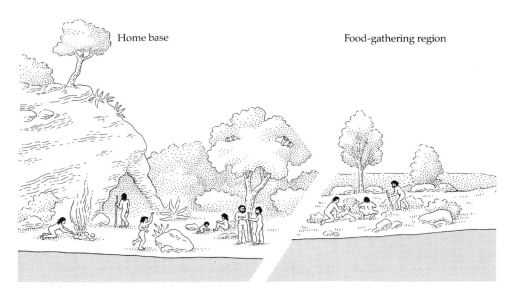

FIGURE 16–17   The term *unearned resources* refers to migratory herds that live for part of the year outside the home range of the hunting bands. Herds that feed in the mountains during the summer may, during the winter, come down to the valleys, where they are hunted. Thus the valley hunters are drawing on food resources of the entire region without actually traveling through it. The figure shows the relationship of the zones of food production to the home base.

POSTSCRIPT

In this chapter we have argued that over roughly a 100,000-year period archaic humans were generally replaced worldwide by fully modern people. We believe that, genetically speaking, the replacement was rather clean, although it must be admitted that some interbreeding between resident archaics and invading *Homo sapiens* may have occurred. But precisely what form the replacement process took remains unclear. Were archaic humans violently exterminated by moderns or simply outcompeted ecologically and thus driven to extinction? As it is usually framed with reference to the Neandertals, did they go out with a bang or a whimper?

Several early writers envisioned a violent replacement. Thus Henry Fairfield Osborn in his 1915 classic *Men of the Old Stone Age* wrote as follows:

> We may infer that the new race [anatomically modern humans] competed for a time with the Neanderthals before they dispossessed them of their principal stations and drove them out of the country or killed them in battle. The Neanderthals, no doubt, fought with wooden weapons and with the stone-headed dart and spear, but there is no evidence that they possessed the bow and arrow. There is, on the contrary, some possibility that the newly arriving Cro-Magnon race may have been familiar with the bow and arrow [and thus the Cro-Magnons may have been] armed with weapons which, with their superior intelligence and physique, would have given them a very great advantage in contests with the Neanderthals.

In a similar vein, in his 1921 short story "The Grisly Folk," H. G. Wells describes how modern "true men" hunted down and exterminated the hairy, beetle-browed, low-vaulted Neandertals.

Winter grazing and hunting grounds   Summer feeding grounds

Such scenes of combat and carnage, however, now appear to have been the products of overactive imaginations. There is simply no archaeological evidence of violent replacement of archaics by moderns. Although present-day humans often seem all too ready to engage in warfare and genocide, there is no reason to believe that our species got its start through such violent practices. Most anthropologists now attribute the demise of the Neandertals and other archaics to behavioral differences that allowed them to be outcompeted by early modern humans. William Howells's recent statement in his book *Getting Here* (1993) is a good example of current views:

> We do not have to imagine bloody battles or in fact any serious conflict: a small erosion of Neanderthals in each generation would have quickly led to extinction. Also, the Upper Paleolithic people were manifestly more numerous than their predecessors. Another simple explanation is one of vastly different lifestyles and hunting capacities, with available game going mostly to the new people.

Neandertal society, according to Chris Stringer and Clive Gamble, was characterized by a focus on local self-sufficiency and a general lack of intergroup ties. In contrast, the Cro-Magnons appear to have developed large, complex societies with widespread trade networks and alliances. Outcompeted by *Homo sapiens* in population size, social complexity, and perhaps even hunting skills, the Neandertals may have withdrawn into marginal habitats and experienced increased mortality rates. Archaeologist Ezra Zubrow has calculated that, if the Neandertals suffered from only 2 percent greater mortality than the invading moderns, Neandertal extinction was likely to have followed within about 1,000 years. Similar fates may have awaited archaic populations all across the Old World. In sum, faced with a choice between a whimper and a bang as an explanation for the replacement of archaic humans, most of today's researchers would opt for the whimper.

REVIEW QUESTIONS

1. Summarize the evidence supporting the rapid-replacement hypothesis of the appearance of anatomically modern people. What weaknesses do you see in the model?
2. Summarize the evidence supporting the regional-continuity hypothesis of the appearance of anatomically modern people. What weaknesses do you see in the model? How would widescale phyletic transformation take place?
3. Compare the anatomy of *Homo sapiens* to that of archaic humans and provide explanations for the changes. What anatomical features, if any, are unique to our species?
4. Describe the peopling of the Americas and Australia. When and how were these regions first entered and by whom?

SUGGESTED FURTHER READING

Hammer, M. F. "A Recent Common Ancestry For Human Y Chromosomes." *Nature*, 378, 1995.

Meltzer, D. J. "Pleistocene Peopling of the Americas." *Evolutionary Anthropology*, 1, 1993.

Nitecki, M. H., and D. V. Nitecki, eds. *Origins of Anatomically Modern Humans.* Plenum, 1994.

Stoneking, M. "DNA and Recent Human Evolution." *Evolutionary Anthropology*, 2, 1993.

Stringer, C., and R. McKie. *African Exodus.* Henry Holt, 1996.

INTERNET RESOURCES

PETER BROWN'S AUSTRALIAN AND ASIAN PALEOANTHROPOLOGY
http://metz.une.edu.au/~pbrown3/palaeo.html
   (A descriptive catalog of late Pleistocene and recent human fossils from Australia.)

THE GREAT DNA HUNT
http://www.archaeology.org/9609/abstracts/dna.html
   (Abstracted from *Archaeology* magazine, this website contains information on the mitochondrial DNA, Y chromosome, and other genetic data bearing on the question of modern human origins.)

THE ORIGINS OF MODERN HUMANS: MULTIREGIONAL AND REPLACEMENT THEORIES
http://www.linfield.edu/~mrobert/origins.html
   (Developed by biologist Michael Roberts, this site provides extensive information on the two primary models for the evolution of modern people.)

USEFUL SEARCH TERMS:
   Modern human origins
   Multiregional theory
   Out of Africa (or replacement) theory
   Paleoindians
   Upper Paleolithic

Chapter 16 Timeline

NEOLITHIC AND MESOLITHIC	YEARS B.P.	EMERGENCE OF MODERN HUMANS	TYPES OF HOMININES
— 10,000		Iron Age	
UPPER PALEOLITHIC		Bronze Age: pottery	
— 40,000		Copper Age	
		New Stone Age (Neolithic)	
	10,000 —	Mesolithic	
MIDDLE PALEOLITHIC		First agriculture: domestication of plants and animals	
Archaics in Europe, Asia, and Africa		Monte Verde, Chile	
— 200,000	20,000 —		**MODERN HUMANS** *(Homo sapiens)*
Swanscombe and Steinheim; Levallois technique		Lake Mungo, Australia: skeletons	
		Předmost: robust modern skulls	
		Most recent Mousterian tools; Zafarraya	
		Cro-Magnon, Dordogne	
400,000 Arago	30,000 —	Lake Mungo, Australia artifacts	
		Velíka Pecína, Předmost: robust modern skulls	
500,000		Le Moustier	
	40,000 —	Possible entry into Americas	
		Amud	
		La Chapelle	
		Sipka jaw fragment: blend of archaic and modern features.	
	50,000 —	Monte Circeo, Shanidar: all clearly archaic skulls	
Gran Dolina fossils		Malakunanja, Australia	
	60,000 —		
		La Quina, La Ferrassie, and Spy	
1 million *Paranthropus* extinct	70,000 —	Border Cave	
	80,000 —		**ARCHAICS AND MODERNS**
LOWER PALEOLITHIC			
	90,000 —		
1.5 million Acheulean industry		Skhūl and Qafzeh: modern features	
	100,000 —		
	110,000 —		
Homo habilis at Olduvai			
1.8 million *Homo erectus* in Africa, the Caucasus, and Java			
	120,000 —		
2 million Oldowan industry			**FIRST MODERN HUMANS IN AFRICA AND WESTERN ASIA**
	130,000 —	Omo Kibish and Klasies River Mouth	

THE FINAL TRANSFORMATION

This chart shows the approximate chronology of the Middle to Upper Paleolithic sequence. Many dates are approximate.

TECHNOLOGY, MAGIC, AND ART

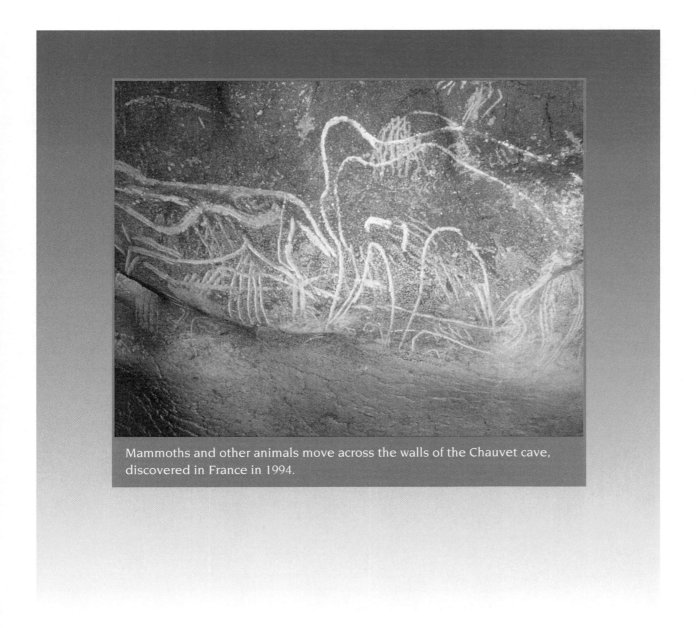

Mammoths and other animals move across the walls of the Chauvet cave, discovered in France in 1994.

Human *life is everywhere a state in which much is to be endured and little to be enjoyed.*

SAMUEL JOHNSON, 1709–1784. Rasselas, Ch. 7.

OVERVIEW

The evolution of anatomically modern humans—*Homo sapiens*—was followed by a significant upswing in cultural complexity, and this chapter is concerned with describing that cultural surge. Increased control was gained over the production and use of fire; improved gathering, fishing, and hunting techniques ensured a dependable food supply and allowed a degree of sedentary living; and technology was broadened by the invention of new tool types and the increased use of bone, antler, and ivory as raw materials. Additionally, there was a strong improvement in artistic skills and endeavors—resulting in beautiful rock-shelter and cave art, carved ivory and bone implements, and clay sculptures—and also the elaboration of funeral rites, very likely reflecting the development of religion. Humankind was now modern not only anatomically, but intellectually as well. Important topics and concepts in this chapter include new fire-making techniques; technological innovations and the use of new raw materials; improvements in subsistence activities; and the development of art and ritual.

AN END TO WANDERING

In the fertile valleys of Egypt, on the frigid plains of Siberia, and along the seacoast of Africa, Upper Paleolithic people were demonstrating that they not only could stay alive but could actually prosper under conditions of extraordinary diversity. Cold was no barrier to their existence; when meat was scarce, their food became fish; and in at least one area we have evidence that with foresight and planning they harvested natural grains. After centuries of nomadism, of moving from place to place in pursuit of game or fresh supplies of plant food, humans were finally able to stay in one place and systematically exploit the seasonal resources of one

 Mini-Timeline

DATE (YEARS B.P.)	EVOLUTIONARY EVENTS OR CULTURAL DEVELOPMENTS
10,000	End of Upper Paleolithic
16,500–11,000	Magdalenian culture (blade tools and harpoons)
20,000	Probable first use of bow and arrow
21,000–16,500	Solutrean culture (laurel-leaf blades)
27,000–21,000	Perigordian culture (female figurines)
33,000–30,000	Oldest cave art (La Grotte Chauvet)
40,000–27,000	Aurignacian culture
40,000	Start of Upper Paleolithic
130,000	Oldest fossils of *Homo sapiens*

locality. They were, in short, gaining ever-increasing control over their relations with the natural world.

A New Lifestyle

A sedentary way of life, and the changes in subsistence that it accompanied, amounted to a minor revolution in human society and lifestyle. More efficient exploitation of resources and the permanence of living quarters brought an increase in the human population. The skeletal evidence also suggests that the life span was extended (perhaps exceeding the Neandertals' life expectancy by 20 percent), which enabled people to accumulate more knowledge and pass on more of that knowledge to their children and grandchildren.

Along with an increasing population, their efficiency as food producers gave them other advantages. Because they were often able to lead a more sedentary life, they could acquire more material goods, objects which would have been impractical to own as long as they were on the move, but which made providing for food and shelter easier. The inhabitants of several Upper Paleolithic sites in central Europe, for instance, were shaping objects from clay and, as we shall see, even firing them in dome-shaped kilns. Even more important than material wealth was the evolution of social behavior—a base for the full development of language, art, and religion and for the complex forms of social and political organization that are the hallmark of all developed human cultures.

During the past 20,000 or so years of their tenure, these people made more technological progress and, in doing so, gained more control over their environment, than had been made or gained in all the million years of human experience that had preceded them. They were the master stoneworkers of all time, improving old techniques to produce stone tools of greater effectiveness and variety. They also exploited other materials—bone, antler, and ivory—that had been little used earlier, selecting and working each to its best advantage in fashioning not only new weapons and new tools but domestic inventions and decorative objects as well. They learned to build better fires more easily and to use them for new purposes. Some shelters were only a step away from real houses; they were more durable than earlier shelters and afforded more protection against the elements. And when the climate changed, these people invented ways to deal with it. Technological innovation and cultural adaptation increasingly reduced the need for physical evolution, and humans' links to their animal past were now beginning to lie more and more behind them. People still depended on nature, but nature's control was being lessened.

Mastery of Fire

These people added new dimensions to the use of fire. For one thing, they were the first to leave proof of their ability to strike a fire quickly whenever they needed one. A cave site in Belgium yielded a beautifully rounded piece of **iron pyrite** (Figure 17–1). This substance is one of the few natural materials from which flint will strike sparks that will set dry tinder on fire; sparks struck from two flints or two ordinary rocks are not hot enough to do so. What is more, the Belgian pyrite has a groove showing where it had been struck again and again with pieces of flint. Because iron pyrite is not easy to find lying about on the ground, each such firestone was undoubtedly a cherished item that would have been carried wherever a band roamed.

Iron pyrite a mineral substance (iron disulfide) that, when struck with flint, makes sparks that will start a fire.

FIGURE 17–1 The oldest known firestone, this iron pyrite is from a Belgian cave, Trou-du-Chaleux. The Upper Paleolithic Magdalenian people were apparently the first to discover that flint and iron pyrite used in combination yielded sparks hot enough to ignite tinder. The stone is here enlarged about two times.

A more dramatic example of the growing mastery of fire, evidence of which has turned up at sites in Russia and France, seems prosaic at first glance: shallow grooves dug into the bottom of a hearth, and a channel curving away from the hearth like a tail. So simple an innovation may well have been overlooked many times in earlier archaeological excavations, but in fact it was the first small step toward the blast furnaces of modern steel mills. The grooves and channels in those prehistoric fireplaces allowed more air to reach the fuel, and fires in them would thus burn hotter.

The people who built the special hearths needed them because of the type of fuel they used. In an area where wood was scarce, they had to turn for fuel to a material that normally does not burn well: bone. Although bone is hard to ignite and burns inefficiently, being only about 25 percent combustible material, it gives off adequate heat. That these people did burn it is proved by the lack of charred wood and the considerable quantities of bone ash found in their specially vented hearths.

The hearth was home, and the Upper Paleolithic people, who changed so much else also changed the concept of home. Though some lived in the same caves and rock shelters that had protected their predecessors, they seem, in some places at least, to have kept cleaner house than those earlier tenants; litter was thrown outside instead of being allowed to pile up inside.

It was in regions that offered no ready-made habitations that the home improvements were most noticeable. Particularly in central and eastern Europe and Siberia, remnants of many sturdily built shelters have been found in open country.

Solutrean Laurel-Leaves

Improvement in stone tools was crucial to the developing Paleolithic technical mastery. It is ironic that, despite all efforts to decipher them, no one really knows what purpose was served by the most beautiful examples of this new skill. Anyone who has ever held and examined a tool such as the magnificent "laurel-leaf" blade (Figure 17–2) must eventually wonder how this implement could have been used. Too delicate for a knife, too big and fragile for a spearhead, so beautifully crafted a piece of flint seems to be a showpiece. Clearly, to produce an object of such daring proportions required craftsmanship bordering on art, and many archaeologists think this masterpiece and others like it may have been just that: works of art that served an aesthetic or ritual function rather than a utilitarian one, and that may even have been passed from one person or group to another as highly prized items.

If the large laurel-leaf blades were made for no useful purpose, they were clearly an instance of technology transcending itself. The smaller, everyday implements on which such showpieces were modeled had strictly practical functions. They are known in the thousands and come in various styles from sites all over the world. Stone points in various sizes have been found in western and central European excavations at cultural levels called **Solutrean**—a style typified by finds from Solutré in France. There is no doubt that many of these points could have served most effectively as spear points or knives with razor-sharp edges. They were significant items in the armory of a people who depended for their existence less and less on the simple strength of their biceps and more and more on their brainpower and the efficacy of their tools.

The small stone blades were unquestionably sharp and efficient. Modern experiments have shown that well-made flint projectile points are sharper than iron points of a similar type and penetrate more deeply into an animal's body. Flint knives are equal, if not superior, to steel knives in their cutting power. The only drawback of flint is that, because of its brittleness, it breaks more easily than metal and has to be replaced more often.

Solutrean an *Upper Paleolithic* culture existing in western Europe between 21,000 and 16,500 years B.P. Best known for its "laurel-leaf" blades.

FIGURE 17–2   A laurel-leaf blade is so delicate that it could have served no practical purpose. This blade—11 inches (28 centimeters) long but only 4/10 inches (1 centimeter) thick—may have been a ceremonial object or even the proud emblem of a master toolmaker. These finely chipped blades are part of the Solutrean tool industry.

The importance of such blades in the lives of hunters lends authority to the theory that the large, nonutilitarian examples, of which at least several dozen have been found, may have been ritualistic objects representing the quintessential spear point. They may, too, have been used as a primitive currency for trade. On the other hand, it has also been suggested that a magnificent laurel-leaf may have simply been a tour de force tossed off by a virtuoso toolmaker as a demonstration of talent. If so, any admiration or praise the work received was well deserved. The laurel-leaf is without doubt a splendid creation, and fewer than a handful of people in the world today are skilled enough in the ancient craft to produce one.

Tool Specialization

However different the various tool industries of this period may have been in style, in character they had much in common. Human groups everywhere produced tools more specialized than any used before. Archaeologists identify sixty to seventy types of tools in the kits of some Neandertals: scrapers meant to be held horizontally, knives with blunted backs, others with double edges, and so on. But they count more than 100 types in the tool kits of Upper Paleolithic humans: knives for cutting meat, knives for whittling wood, scrapers for bone, scrapers for skin, perforators, stone saws, chisels, pounding slabs, and countless others. Among the innovations are two-part composite tools. These people are believed to have begun putting bone and antler handles on many of their stone tools, such as axes and knives. By providing them with a firmer grasp and enabling them to use much more of the muscle power in their arms and shoulders, the handles, through leverage, increased the power the users could put into a blow with a tool by as much as two to three times.

One of the most important tools developed was the cutter called a burin (see Figure 17–3). It is tempting to say that Upper Paleolithic people invented the burin, but it had existed in a few Neandertal tool kits, and a few burinlike tools are sometimes found in the tool assemblages of *Homo erectus*. In the hands of early anatomically modern people, however, the burin was gradually improved and became more important and much more prevalent. A burin was a kind of chisel. Today the name is given to a fine steel cutting tool used by engravers in preparing copper plates. In the Stone Age, it was a tool with a strong, sharply beveled edge or point used to cut, incise, and shape other materials, such as bone, antler, wood, and sometimes stone. It differed from most other stone tools of prehistory in that it was not used by itself to kill animals, cut meat, clean hides, or chop down saplings for tent poles. Rather, like the machine tools of the modern age, its chief function was the manufacture of other tools and implements. With a tool that made other tools, technology could expand many times faster than ever before.

The burin probably helped produce many wooden implements, but only fragments of these have survived. The best record of the object's effectiveness, then, is found in the surviving tools it shaped. These superb tools, like the burin itself, stand out as a mark of sophistication. Besides wood, three organic raw materials— bone, antler, and ivory—helped supply the needs of an ever-expanding economy, and the burin made possible their widespread exploitation. *Homo erectus* and archaic humans had used bone to some extent for scraping, piercing, or digging, but not nearly so much as the Upper Paleolithic people did. At a typical Neandertal site, perhaps 25 out of 1,000 tools turn out to be made of bone; the rest are stone. In some

FIGURE 17–3 This Upper Paleolithic burin is an early chisel, which was a new and important technological development. Its main use was perhaps to make other tools of wood or bone. This photograph is approximately one-half actual size.

Upper Paleolithic encampments, the mix may be as much as half and half, or an even greater proportion of bone.

Bone, antler, and ivory were the wonder materials of those times, much as plastics are today. Less brittle and therefore more workable than flint, much stronger and more durable than wood, they could be cut, grooved, chiseled, scraped, sharpened, and shaped. They could be finely worked into tiny implements like needles, or they could be used for heavy work. A deer antler makes an excellent pick. A mammoth's leg bone cracked lengthwise needs only minor modifications and a handle to become an efficient shovel. Ivory could be steamed and bent, processes adding yet another dimension to toolmaking.

Best of all, the very animals hunted and depended on for food provided these materials in abundance. All animals have bone, of course, and many large animals—red deer, reindeer, mammoth—had antlers or tusks as well. Antlers seemed almost to be nature's gift to humans, because they did not even have to kill an animal to obtain them: every year deer shed their old ones, which lie on the ground for the picking up. Because reindeer and red deer were at one time or another perhaps the most abundant game animals in western Europe, antler was used there more than bone or ivory. In parts of eastern Europe and Siberia, where wood was relatively scarce, the skeletons of giant mammoths that had died natural deaths or had been trapped by hunters were a source of tools. A mammoth tusk might measure more than 9 feet (2.7 meters) and weigh more than 100 pounds (45 kilograms); a lot of implements could be made from that much ivory.

With its strong chisel point, the burin could easily scratch or dig into ivory or bone without breaking. To cut up a bone, the toolmaker could incise a deep groove around the bone and then, with a sharp blow, break it cleanly at the cut, just as a glazier today cuts a groove in a glass pane before breaking it. To get slivers for needles, points, and awls, it was necessary only to draw a burin repeatedly lengthwise down a bone to score two parallel grooves deep enough to hit the soft center. Then the piece of hard material between the grooves was pried out and ground to shape (Figure 17–4). Other pieces of bone could be turned into spatulas, scrapers, beads, bracelets, digging tools, and more.

In addition to domestic utensils, bone and antler provided spear points, lances, and barbed harpoon tips, with which the hunters took advantage of bountiful supplies of game. Probably at no time since have there been so many grazing animals roaming the earth: Europe and Asia had mammoth, horses, red deer, pigs, rein-

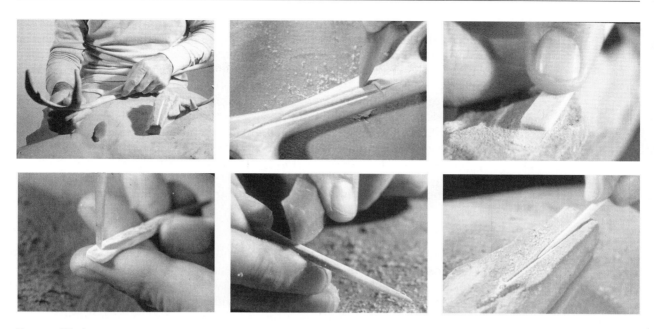

FIGURE 17–4   The slow process of making a needle out of an antler can be broken down into six steps.

deer, and bison. Africa had all the animals known there today, as well as a great many others that are now extinct: enormous relatives of buffalo, hartebeest, and zebra.

The scene was set for hunting-and-gathering humans to reach the peak of successful adaptation. Full exploitation of these rich resources gave an extraordinary amount of control over their environment and formed the stable basis for still further cultural developments.

Hunter Par Excellence

Two dazzling examples of Upper Paleolithic hunting success have been unearthed by archaeologists in Europe. Near the town of Pavlov, in the Czech Republic (Figure 16–1), excavations have revealed the remains of more than 100 mammoths in one giant bone heap; near Solutré, in France (Figure 16–1), an even more staggering bone pile contains the fossils of an estimated 10,000 wild horses lying in a tangled heap at the bottom of a high cliff. The mammoth bones are apparently the remains of the giant beasts trapped in pitfalls; the horses had perhaps been stampeded off the cliff over many years, even generations, by intelligent hunters who were familiar down to the last detail with the terrain of the region and the behavior of their victims.

It is likely that the people of this period all across the world understood as much about hunting large herd animals as any humans in history. They undoubtedly knew just which plants the animals preferred to eat; when seasonal migrations began and how fast the animals traveled; what panicked them and what soothed them. They knew how to drive the animals into pit traps; how to snare them with baited thong nooses; and how to guide them into natural or human-made corrals, either by stampeding them or herding them quietly from a discreet distance. Once trapped, the animals could be dispatched with spears or knives and butchered on the spot. The meat was then taken back to camp, perhaps in processed form, possibly cut up in strips and smoked or sun-dried.

There can also be little doubt that these hunters knew a great deal about the anatomy of their victims and the virtue of eating certain of their organs. Today the inland Alaskan Eskimos save the adrenal glands of slaughtered caribou to give to young children and pregnant women. Chemical analysis of the gland reveals an astonishingly high content of vitamin C, an essential element but one hard to come by in the standard diet of the Eskimo. Without overestimating the earlier hunters' knowledge in these matters, it can be assumed that they, too, knew exactly which parts of the animals they hunted were good, and also which parts were good for them.

Spear Throwers and Points

These people's profound understanding of their prey, combined with significant technical advances in their hunting equipment, paid off in increased food supplies. Hunters had long had wooden spears with fire-hardened tips or sharp stone heads to thrust or throw at their prey, but the effectiveness of a thrown spear against even a young deer, to say nothing of a thick-skinned giant auroch (a kind of extinct wild ox), must have been limited, especially if the animal was in full retreat. Upper Paleolithic hunters made the spear a more effective weapon by inventing the spear thrower (commonly referred to today by its Aztec name, the **atlatl**).

Atlatl Aztec name for the spear thrower, a rodlike device used as an extension of the arm that greatly increases both distance and impact of throw.

The oldest tangible evidence of this rodlike device dates from about 14,000 years B.P., and it comes from the cave of La Placard in France. Here several fragments of spear throwers were discovered, including a length of bone with a hooked end that looks like nothing so much as an oversized crochet needle. All told, more than seventy reindeer-antler spear throwers have turned up in southwestern France and near Lake Constance along the northeastern border of Switzerland. There is a curious dearth of them elsewhere in the Old World, perhaps because they may have been made of perishable wood and rotted away. By about 10,000 years ago, the wooden spear thrower was being used by the Indians of North and South America. The Eskimos used it until recently, and some Australian Aborigines still use it today, calling it a "womera" (Figure 17–5).

The spear thrower is, in the simplest explanation, an extension of the arm. It is 1 to 2 feet (30 to 60 centimeters) long, with a handle at one end and a point or hook at the other that engages the butt end of the spear. Hunters hold the thrower behind their shoulder, hook up, and lay the spear along the thrower so that the spear points forward and slightly upward. During the throw they keep hold of the thrower, which may have a thong tied to its end to go around their wrist. When throwing, they swing their arms forward and snap their wrist, launching the spear with great velocity from the end of the thrower at the top of its arc, in this way taking advantage of the centrifugal force generated. The spear travels faster than if hand-thrown because the extension of the throwing arm provides more leverage; the spear thrower's end moves faster than the hand holding it.

Modern experiments have demonstrated the great advantages a spear thrower gives. A 7-foot (2 meter) spear can be thrown no more than 180 to 210 feet (55 to 65 meters) when launched directly from a hunter's hand, but it can be projected up to

FIGURE 17–5   The method of throwing a spear has not changed since spear throwers were introduced in Magdalenian times, about 14,000 years ago. Here an Australian is shown poised to throw his stone-tipped spear. The womera, or spear thrower, can be clearly seen.

450 feet (135 meters) with a spear thrower, and it can kill a deer at 90 feet (25 meters). Increased distance of throw may not have been the primary benefit, however. Experimental archaeologists W. K. Hutchings and L. W. Bruchert suggest that most hunting with the atlatl was done at distances of 50 to 65 feet (15 to 20 meters) from the prey, with experienced hunters hitting their target almost half of the time. Of particular importance, hits often would have been fatal or disabling since atlatl-thrown spears generate enormous kinetic energy and highly lethal killing impact (surprisingly, the atlatl produces more kinetic energy than arrows shot from either traditional or modern bows). The combination of greater range (compared to hand-thrown spears) and greater impact undoubtedly worked to the Upper Paleolithic hunters' advantage.

The first spear throwers were undoubtedly of wood, as the Australian womeras are today, but soon they were also being made from antler. People of the late Upper Paleolithic **Magdalenian** culture embellished many of their throwers with carved figures and designs and may even have painted them. One ancient Magdalenian thrower bears traces of red ocher in its hollows, and some have black painted into the eyes. Other throwers display exquisite renderings of animals, including horses, deer, ibex, bison, birds, and fish. At least three show an ibex defecating, held still by the art of the engraver in a vulnerable moment, when a kill may be made. These carvings on weaponry represent a combination of aesthetics and utility that is echoed in many aspects of Magdalenian life.

Magdalenian *Upper Paleolithic* culture existing in western Europe from about 16,500 to 11,000 years B.P. Produced many *blade* tools and prototype harpoons.

FIGURE 17–6   This Magdalenian harpoon was beautifully made and was part of a highly developed collection of fishing tackle. This photograph is about 90 percent actual size.

Other functional advances were in the spear itself. By this time hunters had realized that a barbed point does more damage than a smooth one. Harpoon-style points, fashioned from bone or antler, often had several barbs on one or both sides (Figure 17–6). Another development stemmed from the difficulty of killing an animal outright by one spear wound alone; hunters would have to follow their wounded prey for a while until loss of blood made it weak enough for them to kill. To speed this process, some hunters carved bone spearheads with grooves along each side—runnels apparently designed to increase the flow of blood from the wound.

Bow and Arrow

An interesting puzzle is the use of the bow and arrow. There is no clear-cut archaeological evidence that people used such a weapon until the very end of the Upper Paleolithic. But because bows are normally made of wood and sinew or gut, it would be a lucky accident indeed if any had survived the last ice age, and so the lack of evidence cannot be taken as conclusive. A couple of bows have been uncovered in Denmark that date back approximately 8,000 years, and a larger number of stone-tipped wooden arrow shafts, perhaps 10,000 years old, have been found at the campsites of ancient reindeer hunters in northern Germany. In a cave in La Colombière, in France, there have been found small stones, possibly more than 20,000 years old, with pictures scratched on them that may represent feathered projectiles; whether these were arrows or dartlike spears, however, is uncertain. Among the best early evidence of the bow and arrow are approximately 20,000-year-old microliths and bone foreshafts from Africa. These artifacts closely resemble historic arrow points and foreshafts from the region.

Certainly the bow would have given hunters the advantage of increased stealth. The spear thrower, no matter how valuable an aid, required hunters to break cover and stand out in the open where they could be spotted by their prey; an unsuccessful launch would scare off the target. But with the bow, hunters could remain hidden. If they missed with the first arrow, likely they could shoot again. Moreover, the arrow was swifter than the spear and it could be shot at a variety of animals—big and small, standing, running, or on the wing—with a good chance of hitting them.

Fishing Gear

Perhaps even more significant than the invention of the spear thrower or the bow in helping Upper Paleolithic people expand their food supply and make a living in

FIGURE 17–7   The leister is a three-pronged fishing spear, which has been in use for perhaps 12,000 years. The middle prong (not visible here) is shorter than the other two. Here an Australian employs the implement.

varied environments was their development of fishing gear. Human groups had earlier availed themselves of the bounty offered by streams, rivers, and the sea, but for some, fishing now became almost a way of life.

The oldest known bone fishhooks come from European sites about 14,000 years old. A slightly younger development (about 12,000 years B.P.) was a device called the **leister** (Figure 17–7): a tridentlike spear with a point and two curving prongs of bone that held the fish securely after it had been lanced. Another was the fish gorge, a small sliver of bone or wood, perhaps 2 inches (5 centimeters) long, with a leather or sinew line tied around its middle. When the baited gorge was swallowed by a fish, it cocked sideways in its throat in such a way as not to come out easily, and the catch was made.

From a slightly later date, we have evidence suggesting that, in South Africa and perhaps in Europe, people began catching fish in much greater numbers than ever before. Small, grooved cylindrical stones found in South Africa may have been weights on nets made of thongs or plant fibers. With a net, two or three people could catch a whole shoal of fish on one sweep.

The **weir**, a stone corral for trapping fish still used by some modern peoples, was probably also used at this time. This technique would have been especially effective on rivers such as the Dordogne and the Vézère in France, where spawning salmon swarm upstream in great numbers. It seems likely that, at the spawning season, parties went to the fishing grounds to lay in a supply of salmon for the whole band, which may have had its home base miles away. The fish may have been cleaned and perhaps sun-dried or smoked where they were caught, and then carried to camp. At Solvieux, in France, a large rectangular area carefully paved with small stones has been excavated; its placement and design strongly hint that it was a fish-drying platform.

Leister a three-pronged spear used for fishing.

Weir barrier or dam made of stones or sticks set out in a stream or river and used as a fish trap.

Sedentary Life and Sewn Clothing

As modern human groups learned to tap the potential of rivers and seas, climatic changes complemented their improving technologies. The rising sea level that was associated with the retreat of the ice submerged the Atlantic continental shelf and increased the area of warm, shallow sea in which many species of fish could breed. The systematic exploitation of the waters' abundant protein resources—which included great quantities of shellfish as well as fish—was highly significant, not only because it broadened the base of the human diet, but because it helped lead humans toward the next great step in cultural evolution: settled living. With fish and shellfish as a dependable supplement to their regular meat and plant food, people did not have to move around so much in quest of sustenance. With nets they could gather more food with less effort than they could as nomadic hunters-and-gatherers, and thus one place could support a greater number of people. The beginning of a sedentary way of life—**sedentism**—was a crucial development, closely related to what became a rapidly expanding population.

Sedentism a way of life marked by the lack of migratory movements and by the establishment of permanent habitations.

As the last ice age peoples learned to help themselves more efficiently to nature's bounty, they also found ways to protect themselves more effectively from nature's rigors. Carefully sewn, fitted clothing was part of the equipment that enabled them to conquer the far north and eventually to penetrate North America.

The hide clothing of these people was probably much like that of today's Eskimos. A tunic or pullover with tightly sewn seams to keep heat from escaping, pants easily tucked into boots, and some sort of sock, perhaps of fur, would have been warm enough in all but the coldest weather. For frigid days, outer clothing consisting of a hooded parka, mittens, and high boots would have kept a person from freezing. What is our evidence that the people had clothing of this sort? Female figurines from Stone Age Russia look as if they are clothed in fur. Furthermore, even in more moderate climates, well-sewn clothing seems to have been an advantage; the earliest eyed needles discovered to date were fashioned by the same expert Solutrean workers of Europe who produced the laurel-leaf blades between 21,000 and 16,500 years ago.

ART AND RITUAL

Cave Art

Until now, our discussion of Upper Paleolithic peoples has centered on their improvements in working stone and particularly bone, and on the cultural developments furthered by these technological improvements. Notable as these changes were, it is the intellectual and spiritual achievements of these people that make them so impressive to us today. Particularly striking is their astounding artistic ability, a talent that seems to have sprung full-blown out of nowhere and which, if Steve Mithen and others are correct, may have been due to the evolution of a completely modern mind (see Chapter 13). There are dozens of examples of cave art in France alone. These date from more than 30,000 to 10,000 years B.P. and are attributed primarily to the Solutrean and Magdalenian peoples. Equally ancient rock art sites have been found in Tanzania and in the southern African nation of Namibia. At the Namibian site of Apollo Cave, rock slabs painted with the outlines of animals have been recovered that date to between 28,000 and 19,000 years B.P. Similarly aged paintings have come from Australia. Red paint from the Sandy

Creek site in Queensland is reported to date back 26,000 years. Additionally, so-called Bradshaw sticklike figures from the Kimberley region in western Australia have recently been dated by OSL (optically stimulated luminescence; see Appendix II) to more than 17,000 years B.P. By the latest Pleistocene, rock art had also appeared in India and the Americas. All of these sites show that Upper Paleolithic peoples and their contemporaries outside Europe were close observers of the animals they hunted as well as magnificent artists. More than that, the record they left behind shows that they had a sufficiently sophisticated way of life to be able to appreciate and encourage their own talents and to work them into their rituals.

Traditionally, the paintings and carvings of these people have been interpreted as closely associated with their spiritual life. One strong indication is seen in the places they chose to put wall paintings. The caves in the Dordogne are basically of two kinds. The rock overhangs, more or less open and facing out over the valleys, could be made livable by adding barriers of brushwood or animal skins to keep out the wind and snow (Figure 17–8). They are full of the signs of many generations of occupancy; tools lie in all strata in their floors, together with buried skeletons. Hearths abound, tending to become bigger as they become more recent.

Some fragments of wall decoration have been found in the open shelters; perhaps originally there were more that have since been destroyed by exposure to the elements. But the most spectacular wall art is confined to true caves: deep underground fissures with long galleries and passages. These caves have their own subterranean pools, rivers, and festoons of stalactites and stalagmites. They are dark, mysterious, and very cold; they could be entered only by people holding stone lamps or torches. Certainly these caverns were inappropriate as dwelling places,

Figure 17–8 Near the village of Les Eyzies, the Vézère Valley presents a peaceful panorama little changed since Paleolithic people surveyed the scene. In this area, numerous rock shelters and other prehistoric sites are still unexcavated.

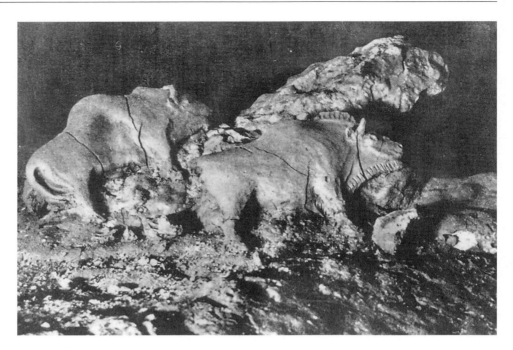

FIGURE 17–9   Clay bison, 24 inches (61 centimeters) long, lean against a limestone block in a remote chamber of Le Tuc d'Audoubert Cave near Ariège, France. They may have been ritual objects.

and they contain little or no evidence of having been lived in. By nature removed from day-to-day life, these caves may well have been used as shrines and for the performance of certain rites (Figure 17–9).

Painting and Hunting Magic

Important observations about the location of cave art were made by the late Abbé Henri Breuil, a French priest who devoted his life to the study of prehistory, and by Johannes Maringer, who also intensively studied this art. The paintings or engravings were often made in the least convenient places for viewing: in narrow niches, behind protrusions of rock, sometimes in areas that must have been not only difficult but actually dangerous for the artist to work in. "It is simply impossible," said Maringer, "that this art should have been invented, in these locations, to give pleasure to the eye of the beholder; the intention must always have been to veil it in mysterious secrecy. "

What was its purpose, then? The traditional explanation, accepted by Maringer and numerous other experts, is that cave art was a vehicle for magic—more specifically, a vehicle for a form known as **sympathetic hunting magic**. Upper Paleolithic people were strong and intelligent, and they were well equipped with all kinds of weapons, from spears and knives to slings. They knew how to make traps for small animals and pitfalls for large ones. They could ambush animals and stampede them. And, as we have seen, they left behind them impressive records of their prowess. Nevertheless, despite their formidable powers, they walked always in the shadow of unpredictable and incomprehensible events, which they may have seen as malign forces. Doubtless they felt it necessary to try to forestall misfortune and injury—and perhaps death, for some of the animals they came up against were

Sympathetic hunting magic the use of rituals (and associated artifacts) that practitioners believed would ensure success and safety in the hunt.

extremely dangerous. Doubtless, too, they believed, like so many people living today, that magic could help them not only dodge misfortune but also gain control over the animals they wanted to kill. By painting the animals' pictures, they became, in effect, the animals' masters and strengthened their chances of dealing the prey a mortal wound during the hunt. Even today, people of many societies believe that creating the likeness of a person or thing gives the person who created it some supernatural power over the subject.

This interpretation of the paintings as hunting magic has a variety of evidence to support it. First, and most direct, is the large number of animals painted with spears lodged in them or marked with the blows of clubs, as though the artists intended to illustrate what they hoped would be the outcome of a chase (Figure 17–10). Less obvious are the drawings of rectangular enclosures with animals seemingly trapped in them. The most frequently seen example of these is in a cave at Font-de-Gaume near Les Eyzies, where a magnificent painted mammoth seems to be caught in a pitfall even though its enormous tusks thrust beyond the snare.

There is also a hint of hunting magic in the practice of superimposing one picture over another. This phenomenon has been observed over and over again in the caves. In one spot at Lascaux in France, the paintings are four layers deep, even though there is plenty of empty wall space nearby. If the painters had meant simply to express themselves or give pleasure to others, they probably would have started with a clean wall surface for each animal depicted. The concentration of paintings in one spot, one atop another, suggests that the placement of the painting was somehow important and that the overpainting was done for a purpose. Certain areas of the cave were favored for some reason, and it would be logical to suppose

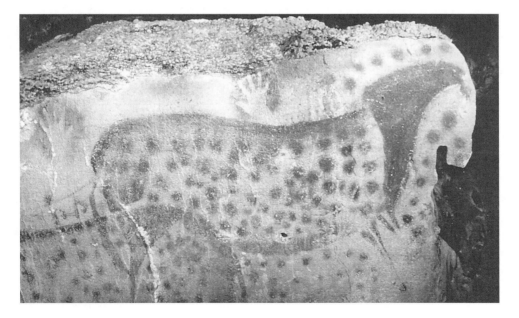

FIGURE 17–10   Pelted with dots, a painting of two horses in the Pech-Merle cave (Dordogne) combines two kinds of symbols for what could be simple decoration, or signs of hunting magic. The dots, in black and red ocher, could represent projectiles; the handprints surrounding the horses, a person's power over the prey. Taken together, the dots and the handprints would then be an invocation to the supernatural, intended to ensure the hunters of a successful kill.

that paintings that had previously brought hunters good luck came, in themselves, to be regarded as good hunting magic. Because all ritual depends on duplicating as closely as possible a procedure that has proved successful in the past, certain spots in the cave would come to be regarded as lucky.

In some instances, entire caves seem to have been imbued with an aura of good fortune. In Les Combarelles in southwestern France, nearly 300 animals crowd onto the cave walls. Perhaps it was this crowding that produced still another phenomenon of wall art: the tendency to overpaint one animal's head on another's body. Where space was at a premium, it would have been more provident to use the magic already available than to start afresh. Or perhaps artists simply looked for a less arduous way of working magic, for many of the cave paintings obviously took time and effort to execute. It is not difficult to imagine wishful hunters contemplating a beautifully painted bison and deciding to take a magical shortcut by substituting a deer's head for the bison's.

Hunting magic may also explain the occasional human-beast figures found in caves, strange-looking creatures with human bodies and animal or bird heads called *therianthropes*. According to South African archaeologist David Lewis-Williams, these creatures represented shamans or sorcerers, who must have played an important part in the lives of the artists. Lewis-Williams believes that many of the paintings were created by shamans in deep trance, and he has made a good case for this supposition. Such a hypothesis would account for many of the curious features of cave art that have no other obvious explanation. His ideas certainly reinforce the belief that the paintings carried powerful magical connotations.

But despite the logic and the long-term popularity of the hunting-magic hypothesis, some researchers believe that it is not the only—and perhaps not even the best—interpretation of cave imagery. For example, Margaret Conkey, of the University of California at Berkeley, and others have pointed out that the cave paintings and sculptures are generally of animal species *other* than those that figured heavily in Upper Paleolithic diets. While roughly 65 percent of the European cave images depict either horses or bison, two other species—red deer and reindeer—actually dominate the food refuse. Thus, if the images were intended to ensure success in the hunt, they didn't work very well—at least as reflected by the remains of ancient meals. Furthermore, the idea that many of the cave sites were shrines whose images accumulated over long periods and repeated visits has been called into question. Recent analyses of pollen in cave sediments and of paint composition ("pigment recipes") suggest that in some cases complex images, including depictions of groups and/or superimposed animals, were painted quickly and on one occasion. Results such as these tend to weaken (though not completely refute) the traditional notion that the caves were used over thousands of years by many generations of hopeful hunters.

Art and Fertility

Thus, although hunting magic may explain a great deal of cave art, that interpretation is not airtight. Some authorities believe that these animals and cryptic geometrical signs are sexual in nature, and the paintings were fertility magic. Pairs of animals were often shown together, sometimes in the act of mating. Horses, does, and cows were painted with swollen bellies (as in Figure 17–11), which have been interpreted as a sign of advanced pregnancy. In other paintings, udders were enlarged, as if to emphasize the rich supply of milk that the mother would be capable of giving to any offspring that might be born.

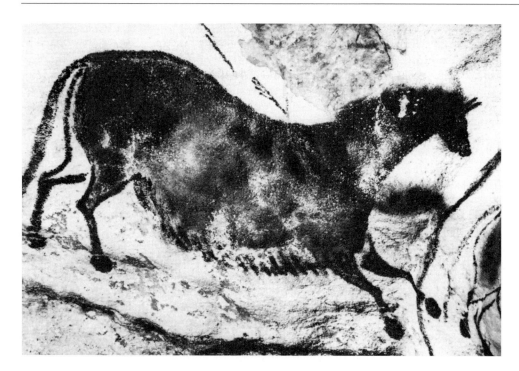

FIGURE 17–11   A pregnant horse gallops across the limestone ceiling of Lascaux. The slash marks above its shoulders may indicate spears. Lascaux, among the finest of all the painted caves of southwestern France, is a Magdalenian masterpiece, dated about 17,000 years B.P. The newly discovered cave of La Grotte Chauvet may surpass even Lascaux in its works of art.

The fertility of prey animals was a natural concern of the hunters. Scarcity of food must have been a periodic problem in many regions. During the colder episodes of the last glacial period, Magdalenian hunters killed mammoths, woolly rhinoceros, ibex, steppe horses, and particularly reindeer, which flourished in large numbers in the tundra environment. When the climate warmed from time to time, they undoubtedly hunted the deer, bison, and wild cattle that replaced the cold-adapted species, but the need to feed increasing numbers may well have led these people to encourage the natural productiveness of their game with fertility magic.

Other authorities think that cave art, though sexual in content, was far less utilitarian in its purpose. Instead of fertility magic, they see it as an attempt to express in visual symbols the dual forces in human nature: male and female. The most notable spokesperson for this post-Freudian point of view is French anthropologist André Leroi-Gourhan, who has made an extensive study of cave art. Leroi-Gourhan charted the frequency of occurrence of the various kinds of animals and signs, along with their locations in the caves and their positions in relation to each other. He thinks that most of the paintings and drawings have specific sexual connotations—that deer and bear are masculine, as are such signs as spears and clubs, whereas cattle and bison, as well as the enclosed figures that other authorities identify as traps in support of the theory of hunting magic, are feminine.

Taking an entirely new approach, Alexander Marshack has examined the smaller portable items of Upper Paleolithic art under a low-powered microscope. He has made many surprising observations and has drawn some startling, if controversial, conclusions. A beautiful horse 2.5 inches (6 centimeters) long, carved in mammoth ivory and from the site of Vogelherd in Germany, is the earliest known example of animal sculpture, dating from about 30,000 years B.P. The carefully carved ear, nose, mouth, and mane have been worn down by persistent handling. At some time during this use, a fresh angle or dart was engraved in its flank, apparently symbolizing an act of actual or ritualized killing. The object was touched and used often and seems to have served some important purpose.

A second example described by Marshack is the image of a horse engraved on a horse's pelvis from the site of Paglicci in Italy. Microscopic examination of the image indicated that the horse had been symbolically killed twenty-seven times. Twenty-seven feathered darts or spears were engraved on and around the horse, each made by a different engraving point and in a different style, possibly over a considerable period of time. This horse was clearly a symbol that could be used in an appropriate way when required.

The large painted horse from the cave of Pech-Merle (Figure 17–10) proves to have somewhat similar characteristics: The black and red dots on its body are made of many pigments and ochers, suggesting that they were applied over a period and that the horse was used continually as an important symbol.

But Marshack has noticed other details. On some portable items he has found small marks, often in series, made at different times by different tools, which seem to indicate some sort of notation or numerical record. One particularly interesting antler fragment, from La Marche in the Dordogne, shows both a pregnant horse (which has been "used" a number of times) and a lengthy notation consisting of small notches in rows made from the tip downward, in lines of eleven (Figure 17–12). Marshack points out that eleven is the number of months in the gestation of a horse. Other notations on other fragments suggest that the phases of the moon were being logged.

Marshack's work has opened our eyes to the fact that these people were very much more sophisticated than anyone had supposed, and that they were not only great artists but also possibly on the brink of developing arithmetic, and even perhaps the beginning of very primitive writing. We do not yet understand the meaning of all the material that they have left us, but we do know that they are ancestors for whom we should have the greatest respect.

When the work of Leroi-Gourhan, Marshack, and others is combined with traditional interpretations, it becomes clear that Upper Paleolithic art may have had multiple functions—as hunting magic or fertility magic, as part of initiation rites, perhaps for communication between groups (see the Postscript to this chapter), and possibly even as a part of complex religious ceremonies (as described below). But how can we tease apart these various functions for a more complete understanding? The first and most important step, according to Margaret Conkey, is to stop viewing Upper Paleolithic imagery as a functionally monolithic phenomenon and to begin disentangling it into its component "sign systems," which can be linked to specific social and historical contexts. Future analyses using this approach promise to produce fascinating results.

But whatever the images' meaning, the skill of the artists and the beauty of their work are astonishing. Every animal is an individual portrait, drawn from life, by painters in complete control of their medium. Their outlines are sure and bold. They painted in various tones of black, red, yellow, and brown obtained from natural clays and mineral oxides. Sometimes they mixed their colors with charcoal and animal fat to make a thick pigment, which they used like a crayon or daubed on with moss, frayed twigs, or even a primitive paintbrush made of hair. At other

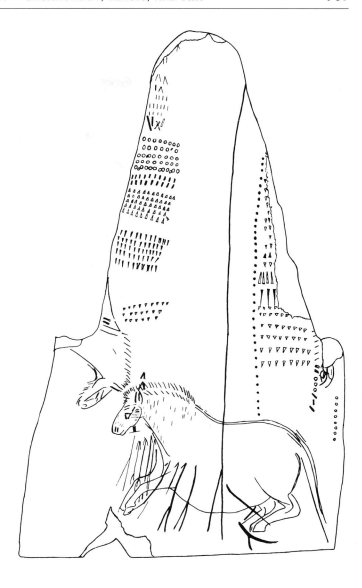

FIGURE 17–12   Fragment of an antler tool from La Marche, France. This is the earliest known artifact containing two types of notations: cumulative markings and naturalistic sketches. The markings may be related to the gestation period of a horse. The line drawing shows the entire surface of the antler fragment.

times, they seem to have blown dry colors directly onto the wall in powder form, possibly through a hollow bird bone. Some researchers even think that Upper Paleolithic artists occasionally masticated their pigments and then spat the paint onto cave walls. Once applied to a wall, the colors were slowly absorbed by the limestone. This absorption begins to explain their phenomenal durability. Thanks to the constant humidity and temperature of the caves, much of Paleolithic art in western Europe has retained its original brilliance for 20,000 to 10,000 years, some of it for even longer.

Spectacular New Painted Cave Found in Southern France (1994)

As if to remind us that even well-explored areas may still hold archaeological secrets, the discovery of a new and spectacular painted cave in the Ardèche region of southern France was announced to the world on December 18, 1994. The cave is called La Grotte Chauvet and it is located near the town of Vallon-Pont-d'Arc, some 40 miles (64 kilometers) northwest of Avignon (see Figure 16–1). Dating from about 33,000 to 30,000 years B.P., the site is particularly valuable to archaeologists because of its undisturbed nature and very early date. Prior to its discovery, the cave apparently had been completely sealed by fallen debris for thousands of years.

Reports suggest that the art of La Grotte Chauvet may surpass even that of the famous caves of Lascaux and Altamira. It is estimated that the cave, which consists of at least four huge halls, contains more than 300 paintings by Upper Paleolithic artists. Included in the vivid images are human hands, bears, mammoths, woolly rhinos, lions, and hyenas, as well as the first known images of owls and a panther. In addition to its art works, the cave is said to contain stone tools, hearths, and numerous bones, including the skull of a cave bear that may have been deliberately displayed amidst a group of bear paintings.

The potential importance of La Grotte Chauvet is shown by the fact that it has been placed under French government protection and at present only archaeologists are allowed to enter the cave. Scientific studies of the site are beginning, and it seems certain that this new painted cave will yield important new insights into Upper Paleolithic life.

Sculpture and Ceramics

In addition to painting, Upper Paleolithic people showed considerable proficiency as sculptors and engravers (see Figure 17–9). In early examples of their skill, they incised the outlines of animals on cave walls. Later artists went on to develop the more advanced technique of carving subjects in high relief, often using the contours of the walls. Le Cap Blanc, near Les Eyzies, has a marvelous set of horses done in this way. The entire frieze is about 40 feet (12 meters) long; the largest horse is 7 feet (2 meters) long. As the bulging sides of the horses' bodies reveal, the artists incorporated the natural curves of the rock into their work with great skill. Apparently more than one artist was guided by the formation and the structure of the rock in carving this frieze, for the animal figures appear to have been worked on at various times.

These artists also made complete statues in the round. In doing so, they left us a means of gaining further insights into Stone Age life and thought. The statues are usually of stone, bone, or ivory, although some were carved out of a mixture of clay and ground bone that had been hardened by firing. The first evidence of firing comes from the site of Dolní Věstonice in the Czech Republic (Figure 16–1). At a settlement dated about 27,000 years B.P. is a kiln where the bone and clay mixture was fired into a new, rock-hard material. This is the first example in technological history of a process that was to become ubiquitous and would eventually be used in producing glass, bronze, steel, nylon, and most of the other materials of everyday life: the combination and treatment of two or more dissimilar substances to make a useful product unlike either starting substance. It would be another 15,000 years or so before other people, living in Japan, learned to turn clay into pots; yet, as the evidence from Dolní Věstonice attests, ceramics had already been invented.

When the kiln hut was first investigated in 1951, its sooty floor was littered with fragments of ceramic figurines. There were animal heads: bears, foxes, lions. In one particularly beautiful lion head was a hole simulating a wound, perhaps intended to help some hunter inflict a similar wound on a real lion. The floor was also cluttered with hundreds of scrap pellets that were probably pinched off the lump of unbaked clay when sculpting began and that still bore the artisan's fingerprints. There also were limbs broken from little animal and human figures. They may have cracked off in the baking or when the ancient ceramist tossed aside a failed work.

Female Figurines

More intriguing than any waste fragments of clay animal figures on the hut floor are the human statuettes found there, particularly the female figures. Unlike the animals, these are not naturalistic but almost surreal. Such figurines have a very wide distribution at Upper Paleolithic sites over much of Europe and eastward as far as western Siberia and Ukraine. Although they vary a good deal in appearance, they have some significant things in common, the most obvious being that the sculptors' interest was focused on the torso. The arms and legs are extremely small in proportion to the trunk, and in some cases they are merely suggested (see Figures 17–13 and 17–14). The heads are also small and typically show little attempt

FIGURE 17–13 This Czech clay figure from Dolní Věstonice shows the Venus's typical traits: huge breasts and belly and shapeless arms. This figure's legs are now broken, but they probably had no feet. The photograph is approximately 80 percent actual size.

FIGURE 17—14   The Venus of Abri Pataud, the armless body of a woman incised in a small piece of rock, is one of the few art objects found at the excavation. It was made some 20,000 years ago.

to portray facial features, although the famous Venus of Willendorf, a four inches (10 centimeters) figurine made of limestone, does have a wavy hairdo executed with considerable care (Figure 17–15). All the emphasis is on the bodies, with their female characteristics—breasts, belly, and buttocks—greatly exaggerated in size. They look like tiny earth goddesses or fertility figures, and a good deal of informed speculation suggests that this is what they were. Many of them show the polish of long use and some the remains of red ocher, which indicates that they were symbolically painted.

Some evidence supporting the idea that they were fertility figures is based on where the statuettes were found and when they are believed to have been made. The majority of them come from the period of the Upper **Perigordian** (or Gravettian), a Paleolithic culture of western Europe that existed between 27,000 and 21,000 years ago. During this period, the weather ranged from cool to very cold. In the cold periods it was bitter in the extreme, especially on the eastern European plains; nevertheless, many people continued to live there. Some made their homes in shallow pits that they dug in the ground and then roofed over with hides or other material. The vague outlines of the walls of many of these sunken

Perigordian *Upper Paleolithic* culture of western Europe dating 27,000 to 21,000 years B.P.

FIGURE 17–15 Small female figures such as the Venus of Willendorf in Austria were widespread in Europe 20,000 years ago. Note the intricate hairdo.

huts may still be seen. The interesting thing is that these sites contain abundant examples of these female figurines, and they are often found lying right next to the walls or buried near hearths. The figurines themselves often taper to a point at the bottom, as if they had been designed to be stuck into the earth or into a base of some sort.

On this evidence, it is fairly clear that the figurines were closely associated with the daily life of the peoples who made them and have a significance utterly unlike that of the wall art that was created in secret, deep in underground caves. Speculating on their purpose, several authorities have proposed various theories. To Johannes Maringer, the figurines seem to point to an enhancement in the status of women. Maringer thinks that a combination of harsh climatic conditions and a relatively sedentary way of life accounts for that change. When people settle down in one place for considerable periods, the home becomes important, and home-making is usually regarded as the woman's prerogative. In the cold of the windswept eastern steppe, it was perhaps the women who had the critical jobs of planning, rationing, storing, and using supplies so that the group could get through the winter. Storage pits were found at many sites, some with animal remains. Women probably also were responsible for making the fur clothing that the people are thought to have dressed in. Sewing carefully with eyed needles of bone, they could have made warm clothing that fitted the body well, particularly around the arms and legs.

But the role of women would also have been important because of their pro-creative function. The mysteries of fertility and birth made women the guardians not only of hearth and home but of life itself. In the minds of some modern experts, the female figurines are cult objects. They represented the tribal ancestresses from whom the group was descended, assuring them of continuity as a group and increasing their population and the population of the animals they hunted. Whether the little figures were worshiped as goddesses or simply venerated as good-luck charms is not known.

Burial Customs and Rites

Upper Paleolithic people were concerned about death as well as life, and their treatment of the dead was careful and thoughtful. The bodies were often placed in graves dug in the ashes of previously occupied living sites, and in many places it was a common practice to sprinkle the deceased with red ocher, perhaps in an effort to bring back the flush of life to pallid skin (Figure 17–16). The practice of including grave offerings, probably begun by archaic humans, was expanded by their successors in Eurasia to extraordinary heights of funerary luxury. An example is the grave of two boys (shown in Figure 17–17) that was excavated during the 1960s in a Paleolithic settlement about 130 miles (210 kilometers) northeast of Moscow, at Sungir (Figure 16–1). The grave suggests either that the boys were very important or that the settlers who lived at Sungir 23,000 years ago had some

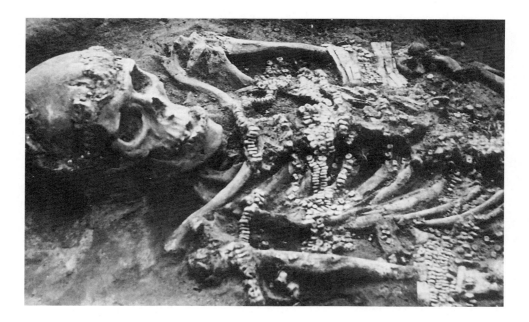

FIGURE 17–16   The skeleton of a man lies just as the body was buried 23,000 years ago in an ocher-sprinkled grave at Sungir, northeast of Moscow. The man was ceremoniously laid to rest, laden with beads, a headband of carved mammoth ivory, and the teeth of arctic foxes, in what appears to have been a burial ground—suggesting that the hunter-gatherers of Sungir lived part of the year in a settled community where they developed complex customs.

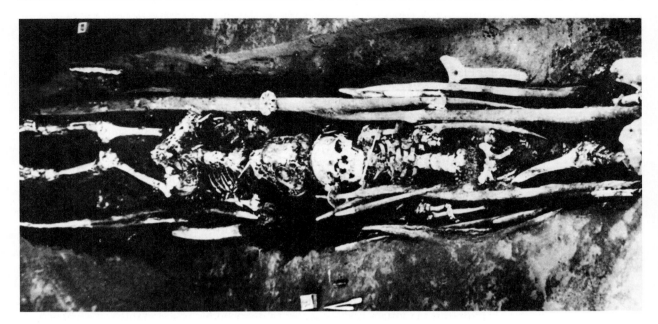

FIGURE 17–17   The skeletons of two boys who died 23,000 years ago lie head to head in a grave at Sungir in Russia. The elaborateness of their grave suggests that the boys were laid to rest amid solemn ritual, perhaps with a view to an afterlife.

fairly elaborate ideas about an afterlife. The boys—one seven to nine years old, the other twelve or thirteen—were laid out in a line, skull to skull. Both had been dressed from head to toe in clothing decorated with ivory beads carved from mammoth tusks, and they wore bracelets and rings of the same material. On the older boy's chest lay a disk of mammoth tusk carved into the shape of a horse, and both boys were equipped with an assortment of ivory weapons, such as lances, spears, and daggers. The lances had been formed from a split mammoth bone that had been warmed over a fire in order to be straightened, a technique that requires considerable sophistication.

Synthesizing Art, Ritual, and Religion in the Upper Paleolithic

American archaeologist D. Bruce Dickson has recently synthesized all of the available evidence on European Upper Paleolithic burial practices and art, and he has reached a set of interesting—and heuristically valuable—conclusions. Dickson believes that the elaborate burials of the Upper Paleolithic indicate a more complex and socially differentiated society than that of the Middle Paleolithic. Furthermore, since complex societies are supported by complex institutions, religious institutions in the Upper Paleolithic probably exceeded the simple shamanistic cult with its part-time religious specialist. Dickson believes that religious rituals, conducted fundamentally in "an attempt to control nature and society by supernatural means," involved shamanistic direction of a community of participants. Community rituals, according to Dickson, were likely to be performed seasonally when, following the rhythms of their subsistence activities, Upper Paleolithic groups aggregated at the painted caves that served as their ceremonial centers. Annual visits to such ceremonial centers may account for the evidence that they were used, and their art added to, repeatedly. Seasonal aggregations and society-wide rituals would have fostered group integrity and continuity, and shared religious beliefs may even have promoted friendly interactions and information sharing among widely separated cultures. Finally, Dickson believes that woven into the ritual practices of Upper Paleolithic people were concepts about the passage of time and about human sexuality, "especially the periodicity and fecundity of women." Thus the Venus figurines and also artifacts suggesting notation systems are seen as facets of a larger, and quite elaborate, belief system.

The more we learn about these early modern people from the evidence of their living sites, the narrower the gap becomes between them and us. But it will never be entirely closed. The intimate details of social life, the games children played, the gestures and courtesies that give a society flavor—all these have necessarily vanished. We have no knowledge of how one addressed another or what words they used. And we will never know.

Some details have enlightened us, however, and some generalizations can be made. As the first modern people stretched their powers, they came to separate themselves from nature's control in ways that their ancestors could not have dreamed of. Spread as they now were throughout the Old and New Worlds, they were adapting to a vast range of environments and developing a host of different cultures and languages. What we have described is based mainly on archaeological research in Europe—a very small part indeed of the whole world. Everywhere culture moved ahead and blossomed in an endless variety of forms, and society developed in a thousand complex ways. The ability to exploit such a variety of environments led to great growth in the numbers of people, and populations increased as much as tenfold in some parts of the world. By the end of this period, some 10,000 years ago, these people had set the stage for the last steps in the emergence of modern culture: agriculture, domestication of animals, metalworking, complex forms of social and political life, writing, and perhaps even war.

SUMMARY

The sedentary lifestyle (sedentism), as distinct from nomadism, was very unusual in human prehistory, but by 30,000 years B.P. sedentism—or at least semisedentism—had become more common with increased control of the environment. People had learned to make fire and had developed a wide range of specialized stone tools. With these they created objects made of wood, bone, antler, and ivory—all invaluable materials available in reasonable quantities. They made beads and bracelets and a whole range of hunting weapons, including spears, spear throwers, spear points, fishing gear of different kinds, tailored clothing, and eventually the bow and arrow.

Ritual life became very important and, with it, art and magic. Cave paintings may have served to influence hunting success and the fertility of game. Sculpture (female figures) and the first ceramics may have been involved in fertility rites. At Magdalenian sites we find the first evidence of numeracy, and an artistic eye can be seen in the design of the artifacts. Considered collectively, the evidence of Upper Paleolithic burials and art suggests an extremely elaborate belief system and complex religious institutions. Clearly, Upper Paleolithic peoples were modern not only anatomically, but intellectually.

POSTSCRIPT

Many students of Upper Paleolithic art believe that the cave paintings and sculptures preserve a kind of "text," and that, if we can once break the "code" of the various symbols, we will be able to reconstruct a good deal of what Upper Paleolithic people thought and how they interacted. Shared symbolism may have facilitated trading or cooperative hunting between widely scattered human groups. Additionally, some artistic symbols may have conveyed complex messages either within or between groups. Consider the case of the handprints.

In several, but by no means all, of the painted caves, images of animals and other objects are accompanied by impressions of human hands (see Figure 17–10). Sites known for their handprints include Gargas, Abri Labatut, Tibiran, and Les Combarelles in France, and El Castillo and El Pindal in Spain. These handprints have several binary features: they are either traced (negative representation) or painted (positive representation); left- or right-handed; red or black in color; whole or "mutilated" (apparently missing digits). As discussed by D. Bruce Dickson, the various attributes combine to produce sixteen distinct types of handprints (e.g., traced-left-red-whole versus painted-right-black-mutilated). Furthermore, as Dickson points out, if one counts fingers, the number of possible combinations rises to forty. Since humans around the world more or less consistently associate the left hand with evil and the right hand with good, and the color red with life and black with death, the handprint code—if that is what it is—seems to be charged with potential meaning. One can imagine handprints being used simply as signatures after the completion of particularly elaborate pieces of cave art ("So-and-so painted this") or as complex, coded messages between groups that routinely visited the same cave sites ("So-and-so was here recently and wishes the reader of this message ill").

Alternately, of course, the handprints may carry no meaning whatsoever, in which case they would fall into the same category as modern doodles. Messages or doodles? Only time and further research will tell. One thing is clear, however: The full meaning of Upper Paleolithic art remains to be revealed, and many surprises lie ahead.

REVIEW QUESTIONS

1. Many researchers argue that Upper Paleolithic people were more sedentary than their Middle Paleolithic predecessors. What sorts of technological and subsistence innovations and/or environmental changes would have allowed the development of sedentism? What sorts of cultural change may have resulted from a less mobile lifestyle?
2. Some of the world's most beautiful flaked stone artifacts were made by Upper Paleolithic artisans. As exemplified by several of the Solutrean blades, however, the artifacts often seem to be too delicate or the wrong size for practical use. Speculate on the possible functions of such "showpiece" artifacts.
3. Describe the evidence of increased hunting efficiency in the Upper Paleolithic.
4. Describe the cave art of the Upper Paleolithic. Speculate on how cave paintings and sculptures may have been incorporated into rituals of various sorts. Compare your speculations with the use of icons in modern religions.

5. Speculate about the relative status of women and men within Upper Paleolithic societies. Which sex do you think made the greater contribution to subsistence activities? To toolmaking? To art? To religion? In each case, explain the basis of your speculations. In particular, do you think the female figurines indicate that European Upper Paleolithic people traced their descent matrilineally or that they worshiped female deities?

SUGGESTED FURTHER READING

Clottes, J., et al. *The Shamans of Prehistory*: *Trance and Magic in the Painted Caves.* Abrams, 1999.

Conkey, M. "Humans as Materialists and Symbolists: Image Making in the Upper Paleolithic," in D. T. Rasmussen, ed., *The Origin and Evolution of Humans and Humanness.* Jones & Bartlett, 1993.

Dickson, D. B. *The Dawn of Belief*. University of Arizona Press, 1990.

Leroi-Gourhan, A. *Treasures of Prehistoric Life*. Abrams, 1967.

Ucko, P. J., and A. Rosenfeld. *Paleolithic Cave Art*. McGraw-Hill, 1967.

INTERNET RESOURCES

AN EXTRAORDINARY ARCHAEOLOGICAL FIND...(CHAUVET CAVE)
http://www.culture.fr/culture/arcnat/chauvet/en/gvpda-d.htm
>(A well-illustrated site describing the newly discovered painted cave in the Ardèche region of France.)

ROCK-LINKS!!!
http://www.geocities.com/Tokyo/2384/links.html
>(This site contains links to over 200 rock art homepages.)

PALEO-PSYCHOLOGY (SIGNS OF CONSCIOUSNESS: SPECULATIONS ON THE PSYCHOLOGY OF PALEOLITHIC GRAPHICS)
http://watarts.uwaterloo.ca/%7Eacheyne/signcon.html
>(Maintained by Al Cheyne at the University of Waterloo, this site probes the meanings behind the various Upper Paleolithic art objects.)

USEFUL SEARCH TERMS:
>*Cave art*
>*Paleolithic art*
>*Rock art*
>*Upper Paleolithic*

Chapter 17 Timeline

NEOLITHIC AND MESOLITHIC	YEARS B.P.	FOSSILS AND ARCHAEOLOGICAL RECORD	MAJOR TOOL INDUSTRIES OF WESTERN EUROPE	
— 10,000			NEOLITHIC AND MESOLITHIC CULTURES	
UPPER PALEOLITHIC				
— 40,000			MAGDALENIAN	
MIDDLE PALEOLITHIC	10,000 —	First farmers Clay pots, Japan Iron pyrite in Belgium, spear thrower at La Placard, France	SOLUTREAN	
		Sungir burials; bow and arrow in Africa Cave art and figurines	PERIGORDIAN (=GRAVETTIAN)	
— 200,000		Lake Mungo, Australia, fossils Zafarraya Neandertals Cro-Magnon		
Swanscombe and Steinheim; Levallois technique Beijing finds Arago		Chauvet cave art St. Césaire Neandertals Modern skull at Niah	AURIGNACIAN/ CHATELPERRONIAN	
400,000		Possible entry into Americas Amud Neandertals La Chapelle Neandertals		
500,000	50,000 —	Monte Circeo skull		
Gran Dolina fossils		Shanidar fossils and flower burial		
LOWER PALEOLITHIC		La Quina and La Ferrassie fossils		
— 1 million *Paranthropus* extinct			MOUSTERIAN	
		Disk-core technique used		
		Skhūl and Qafzeh fossils		
— 1.5 million Acheulean industry	100,000 —			
Homo habilis at Olduvai			ACHEULEAN	
— 1.8 million *Homo erectus* in Africa, the Caucasus, and Java				
— 2 million Oldowan industry	130,000 —	Kabwe, Elandsfontein, Jabel Irhoud, and Klasies River fossils		

TECHNOLOGY, MAGIC, AND ART

Many of the dates given to finds are based on indirect evidence and are estimates; the dates given to cultural phases are approximations.

THE HUMAN CONDITION

A street scene in any modern city reveals humans' biological diversity at a glance.

But man, proud man,
Drest in a little brief authority,
Most ignorant of what he's most assured,
His glassy essence, like an angry ape,
Plays such fantastic tricks before high heaven
As make the angels weep.

             WILLIAM SHAKESPEARE, 1564–1616. *Measure for Measure*, II, ii.

OVERVIEW

Hominid evolution has been under way for an estimated 5 to 7 million years. The earliest phase involved the australopithecines, whose lifeways (although noncultural) and anatomies served them in good stead for millions of years. About 2.4 million years ago, however, a new and significantly brainier type of hominid evolved: the first representatives of the genus *Homo*. The hominines changed rather dramatically after their first appearance. They became bigger and smarter and better communicators; radically broadened their subsistence systems, first by becoming hunters-and-gatherers, and later by domesticating plants and animals; and evolved a tremendously complex cultural lifestyle. Although several extinct hominine species are known, today the subfamily (and indeed the entire family Hominidae) is represented by only one species: modern humans, *Homo sapiens*. This final chapter deals primarily with the extreme physical variability of living humans and with our traditional way of understanding that variability—through the construction of racial classifications. It shows how most anatomical variations can be understood as adaptations to different environments, mere surface features rather than deep lines of division across humanity. It argues that, among humans, race has little or no validity as a biological concept (although it is quite important sociologically) and that therefore biology cannot be used as a justification for racist attitudes and behavior. The chapter concludes with a discussion of some of the challenges that await humans in the future, including limiting global population size and wisely using our growing control over our own evolution. Important concepts and topics in the chapter include human altruism; plant and animal domestication; the beginnings and effects of settled living; physical variation among living humans; human traits as evolutionary adaptations; biological races; sociological races; racism; human population growth; and humans' control over their evolutionary future.

THE STORY OF HUMANKIND

It is hard to realize that the story we have recounted in these chapters took tens of millions of years to enact. The development of technology alone has taken more than 2 million years since the invention of the first stone tools. During this incredibly long period of emergence, the animal that became *Homo sapiens* has been shaped by environment and social experience—both body and culture changing in adaptation.

Evolutionary biology, of which paleoanthropology is a division, makes this much clear to us: each species is a product of its genes and its environment. That is, with few exceptions each characteristic of every species is a product of mutation and natural selection and in a very immediate way *fits* its environment. Fishes have fins, horses have hooves, primates have hands. Each characteristic of the human body is also a direct product of the interaction between genes and environment. This is not to say that natural selection is directed or moved toward any goal, nor does it mean that the characteristics that *have* been selected by the environment are the only ones that could have been. Nature shows us that there is more than one solution to any problem. If in the long run we do not understand the genesis of every human characteristic, we know at least that we can never understand either the genesis or the function of a characteristic without considering the environment in which it evolved.

Environmental History and Adaptation

Taiga northern coniferous forest bordering the *tundra*.

The story of the human environment is relatively clear and forms the first part of the story of human evolution. The tropical rain forest was the womb that held our ape ancestors and from which the earliest hominids emerged into the world. As our ancestors evolved, they left the deep forest to inhabit more open woodlands and tropical savannas throughout the Old World. As they expanded north into the temperate zones, they came to occupy an increasing number of different biomes, or ecological zones. To temperate grassland and woodland alike they adapted, and eventually also to the cool **taiga** (subarctic coniferous forests) and icy tundra. Some populations moved in and out of the northern taiga and followed game to alpine pastures. Other populations began to exploit the regions bordering deserts or they reentered the tropical rain forests. Everywhere humans evolved the flexibility to live in a variety of biomes—and they were the first primate type to do so.

Humankind owed this flexibility to the second part of our story: the evolution of a remarkable and extraordinarily adaptable body and of an astounding brain. We have seen how the australopithecines emerged as the first hominids and that these creatures—at least after *Ardipithecus ramidus*—were both bipeds and had humanlike teeth. By the time of *Australopithecus afarensis*, some 3 to 4 million years ago, hominids were venturing out of the gallery forests and onto the African savanna: a move that probably selected for behavioral flexibility, an omnivorous diet, and social living. Just after 2.5 million years ago, some form of *Australopithecus* gave rise to bigger brained, stone toolmaking creatures that we now classify as hominines: early *Homo*, including *H. rudolfensis* and *H. habilis*. Next in line came *Homo erectus*, the first species modern enough to be called *human* and probably the first hominid type to spread out of Africa and into temperate habitats. *H. erectus*, in turn, gave rise to *Homo heidelbergensis* around 800,000 years B.P. and that archaic species—along with its own descendants, the Neandertals (*H. neanderthalensis*)—continued the expansion into colder regions thanks to increasingly technological cultures (Figure 18–1). Finally, modern people (*Homo sapiens*) evolved around 130,000 years ago—most probably in Africa from another *H. heidelbergensis* population—and ultimately spread throughout the Old World and into the Americas and Australia. With the exception of some remote islands, the entire worldwide expansion was probably completed before the end of the Paleolithic, bringing us almost to the later stone ages, the **Mesolithic** and Neolithic.

Mesolithic a *Stone Age* period recognizable at some European sites and characterized by the use of small stone tools called microliths; lasting at most 2000 years, the Mesolithic followed the *Paleolithic* and preceded the *Neolithic*.

Early *Homo*

Homo erectus

Archaic humans

Homo sapiens

FIGURE 18–1   From bipedal *Australopithecus* on the African savanna to *Homo sapiens* worldwide, from Oldowan choppers to complex technology, human development has been the result of the interaction of environment, body, and culture.

The human organism, miraculous though it may seem in its complexity, was and is a product of natural selection: the human brain was no more than what was needed for survival and successful reproduction in a variety of different physical and social environments. From an average of perhaps 400 cubic centimeters some 4 million years ago, human cranial capacity has risen to vary between 1,000 and 2,000 cubic centimeters. This increase in size has been exceedingly rapid by evolutionary measure and has produced a brain of unprecedented complexity.

Altruism and Bioaltruism Among Humans

The question inevitably arises of whether we are more than a superior kind of animal, and if so, in what way? Have we in some sense escaped from the constraints of our animal ancestry? Are we really different in kind from the animals that share our world? For centuries, philosophers have been trying to define the unique qualities that would set us apart from the animal kingdom. We have language, technology, complex society, even civilization. Some writers have proposed ethics as the most profound characteristic that clearly divides human from beast. Do humans alone show the virtue of unselfishness, or altruism? If they do, does this not finally separate them at a profound level from the selfish and competitive law of natural selection? Altruism—the act of helping others at some cost to oneself—has been claimed to be a unique characteristic of humans, and for many years biologists were unable to see how such a characteristic could possibly emerge as a result of natural selection. The question was discussed by J. B. S. Haldane as long ago as 1932, and he suggested that altruism of a kind would be selected if it prompted the survival of dependents or near relations. This sort of altruism obviously applies to the situation when parents risk their lives for their offspring. Since the essence of natural selection is competition, however, it was not clear how behavior that went against that overriding fact could be selected.

Group selection theoretical model in which natural selection is presumed to operate not on the individual animal but on a social group as a unit.

One hypothesis, put forward originally by Charles Darwin and later developed by the British biologist V. C. Wynne-Edwards, was based on the concept of **group selection**. If natural selection operated on social groups rather than individuals, then any behavior that benefited the social group, even at the expense of the individual, would presumably be selected. This point of view was discussed at length during the 1960s. It was not, however, generally accepted, and it was soon pointed out that other explanations were available that did not depend on the idea of a totally integrated group. Indeed we know that, however well integrated the social group may be, a certain amount of competition continues within it.

Recent work by sociobiologists has, however, thrown light on this difficult question, and their ideas are of immense interest to anthropologists. When W. D. Hamilton introduced the concept of inclusive fitness in 1964, he gave us the key to understanding altruism in many social species (see Chapter 2). The examples of altruism seen among insects and, for example, among birds which give warning calls are not of course what we think of as altruism among humans. This animal type of altruism has been conveniently called bioaltruism. Human altruism is expected to be voluntarily performed and disinterested.

When we come to examine social primates, we can identify a new kind of altruism. When baboons or chimpanzees form alliances, they will often take risks on behalf of one another that look very like human altruism. While in some cases the altruist and the recipient are related, this is not always so. The American biologist Robert Trivers has examined situations of this kind and has introduced the term reciprocal altruism (see Chapter 4). Evidently there is an unspoken understanding between such individuals that "one good turn deserves another." It is in many ways a very human behavior pattern when members of a group of individuals exchange favors. All that is required is that altruism should be reciprocated and that the advantages of such behavior outweigh the disadvantages. It is also necessary that individuals not cheat. Reciprocity is an important basis of much of human social life, and there are strong sanctions against cheating.

Do humans show any kind of altruism that is not based in some biological advantage and is not seen in other species? Edward O. Wilson, who discussed this question at some length in his book *Human Nature*, has concluded that since we, too (with our brains), are a product of natural selection, it is not likely that we should have developed behavior that operates against natural selection. If biological fitness demands altruism, then it will appear in human societies, but if altruism operated to lower individuals' inclusive fitness, then it surely would never become established as a common behavior pattern. Wilson writes:

> Genes hold culture on a leash. The leash is very long, but inevitably values will be constrained in accordance with their effect on the human gene pool. . . . Human behavior—like the deepest capacities for emotional response which drive and guide it—is the circuitous technique by which human genetic material has been and will be kept intact. Morality has no other demonstrable ultimate function.

A review of instances of human altruism produces few examples in which there is not a well-recognized reward for the risks taken, even if the reward is promised in the next life. Human society has developed reciprocal altruism to the point where it is all-pervasive, and society has developed sanctions against failure to act altruistically, that is, against selfishness. Experienced swimmers are expected to save a drowning person even if that person is completely unknown to them, and they frequently do so. So strong is the pressure to act in this way that a police officer recently drowned in England trying to rescue a dog from the waves.

Much human behavior appears nonadaptive or maladaptive: we can choose not to bear children; we can commit suicide. As Wilson says, the genetic leash is long. Reason has given us freedom from the lower brain centers, the limbic system, which makes animals do what they have to do. We can determine our actions without reference to our limbic needs, and we can if we want go against our nature—as individuals. But for the species, such behavior would spell suicide. In this sense we are still held by our genes on that unbreakable leash.

The ultimate human mystery lies perhaps in locating the origin of the dreams that seem so far removed from our biological needs: dreams of dazzling creativity; dreams of a better world founded in equality; dreams of achievements and experience in poetry, music, art, and science. The mystery lies in understanding these new goals that our dreams have set us, goals that arise far from our biological heritage and yet give meaning to the lives of so many people. Human adaptability and reason give us, as individuals, freedom to follow these goals at whatever cost. It is in this sense that we have left the kingdom of animals and gained considerable freedom from our genes.

Cultural History

Adaptability and reason have also led to the third part of our story, the uniquely human characteristic that was also a response to the environment: culture. Culture consists in the first place of those behaviors and ideas which are the property of the society and which are maintained by mutual learning and teaching by its members. In human evolution, language became a new means of transmitting and recording cultural data. Language was a unique and revolutionary organic adaptation, certainly one of the most important developments in human evolution. It opened up new possibilities of existence and allowed a surge in human technology.

The first developments of technology came at an unimaginably slow rate. Any idea of progress would have been entirely foreign to early people; only the very simplest ideas were entering their heads. But progress did occur, however slowly. From using stone flakes they found on the ground as knives, hominids progressed to prepare their own sharp flakes and their own simple choppers. Slowly, over millions of years, they improved the cutting edge and varied the form of their tools for different purposes. The large hand ax and the knifelike blade appeared; manual

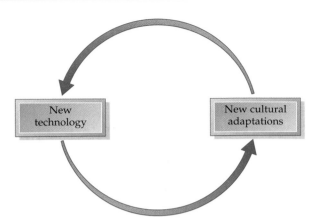

Figure 18–2   Positive feedback loops can be either constructive and creative or destructive. In either case, they tend to accelerate change in their components. This loop brings about accelerating cultural and technological changes.

skill became essential to the development of technology. Fire began to be kept alive in the hearth. The rate of change quickened, and cultural developments came more rapidly (Figure 18–2). In the cold northern winters a relatively complex technology was particularly crucial for human survival. Although we have little direct evidence, we can safely assume that not only containers but also clothing, wood and bone tools, and shelters of different kinds became essential parts of our ancestors' survival kit. People learned from each other, and from time to time an invention was made, but what today we see as a progressive journey was for these early people simply the way things were; their lifestyle was the only one they could imagine.

Domestication of Plants and Animals

Eventually, humans learned to change their environment in a more fundamental way. They became increasingly skilled and effective hunters-and-gatherers. They learned to select and breed animals; they domesticated sheep and cattle. They planted seeds and harvested cereals, becoming farmers.

Identification of the first evidence of the domestication of animals presents problems: the process of turning wild animals into tame ones will generate few identifiable archaeological remains, though after a considerable period of selective breeding, new breeds can be recognized by changes in skeletal structure. Dogs, sheep, goats, and cattle were probably the first animals to be bred selectively, at an approximate date of 10,000 years B.P. in the Middle East (Figure 18–3). By 9,000 years B.P., the domestic goat and sheep had become the principal source of meat and raw materials for the people of this region, and cattle and pigs were almost certainly undergoing domestication at this time. There is some uncertain evidence from cave art in western Europe that horses may have carried bridles at a somewhat earlier time. But the hard evidence comes from a much later period. One of the most significant sites is that of Lukenya Hill, near Nairobi, Kenya, where cattle bones dated 4,000 years B.P. are present on human occupation floors. Earlier sites (circa 6,500 years B.P.) are known from Algeria. Since cattle are not indigenous to sub-Saharan Africa, these animals must have been driven in from Eurasia, which proves that they had reached a certain level of domestication by this time. Indeed, from that date on, domesticated cattle, sheep, goats, and horses are found widely throughout the Old World.

The beginning of agriculture is still a mystery, and its details may always remain so. The first evidence of agriculture—of sowing, harvesting, and selecting wild barleys and wheats—dates from about 10,000 years B.P. and again comes from the Middle East (Figure 18–3). Agriculture also appeared about this time, or soon after, in north China and Mexico, and somewhat later in Peru. The cultivation of rice—a crop that supports an enormous percentage of modern humans—was an early occurrence in eastern Asia. The independent development of agriculture in these different regions is one of the most remarkable events in human prehistory. The plants and animals domesticated in each area were different (Table 18-1), but the techniques were the same: the farmers collected and sowed seeds and then selected the high-yielding varieties for continued planting.

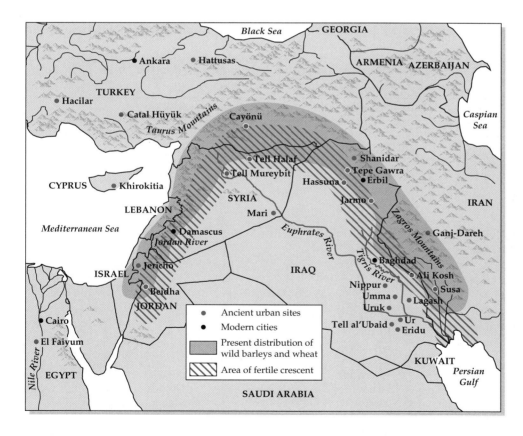

FIGURE 18–3   This map of the Middle East shows the Fertile Crescent, where the domestication of certain plants began about 10,000 years ago. During the past 5,000 years the rainfall of this region has diminished. Now much of the area is no longer suitable for agriculture. The reduction of rainfall was accompanied by the development of the earliest known system of irrigation in the valleys of the Tigris and Euphrates Rivers. The earliest villages and towns also developed in this region of agricultural wealth.

Hunting persisted in many areas, and in some, where humans herded animals, agriculture did not follow until much later, even though the land and the climate were suitable. Clearly the development of agriculture must have been slow, involving a number of steps. Some researchers believe that the development of agricultural techniques brought with it a rapid increase in population; others contend that the increase in population came first (following sedentism) and that the pressures for food which resulted stimulated the development of agriculture and animal husbandry ("Necessity is the mother of invention"). Whichever the order of events, it seems clear that the two factors would soon have come to interact in the manner of positive feedback, which would have resulted in a period of relatively rapid change in both population and culture. Certainly the increase in population that we believe accompanied sedentism would have triggered the need for an even greater and more reliable food supply. And resource domestication occurred only where the appropriate plants and animals existed and the climate was right. One such environment was the Fertile Crescent in the Middle East. Robert Braidwood of the University of Chicago, who worked during the 1960s in northeastern Iraq, described how some 10,000 years ago the climate and plant and animal life were ideal for the innovation of agriculture. Within that zone, he wrote, "occur in nature a remarkable constellation of the very plants and animals which became the basis for the food producing pattern of the Western cultural tradition. Nowhere else in

TABLE 18-1   *Some Wild Vegetables and Animals Domesticated in the Three Primary Zones of Agricultural Development*

ZONE	PLANTS	ANIMALS
Middle East	Almonds	Cattle
	Apricots	Dogs
	Barley	Goats
	Dates	Horses
	Figs	Pigs
	Grapes	Sheep
	Lentils	
	Olives	
	Peas	
	Rye	
	Wheat	
China and Southeast Asia	Bananas	Banteng[a]
	Coconuts	Dogs
	Millet	Pigs
	Rice	Yak
	Soybeans	
	Sugarcane	
South and Central America	Avocados	Alpaca
	Beans	Guinea pig
	Chili	Llama
	Cocoa	
	Corn	
	Gourds	
	Peanuts	
	Potatoes	
	Squashes	

[a] Javanese wild cow.

the world were the wild wheats and barley, the wild sheep, goats, pigs, cattle and horses to be found together in a single environment." The rainfall was right for agriculture without irrigation, but not sufficient to encourage the dense growth of forest, which would have been a stumbling block to primitive farmers.

Civilization

Although the agricultural revolution has not to this day reached all the earth's peoples, just about all the land suitable for agriculture is being farmed. Agriculture has made possible a vast increase in the world's population (see Figure 18–19) and it set the stage for a further cultural development of equal significance: the development of cities and metal technology, the coming of civilization.

The most ancient city known to us is Jericho, which lies on the west bank of the Jordan River (Figures 18–3 and 18–4). This city was first built about 10,000 years B.P. and was no doubt a smaller settlement before then. The surplus food that

FIGURE 18–4   An aerial view of Jericho encompasses the modern city and the dirt mound 50 feet (15 meters) high under which lie buried the many cities and walls of ancient Jericho. One of the more recent excavations can be seen: the trench cutting from left at the bottom of the photograph.

agriculture made available in the region evidently enabled people to live in dense communities where they depended on farmers to supply them with their food—as we do today. This entirely novel situation allowed certain of the the city-dwellers to specialize in arts and crafts of an ever-widening variety, and this kind of specialization was to form, in due time, the basis of modern civilization. Trade flourished: at Jericho, hematite, greenstone, obsidian, seashells, and salt all passed through the city, together with much else of which we have no trace. The north-south trade route on which the city lay was an important stimulus to its development. But civilization probably would not have grown from these early roots without improvements in agriculture. The greatest cities grew in areas of rich agricultural land, where the productivity was greatest; they reflected the agricultural foundation on which they necessarily were based.

The earliest achievements of civilization, including organized religion and government, weaving, writing, and metal technology, are too numerous to list, let alone discuss, but they bring us by an accelerating process of development from prehistory into history. Above all, it was developing technology that brought about the astonishing growth and complexity of human culture.

Environment, human biology, culture: these three are the threads of the human story we have told. During humankind's emergence each acted on the others in mutual feedback (see Figure 18–5); any change in one necessitated adjustment in the others. This relationship was something new in evolution, for learning to change the environment was something no animal had ever done before, beyond building a nest or preparing a small arena for courtship.

The changes in environment brought about by the early farmers were often fatal to the people who initiated them. Gary Rollefson and Ilse Köhler of San Diego State University have uncovered strong evidence that deforestation caused a collapse of early civilization in the Levant (present-day Israel, Jordan, and southern Syria, see Figure 18–3) around 6,000 years B.P. The area was rapidly depopulated at this time, and evidence suggests clearly that this depopulation was due not so much to a change in rainfall as to the extensive felling of woodland. Trees were

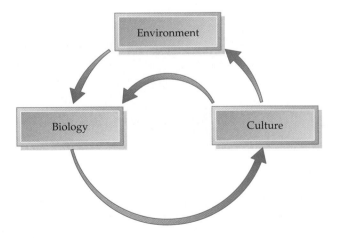

FIGURE 18–5   This feedback loop shows the increasing influence of culture on our biology: our heredity. The biological rate of change always lags behind the cultural rate of change.

used as fuel for, among other things, the production of lime plaster. As time passed, houses were built with smaller and smaller timbers, and the final destruction of the woodland habitat was completed by the herds of goats that ranged over the onetime forest lands and consumed the tender saplings. Then the steep hills eroded rapidly, the soils were lost, and the flourishing communities, which had developed throughout the area, disappeared.

This is just one very significant example of how humans have changed and, in doing so, destroyed their own productive environments. Such changes have occurred in many parts of the world since the coming of animal husbandry and agriculture brought our ancestors to the doors of civilization. The pattern has been repeated the world over but was especially devastating around the Mediterranean basin and in the Middle East, where the goat had been so widely domesticated. Humans may change their environment drastically—and as we can now see, such changes can turn out to be to their ultimate disadvantage. But this was humankind's unique achievement, and it constitutes a central theme in the last phases of human prehistory. Human work and human nature are indeed one. All are directly and systematically related to each other.

HUMAN VARIABILITY

Within this dynamic system unique to humankind, in which the human body and its environment are related through culture, all three components show considerable variability. In our physical variability, humankind is not alone in the animal or plant worlds. Variability in behavior and appearance is characteristic of all living organisms as their environment varies, and it is probably no greater in humans than in many other species. Every individual (except identical twins) carries different genetic material; differences due to age and sex also exist. Beyond this, we find variability that has evolved in response to local (and equally variable) environmental conditions. Humans' physical variations may be found both within and between populations, and in the past such physical differences were often used by anthropologists to construct racial classifications that subdivided humanity. We will argue in a later section that all such classifications have little meaning, and that race is not a useful biological concept when applied to humans. Nonetheless, there are many good reasons for studying human variation apart from race construction, including learning how trait variations correlate with differing environments and susceptibility to certain diseases. Therefore, before addressing the race issue, we will review some of the major physical variations of humankind. We will be concerned with traits of three main kinds: (1) anatomical features, such as skin color, hair form, and body shape; (2) physiological traits, such as metabolic rate and hormone activity, growth rate, color blindness, and genetic diseases; and (3) characteristics of the blood (biochemical traits).

Anatomical Traits

Perhaps the most easily noticed physical characteristic of humans is skin color. Depending on the amount of melanin in the epidermis, human skin varies from very light ("white") to very dark (dark brown or black). As shown in Figure 18–6, skin color is found to be very closely correlated with latitude when analyzed globally. People with dark skin colors are found nearest to the equator, and lighter populations inhabit higher northern and southern latitudes. As explained to some

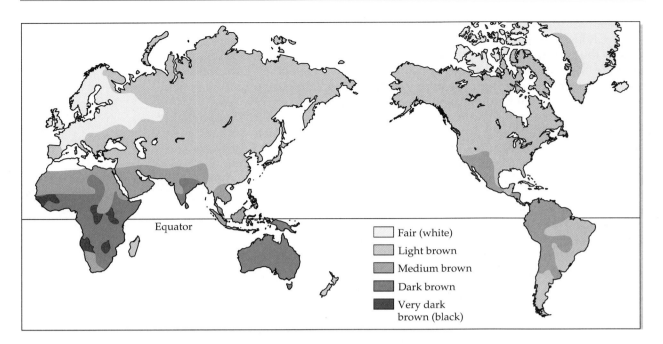

FIGURE 18–6   This global map shows the distribution of skin colors in indigenous populations. Note the clear correlation between skin color and latitude.

extent in Chapter 15, this distribution of skin tones seems to reflect a complex pattern of adaptation by our ancestral populations. In equatorial and subequatorial regions, people are subjected to intense ultraviolet (UV) radiation, and bombardment by UV rays can be extremely harmful. One relatively short-term effect is sunburn, which may result in an inability to sweat efficiently and thus to reduce body heat. Sunburn-induced impairment of sweating may even lead to hyperthermia and death during heavy exercise by light-skinned individuals with a heavy solar heat load. And of course, prolonged exposure to UV radiation may lead to skin cancer and its sometimes deadly consequences. Heavy epidermal concentrations of melanin help to protect tropical people against the ravages of UV radiation. Among equatorial and subequatorial populations, skin cancer rates are relatively low, and sweat glands are protected from UV-induced blockage. Thus there has been strong selection for dark skin colors in regions of intense and prolonged sunlight.

The sun-and-skin problem took on a different dimension in those human populations that migrated north and south away from the sunny regions. In the higher latitudes, sunburn damage and skin cancer became less significant threats, while an inability to produce enough vitamin D gained in importance. As explained in Chapter 15, human populations that inhabited higher latitudes must have experienced selection for lighter skin color (reduced pigmentation) in order to enhance vitamin D production. In contrast, in the tropics natural selection would have favored dark skin for the reasons given above and because, despite heavy pigmentation, the intense sunlight would have caused enough vitamin D to be produced. Skin color thus turns out to be a very clear example of evolutionary adaptation among modern people. It is a very striking trait, but very superficial, both literally and figuratively.

Another trait with clear adaptive consequences is body build. In 1847, Carl Bergmann, a German physiologist interested in the relationships among body mass, surface area, and heat production in warm-blooded animals, observed that populations occupying the coldest parts of a species' range tended to be bulkier, that is, more compact, than those living in the warmer parts ("Bergmann's rule"). In 1877, the American J. A. Allen added that animals with the largest bodies are found not in the coldest part of the range but somewhere in the center. He further stated that the protruding parts of the body, such as limbs, fingers, ears, and tails, tend to be relatively shorter in the cooler parts of the range than in its warmer regions ("Allen's rule"). In cool regions, these adaptations in body build decrease surface area in relation to weight, reducing heat loss. In warm regions, they increase surface area in relation to weight, thus increasing heat loss (Figure 18–7).

FIGURE 18–7 These individuals represent populations that demonstrate Bergmann's and Allen's rules. The African on the left, tall and slim, has long extremities and a high ratio of surface area to weight. The Eskimo on the right has short extremities and a low ratio of surface area to weight, which reduces heat loss. The photographs are of the same scale.

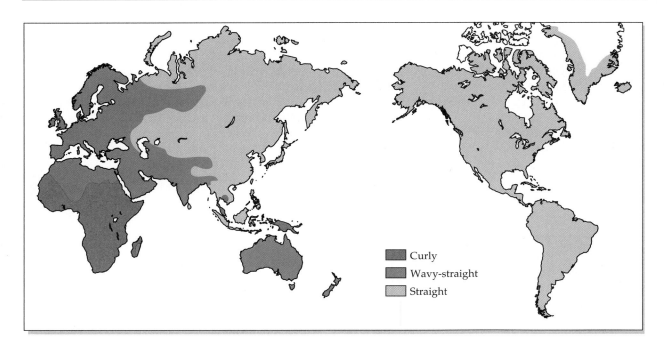

FIGURE 18–8 Hair form varies both within and between human populations. This map shows the distribution of "typical" hair form around the globe.

Epicanthic fold a fold of skin above the inner border of the eye; characteristic of Asiatic, some Native American, and Khoisan people.

Human populations follow these rules derived from animal studies, and it seems clear that populations known only from their fossilized remains did the same (see the description of the Nariokotome *Homo erectus* skeleton in Chapter 10).

Living humans also show variations in hair form, from tight curls to waves to straight hair. Although the adaptive significance, if any, of the various hair patterns has yet to be fully worked out, living populations around the world clearly differ in their typical hair form while also showing much intrapopulational variation (Figure 18–8). Similarly, no clear adaptive function has yet been proved for the fold of skin that occurs in the upper eyelid of some living people, the **epicanthic fold** (Figure 18–9). Epicanthic folds are common among Asian people, some Native Americans, and the Khoisan (Bushmen and Hottentot) people of South Africa (see also Figure 18–14). Research is continuing on the significance of these and other variable human traits. No doubt, in some cases, differences in selection and adaptation will be the correct explanation; for other traits, variation may be the result of more random processes, such as genetic drift.

One of the neatest demonstrations of environmental adaptation is that relating nose shape (expressed as the nasal index: breadth/height × 100) to the humidity of the air (expressed as vapor pressure). Moistening the air is a prime function of the nasal epithelium; the moisture content of the air must be brought up to 95 percent relative humidity at body temperature before the air enters the lungs; otherwise they will be damaged. It seems clear that people adapted to areas of dry air (deserts and high mountains) will tend to have narrow noses, while those adapted to moist

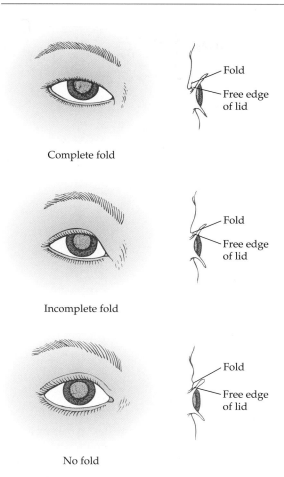

Complete fold

Fold

Free edge of lid

Incomplete fold

Fold

Free edge of lid

No fold

Fold

Free edge of lid

FIGURE 18–9 Asiatic peoples are distinguished by an extra fold of skin in the upper eyelid which covers all or part of its edge. This fold is also found among some Native Americans and among some of the Khoisan peoples of South Africa.

air will usually have broad noses. The correlation can be demonstrated statistically, and the explanation appears valid (see Figure 18–10).

The important thing to remember is that differences are slight. Anatomical traits vary continuously: noses vary from narrow to broad, hair varies by infinitesimal gradations from straight to tightly curled, and skin color varies from very light to black. Anthropologists have recognized as many as thirty-six gradations in this color spectrum. These features are determined by numerous genes and are not discretely segregated into just a few phenotypes.

Physiological Traits

Physiological traits that vary within and between human populations are probably less well known than the more obvious anatomical differences, but they are also significant and reflect adaptation. The basal metabolic rate, which is related to the level of body heat production, varies, as might be predicted, according to the mean annual temperature. Bone growth rate and maturation age also seem to vary, though both are also greatly influenced by nutrition. The age at which teeth appear and their order of eruption vary significantly. Third molars (wisdom teeth), which

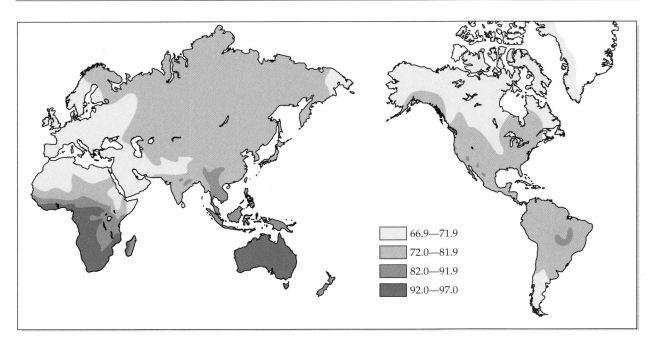

FIGURE 18–10   Nose form varies both within and between human populations. This map shows the distribution of "typical" nasal index (breadth/height × 100) values around the globe.

appear in Europeans between 17 and 20 years of age, appear in East Africans at age 13. Protein structure, keenness of taste, drug sensitivity, balance of urinary substances, color blindness, and sex hormone activity also show measurable differences. And, as we have seen, DNA carries recognizable differences. The better we become able to measure these sometimes trivial differences, the more of them we are likely to find.

Probably the most important physiological differences are those subtle genetic variations that give rise to disease. Because they are based on only one or two genes, these traits are discrete; that is, they are either present or absent. We discussed one of them—sickle-cell anemia—in Chapter 2. Some other genetic diseases are just as dangerous but are limited to small populations. In the Mediterranean region, there is favism, which is a genetically determined allergy to the broad bean and results in severe anemia; the same area also has familial Mediterranean fever, an obscure condition causing acute fever and much pain. Other hereditary disorders are much more widespread and occur more commonly in one population than another. One such disorder is phenylketonuria (PKU), an inability to develop an essential enzyme, which usually results in brain damage and mental retardation. PKU is most common in some areas of Europe. It is rare among persons of African or Asian descent.

A disease like sickle-cell anemia, but appearing mostly in the Mediterranean region and in parts of Asia rather than in Africa, is thalassemia. In the homozygous state (two Th_2 alleles), the resulting anemia is so serious that afflicted individuals rarely reach reproductive age. But homozygous individuals who completely lack the Th_2 allele may die early of serious malaria. It is in the heterozygous state that the trait is present but not serious and provides some protection from malaria. Thus the advantages and disadvantages of the gene in the population have remained in balance while malaria itself continues to thrive. Although most genetic diseases may simply be part of humans' genetic load, it is likely that some, like sickle-cell anemia and thalassemia, are part of such an adaptive equilibrium, termed balanced polymorphism (see Chapter 2).

Blood Groups

The third group of variable traits, the blood groups, have great medical significance. When the possibility of blood transfusions was first investigated during the nineteenth century, it quickly became clear that introducing one individual's blood into another's bloodstream could be fatal. Blood consists of a liquid component, the **blood plasma**, and three main types of cells: the **red blood cells**, which contain the red pigment hemoglobin and carry oxygen to all the parts of the body; the much larger **white blood cells**, or **leukocytes**, which defend against infection; and the smallest cells, the **platelets**, which maintain the circulatory system as a whole. (The liquid remaining after a clot has formed is called the **serum**.) The red cells have a protein coat whose molecules function as **antigens**; when introduced into another individual, antigens trigger the production of specific **antibodies**, other proteins that help protect the body against foreign substances. Microscopic examination of the blood of two people mixed together has shown that difficulties with transfusions come from the reactions between antigens and antibodies.

Safe transfusions now rest on biologist Karl Landsteiner's brilliant discovery in 1901 of the existence of different **blood groups**. Transfusions of the wrong kind of blood can cause the recipient's red blood cells to agglutinate, or clump together, and sometimes to burst. The **agglutination** can result in clots that block the blood's flow. Landsteiner discovered that the blood (actually the antigens) of one individual may trigger the production and agglutination of another individual's antibodies, causing clots. Landsteiner labeled with the letter O the blood of individuals which never agglutinated the blood of other persons, but which would in turn be agglutinated by some foreign blood cells. (Modern labels are given here for Landsteiner's groups.) Blood of yet other individuals that was agglutinated he labeled A. The blood that agglutinated A blood and could itself be agglutinated by A blood, he labeled type B. Thus he had three types: A, B, and O. Blood group A carries antigen A and develops anti-B antibodies. Blood group B contains antigen B and develops anti-A antibodies. Group O contains no antigens but develops both antibodies. Group AB (discovered later) carries antigens A and B but produces neither antibody. Thus type AB people can receive A, B, or O blood, but types A and B can receive only their own groups and type O, and type O people can receive only type O blood. Type O people, then, are universal donors, while type AB people are universal recipients. (The distribution of types A and O throughout the world is shown in Figure 18–11.)

Discovery of the ABO blood groups was followed by the discovery of many others (some of which are listed in Figure 18–12), the most important of which is the rhesus (Rh) system (1940). The rhesus system is responsible for an important disease that can kill newborn babies by destroying their blood cells. The cause of the disease is incompatibility between mother and child for the rhesus antigen D. If the mother is Rh-negative (lacks the D antigen) and the child is Rh-positive (possesses the D antigen), then the mother may form anti-D antibodies at the time of the child's birth, when some of the child's blood may enter the mother's bloodstream. In a second pregnancy, this antibody may pass through the placental barrier,

Blood plasma a clear liquid component of blood that carries the *red blood cells, white blood cells,* and *platelets.*

Red blood cells (corpuscles) vertebrate blood cells lacking nuclei and containing *hemoglobin.*

White blood cells (leukocytes) vertebrate blood cells lacking *hemoglobin.*

Platelets minute blood cells associated with clotting.

Serum the liquid remaining after blood has clotted.

Antigens any organic substances, recognized by the body as foreign, that stimulate the production of an *antibody.*

Antibody a protein produced as a defense mechanism to attack a foreign substance invading the body.

Blood groups groups of individuals whose blood can be mixed without agglutination (e.g., Groups A, B, O, or AB).

Agglutination the clumping of *red blood cells* as a result of the reaction of *antibodies* to an *antigen.*

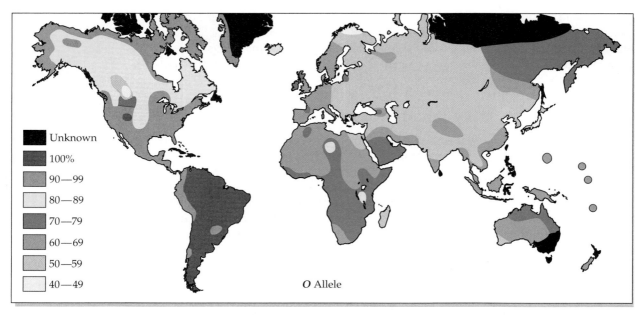

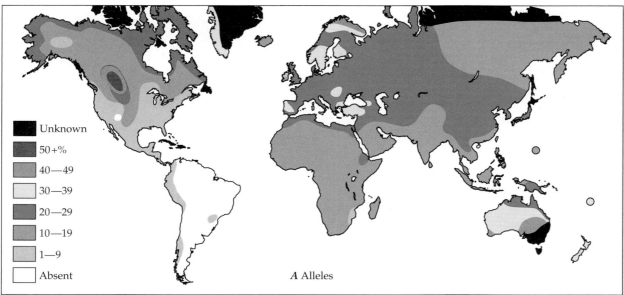

FIGURE 18–11   These maps give some idea of the distribution and frequency of the commonest ABO blood group alleles, *O* and the two *A* alleles (A_1 and A_2, combined for the lower map). This is an example of the kind of genetic data now available for human populations. The upper map charts the distribution of the predominant group O allele, which is common in the New World and especially in South America. The lower map plots the group A alleles, which are reasonably common in the Old World, but rare in many parts of the New World and virtually absent from South America. Remarkable concentrations of the group A alleles are found among the Scandinavian Lapps and the Blackfoot Indians of Western Canada. The latter is possibly the result of a local smallpox epidemic, introduced perhaps by Europeans, in which the alleles were favored.

coating and destroying the red blood cells of the child if it has Rh-positive blood. This second child will have acute anemia at birth (there is no problem if the second child has Rh-negative blood). The anemia can be treated only with extensive blood

Blood group system	Allele	World range	Europeans	Non-Khoisan	Africans Khoisan	Asians	Native Americans	Australians and Oceanics
ABO	A_1	0–45	5–40	8–30	0–15	0–45	0–20	8–38
	A_2	0–37	1–37	1–8	0–5	0–5	0	0
	B	0–33	4–18	10–20	2	16–25	0–4	0–13
	O	39–100	46–75	52–70	75–78	39–68	68–100	51–79
Rhesus	cde–	0–46	25–46	4–29	0	0–5	0	0
	cDe+	0–95	1–5	34–82	84–89	0–4	0–7	1–9
	CDe+	0–95	39–55	0–21	9–14	60–76	32–68	68–95
	cDE+	0–61	6–17	0–19	2	19–31	23–61	2–20
MNS	N	8–78	33–51	39–53	41	37–45	9–35	73–97
	NS	5–74	25–65	22–59	41	38	5–22	69–74
P	P	4–84	41–64	50–84	?	17	15–79	12–67
Lewis	Lewis	0–67	34–50	41	?	39	0–34	0–67
Duffy	Duffy	0-100	37–82	0–6	8	90–100	22–99	100
Diego	Diego	0–34	0	0	0	0–5	0–34	0
Gamma globulin	Gm	23–100	23–37	100	100	100	100	100
Haptoglobin	Hp^1	9–87	9–44	40–87	29	23–28	32–73	46–63

FIGURE 18–12   The frequencies of some blood group alleles present in different populations show the extent of variation in these genetic characters. Three different alleles for the rhesus-positive condition are listed (cDe, CDe, cDE). Alleles of the blood serum components gamma globulin and haptoglobin are also listed.

transfusions, but the disease can now be prevented by giving the mother an injection of powerful anti-D antibody after the birth of the first Rh-positive child. The injection destroys any Rh-positive red cells from the infant remaining in the mother's bloodstream and so inhibits future anti-D antibody production.

The alleles that determine blood types vary widely both within and between populations. Some data on the occurrence of these alleles are given in Figure 18–12. Note how many of the alleles show extensive intrapopulational variation and also overlap between populations.

Genes and Disease

The study of blood groups, an important medical advance, led to an understanding of their role as adaptations to disease antigens. The carrier of blood allele B has some protection against infantile diarrhea, alleles A_1 and B protect against plague, and allele O against bronchial pneumonia. (A_1 and A_2 both fall within blood type A.) Those with rhesus gene D and MNS gene N (see Figure 18–12) are particularly susceptible to smallpox. Type A individuals also seem most liable to stomach cancer and pernicious anemia, while gastric and duodenal ulcers tend to affect persons who are homozygous for allele O. Thus the frequency of genetic diseases and blood group genes may result from selection by the infectious diseases to which different populations have been exposed.

Research into the relationship of disease and human genetics is still in an early stage but is progressing rapidly. One particular medical and genetic problem is presented by people who carry a genetic condition such as sickle-cell anemia in places where malaria is no longer present. Without the malaria to maintain the balance of the polymorphism, the sickle-cell gene should be reduced in the gene pool as a result of natural selection against both homozygotes and heterozygotes. But as long as the sickle-cell allele exists, physicians have little help for those who carry the gene and suffer anemia. A second medical and genetic problem concerns the possibility of a connection between resistance to HIV (the AIDS virus) in some modern human populations and their ancestors' exposure to the bubonic or Black Plague back in the fourteenth century. Roughly 10 percent of people of European descent, and particularly those people from the more northerly parts of the continent, carry a gene that protects them against the AIDS virus. Although common in Europe, the HIV resistance gene becomes scarce around the Mediterranean, and it is absent in modern Africans, Asians, and Native Americans—a distribution that matches the geographic occurrence of the Black Death. Researchers are busy testing the hypothesis that a mutant gene appeared in Europe a few hundred years ago, became a stable part of the regional gene pool because it provided carriers with protection against the Black Plague, and by a stroke of luck also provides their modern descendants with protection against HIV. If future experiments verify the connection between Black Plague survival and HIV resistance, it will provide yet another example of how epidemic diseases can affect the course of human evolution.

THE QUESTION OF RACE

Biological Races

The preceding sections have documented what is widely known: humans, both within their local populations and around the world, vary anatomically and physiologically. In this variation, humans resemble most animal species occupying diverse geographical areas with diverse climates. Such species typically show variation in size and appearance, that is, in superficial (surface) characteristics that respond rapidly to environmental differences. These variations are often described by zoologists as demarcating **races** if they are of a minor nature, or subspecies if they are more striking. In the course of human evolution, populations of our species have adapted to just about every ecological zone on the surface of the earth, excluding Antarctica, and have evolved morphological and physiological adaptations to the temperature, solar radiation, humidity, vegetation, etc., of each zone. The degree of visible difference to be found among members of *Homo sapiens* is striking when we compare, say, Eskimos with sub-Saharan Africans (see Figure 18–7). A zoologist from outer space might well conclude that humans consist of a number of geographic subspecies.

Races divisions of a *species*, usually based on physical or behavioral differences and less well marked than subspecies. Many anthropologists reject the concept of biological races of living humans.

The problem of documenting and classifying human variation fell not to zoologists from Mars, however, but to *Homo sapiens* naturalists (and later, anthropologists) here on earth, and it seems fair to say that the whole process has been a struggle from beginning to end. For more than 200 years, patterns of physical variation have been used by anthropologists (and also by nonspecialists, in the form of "folk concepts") to classify people into races. Typically, races have been viewed as divisions of *Homo sapiens* with the following two main attributes:

1. **Distinctive sets of physical traits**. Although virtually all racial classifications rest mainly on differences in skin color, other characteristics—nose, lip, and eye shapes, hair color and texture, facial shapes, etc.—are typically presented as closely correlated with skin color variations.

2. **Distinctive geographic distributions**. Varying from relatively small areas to entire continents, racial distributions are generally described as they were in the days before sea voyages began to have a major influence on the spread of human populations, that is, before about 1500 A.D. Since then, human populations have extended their ranges and overlapped, and gene flow (which was never fully blocked except for a few unusual cases of prolonged isolation on islands) has increased.

To these physical and spatial attributes, a temporal dimension can be added. Over the centuries, human races have been described or understood to be the products of:

3. **Separate, and probably lengthy, histories of existence**. Early classifiers such as Linnaeus and the German physician, Johann Friedrich Blumenbach (1752–1840), believed that racial differences were established by God during the creation of humans. Modern people more often view races as having long histories of separate evolutionary development.

A typical traditional classification scheme that hypothesizes the existence of nine geographical races prior to the mixing of the past 500 years is shown in Figure 18–13.

The traditional view of human races—as units that are strongly distinctive (and thus easily identified), monolithic (showing only insignificant internal variability in traits), geographically separated, and having lengthy histories—held

FIGURE 18–13   A polar-projection map showing the nine geographic races of humans envisioned by anthropologist Stanley Garn in 1965. (From S. M. Garn, *Human Races*, 2nd edition, 1965. Courtesy of Charles C. Thomas, Publisher, Ltd., Springfield, Illinois.)

sway for more than 200 years. Recently, however, it has begun to break down, at least among anthropologists, as information on human variation (particularly genetic variation) has accumulated and analytical procedures have improved. Over the past few decades, many anthropologists have grown disenchanted with racial classifications and become convinced that race is neither a useful nor a valid biological concept among humans. Admittedly, the discipline is divided on the question. Cultural anthropologists appear to be strongly in favor of abandoning race partitioning. Many physical anthropologists agree, and studies have shown that by the late 1970s most physical anthropology textbooks argued that human races do not exist in a biological sense. Interestingly, one type of physical anthropologists, namely **forensic anthropologists**, continue overwhelmingly to accept the biological race concept. As articulated recently by George Gill of the University of Wyoming, these workers believe that human races not only exist, but that they can be distinguished osteologically with good accuracy (more on this below).

The arguments against the continued application of the biological race concept among humans rest on accumulating evidence that such units are neither easily identified nor monolithic, and actually account for only a small part of our species' overall genetic diversity. Beginning with the problem of identifying races, it is telling that anthropologists have never been able to agree how human races should be defined and delimited. Some workers have relied on a variety of presumably diagnostic genetic or physical differences, while others have argued that the most important measure is reproductive separation. (This involves the interpretation of races as breeding populations, albeit with the potential for interracial reproduction under the right circumstances. Note that this criterion has become increasingly difficult to apply as populations have spread and mixed since 1500 A.D.) In addition to disagreement about which diagnostic tools to apply, there has been confusion about the appropriate level for racial subdivisions. (Should local populations be recognized as microraces, or should only large, geographic races be named?) Collectively, these problems have led to a bewildering array of racial classifications. Harvard's Earnest Hooton, writing in 1946, recognized three primary (large, geographic) races and twenty-one "subraces" or "composite" races. Four years later, Carlton Coon and his colleagues listed six primary races. And in 1965 Stanley Garn identified nine primary races and thirty-two "local" races! This sort of disagreement among competent scientists suggests to many current anthropologists that there is no finite set of human races out there just waiting to be recognized and named. Rather, the varying results suggest that judgements about the identity, size, and diagnostic traits of human races are arbitrary and vary from one researcher to the next.

It follows from the above discussion that most present-day anthropologists have ceased to search for key "marker" traits that will yield a true or "natural" racial subdivision of humans. Although many people have tried (a few are still trying) to base racial classifications on easily observed marker traits, to date all such attempts have proved unsatisfactory because of intrapopulation variation and interpopulation gradation of markers, and because potential marker traits are only loosely correlated with humans' other physical and genetic characteristics. Consider a familiar example. Throughout human history, skin color has undoubtedly been the most commonly used marker trait for racial distinctions. Four skin-color races—black-, white-, yellow-, and red-skinned people—have been listed by many classifiers, with each race being presented (though with little proof) as possessing much internal consistency in its own characteristics while differing extensively from the other three. The fallacy of this view, however, is shown by an

Forensic anthropologists physical anthropologists who apply their expertise to matters of law, e.g., the identification of human remains.

| | | |
| West Africa | Central Africa | South Africa |

Skin: Dark brown/black
Hair: Black, curly
Eyes: Dark brown/black
(no eye fold)
Prognathism: Moderate
Nose: Short, wide
Lips: Thick
Head: CI ≤ 75

Skin: Medium brown
Hair: Black, curly
Eyes: Dark brown/black
(no eye fold)
Prognathism: Little
Nose: Short, wide
Lips: Thin
Head: CI ≥ 80

Skin: Yellowish brown
Hair: Black, tight curly
Eyes: Dark black brown/black
(epicanthic fold present)
Prognathism: Little
Nose: Short, wide
Lips: Thin
Head: CI < 78

FIGURE 18–14   Variation in people traditionally classified as "black." CI = cephalic index (skull breadth/skull length x 100). The CI values are for populations; the other traits are for the individual shown.

examination of Figure 18–6 and comparisons with Figures 18–8, 18–10, and 18–11. Figure 18–6 shows, for example, that "black" people are native to many parts of the Old World (Africa, South Asia, Australia, and the Pacific Islands) rather than to a single geographic homeland, that their dark skin colors show extensive variation (black, dark brown, medium brown), and that their skin shades grade imperceptibly into light brown and thence into white populations. (Note especially the grading of medium-brown Africans into light brown people living around the Mediterranean.) Furthermore, because there is little regular covariance of either genetic or physical traits among humans, dark-skinned people around the world show a wide variety of nose forms, hair forms, and blood types (see also Figure 18–14). Black people, therefore, show extensive variation in their overall set of traits rather than racial consistency (remember that trait uniformity—a monolithic black race—was expected under the old view), and their features grade into those of nonblack populations. The same results can be demonstrated for each of the other skin-color groupings (see Figure 18–15 for trait variation among "whites") and collectively this evidence presents a strong challenge to the old notion of historically distinct, monolithic, and diagnostically different human races. (Forensic anthropologists' reports of diagnostic interracial bony differences are answered by critics who point out that osteological discriminations between people belonging to or descended from different geographic populations do not prove the reality of a limited number of "basic kinds" [that is, races] of humans. As noted below in the discussion of worldwide genetic variation, no one claims that interpopulation differences are zero, only that they are swamped by intrapopulation diversity.)

Middle East	Northern Japan (Ainu)	Europe
Skin: Medium light	Skin: Medium light	Skin: Light
Hair: Dark Brown/black, wavy/straight	Hair: Dark Brown/black, wavy/straight	Hair: Brown/red, wavy/straight
Eyes: Brown (no fold)	Eyes: Brown (fold present)	Eyes: (no fold)
Prognathism: Moderate	Prognathism: Little	Prognathism: Little
Nose: Long, narrow	Nose: Short, wide	Nose: Short, narrow
Lips: Thin/moderately thick	Lips: Moderately thick	Lips: Thin
Head: CI > 80	Head: Mean CI = 77	Head: Mean CI = 76

FIGURE 18–15   Variation in people traditionally classified as "white." CI = cephalic index (skull breadth/skull length x 100). The CI values are for populations; the other traits are for the individual shown.

But, one might argue, if we abandon the traditional strategy of using *single* marker traits and analyze many different characteristics simultaneously—a feat that is easily done today with the aid of computers—surely then we will be able to divide humans into biologically meaningful and consistent groups. In fact, even such multivariate approaches to subdividing humanity have failed to work because there is so little concordance of occurrence (repeated and similar clustering) of humans' genetic and physical features. Figure 18–16 shows the results of a

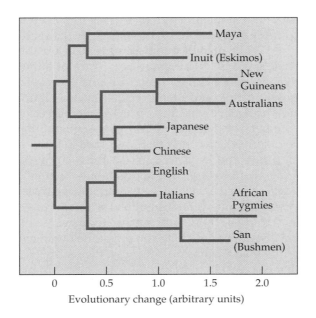

Evolutionary change (arbitrary units)

FIGURE 18–16   This figure shows the linkages calculated between living human populations based on an analysis of fifty-eight different blood group genes. Note the association of Europeans with Africans and Australians with Asians.

multivariate analysis of the occurrence of fifty-eight different human blood group genes. Looking just at the first fork of the linkage tree, the study seems to split humans into two major groups of similar (and, therefore, probably related) populations: Asians, Native Americans, Australians, and New Guineans on one side; Africans and Europeans on the other. In strong contrast to skin-color divisions, this analysis links some black people (New Guineans) with Asians and Native Americans, and black Africans with Europeans!

To make matters even more confusing, a second multivariate analysis—this time using fifty-seven measurements taken on males' skulls—appears to split humans into three biologically linked groups: Europeans by themselves; Polynesians combined with Native Americans and East Asians; and Australo-Melanesians and Africans (see Figure 18–17). This arrangement is distinctly different from the blood gene study, particularly in the substitution of Australo-Melanesians for Europeans as the populations most closely related to Africans. Furthermore, when the skull analysis was repeated using measurements taken on females of the various groups, the linkages changed significantly once again: now Australo-Melanesians were separated from Africans and linked with Polynesians! The fact that different population grouping patterns result from the various multivariate studies, and that simply changing the subjects' sex can alter the linkage trees, has not generated much confidence among anthropologists in the multivariate approach to identifying human races.

The subject of multivariate analyses brings us to a second major reason why most anthropologists now reject race as a valid biological concept among humans. Ironically, while these studies have failed to identify human races, they have succeeded brilliantly in the other direction: that is, multivariate investigations, particularly of genes, have provided seemingly unequivocal proof that human races do

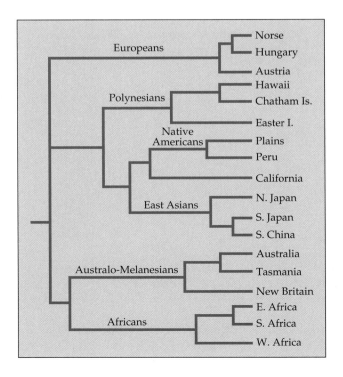

FIGURE 18–17 Here linkages are shown between living human populations based on an analysis of fifty-seven measurements of male skulls. Note the separation of Europeans from Africans and the link between the latter and Australo-Melanesians.

not exist in any biologically meaningful sense. Some of the relevant evidence was discussed above, and additional important material appeared in 1974 when Harvard biologist R. C. Lewontin published the results of a study of genetic diversity within and between several traditionally defined human races (Africans, Native Americans, Mongoloids, Caucasians, South Asian Aborigines, Australian Aborigines, and Oceanians). Lewontin's results, shown in Figure 18–18, revealed that just over 85 percent of human genetic diversity, based on genes for physiological character traits, occurs between individuals belonging to the same population (generally, the same nation or tribe). An additional 8.3 percent of genetic variation is accounted for by differences between populations within the same traditional race (for example, between West Africans and Bantus). This leaves only 6.3 percent of genetic diversity accounted for by interracial differences! Thus, even if one is inclined to believe in the existence of biological races among humans, these data argue strongly that such entities make only a trivial contribution to genetic (and phenotypic) variation among humans. As one non-African geneticist is reported to have said, "There could possibly be more genetic differences between myself and my wife [a member of the same skin-color group] than there are between me and a Kalahari Bushman."

What conclusion, then, do most modern anthropologists reach concerning the question of biological races among living humans? Are we asked to deny the proof of our own eyes that people vary physically, sometimes remarkably so? No, of course not. Nonetheless, the majority of anthropologists—though by no means all—conclude that the human species cannot be broken down scientifically into monolithic races defined by regularly co-occurring trait clusters. To be sure, striking

Gene	Total $H_{species}$	PROPORTION		
		Within populations	Within races between populations	Between races
Hp	.994	.893	.051	.056
Ag	.994	.834	—	—
Lp	.639	.939	—	—
Xm	.869	.997	—	—
Ap	.989	.927	.062	.011
6PGD	.327	.875	.058	.067
PGM	.758	.942	.033	.025
Ak	.184	.848	.021	.131
Kidd	.977	.741	.211	.048
Duffy	.938	.636	.105	.259
Lewis	.994	.966	.032	.002
Kell	.189	.901	.073	.026
Lutheran	.153	.694	.214	.092
P	1.000	.949	.029	.022
MNS	1.746	.911	.041	.048
Rh	1.900	.674	.073	.253
ABO	1.241	.907	.063	.030
Mean		.854	.083	.063

FIGURE 18–18   Analyses such as this one indicate that the vast majority of genetic diversity in humans exists *within* so-called races and not *between* them.

physical differences can be seen all around us—in skin color, facial features, hair form, etc.—and they often give us clues to the place and population of a person's ancestry. Nonetheless, when we look beyond our superficial differences to the genes that code for our traits, we are confronted by overwhelming genetic similarities. The research results are clear: most human genetic diversity (in Lewontin's study, well over 90 percent) occurs *within* the traditional skin-color/geographic groupings, not *between* them. Stanford University geneticist Luca Cavalli-Sforza made the same point when he said, "It is because they are external that [so-called] racial differences strike us so forcibly, and we automatically assume that differences of similar magnitude exist below the surface, in the rest of our genetic makeup. This is simply not so: the remainder of our genetic makeup hardly differs at all." Anthropologist Jonathan Marks of Yale University delivers the message even more forcefully: "You may group humans into a small number of races if you want to, but you are denied biology as a support for it." It seems that in order to understand modern human variation, we must study individual traits, their genetic bases, and their evolutionary histories—not arbitrarily constructed biological races.

Ethnic and Other Social Groups

It would be a wonderful world indeed if anthropologists' repudiation of biological races could put an end to divisions between human populations and bring on an age of global unity. Such a world remains a Utopian dream, however, because race *as a social construct* is alive and well in most modern cultures. This is undoubtedly linked to humans' tendency to focus on all sorts of differences between people and to divide the world into "we-they" groups. Grouping schemes based on real or imagined differences in behavior, customs, or genealogy (descent) result in the identification of **ethnic groups**. This term, which is much less emotionally charged than "race," is now commonly applied both to huge collections of people (for example, Asian-Americans) as well as small populations (for example, Lakota Sioux). Breaking free of our old fixation on physical differences is difficult, however, and people commonly take phenotype into consideration as they (consciously or unconsciously) make ethnic group distinctions.

Ethnic group a group of people perceived as sharing a common and distinctive culture.

Ethnic divisions can serve good and valid purposes. They may foster unity and pride within minority communities, may serve as the focal point for political solidarity, or may facilitate the preservation of a population's cultural heritage. On the other hand, when either the biological race concept or ethnic divisions are combined with another human tendency, our inclination to **xenophobia**, all too often the result is discrimination or **racism**, defined here as the belief that human groups can be ranked as superior or inferior to one another and their members treated accordingly. Racism is responsible for a multitude of evils ranging from job discrimination to genocide (or to use a recently created euphemism, *ethnic cleansing*).

Xenophobia hatred of foreigners.

Racism the assumption of inherent superiority of certain "races", and the consequent discrimination against others.

Perhaps the most strongly held folk belief—and certainly one of the most divisive—is the notion that all other ethnic or racial groups are less intelligent than one's own. In fact, *there is simply no good evidence to support this belief*. Intelligence is such a broad concept that it is impossible to define and measure precisely. So-called **IQ tests** actually tell us little about intellectual differences between individuals even within the same culture because a multitude of factors can influence test scores (for example, genotype, educational history, and family background—particularly parents' socioeconomic status). Furthermore, since none of the IQ tests is culture-free (all operate through linguistic and other cultural modes not shared by

IQ tests tests that supposedly measure an individual's "intelligence quotient." Many consider such tests flawed and of little value, particularly for cross-cultural comparisons.

Box 18-1

CURRENT ISSUE: *Xenophobia, an Outmoded Adaptation*

Why, in the face of overwhelming evidence of humans' biological unity, do we still find superficial physical differences (for example, in skin, hair, and facial features) so striking? And furthermore, why do we so easily develop attitudes of distrust and dislike toward people we classify—based on those same superficial traits—as different from ourselves? Partial answers to these questions can be derived from knowledge of humans' sensory systems and certain of our evolved, but now outmoded, behavioral tendencies. First of all, we are overwhelmingly visual animals. Following in the ancient anthropoid pattern, hominids have always relied for survival mainly on the evidence of their eyes, and consequently, modern humans are masters at noticing visual details. Among the most important visual details, of course, were the physical features of conspecifics. Here our ancestors obtained important information about groupmates' probable kin relations, age, health, and reproductive condition that helped them make decisions about altruistic investments, mate selection, and alliances. Of course, visual clues would also have allowed the identification of strangers (members of other groups or tribes, territorial invaders), a dis-

tinction that—judging from observations of monkeys and apes—often would have triggered a hostile reaction. In humans' prehistoric past, when strangers may have spelled trouble more often than they do today, such xenophobia could have been an adaptive first emotion. In our modern cultures, however, where we are constantly encountering physically and ethnically diverse people, xenophobia has become outmoded and undesirable. No longer the correct first emotion for survival, it has become maladaptive.

Thus the explanation of our modern condition, but how can we change it? (We assume everyone agrees that reducing xenophobia and racism is a worthwhile goal.) Although distrust and dislike of strangers may be an evolved human tendency, this does not make it wise, morally right, or inevitable. Happily, because our behaviors are much more strongly shaped by learning than by genes, it should be possible to remove the basis of xenophobia through determined education by parents, peers, and society. With a strong effort, we should be able to move out of the xenophobic dark ages and into a modern world that accepts and values diversity. ■

all people), none can be used cross-culturally. Unfortunately, anthropology has played a historical role in perpetuating the myth of biological races while psychology has helped in perpetuating the myth of interracial differences in intelligence. It is hoped that by demonstrating that human races are basically the products of our imagination, modern anthropologists can begin to dismantle both myths. In the meantime, although it should go without saying, anthropological studies provide absolutely no justification for any sort of racist attitude or behavior (see also Box 18–1).

CHALLENGES FOR THE FUTURE

Population and Evolutionary Success

The hominid story began some 5 to 7 million years ago in Africa. From rather humble beginnings, our species has evolved to become the dominant force on the planet. Physically and culturally diverse, humans are spread throughout all regions of the globe. Yes, we are a grand evolutionary success, and yet, ironically, our very success may contribute to our undoing. Consider the issue of human population size. Edward S. Deevey estimates that the hominid population of the earth 2 million years ago was little more than 100,000 individuals. By 300,000 years ago, at or near the end of *Homo erectus*'s tenancy, the human population had climbed to 1 million, and by 25,000 years ago, during the Upper Paleolithic, it had jumped to perhaps more than 3 million. (Note that there may have been significant bottlenecks within the broad trend of population growth. As discussed in Chapter 16, modern humans—*Homo sapiens*—may have numbered between 5,000 and 10,000 shortly after their evolutionary origin.) The world population has risen at an increasingly steep pace since the Upper Paleolithic (Figure 18–19). Deevey brings home the extraordinarily rapid mushrooming of today's human population when he shows that about 3 percent of all humans who have ever lived are alive today.

The population, according to Deevey, has not risen in a steady curve. Rather, the increase in the world's population has had a series of surges, reflecting the great cultural innovations associated with hominid evolution. The first cultural innovation, of course, was the development of stone tools. This advance allowed a population increase in two ways: stone tools enabled hominids to venture out into a vast number of environments that people without such tools could not have survived in; it also made populations more efficient, enabling them to exploit those various environments more intensively. The population density of Africa 2 million years ago, in the days of the crude Oldowan industry, has been estimated at only one individual per 100 square miles (260 square kilometers). By the end of the Paleolithic, humans had spread around the world, and their density had probably risen tenfold.

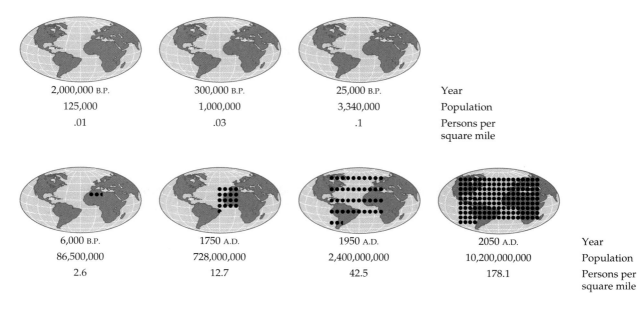

2,000,000 B.P.	300,000 B.P.	25,000 B.P.	Year
125,000	1,000,000	3,340,000	Population
.01	.03	.1	Persons per square mile

6,000 B.P.	1750 A.D.	1950 A.D.	2050 A.D.	Year
86,500,000	728,000,000	2,400,000,000	10,200,000,000	Population
2.6	12.7	42.5	178.1	Persons per square mile

FIGURE 18–19   Until about 25,000 years B.P. humankind was a stable part of the equilibrium existing among animals and plants. With better hunting technology, animal domestication, and agriculture, humans began to increase dramatically and to destroy the wilderness of which they had been a part. The figures given for the populations of the past are, of course, estimates. That for 2050 A.D. is a projection that might be reduced by an effective, worldwide population-control policy or by extensive famines.

The second innovation was the double discovery of how to grow crops and how to domesticate animals. This event came about 10,000 years ago. This second innovation enabled people to settle permanently for the first time, and for the first time to live together in large numbers. Even nomads herding animals could exist in far greater concentrations on a given area of land than could hunters. The effect on world population was extraordinary. In 4,000 years, it jumped from an estimated 5 million to 86 million.

The third innovation was the industrial age. It had its beginnings about 300 years ago, when the human population of the world was in the neighborhood of 550 million. World population has been ballooning ever since and today is 6 billion. If it continues at its present rate of increase, it will double within 50 years.

Although these figures are impressive, even more impressive is the *acceleration* in population growth. It took 2 million years to get through the first phase; the second took only 10,000 years; and the third has been going on for only a few hundred. How long it will continue or what the human population of the earth will ultimately be is anybody's guess. But we can be sure that, because the surface of the earth is finite, as are its resources, present rates of increase will bring us to the limit very soon.

Limits to Growth

It seems clear that the increase in our population is due primarily to making greater and greater use of the available resources. When a forest is cleared and crops are grown in its place, all the sunlight in that area is contributing to synthesis of food for humans. When wild animals grazing in meadows and savanna grasslands are killed and replaced by cattle, sheep, and goats, conversion of plant energy into animal protein is turned fully to human benefit. In these cases we can see that the ultimate limitation is the amount of energy that can be delivered by the sun to the earth's surface and turned into carbohydrates by photosynthesis in green plants. Every green plant needs a place in the sun. Other limiting factors are the other requirements of plants: water, minerals, and appropriate soil. Lack of water in particular has long been a problem for farmers, though they have occasionally overcome it with irrigation. But even with advanced technology, we cannot obtain food from all the earth; the ultimate limits are firm both on land and in the oceans. Eventually, as Thomas Malthus predicted in 1798, these limits will indeed halt human population growth, if we do not bring about stabilization voluntarily.

But the continuing expansion of agriculture and animal husbandry cannot be taken to the ultimate limits set by the area of the earth's landmasses without destroying all the natural wilderness and the miraculous array of wild plants and animals that occupy it. As discussed in Chapter 3, the continued destruction of the tropical forests poses a serious and immediate threat of extinction for many nonhuman primate species and the indigenous humans. The further expansion of agribusiness, or even peasant agriculture, will be destructive to the quality of life we value, and ecologists have made it clear that the continuing loss of forest in particular has very dangerous and irreversible results. We now know that much of the earth's land surface is, in fact, not well suited to agriculture but is best left in its natural state.

In some parts of the world, famine is already becoming a normal condition, and malnutrition is found on many continents. People are dying of hunger by the tens of thousands, partly because the increase in population is due not merely to

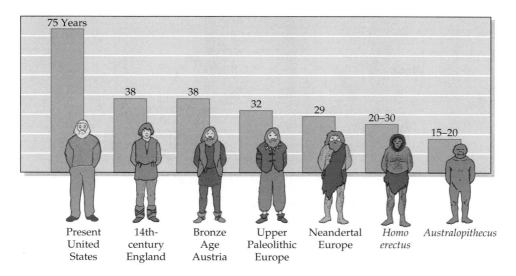

FIGURE 18–20   Since the Upper Paleolithic, life expectancies have doubled in countries with modern medicine and technology. We probably live three to four times as long as *Australopithecus* did. The increased life span has made possible a rapid increase in cultural complexity, skill, and knowledge.

increased resources but also to advances in medicine. These have brought about an increased **life expectancy**. *Australopithecus* may have had an average life expectancy of 15 to 20 years; *Homo erectus* lived for 20 to 30 years; today, a citizen of the United States can expect to live more than 70 years (females 79 and males 72.3 years) (Figure 18–20). A doubling of life expectancy has brought a doubling of population without a corresponding increase in our efficiency in using resources. Thus in many countries people live longer, but not enough food is grown to feed them all.

Large segments of human society have certainly come a long way: in life span, in efficiency in extracting resources, in population density, in technological complexity, and in increased physical comfort. Whether we are really better off as a species, and whether our progress will continue, remains to be seen. For a species like ours, whose survival depends on culture (which is based on knowledge), it is essential to use all available knowledge and understanding to achieve better adaptation to a changing environment. This is perhaps our most difficult problem: each new cultural adaptation we make alters the environment to which we are adapting. New adaptations increase population; greater population densities require further adaptations; new adaptations deplete world resources; resource depletion requires further adaptation. And so it goes on. We find ourselves in a vicious circle of ever-increasing instability (Figure 18–21). Essential now is an all-out attempt to break that accelerating positive feedback loop and bring about new stability in global population size, in technological investment, and in resource consumption.

Population size is certainly a measure of evolutionary success, but another measure that may be more significant is evolutionary longevity. *Homo sapiens*'s 130,000 years is nothing in universal and geologic time, and millions of species have evolved and become extinct in earth history. Compared with most mammals, we are infants of evolution. From this point of view, our apparent present

Life expectancy the average age at death of individuals born into a particular population.

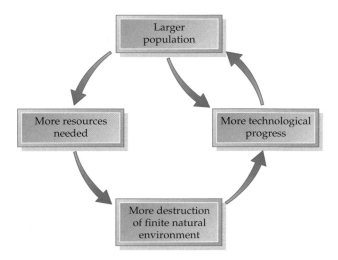

FIGURE 18–21   This positive feedback loop is the most dangerous to us, since it is accelerating very rapidly and involves environmental destruction. With the resource base of our livelihood seriously depleted, the survival of even our present number is threatened.

success can continue only if we can achieve some sort of stability in our relationship with the earth's resources. Otherwise we shall surely perish as a species.

Gaining Control over Our Evolution

The scale of global overpopulation is so great and the solutions so seemingly elusive that most of us have a hard time even imagining, much less dealing with, the problem. Other challenges of the twenty-first century will be much more immediate and personal. For example, with each passing year humans gain more and more control over their health, reproduction, and evolutionary future. With more control, however, will come increasingly difficult choices.

The evolutionary processes described by Charles Darwin and later biologists will, of course, continue to operate in the future. Mutations and new gene combinations will continue to provide the raw material for natural selection. According to British geneticist Steve Jones, the mutation rate due to external agents will probably remain stable in the near future. Mutations due to delayed reproduction, however, may be expected to rise. This rise will be related to the fact that modern people are having children later than has been true during most of human evolution. Jones estimates that today's mean age at first reproduction is about five years later than it was 10,000 years ago (before the agricultural revolution). Because cells (including those that produce sperm and eggs) become increasingly mutation-prone as they age, we can expect an increased number of newborns carrying mutant alleles.

This predicted rise in the mutation rate will coincide with the medical and scientific communities' increased ability to deal with genetic problems. As discussed in Chapter 2 and elsewhere, by using procedures such as amniocentesis, we can already learn not only the sex but also a great deal about the genotype of a developing fetus—information that parents may use to terminate a pregnancy for one reason or another. In the future, prospective parents will be able to learn even more about their unborn children, including genetic predispositions for numerous diseases, and the presence or absence of genes for desired phenotypic traits. How will this information be used? Will we limit ourselves to curing (through such procedures as gene therapy) or preventing diseases? Or will our desire for perfect children result in increased abortions and genetic engineering for cosmetic effects? And looking beyond parents and offspring, how will society use additional genetic information? Science writer Joseph Levine and geneticist David Suzuki have written about how such information might be abused. Here is a chilling real-life case:

> In the early 1970s . . . compulsory screening for sickle-cell trait [i.e., for persons carrying a copy of the gene for sickle-cell anemia] was instituted in at least twelve states. Screening was usually restricted to African-Americans (although 7 percent of subjects with sickle-cell trait were not black), and it was often conducted without informed consent. Inadequate regard for confidentiality, coupled with a preexisting history of racial prejudice, led to denial of insurance coverage and loss of employment for black people, including those who were simply carriers of the sickle-cell trait and showed no symptoms of the disease.

With our already sophisticated medical knowledge, humans have taken several steps down the path of artificial selection within our own species. Increased knowledge of human genetics and improved ability to manipulate the genotype will take us even farther down that path. Many people are very concerned about these developments, and the issue will become even more pressing in the twenty-first century. Natural selection, genetic drift, mutation, and other natural processes got us where we are today. Are we wise enough to meddle with the selection systems of the future? Jeremy Rifkin of the Foundation for Economic Trends and other opponents of genetic engineering believe that the answer is "no." According to Rifkin, "Perhaps none of us is wise enough, has the clairvoyance, the wisdom, to dictate basic changes in millions of years of genetic evolution. I don't think any of us should have that power. I think it's an unwarranted power and should not be exercised."

We are in the midst of a revolution in biological information and medical sophistication that has far-reaching implications for the future of humans. That future will also be affected by our burgeoning global population and by our stressed and deteriorating global environment. Our intelligence and cultural ingenuity—both products of our evolutionary history—brought us this far. We have no choice but to trust them to give us the vision and the tools to cope with our own "success."

SUMMARY

Cultural developments have proceeded at an ever-accelerating pace since the evolutionary appearance of anatomically modern humans. Plant and animal domestication was under way by 10,000 years B.P., and the establishment of modern civilization soon followed. These developments facilitated or accompanied a strong surge in human population growth around the world. Human evolution did not stop with the attainment of modernity, however, and differential adaptation (very likely combined with a bit of genetic drift) led to physical diversity within and between human populations. In contrast to our folk traditions, modern analyses indicate that biological races among humans cannot be demonstrated scientifically. It is now known that most human variation occurs *within* traditionally defined races, and that only a small percentage occurs *between* them. Nonetheless, in line with humans' strong tendency to dichotomize the world into "we-they" units, distinct social groups most definitely exist and may serve good and valid purposes within society. The existence of such groups, however, may also lead to racist and discriminatory attitudes and behaviors, and we must be constantly on guard against these evils.

The primary challenges for humankind in the twenty-first century include gaining control over global population growth, restricting our runaway use of the earth's finite resources, and dealing with the technological, genetic, and medical advances that allow us an ever-increasing measure of control over our evolutionary future.

POSTSCRIPT

This short section brings to an end our history of human evolution. We hope you have enjoyed it and that this is only one of many anthropology books you will read during your college years and beyond. The story of humankind, whether read from the viewpoint of physical or cultural anthropology, is endlessly fascinating, and new discoveries are constantly being made. It is fascinating partly because it tells of a mammalian family that began with only one outstanding attribute—bipedalism—and that evolved the intelligence and the behavioral complexity to hold the fate of the world in its prehensile hands. But primarily, of course, it is fascinating because it is *our* story and ends with modern humans representing the sole surviving twig of the hominid evolutionary bush.

But the hominid story goes beyond being merely fascinating. It is also *important* because it gives us a clear picture of modern human equality and thus allows us to look to the future with a degree of optimism. Optimism is sometimes a rare commodity. As we prepare the eighth edition of this textbook, the world has just commemorated the final events of World War II, a conflict that included one of history's most horrendous examples of genocide; in the African nation of Rwanda people have recently massacred each other in staggering numbers; and in the former Yugoslavia "ethnic cleansing" has made the headlines. How, one might ask, in the light of these events, can we speak of optimism?

We are optimistic because of our deep belief in the unity of humankind. The fossil record shows that all modern people are the descendants of African or Middle Eastern ancestors who lived a short 100,000 to 150,000 years ago. Although in the intervening years people have spread all over the globe, adapted to a variety of environments, and have developed substantial genetic and physical diversity, that diversity is swamped by our overwhelming similarities. As noted in this chapter, only 6.3 percent of genetic diversity occurs between traditionally defined human "races." Recent common ancestry and overwhelming genetic similarities—from these two facts flows the inescapable inference of *human unity*.

We are certainly not the first to make this inference, nor will we be the last. Human unity is a principle worth discovering and describing over and over, in the hope that humanity will finally get the message and move from genocide and international confrontation to peaceful coexistence and cooperation. The challenges facing humankind in the twenty-first century will put a premium on human unity and cooperation as never before. In order to make any significant headway against population growth, resource depletion, and human misery, we must act as a global community. But the development of such a community clearly hinges on our acceptance of one another as absolute equals. It will take massive teamwork, and we implore every reader of this book to contribute to that effort.

REVIEW QUESTIONS

1. Discuss the connection between genes and culture. Specifically, discuss how humans' moral systems may have evolved.
2. Humans' global population is currently burgeoning. Describe the various developments over the course of human evolution that have allowed massive population growth.
3. Argue for or against the proposition that humans can be subdivided into biological races. Be sure to provide supporting evidence for your argument.
4. What is the difference between race and racism? Can races exist without racist attitudes and behavior?
5. Argue for or against the proposition that future human evolution will be controlled mainly by self-directed artificial selection, not by natural selection.
6. What, if anything, can we learn from the study of human evolution that will help guide our individual and societal decisions in the future?

SUGGESTED FURTHER READING

Campbell, B. G. *Human Ecology: The Story of Our Place in Nature from Prehistory to the Present*, 2nd ed. Aldine de Gruyter, 1995.

Cavalli-Sforza, L. L., P. Menozzi, and A. Piazza. *The History and Geography of Human Genes*. Princeton University Press, 1994.

Diamond, J. *Guns, Germs, and Steel*. W. W. Norton, 1997.

Lewontin, R. *Human Diversity*. Scientific American Library, 1982.

Marks, J. *Human Biodiversity: Genes, Race, and History*. Aldine de Gruyter, 1995.

Shanklin, E. *Anthropology and Race*. Wadsworth, 1994.

Smith, B. D. "The Origins of Agriculture in the Americas." *Evolutionary Anthropology*, 3, 1994–1995.

Templeton, A. R. "Human Race: A Genetic and Evolutionary Perspective." *American Anthropology*, 100, 1998.

INTERNET RESOURCES

Surprisingly, authoritative factual material regarding human biological diversity is very limited on the Internet, although personal statements about race and racism are abundant. A few websites and search terms are offered below.

AN INTRODUCTION TO BLOOD GROUPS

http://www.umds.ac.uk/tissue/bludgrp.html

(Maintained by the United Medical and Dental Schools of Guy's and St. Thomas's Hospitals in England, this site provides a basic description of the ABO blood groups, with links to other blood systems.)

ETHNICITY AND RACE

http://daphne.palomar.edu/ethnicity/Default.htm

(Maintained by Dennis O'Neil, Palomar College, this site opens with a discussion of the biological race concept as applied to modern humans.)

NEW PERSPECTIVES ON AGRICULTURAL ORIGINS IN THE ANCIENT NEAR EAST

http://www.mc.maricopa.edu/academic/cult_sci/anthro/lost_tribes/agriculture.html

(This paper by Melinda Zeder discusses the development of farming and herding in the Khabur Basin of ancient Mesopotamia.)

USEFUL SEARCH TERMS:

Animal domestication
Blood groups
Human biological races
Plant domestication
Population growth
Race
Racism

THE GENETIC CODE

DNA Codon	Amino Acid	DNA Codon	Amino Acid
GCA	alanine	AGA	arginine
GCG	alanine	AGG	arginine
GCT	alanine	CGA	arginine
GCC	alanine	CGG	arginine
		CGT	arginine
GAT	aspartic acid	CGC	arginine
GAC	aspartic acid		
		AAT	asparagine
TGT	cysteine	AAC	asparagine
TGC	cysteine		
		GAA	glutamic acid
CAA	glutamine	GAG	glutamic acid
CAG	glutamine		
		GGA	glycine
CAT	histidine	GGG	glycine
CAC	histidine	GGT	glycine
		GGC	glycine
ATA	isoleucine		
ATT	isoleucine	TTA	leucine
ATC	isoleucine	TTG	leucine
		CTA	leucine
AAA	lysine	CTG	leucine
AAG	lysine	CTT	leucine
		CTC	leucine
ATG	methionine/**start**		
		TTT	phenylalanine
CCA	proline	TTC	phenylalanine
CCG	proline		
CCT	proline	AGT	serine
CCC	proline	AGC	serine
		TCA	serine
ACA	threonine	TCG	serine
ACG	threonine	TCT	serine
ACT	threonine	TCC	serine
ACC	threonine		
		TGG	tryptophan
TAT	tyrosine		
TAC	tyrosine	GTA	valine
		GTG	valine
TAA	**stop**	GTT	valine
TAG	**stop**	GTC	valine
TGA	**stop**		

DATING PROCEDURES FOR FOSSIL REMAINS

The problem of determining the age of fossils is handled in several ways. The first is through geology, the study of the earth itself. This branch of science is concerned with the location, size, and nature of the various layers of clay, silt, sand, lava, limestone, and other kinds of rock that constitute the earth's surface, and with their relationship to one another. It examines certain processes, such as continental drift, erosion, the accumulation of layers of silt at the bottom of the sea, and their compaction into rock again by heat and pressure; it notes that these processes take place now at measurable rates and assumes that the same processes took place at approximately comparable rates in the past, just as Charles Lyell suggested. Analysis of these layers, or strata—a scientific discipline known as stratigraphy—permits the working out of a rough picture of past earth history (Figures 5–1, 5–5). From this information the fossils found in different rock structures can be arranged in order of age. The deepest strata are the oldest, and the more recent levels are laid down above them. Thus fossils in the upper strata are relatively younger than those in the lower strata. These data, however, do not give us the absolute age of the fossils in years.

The second way to determine relative age is by studying the fossils themselves. Fossil types are usually not the same in different layers. Animals evolved through time, and since all species have finite lifetimes (ultimately go extinct), their fossils provide clues of their own, particularly if the time sequence can be worked out. The evolution of the horse, for example, is very well known through fossils. Over a period of about 60 million years, the creature developed from an animal the size of a dog with four toes on each foot to the modern large animal with one toe per foot; the numerous intermediate fossil stages located in various geological strata tell this story with great clarity. Fossils of ancestral horses become tools for dating, because any other animal or plant fossil that occurs in the same layer as one of the ancestral horses can be considered of the same age. Once relative ages are established, one fossil can help date another. This method is called dating by faunal correlation.

One problem paleontologists have had to face is establishing contemporaneity when fossils from the same site are said to be associated but their association is questioned. This problem is now less serious than in earlier days, for two reasons. First, today we can check claims of contemporaneity and association by chemically analyzing the bone: bones of roughly the same age should have roughly the same chemical analyses. The chemicals usually assayed are nitrogen (which occurs in bone in the form of the protein collagen and is lost slowly during fossilization) and uranium and fluorine (both of which frequently enter bone from the surrounding groundwater and increase in concentration over a long period). Such analyses can be very valuable in establishing contemporaneity at a site: they are especially valuable if it is suspected that a skeleton has been buried within a deposit that is substantially older than the skeleton itself.

The second reason that contemporaneity can be more clearly established today is that more careful records of excavations are now being kept. Early investigators usually failed to realize the importance of carefully analyzing fossil sites and the position of fossils. Too often they dug with reckless abandon, recovering only the largest bones and major pieces of worked stone. They did not appreciate the information they could get from the position of things relative to one another—and from the surrounding earth itself. Many questions will occur to the curious and well-trained observer. Is there evidence of fire? If so, was it natural or controlled by humans? Do certain kinds of animal bones predominate at one level and decrease at another, indicating a change of diet or climate? Do the deposits preserve snails, or perhaps pollen grains, which are more sensitive clues to vegetation, and hence climate, than the mineral deposits themselves? With the careful plotting of finds and sites, paleontologists can come closer to answering these questions.

Through the constant cross-checking and fitting together of enormous amounts of both rock and fossil evidence, geologists have been able to fit together quite a detailed succession of rock formations and fossils from the present back to the distant Cambrian period (Figure 5–5). But this succession provides only the relative dating of fossils; the absolute, or chronometric dating, of the fossils is still lacking.

Fortunately, atomic physics provides us with some very valuable techniques for obtaining chronometric dates of geological formations (and, in some cases, bones), which have revolutionized our study of human evolution. We know that certain radioactive elements discharge energy at a constant rate, known as the decay rate. Radium, for example, turns slowly but steadily into lead. Once this steady decay rate is known, it is only a matter of using laboratory technique to determine how old a piece of radium is by measuring how much of it is still radium and how much is lead.

One long-lasting radioactive substance used for chronometric dating is potassium 40. This material breaks down into the gas argon at the relatively slow rate of one-half of the original potassium every 1,250 million years (this is known as potassium 40's **half-life**). Because potassium 40 is found in volcanic ash and lava, **potassium-argon** (abbreviated K/Ar) **dating** can be used to date fossils located in volcanic rock or ash or sandwiched between two layers of volcanic matter. The "clock" starts as the lava or ash cools (argon produced previously escaped while the lava was heated in the volcano), and it continues to run steadily with the breakdown of potassium 40. The age of the rock can therefore be calculated with remarkable precision by determining the ratio of argon gas to potassium 40. Problems arise when the rock sample containing the potassium also contains air (which itself contains small quantities of argon), or if the rock has been reheated by later volcanic eruptions, which may have driven off the argon already produced by radioactive decay. The other, more general difficulty is that the method can be used to date fossils only from areas where volcanic eruptions occurred at about the same time as the fossils were deposited. Fortunately, many of the most important fossil sites in East Africa are in areas where volcanic activity was widespread (see Chapters 7 and 8), but in much of Asia, the Americas, and Europe, this method cannot be used.

An important development that supports this technique involves recognizing ash layers that have been deposited over wide areas. It has been shown by Frank Brown of the University of Utah that each ash layer (or **tuff** as such a layer is often

Half-life the time taken for half of any quantity of a radioactive element to decay to its fission products.

Potassium-argon dating *chronometric dating* in which age is determined by measurement of the decay of radioactive potassium 40.

Tuff a rocklike substance formed from volcanic ash.

called) can be recognized by a unique analysis of its mineral components; that is, each tuff has its own "chemical signature." Because of this characteristic, dated tuffs can be recognized over very great distances; their spread may be thousands of miles in extent. Thus it is possible to correlate tuffs from sites as far apart as Kenya, Ethiopia, and the Indian Ocean, where they can be recognized in deep-sea cores. In this way, dated tuffs may be widely mapped, and their K/Ar dates in one area checked against their K/Ar dating in another.

A derivation from K/Ar dating is the Ar^{40}/Ar^{39} procedure. In this test, previously irradiated crystals are melted with a laser beam in order to release argon. The procedure has the advantage of being extremely precise even when very small mineral samples are tested. Together, the K/Ar and Ar^{40}/Ar^{39} procedures can date rocks over a wide span of time, from only a few tens of thousands to many millions of years ago.

Another useful radioactive element is carbon 14, which reverts to atmospheric nitrogen (Figure 5–2). Physicist Willard Libby showed that carbon 14 is present in the atmosphere as carbon dioxide (CO_2) and is incorporated into all plant material. In the plant, the proportion of carbon 14 to the stable atom carbon 12 is the same as the proportion of the two in the atmosphere. The clock starts when the CO_2 is taken into the plant (which animals may feed on) and is buried as either fiber or wood, or as the collagen in bone, or as charcoal left by a fire. After an organism's death, the carbon 14 it contains breaks down, and the proportion of carbon 12 increases. The laboratory technique measures the ratio of carbon 14 to carbon 12 in these prehistoric samples. Carbon 14 has a half-life of only 5,730 years and therefore measurements of the age of carbon compounds cover a relatively short period. The method is most useful between 500 and 40,000 years ago, although its range can be extended somewhat farther into the past.

Errors in this method arise from a number of factors. It was originally supposed that the carbon 14 level in the atmosphere was constant, but we now known that it is not. Volcanoes produce CO_2 without carbon 14, which causes local reductions in the level of carbon 14 in the atmosphere. A more serious variation is in the atmospheric level itself, which alters according to variations in the chemical reactions in the upper atmosphere that create the carbon 14 in the first place. Samples may also become contaminated by modern organic compounds (such as the inks with which the fossils are labeled) or by modern CO_2 from the atmosphere. Although these factors somewhat limit the value of carbon 14 dating, the method has great value to paleoanthropologists when it is carefully used.

Another dating method that depends in a different way on radioactive decay is the fission-track method. The rare radioactive element uranium 238 splits spontaneously to create a minute region of crystal disruption in a mineral. The disruption is called a track. In the laboratory, microscopic examination can determine track densities in mineral crystals containing uranium 238, in proportion to total uranium content. Since the rate of spontaneous fission is known, the age of the crystal can be calculated. The clock is started with the eruption of volcanoes, and so this method has the same geographic limitations as the potassium-argon method.

The main value of the fission-track method at present is as a cross-check on the potassium-argon method. The same volcanic samples can often be used, and the comparison aids in the detection of errors. The fission-track method itself has other problems. With low uranium content and rather recently formed minerals, the track density will be low. Heating eliminates tracks (as we have seen, heating also causes problems in potassium-argon dating). Fission-track dating, however, has proved of great value in dating samples from the beginning of the earth to about 300,000 years ago. It is now being used quite widely in dating early periods of human evolution in volcanically active regions.

Two additional methods of dating that depend on radioactivity are thermoluminescence (TL) and optically stimulated luminescence (OSL). Both procedures measure the emission of light from crystalline materials that have been stimulated in some way: in TL, the stimulation is by heat, while in OSL, it is by exposing the sample to intense light of narrow wavelength. Both types of stimulation release electrons trapped in the sample and this produces measurable light. To further understand luminescence dating, here is how TL works. Over a period of time, electrons become trapped in the crystal structure of buried substances (including pottery and stone tools) as they are irradiated by naturally occurring uranium, thorium, and potassium 40 (for accurate dating, the "traps" must have been emptied prior to electron accumulation by a "zeroing event," such as heating by fire). When the irradiated substances are reheated in the laboratory, the electrons are released with a quantity of light proportional to the number of electrons trapped. If the rate of electron accumulation can be established, the amount of light emitted can be used to measure the time elapsed since the test substance was originally heated. TL works best with pottery, but it can also be used on burnt flints and hearth stones (OSL is used to date sediments, and it works best with wind-blown deposits since the OSL zeroing event is exposure to light). Both types of luminescence dating have remaining problems—such as estimating the rate of electron entrapment and controlling for "fading," the natural and gradual loss of trapped electrons—but they have great potential and have recently been used to establish some important dates. Of particular importance is the fact that the range of usefulness of luminescence dating overlaps those of carbon 14 and potassium-argon (see Figure 5–4).

Finally, the value of radioactive dating has been greatly increased by its use to date periodic changes in the global magnetic field. It appears that the north-south magnetic field of our planet has reversed its direction many times during the earth's history. (During periods of "reversal," a compass needle would point south instead of north.) The direction of an ancient magnetic field can be detected by laboratory measurements of the "fossilized" magnetism in rocks, combined with information on how those rocks were oriented (north-south) at the site of their collection. Such paleomagnetism dates from around the world have enabled geophysicists to construct detailed time charts of normal and reversed periods (see Figure 5–3). These data help scientists determine the age of sites that lack independent chronometric dates, but whose paleomagnetism profiles are known.

DIAGNOSTIC TRAITS OF THE HOMINIDS

This appendix lists selected general and species-specific diagnostic traits for the various hominid species. These lists (which vary in length depending on our knowledge of the different species) are intended to supplement the general anatomical descriptions provided in boxes throughout the text. The characteristics listed here refer to certain anatomical details not described in the main text. For further elucidation of these traits, interested readers are directed to the publications cited at the head of each species' list. To assist students in using the following technical material, a set of illustrative diagrams are provided at the end of the appendix. Throughout the appendix, we follow the standard procedures of labeling the permanent teeth with capital letters, the deciduous teeth with lower case letters, and using superscript/subscript numbers to designate specific upper and lower teeth, respectively.

Diagnostic traits of *Ardipithecus ramidus* (White, Suwa, and Asfaw, 1994)
A. Traits distinguishing this species from other hominids:
- upper and lower canines larger relative to postcanine teeth
- dm_1 narrow and obliquely elongate, with large protoconid, small metaconid that is distally placed, no anterior fovea, and small, low talonid with little cuspule development
- temporomandibular joint lacks clear articular eminence
- enamel on canines and molars absolutely and relatively thinner
- P^3 more asymmetrical, buccal cusp tall and dominant, and with steep transverse crest posterolingually oriented
- P^3 more asymmetrical, with buccal cusp relatively larger, taller, and more dominant

B. Traits distinguishing this species from living and fossil apes:
- canines more incisiform, with crowns less projecting
- P_3 generally smaller, with weaker mesiobuccal projection of crown base and lacking a functional honing facet
- lower molars generally relatively broader
- foramen magnum anteriorly placed relative to the carotid foramen

Diagnostic traits of *Australopithecus afarensis* (Johanson and White, 1979; Conroy, 1997)
General diagnostic traits:
- I^1 wide, I^2 diminutive; both with flexed roots
- permanent canines large, asymmetric, pointed, and projecting slightly above the toothrow

- P_3 with dominant, elongated buccal cusp and usually a small lingual cusp; lacks evidence of sectorial honing characteristic of apes
- relatively small diastemata often present in both upper and lower jaws
- dental arcade generally long, narrow, and with straight sides (not parabolic)
- strong alveolar prognathism with convex clivus
- face includes strong canine juga separated from zygomatic processes by strong depressions
- zygomatic processes are large, with anterior margins located above P^4/M^1 and with inferior margins that flare to front and side
- compound temporonuchal crest on some specimens
- temporomandibular joint is broad and poorly defined
- mandibular ramus broad, but not high
- mandibular corpus rounded and bulbous anteriorly, and relatively deep in larger specimens
- mandibular symphysis slopes strongly to rear
- ilia are low, broad, and show a deep sciatic notch
- large anterior inferior iliac spines
- distinctly oval pelvic girdle that is quite wide both at the level of the iliac crests and the hip joints
- iliac crests (including the anterior superior iliac spines) more laterally flared than in modern humans
- femurs relatively short, but with a long neck
- knees positioned close together near the midline of the body
- patellar groove has a raised lateral lip
- proximal phalanges are longitudinally curved in both hands and feet
- hallux (big toe) is not opposable

Diagnostic traits of *Australopithecus africanus* (Grine, 1993)

A. General diagnostic traits:
- high glabella separated from nasion
- prognathic but flattened nasoalveolar clivus
- anteriorly deep (shelved) palate
- deep glenoid fossa with a distinct articular eminence
- vertically steep tympanic plate
- P_3 bicuspid

B. Traits distinguishing this species from *Australopithecus afarensis*:
- cranium more globular and less pneumatized
- forehead more pronounced
- greater separation of lambda and inion

Diagnostic traits of *Australopithecus anamensis* (Leakey, Feibel, McDougall, and Walker, 1995)

A. Traits distinguishing this species from all other *Australopithecus* (and *Paranthropus*) types (unless otherwise noted):
- external acoustic meatus is small and has a narrow, elliptical outline
- dental arcade shows toothrows nearly parallel and close together (note: this trait does not distinguish *A. anamensis* and *A. afarensis*)
- mental region of mandible not strongly convex

- mandibular symphysis slopes strongly back and down
- very long, robust canine roots
- distal humeral shaft shows a thick cortex that encloses a small marrow cavity

B.   Traits distinguishing this species from *Australopithecus afarensis*:
- less posterior inclination of upper canine root and associated facial skeleton
- lower molars with more sloping buccal sides and upper molars with more sloping lingual sides
- tympanic plate horizontal and lacking defining grooves

C.   Traits distinguishing this species from *Ardipithecus ramidus*:
- absolutely and relatively thicker tooth enamel
- upper canine buccal enamel thickens toward the tip
- molars expanded buccolingually
- M_1 and M_2 similar in size
- tympanic tube extends only to the medial edge of the postglenoid process

Diagnostic traits of *Australopithecus bahrelghazali* (Brunet, et al., 1996)

A.   Traits distinguishing this species from all other hominids:
- mandibular toothrow is parabolic; at the level of P_4 the internal contour is wider than the corpus thickness; symphyseal axis subvertical; corpus of medium height and narrow with a low mental foramen
- anterior teeth large; I_2 and lower C have tall crowns and long roots; lower C also asymmetrical, with long distal cuspule and lingual crest
- lower premolars buccolingually broad with buccal cingula, three entirely distinct roots, and relatively thin enamel
- P_3 bicuspid with a strong metaconid; P_4 molarized with small talonid
- P^3 with three roots and asymmetrical crown

B.   Traits distinguishing this species from *Ardipithecus ramidus*:
- enamel thickening at the canine tips
- thicker enamel on premolars

C.   Traits distinguishing this species from *Paranthropus*:
- more gracile mandibular corpus
- much larger anterior dentition
- asymmetrical and non-oval P^3

Diagnostic traits of *Paranthropus aethiopicus* (Grine, 1993)

A.   General diagnostic traits:
- "dished" midface (note: this trait distinguishes *P. aethiopicus* from *Ardipithecus, Australopithecus*, and *Homo*, but not from the other *Paranthropus* species)
- nasoalveolar clivus that passes smoothly into the nasal floor
- vertically deep and mediolaterally concave tympanic plate
- palate medially thickened and anteriorly shallow
- heart-shaped foramen magnum with a straight anterior margin
- enlarged premolars and molars

B.   Traits distinguishing this species from other *Paranthropus* forms (although not from *Australopithecus afarensis*):
- elongate, unflexed cranial base
- marked alveolar prognathism
- shallow glenoid (mandibular) fossa lacking a clearly discernible articular eminence

Diagnostic traits of *Paranthropus boisei* (Grine, 1993)

A. General diagnostic traits:
- "dished" midface (note: this trait distinguishes *P. boisei* from *Ardipithecus*, *Australopithecus*, and *Homo*, but not from the other *Paranthropus* species)
- high hafting of the facial skeleton (note: also found in *P. robustus*)
- high incidence of occipital/marginal sinus rather than transverse sinuses
- absolutely and relatively small incisors and canines
- absolutely and relatively large premolars and molars

B. Traits distinguishing this species from *Paranthropus robustus*:
- greater maxillary depth
- anteriorly deep (shelved) palate
- laterally bowed and "visorlike" zygomatics
- heart-shaped foramen magnum with a straight or posteriorly convex anterior margin
- temporoparietal overlap at asterion
- larger premolars and molars

Diagnostic traits of *Paranthropus robustus* (Grine, 1993)

General diagnostic traits:
- "dished" midface (note: this trait distinguishes *P. robustus* from *Ardipithecus*, *Australopithecus*, and *Homo*, but not from the other *Paranthropus* species)
- high hafting of facial skeleton (note: also found in *P. boisei*)
- low forehead (receding frontal)
- prominent glabella situated below level of supraorbital margin
- flattened nasoalveolar clivus grading smoothly into nasal floor
- anteriorly shallow palate
- deep glenoid fossa with a distinct articular eminence
- vertically deep tympanic plate
- bulbous mastoid region inflated beyond the supramastoid crest
- canines in the same coronal plane as the incisors
- absolutely and (especially) relatively small incisors and canines
- enlarged premolars and molars

Diagnostic traits of *Homo habilis* (Wood, 1992)

A. Traits distinguishing this species (and all other hominines) from *Ardipithecus*, *Australopithecus*, and *Paranthropus*:
- increased cranial vault thickness
- reduced postorbital constriction
- increased contribution of the occipital bone to cranial sagittal arc length
- increased cranial vault height
- more anteriorly situated foramen magnum
- reduced lower face prognathism
- narrow tooth crowns, particular in the lower premolars
- reduced molar toothrow length

B. Traits distinguishing this species from *Homo rudolfensis*:
- smaller mean brain size
- greater occipital contribution to the sagittal arc
- complex suture pattern of skull
- incipient supraorbital torus
- upper face exceeds midface in breadth
- nasal margins sharp and everted

- zygomatic surface vertical or nearly so
- palate foreshortened
- relatively deep mandibular fossa
- rounded base on body of mandible
- lower premolars and molars show more buccolingual narrowing
- reduced talonid on P_4
- lower premolars mostly single-rooted

C. Traits distinguishing this species from *Homo erectus* and all later hominines:
  - elongated anterior basicranium
  - mesiodistally elongated M_1 and M_2
  - narrow mandibular fossa

Diagnostic traits of *Homo rudolfensis* (Wood, 1992)

A. Traits distinguishing this species from *Ardipithecus, Australopithecus*, and *Paranthropus*:
  - (see the "A list" under *Homo habilis*)

B. Traits distinguishing this species from *Homo habilis*:
  - greater mean brain size
  - lesser occipital contribution to the sagittal arc
  - simple suture pattern of the skull
  - supraorbital torus absent
  - midface exceeds upper face in breadth
  - less everted nasal margins
  - zygomatics anteriorly inclined
  - large palate
  - shallow mandibular fossa
  - everted base on body of mandible
  - broader lower premolars and molars
  - relatively large P_4 talonid
  - twin and/or bifid platelike lower premolar roots

C. Traits distinguishing this species from *Homo erectus* and all later hominines:
  - (see the "C list" under *Homo habilis*)

Diagnostic traits of *Homo erectus* (Aiello and Dean, 1990; Rightmire, 1990; Conroy, 1997)

General diagnostic traits:
- brain sizes range between 750 and 1,251 cubic centimeters (including Ngandong and Sambungmacan)
- crania long and low in outline, with relatively flat basicranial axis
- pronounced alveolar prognathism
- relatively broad nasal aperture; nasoalveolar clivus is flattened
- large supraorbital tori
- midline keeling of the frontal bone is common; such keeling may continue onto the parietal vault
- parasagittal depressions on either side of the parietal keeling
- marked postorbital constriction
- superior temporal line may produce an angular torus at the parietal mastoid angle
- variable supramastoid crest, prominent in some Indonesian individuals

- transverse torus of the occipital
- zygomatic arch lacks raised articular tubercle
- mandible large and robust, with broad ramus
- mandibular symphysis receding
- thick cranial bones

Diagnostic traits of *Homo heidelbergensis* (Groves, 1989; Aiello and Dean 1990; Rightmire, 1990)
General diagnostic traits:

- brain sizes range between 1,100 and 1,450 cubic centimeters
- wide parietal bones
- upper portion of the occipital is vertical and expanded relative to the nuchal plane; relatively great occipital angulation
- well-developed horizontal supramastoid crest
- barlike articular tubercle
- inferior border of the tympanic plate is thin
- broad frontal bone that recedes strongly
- reduced postorbital constriction
- shortened cranial base
- large supraorbital tori, thickened in the middle and thinning laterally
- external auditory meatus above the level of the glenoid cavity and located between the two posterior branches of the zygomatic root

Diagnostic traits of *Homo neanderthalensis* (Conroy, 1997; Stringer and Gamble, 1993; Stringer, et al.,1984; Tattersall, 1995)
General diagnostic traits:

- brain sizes range between 1,125 and 1,750 cubic centimeters
- skull long and low in profile, with retreating forehead and relatively flat cranial base
- double-arched supraorbital torus characterized by extensive pneumatization
- massive facial skeleton, with midfacial prognathism and a very large nasal opening
- rim of raised bone projecting medially from anterior nasal aperture, forming a secondary "internal nasal margin"
- cheekbones "swept back" toward rear of skull
- high, rounded orbits
- pronounced occipital "bun"
- occipital includes suprainiac fossa
- mandibular dentition is forwardly positioned producing a retromolar gap between M_3 and the ramus
- mental foramen under M_1
- broad scapula with strong muscle attachments
- lateral bowing of the radius
- massive head of humerus
- iliac blades show pronounced dorsal rotation
- thin and elongated superior pubic ramus
- femur and tibia robust and thick-walled
- short distal limb segments (tibia, radius)

Diagnostic traits for *Homo sapiens* (Conroy, 1997; Stringer, et al., 1984)

A. General diagnostic traits:
- brain sizes range between 1,000 and 2,000 cubic centimeters
- cranial vault relatively short and high (sharply rising forehead)
- cranial bones reduced in thickness
- weak supraorbital tori
- biparietal breadth greater than, or equal to, the breadth across the ear region (biauricular breadth)
- occipital region rounded; nuchal area reduced
- reduction/loss of sagittal keeling and parasagittal flattening
- shortened and flexed cranial base
- little facial prognathism (nose may still be large)
- canine fossa present (hollowed cheeks)
- mandible with reduced robusticity and a distinct chin

B. Traits distinguishing this species from *Homo neanderthalensis*:
- cheekbones lack "swept back" appearance
- midfacial prognathism lacking
- lower, squarer orbits
- smaller supraorbital tori
- reduced mean brain size
- prominent mastoid processes
- smaller anterior teeth
- hip sockets are less laterally (more ventrally) oriented
- superior pubic ramus shorter and thicker
- postcranial skeleton generally less robust

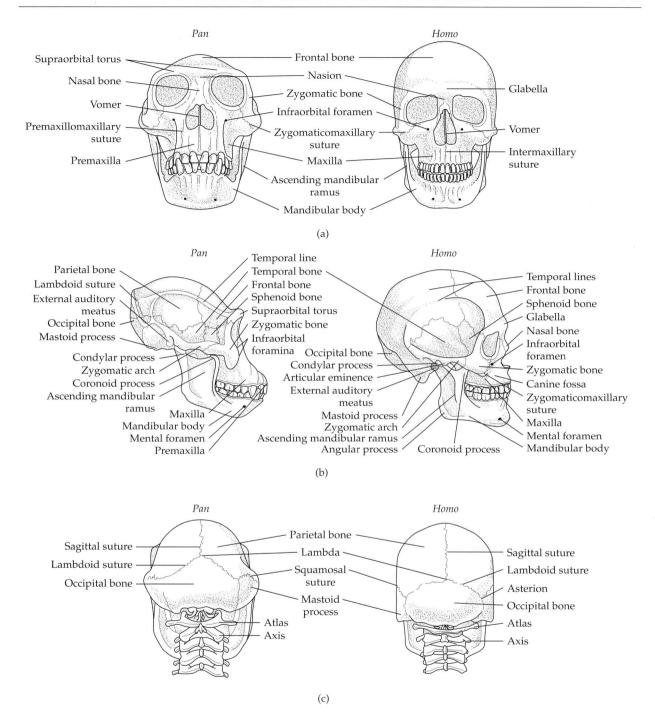

FIGURE A–1   Comparison of the skull in chimpanzees (left) and modern humans (right) with the major bones and bony landmarks identified. (a) Frontal view. (b) Lateral view. (c) Posterior view. (From *Reconstructing Human Origins: A Modern Synthesis* by Glenn C. Conroy. Copyright © 1997 by W. W. Norton & Company, Inc. Reprinted by permission of W. W. Norton & Company, Inc.)

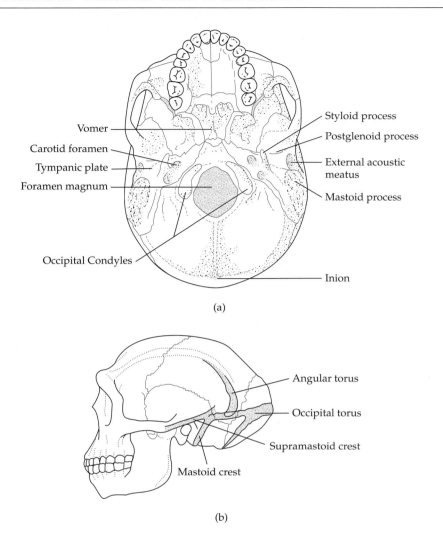

(a)

(b)

FIGURE A–2 (Top) Selected features of the cranial base of modern humans. (Bottom) Reconstructed *Homo erectus* skull showing several bony markings. (From L. Aiello and C. Dean, *An Introduction to Human Evolutionary Anatomy*, Academic Press, 1990. Reprinted by permission of Academic Press, Ltd.)

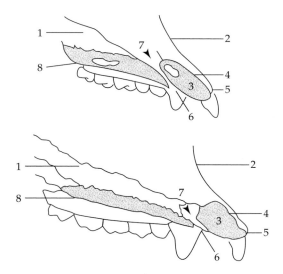

FIGURE A–3   Anatomy of the lower face in two living hominoids. Sagittal sections through the pre-maxilla and palate (shaded areas): *Pan* (top) and *Gorilla* (bottom). Anatomical parts: 1, vomer; 2, lateral margin of nasal aperture; 3, subnasal alveolar process; 4, nasoalveolar clivus; 5, prosthion; 6, oral incisive fossa; 7 and arrowhead, nasal incisive fossa; 8, hard palate. (From *Reconstructing Human Origins: A Modern Synthesis* by Glenn C. Conroy. Copyright © 1997 by W. W. Norton & Company, Inc. Reprinted by permission of W. W. Norton & Company, Inc.)

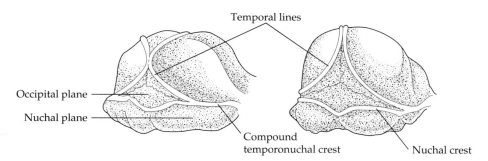

FIGURE A–4   Posterior view of australopithecine skulls and temporanuchal crest. *Aust. afarensis* is shown on the left and *Aust. africanus* on the right. (From *Reconstructing Human Origins: A Modern Synthesis* by Glenn C. Conroy. Copyright © 1997 by W. W. Norton & Company, Inc. Reprinted by permission of W. W. Norton & Company, Inc.)

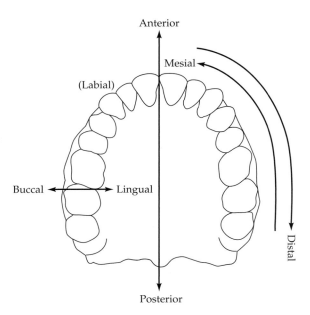

FIGURE A–5   Schematic representation of an upper jaw showing dental terminology for defining position and direction. (Figure redrawn from *Skeleton Keys* by Jeffrey H. Schwartz, Oxford University Press, 1995. Reprinted by permission of the artist John C. Anderton.)

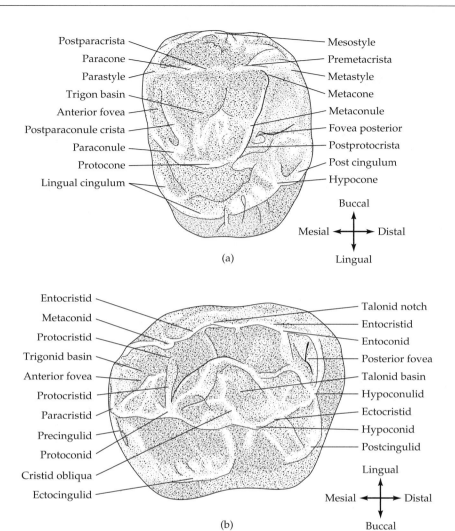

Postparacrista
Paracone
Parastyle
Trigon basin
Anterior fovea
Postparaconule crista
Paraconule
Protocone
Lingual cingulum

Mesostyle
Premetacrista
Metastyle
Metacone
Metaconule
Fovea posterior
Postprotocrista
Post cingulum
Hypocone

Buccal
Mesial ← → Distal
Lingual

(a)

Entocristid
Metaconid
Protocristid
Trigonid basin
Anterior fovea
Protocristid
Paracristid
Precingulid
Protoconid
Cristid obliqua
Ectocingulid

Talonid notch
Entocristid
Entoconid
Posterior fovea
Talonid basin
Hypoconulid
Ectocristid
Hypoconid
Postcingulid

Lingual
Mesial ← → Distal
Buccal

(b)

FIGURE A–6   Main features of the upper molars (top) and lower molars (bottom) of hominoids. (Figure redrawn from *Primate Evolution* by Elwyn Simons, Macmillan, 1972. Reprinted by permission of the author.)

GLOSSARY

Note: Words in *italics*, except some Latin names and self-explanatory terms, are defined elsewhere in the glossary.

Absolute dating: determining the actual age of geologic deposits (and the fossils in them) by examining the chemical composition of rock fragments containing radioactive substances which decay at known rates. Also known as *chronometric dating*. (Compare with *relative dating*.)

Acheulean industry: stone tool tradition that appeared 1.7 to 1.4 million years ago in Africa and originated with *Homo erectus*.

Adapidae: one of the two families of *Eocene prosimians*, now extinct.

Adaptation: an evolutionary change, generally resulting from *natural selection*, which better suits a *population* to its environment, thus improving its chances of survival; a characteristic resulting from such a change.

Aegyptopithecus: a basal catarrhine from the Fayum in Africa; dated to the *Oligocene* epoch.

Agglutination: the clumping of *red blood cells* as a result of the reaction of *antibodies* to an *antigen*.

Algeripithecus: tentatively, the oldest known *anthropoid primate*, from the early-middle *Eocene* epoch of North Africa.

Alleles: *genes* occupying equivalent positions in paired *chromosomes*, yet producing different effects in the *phenotype* when they are *homozygous*. They are alternative states of a gene, originally produced by *mutation*.

Allomothering: typically, care or attention directed toward an infant by a female other than its mother (also called *aunting behavior*).

Allopatric speciation: the production of new *species* through the branching or splitting of existing ones. The process begins with the geographic isolation of one or more *populations* from the bulk of the parent species.

Altiatlasius: the oldest known *primate fossil*; a *prosimian* from the late *Paleocene* of North Africa.

Altricial: the state of being born helpless and requiring parental care.

Alveolar: referring to the toothbearing portion of the jaws.

Amino acids: a group of organic compounds that act as building blocks for *proteins*.

Amphipithecus: a possible *anthropoid* from the late *Eocene* of Burma.

Angular gyrus: part of the human *cerebral cortex* that allows information received from different senses to be associated.

Anterior fovea: a *mesially* positioned depression on the surface of a tooth.

Anterior inferior iliac spine: a projection from the *ilium* that serves as an attachment point for certain thigh muscles and for the *iliofemoral ligament*.

Anthropoid: relating to humans, *apes*, and *monkeys*.

Anthropology: the science of humankind; the systematic study of human evolution, human variability, and human behavior, past and present.

Antibody: a *protein* produced as a defense mechanism to attack a foreign substance invading the body.

Antigens: any organic substances, recognized by the body as foreign, that stimulate the production of an *antibody*.

Ape: among living animals, a large, tailless, semierect mammal of the order *Primates*. Living types are the *chimpanzee, bonobo, gorilla, gibbon, siamang,* and *orangutan*.

Aphasia: the loss or distortion of speech.

Apidium: *primate* of the *Oligocene* epoch, found in Egypt; possibly a basal *anthropoid*.

Arboreal: adapted for living in or around trees, as are most *monkeys* and *apes*.

Archaeology: the systematic study of prehistoric human *cultures*; finding and interpreting the cultural products of prehistoric people.

Archaic humans: collectively, *Homo heidelbergensis* and the Neandertals (*Homo neanderthalensis*).

Arcuate fasciculus: a bundle of nerve fibers in the human brain transmitting signals from *Wernicke's area* to *Broca's area*, making possible vocal repetition of words heard and memorized.

Ardipithecus ramidus: provisionally, a new *genus* and *species* of the family Hominidae, subfamily Australopithecinae; known from East Africa and dating 4.4 million years ago.

Articular eminence: a swelling of the zygomatic arch just anterior to the jaw joint.

Articulation: in anatomy, the joint between two bones; in linguistics, the action of the tongue and lips to form the consonants of *speech*.

Asterion: juncture of the temporal, parietal, and occipital bones.

Artifact: a purposefully formed object.

Assortative mating: the tendency of like to mate with like.

Atlatl: Aztec name for the spear thrower, a rodlike device used as an extension of the arm that greatly increases both distance and impact of throw.

Attractiveness: in *primate* studies, the aspect of female sexuality reflected by attention from males.

Auditory bulla: the bulbous bony development that houses the middle ear region.

Aurignacian: an *Upper Paleolithic*, mainly European, tool culture that existed from about 40,000 to 27,000 years ago.

Australopithecus: a *genus* of the family Hominidae, subfamily Australopithecinae; contains four *species*: *A. afarensis, A. africanus, A. anamensis,* and *A. bahrelghazali* (provisional).

Australopithecus aethiopicus: the original name for the robust australopithecine *species* now called *Paranthropus aethiopicus.*

Australopithecus afarensis: a gracile australopithecine *species* that inhabited East Africa from 4.2 to 2.5 million years ago.

Australopithecus africanus: a gracile australopithecine *species* that inhabited South Africa from 3.5–2.5 million years ago.

Australopithecus anamensis: a *species* of australopithecines that inhabited East Africa from 4.2 to 3.9 million years ago.

Australopithecus bahrelghazali: provisionally, a *species* of australopithecines known from Chad and dating 3.5 to 3.0 million years ago.

Autosome: a *chromosome* other than the *sex chromosomes.*

Baboon: a large *monkey* with a long, doglike muzzle; most baboons have short tails and live on the ground in troops. They live close to the trees in East and Central Africa and in rocky desert in Ethiopia (see also *gelada* and *hamadryas*).

Balanced polymorphism: maintenance in a *population* of different *alleles* of a particular *gene* in proportion to the advantages offered by each (e.g., *sickle-cell* and normal *hemoglobin*).

Band: a small, economically independent group of *primates*, smaller than a troop.

Basicranium: base of the skull.

Beijing man: see *Sinanthropus pekinensis.*

Biface: a tool made by chipping *flakes* off both sides of a core, producing an edge straighter and sharper than those made in earlier cultures, which were chipped on one edge only. A common tool of the *Acheulean industry.*

Bilophodonty: the molar cusp pattern of *Old World monkeys*, featuring four *cusps* arranged in front and rear pairs.

Bioaltruism: behavior that appears to be altruistic, but that in fact is believed to benefit the animal indirectly, by increasing its *inclusive fitness.*

Bioethicist: a person who specializes in exploring the ethical dimensions of biological decisions.

Biomass: the total weight of living material of a *species* or *population.*

Biome: an area characterized by a broadly uniform climate and consisting of a distinctive combination of plants and animals.

Bipedal: moving erect on the hind limbs only.

Biretia: a late Eocene *anthropoid* from Algeria.

Birth canal: the passage through the mother's pelvis by means of which infants are born.

Blade tools: slender, razor-sharp *flake tools* at least twice as long as they are wide.

Blending inheritance: an outmoded theory stating that offspring receive a combination of all characteristics of each parent through the mixture of their bloods; superseded by Mendelian genetics.

Blood groups: groups of individuals whose blood can be mixed without *agglutination* (e.g., Groups A, B, O, or AB).

Blood plasma: a clear liquid component of blood that carries the *red blood cells, white blood cells,* and *platelets.*

Bola: two or more stones connected by thongs or a cord and used as a weapon.

Bonobo: Central African *apes* very similar to the common *chimpanzee* and sometimes called *pygmy chimpanzees*; display some behavioral similarities to humans.

Brachiation: an arboreal locomotor pattern featuring manual swinging from branch to branch.

Branching: the splitting of a family tree into separate evolutionary lines. The *monkeys*, *apes*, and living *prosimians* diverged from a common prosimianlike ancestor; the *hominid* line diverged from the apes.

Branisella: Oligocene platyrrhine monkey from Bolivia.

Broca's area: part of the human *cerebral cortex* involved with the hierarchical organization of grammar and the manual combination of objects.

Brow ridge: a continuous ridge of bone in the skull, curving over each eye and connected across the bridge of the nose. An extremely prominent brow ridge is characteristic of the Neandertal people.

Buccal: within the mouth, toward the cheek (see also *lingual*).

Budding: the gradual expansion of a *species* into new areas, accomplished by a group splitting off from a prospering *population* to set up in an unexploited area near the original *territory*.

Burin: a chisel-like tool used to shape other materials such as bone, antler, and wood; a tool for making other tools.

Calvaria: a braincase; that is, a skull minus the facial skeleton and lower jaw (plural, *calvariae*).

Canines: pointed teeth in the front of the mouth between the incisors and the premolars. In *monkeys* and *apes*, canines are usually large, projecting beyond the other teeth, and are used for tearing up vegetation and for threats and fights. *Hominid* canines are much smaller.

Canine fossa: concavity in the maxilla just behind the *canine jugum*.

Canine jugum: vertical ridge or bulge in the maxilla caused by a large *canine* root (plural, *juga*).

Carbon 14 (C14): a radioactive form of carbon present in the atmosphere as CO_2 that disintegrates at a predictable rate. The amount of carbon 14 remaining in fossils indicates their age.

Carotid foramen: opening for the carotid artery.

Catarrhines: an infraorder of the *anthropoids* that includes *Old World monkeys*, *apes*, and *hominids*.

Catastrophism: Georges Cuvier's theory that vast floods and other disasters wiped out ancient life forms again and again throughout the earth's history.

Catopithecus: a particularly well-known *oligopithecine* from the Fayum in Africa.

Cenozoic: geologic era that began about 65 million years ago.

Centrioles: minute granules present in many cells outside the nuclear membrane. The centriole divides in cell division, and the parts separate to form the poles of the spindle.

Cephalic index: a skull measurement sometimes used by anthropologists; defined as skull breadth/length x 100.

Cerebral cortex: gray, wrinkled, outer layer of the brain; largely responsible for memory and, in humans, reasoned behavior and abstract thought. (Also referred to as the *neocortex*.)

Chain of Being: pre-Darwinian theory of a hierarchy ranking living things from lowest to highest, with humankind at the top; the chain was thought to have been fixed forever at Creation, which meant that no species could change into other forms.

Chatelperronian: an *Upper Paleolithic* tool culture of western Europe, largely contemporaneous with the *Aurignacian culture* (40,000 to 27,000 years B.P.).

Chemical signature: unique chemical nature of a geologic deposit; for volcanic rocks, it is usually determined by an analysis of the ash and lava content.

Chiasmata: points where the *chromatids* of a tetrad overlap and segment exchange may occur; *crossover* points (singular, *chiasma*).

Chimpanzee: African great *ape* thought to be somewhat like the ancestor from which apes and humans are descended. In the trees it climbs; on the ground it usually moves by *knuckle-walking*.

Choppers: small, generally ovoid stones with a few *flakes* removed to produce a partial cutting edge.

Chordata: the *phylum* of animals characterized by the possession of a notochord (a gelatinous dorsal stiffening rod) at some stage of life.

Chromatid: one of the two elements in a duplicated *chromosome*.

Chromosomes: coiled, threadlike structures of *DNA*, bearing the *genes* and found in the nucleus of all plant and animal cells. (See also *meiosis* and *mitosis*.)

Chronometric dating: see *absolute dating*.

Chronospecies: the sort of "*species*" that are created when an unbroken evolutionary continuum is arbitrarily divided into time-defined units.

Cingulum: shelf of enamel running around the periphery of a tooth (plural, *cingula*).

Clade: members of an evolutionary cluster (e.g., sister *species*) plus their common ancestor.

Cladistic analysis: the grouping of *species* by their shared derived traits, with the aim of identifying groups of organisms descended from a common ancestor.

Cladistic classification: evolution-based *taxonomy* that gives equal weight to traits and requires *sister groups* to be similarly ranked.

Cladogenesis: branching evolution involving the splitting of a *species* or lineage.

Class: a *taxonomic* rank in biology. Humans belong to the class *Mammalia*.

Cleaver: an *Acheulean* stone implement with a straight cutting edge at one end; probably used for butchering animal carcasses.

Cline: the gradual change in frequency of a trait or *gene* across a geographic range.

Clivus: see *nasoalveolar clivus*.

Clone: a genetically identical organism asexually reproduced from an ancestral organism.

Close-knee stance: standing with the feet and knees closer together than the hip joints.

Cobble: stone worn smooth by sand and water in running streams or on a rocky seashore. Often used as a core for making a stone tool.

Coccyx: the bones at the end of the human and *ape* spine, the remnants of an ancestral tail.

Co-dominant: the term for *alleles* that, in *heterozygous* combination, produce a *phenotype* distinct from either type of homozygote.

Codon: a *nucleotide* triplet that codes for the production of a particular *amino acid* during *protein* production.

Collective phenotype: the set of phenotypic averages and norms that characterize a *population* or *species*.

Colugos: nonprimate mammals from Asia known for arboreal gliding; misnamed "flying lemurs."

Condyle: the part of a bone that fits into another bone, forming a movable, hingelike joint, like the part of the lower jaw that bears on the skull.

Consortship: generally, a period of exclusive sexual association and mating between a female and a male.

Conspecifics: members of the same *species*.

Continental drift: a theory that describes the movements of continental landmasses throughout the earth's history.

Core area: a portion of the *home range* that is used frequently.

Core tool: implement made from the core of a rock nodule. (Compare with *flakes*.)

Coronal plane: any plane that divides the body into front and rear portions.

Cranium: the skull without the jaw.

Creationism: the belief that humans and all life forms were specially created by God or some other divine force.

Creation myth: a story describing the origins, usually supernatural, of the earth and life (including humans).

Cro-Magnon: anatomically modern humans living in Europe between about 40,000 and 10,000 years ago.

Crossing-over: the exchange of sections between *homologous chromosomes*.

Cultural evolution: changes in human *culture* resulting from the accumulated experience of humankind. Cultural evolution can produce *adaptations* to the environment faster than organic *evolution* can.

Cultural swamping: overwhelming of one *culture* by a technologically more powerful one, often leaving the culture with the weaker technology extinct or nearly so.

Culture: humans' systems of learned behavior, symbols, customs, beliefs, institutions, artifacts, and technology, characteristic of a group and transmitted by its members to their offspring.

Cusps: conical projections on the biting surfaces of teeth. On the molar teeth of primates these include mainly the metacone, hypocone, protocone, and paracone (upper molars), and the metaconid, hypoconid, hypoconulid, entoconid, and protoconid (lower molars). (See also *molars*).

Cytoplasm: the contents of a cell excluding the nucleus.

Darwinian fitness: see *fitness*.

Débitage: debris produced during stone tool manufacture.

Deep time: the theory that the earth is billions of years old and thus has a long history of development and change.

Deme: the community of potentially interbreeding individuals at a locality.

Demography: study of the size, density, distribution, and other vital statistics of *populations*.

Dental formula: the numbers of incisors, *canines*, premolars, and *molars* in half of the upper and lower toothrows.

Denticulates: stone implements made with toothed or notched edges.

Deoxyribonucleic acid: see *DNA*.

Derived traits: recently evolved characteristics shared by a small number of closely related *species*.

Diastema: space in the toothrow that accommodates one or more teeth in the opposite jaw when the mouth is closed (plural, *diastemata*).

Differential reproduction: the effect of *natural selection* that individuals with certain traits are less *fit* than those with other traits.

Diploid number: the full *chromosome* count in somatic cells (all cells other than *gametes*). (Compare with the *haploid* number.)

Directional natural selection: *natural selection* that operates in response to environmental change and produces shifts in the composition of a *population's gene pool* and *collective phenotype*.

Disk-core technique: *Neandertal* stone-knapping method in which a core is trimmed to disk shape and numerous *flakes* are chipped off; the flakes are then generally retouched.

Distal: farther away from a point of reference; in the jaw, farther away from the anterior midline and toward the back of the mouth (see also *mesial*).

Diurnal: active during the day, as *apes*, *monkeys*, and humans are.

DNA (deoxyribonucleic acid): chemical substance found in *chromosomes* and *mitochondria* which reproduces itself, and carries the *genetic code*.

Dominance hierarchy: rank structuring of a *primate* group, usually based on winning and losing fights. For some purposes, the ranks within a subset of animals, such as the adult males, may be analyzed separately.

Dominant: in genetics describes a trait that is expressed in the *phenotype* even when the organism is carrying only one copy of the underlying hereditary material (one copy of the responsible *gene*).

Dorsal: pertaining to the back of an animal or one of its parts; opposite of *ventral*.

Dragon bones: the ancient Chinese term for *fossils* of various sorts that were collected and ground into medicines.

Drift: see *genetic drift*.

Dryopithecus: *ape genus* from Europe dating to the mid-to-late *Miocene*.

Early *Homo*: general term referring collectively to *Homo habilis* and *Homo rudolfensis*.

Ecological niches: the set of resources and habitats exploited by a *species*.

Ecosystem: ecological system; the interacting community of all the organisms in an area and their physical environment, together with the flow of energy among its components.

Ecotone: an area where two or more ecological zones meet.

Emissary veins: veins that pass through the bones of the skull by means of small openings called *foramina*.

Encephalization quotient (EQ): in mammals, a number expressing observed brain size in a particular species relative to expected brain size calculated from body weight.

Endocast: a fossilized cast of the interior of a skull; may reveal much about brain size and shape.

Endogamy: selecting a mate from inside one's own group.

Eocene: the geologic epoch extending from 58 to 35 million years B.P.

Eosimias: probable basal *anthropoid* from the mid-*Eocene* of China.

Epicanthic fold: a fold of skin above the inner border of the eye; characteristic of Asiatic, some Native American, and the Khoisan people.

Estrus: the period, usually around ovulation, of sexual *attractiveness* and activity by *primate* and other mammalian females.

Estrus cycle: the interval between periods of sexual *attractiveness* and activity by *primate* females; correlated with ovulation and the *menstrual cycle*, but with great flexibility among *catarrhines*.

Ethnic group: a group of people perceived as sharing a common and distinctive *culture*.

Ethnographic analogy: an analogy between the ethnography of a society and the supposed ethnography of a prehistoric one.

Ethology: study of the social behavior of animal *species* in their natural environment.

Evolution: cumulative changes in the average characteristics of a *population* that occur over many generations (see also *natural selection*).

Exogamy: among modern humans, the pattern of marrying (and mating) between individuals of different social groups.

Exons: segments of a *gene*'s *DNA* that code for *protein* production.

External acoustic meatus: auditory tube (ear) opening.

Extinction: the loss of a *species* due to the deaths of all its members.

Family: in human society, generally a unit marked by subsistence interdependence, sexual relationships among adults, and parent-offspring relationships.

Fauna: animal component of the *ecosystem* at a given place and time.

Faunal correlation: dating a site by the similarity of its animal *fossils* to those of another site that may carry a reliable *absolute date*.

Feedback: process by which a change in one component in a system affects other components, which in turn bring about changes in the first component.

Femur: the thighbone (plural, *femora*).

Fish gorge: device for catching fish on a line using a moving part that opens at right angles and sticks in the fish's mouth.

Fission-track dating: method of dating rocks from tracks left by the spontaneous splitting of uranium238 atoms.

Fitness: individuals' relative degrees of success in surviving and reproducing, and thus in gaining genetic representation in succeeding generations.

Flakes: sharp-edged fragments struck from a larger stone; the flake may then be used as a cutting tool. (Compare with *core tool*.)

Flake tool: implement made from a *flake* struck from a stone.

Folivore: a leaf-eating animal.

Foramen magnum: large opening in the cranial base, through which the spinal cord passes to the brain.

Forensic anthropologists: physical anthropologists who apply their expertise to matters of law, e.g., the identification of human remains.

Fossil: the remains of an organism, or direct evidence of its presence, preserved in rock. Generally only the hard parts of animals' teeth and bones are preserved.

Fossil magnetism: naturally occurring property of rocks indicating the polarity of the earth's magnetic field when they were laid down. By a comparison of the polarity of one layer with that of others, the age of a rock can, under certain conditions, be approximated.

Founder effect: genetic difference between a newly founded, separated *population* and its parent group. The founding population is usually different because its *gene pool* is only a segment of the parent group's.

Founder principle: the fact that founders of a new colony, if few in number, will contain only a fraction of the total genetic variation of the parental *population* or *species*. The founder colony will therefore most likely differ genetically from the parent population.

Fovea: an area of the *anthropoid* retina that allows extremely detailed vision.

Frenulum: the flap of skin that tethers the upper lip to the jaw in *prosimians*. It is reduced or absent in *anthropoids* and *tarsiers*.

Frontal bone: bone of the *primate* skull that constitutes the forehead and comes down around the eye sockets (orbits).

Frugivore: a fruit-eating animal.

Fusion-fission community: a society that includes several individuals of both sexes and all ages and is characterized by the formation and dissolution of temporary subgroups.

Gametes: reproductive *haploid* sex cells generated by *meiosis*, which fuse with gametes of the opposite sex in fertilization. In animals, the female gamete is the ovum; the male gamete, the sperm.

Gelada: *species* of terrestrial *monkey* related to *baboons*, found in the mountains of Ethiopia; *Theropithecus gelada*.

Gene: primarily, a functional unit of the *chromosomes* in cell nuclei, which controls the coding and inheritance of *phenotypic* traits; some genes also occur in a closed loop in the *mitochondria*.

Gene flow: transmission of genes between *populations* which increases the variety of genes available to each and creates or maintains similarities in the genetic makeup of the populations.

Gene frequency: the number of times a gene occurs in proportion to the size of a *population*.

Gene pool: all the *genes* of a *population* at a given time (summing genes within a *species* yields the species' gene pool).

Genetic code: the chemical code based on four *nucleotides*, carried by *DNA* and *RNA*, which specifies *amino acids* in sequence for *protein* synthesis.

Genetic drift: genetic changes in *populations* caused by random phenomena rather than by *natural selection*.

Genetic load: *recessive genes* in a *population* that are harmful when expressed in the rare *homozygous* condition.

Genetic swamping: the overrunning and absorption of a small *population* by a larger one; the *genes* of the minority are preserved but contribute little to the successors' physical characteristics.

Genome: the totality of the *DNA* unique to a particular organism or *species*.

Genotype: the genetic makeup of a plant or animal; the total information contained in all *genes* of the organism. (Compare with *phenotype*.)

Genus: *taxonomic* category composed of a group of *species* that are similar because of common ancestry.

Geology: study of the earth's physical formation, its nature, and its continuing development.

Gibbon: small, long-armed, tree-dwelling, brachiating *ape* of Southeast Asia.

Gigantopithecus: extinct giant *ape* dating from *Pliocene* and *Pleistocene* epochs. Found in Asia.

Glabella: anteriormost point on the frontal bone, usually between the *brow ridges*.

Glenoid fossa: another name for the *mandibular fossa*.

Gluteus medius: one of the muscles of the hip; a lateral stabilizer of the pelvis in modern humans.

Gluteus minimus: one of the muscles of the hip; a lateral stabilizer of the pelvis in modern humans.

Gorilla: the largest *ape*; a social, terrestrial, *knuckle-walking* vegetarian living in the rain forests and mountain forests of equatorial Africa.

Grades: arbitrarily defined levels of evolutionary development (e.g., *prosimians* versus *anthropoids*).

Gradualism: the hypothesis that *evolution* has consisted for the most part of gradual, steady change. (Compare with *punctuated equilibrium*.)

Gravettian: see *Perigordian*.

Group selection: theoretical model in which *natural selection* is presumed to operate not on the individual animal but on a social group as a unit.

Half-life: the time taken for half of any quantity of a radioactive element to decay to its fission products.

Hamadryas: a *species* of *baboon* adapted to the desert regions of Ethiopia.

Hamstrings: muscles of the hips and the back of the thigh; thigh extensors.

Hand ax: a bifacially flaked stone implement that characterized the *Acheulean industry*.

Haploid number: the number of *chromosomes* carried by *gametes*; equal to one-half the full chromosome count of somatic cells. (Compare with *diploid number*.)

Harem polygyny: in zoology, a group including one breeding male and multiple females; among humans, one husband and multiple wives and concubines.

Hemispherical asymmetry: the condition in which the two cerebral hemispheres differ in one or more dimensions. In most modern humans, the left hemisphere is somewhat larger than the right.

Hemoglobin: a red *protein* found in *red blood cells* that carries oxygen through the circulatory system of vertebrates and some other animals.

Heritability: a property of *phenotypic* traits; the proportion of a trait's interindividual variance that is due to genetic variance.

Heterodont: having several different types of teeth (incisors, *canines*, etc.), each with a different function.

Heterozygous: having different versions of a *gene* (*alleles*) for a particular trait. (Compare with *homozygous*; see also *dominant*.)

Heuristic devices: devices that facilitate or stimulate further investigation and thought.

Home base: camps where *hominid* groups gathered at evening for socializing, food sharing, and sleeping.

Home range: the area a *primate* group uses for foraging, sleeping, and so on in a year. (Compare with *territory*.)

Hominids: living or fossil members of the *primate* family Hominidae, which includes *Homo sapiens*, earlier species of the genus *Homo*, *Ardipithecus*, *Australopithecus*, and *Paranthropus*.

Hominoid: a *primate* of the superfamily Hominoidea, including the *apes* and humans.

Homo: a *genus* of the family Hominidae, subfamily Homininae; contains at least six *species*: *H. habilis, H. rudolfensis, H. erectus, H. heidelbergensis, H. neanderthalensis,* and *H. sapiens.*

Homo antecessor: proposed new *species* name for certain fossils from the site of Gran Dolina, Spain; taxon not recognized as valid in this book.

Homo erectus: hominid species that inhabited much of the Old World between 1.9(?) million and at least 300,000 years B.P.; successor to "early *Homo.*"

Homo ergaster: species name given by some paleoanthropologists to certain African *fossils* regarded by most workers as early *Homo erectus.* The authors of this text side with the majority.

Homo habilis: one of the two *species* of "early *Homo*"; inhabited South and East Africa 2.0 to 1.6 million years ago, and perhaps as early as 2.3 million years ago.

Homo heidelbergensis: the successor to *Homo erectus*, first appearing about 800,000 to 600,000 years B.P.; ancestral to both *Homo sapiens* and the *Neandertals.*

Homologous chromosomes: *chromosomes* that are similar in shape, size, and sequence of *genes.*

Homo neanderthalensis: a *species* of humans that inhabited Europe and the Middle East from about 300,000 to 30,000 years B.P. Descended from *Homo heidelbergensis*, the species' common name is usually spelled *Neandertal.*

Homo rudolfensis: one of the two *species* of "early *Homo*"; inhabited East Africa 2.4 to 1.6 million years ago.

Homo sapiens: among living *primates*, the scientific name for modern humans; members of the *species* first appeared about 130,000 years ago.

Homozygous: having identical versions, of a *gene* (*alleles*) for a particular trait. (Compare with *heterozygous.*)

Hybrid speciation: speciation through hybridization between two good *species.*

Hyoid: a bone of the throat positioned just above the *larynx* and just below the *mandible.* The hyoid provides attachment for one of the muscles of the tongue and for certain muscles at the front of the neck.

Hypoglossal Canal: an opening in the *occipital bone* just anterior to the *occipital condyle*; allows the passage of the hypoglossal nerve to the tongue musculature.

Ignacius: a *genus* of the *plesiadapiforms.*

Iliac blade: the broad portion of the *ilium*, one of the bones of the pelvis.

Iliofemoral ligament: ligament that prevents backward movement of the trunk at the human hip.

Ilium: the hipbone, part of the *pelvis.*

Inbreeding: mating among related individuals.

Incest: legally prohibited sexual relations between kin. How closely related individuals must be for mating to be considered incestuous differs from culture to culture.

Inclusive fitness: the sum total of an organism's individual reproductive success (number of offspring) plus portions of the reproductive success of genetic kin.

Infanticide: the killing of infants.

Inion: midline point of the superior nuchal lines.

Interglacial: a period in which glaciers retreat and the climate warms.

Introns: segments of a gene's *DNA* that do not code for *protein* production (so-called noncoding DNA).

IQ tests: tests that supposedly measure an individual's "intelligence quotient." Many consider such tests flawed and of little value, particularly for cross-cultural comparisons.

Iron pyrite: a mineral substance (iron disulfide) that, when struck with flint, makes sparks that will start a fire.

Ischium: one of the bones of the *pelvis.*

Java man: see *Pithecanthropus.*

Kin selection: the selection of characteristics (and their *genes*) that increase the probability of the survival and reproduction of close relatives.

Knuckle-walking: *quadrupedal* walking on the knuckles of the hands and the soles of the feet, used by *bonobos, chimpanzees,* and *gorillas* on the ground.

Lambda: midline juncture of the sagittal and lambdoidal sutures.

Language: the cognitive aspect of human communication, involving symbolic thinking structured by grammar.

Langur: slender, long-tailed Asian *monkey*.

Larynx: the voice box; the organ in the throat containing the vocal cords, important in human speech production.

Laurel-leaf blade: *Upper Paleolithic* stone artifact so finely worked that it may have had an aesthetic or ritual function. Associated with *Solutrean* tool kits.

Leister: a three-pronged spear used for fishing.

Levallois technique: stone-knapping method in which a core is shaped to allow a *flake* of predetermined size and shape to be detached; originated at least 250,000 years B.P.

Life expectancy: the average age at death of individuals born into a particular population.

Limbic system: the emotional brain; a group of structures in the brain important in regulating such behavior as eating, drinking, aggression, sexual activity, and expressions of emotion. Proportionately smaller in humans than in other *primates*, it operates below the level of consciousness.

Lingual: in the mouth, toward the tongue (see also *buccal*).

Lithic technology: stone-tool technology.

Locus: position of a nuclear *gene* on a *chromosome*; each locus can carry only one *allele* of a gene.

Loris: a *prosimian* of India, Southeast Asia, and Africa that is small, solitary, *quadrupedal*, and slow moving.

Lower Paleolithic: the earliest part of the Old Stone Age, lasting from more than 2 million to about 200,000 years ago.

Lumbar curve: forward curvature of the vertebral column in the lower back that helps bring the *hominid* trunk over the hip joints.

Macromutation: a large and genetically inherited change between parent and offspring.

Magdalenian: *Upper Paleolithic* culture existing in western Europe from about 16,500 to 11,000 years B.P. Produced many *blade* tools and prototype harpoons.

Mammalia: the class of four-legged vertebrates—including humans—having hair or fur, milk glands for suckling their young, and warm blood.

Mandible: the lower jaw.

Mandibular fossa: concave portion of the jaw joint; part of the temporal bone (see *glenoid fossa*).

Mandibular symphysis: the midline connecting the right and left halves of the lower jaw.

Manuports: Unmodified stones that could not have occurred naturally at an archaeological site and must have been carried there; how manuports were used is unknown.

Mastoid process: bony projection of the temporal bone posterior to the *external acoustic meatus*.

Mastoid region: the area around the *mastoid process* of the temporal bone.

Matrilineal kinship: kinship traced through the maternal line.

Meiosis: cell division resulting in the formation of sex cells, each of which will have half the number of chromosomes present in the original cell (the *haploid number*).

Melanocyte: a kind of cell in the skin that produces pigment, giving the skin color.

Menstrual cycle: the interval (generally, monthly) between periods of menstrual bleeding; especially characteristic of catarrhine females.

Mental region of mandible: the front, lower edge of the mandibular body.

Mesial: toward the anterior side of a tooth (i.e., toward the midline at the front of the jaw; see also *distal*).

Mesolithic: a *Stone Age* period recognizable at some European sites and characterized by the use of small stone tools called microliths; lasting at most 2000 years, the Mesolithic followed the *Paleolithic* and preceded the *Neolithic*.

Metaconid: see *cusps*.

Microwear: the microscopic pattern of scratches, pits, and polish produced during the use of a stone tool.

Midden: a refuse heap or dunghill at an archaeological site in which artifacts and food remains may be preserved.

Middle Paleolithic: a period of stone tool manufacture in the Old World (mainly Europe, Africa, and western Asia) that lasted from about 250,000 to 35,000 years B.P.

Midfacial prognathism: forward protrusion of the upper jaw, the midface and the nasal regions; characteristic of *Neandertals*.

Miocene: the geologic epoch extending from 25 to 5 million years B.P.

Mitochondria: granular or rod-shaped bodies in the cytoplasm of cells that function in the metabolism of fat and *proteins*. Probably of bacterial origin.

Mitosis: cell division in somatic cells; two identical *diploid* cells result.

Molars: grinding teeth, which bear many *cusps*. *Primate* molars have three to five cusps, depending on the animal; premolars normally have two.

Molecular clocks: a variety of molecular measures for estimating the time of divergence of living *species* from their common ancestor.

Monkey: usually a small or medium-sized, long-tailed arboreal, *quadrupedal*, vegetarian *primate*. The two groups are *New World monkeys* and *Old World monkeys*.

Monogamy: among humans, having only one spouse. (Compare with *polygamy*.)

Monogyny: in zoology, generally having only one mate. (Compare with *polygyny*.)

Monomorphic: both sexes showing the same trait (e.g., similar body size).

Monophyletic clade: a group of *species* sharing a common ancestor that would be included in the group.

Morotopithecus: a *genus* of *apes* that inhabited East Africa during the early *Miocene*.

Morphological pattern: the distinctive form of a *species*; those anatomical features common to members of a species, which as a group distinguish them from other animals.

Mosaic evolution: *evolution* of different parts of the body at different rates over long periods.

Mousterian industry: a *Middle Paleolithic* tool industry from Europe and the Middle East; primarily associated with the *Neandertals*.

Mousterian of Acheulean tradition (MAT): a variety of the *Mousterian industry* that included very diverse tools, including numerous *hand axes*; associated with *Neandertals* in western Europe during the *Middle Paleolithic* period.

Movius Line: the geographic dividing line between the *Acheulean* tradition in the west and non-Acheulean lithic traditions in eastern and southeastern Asia.

mtDNA: genetic material found in the *mitochondria* of cells.

Mutation: generally, spontaneous change in the chemistry of a *gene* that can alter its *phenotypic* effect. The accumulation of such changes may contribute to *evolution* of a new *species* of animal or plant. (See also *point mutation*.)

Nasion: midline juncture of the frontonasal and nasal sutures.

Nasoalveolar clivus: anterior edge of the premaxilla.

Natural selection: the principal mechanism of Darwinian *evolutionary* change, by which the individuals best adapted to the environment contribute more offspring to succeeding generations than others do. As more of such individuals' characteristics are incorporated into the *gene pool*, the characteristics of the *population* evolve.

Neandertals: (often spelled Neanderthal) members of the species *Homo neanderthalensis*; archaic humans who lived in Europe and the Middle East between 300,000 and 30,000 years ago.

Neocortex: See *cerebral cortex*.

Neolithic: the New Stone Age; a late stage of stone tool making that began about 10,000 years ago. (See *Stone Age*.)

Neurons: nerve cells; the basic units of the nervous system.

New World monkeys: members of the *Primate order* belonging to the superfamily Ceboidea, including marmosets and howler, spider, and squirrel monkeys, among other *species*. (Compare with *Old World monkeys*.)

Niche: precise environment and resource base of a *species* or *population*.

Nocturnal: active during the hours of darkness.

Nuchal area: area of attachment of the muscles of the back of the neck, low on the occipital bone.

Nuclear family: a *family* group of two parents and their children.

Nucleic acid: a long, chainlike compound formed by a large number of *nucleotides*; present in all organisms in one or both of two forms: *DNA* and *RNA*.

Nucleotides: organic compounds, consisting of bases, sugars, and phosphates; found in cells either free or as part of polynucleotide chains.

Occipital bun: a bunlike posterior projection of the occipital bone.

Occipital condyles: pads of bone on the base of the skull that articulate with the uppermost vertebra.

Occipital torus: a ridge running side to side across the occipital bone.

Occlusal plane: the plane lying parallel to the biting surfaces of the teeth.

Occupation level: land surface occupied by prehistoric *hominids*.

Oldowan tool industry: earliest known stone-tool culture, dating 2.5 million years into the past and first made by early *Homo*. The products were very crude stone *choppers* and *flakes*.

Old World monkeys: members of the *Primate order* belonging to the superfamily Cercopithecoidea, including langurs, baboons, and macaques, among other *species*. (Compare with *New World monkeys*.)

Oligocene: the geologic epoch extending from 35 to 25 million years B.P.

Oligopithecines: late *Eocene anthropoids*; many have been collected from Egypt's Fayum Depression.

Omnivore: an animal that eats both meat and vegetation.

Omomyidae: one of the two families of *Eocene prosimians*, now extinct.

Open words: words that can be used alone by children to convey meaning; that is, nouns and some verbs. (Compare with *pivot words*.)

Opportunistic mating: mating done whenever and wherever the opportunity presents itself, and with whatever partner is available.

Opposable thumb: ability to hold thumb and index finger together in opposition, giving a *precision grip*.

Optically stimulated luminescence: a method of dating sediments by stimulating them with intense light; such stimulation causes the sediments to release trapped electrons and thus measurable light.

Orangutan: a tree-dwelling *ape* of Borneo and Sumatra. Has *prehensile* hands and feet for seizing and grasping; limbs articulated for reaching in any direction; and very long arms. Orangutans move on the ground rarely but are then *quadrupedal*.

Order: a *taxonomic* rank. Humans belong to the order *Primates*.

Oreopithecus: a *genus* of *apes* that inhabited Europe during the mid-to-late *Miocene*.

Osteodontokeratic culture: the *culture* of bone, tooth, and horn tools hypothesized by Raymond Dart for *A. africanus*; now largely dismissed.

Otavipithecus: a recently discovered *fossil ape* from the mid-*Miocene* of southern Africa.

Outbreeding: mating among unrelated individuals. (Compare with *inbreeding*.)

Pair bond: a psychological relationship between mates; thought to be marked by sexual faithfulness.

Palate: the bony plate separating the mouth from the nasal cavity. It is arched in humans and flat in *apes*.

Paleoanthropology: the study of the *fossil* and *cultural* remains and other evidence of humans' extinct ancestors.

Paleocene: the geologic epoch extending from 65 to 58 million years B.P.

Paleolithic: the Old Stone Age; the earliest stage of stone tool making, beginning about 2.5 million years ago. (See *Stone Age*.)

Paleomagnetism: magnetism preserved in rock and originally generated by the earth's magnetic field. Past fluctuations in the intensity and direction of this field allow correlation between strata; a form of *relative dating* that can be used for *absolute dating* because the historic pattern of magnetic fluctuations and reversals is known and dated.

Paleontology: the study of the *fossil* remains and biology of organisms that lived in the past.

Parallel evolution: the *evolution* of similar but not identical *adaptations* in two or more lineages.

Paranthropus: a *genus* of the family Hominidae, subfamily Australopithecinae; contains three *species*: *P. robustus*, *P. boisei*, and *P. aethiopicus*.

Paranthropus aethiopicus: robust australopithecine *species* that inhabited East Africa 2.7 to 2.3 million years ago.

Paranthropus boisei: robust australopithecine *species* from East Africa that lived 2.4 to 1.3 million years ago; also known as *Australopithecus boisei*.

Paranthropus robustus: robust australopithecine *species* that lived in South Africa 2.0–1.0 million years ago; also known as *Australopithecus robustus*.

Parapatric speciation: speciation among *populations* of sedentary organisms with adjacent ranges.

Parapithecus: a *primate* of the *Oligocene* epoch, from Egypt; probably a basal *anthropoid*.

Parental investment: any behavior toward offspring that improves the chance of the offspring's survival.

Parietal mastoid angle: angular connection between the parietal and temporal bones near the *mastoid process*.

Particulate inheritance: the transmission of hereditary characteristics by discrete units of genetic material; first proposed by Gregor Mendel (see also *genes*).

Patellar groove: groove separating the femoral condyles, particularly on the ventral aspect of the bone. The lateral lip of the patellar groove is an anterior projection from the lateral condyle that probably functions to prevent dislocation of the kneecap (patella).

Pelvis: a bony structure forming a basinlike ring at the base of the vertebral column with which the legs articulate.

Perigordian: an *Upper Paleolithic* culture of Western Europe, dating 27,000 to 21,000 years B.P.

Persistence hunting: hunting by chasing the prey until it stops, exhausted, when it can be killed.

Pharynx: the throat, above the *larynx*.

Phenetic classification: *taxonomy* based on physical similarities or differences between *species* or other taxa.

Phenotype: the observable characteristics of a plant or an animal; the expression of the *genotype*.

Phonation: the production of vowel sounds by the passage of air through the *larynx* and the *pharynx*.

Phonemes: the smallest sound components of *language*.

Phyletic transformation: the conversion (mainly through *natural selection*) of an entire *species* into a new species.

Phylogenetic classification: *taxonomy* that reflects evolutionary descent and is based on the pattern of primitive and *derived traits*; in traditional evolutionary classifications, traits may be given different weights.

Phylogeny: the evolutionary lineage of organisms; their evolutionary history.

Phylum: a major *taxonomic* rank. Humans are in the phylum *Chordata*.

Piltdown man: a "doctored" modern human skull and ape jaw "discovered" in 1911 and supposed to represent a very primitive human, *Eoanthropus dawsoni*, but exposed as a hoax in 1953.

Pithecanthropus: the original *genus* name given by Eugene Dubois to *fossil* material from Java now classified as *Homo erectus*.

Pivot words: words—prepositions, adjectives, and some verbs—used by children to modify *open words* to make two-word sentences.

Platelets: minute blood cells associated with clotting.

Platycephalic: a term describing a skull that is long, low-vaulted, and wide.

Platyrrhines: an infraorder of the *anthropoids* that includes the *New World monkeys*.

Pleistocene: the geologic epoch that lasted from about 1.6 million to 10,000 years ago.

Plesiadapiformes: *fossil* mammals of the *Paleocene* and *Eocene* that were once thought to be primitive *primates* but are now classified as relatives of *colugos*.

Pliocene: the geologic epoch extending from 5 to 1.6 million years B.P.

Plio-Pleistocene: a combination of the last two epochs of the Cenozoic era; the *Pliocene* lasted from 5 to 1.6 million years B.P. and the *Pleistocene* from 1.6 million to 10,000 years B.P.

Pneumatized: filled with air spaces.

Point mutation: usually the substitution of one *nucleotide* in a single *codon* of a *gene* that affects *protein* synthesis and *genotype*; gene *mutation*.

Polyandry: a female having multiple male sexual partners (among humans, multiple husbands).

Polygamy: having many spouses. (Compare with *monogamy*.)

Polygenic traits: traits determined by more than one *gene*.

Polygyny: in zoology, the tendency for a male to have regular sexual access to two or more females.

Polymerase chain reaction (PCR): a technique for making an infinite number of copies of a *DNA* molecule from a single precursor.

Polymorphism: the appearance of a *gene* in more than one form among individuals of a *population*.

Pondaungia: possible *anthropoid* from the late *Eocene* of Burma.

Population: usually, a local or breeding group; a group in which any two individuals have the potential of mating with each other.

Positive feedback: a process in which a positive change in one component of a system brings about changes in other components, which in turn bring about further positive changes in the first component.

Postcranial: referring to any anatomical feature that is behind the head (in *quadrupeds*) or below the head (in bipeds).

Postglenoid process: bony projection that bounds the *mandibular fossa* laterally and posteriorly.

Postorbital bar: a bar of bone running around the outside margin of the orbits of *prosimians*.

Potassium-argon dating: *chronometric dating* in which age is determined by measurement of the decay of radioactive potassium 40.

Power grip: a grip involving all fingers of the hand equally, as in grasping a baseball. (Compare with *precision grip*.)

Precision grip: a grip that involves opposing the tip of the thumb to the tips of the other fingers, allowing fine control of small objects. (Compare with *power grip*.)

Prehensile: adapted for grasping.

Primates: an *order* of placental mammals, mostly arboreal, with two suborders: the *anthropoids* and the *prosimians*.

Proceptivity: the aspect of female sexuality reflected by inviting copulation.

Proconsul: an *ape* from East Africa that lived during the *Miocene* epoch.

Prognathic: having the lower face and jaws projecting in front of the upper parts of the face.

Promiscuous: both females and males having multiple sexual partners.

Propliopithecus: an *Oligocene fossil* from Egypt believed to be a basal *catarrhine*.

Prosimians: the "premonkeys"; Old World arboreal mammals, including the small lemurs, *lorises*, and *tarsiers*. Less closely related to humans than other *primates*, some have survived with little change for nearly 50 million years.

Protein clock: a method for determining evolutionary relationships by using variations in the *proteins* of different living animal species to indicate the length of time since they diverged in their *evolution*. The method assumes a fairly constant rate of protein evolution, an assumption still open to some doubt.

Proteins: molecules composed of chains of *amino acids*.

Proteopithecus: a *genus* of late Eocene *anthropoids* from Africa.

Protoconid: see *cusps*.

Punctuated equilibrium: the hypothesis that most *species* have long periods of *stasis*, interrupted by episodes of rapid evolutionary change and *speciation* by *branching*. (Compare with *gradualism*.)

Quadrupedal: moving on four limbs.

Races: divisions of a *species*, usually based on physical or behavioral differences and less well marked than subspecies. Many anthropologists reject the concept of biological races of living humans.

Racism: the assumption of inherent superiority of certain "races," and the consequent discrimination against others.

Ramapithecus: a *fossil ape* now subsumed within the genus *Sivapithecus*; thought to be an ancestor of the *orangutan*.

Ramus: the vertical portion of the *mandible*; as opposed to the mandibular body, which bears the teeth.

Rapid-replacement hypothesis: a theoretical model for the evolution of anatomically modern humans which proposes that the existing *populations* all evolved from a single ancestral population that probably appeared in Africa or the Middle East perhaps 150,000 to 100,000 years ago. (Compare with *regional-continuity hypothesis*.)

Receptivity: the aspect of female sexuality reflected by cooperating in copulation.

Recessive: describes a trait that is expressed only when the organism is carrying two copies of the underlying hereditary material (two copies of the responsible *gene*).

Reciprocal altruism: trading of apparently altruistic acts by different individuals at different times; a variety of *bioaltruism*.

Reconciliation: the act of restoring friendly relations.

Rectus femoris: one of the muscles that flexes the hominid thigh.

Red blood cells (corpuscles): vertebrate blood cells without nuclei and containing *hemoglobin*.

Red ocher: powdered mineral and earth mixture used as a red pigment.

Regional-continuity hypothesis: a theoretical model of the evolution of anatomically modern humans which proposes that the existing *populations* evolved from ancestral populations of *Homo erectus* that already existed in the various geographic areas of their range. (Compare with *rapid-replacement hypothesis*.)

Relative dating: estimating the age of geologic deposits (and the fossils in them) by determining their stratigraphic level in relation to that of other deposits whose relative or absolute age is known. (Compare with *absolute dating*.)

Replication: the capacity of *DNA* to generate copies of itself in the nucleus of a cell.

Reproductive success: the production of viable offspring that reproduce in turn; levels of reproductive success may differ between individuals.

Retromolar gap: a space between the lower M3 and the mandibular *ramus* of *Neandertals*.

Rhinarium: the moist, hairless nose characteristic of all *prosimians* except *tarsiers*, and of most nonprimate mammals.

Ribonucleic acid: see *RNA*.

Ribosomes: cellular organelles that contribute to *protein* synthesis.

Rickets: a pathological condition involving curvature of the bones; caused by insufficient vitamin D.

RNA (ribonucleic acid): a compound found with *DNA* in cell nuclei and chemically close to DNA; transmits *genetic code* from DNA to direct the formation of *proteins*. May take two forms: messenger RNA (mRNA) or transfer RNA (tRNA).

Sacrum: the part of the vertebral column that articulates with the *pelvis* and forms the dorsal portion of the pelvic girdle.

Sagittal crest: a ridge of bone running front to rear along the midline of the skull; serves to attach certain jaw muscles. (Compare *sagittal keel*.)

Sagittal keel: a slightly raised ridge running down the midline of a skull; smaller than a *sagittal crest*.

Sagittal suture: the line of union joining the two main side bones of the braincase.

Sangoan: *Middle Paleolithic* tool industry from East and Central Africa; associated with *Homo heidelbergensis*.

Satellite DNA: tandem repetitions of *DNA* sequences that accumulate at certain locations on *chromosomes* and are usually noncoding.

Savanna: tropical or subtropical grassland, often with scattered trees (woodland savanna).

Sciatic notch: a deep indentation of the *dorsal* edge of the hominid ilium.

Scraper: a stone or bone tool for preparing hides and leather, used to scrape the fat and other tissues from the inner surface of the skin.

Secondary altriciality: the phenomenon of an infant's motor skills requiring a lengthy period of postnatal development, as opposed to its sensory systems, which are functional at birth or soon after; characteristic of *H. erectus* and later hominids. See *altricial*.

Secondary sites: archaeological sites in which the artifacts have been disturbed by natural forces and then redeposited.

Sectorial: literally, "cutting"; refers to the first lower premolar of *apes* and some *monkeys*, which acts as a cutting edge in moving against the upper *canine*.

Sedentism: a way of life marked by the lack of migratory movements and by the establishment of permanent habitations.

Selection: see *natural selection*.

Selective pressure: the influence exerted by the environment that promotes the maintenance of traits that facilitate survival in that environment and eliminates other, nonadaptive traits (see also *natural selection*).

Semicircular canals: fluid-filled canals of the inner ear that control balance and coordination.

Serum: the liquid remaining after blood has clotted.

Sex chromosomes: those *chromosomes* that carry *genes* that control gender (maleness or femaleness).

Sex-linked trait: an inherited trait coded on the sex *chromosomes*, and thus having a special distribution related to sex.

Sex swellings: hormone-induced swellings on the hindquarters of certain *primate* females; generally correlated with ovulation.

Sexual dimorphism: characteristic anatomical (and behavioral) differences between the males and females of a *species*.

Sexual selection: a category including intrasexual competition for mates (usually aggressive and among males) and intersexual mate selection (usually of males by females).

Siamang: a large-bodied *gibbon* of Asia; formerly placed in its own *genus*, *Symphalangus*, it is now classified as a *species* of Hylobates.

Siamopithecus: late *Eocene anthropoid* from Thailand.

Sickle-cell anemia: a genetically caused disease that can be fatal, in which the *red blood corpuscles* carry insufficient oxygen.

Sinanthropus pekinensis: the original name given by Davidson Black to ancient *fossils* from Zhoukoudian, near Beijing. These fossils are now classified as *Homo erectus.*

Sister groups: in *cladistics*, the groups resulting from a dichotomous evolutionary branching event; initially ranked as sister species, these groups may change rank because of subsequent branching, but must always maintain the same taxonomic level.

Sivapithecus: a *genus* of *Miocene apes* that includes *Ramapithecus* and was probably ancestral to *orangutans.*

Sociobiology: science of the biological (especially, genetic) basis of social behavior.

Socioecology: the connection between species' ecological relations and their social behavior; also the study of this connection.

Solutrean: an *Upper Paleolithic* culture existing in western Europe between 21,000 and 16,500 years B.P. Best known for its laurel-leaf blades.

Speciation: the production of new *species*, either through gradual transformation or the splitting or branching of existing species.

Species: following the biological species concept, a group of interbreeding natural *populations* that are reproductively isolated from other such groups.

Speech: the oral expression of *language*, or "spoken language" (other expressions include gestural or written language).

Spheroids: spherical stone tools probably used as hammers or missiles or to pound food.

Splicing: the action of messenger *RNA* that removes *intron* information, leaving only information from *exons.*

Stabilizing natural selection: *natural selection* that operates during periods when the environment is stable and maintains the genetic and phenotypic status quo within a *population.*

Stasis: a period of evolutionary equilibrium or inactivity.

Stereoscopic vision: vision produced by two eyes with overlapping fields, giving a sense of depth and distance; most highly evolved in hunting animals and *primates.*

Stone Age: the earliest period in cultural evolution, from more than 2 million to 5,000 years ago. Recognizable periods are the *Paleolithic*, or Old Stone Age; the *Mesolithic*, or Middle Stone Age; and the *Neolithic*, or New Stone Age (see also *Lower Paleolithic, Middle Paleolithic*, and *Upper Paleolithic*).

Stone knapping: stone flaking; generally, the production of *flake* and *core tools* by striking a stone nodule with a hammer stone or other object.

Strategy: in the special zoological sense, a complex of *adaptations* that brings about an effective and efficient means of reproduction or resource use (e.g., a species' reproductive strategy or feeding strategy). No conscious choice is implied.

Stratigraphy: the sequence of geologic strata, or rock layers, formed by materials deposited by water or wind; also, the study of this sequence.

Superior pubic ramus: portion of the pubic bone that runs between the pubic symphysis and the acetabulum.

Suprainiac fossa: a characteristic depression in the occipital bone of *Neandertals.*

Sympathetic hunting magic: the use of rituals (and associated artifacts) practitioners believed would help ensure success and safety in the hunt.

Sympatric speciation: *speciation* among *populations* with the same or overlapping geographic ranges.

Syntax: the rules of structure in *language.*

Szalatavus: *Oligocene platyrrhine monkey* from Bolivia.

Taiga: northern coniferous forest bordering the *tundra.*

Talonid: distal, heel-like portion of lower *molars.*

Taphonomy: the scientific study of the conditions under which objects are preserved as *fossils.*

Tarsier: a small Asian *prosimian* with large eyes and a long tail.

Taxonomy: classification of plants or animals into groups according to their relationships, and the ordering of these groups into hierarchies. *Taxonomic* levels are ranks within these classifications, e.g., *species* or *genus.*

Temporomandibular joint: jaw joint.

Temporonuchal crest: bony crest running around the posterior and lateral edges of the braincase.

Terrestrial: adapted to living on the ground.

Territoriality: an animal's distinctive behavior toward and tendency to defend a recognizable area of land.

Territory: the area occupied and defended by individuals or groups of animals against *conspecifics*. (Compare with *home range*.)

Thermoluminescence: a method of dating pottery and stone tools by heating them to release trapped electrons; the electrons produce measurable light.

Theropithecus oswaldi: an extinct *species* of gelada *baboon*.

Thorax: the region of the rib cage.

Tool kit: all the tools or implements used by a primitive culture; its technology. *Neandertals* had 60 or 70 kinds of known tools; *Cro-Magnons* had more than 100.

Toothcomb: a dental specialization of *prosimians* in which the lower front teeth are closely spaced and forwardly inclined.

Triangulation: in the context of anthropology, the process of interpreting the behavior of extinct *hominids* by using both *apes* and modern humans as analogue models.

True breeding (breeding true): situation in which the members of a genetic strain resemble each other in all important characteristics and show little variability.

Tuff: a rocklike substance formed from volcanic ash.

Tundra: treeless, low-vegetation arctic or subarctic plain, swampy in summer, with permanently frozen soil just beneath the surface.

Turnover pulse: the hypothesis that organisms periodically experience spurts of *speciation, extinction,* and dispersion in response to relatively rapid changes in the physical environment.

Tympanic plate: the cranial base surface of the tubular *external acoustic meatus.*

Type specimen: the *fossil* specimen that serves as the basis for identifying all other individuals in a *species,* usually the original specimen to be found.

Unearned resources: resources that are outside a predator's range, but to which it nonetheless gains secondary access by consuming prey animals with larger ranges.

Uniformitarianism: Charles Lyell's theory that the forces now affecting the earth—water and wind erosion, frost, volcanism—acted in a similar way in the past, and that change is always gradual and nondirectional.

Upper Paleolithic: a period of stone tool manufacture in the Old World that lasted from about 40,000 to 10,000 years B.P.; associated primarily with anatomically modern humans.

Veld (or veldt): South Africa's open savanna grassland, which has few bushes or trees.

Ventral: pertaining to the belly side of an animal or one of its parts; the opposite of *dorsal.*

Vertebrata: a subphylum of the chordates containing all animals with backbones; comprising fishes, amphibians, reptiles, birds, and mammals.

Victoriapithecinae: extinct subfamily of the earliest *catarrhine monkeys.*

Weir: barrier or dam made of stones or sticks set out in a stream or river and used as a fish trap.

Wernicke's area: part of the human *cerebral cortex* essential in comprehending and producing meaningful *speech.*

White blood cells (leukocytes): blood cells of vertebrates containing no hemoglobin.

Wide-knee stance: standing with the feet and knees about as far apart as the hip joints.

Xenophobia: hatred of foreigners.

Y-5 pattern: an arrangement of the cusps and grooves of the lower *molars* that is characteristic of living *hominoids.*

Zinjanthropus boisei: original name of the australopithecine *species* now called *Paranthropus boisei.*

SELECTED BIBLIOGRAPHY

PART I: EVOLUTION

General References for Further Reading

Campbell, Bernard. *Human Evolution*, 4th ed. Aldine, 1998.

Ciochon, R. L., and J. Fleagle, eds. *The Human Evolution Source Book*. Prentice Hall, 1993.

Dobzhansy, Theodosius. *Mankind Evolving*. Yale University Press, 1962.

————. *Genetics and the Origin of Species*. Columbia University Press, 1969.

————, Francisco J. Ayala, G. Ledyard Stebbins, and James W. Valentine. *Evolution*. W. H. Freeman, 1977.

Ebert, James D., et al. *Science and Creationism: A View from the National Academy of Sciences*. National Academy Press, 1984.

Gould, Stephen J. *Time's Arrow, Time's Cycle*. Harvard University Press, 1987.

Grant, Verne. *The Evolutionary Process*. Columbia University Press, 1985.

Jones, S., R. Martin, and D. Pilbeam, eds. *The Cambridge Encyclopedia of Human Evolution*. Cambridge University Press, 1992.

Mayr, Ernst. *Populations, Species and Evolution*. Harvard University Press, 1970.

Sources

Aitken, M. J. *Science-Based Dating in Archaeology*. Longmans, 1990.

Alroy, J. "Cope's Rule and the Dynamics of Body Mass Evolution in North American Fossil Mammals." *Science*, 280, 1998.

Ayala, Francisco J. "The Mechanisms of Evolution." *Scientific American*, 234, no. 3, 1978.

Brothwell Don, and Eric Higgs, eds. *Science in Archeology*, 2nd ed. Praeger, 1970.

Burckhardt F., and S. Smith. *The Correspondence of Charles Darwin*. Cambridge University Press, 1988.

Chapman, Frank M. *Handbook of Birds of Eastern North America*. Dover, 1966.

Darwin, Charles. *The Descent of Man and Selection in Relation to Sex*. John Murray, 1871.

————. *On the Origin of Species* (facsimile of 1st ed.). Harvard University Press, 1966.

————, and Alfred R. Wallace. *Evolution by Natural Selection*. Cambridge University Press, 1958.

Darwin, Francis, ed. *The Life and Letters of Charles Darwin*, 2 vols. Basic Books, 1959.

————, and A. C. Seward, eds. *More Letters of Charles Darwin*, 2 vols. John Murray, 1903.

De Vries, Hugo. *Species and Varieties*. Open Court, 1905.

————. *The Mutation Theory*, 2 vols. Open Court, 1909–1910.

Eisley, Loren. *Darwin's Century: Evolution and the Men Who Discovered It*. Doubleday, 1958.

Fisher, Sir Ronald Aylmer. *The Genetical Theory of Natural Selection*. Clarendon Press, 1930.

Gould, S. J. *Full House*. Harmony Books, 1996.

Grant, V. *The Evolutionary Process*, 2nd ed. Columbia University Press, 1991.

Grayson, D. K. "Differential Mortality and the Donner Party Disaster" *Evolutionary Anthropology*, 2, 1993.

Haldane, J. B. S. *The Causes of Evolution*. Longmans, Green, 1932.

Huxley, Julian. *Evolution: The Modern Synthesis*. Allen & Unwin, 1942.

Huxley, Thomas Henry. *Man's Place in Nature*. University of Michigan Press, 1959.

Joblonski, D. "Body-Size Evolution in Cretaceous Molluscs and the Status of Cope's Rule." *Nature*, 385, 1997.

Kolata, G. "Mutant-Gene Study Alters Estimate of Risks to Women." *The New York Times*, May 15, 1997.

Losos, J., K. I. Warheit, and T. W. Schoener. "Adaptive Differentiation Following Experimental Island Colonization in *Anolis* Lizards." *Nature*, 387, 1997.

Maynard Smith, J. "Bacteria Break the Antibiotic Bank." *Natural History*, 103, 1994.

Mayr, E. *The Growth of Biological Thought: Diversity, Evolution, and Inheritance*. Harvard University Press, 1982.

————. *One Long Argument*. Harvard University Press, 1991.

————. "What is a Species, and What is Not?" *Philosophy of Science*, 63, 1996.

Morgan, Thomas Hunt, *Evolution and Adaptation*. Macmillan, 1903.

————. *The Physical Basis of Heredity*. Lippincott, 1919.

————. *The Mechanism of Mendelian Heredity*. Constable, 1915.

Muller, Hermann J. *Genetics, Medicine and Men*. Cornell University Press, Oxford University Press, 1947.

Numbers, R. L. *The Creationists*. Knopf, 1992.

Prescott, D. M. *Cells*. Jones & Bartlett, 1988.

Price, P. W. *Biological Evolution*. Saunders College Publishing, 1996.

Raup, D. M. *Extinction, Bad Genes or Bad Luck?* W. W. Norton, 1991.

Ridley, Mark. *Evolution*, 2nd ed. Blackwell Science, 1996.

Simpson, George Gaylord. *The Meaning of Evolution*. Oxford University Press, 1950.

———. *The Major Features of Evolution*. Simon & Schuster, 1953.

Singer, M., and P. Berg. *Genes and Genomes*. University Science Books, 1991.

Strickberger, M. W. *Evolution*, 2nd ed. Jones and Bartlett, 1996.

Wallace, Alfred Russel. *My Life: A Record of Events and Opinions*, 2 vols. Chapman & Hall, 1905.

Weiner, Jonathan. *The Beak of the Finch*. Vintage Books, 1994.

Woodward, V. *Human Heredity and Society*. West, 1992.

PART II: THE ORIGIN OF HUMANKIND

General References for Further Reading

Ciochon, R., and J. Fleagle. *Primate Evolution and Human Origins*. Benjamin/Cummings, 1986.

———, (eds.) *The Human Evolution Source Book*. Prentice Hall, 1993.

Conroy, G. C. *Primate Evolution*. W. W. Norton, 1990.

Day, Michael H. *Guide to Fossil Man*, 4th ed. Cassell, 1986.

Delson, Eric, ed. *Ancestors: The Hard Evidence*. Alan R. Liss, 1985.

Fleagle, J. *Primate Adaptation and Evolution*. Academic Press, 1988.

Fobes, James, and James King, eds. *Primate Behavior*. Academic Press, 1982.

Fossey, Dian. *Gorillas in the Mist*. Houghton Mifflin, 1983.

Galdikas, B. M. F. *Reflections of Eden: My Years With the Orangutans of Borneo*. Little, Brown, 1995.

Goodall, Jane. *The Chimpanzees of Gombe*. Harvard University Press, 1986.

Hamburg, David A., and Elizabeth R. McCown. *The Great Apes*. Benjamin/Cummings, 1979.

Jones, S., R. Martin, and D. Pilbeam, eds. *The Cambridge Encyclopedia of Human Evolution*. Cambridge University Press, 1992.

Kinzey, W. G., ed. *The Evolution of Human Behavior: Primate Models*. State University of New York Press, 1987.

Kummer, Hans. *In Quest of the Sacred Baboon*. Princeton University Press, 1995.

Larson, S. G. "Parallel Evolution in the Hominoid Trunk and Forelimb." *Evolutionary Anthropology*, 6, 1998.

Le Gros Clark, W. E. *The Antecedents of Man*. Edinburgh University Press, 1959.

———. *Man-Apes or Ape-Men?* Holt, Rinehart & Winston, 1967.

———, and Bernard G. Campbell, *The Fossil Evidence for Human Evolution*. University of Chicago Press, 1978.

Loy, J. D., and C. B. Peters, eds. *Understanding Behavior: What Primate Studies Tell Us About Human Behavior*. Oxford University Press, 1991.

Szalay, Frederic S., and Eric Delson. *Evolutionary History of the Primates*. Academic Press, 1979.

Waal, Frans de. *Chimpanzee Politics: Power and Sex Among Apes*. Harper & Row, 1982.

Wrangham, R. W., W. C. McGrew, F. B. M. de Waal, and P. G. Heltne, eds. *Chimpanzee Cultures*. Harvard University Press, 1994.

Sources

Aiello, L., and C. Dean. *An Introduction to Human Evolutionary Anatomy*. Academic Press, 1990.

———, and P. Wheeler, "The Expensive-Tissue Hypothesis." *Current Anthropology*, 36, 1995.

Alpagut, B., P. Andrews, M. Fortelius, J. Kappelman, I. Temizsoy, H. Celebi, and W. Lindsay. "A New Specimen of *Ankarapithecus meteai* From the Sinap Formation of Central Anatolia." *Nature*, 382, 1996.

Asfaw, B., T. White, O. Lovejoy, B. Latimer, S. Simpson, and G. Suwa. "*Australopithecus garhi*: A New Species of Early Hominid from Ethiopia." *Science*, 284, 1999.

Bailey, W. J. "Hominoid Trichotomy: A Molecular Overview." *Evolutionary Anthropology*, 2, 1993.

Bartlett, T., R. Sussman, and J. Cheverud. "Infant Killing in Primates: A Review of Observed Cases with Specific Reference to the Sexual Selection Hypothesis." *American Anthropologist*, 95, 1993.

Beard, K. C., Tao Qi, M. R. Dawson, Banyue Wang, and Chuankuei Li. "A Diverse New Primate Fauna from Middle Eocene Fissure-Fillings in Southeastern China." *Nature*, 368, 1994.

———, Yongsheng Tong, M. R. Dawson, Jingwen Wang, and Xueshi Huang. "Earliest Complete Dentition of an Anthropoid Primate From the Late Middle Eocene of Shanxi Province, China." *Science*, 272, 1996.

Begley, S. "Out of Africa, A Missing Link." *Newsweek*, October 3, 1994.

Begun, D. R. "Relations Among the Great Apes and Humans: New Interpretations Based on the Fossil Great Ape *Dryopithecus*." *Yearbook of Physical Anthropology*, 37, 1994.

Behrensmeyer, A. K., N. E. Todd, R. Potts, and G. E. McBrinn. "Late Pliocene Faunal Turnover in the Turkana Basin, Kenya and Ethiopia." *Science*, 278, 1997.

Beneviste, R. E., and G. J. Todaro. "Evolution of Type C Viral Genes: Evidence for an Asian Origin of Man." *Nature*, 261, 1976.

Berger, L. R., and P. V. Tobias. "A Chimpanzee-like Tibia from Sterkfontein, South Africa and its Implications for the Interpretation of Bipedalism in *Australopithecus africanus*." *Journal of Human Evolution*, 30, 1996.

Blumenschine, R. J. "Percussion Marks, Tooth Marks, and Experimental Determinations of the Timing of Hominid and Carnivore Access to Long Bones at FLK *Zinjanthropus*, Olduvai Gorge, Tanzania." *Journal of Human Evolution*, 29, 1995.

Boesch-Achermann, H., and C. Boesch. "Hominization in the Rainforest: The Chimpanzee's Piece of the Puzzle." *Evolutionary Anthropology*, 3, 1994.

Bromage, T. G., F. Schrenk, and F. W. Zonneveld. "Paleoanthropology of the Malawi Rift: An Early Hominid Mandible From the Chiwondo Beds, Northern Malawi." *Journal of Human Evolution*, 28, 1995.

Broom, Robert. *Finding the Missing Link*. Watts, 1950.

Brown, B., A. Walker, C. V. Ward, and R. E. Leakey. "New *Australopithecus boisei* Calvaria from East Lake Turkana, Kenya." *American Journal of Physical Anthropology*, 91, 1993.

Brunet, B., A. Beauvilain, Y. Coppens, E. Heintz, A. H. E. Moutaye, and D. Pilbeam. "*Australopithecus bahrelghazali*, Une Nouvelle Espece d'Hominide Ancien de la Region de Koro Toro (Tchad)." *Paleontology* (Academy of Sciences, Paris), 322, 1996.

———."The First Australopithecine 2,500 Kilometres West of the Rift Valley (Chad)." *Nature*, 378, 1995.

Butzer, Karl W. *Environment and Archeology: An Ecological Approach to Prehistory*. Aldine-Atherton, 1971.

Cartmill, M. "New Views on Primate Origins." *Evolutionary Anthropology*, 1, 1992.

———. "Rethinking Primate Origins." *Science*, 184, 1974.

Chalmanee, Y., V. Suteethorn, J.-J. Jaeger, and S. Ducrocq. "A New Late Eocene Anthropoid Primate From Thailand." *Nature*, 385, 1997.

Cheney, D. L. "Interactions and Relationships Between Groups," in B. Smuts et al., eds., *Primate Societies*. University of Chicago Press, 1987.

———, and R. M. Seyfarth. *How Monkeys See the World*. University of Chicago Press, 1990.

Chivers, David L., Bernard W. Wood, and Alan Bilsborough, eds. *Food Acquisition and Processing in Primates*. Plenum Press, 1984.

Ciochon, Russell L., and Robert S. Corrucini. *New Interpretations of Ape and Human Ancestry*. Plenum Press, 1983.

Clark, J. Dresmond. *The Prehistory of Africa*. Praeger, 1970.

Clarke, R. J., and P. V. Tobias. "Sterkfontein Member 2 Foot Bones of the Oldest South African Hominid." *Science*, 269, 1995.

Coffing, K. C. Feibel, M. Leakey, and A. Walker. "Four-Million-Year-Old Hominids from East Lake Turkana, Kenya." *American Journal of Physical Anthropology*, 93, 1994.

Conroy, G. C. *Reconstructing Human Origins*. W. W. Norton, 1997.

———, G. W. Weber, H. Seidler, P. V. Tobias, A. Kane, and B. Brunsden. "Endocranial Capacity in an Early Hominid Cranium from Sterkfontein, South Africa." *Science*, 280, 1998.

———, M. Pickford, B. Senut, and P. Mein. "Diamonds in the Desert: The Discovery of *Otavipithecus namibiensis*." *Evolutionary Anthropology*, 2, 1993.

Coppens, Y. "East Side Story: The Origin of Humankind." *Scientific American*, 270, 1994.

———, F. Clark Howell, G. L. Isaac, and Richard E. F. Leakey, eds. *Earliest Man and Environments in the Lake Rudolf Basin*. University of Chicago Press, 1976.

Dart, Raymond. *Adventures with the Missing Link*. Viking Press, 1959.

Dalh, J. F. "Cyclic Perineal Swelling During the Intermenstrual Intervals of Captive Female Pygmy Chimpanzees (*Pan paniscus*)." *Journal of Human Evolution*, 15, 1986.

Doran, D. M., and A. McNeilage. "Gorilla Ecology and Behavior." *Evolutionary Anthropology*, 6, 1998.

Dunbar, R. I. M. "Neocortex Size as a Constraint on Group Size in Primates." *Journal of Human Evolution*, 20, 1992.

———. "The Price of Being at the Top." *Nature*, 373, 1995.

Falk, D. *Braindance*. Henry Holt, 1992.

Feathers, J. K. "Luminescence Dating and Modern Human Origins." *Evolutionary Anthropology*, 5, 1996.

Fischman, J. "Putting a New Spin on the Birth of Human Birth." *Science*, 264, 1994.

Fleagle, J. G., D. T. Rasmussen, S. Yirga, T. M. Brown, and F. E. Grine, "New Hominid Fossils from Fejej, Southern Ethiopia." *Journal of Human Evolution*, 21, 1991.

Friday, A. E. "Human Evolution: The Evidence From DNA Sequencing," in S. Jones, R. Martin, and D. Pilbeam, eds. *The Cambridge Encyclopedia of Human Evolution*, Cambridge University Press, 1992.

Furuichi, T. "The Prolonged Estrus of Females and Factors Influencing Mating in a Wild Group of Bonobos (*Pan paniscus*) in Wamba, Zaire," in N. Itoigawa et al., eds., *Topics in Primatology, vol. 2: Behavior, Ecology, and Conservation*. University of Tokyo Press, 1992.

Gabunia, L., and A. Vekua. "A Plio-Pleistocene Hominid from Dmanisi, East Georgia, Caucasus." *Nature*, 373, 1995.

Gagneux, P., D. S. Woodruff, and C. Boesch. "Furtive Mating in Female Chimpanzees." *Nature*, 387, 1997.

Gebo, D. L. "Climbing, Brachiation, and Terrestrial Quadrupedalism: Historical Precursors of Hominid Bipedalism." *American Journal of Physical Anthropology*, 101, 1996.

———, L. MacLatchy, R. Kityo, A. Deino, J. Kingston, and D. Pilbeam. "A Hominoid Genus From the Early Miocene of Uganda." *Science*, 276, 1997.

Giacobini, G. *Hominidae: Proceedings of the Second International Congress of Human Paleontology, Turin, September–October 1987*. Jaca Book, 1989.

Goodman, M. "Protein Sequencing and Immunological Specificity," in W. Luckett and F. Szalay, eds. *Phylogeny of the Primates*, Plenum, 1975.

Greenfield, L. O. "Origin of the Human Canine: A New Solution to an Old Enigma." *Yearbook of Physical Anthropology*, 35, 1992.

Grine, F. E. "Australopithecine Taxonomy and Phylogeny: Historical Background and Recent Interpretation," in R. L. Ciochon and J. G. Fleagle, eds. *The Human Evolution Source Book*. Prentice Hall, 1993.

———, B. Demes, W. L. Jungers, and T. M. Cole, III. "Taxonomic Affinity of the Early *Homo* Cranium from Swartkrans, South Africa." *American Journal of Physical Anthropology*, 92, 1993.

Harris, Jack W. K. "Cultural Beginnings: Plio-Pleistocene Archaeological Occurrences from the Afar, Ethiopia." *African Archaeological Review*, 1, 1983.

Hartwig-Scherer, S. "Body Weight Prediction in Early Fossil Hominids: Towards a Taxon-Independent Approach." *American Journal of Physical Anthropology*, 92, 1993.

Hausfater, G. *Dominance and Reproduction in Baboons (Papio cynocephalus)*. S. Karger, 1975.

———, and Sarah Blaffer-Hrdy, eds. *Infanticide: Comparative and Evolutionary Perspectives*. Aldine, 1984.

Hawkes, N. "'Missing Link' Ate Fruit and Leaves." *The Times (London)*, September 22, 1994.

Heltne, P. G., and L. A. Marquardt, eds. *Understanding Chimpanzees*. Harvard University Press, 1989.

Hill, Andrew, and S. Ward. "Origin of the Hominidae: The Record of African Large Hominoid Evolution Between 14 My and 4 My." *Yearbook of Physical Anthropology*, 31, 1988.

———, and B. Brown. "Anatomy and Age of the Lothagam Mandible." *Journal of Human Evolution*, 22, 1992.

Hohmann, G., and B. Fruth. "Field Observations on Meat Sharing Among Bonobos (*Pan paniscus*)." *Folia Primatologica*, 60, 1993.

Howells, W. *Getting Here*. Compass Press, 1993.

Hrdy, Sarah B. *The Langurs of Abu: Female and Male Strategies of Reproduction*. Harvard University Press, 1977.

Huffman, M. A., and R. Wrangham. "Diversity of Medicinal Plant Use by Chimpanzees in the Wild," in R. Wrangham et al., eds., *Chimpanzee Cultures*. Harvard University Press, 1994.

Ingmanson, Ellen J. "Tool-using Behavior in Wild *Pan paniscus*: Social and Ecological Considerations," in A. E. Russon et al., eds., *Reaching Into Thought: The Minds of the Great Apes*. Cambridge University Press, 1996.

Isaac, G. L., and Elizabeth R. McCrown, eds. *Human Origins*. Staples Press, 1976.

Isbell, L. A., and T. P. Young. "The Evolution of Bipedalism in Hominids and Reduced Group Size in Chimpanzees: Alternative Responses to Decreasing Resource Availability." *Journal of Human Evolution*, 30, 1996.

Jablonski, N. G., and G. Chaplin. "The Origin of Hominid Bipedalism Re-examined." *Perspectives in Human Biology, 2/Archaeology in Oceania*, 27, 1992.

Johanson, Donald C., and Maitland A. Edey. *Lucy: The Beginnings of Humankind*. Simon and Schuster, 1981.

———, and Blake Edgar. *From Lucy to Language*. Simon and Schuster, 1996.

———, and Tim D. White. "A Systematic Assessment of Early African Hominids." *Science*, 203, 1979.

Jolly, Clifford. "The Seed-Eaters." *Man*, 5, no. 1, March 1970.

Kappelman, J., G. C. Swisher, J. G. Fleagle, S. Yirga, T. M. Bown, and M. Feseha. "Age of *Australopithecus afarensis* From Fejej, Ethiopia." *Journal of Human Evolution*, 30, 1996.

Kay, R. F., C. Ross, and B. A. Williams. "Anthropoid Origins." *Science*, 275, 1997.

———, J. G. M. Thewissen, and A. D. Yoder. "Cranial Anatomy of *Ignacious graybullianus* and the Affinities of the Plesiadapiformes." *American Journal of Physical Anthropology*, 89, 1992.

Kerr, R. A. "New Mammal Data Challenge Evolutionary Pulse Theory." *Science*, 273, 1996.

Kidd. R. S., P. O'Higgins, C. E. Oxnard. "The OH8 Foot: A Reappraisal of the Functional Morphology of the Hindfoot Utilizing a Multivariate Analysis." *Journal of Human Evolution*, 31, 1996.

Kimbel, W. H., R. C. Walter, D. C. Johanson, K. E. Reed, J. L. Aronson, Z. Assefa, C. W. Marean, G. G. Eck, R. Bobe, E. Hovers, Y. Rak, C. Vondra, T. Yemane, D. York, Y. Chen, N. M. Evensen, and P. E. Smith. "Late Pliocene *Homo* and Oldowan Tools From the Hadar Formation (Kada Hadar Member), Ethiopia." *Journal of Human Evolution*, 31, 1996.

Kummer, Hans. *Social Organization of Hamadryas Baboons*. University of Chicago Press, 1968.

Lancaster, Jane B., and C. S. Lancaster. "Parental Investment: The Hominid Adaptation," in D. J. Ortner, ed., *How Humans Adapt: A Biocultural Odyssey*. Smithsonian Institute Press, 1983.

Leakey, Mary D. *Olduvai Gorge*, vol. 3. Cambridge University Press, 1971.

Leakey, Meave. "The Dawn of Humans: The Farthest Horizon." *National Geographic*, 188, 1995.

———, and A. Walker. "Early Hominid Fossils From Africa." *Scientific American*, 276, 1997.

———, C. S. Feibel, I. McDougall, and A. Walker. "New Four-Million-Year-Old Hominid Species from Kanapoi and Allia Bay, Kenya." *Nature*, 376, 1995.

Leonard, W. R., and M. L. Robertson. "Energetic Efficiency of Human Bipedality." *American Journal of Physical Anthropology*, 97, 1995.

Lieberman, D. E., B. A. Wood, and D. R. Pilbeam. "Homoplasy and Early *Homo*: An Analysis of the Evolutionary Relationships of *H. habilis sensu stricto* and *H. rudolfensis*." *Journal of Human Evolution*, 30, 1996.

Lovejoy, C. Owen. "Evolution of Human Walking." *Scientific American*, 259, 1988.

———. "Modeling Human Origins: Are We Sexy Because We're Smart, or Smart Because We're Sexy?" in D. T. Rasmussen, ed., *The Origin and Evolution of Humans and Humanness*. Jones & Bartlett, 1993.

———. "The Origin of Man." *Science*, 211, no. 4480, 1981.

Martin, R. D. *Primate Origins and Evolution: A Phylogenetic Reconstruction*. Chapman & Hall, 1990.

———. "Primate Origins: Plugging the Gaps." *Nature*, 363, 1993.

McCrossin, M. L. "Bridging the Gap: Connecting the Origin of Bipedalism in Pliocene Hominidae With the Advent of Semi-terrestrial Adaptations Among African Miocene Hominoidea." *Journal of Human Evolution*, 32, 1997.

———. "New Postcranial Remains of *Kenyapithecus* and Their Implications for Understanding the Origins of Hominoid Terrestriality." *American Journal of Physical Anthropology*, Suppl. 24, 1997.

McGrew, W. C. *Chimpanzee Material Culture*. Cambridge University Press, 1992.

McHenry, H. M. "How Big Were Early Hominids?" *Evolutionary Anthropology*, 1, 1992.

———. "Behavioral Ecological Implications of Early Hominid Body Size." *Journal of Human Evolution*, 27, 1994.

———, and L. R. Berger. "Body Proportions in *Australopithecus afarensis* and *A. africanus* and the Origin of the Genus *Homo*." *Journal of Human Evolution*, 35, 1998.

McKee, J. K. "Faunal Dating of the Taung Hominid Fossil Deposit." *Journal of Human Evolution*, 25, 1993.

Melnick, D. J., and M. C. Pearl. "Cercopithecines in Multimale Groups: Genetic Diversity and Population Structure," in B. Smuts et al., eds., *Primate Societies*. University of Chicago Press, 1987.

Mithen, S. *The Prehistory of the Mind*. Thames and Hudson, 1996.

"Moyá-Solà, S., and M. Köhler. "A *Dryopithecus* Skeleton and the Origins of Great-ape Locomotion." *Nature*, 379, 1996.

Napier, John. *The Roots of Mankind*. Smithsonian Institution Press, 1970.

———, and P. H. Napier. *Handbook of Living Primates*. Academic Press, 1967.

———, and ———. *The Natural History of the Primates*. British Museum (Natural History) and Cambridge University Press, 1985.

Nishida, T. *Chimpanzees of the Mahale Mountains*. University of Tokyo Press, 1990.

———, and M. Hiraiwa-Hasegawa. "Chimpanzees and Bonobos: Cooperative Relationships Among Males," in B. Smuts et al., eds., *Primate Societies*. University of Chicago Press, 1987.

Oakley, Kenneth, Bernard G. Campbell, and Theya L. Mollison, eds. *Catalogue of Fossil Hominids: Part I*, 2nd ed. Trustees of the British Museum (Natural History), 1977.

Oxnard, Charles. *The Order of Man*. Yale University Press, 1984.

Packer, C., D. A. Collins, A. Sindimwo, and J. Goodall. "Reproductive Constraints on Aggressive Competition in Female Baboons." *Nature*, 373, 1995.

Palombit, Ryne. "Dynamic Pair Bonds in Hylobatids: Implications Regarding Monogamous Social Systems." *Behavior*, 128, 1994.

Parish, A. R. "Sex and Food Control in the 'Uncommon Chimpanzee': How Bonobo Females Overcame a Phylogenetic Legacy of Male Dominance." *Ethology and Sociobiology*, 15, 1994.

Pilbeam, D. "Genetic and Morphological Records of the Hominoidea and Hominid Origins: A Synthesis." *Molecular Phylogenetics and Evolution*, 5, 1996.

Plavcan, J. M., and J. Kelley. "Evaluating the 'Dual Selection' Hypothesis of Canine Reduction." *American Journal of Physical Anthropology*, 99, 1996.

Potts, R. "Archeological Interpretations of Early Hominid Behavior and Ecology," in D. T. Rasmussen, ed. *The Origin and Evolution of Humans and Humanness*. Jones & Bartlett, 1993.

———. *Early Hominid Activities at Olduvai*. Aldine de Gruyter, 1988.

———. *Humanity's Descent*. William Morrow, 1996.

Price, Peter W. *Biological Evolution*. Saunders College Publishing, 1996.

Pusey, A., J. Williams, and J. Goodall. "The Influence of Dominance Rank on the Reproductive Success of Female Chimpanzees." *Science*, 277, 1997.

Rasmussen, D. T., and E. L. Simons. "Paleobiology of the Oligopithecines, the Earliest Known Anthropoid Primates." *International Journal of Primatology*, 13, 1992.

Reichard, Ulrich. "Extra-pair Copulations in a Monogamous Gibbon (*Hylobates lar*)." *Ethology*, 100, 1995.

Richmond, B. G., and W. L. Jungers. "Size Variations and Sexual Dimorphism in *Australopithecus afarensis* and Living Hominoids." *Journal of Human Evolution*, 29, 1995.

Rightmire, G. P. "Variation Among Early *Homo* Crania from Olduvai Gorge and the Koobi Fora Region." *American Journal of Physical Anthropology*, 90, 1993.

Roberts, N. "Climatic Change in the Past," in S. Jones et al., eds., *The Cambridge Encyclopedia of Human Evolution*. Cambridge University Press, 1992.

Rodman, P. S., and J. C. Mitani, "Orangutans: Sexual Dimorphism in a Solitary Species," in B. Smuts et al., eds., *Primate Societies*. University of Chicago Press, 1987.

Rogers, L. J., and G. Kaplan. "A New Form of Tool Use by Orang-Utans in Sabah, East Malaysia." *Folia Primatologica*, 63, 1994.

Rose, L., and F. Marshall. "Meat Eating, Hominid Sociality, and Home Bases Revisited." *Current Anthropology*, 37, 1996.

Ruff, C. B. "Biomechanics of the Hip and Birth in Early *Homo*." *American Journal of Physical Anthropology*, 98, 1995.

Sarich, V. M., and J. E. Cronin. "Generation Length and Rates of Hominoid Molecular Evolution." *Nature*, 269, 1977.

———, and A. C. Wilson. "Immunological Time Scale for Hominoid Evolution." *Science*, 158, 1967.

van Schaik, C. P., E. A. Fox, and A. F. Sitompul. "Manufacture and Use of Tools in Wild Sumatran Orangutans." *Naturwissenschaften*, 83, 1996.

———, and J. A. R. A. M. van Hooff. "Toward an Understanding of the Orangutan's Social System," in W. C. McGrew et al., eds., *Great Ape Societies*. Cambridge University Press, 1996.

Schaller, George B. *Year of the Gorilla*. University of Chicago Press, 1964.

———, and Gordon Lowther. "The Relevance of Carnivore Behavior to the Study of Early Hominids." *Southwestern Journal of Anthropology*, 25, 1969.

Schick, K. D., and N. Toth. *Making Silent Stones Speak*. Simon & Schuster, 1993.

Schrenk, F., T. G. Bromage, C. G. Betzler, U. Ring, and Y. M. Juwayeyi. "Oldest *Homo* and Pliocene Biogeography of the Malawi Rift." *Nature*, 365, 1993.

Schultz, Adolph H. *The Life of Primates*. Universe Books, 1969.

———. "The Recent Hominoid Primates," in S. L. Washburn and P. C. Jay, eds., *Perspectives on Human Evolution 1*. Holt, Rinehart and Winston, 1968.

Schwartz, J. H. *Skeleton Keys*. Oxford University Press, 1995.

Semaw, S., P. Renne, J. W. K. Harris, C. S. Feibel, R. L. Bernor, N. Fesseha, and K. Mowbray. "2.5-Million-Year-Old Stone Tools From Gona, Ethiopia." *Nature*, 385, 1997.

Senut, B. "New Ideas on the Origins of Hominid Locomotion," in T. Nishida, W. McGrew, P. Marler, M. Pickford, and F. de Waal, eds., *Topics in Primatology: Vol. 1. Human Origins*. University of Tokyo Press, 1992.

Shreeve, J. "Sunset on the Savanna." *Discover*, 17, 1996.

Simons, E. L. *Primate Evolution*. Macmillan, 1972.

———. "Egypt's Simian Spring." *Natural History*, 102, 1993.

———, and D. T. Rasmussen. "Skull of *Catopithecus browni*, an Early Tertiary Catarrhine." *American Journal of Physical Anthropology*, 100, 1996.

Shipman, Pat. "Scavenging or Hunting in Early Hominids: Theoretical Framework and Tests." *American Anthropologist*, 88, 1986.

Skelton, R. R., and H. M. McHenry. "Evolutionary Relationships Among Early Hominids." *Journal of Human Evolution*, 23, 1992.

Small, M. F. *Female Choices*. Cornell University Press, 1993.

Sponheimer, M., and J. A. Lee-Thorp. "Isotopic Evidence for the Diet of an Early Hominid, *Australopithecus africanus*." *Science*, 283, 1999.

Spoor, F., B. Wood, and F. Zonneveld. "Implications of Early Hominid Labyrinthine Morphology for Evolution of Human Bipedal Locomotion." *Nature*, 369, 1994.

Stanford, Craig B. "The Hunting Ecology of Wild Chimpanzees: Implications for the Evolutionary Ecology of Pliocene Hominids." *American Anthropologist*, 98, 1996.

———. "The Social Behavior of Chimpanzees and Bonobos." *Current Anthropology*, 39, 1998.

Steudel, K. "Limb Morphology, Bipedal Gait, and the Energetics of Hominid Locomotion." *American Journal of Physical Anthropology*, 99, 1996.

Stewart, I. "Real Australopithecines Do Eat Meat." *New Scientist*, 134, 1992.

Stewart, K. I., and A. H. Harcourt. "Gorillas: Variation in Female Relationships," in B. Smuts et al., eds., *Primate Societies*. University of Chicago Press, 1987.

Strum, Shirley C. *Almost Human: A Journey into the World of Baboons*. Elm Tree Books, 1987.

Susman, R. L., ed. *The Pygmy Chimpanzee: Evolutionary Biology and Behavior*. Plenum Press, 1984.

———. "Fossil Evidence for Early Hominid Tool Use." *Science*, 265, 1994.

Sussman, R. W. "Primate Origins and the Evolution of Angiosperms." *American Journal of Primatology*, 23, 1991.

Suwa, G., T. D. White, and F. C. Howell. "Mandibular Postcanine Dentition From the Shungura Formation, Ethiopia: Crown Morphology, Taxonomic Allocations, and Plio-Pleistocene Hominid Evolution." *American Journal of Physical Anthropology*, 101, 1996.

Szalay, Frederic S., and Eric Delson. *Evolutionary History of the Primates*. Academic Press, 1979.

Tanner, Nancy M. *On Becoming Human*. Cambridge University Press, 1981.

Tattersall, Ian. "Out of Africa Again . . . and Again?" *Scientific American*, 276, 1997.

———. *The Fossil Trail*. Oxford University Press, 1995.

Tobias, P. V. *Hominid Evolution*. Alan R. Liss, 1985.

———. *The Brain in Hominid Evolution*. Columbia University Press, 1971.

———. "The Brain of *Homo habilis*: A New Level of Organization in Cerebral Evolution." *Journal of Human Evolution*, 16, 1987.

Trevathan, W. *Human Birth: An Evolutionary Perspective*. Aldine de Gruyter, 1987.

———. "Fetal Emergence Patterns in Evolutionary Perspective." *American Anthropologist*, 90, 1988.

Turner, A., and B. Wood. "Comparative Palaeontological Context for the Evolution of the Early Hominid Masticatory System." *Journal of Human Evolution*, 24, 1993.

Tuttle, Russell, ed. *The Functional and Evolutionary Biology of Primates*. Aldine-Atherton, 1972.

Vrba, E. S. "Ecological and Adaptive Changes Associated with Early Hominid Evolution" in R. L. Ciochon and J. G. Fleagle, eds., *The Human Evolution Source Book*. Prentice Hall, 1993.

———. "The Pulse That Produced Us." *Natural History*, 102, 1993.

Waal, F. de *Peacemaking Among Primates*. Harvard University Press, 1989.

———, and F. Lanting. *Bonobo: The Forgotten Ape*. University of California Press, 1997.

Walker, Alan, Richard E. Leakey, John M. Harris, and Frank H. Brown. "2.5 myr *Australopithecus boisei* from West of Lake Turkana, Kenya." *Nature*, 322, 1986.

Ward, C. V., A. Walker, M. F. Teaford, and I. Odhiambo. "Partial Skeleton of *Proconsul nyanzae* from Mfangano Island, Kenya." *American Journal of Physical Anthropology*, 90, 1993.

Wheeler, P. "The Influence of Bipedalism on the Energy and Water Budgets of Early Hominids." *Journal of Human Evolution*, 21, 1991.

———. "The Thermoregulatory Advantages of Hominid Bipedalism in Open Equatorial Environments: The Contribution of Increased Convective Heat Loss and Cutaneous Evaporative Cooling." *Journal of Human Evolution*, 21, 1991.

———. "Human Ancestors Walked Tall, Stayed Cool." *Natural History*, 102, 1993.

White, F. J. "Activity Budgets, Feeding Behavior, and Habitat Use of Pygmy Chimpanzees at Lomako, Zaire." *American Journal of Primatology*, 26, 1992.

White, T. D., G. Suwa, and B. Asfaw. "*Australopithecus ramidus*, A New Species of Early Hominid from Aramis, Ethiopia." *Nature*, 371, 1994 (also 375, 1995).

———, G. Suwa, W. K. Hart, R. C. Walter, G. WoldeGabriel, J. de Heinzelin, J. D. Clark, B. Asfaw, and E. Vrba. "New Discoveries of *Australopithecus* at Maka in Ethiopia." *Nature*, 366, 1993.

———, Donald C. Johanson, and William H. Kimbel. "*Australopithecus africanus*: Its Phyletic Position Reconsidered." *South African Journal of Science*, 77, 1981.

Wilford, J. N. "Near-intact Skeleton Offers Clues to Human Tree's Roots." *The New York Times*, December 10, 1998.

———. "New Fossils Take Science Close to Dawn of Humans." *The New York Times*, September 22, 1994.

WoldeGabriel, G., T. D. White, G. Suwa, P. Renne, J. de Heinzelin, W. K. Hart, and G. Helken. "Ecological and Temporal Placement of Early Pliocene Hominids at Aramis, Ethiopia." *Nature*, 371, 1994.

Wolpoff, M. H. *Human Evolution* (1996–1997 edition). McGraw-Hill, 1996.

Wood, B. "Origin and Evolution of the Genus *Homo*." *Nature*, 355, 1992.

———. "The Oldest Hominid Yet." *Nature*, 371, 1994.

Wrangham, Richard, and Dale Peterson. *Demonic Males*. Houghton Mifflin, 1996.

Yamakoshi, Gen, and Yukimaru Sugiyama. "Pestle-Pounding Behavior of Wild Chimpanzees at Bossou, Guinea: A Newly Observed Tool-Using Behavior," *Primates*, 36, 1995.

PART III: THE EVOLUTION OF HUMANKIND

General References for Further Reading

Flint, Richard Foster. *Glacial and Quaternary Geology*. Wiley, 1971.

Howells, William E. "*Homo erectus*—Who, When, and Where: A Survey." *Yearbook of Physical Anthropology*, 23, 1980.

Le Gros Clark, Wilfrid E., and Bernard G. Campbell. *The Fossil Evidence for Human Evolution*. University of Chicago Press, 1978.

Savage-Rumbaugh, S., and R. Lewin. *Kanzi: The Ape at the Brink of the Human Mind*. Wiley, 1994.

Sources

Aiello, L., and C. Dean. *An Introduction to Human Evolutionary Anatomy*. Academic Press, 1990.

———, and P. Wheeler. "The Expensive-Tissue Hypothesis." *Current Anthropology*, 36, 1995.

———, and R. I. M. Dunbar. "Neocortex Size, Group Size, and the Evolution of Language." *Current Anthropology*, 34, 1993.

Ascenzi, A., I. Biddittu, P. F. Cassoli, A. G. Segre, and E. Segre-Naldini. "A Calvarium of Late *Homo erectus* From Ceprano, Italy." *Journal of Human Evolution*, 31, 1996.

Aschoff, J., B. Gunther, and K. Kramer. *Energiehaushalt und Temperaturregulation*. Urban and Schwarzenberg, 1971.

Begun, D., and A. Walker. "The Endocast," in A. Walker and R. Leakey, eds., *The Nariokotome Homo erectus Skeleton*. Harvard University Press, 1993.

Bellomo, R. V. "Methods of Determining Early Hominid Behavioral Activities Associated with the Controlled Use of Fire at FxJj 20 Main, Koobi Fora, Kenya." *Journal of Human Evolution*, 27, 1994.

Binford, Lewis R. *Bones: Ancient Men and Modern Myths*. Academic Press, 1981.

———. *Faunal Remains from Klasies River Mouth*. Academic Press, 1984.

———, and C. K. Ho. "Taphonomy at a Distance. Zhoukoudian, 'The Cave of Beijing Man'?" *Current Anthropology*, 26, 1985.

———, and N. M. Stone. "Zhoukoudian: A Closer Look." *Current Anthropology*, 27, 1986.

Borja, C., M. Garcia-Pacheco, E. G. Olivares, G. Scheuenstuhl, and J. M. Lowenstein. "Immunospecificity of Albumin Detected in 1.6 Million-Year-Old Fossils From Venta Micena in Orce, Granada, Spain." *American Journal of Physical Anthropology*, 103, 1997.

Braga, J., and C. Boesch. "Further Data About Venous Channels in South African Plio-Pleistocene Hominids." *Journal of Human Evolution*, 33, 1997.

Brauer, G., and M. Schultz. "The Morphological Affinities of the Plio-Pleistocene Mandible From Dmanisi, Georgia." *Journal of Human Evolution*, 30, 1996.

Brown, Frank, John Harris, Richard E. Leakey, and Alan Walker. "Early *Homo erectus* Skeleton from West Lake Turkana, Kenya" *Nature*, 316, 1985.

Butzer, Karl W. "Acheulian Occupation Sites at Torralba and Ambrona, Spain: Their Geology." *Science*, 150, no. 3704, 1965.

———, and G. L. Isaac, eds. *After the Australopithecines: Stratigraphy, Ecology, and Culture Change in the Middle Pleistocene*. Mouton, 1975.

Campbell, Bernard G., ed. *Sexual Selection and the Descent of Man, 1871–1971*. Aldine, 1972.

Cartmill, M. *A View to a Death in the Morning*. Harvard University Press, 1993.

Chang, Kwang-chih. *The Archaeology of Ancient China*. Yale University Press, 1968.

Cheney, D. L., and R. Seyfarth. *How Monkeys See the World*. University of Chicago Press, 1990.

Conroy, G. C. *Reconstructing Human Origins*. W. W. Norton, 1997.

Convey, Curt. "Earth's Orbit and the Ice Ages." *Scientific American*, 250, 1984.

de Lumley, Henry. "A Paleolithic Camp at Nice." *Scientific American*, 220, no. 5, 1969.

Dronkers, N. F. "A New Brain Region for Coordinating Speech Articulation." *Nature*, 384, 1996.

Duchin, Linda E. "The Evolution of Articulate Speech," *Journal of Human Evolution*, 19, 1990.

Dunbar, R. I. M. "The Social Brain Hypothesis." *Evolutionary Anthropology*, 6, 1998.

Falk, D. *Braindance*. Henry Holt, 1992.

Gardner, R. Allen, and Beatrice T. Gardner. "Teaching Sign Language to a Chimpanzee." *Science*, 165, no. 3894, 1969.

Gee, H. "Box of Bones 'Clinches' Identity of Piltdown Palaeontology Hoaxer." *Nature*, 381, 1996.

Geschwind, Norman. "The Neural Basis of Language," in K. Salzinger and S. Salzinger, eds., *Research in Verbal Behavior and Some Neurophysiological Implications*, Academic Press, 1967.

Gibson, K. R. "Continuity Theories of Human Language Origins Versus the Lieberman Model." *Language and Communication*, 14, 1994.

Gould, Stephen J. *The Mismeasure of Man*. Norton, 1981.

———. *Hen's Teeth and Horse's Toes: Further Reflections on Natural History*. Norton, 1983.

Gouzoules, H., S. Gouzoules, and P. Marler. "Vocal Communication: A Vehicle for the Study of Social Relationships," in R. Rawlins and M. Kessler, eds., *The Cayo Santiago Macaques*. State University of New York Press, 1986.

Greenfield, P. M. "Language, Tools and Brain: The Ontogeny and Phylogeny of Hierarchically Organized Sequential Behavior." *Behavioral and Brain Sciences*, 14, 1991.

Groves, C. P. *A Theory of Human and Primate Evolution*. Clarendon Press, 1989.

Harrison, T. "Cladistic Concepts and the Species Problem in Hominoid Evolution," in W. H. Kimbel and L. B. Martin, eds., *Species, Species Concepts, and Primate Evolution*. Plenum Press, 1993.

Hockett, Charles F. "The Origin of Speech." *Scientific American*, 203, no. 3, 1960.

Holloway, Ralph L. "The Evolution of the Primate Brain: Some Aspects of Quantitative Relations." *Brain Research*, 7, 1968.

Hood, Dora. *Davidson Black: A Biography*. University of Toronto Press, 1971.

Howell, F. Clark. "Observations on the Earliest Phases of the European Lower Paleolithic." *American Anthropologist*, 68, no. 2, 1966.

Howells, W. *Getting Here*. Compass Press, 1993.

Isaac, Glynn L. "Studies of Early Culture in East Africa." *World Archaeology*, 1, no. 1, 1969.

———. "The Diet of Early Man: Aspects of Archaeological Evidence from Lower and Middle Pleistocene Sites in Africa." *World Archaeology*, 2, no. 3, 1971.

Jelinek, A. J. "The Lower Paleolithic: Current Evidence and Interpretations." *Annual Review of Anthropology*, 6, 1977.

Jellema, L. M., B. Latimer, and A. Walker. "The Rib Cage," in A. Walker and R. Leakey, eds., *The*

Nariokotome Homo erectus Skeleton. Harvard University Press, 1993.

Jerison, Harry J. *Evolution of the Brain and Intelligence.* Academic Press, 1973.

Jia, Lanpo, and Huang Weiwen. *The Story of Peking Man.* Oxford University Press, 1990.

Jones, S., R. Martin, and D. Pilbeam, eds. *The Cambridge Encyclopedia of Human Evolution.* Cambridge University Press, 1992.

Ju-kang, Woo. "The Skull of Lantian Man." *Current Anthropology,* 7, no. 1, 1966.

Kay, R. F., M. Cartmill, and M. Balow. "The Hypoglossal Canal and the Origin of Human Vocal Behavior." *Proceedings of the National Academy of Sciences USA,* 95, 1998.

Kim, K. H. S., N. R. Relkin, K.-M. Lee, and J. Hirsch. "Distinct Cortical Areas Associated With Native and Second Languages." *Nature,* 388, 1997.

Klein, R. G. *The Human Career.* University of Chicago Press, 1989.

Kramer, A. "A Critical Analysis of Claims for the Existence of Southeast Asian Australopithecines." *Journal of Human Evolution,* 26, 1994.

Krantz, Grover S. "Brain Size and Hunting Ability in Earliest Man." *Current Anthropology,* 9, no. 5, 1966.

Kurtén, Björn. *Pleistocene Mammals of Europe.* Aldine, 1968.

Laitman, Jeffrey T., and Raymond C. Heimbuch. "The Basicranium of Plio-Pleistocene Hominids as an Indicator of Their Upper Respiratory Systems." *American Journal of Physical Anthropology,* 59, 1982.

——, ——, and E. S. Crelin. "The Basicranium of Fossil Hominids as an Indicator of Their Upper Respiratory Systems." *American Journal of Physical Anthropology,* 51, 1979.

Lancaster, Jane B. "Primate Communication Systems and the Emergence of Human Language," in Phyllis C. Jay, ed. *Primates: Studies in Adaptation and Variability.* Holt, Rinehart & Winston, 1968.

Lewin, Roger. *Human Evolution: An Illustrated Introduction.* Blackwell Scientific Publications, 1993.

Lieberman, Philip. *On the Origins of Language.* Macmillan, 1975.

——, Edmund S. Crelin, and Dennis H. Klatt. "Phonetic Ability and Related Anatomy of the Newborn and Adult Human, Neanderthal Man, and the Chimpanzee." *American Anthropologist,* 74, no. 3, 1972.

MacLarnon, A. "The Vertebral Canal," in A. Walker and R. Leakey, eds., *The Nariokotome Homo erectus Skeleton.* Harvard University Press, 1993.

McHenry, H. "How Big Were Early Hominids?" *Evolutionary Anthropology,* 1, 1992.

Mithen, S. *The Prehistory of the Mind.* Thames and Hudson, 1996.

Morwood, M. J., P. B. O'Sullivan, F. Aziz, and A. Raza. "Fission-track Ages of Stone Tools and Fossils on the East Indonesian Island of Flores." *Nature,* 392, 1998.

Moyá-Solà, S., and M. Köhler. "The Orce Skull: Anatomy of a Mistake." *Journal of Human Evolution,* 33, 1997.

Murrill, R. I. *Petralona Man.* Charles C. Thomas, 1981.

Myers, Ronald E. "Comparative Neurology of Vocalization and Speech," in S. L. Washburn and E. R. McCown, eds., *Human Evolution: Biosocial Perspectives.* Benjamin/Cummings, 1978.

Napier, John. "The Evolution of the Hand." *Scientific American,* 207, no. 6, 1962.

Oakley, Kenneth P. *Man the Tool-Maker,* 6th ed. Trustees of the British Museum (Natural History), 1972.

Palmqvist, P. "A Critical Re-evaluation of the Evidence for the Presence of Hominids in Lower Pleistocene Times at Venta Micena, Southern Spain." *Journal of Human Evolution,* 33, 1997.

Passingham, Richard L. *The Human Primate.* Freeman, 1982.

Petersen, S. E., P. T. Fox, M. I. Posner, M. Mintum, and M. E. Raichle. "Positron Emission Tomographic Studies of the Cortical Anatomy of Single-word Processing." *Nature,* 331, 1988.

Pope, G. G. "Bamboo and Human Evolution." *Natural History,* 98, 1989.

——. "Ancient Asia's Cutting Edge." *Natural History,* 102, 1993.

Povinelli, D. J. "What Chimpanzees (Might) Know About the Mind," in R. Wrangham et al., eds., *Chimpanzee Cultures.* Harvard University Press, 1994.

Rightmire, G. P. "Evidence From Facial Morphology for Similarity of Asian and African Representatives of *Homo erectus.*" *American Journal of Physical Anthropology,* 106, 1998.

——. *The Evolution of Homo erectus.* Cambridge University Press, 1990.

——. "*Homo erectus:* Ancestor or Evolutionary Side Branch?" *Evolutionary Anthropology,* 1, 1992.

Rosenberg, K. R. "The Evolution of Modern Human Childbirth." *Yearbook of Physical Anthropology,* 35, 1992.

——, and W. Trevathan. "Bipedalism and Human Birth: The Obstetrical Dilemma Revisited." *Evolutionary Anthropology,* 4, 1995/96.

Ruff, C. B. "Biomechanics of the Hip and Birth in Early *Homo.*" *American Journal of Physical Anthropology,* 98, 1995.

——, E. Trinkaus, T. W. Holliday. "Body Mass and Encephalization in Pleistocene *Homo.*" *Nature,* 387, 1997.

Savage-Rumbaugh, S. "Language Training of Apes," in S. Jones et al., eds., *The Cambridge Encyclopedia of Human Evolution.* Cambridge University Press, 1992.

———, and R. Lewin. "Ape at the Brink." *Discover*, 15, 1994.

Schick, K., and N. Toth. *Making Silent Stones Speak*. Simon & Schuster, 1993.

Schwartz, J. H. *Skeleton Keys*. Oxford University Press, 1995.

Semenov, S.A. *Prehistoric Technology*. Cory, Adams & Mackay, 1964.

Seyfarth, Robert M., Dorothy L. Cheney, and Peter Marler. "Monkey Responses to Three Different Alarm Calls: Evidence of Predator Classification and Semantic Communication." *Science*, 210, 1980.

———. "Vervet Monkey Alarm Calls: Semantic Communication in a Free-Ranging Primate." *Animal Behavior*, 28, 1980.

Shapiro, Harry, L. *Peking Man*. Simon & Schuster, 1974.

Spencer, Frank. *Piltdown: A Scientific Forgery*. Natural History Museum, London and Oxford University Press, 1990.

Stringer, C., and C. Gamble. *In Search of the Neanderthals*. Thames & Hudson, 1993.

———, J. J. Hublin, and B. Vandermeersch. "The Origin of Anatomically Modern Humans in Western Europe," in F. Smith and F. Spencer, eds., *The Origins of Modern Humans: A World Survey of the Fossil Evidence*. A. R. Liss, 1984.

———, and R. McKie. *African Exodus*. Henry Holt, 1996.

Swisher, C. C., G. H. Curtis, T. Jacob, A. G. Getty, A. Suprijo, Widiasmoro. "Age of the Earliest Known Hominids in Java, Indonesia." *Science*, 263, 1994.

———, W. J. Rink, S. C. Anton, H. P. Schwarcz, G. H. Curtis, A. Suprijo, Widiasmoro. "Latest *Homo erectus* of Java: Potential Contemporaneity With *Homo sapiens* in Southeast Asia." *Science*, 274, 1996.

Tattersall, I. *The Last Neanderthal*. Macmillan, 1995.

Theunissen, B. *Eugene Dubois and the Ape-man from Java*. Kluwer, 1989.

Thieme, H. "Lower Palaeolithic Hunting Spears From Germany." *Nature*, 385, 1997.

Tobias, Phillip V. *The Brain in Hominid Evolution*. Columbia University Press, 1971.

———. "The Brain of *Homo habilis*: a New Level of Organization in Cerebral Evolution." *Journal of Human Evolution*, 16, 1987.

Trevathan, W. *Human Birth: An Evolutionary Perspective*. Aldine de Gruyter, 1987.

von Koenigswald, G. H. R. *Meeting Prehistoric Man*. Harper, 1956.

Vygotskii, L. S. *Mind in Society: The Development of Higher Psychological Processes*. Harvard University Press, 1978.

Walker, A. "The Origin of the Genus *Homo*," in D. T. Rasmussen, ed., *The Origin and Evolution of Humans and Humanness*. Jones & Bartlett, 1993.

———, and C. Ruff. "The Reconstruction of the Pelvis," in A. Walker and R. Leakey, eds., *The Nariokotome Homo erectus Skeleton*. Harvard University Press, 1993.

———, and R. Leakey, eds. *The Nariokotome Homo erectus Skeleton*. Harvard University Press, 1993.

Wallace, Alfred Russel. *Darwinism: An Exposition of the Theory of Natural Selection*. Macmillan, 1889.

Wanpo, Huang, R. Ciochon, G. Yumin, R. Larick, F. Qiren, H. Schwarcz, C. Yonge, J. de Vos, and W. Rink. "Early *Homo* and Associated Artifacts From Asia." *Nature*, 378, 1995.

Washburn, Sherwood L. *Social Life of Early Man*. Aldine, 1961.

———, and Phyllis Dolhinow, eds. *Perspectives on Human Evolution*, 4 vols. Holt, Rinehart & Winston, 1968–1976.

Weidenreich, Franz. *Apes, Giants, and Man*. University of Chicago Press, 1946.

Wood, Bernard A., Lawrence Martin, and Peter Andrews, eds. *Major Topics in Human and Primate Evolution*. Cambridge University Press, 1986.

Wu, Rukand, and Lin Shenglong. "Peking Man." *Scientific American*, 248, 1983.

PART IV: MODERN HUMANITY

General References for Further Reading

Bordes, Francois. *The Old Stone Age*. McGraw-Hill, 1968.

Campbell, Bernard G. *Human Ecology: The Story of Our Place in Nature from Prehistory to the Present*. 2nd ed. Aldine, 1995.

Cavalli-Sforza, L. L., P. Menozzi, and A. Piazza. *The History and Geography of Human Genes*. Princeton University Press, 1994.

Clutton-Brock, Juliet. *A Natural History of Domesticated Animals*. British Museum (Natural History) and Cambridge University Press, 1987.

Corruccini, R. S., and R. L. Ciochon, eds. *Integrative Paths to the Past: Paleoanthropological Advances in Honor of F. Clark Howell*. Prentice Hall, 1994.

Jones, S., R. Martin, and D. Pilbeam, eds. *The Cambridge Encyclopedia of Human Evolution*. Cambridge University Press, 1992.

Leakey, L. S. B., and Vanne Morris Goodall. *Unveiling Man's Origins*. Schenkman, 1969.

Marks, J. *Human Biodiversity: Genes, Race, and History*. Aldine de Gruyter, 1995.

Nitecki, M. H., and D. V. Nitecki, eds. *Origins of Anatomically Modern Humans*. Plenum, 1994.

Service, Elman R. *The Hunters*. Prentice-Hall, 1966.

Smith, Fred H., and Frank Spencer, eds. *The Origins of Modern Humans: A World Survey of the Evidence*. Alan R. Liss, 1984.

Wilson, Edward O. *On Human Nature.* Harvard University Press, 1978.

Sources

Aiello, L., and C. Dean. *An Introduction to Human Evolutionary Anatomy.* Academic Press, 1990.

———, and R. I. M. Dunbar. "Neocortex Size, Group Size, and the Evolution of Language." *Current Anthropology,* 34, 1993.

Anonymous. "'Not a Love Child.' Skeleton Shows Neanderthals, Early Humans Interbred." *Reuters,* April 20, 1999.

Arens, W. *The Man-Eating Myth.* Oxford University Press, 1979.

Arsuaga, J. L., I. Martinez, A. Garcia, J.-M. Carretero, and E. Carbonell. "Three New Human Skulls from the Sima de los Huesos Middle Pleistocene Site in Sierra de Atapuerca, Spain." *Nature,* 362, 1993.

———, I. Martinez, A. Garcia, and C. Lorenzo. "The Sima de los Huesos Crania (Sierra de Atapuerca, Spain). A Comparative Study." *Journal of Human Evolution,* 33, 1997.

———, I. Martinez, A. Garcia, J.-M. Carretero, C. Lorenzo, N. Garcia, and A. I. Ortega. "Sima de los Huesos (Sierra de Atapuerca, Spain). The Site." *Journal of Human Evolution,* 33, 1997.

Bada, Jeffrey L. "Aspartic Acid Racemization Ages of Californian Paleoindians." *American Antiquity,* 50, 1979.

Bahn, P. G. "Cannibalism or Ritual Dismemberment?" in S. Jones, R. Martin, and D. Pilbeam, eds., *The Cambridge Encyclopedia of Human Evolution.* Cambridge University Press, 1992.

Bermudez de Castro, J. M., J. L. Arsuaga, E. Carbonell, A. Rosas, I. Martinez, and M. Mosquera. "A Hominid From the Lower Pleistocene of Atapuerca, Spain: Possible Ancestor to Neandertals and Modern Humans." *Science,* 276, 1997.

Bischoff, J. L., J. A. Fitzpatrick, L. Leon, J. L. Arsuaga, C. Falgueres, J. J. Bahain, and T. Bullen. "Geology and Preliminary Dating of the Hominid-bearing Sedimentary Fill of the Sima de los Huesos Chamber, Cueva Mayor of the Sierra de Atapuerca, Burgos, Spain." *Journal of Human Evolution,* 33, 1997.

Bordes, Francois. *A Tale of Two Caves.* Harper & Row, 1972.

Bowcock, A. M., A. Ruiz-Linares, J. Tomfohrde, E. Minch, J. R. Kidd, and L. L. Cavalli-Sforza. "High Resolution of Human Evolutionary Trees with Polymorphic Microsatellites." *Nature,* 368, 1994.

Brace, C. L. "A Nonracial Approach Towards the Understanding of Human Diversity," in A. Montagu, ed., *The Concept of Race.* Free Press, 1964.

Brauer, G., Y. Yokoyama, C. Falgueres, and E. Mbua. "Modern Human Origins Backdated." *Nature,* 386, 1997.

Breuil, Abbé H. *Four Hundred Centuries of Cave Art.* Centre d'Études et de Documentation Préhistoriques, 1952.

Brose, David S., and Milford H. Wolpoff. "Early Upper Paleolithic Man and Late Middle Paleolithic Tools." *American Anthropologist,* 73, 1971.

Cann, Rebecca L., Mark Stoneking, and Allan C. Wilson. "Mitochondrial DNA and Human Evolution." *Nature,* 325, 1987.

Carbonell, E., J. M. Bermudez de Castro, J. L. Arsuaga, J. C. Diez, A. Rosas, G. Cuenca-Bescos, R. Sala, M. Mosquera, and X. P. Rodriguez. "Lower Pleistocene Hominids and Artifacts From Atapuerca-TD6 (Spain)." *Science,* 269, 1995.

Cavalli-Sforza, L. L., and F. Cavalli-Sforza. *The Great Human Diasporas.* Addison-Wesley, 1995.

Chu, J. Y., W. Huang, S. Q. Kuang, J. M. Wang, J. J. Xu, Z. T. Chu, Z. Q. Yang, K. Q. Lin, P. Li, M. Wu, Z. C. Geng, C. C. Tan, R. F. Du, and L. Jin. "Genetic Relationships of Populations in China." *Proceedings of the National Academy of Sciences,* 95, 1998.

Clark, J. Desmond. *The Prehistory of Africa.* Praeger, 1970.

Clark, J. Grahame D. *Prehistoric Europe: The Economic Basis.* Philosophical Library, 1952.

Conkey, M. "Humans as Materialists and Symbolists: Image Making in the Upper Paleolithic," in D. T. Rasmussen, ed., *The Origin and Evolution of Humans and Humanness.* Jones & Bartlett, 1993.

Conroy, G. C. *Reconstructing Human Origins.* W. W. Norton, 1997.

Daniel, Glyn A. *A Hundred and Fifty Years of Archaeology.* Duckworth, 1975.

D'Errico, F., P. Villa, A. C. Pinto Llona, and R. Ruiz Idarraga. "A Middle Palaeolithic Origin of Music? Using Cave-bear Bone Accumulations to Assess the Divje Babe I Bone 'Flute'." *Antiquity,* 72, 1998.

Diamond, J. *Guns, Germs, and Steel.* W. W. Norton, 1997.

Dickson, D. B. *The Dawn of Belief.* University of Arizona Press, 1990.

Eiseley, Loren. "Neanderthal Man and the Dawn of Human Paleontology." *Quarterly Review of Biology,* 32, no. 4, 1957.

Falk, D. *Braindance.* Henry Holt, 1992.

Frison, G. C. "Modern People in the New World," in G. Burenhult, ed., *The First Humans: Human Origins and History to 10,000 B.C.* HarperCollins, 1993.

Garn, S. M. *Human Races,* 2nd ed. Charles C. Thomas, 1965.

Gibbons, Ann. "Ideas on Human Origins Evolve at Anthropology Gathering." *Science,* 276, 1997.

Gill, G. W. "The Beauty of Race and Races." *Anthropology Newsletter*, 39, no. 3, 1998.

Glover, I. C. "Tools and Cultures in Late Paleolithic Southeast Asia," in G. Burenhult, ed., *The First Humans: Human Origins and History to 10,000 B.C.* HarperCollins, 1993.

Gould, S. J. *The Mismeasure of Man*. W. W. Norton, 1981.

———. "Human Equality Is a Contingent Fact of History." *Natural History*, 93, 1984.

Grun, R., J. S. Brink, N. A. Spooner, L. Taylor, C. B. Stringer, R. G. Franciscus, and A. S. Murray. "Direct Dating of Florisbad Hominid." *Nature*, 382, 1996.

Hammer, M. F. "A Recent Common Ancestry For Human Y Chromosomes." *Nature*, 378, 1995.

———, and S. L. Zegura. "The Role of the Y Chromosome in Human Evolutionary Studies." *Evolutionary Anthropology*, 5, 1996.

Harris, D. R. "Aboriginal Subsistence in a Tropical Rain Forest Environment: Food Procurement, Cannibalism, and Population Regulation in Northeastern Australia," in M. Harris and E. Ross, eds., *Food and Evolution*. Temple University Press, 1987.

Holliday, T. W. "Postcranial Evidence of Cold Adaptation in European Neandertals." *American Journal of Physical Anthropology*, 104, 1997.

Hooton, E. A. *Up from the Ape*. Macmillan, 1946.

Howell, F. Clark. "European and Northwest African Middle Pleistocene Hominids." *Current Anthropology*, 1, 1960.

———. "Recent Advances in Human Evolutionary Studies." *Quarterly Review of Biology*, 42, 1967.

Howells, W. "The Dispersion of Modern Humans," in S. Jones, R. Martin, and D. Pilbeam, eds., *The Cambridge Encyclopedia of Human Evolution*. Cambridge University Press, 1992.

———. *Getting Here*. Compass Press, 1993.

Hutchings, W. K., and L. W. Bruchert. "Spearthrower Performance: Ethnographic and Experimental Research." *Antiquity*, 71, 1997.

Johanson, D., and B. Edgar. *From Lucy to Language*. Simon and Schuster, 1996.

Jolly, C. J., and R. White. *Physical Anthropology and Archaeology*, 5th ed. McGraw-Hill, 1995.

Jones, S. "Genetic Diversity in Humans," in S. Jones, R. Martin, and D. Pilbeam, eds., *The Cambridge Encyclopedia of Human Evolution*. Cambridge University Press, 1992.

———. "The Evolutionary Future of Humankind," in S. Jones, R. Martin, and D. Pilbeam, eds., *The Cambridge Encyclopedia of Human Evolution*. Cambridge University Press, 1992.

Klein, Richard G. *Man and Culture in the Late Pleistocene*. Chandler, 1969.

———. "The Archaeology of Modern Human Origins." *Evolutionary Anthropology*, 1, 1992.

———. *The Human Career*. University of Chicago Press, 1989.

Kolata, G. "Frequency of AIDS Resistant Gene and Progress of Black Plague From 1347 to 1352." *The New York Times*, May 26, 1998.

Kranzberg, Melvin, and Carroll W. Pursell, Jr., eds. *Technology in Western Civilization*, vol. 1. Oxford University Press, 1967.

Krings, M., A. Stone, R. W. Schmitz, H. Krainitzki, M. Stoneking, and S. Paabo. "Neandertal DNA Sequences and the Origin of Modern Humans." *Cell*, 90, 1997.

Kurtén, Björn. *The Ice Age*. Putnam's, 1972.

———. *The Cave Bear Story*. Pantheon, 1977.

Lahr, M. M. "The Multiregional Model of Modern Human Origins: A Reassessment of Its Morphological Basis." *Journal of Human Evolution*, 26, 1994.

———. "Patterns of Modern Human Diversification: Implications for Amerindian Origins." *Yearbook of Physical Anthropology*, 38, 1995.

Laming, Annette. *Lascaux*. Penguin, 1959.

Lee, Richard B. *Studies of the !Kung San and Their Neighbors*. Harvard University Press, 1976.

———, and Irven De Vore, eds. *Man the Hunter*. Aldine, 1968.

Leroi-Gourhan, André. *Treasures of Prehistoric Art*. Abrams, 1967.

Levin, J., and D. Suzuki. *The Secret of Life*. WGBH Boston, 1993.

Lewis-Williams, J. D. *The Rock Art of Southern Africa*. Cambridge University Press, 1983.

Lewontin, R. *Human Diversity*. Scientific American Library, 1982.

Lieberman, D. E. "Sphenoid Shortening and the Evolution of Modern Human Cranial Shape." *Nature*, 393, 1998.

Littlefield, A., L. Lieberman, and L. T. Reynolds. "Redefining Race: The Potential Demise of a Concept in Physical Anthropology." *Current Anthropology*, 23, 1982.

Marean, C. W., and Soo Yeun Kim. "Mousterian Large-Mammal Remains from Kobeh Cave." *Current Anthropology*, 39 (Supplement), 1998.

Maringer, Johannes. *The Gods of Prehistoric Man*. Knopf, 1960.

———, and Hans-Georg Bandi. *Art in the Ice Age*. Praeger, 1953.

Marks, J. "Black, White, Other." *Natural History*, 103, 1994.

Marshack, Alexander. *The Roots of Civilization*. McGraw-Hill, 1972.

McKie, R. "The People Eaters." *New Scientist*, 157, 1998.

Mellars, P., and C. Stringer, eds. *The Human Revolution.* Edinburgh University Press, 1989.

Meltzer, D. J. "Monte Verde and the Pleistocene Peopling of the Americas." *Science,* 276, 1997.

———. "Pleistocene Peopling of the Americas." *Evolutionary Anthropology,* 1, 1993.

Mithen, S. *The Prehistory of the Mind.* Thames and Hudson, 1996.

Molnar, S. *Human Variation,* 3rd ed. Prentice Hall, 1992.

Mulvaney, D. J., and J. Gordon. *Aboriginal Man and Environment in Australia.* Australian National University Press, 1971.

Oakley, Kenneth P., Bernard G. Campbell, and Theya I. Mollison. *Catalogue of Fossil Hominids,* 3 vols. Trustees of the British Museum (Natural History), 1967–1977.

Osborn, H. F. *Men of the Old Stone Age.* Scribner's, 1915.

Ovey, C. D., ed. "The Swanscombe Skull." *Occasional Papers of the Royal Anthropological Institute,* 20. London, 1964.

Rightmire, G. P. "Human Evolution in the Middle Pleistocene: The Role of *Homo heidelbergensis.*" *Evolutionary Anthropology,* 6, 1998.

———. "The Human Cranium from Bodo, Ethiopia: Evidence for Speciation in the Middle Pleistocene?" *Journal of Human Evolution,* 31, 1996.

Roberts, M. B., C. B. Stringer, and S. A. Parfitt. "A Hominid Tibia from Middle Pleistocene Sediments at Boxgrove, UK." *Nature,* 369, 1994.

Roberts, R., G. Walsh, A. Murray, J. Olley, R. Jones, M. Morwood, C. Tuniz, E. Lawon, M. Macphail, D. Bowdery and I. Naumann. "Luminescence Dating of Rock Art and Past Environments Using Mud-Wasp Nests in Northern Australia." *Nature,* 387, 1997.

Robins, A. H. *Biological Perspectives on Human Pigmentation.* Cambridge University Press, 1991.

Roosevelt, A. C., M. Lima da Costa, C. Lopes Machado, M. Michab, N. Mercier, H. Valladas, J. Feathers, W. Barnett, M. Imazio de Silveira, A. Henderson, J. Silva, B. Chernoff, D. S. Reese, J. A. Holman, N. Toth, and K. Schick. "Paleoindian Cava Dwellers in the Amazon: The Peopling of the Americas." *Science,* 272, 1996.

Ross, C., and M. Henneberg. "Basicranial Flexion, Relative Brain Size, and Facial Kyphosis in *Homo sapiens* and Some Fossil Hominids." *American Journal of Physical Anthropology,* 98, 1995.

Schepartz, L. A. "Language and Modern Human Origins." *Yearbook of Physical Anthropology,* 36, 1993.

Semenov, S. A. *Prehistoric Technology.* Cory, Adams & Mackay, 1964.

Shanklin, E. *Anthropology and Race.* Wadsworth, 1994.

Shea, J. J. "Neandertal and Early Modern Human Behavioral Variability." *Current Anthropology,* 39 (Supplement), 1998.

Smith, B. D. "The Initial Domestication of *Cucurbita pepo* in the Americas 10,000 Years Ago." *Science,* 276, 1997.

———. "The Origins of Agriculture in the Americas." *Evolutionary Anthropology,* 3, 1994/95.

Smith, G. Elliott. "Neanderthal Man Not Our Ancestor." *Scientific American,* August, 1928.

Sohn, S., and M. H. Wolpoff. "Zuttiyeh Face: A View from the East." *American Journal of Physical Anthropology,* 91, 1993.

Solecki, Ralph S. *Shanidar: The First Flower People.* Knopf, 1971.

Stoneking, M. "DNA and Recent Human Evolution." *Evolutionary Anthropology,* 2, 1993.

Stringer, C. "A Metrical Study of the WLH-50 Calvaria." *Journal of Human Evolution,* 34, 1998.

———. "New Views on Modern Human Origins," in D. T. Rasmussen, ed., *The Origin and Evolution of Humans and Humanness.* Jones & Bartlett, 1993.

———, and C. Gamble. *In Search of the Neanderthals.* Thames & Hudson, 1993.

———, and P. Andrews. "Genetic and Fossil Evidence for the Origin of Modern Humans." *Science,* 239, 1988.

———, and R. McKie. *African Exodus.* Henry Holt, 1996.

Tacon, P. "Art of the Land," in G. Burenhult, ed., *The First Humans: Human Origins and History to 10,000 B.C.* HarperCollins, 1993.

Tattersall, I. *The Human Odyssey.* Prentice Hall, 1993.

———. *The Fossil Trail.* Oxford University Press, 1995.

———. *The Last Neanderthal.* Macmillan, 1995.

Trinkaus, E., and P. Shipman. *The Neandertals.* Knopf, 1993.

———, and William W. Howells. "The Neanderthals." *Scientific American,* 241, no. 6, 1979.

Turnbaugh, W. A., R. Jurmain, H. Nelson, L. Kilgore. *Understanding Physical Anthropology and Archaeology,* 6th ed. West, 1996.

Turner, C. G., II, and J. A. Turner. *Man Corn.* University of Utah Press, 1999.

Ucko, Peter J., and André Rosenfeld. *Palaeolithic Cave Art.* McGraw-Hill, 1967.

Villa, P. "Cannibalism in Prehistoric Europe." *Evolutionary Anthropology,* 1, 1992.

Waddle, D. M. "Matrix Correlation Tests Support a Single Origin for Modern Humans." *Nature,* 368, 1994.

Ward, N. "To People the World, Start With 500." *The New York Times,* November 11, 1997.

Ward, R., and C. Stringer. "A Molecular Handle on the Neanderthals." *Nature*, 388, 1997.

Wells, H. G. "The Grisly Folk." Original 1921, reprinted in Well's *Selected Short Stories*. Penguin, 1958.

White, J. P. "The Settlement of Ancient Australia," in G. Burenhult, ed., *The First Humans: Human Origins and History to 10,000 B.C.* HarperCollins, 1993.

White, T. D. *Prehistoric Cannibalism at Mancos 5MTUMR-2346*. Princeton University Press, 1992.

Wilford, J. N. "Discovery of Flute Suggests Neanderthal Caves Echoed With Music." *The New York Times*, October 29, 1996.

————. "Evidence Indicates Humans Inhabited Siberia 300,000 Years Ago." *The New York Times*, February 28, 1997.

————. "Fossil May Link Neanderthal and Modern Humans." *The New York Times*, May 30, 1997.

Willermet, C. M., and B. Hill. "Fuzzy Set Theory and Its Implications for Speciation Models" in G. A. Clark and C. M. Willermet, eds., *Conceptual Issues in Modern Human Origins Research*. (Aldine de Gruyter, 1997.

Wolpoff, M. H. *Human Evolution* (1996–1997 edition). McGraw-Hill, 1996.

ACKNOWLEDGMENTS

PHOTO CREDITS

Chapter One

1: Mary Evans Picture Library;   5: The Natural History Museum, London;   6: Wm. Buckland, Reliquiae Diluvianae, 1823;   8 *top:* James Hutton, *Theory of the Earth,* 1795.;   8 *bottom:* Corbis-Bettmann;   11: Corbis;   14 *top:* Bettmann Archive;   14 *bottom:* Bettmann Archive;   17: Mary Evans Picture Library/ Photo Researchers;   20: Bettmann Archive;   27: Brown Brothers;   28: Courtesy Department Library Services, American Museum of Natural History, Photo by Jules Kirschner #311414;   29 *top left:* UPI/Corbis-Bettmann;   29 *top right:* AP/Wide World;   29 *bottom:* AP/Wide World.

Chapter Two

33: Oscar Miller/SPL/Photo Researchers;   37: © Biofoto/ Photo Researchers;   44: © Oliver Meckes/Photo Researchers;   58 *top:* Photo Researchers;   58 *bottom:* Photo Researchers

Chapter Three

75: © 1984 Gregory Dimijian/Photo Researchers;   84: Sarah Blaffer Hrdy/Anthro-Photo;   85: David Haring;   86 *top:* Wildlife Conservation Society;   86 *bottom:* A.W. Ambler/ National Audubon Society/Photo Researchers;   87: A.W. Ambler/National Audubon Society/Photo Researchers;   92 *top left:* D. J. Chivers/Anthro-Photo;   92 *top right:* Werner H. Muller/Peter Arnold;   92 *bottom left:* Werner H. Muller/Peter Arnold;   92 *bottom right:* D. J. Chivers/Anthro-Photo;   93 *top left:* Michael Rougier;   93 *top right:* Ralph Morse/Time Magazine © Time Warner;   93 *bottom left:* © Wildlife Conservation Society;   93 *bottom right:* Richard Wrangham/Anthro-Photo;   96: Fritz Goro;   97: Ralph Morse/Life Magazine © Time Inc.;   99: Dr. Geza Teleki/Committee for Conservation and Care of Chimpanzees;   100: Gibbs Gately;   104: Julie O'Neil;   105 *left:* Laima Druskis/Photo Researchers;   105 *right:* Roberta Hershenson/ Photo Researchers;   106 *right:* J. R. Napier and P.H. Napier, *A Handbook of Living Primates* Academic Press, Inc. (London, Ltd.);   107: Lester Bergman & Associates;   112: Terrence Spencer/Paul Popper Ltd.

Chapter Four

113: © 1979 TomMcHugh/Photo Researchers;   119: © Wildlife Conservation Society;   123: Richard Wrangham/Anthro-Photo;   124 *left:* Sarah Blaffer Hrdy/Anthro-Photo;   124 *right:* Anthro-Photo;   125: © Walter Gotz, Courtesy of Hans Kummer;   126: Anthro-Photo;   130: Irven DeVore/Anthro-Photo;   132: Joseph Popp/Anthro-Photo;   134: Irven DeVore/Anthro-Photo;   137: Anthro-Photo;   140: David Chivers/Anthro-Photo;   141: Irven DeVore/Anthro-Photo ;   143: Robert M. Campbell/National Geographic Image Sales;   146: Sarah Blaffer Hrdy/Anthro-Photo;   148: Hugo Van Lawick/National Geographic Image Sales;   152: Dr. Geza Teleki/Committee for Conservation and Care of Chimpanzees;   154 *left:* Irven DeVore/Anthro-Photo;   154 *right:* Irven DeVore/Anthro-Photo ;   156: Alison Hannah;   159: From de Waal (1989) *Peacemaking among Primates;*   160: From de Waal (1989) *Peacemaking among Primates.*

Chapter Five

166: Courtesy Department Library Service, American Museum of Natural History Photo C. Chesek (1994)/#2A2 1279;   174: Zoological Society of San Diego;   179: D. Rasmussen/Courtesy of Duke University Primate Center;   180 *top:* Dr. E. L. Simons/Duke University Primate Center;   181 *top:* Dr. E. L. Simons/ Duke University Primate Center;   181 *bottom:* Dr. E. L. Simons/Duke University Primate Center;   186: The Natural History Museum, London;   188: William Sacco/Anthro-Photo;   190: Salvador Moya-Sola.

Chapter Six

202: David L. Brill/Atlanta;   204: David L. Brill/Atlanta;   208: Ernest Shirley;   210: William B. Terry, *Early Man;*   212: Glen Conroy/Washington University Medical School, St. Louis;   215 *top:* Transvaal Museum, D.C. Panagos;   215 *bottom:* Transvaal Museum;   219 *top:* Transvaal Museum, D.C. Panagos;   219 *bottom:* Transvaal Museum, D.C. Panagos;   220: Transvaal Museum, D.C. Panagos;   221: Ronald J. Clarke;   223: Ken MacLeish, *Early Man.*

Chapter Seven

232: Des Bartlett/Photo Researchers;   235: Donald Johanson/ Institute of Human Origins;   236: Bob Campbell/ © National Geographic Society;   237: Gordon Gahan/National Geographic Image Sales;   239: Des Bartlett/Photo Researchers;   240: F. Clark Howell;   242: John Reader/*Life* Magazine © 1969/ Time Inc.;   243: National Museums of Kenya;   246: Alan Walker/National Museums of Kenya;   248 *top left:* Don Johanson/Institute of Human Origins;   248 *bottom left:* Institute of Human Origins;   248 *bottom center:* Nanci Kahn/Institute of Human Origins;   248 *bottom right:* © David L. Brill/Atlanta;   249: Don Johanson/Institute of Human Origins;   252: © 1993 David L. Brill;   253: Institute of Human Origins;   257: From Olduvai Gorge, vol. III © 1971 by Mary Leakey and Cambridge University Press. Reprinted with permission of the publisher;   258: John Reader/Science Source/Photo Researchers;   259: Kenneth Garrett/National Geographic Image Sales;   261: National Museums of Kenya;   262: National Museums of Kenya;   264: © Tim White/David L. Brill.

Chapter Eight

278: John N. Richards;   281: The Natural History Museum, London;   282: © 1997 David L. Brill;   287: © 1994 David L. Brill

Chapter Nine

294: © John Reader/Science Source/Photo Researchers; 310: National Museums of Kenya; 311 *top:* R. Potts; 311 *bottom:* Kathy D. Schick and Nicholas Toth, CRAFT Research Center, Indiana University (From Schick and Toth, 1993, p. 163); 312: Kathy D. Schick and Nicholas Toth, CRAFT Research Center, Indiana University (From Schick and Toth, 1993, p. 171); 316 *top:* From Olduvai Gorge, vol. III © 1971 by Mary Leakey and Cambridge University Press. Reprinted with permission of the publisher.

Chapter Ten

323: Courtesy Department Library Services, American Museum of Natural History #335797; 324: From an unpublished manuscript: *Trinil, A Biography of Professor Dr. Eugene Dubois, the discoverer of* Pithecanthropus Erectus, by Dubois's son, Jean M. F. Dubois; 327: Culver; 330: Courtesy Department Library Services, American Museum of Natural History, photo by Dr. von Koenigswald #298897; 331 *top:* Courtesy of Rijksmuseum van Natuurlijke Historie, Leiden; 331 *bottom:* From an unpublished manuscript: *Trinil, A Biography of Professor Dr. Eugene Dubois, the discoverer of* Pithecanthropus Erectus, by Dubois's son, Jean M. F. Dubois; 335: From an unpublished manuscript: *Trinil, A Biography of Professor Dr. Eugene Dubois, the discoverer of* Pithecanthropus Erectus, by Dubois's son, Jean M. F. Dubois; 337: Courtesy Department Library Services, American Museum of Natural History, Copied by J. Coxe #336414; 338: Courtesy Department Library Services, American Museum of Natural History #335797; 339: Bettmann Archive; 341: Peabody Museum, Harvard University; 342: Bettmann Archive; 344: Courtesy Department Library Services, American Museum of Natural History #333193; 346: National Museums of Kenya; 347: David L. Brill; 350: Russell Ciochon; 360: The Natural History Museum, London.

Chapter Eleven

364: Kathy D. Schick and Nicholas Toth, CRAFT Research Center, Indiana University. (From Schick and Toth 1993, p. 236); 371: M. Riboud/Magnum Photos; 372: M. Riboud/Magnum Photos; 374: Kathy D. Schick and Nicholas Toth, CRAFT Research Center, Indiana University. (From Schick and Toth 1993, p. 245); 377: Nicholas Toth, CRAFT Research Center, Indiana University, and Giancarlo Ligabue From Ligabue missions 1986–1990. (From Schick and Toth 1993, p. 277); 378: DeVore/Anthro-Photo; 379: Henry de Lumley; 380: The Natural History Museum, London.

Chapter Twelve

391: © Kenneth Good; 398: F. Clark Howell; 402: Shostak/Anthro-Photo; 404: DeVore/Anthro-Photo; 407: From G. H. R. Koenigswald, Begegnung mit dem Vormenschen © 1956, Eugen Diederichs Verlag, Cologne.

Chapter Thirteen

412: John Reader/SPL/Photo Researchers; 415 *top left:* DeVore/Anthro-Photo; 415 *top center:* Anthro-Photo; 415 *top right:* DeVore/Anthro-Photo; 415 *bottom left:* Leo de Wys, Inc.;

415 *bottom center:* Alex Bordulin/Leo de Wys, Inc.; 415 *bottom right:* Leo de Wys, Inc.; 416: From *In the Shadow of Man* by Jane van Lawick-Goodall, © 1971 by Hugo and Jane van Lawick-Goodall. Reprinted with permission of Houghton Mifflin Company and Hugo van Lawick.; 417: From *In the Shadow of Man* by Jane van Lawick-Goodall, ©1971 by Hugo and Jane van Lawick-Goodall. Reprinted with permission of Houghton Mifflin Company and Hugo van Lawick.; 418: R. Wrangham/Anthro-Photo; 421: H.S. Terrace/Anthro-Photo; 427: Pictor Uniphoto.

Chapter Fourteen

446: © Erik Trinkaus; 450: Rheinisches Landesmuseum Bonn; 452: Courtesy Department Library Services, American Museum of Natural History, Photo J. Kirschner #27935; 454 *top:* Musee de l'Homme; 454 *bottom:* Musee de l'Homme; 459: Peabody Museum, Harvard University, Photograph by Hillel Burger; 461: Javier Trueba/Madrid Scientific Films; 464 *left:* Peabody Museum, Harvard University, Photograph by Hillel Burger; 464 *right:* Musee de l'Homme; 465 *top:* © Erik Trinkaus; 465 *bottom:* Courtesy Department Library Services, American Museum of Natural History #338383; 467: The Natural History Museum, London; 468: © Institute of Human Origins/Don Johanson; 471: Javier Trueba/Madrid Scientific Films.

Chapter Fifteen

481: The Field Museum, # CK30T, Chicago; 493: The Field Museum, # GEO 82369, Chicago; 495: Lee Boltin; 500 *top:* Used by permission from *The Old Stone Age*, by Francois Bordes. © 1968 by Francois Bordes. Published by Weidenfeld and Nicolson.; 500 *bottom:* © Alexander Marshack; 503: Ralph S. Solecki; 504: Ralph S. Solecki; 506: Richard Schlecht/National Geographic Image Collection; 507: Musee de l'Homme.

Chapter Sixteen

513: © Ian Tattersall; 517: Peabody Museum, Harvard University, Photograph by Movius; 518: The Natural History Museum, London; 525: Ian Tattersall: *The Fossil Train,* Oxford University Press, 1995.; 531: K. Porter/Photo Researchers; 538 *top left:* Musee de l'Homme; 538 *top right:* Musee de l'Homme; 538 *bottom left:* Peabody Museum, Harvard Unversity; 538 *bottom right:* Courtesy Department Library Services, American Museum of Natural History, Photo J. Kirschner #310724.

Chapter Seventeen

548: © Jean Clottes/Ministerere/Sygma; 551: Royal Belgian Institute of Natural Sciences; 552: Pierre Boulat/Cosmos; 554: Riuchard Jeffrey/Courtesy J. Tixier; 555: Pierre Boulat/Cosmos; 557: Axel Poignant Archive; 558: Courtesy Department Library Services, American Museum of Natural History, Photo J. Kirschner #39686; 559: Axel Poignant Archive; 561: © 1985 David L. Brill; 562: Courtesy Department Library Services, American Museum of Natural History, Photo H. S. Rice #273695; 563: © Alexander Marshack; 565: Ralph Morse, *Early Man;* 567: © Alexander Marshack; 569: Courtesy Department Library Services, American Museum of Natural History, Photo Jim Coxe #336871; 570: Gordon Tenney; 571: Courtesy Department Library Services, American Museum of Natural History, Photo

Lee Boltin #326474; 572: G. Shilonsky/Sovfoto/Eastfoto; 573: Novosti Press Agency/Sovfoto/Eastfoto.

Chapter Eighteen

578: Jeff Dunn/Stock Boston; 587: David Rubinger, Israel; 591 *left:* Smucker/Anthro-Photo; 591 *right:* 601 *left:* © Betty Press/Woodfin Camp; 601 *center, right* Hooten, E.A. *Up From the Ape,* Macmillan, New York 1946; 602: Hooten, E.A. *Up From the Ape,* Macmillan, New York 1946.

Photo Essays

The Living Apes: 1: Painting "Darwin and Friends" by Stephen D. Nash. Reproduced with permission of the Department of Physical Anthropology, University College, London; 2: © Tom McHugh, Photo Researchers; 3: © Tom McHugh, Photo Researchers; 4: Mike Nichols/Magnum; 5: Mike Nichols/Magnum; 6: © 1979 Tom McHugh, Photo Researchers; 7: Robert Hynes, © Cartographic Division, National Geographic Society; 8: Robert Hynes, © Cartographic Division, National Geographic Society; Fossil Hominids: 1: William H. Kimbel/Institute of Human Origins; 2: © 1985 David L. Brill/Atlanta; 3: Courtesy Department Library Services, American Museum of Natural History, D. Finnan/C. Chesek; 4: © 1985 David L. Brill/Atlanta; 5: © 1993 John Reader; 6: © 1985 David L. Brill/Atlanta; 7: From Ian Tattersall, *The Human Odyssey,* Prentice Hall, 1993. Photo of casts by Willard Whitson; 8: Alan Walker © National Museums of Kenya; 9: From Ian Tattersall, *The Human Odyssey,* Prentice Hall, 1993. Photo of casts by Willard Whitson; 10 *top left:* © 1985 David L. Brill\Atlanta; *top right:* Israel Antiquities Authority; *bottom:* © 1985 David L. Brill\Atlanta; 11: From Ian Tattersall, *The Human Odyssey,* Prentice Hall, 1993. Photo of casts by Willard Whitson; The Faces of Physical Anthropology and Archeology: 1: Mark Schmidt, University at Albany; 6: Photo by and courtesy of T. White, 1995.

TEXT AND ILLUSTRATION CREDITS

Chapter One

p. 1: Caricature of Darwin as a Monkey. Reprinted by permission of Mary Evans Picture Library; Fig. 1–12, p. 16: Reprinted by permission of the publisher from *One Long Argument: Charles Darwin and the Genesis of Modern Evolutionary Thought by* Ernst Mayr, Cambridge, Mass: Harvard University Press, copyright © 1991 by the President and Fellows of Harvard College; Fig. 1–14, p. 18: T.H. Huxley, *Evidence as to Man's Place in Nature,* frontispiece (London, 1863).

Chapter Two

Fig. 2–1, p. 36: Animal cell from *Genes & Genomes* by Maxine Singer and Paul Berg, 1991, p. 4. Reprinted by permission of University Science: 55 D Gate Five Road, Sausalito, CA 94965; Fig. 2–4, p. 40: Protein Synthesis from *Genes & Genomes* by M. Singer and P. Berg, 1991, p. 27. Reprinted by permission of University Science: 55 D Gate Five Road, Sausalito, CA 94965;

Fig. 2–5, p. 41: DNA-RNA from *Genes & Genomes* by M. Singer and P. Berg, 1991, p. 432. Reprinted by permission of University Science: 55 D Gate Five Road, Sausalito, CA 94965; Fig. 2–6, p. 41: RNA Splicing from *Genes & Genomes* by M. Singer and P. Berg, 1991, p. 437. Reprinted by permission of University Science: 55 D Gate Five Road, Sausalito, CA 94965; Fig. 2–7, p. 42: Ribosomes Engaging mRNA from *Genes & Genomes* by M. Singer and P. Berg, 1991, p. 33. Reprinted by permission of University Science: 55 D Gate Five Road, Sausalito, CA 94965; Fig. 2–9, p. 45: Meiosis from *Genes & Genomes* by M. Singer and P. Berg, 1991, p. 9. Reprinted by permission of University Science: 55 D Gate Five Road, Sausalito, CA 94965; Fig. 2–10, p.46: Crossing Over from *Genes & Genomes* by M. Singer and P. Berg, 1991, p. 20. Reprinted by permission of University Science: 55 D Gate Five Road, Sausalito, CA 94965; Fig. 2–13, p. 51: Gene Frequency Changes from *Evolution,* 2/e by Mark Ridley, p. 74, © 1996. Reprinted by permission of Blackwell Science, Inc.; Fig. 2–15, p. 52: Two Kinds of Selection from *Evolution,* 2/e by Mark Ridley, p. 102, © 1996. Reprinted by permission of Blackwell Science, Inc.; Fig. 2–16, p. 57: Genetic Drift from *The Genetics of Human Population* by L.L. Cavalli-Sforza and W.F. Bodmer, p. 392, © 1971 by W.H. Freeman and Company. Used with permission; p. 62: Data from *The Human Species: An Introduction to Physical Anthropology* second edition, by F. S. Hulse. Copyright © 1963, 1971 by Random House, Inc. Adapted by permission of Random House, Inc.

Chapter Three

Fig. 3–2, p. 81: Primate Distribution Map from *Handbook of Living Primates,* p. 378 by J. Napier and P. Napier, 1967; Fig. 3–3, p. 82: Map of Vegatational Zones from *Handbook of Living Primates,* p. 378 by J. Napier and P. Napier, 1967; Fig. 3–9, p. 89: Comparative Skull Anatomy from *Physical Anthropology and Archaeology,* 5/e by C. Jolly and S. Plog, 1986. Reprinted by permission of McGraw-Hill Companies; Fig. 3–10, p. 90: Dental Formulae and Teeth from *The Cambridge Encyclopedia of Human Evolution,* p. 57 by Steve Jones, Robert Martin, and David Pilbeam, editors, 1992. Reprinted with the permission of Cambridge University Press; Fig. 3–11, p. 91: Primate, Opossum, Squirrel Hands, p. 24 from *The Cambridge Encyclopedia of Human Evolution* by Steve Jones, Robert Martin, and David Pilbeam, editors, 1992. Reprinted with the permission of Cambridge University Press; Fig. 3–15, p. 94: Primate Skeletons from *Primate Adaptation & Evolution* by J.G. Fleagle, p. 245–251, 1988. Copyright © Academic Press, 1988. Reprinted by permission.

Chapter Four

Fig. 4–2, p. 122: Primate Society from *Primate Adaptation and Evolution* by John Fleagle, p. 57, 1988. Copyright © Academic Press, 1988. Reprinted by permission; Fig. 4–18, p. 149: Chimpanzee and Bonobo Habitats map based on Jane Goodall's *Chimpanzees of Gombe,* Fig. 31, p. 45, © 1986 Harvard University Press. Reprinted by permission of The Lazear Agency.

Chapter Five

Fig. 5–7, p. 174: Redrawn from *Primate Evolution* by Glenn C. Conroy, p. 45 Copyright © 1990 by W.W. Norton & Company, Inc.; Reprinted by permission of W.W. Norton & Company,

Inc.; Fig 5–10, p. 176: Early Prosimian Skulls, p. 204 from *The Cambridge Encyclopedia of Human Evolution* by Steve Jones, Robert Martin, and David Pilbeam, editors, 1992. Reprinted with the permission of Cambridge University Press; Fig. 5–17, p. 184: Miocene Ape Fossils Map, p. 224 from *The Cambridge Encyclopedia of Human Evolution* by Steve Jones, Robert Martin, and David Pilbeam, editors, 1992. Reprinted with the permission of Cambridge University Press; Fig. 5–19, p. 186: Proconsul Skeleton from *Primate Adaptation & Evolution* by J.G. Fleagle, p. 369, 1988. Copyright © Academic Press, 1988. Reprinted by permission; Fig. 5–20, p. 187: Time Ranges of Extinct Apes, p. 229 from *The Cambridge Encyclopedia of Human Evolution* by Steve Jones, Robert Martin, and David Pilbeam, editors, 1992. Reprinted with the permission of Cambridge University Press; Fig. 5–22, p. 189: Oreopithecus Reconstruction from *Primate Adaptation & Evolution* by J.G. Fleagle, p. 381, 1988. Copyright © Academic Press, 1988. Reprinted by permission; Fig. 5–28, p. 194: Human & Ape Skeleton and Femurs from *An Introduction to Human Evolutionary Anatomy* by L. Aiello and C. Dean, p. 457, ©1990 Academic Press; Fig. 5–28, p. 194: Human & Ape Skeleton and Femurs adapted from *The Life of Primates* by A. H. Schultz, p. 77, 1969, Universe Books; Fig. 5–29, p. 195: Human Pelvic Bones from Atlas der Anatomie des Menschen, 20th Edition by Sobotta. Reprinted by permission of Urban & Fischer Verlag; Fig. 5–29, p. 195: Ape and Human Pelvic Girdles from *The Antecedents of Man* by Le Gros Clark, 1962, Edinburgh University Press; Fig. 5–30, p. 196: Ape and Human Center of Gravity from *Introduction to Human Evolutionary Anatomy* by C. Dean ad L. Aiello. Academic Press London, 1990; Fig. 5–31, p. 196: Human and Ape Bipedal Walking from *Introduction to Human Evolutionary Anatomy* by C. Dean and L. Aiello. Academic Press London, 1990; Fig. 5–31, p. 196: Human and Ape Bipedal Walking from *The Ascent of Man* by David Pilbeam, p. 67. Copyright © 1972 by Allyn & Bacon. Reprinted/adapted by permission; Fig. 5–32, p. 197: Minor Gluteal Muscles and Iliofemoral Ligament from *The Ascent of Man* by David Pilbeam, p. 67. Copyright © 1972 by Allyn & Bacon. Reprinted/adapted by permission; Fig. 5–32, p. 197: Minor Gluteal Muscles and Iliofemoral Ligament from *An Introduction to Human Evolutionary Anatomy* by L. Aiello and C. Dean, p. 437. Academic Press, London, 1990.

Chapter Six

Fig. 6–14, p. 220: *Australopithecus africanus* Pelvic Girdle adapted from *Early Hominid Posture and Locomotion* by John T. Robinson, University of Chicago Press, 1972. Reprinted by permission of the author; Fig. 6–17, p. 224: Sterkfontein Stone Choppers. Figure redrawn from *South African Archaeological Bulletin*, Vol. 17, #66, 1962, p. 111; Fig. 6–18, p. 225: From *Reconstructing Human Origins: A Modern Synthesis* by Glenn C. Conroy. Copyright © 1997 by W.W. Norton & Company, Inc. Reprinted by permission of W.W. Norton & Company, Inc.

Chapter Seven

Fig. 7.1, p. 244. Skulls and Brain Size from *The Antecedents of Man* by W.E. Le Gros Clark, Fig. 69, 1959. Reprinted by permission of Edinburgh University Press; Fig. 7–12, p. 250: Stratigraphic Column from Hadar. Drawn by Bobbie Brown; Fig. 7–15, p. 254: Chimp, Hadar, Human dental comparisons. Redrawn

from original drawings by Luba Dmytryk Gudz from *Lucy: The Beginnings of Humankind* by Donald C. Johanson and Maitland Edey, 1981, Simon & Schuster.

Chapter Eight

Fig. 8–4, p. 287. *H. habilis* drawing from *Lucy's Child* by D. Johanson and J. Shreeve, p. 15, 1989. Copyright © 1989 by Douglas Becker. Reprinted by permission of William Morrow and Company, Inc.

Chapter Nine

Fig. 9–1, p. 300: Hominids Under the Sun by Pete Wheeler from *Natural History*, 102 (8), p. 66, 1993. Reprinted by permission of the author; Fig. 9–3, p. 304: Fetal Heads and Birth Canals from "Evolution of Human Walking" by C. Owen Lovejoy in *Scientific American*, p. 125, November 1988, vol. 259. Reprinted by permission of Carol Donner, the artist; Fig. 9–9, p. 315: Stone and Bones in Bed I from *Olduvai Gorge*, vol. III, 1971 by Mary Leakey. Reprinted by permission of Cambridge University Press; Fig. 9–11, p. 316: Butchery Site in Bed I from *Olduvai Gorge*, vol. III, 1971 by Mary Leakey. Reprinted by permission of Cambridge University Press.

Chapter Ten

Box 10–2, p. 357: Two Modes of Evolution from *Human Evolution: An Illustrated Introduction*, 3/e by Roger Lewin, p. 18, © 1993. Reprinted by permission of Blackwell Science, Inc.; Fig. 10–11, p. 340: Redrawn with permission from original drawings by Janis Cirulis from *Mankind in the Making* by William Howells, © 1959, 1967; Fig. 10–19, p. 352: *Homo erectus* skulls from *Introduction to Human Evolutionary Anatomy* by C. Dean and L. Aiello, p. 437, © 1990 Academic Press; Fig. 10–19, p. 532: *Homo erectus* skulls from *The Cambridge Encyclopedia of Human Evolution* by Steve Jones, Robert Martin, and David Pilbeam, editors, 1992. Reprinted with the permission of Cambridge University Press; Fig. 10–20, p. 353: Cladistics Concepts and the Species Problem from T. Harrison in *Species, Species Concepts & Primate Evolution*, R. Kimbel and Martin, eds., 1993. Reprinted by permission of the author and Plenum Publishing; Fig. 10–21, p. 355: *Homo erectus* Brain Size Chart. Reprinted by permission of the publisher from "The Endocast" by D. Begun and A. Walker in *The Nariokotome* Homo erectus *Skelton*, p. 351, A. Walker and R. Leakey, eds. Cambridge, Mass: Harvard University Press, copyright © 1993 by the President and Fellows of Harvard College; Fig. 10–22, p. 358: Human Vertebra Chart Data from "The Vertebral Canal" by Anne MacLarnon in *The Nariokotome* Homo erectus *Skeleton*, p. 378, by Anne MacLarnon, A. Walker and R. Leakey, eds., Cambridge, Mass:, Harvard University Press, copyright © 1993 by the President and Fellows of Harvard College; Fig. 10–22, p. 358: Figure adapted from Atlas der Anatomie des Menschen, 20th Edition by Sobotta. Reprinted by permission of Urban & Fischer Verlag.

Chapter Eleven

Fig. 11.1, p. 383: Mass-Specific Organ Metabolic Rates in Humans from L.C. Aiello and P. Wheeler in *Current Anthropology*, 36, no. 2, pp. 210, April 1995. Reprinted by permission of University of Chicago Press; Fig. 11–3, p. 368: Glacial Cycle Chart

"Climatic Change in the Past" by N. Roberts, p. 175 from *The Cambridge Encyclopedia of Human Evolution* by Steve Jones, Robert Martin, and David Pilbeam, editors, 1992. Reprinted with the permission of Cambridge University Press; Fig. 11–4, p. 369: Acheulean Artifacts redrawn by R. Freyman and N. Toth from *Olduvai Gorge*, Vol. 3. ©1971 by Mary Leakey. Reprinted by permission of Cambridge University Press; Fig. 11–6, p. 371: Choppers to Bifacial Tools Sequence figure redrawn by permission from *The Old Stone Age* by Frances Bordes, copyright © 1968 Frances Bordes, Weidenfeld & Nicolson publishers; Fig. 11–9, p. 375: Map of Movius Line, p. 352 from *The Cambridge Encyclopedia of Human Evolution* by Steve Jones, Robert Martin, and David Pilbeam, editors, 1992. Reprinted with the permission of Cambridge University Press and Joe LeMonnier from *Natural History*, October 1989, p. 50; Fig. 11–10, p. 376: East Asian Chopping Tools redrawn by R. Freyman and N. Toth from *Olduvai Gorge*, Vol. 3, ©1971 by Mary Leakey. Reprinted with the permission of Cambridge University Press; Fig. 11–15, p. 384: Typical Primate Organ Sizes by L. C. Aiello and P. Wheeler from *Current Anthropology*, 36, no. 2, pp. 204, April 1995. Reprinted by permission of University of Chicago Press; Fig. 11–16, p. 388: Chimp/Human Split Figure, p. 340 from *The Cambridge Encyclopedia of Human Evolution* by Steve Jones, Robert Martin, and David Pilbeam, editors, 1992. Reprinted with the permission of Cambridge University Press; Fig. 11–17, p. 389: Diagram of Analogue Models, p. 339 from *The Cambridge Encyclopedia of Human Evolution* by Steve Jones, Robert Martin, and David Pilbeam, editors, 1992. Reprinted with the permission of Cambridge University Press.

Chapter Twelve

Fig. 12–4, p. 403: Hunting Dependence Chart, p. 335 from *The Cambridge Encyclopedia of Human Evolution* by Steve Jones, Robert Martin, and David Pilbeam, editors, 1992. Reprinted with the permission of Cambridge University Press.

Chapter Thirteen

Fig. 13–8, p. 426: Four Brains in Partial Section redrawn from *Electrical Stimulation of the Brain* edited by Daniel E. Sheer, p. 167, Figure 15.1. Copyright ©1961, renewed 1989. Reprinted by permission of the University of Texas Press; Fig. 13–16, p. 438: Blood Flow Chart adapted from *Braindance*, pp. 134 and 155 by Dean Falk. Copyright ©1992. Reprinted courtesy of Dean Falk; Fig. 13–17, p. 439: The Brain of a Chimpanzee from *The Prehistory of the Mind* by Steven Mithen, p. 89, 1996. Reprinted by permission of the author; Fig. 13–18, p. 440: Technical Intelligence and Full Cognitive Fluidity from *The Prehistory of the Mind* by Steven Mithen, pp. 145 and 153, 1996. Reprinted by permission of the author.

Chapter Fourteen

Fig. 14–5, p. 455: Reconstruction of Neanderthal Skeleton. Courtesy Masson S.A. Editeur, Paris; from M. Buole and H. Vallois in *Les Hommes Fossiles*, 1952; Fig. 14–9, p. 463: Skeleton Comparisons from *The Last Neanderthal* by Ian Tattersall, p. 14, 1995. Westview Press, 1999. Reprinted by permission of the author; Fig. 14–16, p. 470: Figure redrawn with permission from original drawings by Janis Cirulis from *Mankind in the Making* by William Howells © 1959, 1967.

Chapter Fifteen

Fig. 15–2, p. 487: Pleistocene Ice Ages Chart redrawn from "The Earth's Orbit and the Ice Ages" by Curt Covey, *Scientific American*, 250:2. Copyright © 1984 Scientific American, Inc; Fig. 15–3, p. 490: Brain Sizes from *The Last Neanderthal* by Ian Tattersall, p. 12, 1995. Westview Press, 1999. Reprinted by permission of the author; Fig. 15–10, p. 499: Redrawn by permission from *The Gods of Prehistoric Man* by Johannes Maringer, edited and translated from the German by Mary Ilford, © 1960 by Alred A. Knopf, Inc.

Chapter Sixteen

Fig. 16–5, p. 521: Aurignacian tools. Figure redrawn by permission from *The Old Stone Age* by Frances Bordes, ©1968 Frances Bordes, Weidenfeld & Nicolson publishers; Fig. 16–6, p. 522: Chatelperronian tools. Figure redrawn by permission from *The Old Stone Age* by Frances Bordes, 1968 Frances Bordes, Weidenfeld & Nicolson publishers; Fig. 16–7, p. 524: Neanderthal and Modern Human Skulls Compared. Figure redrawn from "The Neadertals" by Erik Trinkaus & William Howells in *Scientific American*, 241:6, 1979; Fig. 16–12, p. 533: Redrawn by permission of Allan Wilson.

Chapter Eighteen

Fig. 18–6, p. 590: Skin Color Map from *Biological Perspectives on Human Pigmentation*, by A.H. Robins, p. 187, 1991. Reprinted with the permission of Cambridge University Press; Fig. 18–8, p. 592: Hair Form Distribution Map from *The Concept of Race*, pp. 120–121, edited by Ashley Montagu. Reprinted with permission of The Free Press, a Division of Simon & Schuster, Inc. Copyright © 1964 by Ashley Montagu; Fig. 18–9, p. 593: Eye Fold Variants from *Human Biology and Behavior: An Anthropological Perspective*, 3/e, p. 421 by Mark L. Weiss and Alan E. Mann, 1981. Reprinted by permission of Addison Wesley ducational Publishers, Inc.; Fig. 18–10, p. 594: Nose Form Map from *The Concept of Race*, pp. 120-121, edited by Ashley Montagu. Reprinted with permission of The Free Press, a Division of Simon & Schuster, Inc. Copyright © 1964 by Ashley Montagu. Fig. 18–11, p. 596: O and A Blood Group Alleles Maps from *The Living Races of Man* by Carleton S. Coon and Edward E. Hunt, Jr. Copyright © 1965 by Carleton S. Coon. Reprinted by permission of Alfred A. Knopf, Inc.; Fig. 18–12, p. 597: Blood Group Alleles Table adapted from *The Human Species: An Introduction to Physical Anthropology*, 2/e by Frederick S. Hulse, Copyright © 1963 by Random House, Inc. Reprinted by permission of Random House, Inc.; Fig. 18–13, p. 599: Racial Map from *Human Races*, 2/e by S.M. Garn, p. 129, 1965. Courtesy of Charles C. Thomas, Publisher, Ltd., Springfield, Illinois; Fig. 18–16, p. 602: Linkage Tree from Blood Group Genes, p. 395 from *The Cambridge Encyclopedia of Human Evolution* by Steve Jones, Robert Martin, and David Pilbeam, editors, 1992. Reprinted with the permission of Cambridge University Press; Fig. 18–17, p. 603: Linkage Tree from Male Skull Measurements, p. 396 from *The Cambridge Encyclopedia of Human Evolution* by Steve Jones, Robert Martin, and David Pilbeam, editors, 1992. Reprinted with the permission of Cambridge University Press; Fig. 18–18, p. 604: Genetic Diversity Table, from *Genetic Basis of Evolutoinary Change* by Richard C. Lewontin. Copyright © 1974 Columbia University Press. Reprinted with permission of the publisher.

INDEX